THE LETTERS
OF
KING GEORGE IV
1812–1830

IN THREE VOLUMES
VOLUME III

LONDON
Cambridge University Press
BENTLEY HOUSE

NEW YORK · TORONTO
BOMBAY · CALCUTTA · MADRAS
Macmillan

TOKYO
Maruzen Company Ltd

THE LETTERS
OF
KING GEORGE IV
1812–1830

Published by authority of
HIS LATE MAJESTY KING GEORGE V

═══════════

Edited by

A. ASPINALL
M.A., Ph.D.
Lecturer in Modern History,
University of Reading

With an Introduction by

PROFESSOR C. K. WEBSTER
M.A., Litt.D., F.B.A.
Stevenson Professor of International History,
London School of Economics, University of London

IN THREE VOLUMES
VOLUME III
February 1823—June 1831

CAMBRIDGE
AT THE UNIVERSITY PRESS
1938

PRINTED IN GREAT BRITAIN

NOTE

A detailed list of the complete contents, arranged chronologically, is included at the beginning of Volume I. The Index to the complete work is at the end of Volume III.

1823—1831

Fife House, Feb. 28, 1823.

LORD LIVERPOOL has had the honour of receiving your Majesty's letter, and he can assure your Majesty that he feels most anxious to relieve your Majesty's Privy Purse from an amount equivalent to that which is unfortunately thrown upon it by your Majesty's gracious intention of continuing to Sir B. Bloomfield the amount of his pension upon the Civil List which, by law, is dormant as long as he holds the mission in Sweden.

Lord Liverpool enters most cordially into all your Majesty's kind feelings with respect to Mr. Watson, and feels the justice of some permanent provision being made for him, but he humbly submits to your Majesty whether it would not be more advisable to give him a seat at the Customs, or at one of the Revenue Boards, which can now be done, rather than appoint him Auditor of the Civil List.[1]

Lord Liverpool is quite satisfied that no person would discharge the duties of the Civil List more conscientiously than Mr. Watson, and he can assure your Majesty that the Treasury would not feel any repugnance, as far as they were concerned, to the appointment, but the circumstance of appointing any person to this situation who had been for so many years so intimately connected with your Majesty's Household would very probably become matter of comment in Parliament, and in the public, and this would be particularly unfortunate at a moment when there is not any disposition nor pretence to interfere in any way in the concerns of your Majesty's Royal and domestick establishment. Lord Liverpool ventures further to observe that the arrangement which he has proposed would be more advantageous to Mr. Watson.

Lord Liverpool is apprehensive that a message from your Majesty to the two Houses of Parlt is absolutely necessary in point of form to the introduction of the Bill relative to your Majesty's private property, but the Bill will be introduced by the Attorney Genl, and Lord Liverpool has

1 Watson was appointed a Commissioner of the Customs for the United Kingdom on 29 September.

no reason for believing that it can meet with any serious objection from any quarter.[1]

Lord Liverpool has received the most sincere gratification from the account your Majesty has had the condescension to give him of the improvement in your Majesty's health; he is very happy in being able to assure your Majesty that the progress of all business in Parlt has hitherto been most satisfactory.

1063 THE EARL OF LIVERPOOL *to the* KING

Fife House, April 7, 1823.

LORD LIVERPOOL has had the honour of receiving your Majesty's letter, and he will not fail to recollect your Majesty's wishes respecting the Dean of Hereford,[2] when the opportunity offers.

Lord Liverpool would humbly submit to your Majesty that it might be better that your Majesty should be pleased to abstain from making any positive promise to the Dean of Hereford, as events sometimes occur which render promises of this nature particularly inconvenient.

Lord Liverpool is most truly sensible of your Majesty's great kindness in alluding to the severe loss which Lord Liverpool has sustained by the death of his cousin Col. Jenkinson.

1 On 6 March the following message from the King was presented to the House of Commons: "His Majesty being informed that doubts have arisen touching the powers vested in his Majesty to dispose of any real, copyhold, or leasehold property to which his Majesty was entitled before and at the time of his accession to the Crown, and also concerning the powers of his Majesty's successors to dispose of the real, copyhold, or leasehold property to which they at the time of their accession to the Crown may be entitled, his Majesty recommends to his faithful Commons to take this subject into their consideration, and to make such provision respecting the same as may appear to them to be proper."

2 The Rev. Robert James Carr (1774–1841), Bishop of Chichester, 1824–31; Bishop of Worcester, 1831–41. The King wrote to Liverpool on the 6th: "...The name of Chichester reminds me of a wish that I have long had and which I believe I have before mentioned to you, namely, that whenever that diocese shall become vacant, to promote the Dean of Hereford to that See. You know him to be an excellent and exemplary man, and is much esteemed, respected and looked up to by all our most respectable friends in this country, and I confess I take a great interest in this...." (Add. MSS. 38190, fo. 70.)

Fife House, May 1, 1823.

LORD LIVERPOOL begs leave most humbly to acknowledge your Majesty's goodness in acquainting him with the arrangement which your Majesty has been graciously pleased to make as to the office of Rec^r Genl of the Duchy of Cornwall, vacant by the death of Lord Wm Gordon,[1] and to assure your Majesty that Lord Liverpool is fully sensible of the justice of your Majesty's decision in favour of Sir Wm Knighton, as well as of your Majesty's kind consideration of Mr. George Harrison.[2]

1065 THE DUKE OF WELLINGTON *to the* KING

London, May 2d 1823.

I HAD the honor of receiving your Majesty's commands yesterday evening, and I have communicated to Mr. Arbuthnot your Majesty's most gracious intentions. He is truly sensible of your Majesty's kindness towards him, and will himself express his gratitude to your Majesty.

I cannot report my execution of your Majesty's commands upon this occasion without at the same time expressing how sensible I am of your Majesty's kindness in selecting me as the channel of communicating to Mr. Arbuthnot your Majesty's gracious intentions in his favour.[3]

All which is submitted by your Majesty's most devoted and faithful subject and servant.

1 Second son of the third Duke of Gordon, by Catherine, daughter of the second Earl of Aberdeen (1761–1823).

2 He had been Assistant Secretary of the Treasury since 1805. The King wrote to Liverpool on 1 May: "Although the Duchy of Cornwall is my own little private concern, yet I do not choose to make my appointments without acquainting you with what I have done. Lord William Gordon is dead: since the death of McMahon, Sir William has been the Auditor of the Duchy. I therefore make him succeed, as McMahon had before done, to the Receiver-Generalship, and I have appointed that old and valuable servant of the Crown and the Government, Mr. George Harrison, to be the Auditor. As the Duchy is now managed, it is absolutely necessary to have effective officers, not only on account of the revenues of the Duchy, but more especially as poor Mr. Gray is worn out. The *little* stipend attached to this, will also help poor Harrison's retirement, when he is no longer able to work at the Treasury...." (Add. MSS. 38190, fo. 72.)

3 See No. 1116 n.

1066 Dr. John Keate[1] *to* Sir William Knighton

Eton, May 18, 1823.

I BEG leave to acknowledge the receipt of your letter of this morning with the magnificent enclosure from His Majesty, which will be received by the captain of the school on Tuesday with all the gratitude which so gracious an act merits.

We are very much flattered by His Majesty's condescension in expressing his regret at not being able to be present at Montem. His Majesty's absence, as well as the cause of it, is severely felt and sincerely lamented by all Etonians, and by none more than by him who has the honor to subscribe himself [etc.].

1067 Dr. John Keate *to* Sir William Knighton

Eton, May 19, 1823.

I HAVE always been in the habit of drawing out the order of the Montem procession, and presenting it to His Majesty upon his arrival at Eton, and as His Majesty takes so kind an interest in the ceremony, I have thought it possible that, though absent from the scene, he might still deign to cast his eyes upon the description of it. You will therefore greatly oblige me by laying the enclosed with my humble duty before His Majesty.

1068 The King *to* Sir Benjamin Bloomfield
Copy.

C[arlton] H[ouse], May 19, 1823.

YOUR friend Sir William Knighton has approached me this morning upon the contents of your letter, which I desired to see. As your outfit has been expensive, I have directed him to pay into your bankers £1500. But it never was my intention (and I am satisfied that you must have known that it was so) to continue your salary, as Private Secretary to me, when appointed to a foreign mission. In short, there is no circumstance under which I should have thought such a proceeding proper or admissible. Sir William represented to me that the salary of your mission would render your pension dormant; I therefore ordered him to acquaint

1 Headmaster of Eton, 1809–34. [1773–1852.]

you that should be paid from the Privy Purse, and I received your grateful thanks for it. Your representation respecting the Receiver General (I dare say unintentionally) but is not correct [*sic*]. When I gave you the fourteen thousand pounds, it was a full *compensation* for that situation, which I must after all, and in justice to myself, say you were in no way entitled to. When, therefore, I look back to the period when you were first introduced to me by poor Thornton, when I look to your situation and the date of your first becoming my servant, and compare it to your situation and income at this moment, neither you nor your family, I feel, can have the smallest reason to complain of my want of generosity to you.

P.S. The Duke of Wellington and Lord Stewart were both acquainted, and felt it was highly proper to my character, that all further salary from my Privy Purse to you should cease upon your obtaining the mission. Since which I must in justice to myself recall your attention to my spontaneous donation in *lieu* of the *dormant* pension as mentioned above.

1069 SIR BENJAMIN BLOOMFIELD *to the* KING

Edinburgh, 23rd May, 1823.

I SCARCELY feel yet to have recovered my senses since that day, fatal to my peace of mind for ever, when I had the honor to receive your Majesty's letter.

It would ill become me to offer any explanation of the unhappy circumstances which have drawn upon me your Majesty's high displeasure; still, I trust that your Majesty's indulgence will permit me to declare, in the presence of my God, that to give offence to your Majesty, or to state any circumstance differing from that which I believed to be true were incompatible with my nature.

I will not presume to trespass further upon your Majesty than to offer up my fervent prayers to Heaven for your Majesty's long life, glory and happiness.

Rome, July 8th 1823.

YOUR MAJESTY has always expressed so great an interest about His Holiness the Pope, that I flatter myself that these few lines independent of what the Baron de Reden will have written, may be acceptable to you, tho' alas their contents are of a melancholy nature. On Sunday evening the Pope remark'd to a person or persons who were with him, that it was the anniversary of the breaking into his Palace by the French, when Radet carried him off to France, he added "pur ci siamo bene". The gentlemen who were on a visit soon after this took leave of H.H. & the gentleman usher conducted them to the door of the apartment—in this moment the Pope leaning on the table with one hand, rose from his seat & with the other meant to lay hold of the rope which has been placed for him to lean upon it, when he wishes to walk, but he miss'd of it & fell— he call'd out "ajuto a me" & the gentleman usher who was returning, hurried back & with help lifted the Pope into his chair, but the pain which he felt soon alarm'd them, the Cardinal Consalvi was sent to who hurried to the Pope's room & sent for the surgeon. The night was restless, but the next day was tranquil tho' two other surgeons who were summon'd, declar'd the bone to be broken, I think they call it the femur—to day fever has come on, frequent delirium, & as H.H. is extremely weak the apprehensions are very great that he must sink under it. For the publick it will be an irreparable loss, for Consalvi it is the loss of a friend, & of a Sovereign to whom he had devoted himself, & from whom he receiv'd every possible mark of affection & confidence—to the world in general it will be the loss of a most virtuous, firm, yet mild and conciliatory head of the Catholick Church.[1]

Cardinal Consalvi is much better, but has still some pain, only now he don't attend to himself—he was touch'd to the extreme at your Majesty's kind interest about his health w^h you express'd Sir to Sr Henry Halford. I have been most happy to hear so good an account of your Majesty's looks & health, which Lord Lauderdale wrote to Lady Mary Deerhurst last post. Your kindness to me dear Sire during my stay at Brussells & my vis^t to England I can never forget. I am with the utmost respect & attachment your Majesty's most faithfull humble servant & subject.

1 Pope Pius VII died on 20 August.

96 Great Russell Street,
July 9th 1823.

I N my own name and that of the other executors of the late Lord Keith
I beg to mention that there is now in the warehouses of the East India
Company a magnificent model, seven feet high by four feet square, of an
Indian temple, sent by his nephew Mr. Elphinstone[2] to his Lordship.
The figures move by clock work.

Conceiving that, as executors, we cannot with propriety pay the duties
on it, and thinking that it may form an addition to His Majesty's collection at Brighton, we have felt it to be our duty to mention the circumstance to you, in case it might meet His Majesty's wishes to possess it.
It has just arrived on the Duchess of Athol East Indiaman.

In placing it at His Majesty's command, we are not only doing what
is most agreeable to ourselves, but what we believe would have been so
to Lord Keith, if he had been alive, and what is most agreeable to his
daughter and M. de Flahault and all the other branches of his family.

George Canning to the King, 11 July 1823. (*Stapleton*, p. 370.)

1072 THE MARQUIS OF LONDONDERRY *to the* KING

Holdernesse House, July 12th 1823.

W HEN your Majesty was graciously pleased to grant me an audience
at the Cottage, I hesitated not to lay open to your Majesty my most
secret thoughts, and the painful predicament in which I felt myself with
respect to my adored brother's Irish honours being transferred to another
family.[3] Your Majesty, abounding in that condescension and favor which

1 The Marquis of Stafford's estate agent. He acted in a similar capacity to other noblemen,
and was in Parliament after 1827. [1780–1855.]

2 Mountstuart Elphinstone (1779–1859), Governor of Bombay.

3 There is much correspondence in the Londonderry family archives on the subject of
Castlereagh's "Irish honours", and the incident led to great bitterness between the third
Marquess of Londonderry and Lord Liverpool. These "Irish honours" consisted of, first,
the command of the regiment of Derry Militia; second, the office of Governor of Derry
County (an office corresponding to that of Lord Lieutenant in England); and third, the office
of Custos Rotulorum of that County. Wellesley, the Lord Lieutenant of Ireland, explained
the matter to Lord Londonderry on 18 August 1823:

"Your Lordship must be satisfied that the unfortunate result of the arrangements for the
disposal of the regiment of Derry Militia has deeply afflicted me, and is entirely contrary
to my most anxious wishes and declared, unequivocal intentions.

[Upon hearing of Castlereagh's death] "...it was my immediate object to confer upon
your Lordship without delay every office and distinction enjoyed in Ireland by your brother,
which could properly be held by your Lordship....I therefore ordered the appointment of

I have never ceased to experience at your hands, was so kind as to assure me that the business being left in your hands, it should be adjusted. As the Session is now rapidly drawing to a close, and my departure for Ireland very near, and as I hear of no settlement of this matter, I venture humbly to implore your Majesty by your recollection of my poor brother's services during the whole of his laborious life, to interfere so far in this question as to see Sir George Hill[1] and Lord Beresford and to express to them your Royal regret that in the moment of the heavy calamity and without any communication with me (abroad on your Royal service), so great an object of political influence and importance in a County which I had so long represented was transferred by the Govt. in Ireland to another family.

I can entertain no doubt that they would instantly attend to your Majesty's sentiments, delivered by yourself, upon this distressing affair, and I feel a perfect confidence, Sire, that your *just* mind will see in this my humble appeal to you that I can be directed by no other motives than the duty imposed upon me to uphold the memory and position of a statesman who loved your Majesty as devotedly as he served you, and whose every act in life was self-disinterestedness, purity and immolation of himself for those he desired (for your Majesty's service) to uphold.

Your Majesty as a brother would feel as I do—your Majesty as the head of a family would not quietly acquiesce in seeing the few just

Governor to be made out, and application to be made to the Lord Chancellor for that of Custos Rotulorum, and I sincerely believed that both appointments had been then completed. I find however that some unaccountable delay had arisen in the offices. Both appointments however have for some time been complete and are now at your Lordship's command. With respect to the regiment of militia no mention was made by the friends of your family, of your Lordship's particular wishes on that subject; and some doubt was entertained whether personally the command of that regiment was compatible with your high military rank and station.

" In this state of the question it was strongly represented that Sir George Hill's promotion would be the most acceptable arrangement to your Lordship; and that, if your brother had ever resigned the militia, Sir George Hill would have been the object of his selection as his successor in that command.

"It therefore appeared to me that the appointment of Sir George Hill (securing at the same time the command of Lieutenant Colonel for Mr. Stewart) would be the arrangement most respectful to the memory of your brother, and most conformable to your Lordship's wishes and interests.

"With all reasonable respect and consideration for Sir George Hill, I certainly never can admit that his claim to the militia rested on any grounds, independent of his connection with your Lordship's family, and of the supposed wishes and interests of your brother and of your Lordship. It never could have entered into my contemplation to offer him what he has received, as the reward of his own merits or the satisfaction of his own rights; and if the appointment be now considered injurious to your Lordship's rights or interests, as the representative of your brother, it is perverted to a purpose diametrically opposite to my intention; indeed contrary to my positive duty towards your Lordship and your family...." (*Londonderry MSS.*)

1 Sir George Fitzgerald Hill (1763–1839), Vice-Treasurer for Ireland, 1817–30.

honors obtained by my brother during a course of life as unexampled in exertion as rich in success, transferred by the Executive of the country to a man of comparatively no importance; and lastly your Majesty, from every feeling of your exalted and generous nature would never desire that the name of Londonderry should be stripped in Ireland and in our own County of any of those fair honors from the Crown, which have been won and accorded by your Majesty and your Royal father for services which England and Europe have universally admitted and which posterity will do ample justice to. If your Majesty will graciously grant me an audience on this subject, I will obey your Majesty's gracious summons instantly. But to save your Majesty's precious time, I have stated in these lines the substance of what I wish to convey to your Majesty's Royal ear and I have the honor to be ever [etc.].

1073 THE KING *to the* EARL OF LIVERPOOL

C. H., July 16th 1823.

YOU are already acquainted with my feelings relative to the admission of my invaluable friend Sir Wm. Knighton, into the Privy Council. The thing is so proper and so just that I wish to have no conversation on the subject; as my first Minister, I wish to do nothing but what is in unison with your feelings, as far as I can; nevertheless, there are occasions in which I must use my own judgment. I feel satisfied, however, the more you consider this matter, the more you will be convinced of its propriety.[1] I have not strength in my limbs (which the result of last night has taught me) to prorogue the Parliament in person; I will therefore hold another Council on Saturday at one o'clock.

1 Lord Liverpool said that Knighton's admission into the Privy Council might be necessary "to avoid ill humour and other inconveniences", but that it was "most objectionable in principle and precedent". "No King ever had a private secretary till George the Third was blind. Sir H. Taylor was then in that situation, and the late King, who understood these matters better than any one, decided that he should be put upon exactly the footing of an Under-Secretary of State", who was never a Privy Councillor. Wellington would have given way, but Liverpool held out and Knighton was not called to the Privy Council. (*W.N.D.* II, 103, 105.)

Kensington, July 17th 1823.

ON my return from the country I have just now had the great pleasure to receive your announcement of the very distinguished honor that has been conferred upon me by the appointment of Limner to the King for Scotland, in the room of Sir Henry Raeburn.[1]

Such a token of His Majesty's most gracious condescension towards me as a Scottish artist, conferred in so unexpected and so flattering a manner, I receive with the deepest feeling of respect and devotion, and can only wish the considerations by which a great Sovereign is thus pleased to honor a humble subject, whom his Royal patronage has upon former occasions so materially advanced, were more fully justified by my deserts as I feel they would be by my endeavours.

1075 THE MARQUIS OF HASTINGS *to* SIR WILLIAM KNIGHTON

Campden Hill, July 23d 1823.

UPON emptying a trunk, supposed to contain only clothes, there was found at the bottom the original translation which the Council at Calcutta caused to be made from the King of Oude's letter to our Sovereign. Not having been able to discover it at Genoa, I had imagined that my servant had neglected to put it up when I was leaving India, and in that persuasion I sent to His Majesty the copy which had been taken from it for myself. As the original is in a more becoming form for preservation in a record room than that document which I forwarded, I now have the honor to transmit the former.

From the newspapers I learn that the King purposes setting out on his marine expedition as early as the 3d. of August. I shall not have returned from Leicestershire, whither I am called for a week on business, by that time; nor will His Majesty probably be in town before the day, Tuesday next, which I have fixed for running down to Donington. As my plan is not to stay more than a week in England after I get back to London, I shall not have the chance of again seeing the King: therefore I beg leave to request that you will have the goodness to inform yourself whether His Majesty has any objection to my proceeding to the Continent at the period which I have mentioned. It is requisite that I should

---

1 Sir Henry Raeburn (1756–1823) had received this appointment only a few days before his death (6 July). Peel's letter to Wilkie, dated 15 July, is in Cunningham's *Life of Wilkie*, II, 103.

not delay, lest I should not reach the Alps before the snows are to be apprehended. As, in these circumstances, I am not likely to see the King again, I will entreat you to assure His Majesty that my fervent prayers for his health and comfort will be unremitting.

1076 THE EARL OF LIVERPOOL *to* SIR WILLIAM KNIGHTON

Coombe Wood, Augst. 6, 1823.

I HAVE this moment received your letter, informing me that it is His Majesty's gracious intention to subscribe one thousand pounds to the intended improvements at Trinity College, Cambridge.

I will lose no time in transmitting to the Master and Fellows of Trinity College this information, and I have no doubt that they will feel deeply sensible of His Majesty's kindness and munificence towards this Royal institution.[1]

1077 THE MARQUIS OF LONDONDERRY *to the* KING

Aug. 7th 1823.

THE DUKE OF WELLINGTON has transmitted to me the substance of the letter which your Majesty was graciously pleased to write to him on the affair with Sir Geo. Hill. Although the efforts in this unfortunate business are still wholly unsuccessful, it is impossible I can refrain from offering to your Majesty the homage of a grateful heart for your having deigned to interest yourself personally upon a point so mortifying to all my family and myself. I can never forget this last act of your goodness, and I still confidently rely that your Majesty's servants, knowing the interest your Majesty has personally expressed, will in the end afford a retributive act of justice for the memory and for the services of him on whose account I have thought it my duty to prefer and uphold, as far as possible, my humble petition.

For myself, Sire, although removed by our irreparable loss further from your Majesty's sacred person and presence, I trust you will permit me to declare from every feeling of my existence that you have not in your realms a *more gratefull*, devoted and dutiful subject than your Majesty's [etc.].

1 On 12 August, the King's birthday, the first stone of the new quadrangle at Trinity College, which was to be called *The King's Court*, was laid by the Speaker of the House of Commons, whom the King had nominated for this purpose.

London, August 11th 1823.

YOUR MAJESTY's goodness has been so repeatedly manifested towards me that I feel a difficulty in addressing you upon a subject that has occurred to me upon seeing the death of Lord Cornwallis[1] in the papers of this day. But there are certain circumstances connected with my name which make me feel naturally most desirous to draw as near your Majesty's sacred person as possible, and knowing the high distinction and honour of the office Lord Cornwallis held, and feeling that from circumstances my diplomatick career has been arrested,[2] I humbly venture to express to your Majesty how gratified I should feel by your consideration of me on the present occasion, if it shd. not interfere with your Majesty's more important considerations and views.

1079 THE EARL OF LIVERPOOL *to the* KING

Coombe Wood, Augst. 11, 1823.

LORD LIVERPOOL has just received the intelligence of the death of the Marquis Cornwallis.

In consequence of the melancholy event, Lord Liverpool ventures most humbly to represent to your Majesty that it would be a great accommodation to your Majesty's Govt, if it should not be disagreable or inconvenient to your Majesty, to allow Lord Liverpool to make the offer of the office [of] Master of the Buck Hounds to Lord Maryborough, whereby (if accepted by him) the office of Master of the Mint would become vacant, and Lord Liverpool would be enabled to reward the indefatigable exertions of Mr. Wallace,[3] as Chairman of the Parliamentary Commission,[4]

---

1 Charles, second Marquis Cornwallis (1774–1823). Master of the King's Buckhounds since 1807.

2 He had resigned the Vienna Embassy upon hearing of Canning's appointment as Foreign Secretary. His application was unsuccessful, the appointment being given to Lord Maryborough.

3 Lord Liverpool had grievously offended him in December 1822 by promoting Huskisson over his head to the office of President of the Board of Trade—a situation for which, thought Wallace, he had no peculiar aptitude; and on 9 January 1823 Wallace had written to Liverpool a letter of resignation.

Though appointed to Maryborough's office of Master of the Mint, Wallace was not allowed to succeed him in the Cabinet, the King having resolved that the Mint should never again be a Cabinet office. It never would have been made such but for the fact that this was the only favour which Wellington asked, on his brother's behalf, upon his return from the Peninsular War in 1814. (Add. MSS. 38291, fos. 335, 344, 399.)

4 A Commission originally appointed in 1821 to inquire into the collection and management of the Irish revenue, with the view of assimilating it to the system established in England.

and repair in some degree the injury which he thought he received last year, when he was compelled to relinquish the Vice-Presidentcy of the Board of Trade.

Lord Liverpool has less scruple in submitting this proposal for your Majesty's gracious consideration as, in other instances when the offices of the Household have been generally kept distinct from the political arrangements, this principle has not been applied to the office now vacant, Lord Grenville having been allowed by His late Majesty to recommend Lord Albemarle (at the desire of Mr. Fox) for the situation in 1806, and the Duke of Portland, as Lord Liverpool knows, having recommended the Marquis Cornwallis upon the change of Administration in the year succeeding.

1080 THE EARL OF LIVERPOOL *to the* KING

Coombe Wood, Augst 18, 1823.

LORD LIVERPOOL has the honour to send your Majesty the answer which he has just received from Lord Maryborough, and Lord Liverpool trusts your Majesty will allow him to appoint Lord Maryborough to attend at Windsor Castle on Thursday at two o'clock. Lord Liverpool begs to be permitted again to return your Majesty his most grateful thanks for the kindness with which your Majesty has consented to make this arrangement.

1081 COUNT MÜNSTER *to* SIR WILLIAM KNIGHTON

Barnes Terrace, 19th August, 1823.

THE riots which have taken place amongst the students of the University of Göttingen have happily subsided. In fact the public lectures have never been interrupted. I enclose for your information the reports I have received on this unpleasant subject. You will find that the broil arose from the imprudence of a beadel of the University who, seeing that a student, who accompanied to her lodgings a milliner, had attracted a great crowd, had desired the student to let the lady go on her way alone. This interference was complained of by the students en masse, and on their not obtaining redress they proceeded to break the beadel's windows. The punishment incurred by some on this account brought about 7 or 8 hundred students to the resolution of leaving the University. Seeing however that Government was not inclined to yield, the students, perhaps with a few exceptions, have returned. Two have been punished with relegation and 5 with consilium abeundi. I hope that your friend may have met with no unpleasant accident. Should I hear further particulars I shall communicate them to you.

Pray return the enclosed papers. I have the honor to be, dear Sir William, [etc.].

P.S. I intend to settle in town tomorrow for Countess Munster's confinement. I hope I may soon have the happiness of waiting on the King, having asked permission to bring some reports for His Majesty's decision.

1082 SIR HERBERT TAYLOR *to* SIR WILLIAM KNIGHTON

Horse Guards, August 20, 1823.

MY old friends, the Corporation of Windsor, are extremely anxious to pay every tribute of duty and devotion to the King upon the occasion of his making Windsor Castle his residence, and have applied privately to me, in the absence of Mr. Disbrowe, to endeavor to learn whether they may be permitted to present an Address to His Majesty upon the occasion, for which they assure me that there are precedents. I have rather discouraged their expectation that His Majesty would subject himself to the inconvenience of receiving their Address in person, and if I should have judged correctly in so doing, they would offer their Address by a deputation through the Lord Steward or any other officer of the Household whom His Majesty would be graciously pleased to authorize to receive it.

Might I therefore request the favor of you to acquaint me what course it would be most proper and most agreable that they should pursue, and towards what period they should be prepared with their Address.

Pray forgive my giving you this trouble, and believe me to be, with great regard [etc.].

1083 LORD BEXLEY *to the* KING

Blackheath, 25 Augt. 1823.

LORD BEXLEY begs leave dutifully to acknowledge the honor of your Majesty's commands respecting the Marquis of Hastings, and will take the earliest opportunity of communicating with Mr. Grant[1] on the subject. Lord Bexley conceives that it will be more desirable that he should see Mr. Grant, if possible, than write to him, and he will also speak to Mr. Parry,[2] with whom from family connection he is much more intimate than with Mr. Grant, and who is Mr. G.'s particular friend.

Lord Bexley hopes your Majesty will pardon him for adding that the high sense he entertains of Lord Hastings's services will make it a particular pleasure to him if he can be of any service on this occasion.

1084 LORD BEXLEY *to the* KING

Great George Street, 26 Augt. 1823.

IN obedience to your Majesty's commands I this morning saw Mr. Grant, and made to him the communication with which your Majesty did me the honor to charge me. I was desired by him to express every sentiment of duty and affection to your Majesty, but to represent the difficulties under which he was placed, with respect to Lord Hastings, by his declared sentiments with respect to some of the leading measures of that nobleman's government, and by the apprehension that the proposition of a second grant to Lord Hastings would lead to a similar proposition in favor of Lord Wellesley, and possibly of other persons.[3] I endeavoured, as far as I was able, to take off the force of these objections, and particularly that which relates to his own consistency, which is evidently what presses most upon his mind. Much, therefore, will depend upon the mode and form in which the proposition may be brought forward; and as the grace and credit of the measure must so much depend upon its being passed by a large majority, if not unanimously, I hope the friends of Lord Hastings will very cautiously avoid any circumstances which can provoke opposition.

I have spoken to Mr. Parry, who I am convinced will do what lies in his power to conciliate Mr. Grant, with whom he almost uniformly has acted. I have the honor to be, Sir, with every sentiment of gratitude and duty [etc.].

1 Charles Grant, senior, the Director of the East India Company.
2 Lord Bexley's sister Emilia married Edward Parry, a Director of the East India Company.
3 In 1819 the Company had made him a grant of £60,000 for the purchase of an estate to be held in trust for the benefit of his family. The question of a second grant was not placed before the Court of Proprietors until 1824, and was then postponed.

London, September 1st 1823.

FROM your kind and affectionate letter, which has just reached me, I learn with great satisfaction that you are gratified with the flattering and distinguished attentions which are paid to you by the Court of Stockholm and the Swedish nation. The King[2] seems to be truly sensible of the advantage which his Kingdom derives from having a person of such high character as yourself accredited to him as the representative of the great Monarch of this powerful country. On your part I have no doubt that it will be your study to fulfill the trust reposed in you to the entire satisfaction of the Swedish Court and of your own Sovereign.

Your affectionate expressions of friendship and of attachment are very sensibly felt by me, and with an entire reciprocity of regard. Indeed, I should be most ungrateful if I could for a moment cease to remember the many acts of kindness which I have, at various times, received from you. You may believe me, therefore, when I assure you that you shall always find in me a true friend and adviser, ever watchful to promote your *real* welfare and best interests.

It is in this character that I now express my unfeigned regret and *surprise* that the name of our excellent friend, Sir William Knighton, does not once occur in your letter. I think that you ought to have written to him the moment that you knew the effect which your unfortunate letter had produced on his mind, and I honestly confess that I have daily been expecting to hear from him that such a letter had arrived.

I am sure that his never-ceasing endeavours to serve you and your son deserve, not only this attention, but the most affectionate feelings towards him on your part. I do not assert this at a venture, but I speak from an accurate knowledge of all that has passed, and, as I made Minutes at the time, I will give you a rapid sketch of all the circumstances connected with the subject of your letter. You may remember, when this unfortunate letter first arrived, it was my decided opinion that if your mutual friendship was to be preserved, it was most advisable, nay absolutely necessary, that I should answer it. At the same time I was decidedly of opinion that there was no alternative but to lay the letter before His Majesty, in justice both to Knighton and to yourself. What the King wrote on that occasion I was not made acquainted with. Sir William told me that the King talked over the subject with great vehemence, then wrote his letter which Sir William neither saw nor even sealed, but that when your answer to the King arrived, which was

1 Tory M.P. for Bristol.
2 Bernadotte had succeeded Charles XIII as Charles XIV in 1818.

deemed highly improper, then His Majesty recapitulated what he had written.

Poor Mr. R. Gray, as you probably know, is dead. I am completely in the secret of the importance of that most invaluable servant to the King. Before Lord Wm. Gordon's death our friend George Harrison applied for his situation, as did Sir Wm. Keppel, in the most urgent manner, by a letter addressed directly to the King, as also did Sir Hilgrove Turner. The Government were anxious, on the expected death of Mr. Gray, that there should be a superintending man of business in the Dutchy office, whom not only the King but the Treasury might rely on. When this was mentioned our friend K[nighton] saw the great importance of this arrangement to all the King's concerns, and more especially in re-lation to His Majesty's private affairs, because such a person was absolutely necessary for the purpose of becoming, as it were, a voucher for his (Sir William's) own transactions.

In the midst of all this, however, he told me at the time that he had ventured to submit your name, as a suggestion, to the King; & that the answer was—"Are you mad? Otherwise, how is it possible that such a suggestion could enter into your head?"

I can truly assure you that K— never dreamt of or wished for the appointment himself of Receiver General of the Dutchy. There is not I believe more than £200 per annum difference in the salary, but the King very kindly said to Knighton "I will move you up in the Dutchy; for the place of Auditor will be more appropriate for Mr. Harrison, since the Treasury think it desirable that he should be there."

In relation to the suspension of your salary, it took place, I believe, about the close of the time that Mr. Gray was executing the office of Privy Purse, under your power of attorney. Our friend Sir William, when he came into office, mentioned to me his distress that the King would no longer continue your salary as Private Secretary; and I will honestly confess to you that, friendly as I am to your interests, my answer was *"Bloomfield ought not to expect this allowance to be con-tinued."* He then repeated to me the particulars of the last conversation which he had had with you on this subject; for at one time Sir William had hoped that it was His Majesty's intention to have continued your salary. I again confess that, under all the circumstances, my advice to him then was to say nothing further on the subject, either to the King or to yourself.

Some time after this arose the question about your pension which be-came dormant on your receiving the salary as Ambassador. There again I can truly say that I never witnessed more eager and affectionate anxiety than was manifested by Knighton on that occasion. He saw Arbuthnot, Lushington,[1] Herries,[2] Harrison and the whole kit, and subsequently *Lord Liverpool*, but it was impossible to do anything with them. He then approached the King who has always been your best friend. His Majesty was kind and, as K. said, *"comfortable"* towards you, and finally consented to have the pension paid out of the Privy Purse, and the very day previous to my receiving your last letter, so full of inquietude and uncomfortable feeling, dear Knighton told me that he had succeeded in being allowed to pay your pension *in full*, namely the twelve hundred pounds per annum, without the deductions attendant upon it when paid from the Exchequer. About a fortnight before this, when some move or alteration respecting the diplomacy at Frankfort and elsewhere took place, Mr. Canning was graciously reminded by the King, *under his own hand* (which letter Knighton himself delivered), respecting your son, who is, I understand, at present a paid attaché at £250 per annum at Vienna. This, Mr. C. did for him some short time since, at the desire of the King, there being, as I understand, only four that are paid. Independently of this, there is no effort which K. has omitted to get you removed to a warm climate in the most eligible part of Italy. This endeavour he has pursued and still does follow up in a most satisfactory and steady manner, and my own impression is that he will, by and by, succeed.

What you state respecting the silly opinions of individuals, namely, that you had made a fortune whilst you were in your late situation, is best answered by the release which the King gave you on the close of your accounts, the draught of which K[nighton] drew himself & desired me to consider whether stronger and more secure words could be devised. I should certainly say not, for it was perfect in all its parts as an effectual and ample release. There is, as you know, a heavy debt in the Lord Chamberlain's department, arising out of the wants of the Crown, which must no doubt have made the Government uneasy as it was contracted illegally, that is, by an infringement of an Act of Parliament; but to my knowledge K[nighton] has taken this delicate affair into his own hands, that it may not become the subject of any observation.

Now my dear friend, *having stated these facts*, and feeling as I do towards you, what must have been my reflections on perusing your querulous and, I must say, wrong-headed letter.

Let us consider the usual course of politics and the common events of

---

1 Joint Secretary of the Treasury.
2 John Charles Herries (1778–1855), Joint Secretary of the Treasury, February 1823–September 1827.

life, as connected with Courts, and then let me fairly put this question to you. What is there remarkable in your lot except the most extraordinary and most unlooked-for good fortune, both in the rise and progress, AND EVEN IN THE DECLINE, OF THE ROYAL FAVOUR.

Has not H.R.H. the Duke of York found it convenient to change his Private Secretaries five times over, and what is their distinction and reward when compared with yours? Sir H. Taylor was, I believe, fifteen years with the late King, and is now a daily drudge at the Horse Guards for less than £2,000 per annum. What answer can be made to these and similar cases except that *your Sovereign* has been *most gracious*, and *that your friends have never ceased in their anxious endeavours to serve you.*

As to K[nighton] until I knew him I did not rightly estimate the extent of the term *friendship*, nor what duties it comprised. When I look back upon his constant, disinterested, and most affectionate attentions to me whilst I was suffering under the severe pressure of a cruel and *most unexpected* reverse of fortune, I can inform you *from practical experience* what his feelings always have been, what they are, and what I believe they ever will be, towards yourself. I am confident you will now feel that your apparently neglectful silence towards one of your best friends has neither been proper nor just.

After you had received my letter I fully expected that he would have heard from you. He always speaks of you with the kindest feelings, and only suspends writing until he hears from yourself that your friendship is unaltered towards him.

If, after this full explanation, you should still prefer that your correspondence should pass through me, I shall accept your confidence with pleasure.

The length of this letter will have strongly manifested to you my sincere desire to set your mind right on many points *deeply interesting to your future welfare and happiness*. I shall be much gratified to learn from you in reply that this attempt has not entirely failed of success.

1086 THE MARQUIS OF HASTINGS *to* SIR WILLIAM KNIGHTON

Calais, September 7th 1823.

EXPECTING to have quitted England earlier, I wished to delay answering your letter until I should have effected that purpose; for I feared that otherwise I might be supposed as seeking indirectly to obtrude myself further on the King's notice.

I may now allow myself to observe that no strength of expression was requisite to make me discard a wish which I had never submitted with any degree of earnestness or with a conception that it could be regarded as possessing any significance beyond its being the means to do away the unfavourable inferences which might be drawn from my recent disappointment.[1] Your simple silence would have implied that the King had not met the suggestion, and I should have thought of it no more. You will have the goodness to recollect that the topic arose suddenly out of a conversation between us. I had professed the belief, in commenting upon a paper which you read to me, of its being as interesting for the King as for myself that something should be done to counterbalance the appearance of an unmerited slight inflicted on me, however unintentionally, on my arrival from India. Imminent peril of long embarrassment and financial distress, if not of more serious consequences, to the British interests in India had been dissipated by my exertions: and this too was achieved when the enterprise seemed so unpromising that all the authorities with which I had connection avowed the disposition to await the maturity of the mischief rather than take what I thought the better chance of encountering it before it had attained the full vigor of complete organization. To have dispelled such a danger, even at heavy cost, would have had some pretension to acknowledgment; therefore the claim was sufficiently distinct when the object had been accomplished, not only without incurrence of charge, but with the addition of an indisputable future security and an augmented affluence such as the fondest hope could not have anticipated. The hazards which had been impending are stated by me as having menaced British interests generally, not the Company's alone, because that description is the unquestionable truth of the case. To my Sovereign, consequently, I humbly looked for a recognition of what I could not but have some consciousness was not a commonplace effort. If my vanity overrated the service, that recognition might have been withheld: but assuredly it was not an instance in which a marked disregard was deservedly applied. I sought to evoke the King's own feelings under what I knew to have proceeded from his inadvertence not from his purpose. Still, the awkwardness was not the less for me who stood in the eyes of the public treated with something more positive than indifference.

I did believe that the King comprehended how painful the circumstance must have been to me and that His Majesty was graciously solicitous to repair the undesigned grievance. The persuasion referred itself to His Majesty's equity, since it was visible that a disparagement of me mani-

1 In being refused a Dukedom.

fested in that high quarter would fix elsewhere the estimate of attention due to me. It is impossible that you should not be sensible that the apparent neglect of me by the King gave the tone to the Court of Directors and produced a decision as unsatisfactory, I am convinced, to the King as it will probably be to others. This was easy to be foreseen; and the perception of it caused, in the unpremeditated conversation between you and me, the pointing at what occurred solely as the very lowest expedient by which His Majesty could avoid letting me return to the Continent under a discredit which I must be confident it could not be the King's desire should rest upon me.

That any importance could be attached to the name beyond its being a mark of favor, if conferred, was never surmised by me. If that name can be a doubtful encroachment the name of Stuart is open to the same objection. So little, indeed, could an impropriety be imagined that the Duke of Buckingham,[1] the Earl of Huntingdon,[2] and Lord Charles Somerset[3] have each of them added Plantagenet to the Christian name of children as indication of descent. That I, therefore, should be deemed guilty of an indecent presumption, when the imputation is, in its particular nature, so irreconcileable to the tenor of my life, is a singular misfortune. In another, I might apprehend that the forced construction was to justify the antecedent procedure, however inapplicable in order of time.

The soul of the King is known to me to be proudly incapable of such a policy. His Majesty has used the phrase from a hasty and unexamined impression: yet it is used; and, while I bow with unqualified submission to His Majesty's pleasure regarding the matter itself, I should be disingenuous were I to conceal that the wound from those words is far deeper than the former.[4]

1 His wife, Anna Eliza Brydges, daughter of the third and last Duke of Chandos, claimed descent from Henry VIII's sister Mary, Duchess of Suffolk.

2 Hans Francis Hastings, eleventh Earl of Huntingdon (1779–1828). He claimed descent, through Katherine, wife of the second Earl of Huntingdon (1514–1561), and grand-daughter of Margaret, Countess of Salisbury, from Edward IV's brother, the Duke of Clarence, who was the father of the Countess of Salisbury.

3 The second son of the fifth Duke of Beaufort (1767–1831). Descended, illegitimately, from John of Gaunt.

4 Lord Hastings assumed, by royal permission, his maternal surname of "Hastings" in addition to that of Rawdon. His mother, Elizabeth Hastings, was the daughter of the ninth Earl of Huntingdon.

Copy.

September 24, 1823.

M Y regard for you has arisen not only out of circumstances connected with yourself, but is also blended with feelings of the warmest affection to the memory of our much lamented friend, poor Lord Londonderry, for I well know the sincere estimation in which he held you, and that his friendship towards you was of the strongest character.

I do, therefore, for you on the present occasion what poor Londonderry would have done, had he been alive; and hence it is that I cannot refrain from making the present communication to you with my own hand, for the purpose of acquainting you with what indeed came to my knowledge some time since, but through a secret channel, *quite independent of any member of my Cabinet*, and which alone prevented me sooner naming it to you.

The King of the Netherlands has, from some caprice or other, an uncomfortable feeling towards you, and to such a degree as to suspend that confidence which you have, and unquestionably to his great advantage, for so many years so justly enjoyed.[1]

It is in vain to enquire what infirmity of mind, or what unhappiness of temper in the King has led to this unfortunate change, but the fact is so.

You will see that what I state is not mere surmise, for the King's feelings already develope themselves in the settled determination H.M. has taken to recall Baron Fagel[2] on the first of the New Year, under the immediate pretext of making him his First Minister. But the scheme is evidently framed solely for the purpose, my dear Lord, of getting rid of you; for on Baron Fagel's recall the King of the Netherlands intends to send to this Court *simply* a mission. Now in the present state of Europe this is decidedly wrong, as well as disreputable in the greatest degree.

Under these circumstances, and with my feelings towards you, I could not remain silent, and I therefore recommend to you what our poor Londonderry would have done, namely, to advise you to desire your recall without delay.

No one, you may believe, regrets the necessity of this more than I do, and it is but fair and just most distinctly to state that Mr. Canning regrets it equally with myself; for when I conversed with him on the subject, which I thought it right to do, he said that your conduct as a Minister, since he,

1 Canning's friend Bagot later said that "in the latter years of Ld. Clancarty's reign much mischief was done by the obtrusion of familiar intercourse and advice without management, and without proper deference to the King's temper, dignity, and established position". (*Bagot*, II, 343. See also p. 223.)
2 Netherlands Minister in London.

Mr. Canning, had held the seals of the Foreign Department, was everything he could wish, and that you had his entire confidence.

The peculiar and unfortunate temper of the King of the Netherlands we need not again refer to, as it has more than once given rise to the most painful vexations.

I shall, however, do all in my power to mark my decided approbation of your conduct, and the estimation in which I have and do hold your public services.

Your pension will await you on your return to this country, and I propose also to rise [*sic*] you a step in the English peerage, and, as a further mark, should it be acceptable to you, the first Irish Ribbon shall be at your service.[1]

1088 EARL BATHURST *to the* KING

Cirencester, Sept. 28th 1823.

I HAD the honour of receiving yesterday the letter[2] which your Majesty was graciously pleased to address to me on the 26th inst., and will obey your Majesty's commands in writing to Lt. Col. Brown to inform him that your Majesty's previous engagements will put it quite out of your Majesty's power to place him in the Household, and that by your Majesty's commands I have placed his name down for some colonial situation.

With regard to Sir Robert Farquhar, I think it my duty to submit to your Majesty that the report which the Treasury is about to make on Mr. Theodore Hook's[3] accounts will implicate some other persons in high official situations at the Mauritius, but I am happy to say that Sᵣ Robert Farquhar will stand clear of any charge except what may arise from the facility with which his amiable disposition allowed others to practise upon him; and in all the proceedings which may take place I will not fail to bear in mind the interest which your Majesty has been graciously pleased to express in his behalf.

1 His earldom of Clancarty was in the Irish peerage; he was created a peer of the United Kingdom, as Baron Trench, in 1815, and was raised to an English Viscounty in November 1823.

2 See *Bathurst Papers*, p. 544. Lieutenant-Colonel Browne was putting forward claims to recompense for his services in the matter of the Milan Commission. The King considered his conduct "altogether wrong-headed", but was prepared to give him a Privy Purse pension of £250 a year "until he is employed on full pay or has some employment to give him an increase of income".

3 He had been held responsible, as Accountant General at the Mauritius, for a deficiency of £12,000 in his accounts and had been sent home a prisoner in 1818. Began to edit the Tory weekly paper, *John Bull*, 1820; imprisoned, 1823–25. See No. 1148.

I take the liberty of adding, knowing the interest which your Majesty takes in those who have been under your Majesty's protection, that Sir Robert Barclay, whom I placed by your Majesty's commands in a good situation in the Mauritius,[1] is not implicated in the Report of the Lords of the Treasury, and that the situation he has held has enabled him to get over many of his pecuniary difficulties. It is the expectation that this Report will ultimately lead to the dismissal of others, which will enable me to hold out to Lt. Col. Brown an expectation of a provision, without the fear of disappointing him.

Lady Bathurst and my daughters are most grateful for your Majesty's gracious remembrance of them, and I beg to subscribe myself [etc.].

The Earl of Clancarty to the King, 3 October 1823. (*W.N.D.* II, 144–45.)

1089 THE DUKE OF MONTROSE *to the* KING

Buchanan, near Dumbarton, 5th Octr. 1823.

YOUR MAJESTY'S communication of the 30th of September has been received by the Duke of Montrose, who is gratified that the Chamberlain's department (considering the state of the demands on it) has been able to render the noble Castle of Windsor comfortable for your Majesty's reception. Your Majesty's gracious expression of desiring to see your Majesty's humble servant will be taken advantage of as soon as lies in the Duke's power; but, Sir, be assured this country requires to be attended to, as do the tenantry, that they may not be pressed too hard, and yet that rents may be obtained from them, such as they can afford to pay, without depressing and injuring good tenants. The Duke of Montrose can safely state to your Majesty that, personally, he would be delighted that a French theatre was licensed by your Majesty's authority, but he doubts the policy as regarding the State or your Majesty's service; the institution would undoubtedly occasion riots in London, founded on dislike to the French, and on the supposed interests of the other theatres.

The topick might also be made a popular handle to run down the Government as too much connected with France, and might even be worked up to be very disagreeable personally to your Majesty; so it strikes your Majesty's Chamberlain, and therefore the Duke humbly requests that your Majesty will have the goodness to consult the

1 As Collector of the internal revenues of the Mauritius.

Secretary of State for the Home Department, and even the Cabinet, before your Majesty is pleased to give your commands on this subject.

The gentleman your Majesty recommends shall be attended to, if your Majesty should finally be of opinion that a French theatre should be licensed. The Duke of Montrose trusts for your Majesty's forgiveness, whilst he presumes to take this liberty, which he conceives founded on his duty, always remaining, Sir, [etc.].

1090 GEORGE CANNING *to the* KING

Foreign Office, Oct. 6, 1823.

MR CANNING thinks it his duty to lose no time in forwarding to your Majesty Lord Clancarty's answer to your Majesty's gracious letter of the 24th Septr, to which he humbly takes the liberty to add a letter received by himself from Ld. Clancarty at the same time.

Tomorrow being post day for Holland, Baron Fagel will, no doubt, call on Mr. Canning, when Mr. Canning proposed (subject to your Majesty's gracious approbation) to state to Baron Fagel the substance of what has passed, and to ground thereon the expression of your Majesty's hope and expectation that Baron Fagel may be allowed to remain near your Majesty, or that, at least, no change shall take place in the character of the Netherland mission.

A doubt, however, has occurred to Mr. Canning whether Lord Clancarty might not possibly think it unkind that a previous, or even simultaneous communication should be made to the King of the Netherlands, through his Ambassador, and whether it might not be fairer to Ld Clancarty to give him notice tomorrow that such a communication will be made to Baron Fagel on Friday.

To save your Majesty the trouble of writing at least in one case, Mr. Canning will, *if he does* NOT hear from your Majesty tomorrow, adopt the *latter* course, and only assure Baron Fagel that he shall be enabled to write fully to his Court by the next post.

1091 THE DUKE OF MONTROSE *to the* KING

Buchanan, near Dumbarton, 6th Octr. 1823.

YOUR MAJESTY, in the letter of the 30th of Septr., with which your Majesty was pleased to honor the Duke of Montrose, alluded to a little more being done for the Hay Market theatre. It will always be the desire, as well as the duty of the Duke of Montrose to attend to the slightest hint from your Majesty, but when the proprietors of the great theatres, and the proprietors of the Hay Market theatre attended the Chamberlain's office on the subject of the Hay Market licence, and stated all their interests and claims, it appeared to the Duke that the utmost that could be done for the Hay Market theatre was the term granted, with the declaration of the proprietors of the great theatres, that they would not put any clause into their agreements with the actors on their establishments that the actors should not play at the Hay Market theatre, or otherwise obstruct such engagements with the Hay Market theatre; for such a clause one of the theatres had actually adopted.

Any extension of the term of the Hay Market licence would not only be injurious to the great theatres, both in the receipts at the commencement and latter end of the season, but would enable the Hay Market theatre to make engagements with the principal actors which would enable these actors to play at the Hay Market theatre, and afterwards make engagements with the country theatres for the winter months, an object much desired by the country theatres and by the actors; and this would be highly injurious to the great theatres, and frequently deprive the capital of the best actors during the winter months.

For these reasons the licence was granted with the limitation to certain months, and which it is humbly hoped will meet with your Majesty's approbation, for it was well considered and decided without partiality, for the advantage of the public, and the relative interests of the respective establishments, by your Majesty's dutiful, and I may venture to say well-intentioned Chamberlain, who has the honor [etc.].

1092 GEORGE CANNING *to the* KING

Cirencester, Oct. 16, 1823.

MR. CANNING humbly acquaints your Majesty that considerations arising out of despatches received from India (a few days after Mr. Canning paid his duty to your Majesty at Windsor) are understood to have prevented Lord Hastings's friends from renewing the motion in Lord H.'s favour at the E. India House last week (as was intended) and that (as Mr. Canning is informed) that motion is like to be deferred until a more propitious opportunity.

Mr. Canning humbly conceives that it may be more agreeable to your Majesty that he should not stir in that part of the arrangement which relates to the embassy at St. Petersburgh until the success of the vote at the India House shall have been ascertained.[1]

In the mean time, as it would be highly inconvenient that The Hague should be left open after Lord Clancarty's resignation is known, (especially as Baron Fagel's projected change of destination was to take place on the first day of the New Year) Mr. Canning humbly submits to your Majesty that it may be expedient to appoint Lord Granville,[2] in the first instance, to The Hague—subject to removal to Paris when the further arrangements can be carried into effect.

1093   EARL BATHURST *to the* KING

Cirencester, Oct. 16, 1823.

LORD BATHURST cannot sufficiently express to your Majesty his mortification at finding that the dispatches recently received from the West Indies regarding the insurrection at Demerara have not been submitted to your Majesty.[3]

This mistake arose from Mr. Wilmot Horton[4] (the Under Secretary) having come down to Cirencester on a visit to Lord Bathurst the day before the first dispatches had arrived. Lord Bathurst trusts to your Majesty's great indulgence for pardoning this oversight.

It is submitted that two regiments at least should be sent out to the West Indies, without diminishing the force in Ireland, and measures are taking to accomplish this important object with all the dispatch which the present military establishment of the country will permit.

1 Canning's friend Sir Charles Bagot was British Ambassador at Petersburg from 1820 to 1824.

2 Lord Granville Leveson-Gower, first Earl Granville (1773–1846); Canning's close friend. Minister at The Hague, February to November, 1824; Ambassador at Paris, 1824–28.

3 On 18 August the Demerara negroes, erroneously believing that the Imperial Government had decreed the emancipation of all slaves in the Empire and that their masters had frustrated the execution of the decree, broke out into an almost general insurrection; but it was speedily suppressed.

4 Sir Robert John Wilmot Horton (1784–1841). Under-Secretary for War and the Colonies, 1822–28; Governor of Ceylon, 1831–37; knighted, 1831; succeeded to baronetcy, 1834.

The Hague, 17 Octr. 1823.

YOUR MAJESTY's most gracious condescension in again addressing me for the purpose of expressing your Majesty's approbation of the conduct I have pursued on a late occasion has afforded me the most heartfelt satisfaction, and furnished an additional motive for my entire and never ending gratitude.

Believe me, Sire, although, since I had the honour of laying my resignation at your Majesty's feet, much has passed between the King of the Netherlands and me, with the substance of which your Majesty has doubtless been made acquainted by Mr. Canning, I have never for one instant repented the course then taken by me, or have felt the slightest desire that that resignation should be recalled.

Assured of your Majesty's approbation of my feeble services in a manner and in terms which under no circumstances I could have had the presumption to expect, and honoured by such gracious public testimonies of your Majesty's regard, rendered additionally valuable as proceeding from your Majesty's mere motion, I could never retire from the public service with greater honour or satisfaction to myself; and I shall retire from it, Sire, with a heart filled with continual gratitude, devotion and attachment to your Majesty's person.

As to the remaindership in the English honour which I took the liberty of suggesting—I am far indeed from wishing that any rule established for the exercise of your Majesty's Royal Prerogative should be violated upon my account.

With sentiments of the most profound and sincere respect and gratitude inseparable from my existence I have the honour to subscribe myself [etc.].

1095 THE EARL OF LIVERPOOL *to the* KING

Walmer Castle, Octr. 18, 1823.

LORD LIVERPOOL has this moment received your Majesty's letter, and will lose no time in obeying your Majesty's commands, by making the communication you desire to Col. Stephenson.

It will be Lord Liverpool's duty, in conformity to your Majesty's commands, to consider what new arrangement can be made for conducting the business of the Board of Works in a way most advantageous to your Majesty's service, and most agreable to your Majesty; but Lord

Liverpool trusts he shall meet with your Majesty's forgiveness if he humbly solicits you, before such a step is irretrievably taken, to require from Col Stephenson some explanation and apology, as Lord Liverpool can never suppose that any person in Col Stephenson's situation could intend to question any commands or wishes on such a subject which he had any reason to suppose were conveyed by your Majesty.

Lord Liverpool can have no personal nor political object in venturing to solicit your Majesty's kind consideration of this request, but he is willing to entertain the hope that the incident which has given offence to your Majesty must have arisen from some misunderstanding.

1096 THE DUKE OF YORK *to the* KING

Cheveley, October 19, 1823.

I HAVE the honor to report to your Majesty that in consequence of the insurrection which has broken out in Demarara, and of the probability of its spreading through the whole of your Majesty's West India possessions, a reinforcement of two batallions has been urgently called for by your Majesty's Government, one of which it has been easy to detach from Ireland without diminishing the force stationed there, as a relief happened to be going forwards, and the 93rd regiment has been ordered, in consequence, to embark immediately, but without the greatest inconvenience it is very difficult to find another batallion, as it must ultimately be taken from the force in this country, where there is, alas, but one batallion really fit for service, which is the Fuziliers.

Under these circumstances I trust that your Majesty will approve of their being sent abroad, but as I am sure that your Majesty would wish so fine and respectable a corps to be placed in a good climate and not too far from home, should any service arise in Europe, I therefore propose that they should relieve the 27th regiment at Gibraltar, which corps may be immediately sent from there to the West Indies.

As the necessity for the early reinforcement of the West Indian garrison is urgent, I trust that your Majesty will approve of a detachment of the brigade of Guards relieving the Fuziliers upon your Majesty's duty at Windsor, which they will be able to do for a short time till I can pick out the best of the batallions of the line in England to attend your Majesty.

Walmer Castle, Octr. 20, 1823.

LORD LIVERPOOL has had the honour of receiving your Majesty's letter[1] on the subject of the claim advanced by the Dean[2] and Chapter of Windsor.

Lord Liverpool felt it to be his duty to lay this letter and its enclosure before your Majesty, but he has not informed the Dean and Chapter of Windsor that he has so done, and he requests your Majesty's permission not to return any answer to this letter until the Lord Chancellor comes to town, and Lord Liverpool has had an opportunity of communicating with him.

In the mean time, your Majesty may continue to enforce any orders your Majesty may have given respecting the Terrace. Lord Liverpool can never believe that the Dean and Chapter of Windsor (whatever their strict right may be) can think of obtruding on your Majesty's privacy whilst your Majesty is actually residing in Windsor Castle.

Lord Liverpool is ready to take all the responsibility upon himself of having withheld the official communication of the letter of the Dean and Chapter of Windsor for the present.

1098 COLONEL STEPHENSON *to the* EARL OF LIVERPOOL

Office of Works, 20th Oct. 1823.

IT is with feelings of the greatest concern that I have the honor of acknowledging the receipt of your Lordship's letter of the 18th instant, communicating His Majesty's commands for dismissing me from the situation I have the honor of holding in this department. And in justice

1 "I seem to be exposed to impertinence, and from them who eat my bread", he wrote on the 19th. "Neither my father nor my predecessors would tolerate such conduct, nor will I." In an enclosed memorandum he declared: "The King will not admit the privilege claimed by the Dean and Chapter of Windsor. They will share the same indulgence as is granted to the inhabitants in general. The Terrace will be open on a Sunday, but on a Sunday *only*; without *this*, it would be impossible for the King to reside in the Castle without being exposed to public intrusion from morning till night. King Charles may have done a silly thing, but which *can* not, nor *shall* not bind the present King.

"The King desires that Lord Liverpool will acquaint him in the most *scrupulous* manner, what real power the King has over the Dean and Chapter of Windsor, for a more offensive and troublesome set of individuals to the King personally it is impossible to imagine. This was illustrated by what happened, and which Lord Liverpool can not forget, their indecent conduct both at the funeral of the King's poor sister Amelia, poor Charlotte, and above all, the King's poor mother." (Add. MSS. 38190, fos. 79–80.)

2 Henry Lewis Hobart, D.D. (1774–1846), fourth son of the third Earl of Buckinghamshire (1731–1804).

to myself and family [I] must entreat your Lordship will take an early opportunity of most humbly representing to His Majesty how deeply I feel his Royal displeasure, and how sincerely I lament that any act of mine could ever have been so represented to His Majesty as to incur the severe sentence of dismissal from a situation upon which the support of myself and numerous family almost entirely depends.

Most faithfully and solemnly can I assure His Majesty that the whole of my official attention has unceasingly been directed towards discharging my duties upon every occasion in the way I deemed best calculated to secure His Majesty's approbation, and promote the good of his service, within the limits of my department.

With reference to my general practice I must observe that my directions to the Clerks of the Works at Windsor have been invariably to execute without delay all orders for alterations and repairs that may come to him in His Majesty's name, by whomever such orders may be conveyed; but that unless there was His Majesty's sanction, nothing was to be done, excepting such repairs and trifling works as appeared necessary for the immediate comfort and convenience of His Majesty's Household. These are the general rules to which I have endeavoured always strictly to adhere. With regard to the note of the 16th instant I admit most fully that I acted incautiously in writing it without having previously ascertained whether the orders for the removal of the pulpit, to which it refers, were given by His Majesty or not. But my error is one of inadvertence, and my conscience acquits me of intentional disrespect to His Majesty. Had I had the slightest conception that His Majesty had personally directed the removal of the pulpit, so far from appearing to question the authority, I would have done everything in my power to promote an immediate compliance with His Majesty's wishes.

I cannot conclude without assuring your Lordship that deeply as the interests of myself and of my family are now at stake, the greatest grief which I shall suffer will arise from the painful reflection that I have incurred His Majesty's displeasure.

I have been honored with many marks of His Majesty's most gracious goodness. It will be of those marks of goodness, no otherwise merited by me than by my sincere and dutiful attachment to his Royal person, that I shall, when dismissed from his service, cherish an unceasing recollection; and with truth may I add that no subject of His Majesty could feel more gratitude than I shall for all past favours.

Horse Guards, October 21, 1823.

SIR HENRY TORRENS has communicated to me a letter with which he was honored by the King, early this morning, disapproving of the arrangements made, at the pressing requisition of His Majesty's Government, and in pursuance of instructions from the Commander-in-Chief, for the purpose of sending a reinforcement to the West Indies.

I feel, therefore, anxious not to lose a moment in requesting that you will submit to His Majesty, with the humble expression of my duty, that the arrangement made had been the subject of much communication with Lord Bathurst and the Commander-in-Chief, and one of extreme difficulty and embarrassment, in consequence of the reduced state of the infantry in Great Britain, and of the objections which unfortunately occur to drawing more than one battalion from Ireland, and that, after much hesitation and various proposals, the arrangement which has, I grieve to learn, experienced His Majesty's disapproval, was suggested by myself as the only practicable expedient in the extreme urgency of the moment. To effect even this, it has become necessary to apply to the Ordnance and the Admiralty to provide the means of relieving the 12th regt. in the duties at Chatham and Sheerness.

It was unadvisable to order that regt. for immediate embarkation as, in consequence of its station at Sheerness, it had become unhealthy, and there is not another corps of infantry in Great Britain which, in respect of numbers or in any other view is fit for embarkation for *any* station.

The orders from His Majesty's Government were most pressing and appeared to admit of no delay whatever, and the Commander-in-Chief, when this arrangement was finally suggested, immediately wrote from Cheveley to His Majesty the letter which I received from H.R.H., with the intimation of his approval, and which I had the honor of forwarding to His Majesty yesterday morning.

If there has been any omission of due form, and any unjustifiable haste upon this occasion, the blame rests with me only, for having proceeded upon the presumption of the King's approval of what was submitted in H.R.H.'s letter, and I must, in the absence of the Commander-in-Chief, take it wholly to myself and throw myself upon His Majesty's mercy, trusting that His Majesty will be graciously pleased, with that indulgence which I have so often experienced, to make allowance for the anxiety which I felt to give immediate effect to the instructions I had received, under circumstances so urgent, as also for the difficulty and embarrassment to which the military department are subject from the unprecedented want of means. These have of late been quite unequal to the *ordinary* duties at home and it has been impossible, in many instances, to provide for those most indispensable without resorting to expedients very inconvenient to the service in general, and ruinous to the discipline of the troops. One effect of this reduction of means has recently been the suspension of the reliefs to foreign stations, and the difficulties attending *extraordinary* cases have unfortunately become too apparent upon this occasion. I have *personally* to lament, as a painful consequence of such a state of things, His Majesty's displeasure in respect to the measures suggested to meet the evil.

1100 SIR HENRY TORRENS *to the* KING

Fulham, Oct. 21, 1823.
½ past three o'clock.

I HAVE this moment been honored by your Majesty's commands, conveyed to me in your Majesty's letter of the 20th instant; and without presuming to trouble your Majesty by any explanation of the circumstances of extreme emergency which have led to an anticipation of your Majesty's approval of the arrangement for reinforcing the West Indies, I hasten humbly to assure your Majesty that, in obedience to your Majesty's commands, I have given the necessary orders for countermanding the march of the Fuziliers, as well as that of the detachment of Guards which were intended to relieve that corps at Windsor.

I have the honor to be, Sir, with the most profound devotion and respect [etc.].

1101 THE EARL OF LIVERPOOL *to the* KING

Walmer Castle, Octr. 22, 1823.

LORD LIVERPOOL feels it to be his duty to lose not a moment in laying before your Majesty the enclosed letter, which he has this moment received from Col. Stephenson.

Lord Liverpool has such reliance on the kindness of your Majesty's disposition, that he would fain hope that your Majesty may be induced to overlook what has passed, and not insist upon the execution of the order which your Majesty has given Lord Liverpool for the dismissal of Col. Stephenson. But whatever may be your Majesty's final determination, after your Majesty shall have been so good as to consider the humble apology of Col. Stephenson, which Lord Liverpool cannot do otherwise than lay before you, it will be Lord Liverpool's duty, as well as inclination to obey your Majesty's commands, and if your Majesty shall continue to require the removal of Col. Stephenson, to endeavour to make the arrangement for the discharge of the duties of the Board of Works which may be likely to be, in all respects, most satisfactory to your Majesty.

1102 THE EARL OF LIVERPOOL *to the* KING

Walmer Castle, Octr. 23, 1823.

LORD LIVERPOOL requests your Majesty's permission to acknowledge in the most humble and dutiful terms, his deep sense of your Majesty's goodness in permitting Col. Stephenson, at Lord Liverpool's solicitude, to remain in his situation at the head of the Board of Works.

Your Majesty may rely upon Lord Liverpool giving Col. Stephenson a proper reproof, and making him duly sensible of your Majesty's kindness, and Lord Liverpool will lose no time in endeavouring, in conjunction with Mr. Arbuthnot, according to your Majesty's commands, to make such arrangements as to the conduct of the business of the Board of Works as may relieve your Majesty from any further inconvenience or trouble.

1103 GEORGE CANNING *to the* KING

Saltram, Oct. 23, 1823.

MR. CANNING has signified to Lord Granville your Majesty's gracious pleasure as to his appointment to succeed Lord Clancarty at The Hague, and as to his further eventual destination, and he is desired by Lord Granville to lay him, in all humility, at your Majesty's feet, with the expression of his humble and dutiful acknowledgments for your Majesty's grace and favour.

Mr. Canning took the liberty of sending for your Majesty's perusal, to Ld. Francis Conyngham, the last private letter which he received from Lord Clancarty. He now presumes to lay before your Majesty the copy of the answer which he has returned to it. He thought it much most advisable to avoid entering into any discussion, *after the event*, either of Lord Clancarty's reasons for seeking an explanation with the King of the Netherlands, or of the result of that explanation.

1104 GEORGE CANNING *to the* EARL OF CLANCARTY

Saltram, Oct. 22, 1823.

YOUR letter of the 14th has followed me to this distant part of the country, where, finding myself under the same roof with Lord Granville, I have had an opportunity of communicating to him generally the topicks of your letter to Planta; and I have the pleasure to inclose a letter from Lord Granville to your Lordship, which I hope will be satisfactory to you in all those respects.

Your Lordship will, of course, consult your own convenience entirely as to the time of your return. Your appointments will, equally of course, continue till the end of the current quarter. Lord Granville will be at The Hague in January.

The King, I know, has written to your Lordship, in answer to your letter to His Majesty, and, no doubt, has touched upon the points to which you refer. But, as I had obtained H.M.'s permission to leave town for a short time before H.M. wrote, I did not in this instance see His My's letter.

I can as confidently vouch for Baron Fagel as for myself (and as it is impossible to vouch a negative)—that he was not any more than myself the channel of any communication to His Majesty.

Your Lordship will, I am sure, have found reason to be quite satisfied that he knew nothing of what has been passing since. I am ever, my dear Lord [etc.].

1105 GEORGE CANNING *to the* KING

Saltram, Oct. 23, 1823.

MR. CANNING humbly apprehends that, in his desire to avoid troubling your Majesty with unnecessary detail respecting the matter pending at the India House, he may have occasioned your Majesty a greater degree of solicitude on Lord Hastings's account than the circumstances of the case warrant.

There is no imputation of personal corruption against Lord Hastings. The extent of the blame imputed to his Lordship is that of a too kind and anxious protection of a person concerned in the transactions carried on at Hyderabad, which, unluckily, turn out to be much greater in amount, and to implicate a greater number of individuals than was originally known. It was the arrival of despatches, containing some aggravating particulars of this sort the week before last that induced (as was supposed) the friends of Lord Hastings in the Court of Directors to postpone the renewal of the motion in his Lordship's favour. Such a motion was expected to be made by Mr. Elphinstone[1] on the Wednesday after Mr. Canning waited upon your Majesty at Windsor Castle. And Mr. Canning had reason to be assured that, if brought forward on that day, the motion would be carried, though not, perhaps by a large majority. On Wednesday Mr. Canning was informed that the above-mentioned despatches had arrived, and that they were to be "read in Court" (according to the custom of the India House) that day, which Mr. Canning's informant thought an unlucky coincidence. On the following day he received the further information that Mr. Elphinstone had left the Court during the reading of the despatches, so that his expected motion dropped, without the formality of a postponement. The inference was that Mr. Elphinstone had also thought that the coincidence of the topicks suggested by the despatches with those by which his motion was to be introduced would be unfavourable, not, perhaps, to its positive success, but to the temper of the discussion. Mr. Canning's informant had no direct communication with Mr. Elphinstone, and could not therefore, state as a *fact* that such *were* Mr. Elphinstone's motives. But it appears highly probable; and the course pursued by that gentleman appears to have been more judicious than if he had suffered, on that occasion, any discussion to arise, even on a question of postponement. The motion is now considered as still pending, and Mr. Canning sees no reason to fear but that, brought forward at a proper time, it will be carried. That time, however, may possibly not arrive until the instructions to the Bengal Governm^t on the subject of the despatches in question, which Mr. Canning understands to be in preparation, and which will probably be the last that will have reference to the conduct of Lord Hastings's Government in the affair of Hyderabad, shall have passed the Court of Directors.

1106 THE EARL OF LIVERPOOL *to the* KING

Walmer Castle, Oct. 23rd 1823.

LORD LIVERPOOL has the honour to enclose the copy of a letter which he has address'd to the Dean and Chapter of Windsor, in obedience to your Majesty's commands.

1 William Fullerton Elphinstone.

Lord Liverpool has been quite *positive* and *distinct* upon the subject of your Majesty's order, but it has been necessary for him to be cautious in the manner of expressing himself, as your Majesty will recollect that the Dean and Chapter rest their application on the ground of a sort of *legal right* for which, they say, they gave up an equivalent in the time of King Charles the Second. It was upon this account *only* that Lord Liverpool hesitated whether he should return any answer to the letter before he had consulted the Chancellor, but he is quite satisfied the answer now returned is safe, and ought to answer every purpose.

1107 THE EARL OF LIVERPOOL *to the* DEAN AND CHAPTER OF WINDSOR

Copy.

Walmer Castle, Oct. 23d 1823.

LORD LIVERPOOL has laid before the King the letter of the Dean of Windsor, written on behalf of himself and of the Chapter, on the subject of their privilege to have access at all times to the Terrace at Windsor Castle.

Lord Liverpool is commanded by the King to inform the Dean and Chapter of Windsor that, as His Majesty could never have chosen Windsor Castle for his Royal residence unless the privacy of the Terrace could have been secured, and His Majesty thereby not exposed to be overlooked and interrupted at all periods of the day, it is impossible for His Majesty to make any relaxation or alteration in the order which he has directed to be enforced during the time he may think proper to reside in Windsor Castle.

1108 THE EARL OF ELDON *to the* KING

Hamilton Place, Oct. 29, 1823.

THE LORD CHANCELLOR, after offering to your Majesty his most humble duty, has the honor to mention that Mr. Alderman Waithman is to be presented to the Chancellor for your Majesty's approbation of the choice by which he has become Lord Mayor elect. The Lord Chancellor humbly thinks that it is adviseable that your Majesty should grant that approbation, as it cannot but be attended, he thinks with great inconvenience to withhold it, and the Chancellor is not aware of any instance of withholding it.

Walmer Castle, Novr. 3, 1823.

LORD LIVERPOOL presents his humble duty to your Majesty, and begs your Majesty's permission to be allowed to recall to your Majesty's recollection that when, in the month of Jany. last, your Majesty was pleased to sanction the new arrangements in your Government respecting the offices of Chancellor of the Exchequer and President of the Board of Trade,[1] your Majesty was pleased to say "that if Lord Liverpool should think the admission of Mr. Huskisson into the Cabinet for the good of the publick service, Lord Liverpool need not hesitate in summoning him to it".

Lord Liverpool was duly sensible of your Majesty's goodness, and requested your Majesty's permission "to assure Mr. Huskisson that, in consideration of his services and of the many years which he had held official situations of trust and confidence under the Crown, your Majesty would have no objection to authorize the admission of Mr. Huskisson into the Cabinet, after he shall have held the Presidency of the Board of Trade for a twelvemonth, or sooner, if from any circumstances the present numbers of the Cabinet should be reduced".

Lord Liverpool ventures, therefore, to submit to your Majesty that, as Lord Bathurst has summoned a Cabinet for the 18th of this month, principally for the consideration of the present state of the West Indies, and as the business for which the Cabinet is summoned is materially connected with the business of the department of which Mr. Huskisson is the head, your Majesty will be so kind as to authorise Lord Liverpool to direct a summons to be sent to Mr. Huskisson.

1110 THE KING *to the* EARL OF LIVERPOOL

Windsor Castle, 6 November 1823.

A correct copy G.R.

THE KING does not hesitate to give his consent to the admission of Mr. Huskisson into the Cabinet, for the King acquiesced in the proposal soon after the arrangement was made for putting into the hands of Mr. Canning the seals as Secretary of State for the Foreign Department.

The King should have there suffered the renewal of this subject to have passed sub silentio but for the recent retirement of Lord Maryborough,

1 Robinson succeeding Vansittart, and Huskisson succeeding Robinson as President of the Board of Trade, without, however, being admitted to the Cabinet.

whom the King at the time supposed Lord Liverpool to have removed from the Cabinet for the purpose of lessening the numbers of which it is composed; this might have been, perhaps, a reason, altho' a very questionable one, especially as that individual had been sitting in the same Cabinet, with the same members, for the last nine years. But there was a graver consideration, as it appeared to the King, namely, that delicacy and propriety of feeling which should have been observed in relation to the Duke of Wellington, whose extraordinary services to this country puts everything, when brought into competition, entirely in the shade.

It would be difficult to find a man of such consummate integrity, possessing such straightforward, *true* political wisdom, or such unsullied principles, that comprehend everything that is noble, everything that is great. There is in him no weak ambition, no narrowness of mind, no desire but to serve by the best and most honest means his King and his country. Can it be supposed that the Duke of Wellington can view with indifference and without silently feeling what must, indeed, be considered ungracious conduct towards his brother?

The King's letter therefore, to Lord Maryborough upon his appointment as Master of the Buckhounds was written with a view to place him, if possible, above the mortified feelings that must naturally have pressed upon him at the time. This the King felt was justly due to the brother of the Duke of Wellington. Mr. Huskisson may be, and no doubt is a very clever man, but he is not always a prudent one.

The misfortune of this Government is that it is a Government of departments; but Lord Liverpool must endeavor to correct this defect by suppressing the passion which seems to exist for speech making out of time and out of proper place.

What would Mr. Pitt have said if, in his days, sub-Ministers and others belonging to the Government had indulged in such inconvenient practices!

The King intends no unkindness nor embarrassment to Lord Liverpool by these observations, quite the contrary; but as the King passes much of his time in quiet retirement, nothing escapes his observation, although the King may not always consider it necessary to express his feelings.

Whenever the King puts upon his memoranda the word *confidential*, the King desires Lord Liverpool will always consider such communications to be strictly so, and that the contents of the papers may rest solely with themselves.

Russell Square, Novm the 11th 1823.

YOU have given me too much happiness by your kind offices on this occasion, and made me too grateful to His Majesty to make me hesitate to promise the fulfilment of your wishes. I am rather *proud* to say that it is just the thing that I should jealously reserve for a near and valued friend.

I can now hardly be content without your effecting both the measures which you have the prospect of realising in the next week, viz. His Majesty's letter to the Duchess,[1] and the implied permission for my communication with the Cardinal,[2] the true lover of His Majesty, and the most high minded gentleman that, next to the King, and of elevated station, I have ever known.

There are reasons for my taking advantage of your liberal consideration as to the time in which my pleasing tasks for you may be completed, but within it, and probably *much* within it, it shall be finished.

Believe me to remain with increased (though previously great) esteem and regard [etc.].

1112 THE EARL OF MOUNTCHARLES *to* SIR WILLIAM KNIGHTON

Malvern Wells, Nov^br. 19th 1823.

MANY thanks for your affectionate letter which has done me a great deal of good: I feel kindness so much that it always affects me much. I am sure you will think it almost unnecessary that I should say one word of the deep impression His Majesty's most gracious conduct towards me, has made upon me, but I should feel myself wanting in respect if I did not request of you to have the goodness to present my humble duty to him, to assure him that while I live I never can forget, or allow to be absent from my recollection for one moment, all I owe him. Without his most kind interference in my favor I never could have endured a six months' residence at this place, as I probably should not have had the pleasure of repeated visits from you. Do pray say how much I feel, more than I can express. Your kindness about the white wine I acknowledge with many thanks, it is just received. Brent has been very kind, as usual —will you in conversation about me just mention that you know I feel his early attentions. I presume this will find you in town, so I shall direct accordingly. *We* have had a most distressing scene since you were

1 The Duchess of Devonshire.   2 Consalvi.

here, our dear mare proves to have the glanders and was obliged to be returned as unsound. This difficulty is therefore removed. Mrs. C. desires me to say that she only wishes she had had it in her power to make you more comfortable on your visits here, or that you would have allowed her to show you more attention. She is very thankful for your kind remembrances. Our plans at present are that she should go up on Monday week, and I follow on Friday. She will by that time be comfortably settled in a house, to which I shall go immediately, *without* first going to Pall Mall. I perfectly agree about Brighton; after what you know, would it not be better for Mrs. C. to arrange to stay in town, she might get a house more readily for a few months than for one only: & I should then propose to you, that if the King's pleasure was that I should pay my respects at the Pavilion at any time, my stay should not exceed the usual visiting time of others, and thus avoid any unpleasant annoyance which I should have to endure. Pray, if you have time, give me a line to say if these things are to be so.

1113 THE DUKE OF DEVONSHIRE *to the* KING

Rome, Nov. 20th 1823.

YOUR MAJESTY'S kindness about the monument to Canova[1] has given the greatest pleasure to the Duchess, and I only waited for seeing her to obey your Majesty's commands that we should name a sum for the subscription. The Duchess agrees with me in wishing it to be £200, concluding that yr Majesty will probably give the same to the other monument at Venice. The Duchess will announce that yr. Majesty subscribes, but without mentioning the sum till it has received your sanction by the necessary orders being given.

I have seen the Cardinal Consalvi, who, I regret to say, is extremely unwell; he was very much delighted with the kind expressions and recollection of yr. Majesty which I conveyed to him; he begged me to say everything to express his devotion and gratitude. He has no share in the new Government; his successor, the Cardinal Sommaglia, is eighty-two years old. Consalvi has, however, been received by Leo the 12th[2] with marked attention and kindness.

I had the pleasure of finding the Duchess at Naples, where Clifford carried me in the Euryalus from Genoa; the voyage was most delightful,

1 The Italian sculptor (1757–1822).
2 Pope, from 1823 to 1829.

though stormy, but in a large ship the difference is wonderful, and I can now understand yr Majesty's fondness for the sea.

Madame de Lieven is staying at Florence, regretting England and not very much pleased with Italy. At Milan we were much together, and her influence with Rossini[1] made him exert himself in the most amusing manner. Her health seemed improved by travelling.

1114 THE DUKE OF YORK *to the* KING

Stable Yard, November 21, 1823.

I HAVE just seen Sir William Knighton, who has made the confidential communication to me which your Majesty was graciously pleased to direct, and I hasten to express to your Majesty the deep sense which I entertain of the affectionate and fraternal feelings which have prompted you to consider my interests in the proposed arrangement for the raising a sum of money upon your Majesty's receipts from Hannover.

I shall ever consider that as a further proof of that kindness and attachment which has subsisted between us since our childhood, and therefore cannot hesitate in availing myself of this offer, and in concurring with your Majesty in any arrangement or settlement which may be required on my part upon this matter.

1115 THE BISHOP OF ST DAVID'S[2] *to* [SIR WILLIAM KNIGHTON]

Abergwelty Palace, Nov. 22, 1823.

THE two notes which I had the pleasure of receiving with your obliging letter this morning I have here returned. For the kind expressions concerning me in your own note to Lord John Townsend[3] I return you many thanks.

The valuable name of Lord John Townsend will add strength to the Royal Society of Literature. I have written by this day's post to the Vice-President, who presided at the meeting on the 19th inst., to desire

1 The Italian composer (1792–1868).
2 Dr Thomas Burgess (1756–1837), Bishop of St David's, 1803–25; subsequently Bishop of Salisbury.
3 Lord John Townshend (1757–1833), second son of the first Marquess Townshend.

him to propose Lord John Townsend at the next meeting of the Society.[1]

I cannot lose this opportunity of informing you that on Monday last I went to Lampeter to inspect the progress of the building of St. David's College, and I have the gratification of adding that one half of the College, including the Chapel, the Master's lodgings and rooms for thirty-one students and one of the lecturers, will be roofed in by Christmas next. His Majesty's very gracious approbation and support of this undertaking continues to have a very beneficial influence on the contributions to it.

I most sincerely participate in the satisfaction expressed by Lord John Townsend at the continuance of His Majesty's health and spirits.

1116 THE KING *to the* DUKE OF WELLINGTON

28 November 1823.

A true copy G.R.

CIRCUMSTANCES are so continually occurring to bring you nearer and nearer to me, that our mutual confidence must now be considered as complete, and can only be separated by the termination of life.

Whenever, therefore, I shall wish to use you as my friend, I shall do so without hesitation, and in the strictest sense of the word.

After conveying to you these sentiments, you will not be surprised that I should make the present communication, as I well know that it will not only be agreeable to the best affections of your heart, but add to your happiness; and I must say that it is the influence of these feelings which have, in a great degree, prompted me to do what I am about to do on the present occasion.

I have reason to know that our poor friend Arbuthnot's affairs are in the most desperate and wretched state, and without some immediate and most material relief his present situation must not only be abandoned, in all probability, but it would be necessary for him to quit (for a time at least) this country.

Under these circumstances, I have resolved, as soon as I can borrow the money, which I believe will be in a few days, to send him, through you, fifteen thousand pounds. I beg, my dear friend, that in doing this,

1 There is an account of the foundation of the Royal Society of Literature in *Gent. Mag.*, 1823, I, 543–46.

you will say everything kind and affectionate to Mr. and Mrs. Arbuthnot, because I know how much you love and regard them.

I wish you would contrive to be in town on Saturday at latest, for reasons which will be explained to you by my confidential friend, who will call at your house on that day.[1]

1117 CHARLES ARBUTHNOT *to* [SIR WILLIAM KNIGHTON]

Whitehall Place, Thursday, 27 Nov. 1823.

YOU have sometimes flattered me by saying that I know how to express what I mean. I am sure that on the present occasion I cannot express what I feel; for who is the person that was ever so treated and so favoured as I am? Lay me at the King's feet, and tell him, I pray you, that he may guess a little from what is passing in his own heart at the effusions of gratitude which pour forth from mine. I cannot feel that I have ever done more in my attempts to serve His Majesty than what my bounden duty required; but strange indeed wd be my disposition were I not rivetted to him heart and soul, and my prayer is that in my obedience to his commands and in devotion to his wishes zeal may be taken in account for my lack of means.

May God shower down every blessing upon him.

I fear that what I wrote to you was ill expressed and ill understood. Knowing as I do how fond you all are of the Duke of Wellington, I thought you wd like to see in what light he considered me and my services to the *Government*. It was in the *restricted* sense as applied to *Ministers alone* that he was expressing himself when he spoke of the claims w[hi]ch I had upon *them*, and it was solely and wholly in that *restricted* sense that I made the communication to you as from one friend to another.

Alas, I never could have so served the King as to give me claims upon him; and even had it been possible that any such claims existed, I should have felt myself to have been repaid a thousandfold by the extraordinary condescension and unmerited goodness with which I am ever treated.

1 Nothing is known about Arbuthnot's financial position at this time. He had resigned the Secretaryship of the Treasury owing to ill-health, in February 1823, and Liverpool had given him the less arduous office of First Commissioner of Woods and Forests. In leaving the Treasury, however, he sacrificed £2000 a year, but at the end of 1823 Lord Bathurst, at Wellington's request, offered him the Ceylon Agency which Huskisson had resigned, and which was worth £1200 a year (£1100 net); and a few weeks earlier, apparently, Mrs Arbuthnot was given a pension of £1200 a year. (*Huskisson Papers*, p. 173.)

Pray, therefore, efface from yr mind the misconception which appears to have arisen. It delighted me that the Duke so thought of me, and I was very sure it wd delight you also. But all this was with reference to my claims, if claims there are any, UPON THE MINISTERS.

I cannot tell you, my dear friend, how much and how strongly I feel your kindness. I can give you no other return than that I am and ever shall be [etc.].

[P.S.] As desired I return the letter. I will be with you tomorrow morning.

1118 COUNT MÜNSTER *to the* KING

Grosvenor Place, 29 November 1823.

I AM going, without a moment's delay, to obey your Majesty's commands at Mr. Harrison's.

The enclosed letter I intended to have layd myself before your Majesty, that I might not apear guilty of having concealed from you the real state of our finances, which, of course, I could not explain to anybody else.

I am, with the profoundest veneration, [etc.].

[*Enclosure.*]

GEORGE HARRISON *to* COUNT MÜNSTER.

4 Spring Garden Terrace, 29 November 1823. (*Copy.*)

Mr. George Harrison has the honor to present his best respects to Count Munster, and to acknowledge the receipt of his Excellency's note of yesterday. Mr. Harrison has in consequence written to Mr. Rothschild to desire he will furnish him, for Count Munster's information, with an accurate account of the present state of the former loan of £50,000, and how much still remains to be paid off.

Mr. Harrison imagines that in point of fact, the *interest* (at the rate of 5 per cent) as well as the principal, of the former loan, has actually been paid out of the Hanoverian funds. But upon this point Mr. Harrison cannot speak with any confidence until he shall have seen Mr. Rothschild.

Mr. Harrison has understood that it is His Majesty's intention *now* to mortgage the Hanoverian income until the proposed loan of £125,000 and *also the interest thereon*, at the rate of 5 per cent shall be repaid. The period which this will require will be about six years, viz. five years for the principal, and about one year more on account of the interest. The payments of interest and principal upon the new loan cannot of course commence until the former loan is completely satisfied. But it does not occur to Mr. Harrison that this circumstance need create any impediment to the *immediate* completion of the arrangements for the new loan—as the only effect of it would be that the application of the Hanoverian income to the liquidation of the *new* loan will be deferred in its commencement for a short period.

If Mr. Harrison had been able, he would, with Count Munster's permission, have done himself the honor of waiting upon his Excellency, as five minutes of conversation often does more to clear up little difficulties in matters of business, than volumes of correspondence. But he has been for several days, and still is, confined to his bedchamber by a severe attack of gout. If Count Munster could, without inconvenience, do Mr. Harrison the honor of calling upon him this morning he will be happy to receive his Excellency at any hour which may be most convenient to him.

1119 CHARLES ARBUTHNOT *to* SIR WILLIAM KNIGHTON

Whitehall Place,
Tuesday night 2nd. Decr. 1823.

I CAME up with a load of misery upon my heart—I go down with one so light and free that I know not my own thoughts and feelings. With everything at home to make me happy, I still was a wretched being; and you have turned me into a most happy one. But you have done more than this—you have made happy one of the very best of women—one whose strength of mind has supported me under the severest trials, and one who will ever join with me in thanks and gratitude to you.

May God bless you.

The King was angelic. Keep him in the feeling that he saved me from perdition, and that in gratitude at least I am nothing wanting. I cannot but think that my short letter did not express all thought [*sic*] it ought to have done. Recollect the painter who, in despair, could not attempt to show the face of anguish, and therefore hid the face altogether. I could show nothing, but I felt a great deal.

I leave town very early tomorrow morning.

I ought to have returned the enclosed some days ago, but has not my mind been so over occupied that I cd do nothing and think of nothing?

I believe that Bates explained that the Act of P[arliamen]t was so in our teeth as to prevent our aiding Lord Conyngham. I am indeed most sorry; but Bates said that you felt there was nothing to be done but to return the papers to you, and therefore I do so. Goodbye, my dear friend [etc.].

I will not rest till I get Col. Hawker's settled; and glad shall I be when there is a vacancy here. Pray let me hear from you.

1120 CHARLES ARBUTHNOT *to the* KING

Carlton House, 2nd Decr. 1823.

YOUR MAJESTY has told me not to say one word. Oh Sir what words could I say? May I not say that my beloved Sovereign has made two beings happy, & that those two beings were even long since devoted to him?

Without you Sir we should have been lost. Your Majesty has saved us & made us most happy.

May God shower down every blessing upon your Majesty, and that I may be allowed to have the means of proving my devotion & my gratitude is the fervent prayer of [etc.].

1121 GEORGE HARRISON *to the* KING

4 *Spring Garden Terrace*,
2^{d} December 1823.

MR. GEORGE HARRISON, presents his most humble duty to your Majesty, and has the honor of transmitting and giving an account to your Majesty, of the sum of one hundred and twenty five thousand pounds, being the amount of a loan contracted for with the House of Rothschild and Sons of Frankfort on your Majesty's Hanoverian income.

This sum Mr. George Harrison received, and therefore now transmits in the following order, namely,

No. 1. Packet containing fifty five thousand pounds.

No. 2. Packet containing fifty thousand pounds.

No. 3. Packet containing fifteen thousand pounds

and five thousand pounds put by as a fund for secret and collateral services connected with your Majesty's service.

Mr. George Harrison humbly hopes that your Majesty's usual affectionate approbation will be extended to him, by beleiving that he has contracted for this loan on the best terms that he was enabled to effect with Mr. Rothschild and it is his duty to observe that this gentleman has behaved with great loyalty and honesty towards your Majesty, as it appears to Mr. Harrison in everything relating to this transaction.

1122 THE KING *to the* DUKE OF YORK

Carlton Palace, 3 December 1823.

I CANNOT sufficiently express to you the pleasure I really feel that I have it in my power to transmit to you the sum of fifty thousand pounds, which I have raised on my Hanover income for your benefit.

You know well the real brotherly affection I have for you, & when I venture to hint to you, to lay aside those collateral expenses which are generally continued from the influence of habit, I am sure you will not take it amiss; because had I myself continued on the turf &c, it might have been difficult, without great inconvenience to the country, for me to have fulfilled the high duties of my present high station.

In this suggestion I have no motive, no feeling, but what arises from the purest source; do not therefore answer this, nor recur to it in conversation, because I wish that the few years which may be left to either of us, should be pass'd in uninterrupted friendship & the warmest affection.

1123 THE DUKE OF YORK *to the* KING

Stable Yard, December 3, 1823.

I HAVE received from Sir William Knighton the sum of fifty thousand pounds. Receive from me all that I can give, my devoted affection.

1124 MRS ARBUTHNOT *to* SIR WILLIAM KNIGHTON

Woodford, Decr. 4, 1823.

MR. ARBUTHNOT has, as you may imagine, communicated to me all that has been passing in London, and, as I find that His Majesty has condescended to name me in the letters which he has written to the Duke of Wellington and to Mr. Arbuthnot, I cannot help requesting that you will lay at His Majesty's feet the warm expression of my gratitude and thanks for the most kind and generous manner in which he has pressed forward to assist Mr. Arbuthnot in his difficulties. I assure you I cannot find words to express my sense of His Majesty's kindness, and I must trust to you to say to His Majesty for me whatever you may judge most right and proper. It is, however, most true that His Majesty's generous kindness could not have been bestowed upon one more sensible of it, and I assure you he has no subjects more loyally and devotedly attached to him than Mr. Arbuthnot and myself.

Let me take this opportunity of expressing to you how much I have felt the kind anxiety you have shewn in this business. I know it will be a reward to you to tell you that you have sent Mr. Arbuthnot back to me the happiest man in England.

1125 SIR HENRY BATE DUDLEY *to* SIR WILLIAM KNIGHTON

Chitterton, Dec. 7th 1823.

MR. ARBUTHNOT having probably left town without seeing you since my interview with him on Tuesday, it may not be improper in me briefly to state to you what passed on this occasion.

The remunerative proposal he had to make was introduced in so kind a manner, that, though it fell short of my expectation, I readily, and I trust not ungratefully acceded to it.—viz. £300 in advance, and the same sum annually on the 1st of December.

On returning to me the letters of Earl Moira and Col. McMahon, he remarked "that it would be handsome in me to put them into the fire", which I instantly did, assuring him, at the same time, that I should have the further satisfaction of destroying the unpleasant correspondence and every other paper connected with so embarrassing a subject.[1]

1 He wrote to Lord Liverpool on 7 February 1823 from Ely College: "...I must entreat your Lordship to consider my application to an exalted personage as totally distinct from any claim for public service, and that my Baronetcy and Church preferment were bestowed upon me by the Prince Regent for the faithful discharge of antecedent duties, under a Royal promise *guaranteed by Lord Moira more than thirty years ago*!

"Sir William [Knighton] will probably inform your Lordship that from a continuance of embarrassing disappointments I am at length rendered incapable of remaining a resident Magistrate for this Isle, or the County of Cambridge." He refers too to the "pecuniary losses and personal privations which I sustained in his [the King's] most confidential service". (Add. MSS. 38292, fo. 152.) He wrote a further letter to the Prime Minister on 19 April 1823:

"I imparted to Sir William Knighton a few days since for the information of an exalted personage, that I was disposed cheerfully to relinquish my pretensions to any higher promotion

Alluding to the long misunderstanding that had arisen between yourself and me, he observed "that from his own personal knowledge your endeavours to serve me had been sincere and unremitting". It was impossible to receive so earnest an assurance from so friendly a quarter without a suitable impression.

Towards the close of our conversation he noticed the gracious intention of an exalted personage respecting my wife, which you stated when he met us at Carlton House, and said that he would see you upon it. This mark of regal favour will perfect his gracious beneficence towards us, and enable us with cheerfulness and comfort to enter upon that more humble state to which a reverse of fortune has destined us.

1126 THE KING *to* GEORGE CANNING
Copy.

Pavilion, December 1823.

THE KING sends his regards to Mr. Canning.

The King approves of the answer to Gen. Mina's[1] very proper letter; but the King desires to observe that expressions of commiseration towards such individuals must be limited, or this country will soon be filled with all those turbulent spirits that seem so ready to seek for a cause to disturb the peace of Europe, and of which description we have, God knows, a sufficient number amongst ourselves.

1127 THE KING *to* GEORGE CANNING
Copy.

Pavilion, December 1823.

THE KING was much surprised to find from his friend Sir William Knighton how entirely the obliging intention of Mr. Canning's note relative to the key of the F.F.F. boxes had been overlooked and mistaken by the King.

in the Church, rather than subject His Majesty's Government to any further embarrassment on this occasion....

"In addition to the common privations attendant on adverse fortune, I have found it necessary to devote the whole property I possessed, together with my professional income, to meet the just demands of my creditors, and also painfully to retire from the Magistracy of this Isle...." (Add. MSS. 38293, fo. 389.)

1 The reactionary rule of the despotic Ferdinand VII of Spain had provoked a revolutionary movement, and General Mina had been placed at the head of the rebel forces. Early in 1823 a French army entered Spain, suppressed the rising, and restored Ferdinand to power.

It is very true that a second key, and which the King *has not,* would often be a matter of great convenience.

Mr. Canning and, indeed, the whole of the King's Government must be aware that the King, from time to time, is under the necessity of calling upon Sir William Knighton to fulfil those duties that would naturally attach to the office of the King's Private Secretary.

The King, as soon as Sir William Knighton was appointed Keeper of the King's Privy Purse, put the whole of his private affairs under his immediate control and management, and the King has had the most substantial reason to be satisfied with that confidence which the King has so implicitly placed in him.

Under these circumstances the King desires that Mr. Canning will send a key of the F.F.F. boxes to be placed in the hands of Sir William Knighton, for purposes connected with the King's private convenience.

1128 GEORGE CANNING *to the* KING

Foreign Office, Decr. 12, 1823.

MR. CANNING, in obedience to your Majesty's commands, humbly transmits to your Majesty a spare key of the F.F.F. boxes.

1129 LORD FRANCIS CONYNGHAM *to* SIR WILLIAM KNIGHTON

Foreign Office, Dec. 13th/23.

THE key, as you know, was sent last night; His Majesty's letter to Mr. C[anning] was a very proper and good one; immediately I read it, I perceived who had helped to write it. Mr. C. made no comment whatsoever upon it. Did not the K. feel some repugnance at confessing that he had mistaken Mr. C.'s letter?

Mr. C. is fearful it must have annoyed him. He certainly is pleased that the affair has ended thus.

Mr. C. is at present confined to his bed by the gout; this has prevented him speaking much on the subject; besides, you are aware how irritable such an attack always makes a person, more especially Mr. C., who is never over cool in his mind. I trust everything is going on well at Brighton.

Will you find out whether I am to send any further invitations for Xmas beyond the list you gave me when you were in town.

Planta is gone on a shooting party for a day or two. I am therefore alone at the office. May I beg you to present my humble duty to the King, and believe me always affly yrs.

1130 SIR WILLIAM KNIGHTON *to* LORD FRANCIS CONYNGHAM

Pavilion, 14 December 1823.

YOUR mother proposes to write to you herself on what may relate to further invitations; all that have hitherto been invited, come, so that your numbers begin to count largely!

I came up to town on Wednesday, and I return on Saturday; if you choose to come down with me the best corner of my carriage will be at your service.

No! There was no disgust excited; some surprise was expressed, and then a voluntary desire to write the letter which you have seen.

We have nothing to do with your friend's[1] irritability, except in taking good care not to be in the slightest degree inconvenienced by it; laws are framed and acted upon by the joint efforts of different individuals, but the happiness and delight of gracious favour, kindness and protection must always emanate from Royal authority and from that only, until such authority be extinguished. That time, I hope, is not yet arrived. It may be as well, perhaps, to remember this. Do you understand me? I hope so.

The King commands me to send you his warm affection, and to express the real pleasure H.M. feels at the prospect of again seeing you here.

1131 THE EARL OF LIVERPOOL *to the* KING

Coombe Wood, Dec. 15, 1823.

LORD LIVERPOOL has had the honour of receiving your Majesty's letter on the subject of the Green Ribbon vacant by the death of Lord Erskine.

Your Majesty may depend upon Lord Liverpool not coming to any conclusion as to the most proper mode of disposing of it before he has had an opportunity of hearing your Majesty's oppinion and wishes.

1 Canning's.

Pavilion, 16 December 1823.

I HAD the honor of reading your letter to the King; His Majesty expressed himself in the most gracious and affectionate terms towards you; entered into all your private feelings and would be truly happy if any opportunity should arise by which your numerous family could be benefitted in the manner you desire.

I am, however, commanded to state that, from the Constitution of this country, it is always inconvenient for the King to name particular individuals to his Ministers for lucrative situations because it is an interference with that patronage which enables the Minister, or at least assists in carrying on the Government for the benefit of the country.

Under these circumstances, His Majesty can only say that whatever the Minister could propose for your benefit would at all times be truly agreeable to H.M.'s feelings.

1133 THE MARQUIS OF HASTINGS's *Memorandum*

[*c*. 1823.]

BY executing the duties of Commander-in-Chief without receiving the salary, I saved to the Company seven thousand pounds ster[ling] annually from the time of Sir G. Nugent's departure. As that salary was a consolidated one, which involved all other allowances, tho' I did not receive it, I regarded myself as precluded from any collateral conveniences by the title of the appointment, and I never even drew forage for my horses.

The Court possesses the statement that during my administration, notwithstanding the unprecedented exertions which took place, the supplies from India to England averaged annually one million three hundred and twelve thousand pounds ster[ling] while the annual average for the twenty preceding years was but four hundred and twenty five thousand pounds. In both cases, the supplies are the balances beyond the supplies received *from* England.

By having attained such a command of the money market as enabled me to restrict drafts upon the Court for the interest of the Indian debt, I saved to the Company about £250,000 annually. A further pecuniary benefit has since been secured for the Company thro' this condition of the

---

1 Thomas North Graves, second Baron Graves (1775–1830). He was driven to suicide by his wife's infidelity. He had four sons and six daughters.

finances, but it was one which I had considered as unadvisable to be pressed in my time.

The actual receipt of 1821–22 exceeded that of 1813–14 (at the termination of which latter official year I deemed my financial administration to commence) by five millions one hundred and seventy thousand pounds ster[ling]. The difference ought to have been greater by above £400,000, the Government of Bombay having erroneously thrown the *receipt*, to that amount, of a sum due in 1821–22 into the ensuing year. I have calculated the receipt of 1822–23 as exceeding that of 1813–14 by more than six millions.

The Nipaul War, instead of costing the Company a rupee, produced a gain of six hundred thousand pounds ster[ling]. I do not refer to the revenue of territory acquired, but to hard cash placed by me in the Company's treasuries.

I left an ostensible addition to the debt amounting to five millions and a half. But on the latest day to which the cash balances could be made up I had accumulated in the Company's coffers six millions two hundred thousand pounds ster[ling] beyond what I set out with at the close of the official year 1813–14. Of course I could have paid off the added debt, still leaving in the Treasury seven hundred thousand pounds more than I found in it. Such a liquidation would have been highly impolitic, when the Company's bonds, which I had found at twelve per cent discount, were left by me floating between fourteen and sixteen per cent premium.

These financial points have been all certified to the Court by the Company's Accountant General in India.

I have stated to the Court, and the soundness of my calculations has been hitherto experienced, that the net Indian surplus ought not henceforth to be short of four millions ster[ling] annually.

1134 THE EARL OF ELDON *to the* KING

Tuesday evening [January 1824].

THE LORD CHANCELLOR is unable to express, in adequate terms, his grateful sense of your Majesty's kindness.

He believes himself to be recovering fast from a fit of the gout, which he suspects that it was thought necessary to inflict upon him, by producing it, in order to remove the causes of that third attack this year by which he so deeply laments that your Majesty was, on the day he had the honor of dining at Carlton House, disturbed. With the exception of a momentary return of that complaint on Sunday last, and extreme gouty pains for some days, he has had little to complain of; and what he has had to complain of has been abundantly recompensed to him by a return of that confidence as to the state of his mind and understanding of which the two attacks in the course of the Summer had deprived him.

Little progress has been made in the law arrangements. The Chancellor mentioned the Chief Baronship to Mr. Alexander[1] who has requested to be allowed two or three days before he makes his determination. It would occur to your Majesty that Lord L[iverpool] postpones taking into consideration the succession to the Solicitor Generalship[2] till it is fixed who is to be Chief Baron, and, upon that succession matters remain as they were when your Majesty left town.

The Lord Chancellor repeats, most earnestly, his grateful and heart-felt thanks for your Majesty's great kindness.

1135 THE BISHOP OF ST DAVID'S (DR BURGESS) *to* [SIR WILLIAM KNIGHTON]

12 *Upper Montagu St.* Jan. 8th 1824.

THE ROYAL SOCIETY of Literature held their first *ordinary* for the year 1824 yesterday; and it appearing that the Society has lately received a large accession of new members, a wish was expressed by some of the members of the Council that the Society should take upon itself the expence of the dye that has been cut for His Majesty's gold medal. If therefore nothing has been intimated by you to His Majesty on the subject the Society will readily take that charge upon themselves. An interesting paper (the conclusion of a dissertation which has occupied three evenings) on the affinities of languages,[3] by Mr. Sharon Turner, was read yesterday. A valuable memoir on the Euphrates will probably extend through our next three or four *ordinary* meetings, which are on the first and third Wednesdays of every month.[4]

1 Sir William Alexander; appointed Lord Chief Baron, and knighted, January 1824. He resigned in 1831.

2 Wetherell succeeded Sir John Copley (who became Attorney-General, vice Sir Robert Gifford) as Solicitor-General, in January 1824.

3 "On the mutual resemblances discoverable in the languages of nations, not related to each other by known origin or by any geographical contiguity."

4 Sir W. Ouseley contributed a paper entitled "Observations on the River Euphrates", which concluded with a discussion of the site of the Garden of Eden.

Dunbar House, 19th January, 1824.

I HAVE not intruded upon you for a length of time because I have uniformly received from various quarters such good accounts of His Majesty's health as to be quite at ease upon that subject. But I am now going to write to you to communicate to you a little invention of my own which it would give me great pleasure to think produced as much ease and comfort to His Majesty as it has done in my case.

You perfectly well know the lint which is prepared in all hospitals, and indeed in all apothecaries' shops. I have found that by cutting a bit of it exactly the shape of the gold in the inside which fits the gum, and after steeping it in a little tincture of myrrh, placing it upon the gold before the teeth are put into the mouth, that it takes off all the irritation arising from the metal being in contact with the gum, whilst at the same time it fixes the teeth much firmer and more comfortably than they can be fixed without it.

My practice is to do this every morning, and every day before dinner, and my servant can cut the thing accurately to the shape when once he has a pattern. That you may see how easily it is managed I send you a duplicate of the pattern I use. If it is applied to the lint doubled of course you know when it is afterwards opened it makes the complete round. You will observe from the shape that it does not go all the way back, but that from experience I feel to be the preferable mode.

1137 THE EARL OF LIVERPOOL *to the* KING

Fife House, January 21st 1824.

LORD LIVERPOOL has the honour to inform your Majesty that he has just received intelligence of the death of the Bishop of Litchfield and Coventry.[1]

The preferment of most importance vacated by this event is the Deanery of Durham, and Lord Liverpool humbly conceives that he is meeting your Majesty's wishes, as well as his own, by recommending for it the present Dean of Christ Church, Dr. Hall.[2]

It is the only preferment which can properly be proposed for him, and

1 James Cornwallis, fourth Earl Cornwallis (1742–1824). Third son of the first Earl. Succeeded as fourth Earl Cornwallis, 1823. Bishop of Lichfield and Coventry since 1781, and Dean of Durham since 1794.

2 Charles Henry Hall (1763–1827). Dean of Christ Church since 1809; Dean of Durham, 1824–27. See No. 1139.

it is a great publick object to place some other person in the station which he holds at Oxford.

Lord Liverpool would feel very much relieved if your Majesty would permit him to offer the Bishoprick of Litchfield to the Bishop of Gloucester.[1] Lord Liverpool would suggest Dr. Bethel,[2] the Dean of Chichester, for the vacant Bishoprick, whatever it may be, and Dr. Slade[3] for the Deanery of Chichester. He was tutor to the late Duke of Dorset[4] [&] chaplain to Lord Whitworth, when Lord L[ieutenan]t of Ireland, who never had an opportunity of adequately providing for him.

Lord Liverpool will request your Majesty's permission to allow him to defer for a few days the suggestion of the arrangement most proper for filling up the Deanery of Christ Church.

1138 SIR WILLIAM KNIGHTON *to the* EARL OF LIVERPOOL

[January 24th 1824.]

SIR WILLIAM KNIGHTON is obliged to write to Lord Liverpool for the purpose of acquainting his Lordship with the King's indisposition.

His Majesty was seized with a general rheumatic affection on Wednesday evening; on Thursday and yesterday it increased, and today, from very acute pain in the back and loins and one arm, H.M. is unable to move, or even to sit up in his bed.

Under these circumstances the enclosed confidential memorandum has been written by Sir William Knighton by command of His Majesty; and of course the words of this note, and the sentiments expressed, are used under the influence of His Majesty's own personal dictation.

His Majesty is at present unable to sign his name. Sir William Knighton has therefore affixed the seal which His Majesty constantly wears attached to his person.

1 Henry Ryder (1777–1836), Bishop of Gloucester, 1815–24; subsequently Bishop of Lichfield and Coventry. He was the son of Nathaniel Ryder, first Baron Harrowby.
2 Christopher Bethell (1773–1859). Dean of Chichester since 1814. Bishop of Gloucester, 1824–30, and later Bishop of Bangor.
3 The Rev. Samuel Slade now became Dean of Chichester.
4 George John Frederick Sackville, fourth Duke of Dorset (1793–1815).

(*Copy.*)

Pavilion, January 24th 1824.

THE KING in conformity with Lord Liverpool's wishes consents, altho' reluctantly, to the offer being made to the Bishop of Gloucester for his translation to Litchfield and Coventry.

The Bishop of Gloucester is no doubt a pious and good man, and the King is acquainted with many acts of his life which bespeak it; but nevertheless the King, without wishing to say anything unkind or harsh of the Bishop of Gloucester, sees objections to his advancement; which objections, were they to become general among the individuals constituting the bench of Bishops, might be attended with great inconvenience to the State.

With this impression on the King's mind, the Bishop's translation to Lichfield and Coventry should be considered *final*, and no expectations held out to him of a further move.

The King has no objection to Dr. Bethel's advancement; on the contrary, from his great learning, orthodox principles, and general good conduct, the King considers him a most fit person; this is much more satisfactory to the King's feelings for making him a Bishop than political motives, or his having been tutor to a Duke.

The proposal respecting the Deanery of Chichester the King assents to with great pleasure as being conferred on a gentleman who has served usefully in Lord Liverpool's own family connections. But on a future occasion, the King reminds Lord Liverpool, that Dr. Hook[1] must not be forgotten; for the King has long had the private means of knowing how essentially that individual has served both the King and the Government.

The King takes this opportunity of again mentioning that the Dean of Hereford must be the next Bishop; a more excellent man does not live, and the King is much and sincerely attached to him.

The King considers the proposed preferment for the Dean of Christ Church to be very proper, but the King hopes that Lord Liverpool will not fail to look with the most scrupulous care as to the individual to be recommended to the King for the Dean's successor.[2]

1 See No. 1001.
2 Writing in 1826 Liverpool said that had there been no special objections to his promotion, Dr Hall would have been a Bishop twelve or fifteen years ago. "The objection to his promotion to the bench was the situation in which he had placed himself from his embarrassed circumstances. This was obviously a source of infinite evil at such a place as Christ Church." He could be removed from Christ Church only by giving him in exchange "some rich & valuable deanery which he could not refuse", and the Deanery of Durham was considered by the Church equivalent to a Bishopric. (*Yonge*, III, 387–88.)

Fife House, January 25th 1824.

LORD LIVERPOOL has just received the memorandum which your Majesty has been graciously pleased to dictate in answer to Lord Liverpool's letter of the 21st. inst.

Lord Liverpool most deeply regrets the severe rheumatic affection under which your Majesty has been labouring, and he sincerely hopes he may be allowed to hear tomorrow a more favourable account of your Majesty's health.

Lord Liverpool is most truly grateful to your Majesty for your kindness in agreeing to the ecclesiastical arrangements which he has ventured to submit to your Majesty and he most sincerely believes that your Majesty will have no reason to regret of them.

Lord Liverpool will attend to your Majesty's wishes as express'd in favour of the Dean of Hereford and Dr. Hook. Lord Liverpool is fully sensible of the merits of the Dean of Hereford. Lord Liverpool is not certain whether he was educated at Oxford or Cambridge, but he conceives your Majesty to mean that if at the former he should be recommended for the first Bishoprick vacant, if at the latter for the first Cambridge turn, unless the Bishoprick of Chichester should be the first vacancy, in which case a departure may very properly be made from the usual rule in obedience to your Majesty's special commands.

1141 THE EARL OF LIVERPOOL *to* SIR WILLIAM KNIGHTON

Fife House, January 26th 1824.

I HAVE received with the deepest regret and concern your account of the very severe attack of gout which His Majesty has experienced, and from which I was in hopes he would have kept free in consequence of the mildness of the season and the general improvement in his health.

I will be obliged to you if you would let me have daily a line to say how His Majesty is, and I request of you to give my humble duty to His Majesty, to assure him how much I am grieved at his indisposition, and that he may rely that his orders as to the Council previous to the meeting of Parlt and the speech shall be punctually obey'd.

Fife House, January 28th 1824.

LORD LIVERPOOL has the honour to inform your Majesty that he has taken the utmost pains to acquire every information which could be necessary for submitting to your Majesty the recommendation of a proper person for the Deanery of Christ Church.

Lord Liverpool has accordingly consulted Lord Grenville and the Bishop of London, and the latter has had a full communication with the Bishop of Llandaff who recently held the situation of Div[inity] Professor and canon of Christ Church for the space of nearly ten years.

Without taking up your Majesty's time with all that has passed at these deliberations, Lord L. can state to your Majesty that in the opinion of the respectable individuals to whom he has alluded as well as of some others to whom Lord Liverpool has spoken, the two names which can most properly be submitted to your Majesty are those of Dr. Smith,[1] now canon of Christ Church and son of the late Master of Westminster, and Dr. Goodenough the present Master of Westminster.

Dr Smith has been known to Lord Liverpool for more than thirty years; he was tutor at the College & censor during the time of Dr. Cyril Jackson;[2] he was afterwards chaplain to the House of Commons; he had the reputation of being a very good scholar; but what would particularly recommend him upon the present occasion, when the discipline of the College requires re-establishing, he always has been, and is now most highly respected for, a manly, highminded and straight-forward character. The advantages of these qualifications in the head of such a body as Christ Church no one is more competent to appreciate than your Majesty.

Dr. Goodenough was recently likewise tutor and censor at Christ Church; he has been between four and five years Master of Westminster School which he is conducting with great ability and to general satisfaction. He is an excellent scholar and his character very much respected. He is many years younger than Dr. Smith which in one sense may be considered as diminishing his claim, but on the other hand must give him some advantages in point of strength of constitution and vigour, though in neither of these respects (as Lord L. understands) is Dr. Smith deficient.

Under all the present circumstances of the College Lord Liverpool, after mature consideration, would be disposed to recommend Dr. Smith for the Deanery of Christ Church, but he has thought it at the same time

1 The Reverend Samuel Smith.
2 Cyril Jackson (1746–1819), Dean of Christ Church, 1783–1809.

to be his duty to bring the pretensions of Dr. Goodenough under your Majesty's consideration.

Lord Liverpool has thought that it might be a satisfaction to your Majesty to see the letters of Dr. Goodenough [and] Dr. Smith to the Bishop of Llandaff, with the Bishop of London's letter in which it was enclosed to Lord Liverpool.

1143 THE EARL OF LIVERPOOL *to* SIR WILLIAM KNIGHTON

Fife House, January 29th 1824.

I SEND enclosed a draft of the intended speech of Lords Commissioners, and I humbly request His Majesty will have the goodness to keep it till I have the honour of seeing him on Saturday.

The Lord President, the Lord Privy Seal, Mr. Canning, the Chancellor of the Exchequer and Lord Liverpool will attend at Brighton on Saturday.

It will save His Majesty the trouble of another Council if he can take upon himself on Saturday the trouble of settling the Sheriffs. I have the Chancellors authority for saying that the pricking might be performed by any of the Lords in the presence and by the direct authority and orders of the King, but I am afraid His Majesty must sign the roll.

In case therefore His Majesty's state of health should not permit his settling the Sheriffs on Saturday a Council must be held in the course of next week as the Sheriffs must be declared in the Gazette of Saturday sennight.

Mr. Buller will attend on Saturday with the roll in case His Majesty shall be sufficiently well to attend the Council to this business after the speech has been read [*sic*].

I shall send this letter by a special messenger and I trust you will be enabled to send me a favourable account of the progress of His Majesty towards recovery.

1144 THE EARL OF LIVERPOOL *to the* KING

Fife House, February 6th 1824.

LORD LIVERPOOL has the honour to inform your Majesty that, in obedience to your Majesty's commands, he communicated to the Lord Chancellor yesterday the correspondence which had passed with the Dean and Chapter of Windsor respecting the Terrace.

The Lord Chancellor will immediately ask for the Statutes and he has desired Lord Liverpool to say that your Majesty need have no difficulty in excluding the Dean and Chapter from the Terrace, as well as all other persons, during your Majesty's residence in Windsor Castle, as necessary for your Majesty's quiet and comfort.

The Lord Chancellor seems to think that if they (the Dean and Chapter) have any claim to walk upon the Terrace, grounded upon any equivalent they may have formerly given up, such claim (considering its nature) may be *bar'd* by some compensation, but the Lord Chancellor would by no means advise such an idea being thrown out until he has had an opportunity of thoroughly investigating the subject.

1145 EARL BATHURST *to the* KING

Downing Street, February 9th 1824.

LORD BATHURST begs most humbly to acknowledge the receipt of the very gracious letter which your Majesty has vouchsafed to address to him, and will take care that some record is preserved of the very flattering circumstances under which Lord Bathurst was enabled to offer to the Rev. Charles Sumner to submit his name to your Majesty for the Bishopric of Jamaica, and that the appointment did not take place, not in consequence of Mr. Sumner's backwardness to engage in so important a duty but from your Majesty being unwilling to dispense with his services at home.

Lord Bathurst deeply regrets that your Majesty had not conveyed your Majesty's wishes in favour of Mr. Atwood's son six weeks ago as an opportunity then existed of enabling Lord Bathurst to obey your Majesty's commands. There is however now no vacancy, or likely to be one, in this office.

1146 THE DEAN OF CHRIST CHURCH (THE REV. SAMUEL SMITH) *to* SIR WILLIAM KNIGHTON

London, February 10th 1824.

I HAVE the honour of your letter of the 6th. instant signifying to me His Majesty's desire that a son of Sir H. Calvert[1] should be nominated to a studentship of Christ Church.

1 General Sir Harry Calvert (1763?–1826). Adjutant-General of the Forces, 1799–1818. Created Baronet, 1818.

I hope that I may be allowed to state that, from the moment of my being acquainted with His Majesty's gracious intention to confer upon me the Deanery of Christ Church, it was my resolution to devote the nominations to studentships which should come within my power to the encouragement of the young men under my care.

During my former residence at Christ Church I had frequent opportunities of observing the beneficial effects of the practice of the late Dr. Cyril Jackson upon this point. It must, I believe, be known to His Majesty that he uniformly resisted all private applications for nominations to studentships and bestowed them upon those who had previously entered as commoners without any other consideration than their merit; and by this course he gave the greatest encouragement to many who have since distinguished themselves in the world.

I humbly beg leave to lay this statement before His Majesty, hoping that he will be graciously pleased to pardon me for presuming to make a representation which I would not have done but for the anxious desire I have to fulfil, to the utmost of my power, the just expectations of His Majesty, communicated to me by the Earl of Liverpool, in the future management of the great establishment committed to my care.

1147 [SIR WILLIAM KNIGHTON] *to the* EARL OF LIVERPOOL

[February 1824]

THE KING has commanded me to write your Lordship a private letter on the subject of H. M's. commands relative to the two studentships of C. C. I explained to H. M. in the most detailed and accurate manner all that your Lordship had said on the subject in conversation with me yesterday; and I, at the same time, mentioned to H. M. what I had humbly presumed to advise the Dean of C. C. to do through your Lordship, and hence the Dean's letter to me.

His Majesty, I am commanded to say, agrees in the general principle laid down by the D. of C. C. as it was urged and supported by your Lordship at our interview on that occasion. But H. M. will not, on this present occasion, forego his commands altho' H. M. may not repeat such commands in future.

Sir H. Calvert's son was promised by the King, three years since, at the earnest and affectionate solicitation of the Duke of York.

The King's word was passed and the young man is under the influence of this promise. Under these circumstances the King is obliged to consult the delicacy due to his own feelings as well as those of his brother the Duke of York.

The King has long had the intention of fulfilling, for a variety of amiable as well as just reasons (which H. M. says it becomes no one to question) to command a studentship for Richard Seymour. He is one of eleven or twelve children, is on the foundation of the Charter House, there placed by the Archbishop of Canterbury and is at the head of the school. Sir M. Seymour,[1] the father of this young gentleman, stands thus in the annals of his country. On the first of June[2] he lost his arm. On commanding the Amethyst, frigate, he took the Thetis, French frigate, of superior force, in single action and had the medual [*sic*].[3] He afterwards, in single action, took the Niemen, French frigate, of much superior force, for which he was created a Baronet.[4] He continued to serve during the whole of the War, with increased reputation, and at the close was made Commander of the Bath. Now Sir M. Seymour commands the King's yatch.[5] It would be invidious to say the King's favor was improperly bestowed on this occasion.

I am further commanded to state to you that it is now seven years since the King has commanded a studentship, which then was for Dr. Hook's[6] son,—the grandson of the late Sir W. Farquhar[7]—and, more-over, this studentship was required of the late Dean by the application of Dr. Cyril Jackson, at His M's. gracious commands.

1148 THEODORE EDWARD HOOK *to* SIR WILLIAM KNIGHTON

London, February 15th 1824.

CONSCIOUS as I am of my presumption in entreating you to be pleased to submit the extraordinary circumstances in which I am placed to the notice of His Majesty, I can only trust to His Majesty's gracious good-

1 Admiral Sir Michael Seymour, first Baronet (1768–1834).
2 1794.
3 He was appointed to the command of the *Amethyst*, a 36-gun frigate, in June 1806, and the *Thétis* was taken on 10 November 1808. Seymour was presented with a gold medal and a sum of £100.
4 The *Niémen* was captured off Ushant on 6 April 1809.
5 The *Prince Regent*. In 1825 he became commander of the King's own yacht, the *Royal George*.
6 The Reverend James Hook. His eldest son, Walter Farquhar Hook (1798–1875), was educated at Winchester and Christ Church, Oxford. He was appointed Dean of Chichester in 1859.
7 Physician in ordinary to the Prince of Wales, 1796; created Baronet, 1796. (1738–1819.) His daughter Anne married Dr Hook.

ness to forgive such a request, should you be kindly disposed to accede to it.

I have been now a prisoner at the suit of the Crown for upwards of nine weeks, having on account of *the same debt* (contracted by an over-confidence in my official subordinates) been deprived of my office and having *twice* suffered the process of extent which swept away every particle of property I possessed, even while the amount of the debt itself is yet undecided.

Through you, Sir, I most humbly and dutifully venture to submit the particular hardship of my case, it being notorious that the difficulties in which I am involved have chiefly arisen from the vindictive measures of the host of enemies I have created because, in a time of peril and when the country was agitated by as desperate a faction as ever disturbed its happiness and repose, I solely and singly without aid or patronage *established* the paper called John Bull.

It would be needless presumption in me to say one word of what that paper has done or what, *under my sole and uncontrouled direction* it is now doing, but with reference to the alleged amount of my debt to the Crown it may not be wrong to observe that the paper has already, since its establishment, produced to the Exchequer upwards of thirty thousand pounds.[1]

In the course of last week an arrangement was proposed from the Audit Office under which I was to have been liberated upon giving security to the amount of twelve thousand pounds, and my friends were ready to enter into such sureties until they were advised that a security to the Crown would interfere with their titles to property and with the conduct of their private affairs. This proposal has therefore fallen to the ground and I am doomed to continued imprisonment.

It is not that under such trying circumstances I presume to lay any specific petition at the feet of the King, but conscious in my heart of the rectitude of my official conduct, I have ventured this statement in the hope, should you see fit to bring it under His Majesty's most gracious consideration, that His Majesty in the known benignity of his heart may condescend to interpose a shield between me and the heavy weight of evils which assail me for no crime but because I have dutifully and fearlessly devoted the indefatigable application of my time and humble talents to the exclusive service of my Sovereign.

I do assure you, Sir, that it is with the deepest regret I feel driven, at a moment when I see no prospect of relief, to address you upon this most delicate subject. It will be superfluous to add to the main request

1 In the form of newspaper stamp duties (fourpence per copy).

contained in this letter another that, with such an exception as you may be disposed to make, you will be pleased to consider *the avowal* it contains as STRICTLY *confidential*.

Should you kindly favour me with any answer the same medium through which you will receive this will, with equal security, bring me your reply, and, in entreating you to pardon the liberty I have taken with you, I have the honour to be, Sir,[1] [etc.].

1149 GEORGE CANNING *to* [SIR WILLIAM KNIGHTON]

F. O., Feb. 24. 1824.
½ p. 11. P.M.

As I imagine that His Majesty will be anxious to know the result of the motion upon the Court of Chancery, I send off a messenger with my report, but with orders not to disturb His Majesty if he should be gone to bed.[2]

1150 THE MARQUIS OF HASTINGS *to the* KING

Rome, March 3rd 1824.

THE gracious letter of the 14th of February with which your Majesty has deigned to honor me claims to be met by my most grateful acceptance of the appointment so generously offered.

It is not with simple thankfulness to the bounty of my Sovereign that I acknowledge the favor. Your Majesty's recollection of former periods will justify me in venturing to express my conviction of your Majesty's belief that no appetence of honors or advantages could lead me to a protestation which did not come from the heart; and it is from that reference alone that I can hope to be understood adequately when I profess feelings on the occasion far beyond what even the immediate act of benignity ought to inspire.[3]

1 He remained in prison until 1825, and was never relieved of his civil responsibility for the deficiency of 62,000 dollars.

2 John Williams' motion for a committee of inquiry into the sources of the delays and expenses of the Court of Chancery was withdrawn, the Government agreeing to the appointment of a commission.

3 His appointment as Governor and Commander-in-Chief of Malta was gazetted on the 22nd.

4 Stanhope St., March 12th 1824.

I CANNOT sufficiently express my thanks to you for the very kind and friendly reception with which you favoured me when last I saw you, and in consequence of what then passed I waited on Lord Grenville on Monday. He approved of my plan and was sanguine as to my success. He suggested the propriety of first apprizing Lord Liverpool of my intentions. I have done so and he replies "If His Majesty should be pleased to communicate with me at any time upon the subject I have no hesitation in assuring you that I shall be most ready to recommend you to His Majesty's favourable consideration for the honour in question." I have not seen Lord G. since for I understand he is not quite as well as he was and yesterday he put off a party who were to dine with him, and I confess I rather anticipated a refusal to transmit my letter to His Majesty on the ground that as he had retired from public life he declines to interfere. I therefore avail myself of your kind offer to present my letter to the King. Will you excuse me for troubling you with a copy of my letter to His Majesty. I am so entirely unaccustomed to letters of that nature that I am not satisfied some alterations may not be necessary. If so, you will greatly oblige me by returning the letter with any suggestions you may think proper. Lady Hereford begs to be most kindly remembered to you.

[P.S.] On Tuesday next we remove to 28 Park St. Grosvenor Square.

1152 VISCOUNT HEREFORD *to the* KING
Copy.

[March 12, 1824.]

TRUSTING to your Majesty's accustomed goodness I presume to obtrude upon your notice with the most profound respect, and while I venture with diffidence to make a tender of my humble services to your Majesty whenever a vacancy may occur among the Lords of your Majesty's Bedchamber I beg to solicit your Majesty's gracious con-descension to pardon this intrusion. With every sentiment of loyalty and attachment, I have the honor to subscribe myself, [etc.].

1 Henry Fleming Devereux, fourteenth Viscount Hereford, Premier Viscount of England (1777–1843). In his early years he was a member of the Whig party, but was later classed as a Tory. He married Frances Elizabeth, daughter of Sir George Cornewall.

1153 The Bishop of St David's (Dr Burgess) *to* Sir William Knighton

Durham, March 20, 1824.

You will much oblige me by informing me if the inclosed application for His Majesty's bounty to the Royal Society of Literature is properly expressed.

As His Majesty has graciously proposed that the Keeper of his Privy Purse should pay the Royal bounty to the President of the Society, it is, I think, desirable that the order which conveys the Royal bounty should direct that the several bounties and medals should be delivered by the President, or, in his absence, by one of the Vice-Presidents, to the persons entitled to them at the commemoration of St. George's Day, on which the Society will hold their anniversary.

1154 The Marquis of Anglesey *to the* King

Windsor Castle, March 24th 1824.

Will your Majesty forgive me for stating that I have just heard from undoubted authority that Sir Thomas Munro[1] will immediately quit Madras, and that his appointment would, if it could be procured for Berkeley, make his fortune.

The kind interest your Majesty has so frequently expressed for him emboldens me to make this communication. Remaining, [etc.].

1155 The Rev. Richard Cattermole[2] *to* Sir William Knighton

Council Room, 61 *Lincoln's Inn Fields,*
March 25th 1824.

The Council of the Royal Society of Literature beg leave to enclose to Sir William Knighton, for the information of His Majesty, a list of the Associates on the Royal foundation whom they have elected pursuant to His Majesty's command, communicated to them on the 15th. Decr last; and the form in which they propose to apply to him, as the Keeper of His Majesty's Purse, for the annual Royal endowment.

The Council have to regret that, from the circumstance of their President, the Bishop of St. Davids, being at a great distance from London and not having yet transmitted to them his signature to the said application according to their request, they have not been able to send

1 Governor of Madras, 1819–27. [1761–1827.]
2 The Secretary of the Royal Society of Literature until 1852. [1795?–1858.]

that application to Sir William Knighton, in due form, at an earlier period; but they beg leave to add, that they propose to do so as soon as they shall receive his Lordship's signature.

By Order of the Council, [etc.].

1156 *List of Associates of the Royal Society of Literature*

THE PRESIDENT and Council of the Royal Society of Literature having, since the gracious sanction given by His Majesty under the Royal sign manual to the Constitution and regulations of the Society, in the month of June 1823, elected the ten following gentlemen, being fit and proper persons to receive His Majesty's annual bounty of one hundred guineas each, Associates of the First Class on the Royal foundation, viz:

Samuel Taylor Coleridge, Esq. James Millingen,[5] Esq.
The Rev. Edward Davies.[1] Sir Wm. Ouseley,[6] Knt.
The Rev. Dr. John Jamieson.[2] William Roscoe,[7] Esq.
The Rev. Thomas Robert Malthus.[3] The Rev. John Henry Todd,[8] and
Thomas James Mathias,[4] Esq. Sharon Turner,[9] Esq.

And having also adjudged the two medals of fifty guineas each, placed by His Majesty annually at the Society's disposal, to

William Mitford,[10] Esq. and Signor Angelo Maï;[11]

do hereby, in obedience to His Majesty's command, empower Archibald Elijah Impey Esq. their Treasurer, to make application to the Keeper of His Majesty's Privy Purse, for £1155, the sum necessary for the payment of this Royal endowment, for the present year.

1 The Welsh antiquary. He published *Celtic Researches on the Origin, Traditions and Language of the Ancient Britons*, in 1804. [1756–1831.]
2 The antiquary and philologist; compiled *Etymological Dictionary of the Scottish Language*, 1808. [1759–1838.]
3 Author of the famous *Essay on Population*, 1798. [1766–1834.]
4 The Italian scholar (1754?–1835).
5 The archaeologist; author of many works on coins, medals, Etruscan vases, etc. [1774–1845.]
6 The orientalist. Published *Persian Miscellanies* (1795) and *Oriental Collections* (1797–99). [1767–1842.]
7 The Liverpool banker and historian. Author of *Life of Lorenzo de Medici*. Whig M.P. for Liverpool, 1806–7. [1753–1831.]
8 He edited the works of Milton and Spenser, and revised Dr Johnson's *Dictionary*. (1763–1845.)
9 An authority on Icelandic and Anglo-Saxon literature. (1768–1847.)
10 For his *History of Greece*. [1744–1827.]
11 For his literary discoveries in the Milan and Vatican libraries. He was Librarian to the Vatican, and an Honorary member of the Society.

Rome, March 30th 1824.

I GRIEVE to address your Majesty for the purpose of informing you of the loss I have sustained. The poor Duchess died this morning; she had been for a week suffering from a most violent inflammation of the lungs, the fever accompanying which it was found impossible to subdue. She did not suffer much, she knew her danger and behaved with the greatest composure and resignation.

I was just beginning to hope that she was recovering her spirits which had almost left her since the great loss she had in Consalvi. Knowing yr Majesty's kind feelings towards her I feel sure that I need not apologise for this intrusion.

1158 The Earl of Liverpool *to the* King

Fife House, April 10, 1824.

LORD LIVERPOOL is under the painful necessity of informing your Majesty of an event at which he is confident your Majesty will be most sincerely grieved, the death of his poor sister the Duchess of Devonshire.[1]

This sad intelligence has just been received by Lady Erne[2] in a letter from the Duke of Devonshire, a week's illness (an inflammation on the lungs) carried her off.

The Duke speaks in the most feeling manner of her composure, her fortitude, and soothing consideration of all around her. When she was sensible of her danger, she desired the attendance of a clergyman of the Church of England, and had a most interesting interview with him.

Lord Liverpool is well aware how your Majesty will feel on the occasion of the loss of a person, so sincerely attached to your Majesty.

Lord Liverpool must ever deplore so near and dear a connection, from whom he never experienced during the course of more than thirty years, any feelings but those of the greatest kindness.

1 Elizabeth, Duchess of Devonshire, was the daughter of the fourth Earl of Bristol. Lord Liverpool's first wife, who died in June 1821, was her younger sister. The sixth Duke of Devonshire was her step-son.
2 The second wife of John Creighton, first Earl Erne. She was the Duchess of Devonshire's eldest sister, and died in 1842.

Fife House, May 3rd 1824.

LORD LIVERPOOL has this instant received the intelligence of the death of the Bishop of Chichester,[1] and he humbly solicits your Majesty's permission to offer it to the Dean of Hereford instead of the Bishoprick of Chester.

Lord Liverpool will not object to his retaining the Deanery of Hereford with it, and it will occasion far less expence to the Dean than removing to Chester.

Lord Liverpool can have no personal interest in the question but he is conscientiously convinced, from all he has heard since he last addressed your Majesty on the subject, that Chester is the most laborious and important diocesce in the Kingdom after London and requires an individual in full health and vigour and, at the same time, possessed of every qualification which will ensure respect from all classes of people.

Lord Liverpool is fully authorised by the Bishop of London to say that Archdeacon Bloomfield[2] is the most proper person, not yet promoted to the bench, for an extensive and populous diocesce [*sic*]. He stands as high as any person in the Kingdom as a divine, is avowedly the first great scholar in the University of Cambridge, and has been now for some years one of the Archdeacons of London and minister of the important and populous parish of Bishopsgate.

1160 THE REV. ROBERT JAMES CARR *to* SIR WILLIAM KNIGHTON

Hanover Square, May 3rd 1824.

MR. HUSKISSON was delayed so late at the Council that I did not get an interview with him in time to be with you at the hour appointed. I have just left him, and as he was requested by Lord Liverpool to offer me the choice of Chester or Chichester I have accepted the latter.

The King's goodness to me, in insisting that I should retain the Deanery of Hereford with the Bishoprick of Chester, has proved the most fortunate occurrence of my life. I should not have been allowed to retain it had Chichester been first vacant; but Lord Liverpool is pleased to say he shall be most happy to attend to His Majesty's commands and I shall be permitted to keep my Deanery also.

1 The Right Reverend John Buckner (1734–1824), Bishop of Chichester since 1797.
2 Charles James Blomfield (1786–1857), Bishop of Chester, 1824–28; Bishop of London, 1828–57.

How can I attempt to express the feelings of gratitude and love that oppress my heart to an almost painful excess. To you my dear kind friend I must leave it to tell that good and gracious master that his benevolence has made the most dutiful and affectionate of his servants the happiest of human beings.

Believe me with the sincerest regard, My dear Sir William, [etc.].

1161 THE DUKE OF WELLINGTON *to* SIR WILLIAM KNIGHTON

London, May 4th 1824.
4 P.M.

I HAVE seen the draft of the letter[1] and I really think it is one which will enable the King to put an end to the discussion and to the whole affair, with becoming dignity.

It is addressed to Lord Liverpool and is very long. The cause for not sending it sooner is the attendance in Parlt and at the Cabinets.[2]

1162 THE EARL OF LIVERPOOL *to the* KING

Fife House, May 5th 1824.

LORD LIVERPOOL has the honour to enclose a letter which he has received from Mr. Canning in consequence of the communication which Lord Liverpool thought it his duty to make to him.

Lord Liverpool trusts that this explanation will prove satisfactory to your Majesty. It will at least prove that Mr. Canning was actuated by no consideration in attending the entertainment at the Mansion House on Easter Monday, except his sense of what might be most advantageous for your Majesty's service, and he is sincerely sorry if his conduct on that occasion has unfortunately met with your Majesty's displeasure.

The Duke of Wellington to Sir William Knighton, 5 May 1824. (*W.N.D.* II, 262–3.)

1 Canning's letter to Lord Liverpool (No. 1163).
2 The King was deeply offended with Canning for attending Lord Mayor Waithman's banquet at the Mansion House and considered that, in view of the prominent part which Waithman had played during the Queen's Trial, Canning ought to have declined the invitation. Wynn was the only other Cabinet Minister present.

Gloucester Lodge, May 5th 1824.

CABINETS and House of Commons have prevented me from sooner replying to the letter which I received from you on Monday. A part of its contents surprised as well as afflicted me. I did not presume, indeed, that the King had *approved* of my determination to attend the dinner at the Mansion House, but certainly I had not the slightest apprehension of what you describe as the circumstance which has "most particularly affected" His Majesty—I mean the circumstance that His Majesty understood me to have received from Lord F. Conyngham an intimation of His Majesty's "lasting displeasure" if I should attend that dinner.

I have no consciousness of having received such an intimation. I commissioned Lord F. C. indeed to mention to the King my intention to go to the dinner, and to explain to His Majesty the reasons why I thought it for His Majesty's service that I should do so. But I had no pretension to ask the sanction of His Majesty, nor to elicit any expression of His Majesty's opinion upon the subject. Had such been my purpose I should have addressed myself to His Majesty either personally or by letter; and certainly should have done so in time to be enabled to act upon His Majesty's decision without the hazard of bringing His Majesty's name into question. I now wish that I had taken that course, but in truth it never occurred to me to give so much importance to the matter. It *did* occur to me that it might be as well that His Majesty should know the fact beforehand rather than learn it from newspapers the next day; and Ld. F. C. being, on other accounts, to go to Windsor some day in the course of the week, I did think it of importance enough to expedite his going. Perhaps in this I may have judged wrong. And at least the error was on the side of attention to His Majesty.

It would not perhaps have occurred to me to assign even this degree of importance to the matter if I had not recollected that the King had expressed to me in November His Majesty's satisfaction that none of his servants had attended the dinner in Guild Hall. His Majesty, I know, does me the justice to recollect that I, on that occasion, took the liberty humbly to declare my opinon upon the subject; and to state to His Majesty the grounds on which I ventured to think it highly inexpedient for His Majesty's service that his Ministers should absent themselves, by common consent, from these publick meetings of the city (whatever might be the personal politicks of the Chief Magistrate for the time being), and should thus leave the tone of such meetings to be given by the Opposition exclusively.

On this principle *I* have attended dinners when in office, both at the Mansion House and at the Guild Hall, on occasions on which it would have been infinitely more agreeable to stay away; occasions when the city were in direct hostile array against the Government.

You must remember the Easter dinner during Lord Melville's[1] unhappy persecution. You may remember also the dinner at Guild Hall, in Novr 1808, when the city were in a ferment of indignation for vengeance on the authors and abettors of the Convention of Cintra.[2]

The distinction between Guild Hall and the Mansion House does not, I confess, appear to me to be a material one. The visit is, in either case, to the Magistrate, not the individual. In some respects, indeed, the Easter meeting is the more important, as taking place during the Session of Parliament, when the Opposition as well as the members of Government are in town.

In the present instance I am morally certain that the attendance of a Minister was of signal use. There is no strong hostility to the Government at this moment, but there are questions in progress which it is of the utmost importance to keep in our own hands, and on which not only the Opposition but many of our supporters (the latter from over zeal, the others perhaps from hope of mischief) are desirous of pushing us faster than we would go. South America and Greece are questions of this sort. Now the Greek question was (*as I told you* it would be) in full preparation for the Easter dinner. The Greek deputies were there in full costume, with their keeper Mr. Bowring, at the head of one of the tables. I have not the smallest doubt that, had I not been there, *their* healths and speeches would have followed those of the Royal family, city and the Ld Mayor, and would have given the tone to the whole meeting.

Our difficulties at Constantinople, arising from causes of this sort, are sufficiently embarrassing already. You know how impossible it is to make the Turks comprehend that the city of London has nothing to say to the

1 Henry Dundas, first Viscount Melville (1742–1811). He was impeached, in 1806, for malversation whilst First Lord of the Admiralty. "No transaction in Mr. Pitt's political life", wrote Liverpool and Wellington to the King, "ever affected his feelings so strongly as the proceedings in the House of Commons, and the subsequent conduct of the City of London in the case of Lord Melville, but immediately after the address presented to the Crown by the City on that occasion, though his own health would not permit his being present at the Mansion House at Easter, Lord Liverpool, as Secretary of State, and the Duke of Montrose went there at his desire, and thereby certainly prevented the expression of public sentiments which would indubitably have been manifested in the absence of any of the King's Ministers, and might have been most inconvenient, if not disastrous, at that period."

2 The Armistice concluded by Sir Hew Dalrymple with the French, after Junot had been soundly beaten by Sir Arthur Wellesley at Vimiero. By its terms the remnants of Junot's army were not to be treated as prisoners of war, but were to be transported by sea to France. (August 1808.)

Government of England, and there are few things that could more inconveniently aggravate those difficulties at the present crisis, and put to hazard the success of Lord Strangford's[1] negotiations, than the report at Constantinople of *such* an Easter dinner as this would have been if no Minister had been present at the Mansion House. That *my* presence did repress this particular mischief I positively know. There *was* a cry for "The Greeks" from one part of the Hall late in the evening, of which the Lord Mayor got the better by giving a farewell toast and breaking up the company; and he afterwards took credit with me for having done so.

I am, I own, decidedly of opinion that the Government should not, on such occasions, leave a clear stage to their opponents. *The city* may be a very inconvenient power in the State. But *there it is.* You cannot put it aside. You cannot even controul it. It has been suffered to slip out of your hands; but I think it would be good policy to endeavour, by all reasonable attentions, to recover it.

I flatter myself that I have as good a right as any publick man of the present day not to be suspected of courting popularity by a compromise with Jacobinism. I have passed near thirty years in fighting the battle with it. I have incurred as much unpopularity at various times, in that contest, as any man, and have braved that unpopularity as fearlessly. But I think that the battle is now fought. I think we have gained the victory. And I think it would be something like a dereliction of publick duty not to reap the full advantages of the present position of the Government; a position which it is for the interest of the King's service to strengthen, and which owes no small part of its present strength to His Majesty's personal popularity.

I have stated my opinions thus at large because I wish His Majesty to know them thoroughly and without reservation. His Majesty will see that the particular case was one in which, according to my view of it, the interest of His Majesty's service was concerned. But I am anxious above all things that His Majesty should be persuaded that nothing could give me so much pain as the apprehension that I had given cause of uneasiness, much more of displeasure, of His Majesty; and that there is no feeling nearer my heart than that of affectionate gratitude to His Majesty for the kindness and confidence with which His Majesty has invariably treated me since he was graciously pleased to recall me to his service.[2]

1 At this time Ambassador at Constantinople.
2 For further correspondence relating to this question see *W.N.D.* II, 250–1, 261; *Yonge,* III, 279–83.

1164 THE BISHOP *of* LINCOLN (DR GEORGE PELHAM)[1] *to the*
REV. CHARLES RICHARD SUMNER

London, May 5th 1824.

I HAVE this morning received His Majesty's commands to appoint you
Deputy Clerk of the Closet vacant by the nomination of the Dean of
Hereford to the see of Chichester. I have much satisfaction in so doing
as it was my full intention to have named you to His Majesty for that
situation on the first vacancy.

1165 SIR BENJAMIN BLOOMFIELD *to* SIR WILLIAM KNIGHTON

Stockholm, 6th May, 1824.

YOUR two affectionate letters of the 17th. and 19th. reached me on the
1st. Thank God I can speak most satisfactorily of my health as, ever since
the attack, my bowels have had much less irritable sensations, and I
trust, by observing your injunctions, to hold on for some time still.
Long ago you ordered me to wear a shammy leather belt which I have
never been without.

Believe me, my excellent friend, to feel most sensibly your unwearied
anxiety in all that concerns my interests. I have, influenced by your
opinions, as well as those of our excellent friend Davis,[2] accepted
Florence, though I have done so in fear and trembling for I anticipate
a second demenagement with the horrors of almost ruin, besides a
diminished salary in a residence said to be the most expensive on the
Continent. When I have found the income of this secluded corner inadequate to its expenditure what am I not to fear at a post the most
resorted by our countrymen of any other? However Lord Francis,[3]
with his accustomed kindness, holds out the hope of John's[4] appointment
to be Secretary of Legation. This is the greatest of all happinesses to me
and, I confess, gladdens my heart. Indeed I persuade myself that His
Majesty would deign to afford his protecting hand to this dear fellow,
who has certainly never offended any human being. I leave this object
in your hands and have no fears for the result.

As to the Peerage, my dear friend, I really am astonished when you
tell me that a *doubtful* Minute has been made of the Duke of Wellington's
communication. Were it *my last breath* I declare his Grace to have stated
that "Judge Downs[5] was to have the first vacancy, and that the second

1 [1766–1827.] Bishop of Lincoln since 1820.   2 R. Hart Davis. See No. 1085.
3 Lord Francis Conyngham.   4 Sir Benjamin Bloomfield's son.   5 See No. 999.

was destined for me". 'Tis true the promise could not be positive as to time, such elevation depending upon 3 vacancies by death, of course uncertain in their occurrence. Surely you yourself recollect these facts as I imparted everything to you at that unhappy period. My letter to the Duke was merely to open the subject, that I might procure myself the opportunity of naming my title. I never will mix up this engagement with any other or make it any condition, and have therefore abstained carefully from the mention of it in my reply to Lord Francis. Should it turn out that my son is as indifferent as his papa to this distinction I shall, if there is any hesitation on the part of the Government, decline the thing altogether. You know I relinquished an English Peerage rather than have a rumpus with the Govt and I do assure you that the proposed distinction has not a single charm for either L[ad]y Bloomfield or myself, save as coming from the hand of my Sovereign.

Tomorrow I leave here for Copenhagen, and, including Norway after the camp, calculate upon a nearly three months absence. I dined, to take leave, with the King this day when he observed that to be the most probable period. His Majesty has sent orders to all the arsenals and to his civil authorities to afford me every possible facility and attention, and has lodged me near to the Prince Royal[1] at the camp. God bless you my dear friend. Believe in the sincerity of my affection.

[P.S.] I fear it will not be possible for me to reply to Davis's kind letter until my next courier. Say so to him with the assurance of my regard. I have had the heaviest days work in correspondence that has befallen me since here.

1166 ROBERT SMIRKE[2] *to* SIR HENRY HALFORD

Stratford Place, May 7th 1824.

THE contractor is unable to proceed with his work for the College of Physicians from the want of sufficient space next the north front of the building. If the Master of [the] Horse would allow the wall to be removed which encloses a small court attached to the mews, so as to give the use of an additional width of ground of 12 or 14 feet in front of the building, there would be no longer any impediment to its immediate and satisfactory progress.

The only inconvenience sustained by the establishment of the Master

1 Bernadotte's son, afterwards Oscar I of Sweden. [1799–1859.]
2 The architect. See No. 62.

of the Horse would be that to get access to this small court they must pass round to Pall Mall East, but as there are only a few detached coach houses in the Court I should hope that the inconvenience would be thought very trifling and it will certainly be only a temporary one.

1167 SIR BENJAMIN BLOOMFIELD *to* SIR WILLIAM KNIGHTON

Copenhagen, 29th May, 1824.

I CANNOT tell you, my dear Knighton, how much and how sensibly I feel your kindness about my boy, as well as your reception of him. It afforded me also a very sincere gratification that he was presented to our worthy friend Davis[1] who, like yourself, has written in cordial terms of the dear fellow, and such as have gladdened poor papa's heart. He is a dear boy and has his first fault yet to commit, with the most enviable temper and disposition I ever beheld. He was himself highly gratified with his visit to you which had been delayed owing to his eternal gallopping about.

I learn from Johnny that the scheme of F[lorence] is no longer upon the cards. This is a sad blow. Nevertheless I equally feel the desire of everyone to improve my position, and look confidently to some favorable chance before I am quite frozen up. To confess the truth however the diminished income of F. frightened me, therefore perhaps all is for the best. As to myself, I consider all as nothing compared to John's promotion, and I am persuaded that you have not let slip the present vacancy at Florence. John is amongst the seniors of his class and his conduct has been exemplary under all his chiefs. You know he was not removed from Vienna by his own seeking, therefore surely Lord Francis[2] could manage the *continuance* of the salary from his first appointment.

I cannot adequately thank you for the print. How like! But I conceive the expression too old. You could not have thought of me in *any way so acceptable to my feelings*, and you do only justice to my value for a resemblance of him whom I shall love to my latest hour. Thank God he is well again. God bless you.

Be assured, my dear friend, of my sincerity and utmost affection.

[P.S.] I have just been presented to His Danish Majesty. He had the grace to receive me though about to set out upon a tour of inspection and to be absent for 2 months. He begins his journey at six this evening.

1 See No. 1085.   2 Lord Francis Conyngham.

June 16th 1824.

HAVING received an intimation through the Earl of Liverpool that your Majesty is now desirous of having the possession of Marlbro' House for the purpose of residing there, I lose no time in assuring your Majesty of my perfect readiness to meet the wishes your Majesty seems to have expressed on this subject, whatever the personal considerations or inconvenience may be.

I have therefore given directions that every information, with respect to this House, shall be forwarded as early as possible to Lord Liverpool.

I have the honor to be,
Sir,
Your Majesty's dutiful humble subject
and son-in-law,
LEOPOLD.

The Earl of Liverpool to the King, 16 June 1824. (*Yonge*, III, 288.)

1169 GEORGE CANNING *to the* KING

Foreign Office, June 18th 1824.
½ past 2 A.M.

MR. CANNING humbly reports to your Majesty that, among the Bills which have passed the House of Commons tonight, is a Bill for repealing that part of the Superannuation Act of 1822 which deducted 5 per cent. from the salaries of clerks in publick offices.

In the course of the debate on this subject it was suggested by Mr. Buxton,[1] and the suggestion was supported by Dr. Lushington, Mr. Spring Rice,[2] Sir Charles Forbes[3] and Mr. Money,[4] that the same principle on which the clerks were to be thus relieved should be considered as applying to the contribution of 10 per cent. on the salaries of Ministers and Officers of State which was levied, by Order in Council, the same year.

Mr. Canning ventures humbly to express to your Majesty the sense of himself and of his colleagues in the House of Commons that (although

1 Sir Thomas Fowell Buxton (1786–1845), the prison reformer and slavery abolitionist. M.P. for Weymouth since 1818. Created Baronet, 1840.

2 Thomas Spring-Rice, first Baron Monteagle (1790–1866), Whig M.P. for Limerick. Held office after 1830 under Grey and Melbourne. Raised to the peerage, 1839.

3 Tory M.P. for Malmesbury. Created Baronet, 1823. (1774–1849.)

4 William Taylor Money, Tory M.P. for St. Michael until 1826, when he was appointed Consul-General at Venice.

they would not presume to mention your Majesty's name in the debate without the previous knowledge that it would not be disagreeable to your Majesty) it will be their duty, when these repeals are carried into effect, to tender to your Majesty their humble opinion and advice that your Majesty should discontinue, from the same period, the onerous sacrifice, voluntarily made by your Majesty in 1822, of a portion of your Majesty's Civil List revenue—a sacrifice which they fear must already have occasioned to your Majesty a degree of inconvenience from which they are most anxious that your Majesty should be relieved.

The Duke of Wellington to the King, 1 July 1824. (*W.N.D.* II, 281–3.)

1170 *Minute of the Cabinet [in* CANNING's *handwriting]. Foreign Office, July 2nd* 1824. ½ *past* 4 P.M.

PRESENT.

The Lord Chancellor	Lord Sidmouth
Lord President	Lord Bexley
Lord Privy Seal	Mr. Peel
Duke of Wellington	Mr. Robinson
Lord Bathurst	Mr. Wynn
Lord Liverpool	Mr. Huskisson
Lord Melville	Mr. Canning

YOUR MAJESTY's confidential servants, having had under consideration the official note delivered to Mr. Canning, the day before yesterday, by the Count de Villa Real,[1] requesting, in the name of His Most Faithful Majesty,[2] an aid to Portugal of from 4,000 to 6,000 troops, British if possible, but if not British, Hanoverian; have agreed to submit to your Majesty their humble opinion and advice that the present amount and distribution of the British army would not admit of such a detachment for foreign service, even if any such detachment could be made without calling Parliament; and that the calling Parliament for this purpose and for the purpose of obtaining an augmentation of force would (in addition to other objections) require a length of time, and give a degree of publicity to the measure, which would defeat all its utility.

Your Majesty's confidential servants have not the means of judging how far it may be in the power of your Majesty's Hanoverian Government to furnish the assistance required. But, supposing it to be so, your

1 The Portuguese Minister in London.
2 John VI, King of Portugal (1767–1826).

[Minute of the Cabinet [in CANNING'S *handwriting], cont.]*

Majesty's servants, without presuming to offer their advice to your Majesty on a matter not of their competence, feel it their duty nevertheless to state their humble opinion that, under the circumstances of the case, as stated in the Ct. de Villa Real's note, there might be great advantage in your Majesty's authorizing Mr. Canning to signify to the Count de Villa Real your Majesty's gracious disposition to direct your Majesty's Hanoverian servants to consider favourably that part of M. de Villa Real's proposition.[1]

1171 *Cabinet Minute [in* CANNING'S *handwriting]. Foreign Office, July 15th* 1824

PRESENT.

The Lord President   Mr. Peel
Lord Privy Seal   Mr. Robinson
Duke of Wellington   Mr. Wynn
Lord Bathurst   Mr. Huskisson
Lord Liverpool   Mr. Canning
Lord Melville
Lord Sidmouth
Lord Bexley

YOUR MAJESTY'S confidential servants deem it their duty to lay before your Majesty the change which has taken place in the grounds of the opinion, humbly submitted to your Majesty on the 2nd. inst. as to the expediency of your Majesty's recommending to your Majesty's Hanoverian Government to consider of the request for an aid of 6000 men for the service of His Most Faithful Majesty.

That opinion of your Majesty's servants was founded on the mixed considerations, suggested by the Count de Villa Real's official note,... 1*st*. of the evil which must result from the introduction of a French force into Portugal (which was distinctly held out as a consequence of your Majesty's refusal to lend the required aid in one or other of your Majesty's Sovereign capacities); 2*ndly*. of the King of Portugal's desire to reform his own army, and to have at hand a friendly foreign force to enable him to set about that salutary measure with safety.[2]

1 In February 1823 a revolt had broken out in Portugal against John VI, who appealed to the British Government for assistance. In April 1824 the rebellion assumed a more serious character and the King's second son, Dom Miguel, joined the movement. John VI again sought British military aid.

2 Wellington writes of the "disposition and habit of mutiny" in the Portuguese army. (*W.N.D.* II, 276.)

Some of your Majesty's servants were influenced by both these considerations; some by the latter chiefly but some solely and singly by the first:—the apprehension of seeing a French army introduced into the Kingdom of your Majesty's Ally, contrary, not indeed to the express letter of Treaties but to the whole tenour of those relations between Portugal and Great Britain which have subsisted for a century and a half; and in defiance of the publick declarations made, in the name of your Majesty, at the period of the French invasion of Spain and since repeatedly recalled to the recollection of the French Government.

It appeared to those of your Majesty's servants who were most particularly impressed with this consideration that almost under any circumstances, but especially after those publick declarations, the presence of a French force in Portugal could not but lead to a collision between France and England.

The verbal assurance indeed of the French Government to your Majesty's Ambassador at Paris, and of the French Ambassador here, had been constant and uniform that no occupation of Portugal was in the contemplation of France. On the other hand it was known to your Majesty's Government, on authority which they could not doubt, that the French Ambassador at Lisbon had repeatedly offered to H[is] M[ost] F[aithful] M[ajesty] the aid of the French army in Spain; and that, after the events of the 30th. of April, he had actually summoned the French garrison of Badajoz to Lisbon. These facts gave to the intimation conveyed in M. de Villa Real's note a character of probability which much impaired the credit of the verbal assurances before received; and it was remarkable that these verbal assurances had never been followed up by any *written* declaration to the same effect on the part of the French Government.

It was under these circumstances that the opinion of the 2nd. of this month was humbly submitted to your Majesty.

On hearing the rumour of an intention on the part of your Majesty's Government to send troops to Portugal, the French Ambassador sought an opportunity of renewing to Mr. Canning the verbal assurances above described respecting the intentions of his Government. But, as the Prince de Polignac[1] professed an entire disbelief of that part of M. de Neuville's[2] proceedings which Mr. Canning cited as justifying suspicion (the summons of the garrison of Badajoz to Lisbon), the P. de Polignac's profession (the veracity of which could not be doubted) only served to strengthen that suspicion; as it showed the P. de Polignac to be ignorant

1 The French Ambassador in London.
2 The French Ambassador in Portugal.

of transactions the existence of which was then known to your Majesty's servants, and is now indeed admitted by the French Government.

The Prince de Polignac promised to write to his Government for such information as should set all suspicion at rest. The result of that reference has been a despatch from his Court which the P. de Polignac read to Mr. Canning *in extenso*, and a memorandum of which he afterwards transmitted to Mr. Canning in writing. This memorandum (which has been laid before your Majesty) admits the facts of M. de Hyde de Neuville's repeated offers of a French force to His M.F.M.; and of his actual summons of the garrison of Badajoz: but it avers that M. Hyde de Neuville's conduct in these proceedings was not only unauthorized but has been *"formellement désapprouvée"*; it declares the positive resolution of the French Government to refuse compliance with any demand for troops which *may be made to them* by Portugal, and to repeat to their Ambassador at Lisbon instructions not to entertain any overture of that nature.

This explanation having satisfactorily removed the grounds upon which the entrance of a French army into Portugal was apprehended, the alleged state of the Portuguese army does not appear to your Majesty's servants, of itself, a sufficient cause for sending, under present circumstances, the military force which it was in contemplation to provide for the service of Portugal.

There is another consideration which weighs with your Majesty's servants against a compliance with the demand for military aid on the sole ground of enabling H.M.F.M. to effect a reform in his own army. They suspect that the state of that army is not the sole, perhaps not the real, motive of the demand. They believe an influencing part of the Portuguese Government to have been actuated by the hope of a refusal, and by the desire and intention to resort to the aid of France when that refusal shall have been received.

It cannot be denied that this suspicion receives a singular confirmation from the opinion of Lord Beresford which is annexed to this Minute; an opinion the rather to be relied upon as it was written after Lord Beresford had declined the command of the Portuguese army.

Had your Majesty's servants however been quite certain that such was the real motive of the demand for your Majesty's military assistance, still, so long as they were without any formal and satisfactory pledge from France that French troops should not be sent into Portugal, your Majesty's servants would have advised a compliance with the demand for the purpose of disappointing its ulterior object. But being now in possession of such a pledge it appears to your Majesty's servants, in addition to all other considerations, that it would be highly unadviseable to comply with a demand which, there is so much reason to suppose, may have been made under the influence and for the purpose described by Lord Beresford.

Your Majesty's servants, while they feel it their indispensable duty to state without reservation to your Majesty their present opinions, cannot forbear humbly to express to your Majesty their grateful sense of the promptitude with which your Majesty was pleased, under many difficulties and inconveniencies, to recommend to the consideration of your Majesty's servants in Hanover the proposition which they first submitted to your Majesty. They greatly regret the trouble and anxiety which may have been thus occasioned to your Majesty and to your Hanoverian Government. But they trust, at the same time, that your Majesty will see, in the altered circumstances of this most delicate and important question, the necessity for such an alteration of counsel as they now venture humbly to submit for your Majesty's Royal approbation.

The Lord Chancellor not having been able to attend the adjourned discussion of the Cabinet today has favoured Mr. Canning with his Lordship's opinion by letter, which Mr. Canning thinks it his duty humbly to lay before your Majesty.

Extract of a letter from Lord Beresford to the Duke of Wellington, dated 8 June 1824: "I understand they have again asked you to send troops, which I suppose you will continue to refuse. So Monsr. Hyde de Neuville expects, and that *then* his favourite object, and one to which all his views and projects tend, will be effected: that of bringing in French troops. The introduction of foreign troops ought to be unnecessary. They have no reason whatever to complain of the army on the 30th. and succeeding days; they obeyed their legal Commander-in-Chief, and I can assure you, when they saw what the thing tended to, they continued their obedience to him against their will." [In Canning's handwriting.]

1172 THE DUKE OF WELLINGTON *to the* KING

London, July 20th 1824.

I BEG leave to submit to your Majesty the expediency of carrying into full operation in the corps of artillery and engineers the arrangement of your Majesty's warrant of the 12th. August 1824, in regard to the removal of officers holding the rank of Major General from their regimental commissions, with the exception of Colonels com[man]d[in]g battallions.

The object of this recommendation is to give promotion immediately to those corps respectively; to remove from the performance of active duties those probably not now the most fit to perform those duties; and to give these corps in future this channel of promotion which exists in all the regts of the line.

I have preferred to recommend to your Majesty this mode of granting promotion to that of forming an invalid battallion, of which I had the option, because at the same time that it is not more expensive it will extend promotion throughout all ranks, and will place the corps of artillery and engineers on the same footing with those of the army upon the occasion of the future periodical promotions by brevet.

The operation of the plan at present will be, first, to place upon the list of unattached General Officers receiving the pay of one pound six shillings per diem the following General Officers who are Colonels of the artillery and engineers respectively: [1]—

Secondly, to promote to the rank of Colonel the following officers of the two Corps respectively.[1]

Thirdly, to promote officers in the several ranks in succession to those above mentioned, whose names I will hereafter submit to yr. Majty.

If your Majesty should be most graciously pleased to approve of this arrangement I will hereafter submit to your Majesty the necessary warrants for its regulation, and for that of other matters connected with the retired pay and allowances to officers of the corps serving under the ordnance, widows pensions &c.

The General Officers who will be removed from their reg[imenta]l commissions under this arrangement will retain their eligibility to employment where their services may be required, and their claims to succeed to the command of battallions under the arrangement approved of by your Majesty of February 1824.

All which is submitted for your Majesty's pleasure by your Majesty's most devoted subject and servant.

1173 SIR BENJAMIN BLOOMFIELD *to* SIR WILLIAM KNIGHTON

Gotheburg, 20th July 1824.

IN the proportion of my delight at your communication, so do I feel this fresh act of your kindness towards my son. I need not, either in his name or my own, entreat your continued watchfulness in his interests nor offer the assurance of all we experience in the anticipation of a promotion, to attain which you have so mainly helped. I cannot suffer myself to doubt, sh[oul]d more power be wanting, the good-will of His Majesty, whose word with Mr. Canning would be conclusive. Mr. Canning's permission

1 The long list of names is omitted.

that John shd remain here is the greatest comfort. He is the only person in charge of the office and I am delighted to observe his method in the conduct of its duties. He is assiduous to a degree quite unusual at his age, is exceedingly clear in all his arrangements, and never allows anything to clash with his business; therefore always before his work. In all other respects I cannot be sufficiently thankful to the Almighty for such a blessing. John deeply feels your interference but intends to speak for himself.

I am thus far on my route for Christiania [*sic*] and have the gratification to assure you that nothing can be more satisfactory than the state of everything connected with my responsibility. The British merchants established at this place give me a dinner tomorrow in testimony of their gratitude for having successfully fought their battle with the Swedish Government and secured for them some highly important benefits. I know that these little histories will give you pleasure.

God bless you. Believe me ever, My dear friend, [etc.].

1174 THE TSAR ALEXANDER I *to the* KING

St Pétersbourg, ce 9 Août 1824.

LE VICOMTE DE STRANGFORD[1] vient de me rendre un service que je croirois ne pas suffisamment reconnoitre si je ne témoignois moi même à Votre Majesté d'une part combien il m'est agréable de devoir principalement à son intervention amicale, un résultat qui remplit tous mes voeux, de l'autre, combien j'apprécie le zèle et les talens qu'a déployés son Ambassadeur près la Porte Ottomane. L'habileté du Vicomte de Strangford lui a valu des succès dont l'Europe entière ne sauroit trop se féliciter.

La paix et les relations qui en sont la suite pourront, je l'espère, se maintenir longtemps entre La Russie et La Porte. Je me flatte surtout que bientôt l'Alliance aura achevé son ouvrage, et que sachant qu'il ne peut être ni parfait ni solide, tant que l'Orient gémira des troubles et des malheurs qui le désolent, elle va se hâter pour y mettre un terme, d'avoir recours aux moyens qu'elle a déjà approuvés d'une voix unanime.

C'est là le seul complément que demandent les heureuses et mémorables négociations du Vicomte de Strangford. Quant à mes déterminations présentes, elles seront telles que je les ai toujours annoncées. La Russie y trouvera le meilleur prix de sa modération, et Votre Majesté l'accomplissement de ses désirs. Mais afin de mieux constater encore

1 Ambassador at Constantinople, 1821–24; at Petersburg, 1825–26.

les sentimens que je lui porte et que je tiens à lui exprimer dans cette circonstance, afin de mieux marquer la satisfaction que j'éprouve du dénoucment qui couronne les longs efforts de son Plénipotentiaire, c'est mon Aide-de-Camp-Général, le Comte Ozarowski, que je charge de déposer cette lettre entre les mains de Votre Majesté. Je sollicite en sa faveur l'accueil bienveillant dont elle l'a honoré dans plus d'une occasion, et je saisis avec d'autant plus de plaisir cette qui s'offre à moi pour lui adresser la présente, qu'elle me met à même de rendre aussi au Chevalier Bagot[1] toute la justice qui lui est dûe. Je me saurois trop me louer de sa conduite et de la manière dont il a rempli les fonctions que Votre Majesté lui avait confiées. Sa loyauté, son esprit de conciliation, son caractère noble et franc, lui ont acquis à jamais ma plus sincère estime, et je me plais à croire, Sire, que ce témoignage sera pour lui un titre de plus à vos bontés.

C'est toujours avec le plus vif empressement que je vous réitère l'assurance de l'attachement inviolable et de la considération la plus distinguée avec les quels, [etc.].

1175 Major-General Hussey Vivian[2] *to* Sir William Knighton

Beechwood, Southampton, August 11th 1824.

THE kindness with which you have ever expressed yourself towards me leads me to hope you will excuse my thus troubling you. It is generally understood that Sir Edward Paget has the offer of the appointment at the Military College at Sandhurst now vacant. It is just possible that the war with the Birmese,[3] or some other consideration, may induce him to decline it. Should he do so, I trust I shall not be considered as too presumptuous in asking you to mention me to His Majesty as a candidate for the situation. My rank (ten years a Major General) is not inadequate to it. Of my claims as a soldier I shall merely state, a constant active service from the commencement of the war in '93 untill the Battle of Waterloo; during which time I can truly say I was never once absent from my duty when my presence was required. (How I performed that duty I could confidently appeal to those under whom I served.) Of my qualifications I must speak with diffidence, but as far as attachment to

1 Sir Charles Bagot, Ambassador at Petersburg, 1820–24.
2 Sir Richard Hussey Vivian, first Baron Vivian (1775–1842). Created Baronet, 1828; elevated to the peerage, 1841.
3 The First Burmese War, 1824–26, caused by repeated violations of the frontier of Bengal in the Chittagong District.

the service, as a thorough acquaintance with the practical part of my profession, and an anxious desire at all times and in all situations properly to discharge my duty, are requisites, I may be allowed to say that I hope I should not be found wanting.

Believe me my dear Sir William I would not through you (and I do it with the utmost reluctance) thus presume to intrude myself on His Majesty (of whose infinite kindness to me on all occasions I am most fully sensible, and for which I hope I have endeavoured ever to shew myself as truly grateful) did not the state of my finances make it absolutely necessary that I should take some steps in order to releive myself from difficulties which will otherwise oppress and inconvenience me during my life. And had I not daily opportunities of seeing that unless a man makes known his wishes (even when the kindest intentions are entertained towards him), he is constantly passed over under the impression that he desires to remain unemployed. Should the acceptance of the appointment I have named by Sir Edward Paget, or should any other cause place it beyond my reach, I venture to add that any command of which with my family I could take advantage would be most acceptable.

Again I must beg of you to excuse my thus trespassing on you, and, should you think it right to mention the purport of this letter to the King, I must at the same time beg of you to lay my humble duty at his feet with the assurance that the difficulties under which I labour (and of which I have before now explained to you the occasion in a great degree) have alone occasioned my taking so great a liberty; and I must entreat you also to beg for me His Majesty's pardon should I have done wrong in making this appeal.

P.S. If you yourself think my request unreasonable or improper pray say nothing of it.

1176 THE REV. LEWIS WAY[1] *to* SIR WILLIAM KNIGHTON

Hotel Marbeuf, Champs Elisées, Paris,
Sept. 20th 1824.

MR. NOEL has been obliged to return to Geneva and therefore I cannot cross the water at present. My affairs on this side of the Channel are also the most urgent and important. I should not have troubled you with

---

1 The advocate of the conversion of the Jews. He founded Marbœuf (an English Protestant) Chapel in Paris. [1772–1840.]

any concern in them but for your own friendly overture, and the mode in which you may render me the most essential service depends on the decision of a question which you alone must resolve, viz:—whether on consideration you determine to be the purchaser of the two fruit farms and as much of the forest as lies divided by a straight fence from the grown timber on the side of the great avenue to the South and by the road from the Lodges to the East. The division of what would remain to Stansted, this would certainly fall within the compass of such a purchase as you propose to make, and, if it did not, as much as you please might be taken off on the side to the East. The price of purchase may be settled by two surveyors, taking the division of their difference. I make you this offer *as from Mic[haelma]s day next* from which time you shall take possession, making the payment and finishing the matter at Xmas. If you cannot make up your mind to this, then I have another offer to make which is that if you will advance or lend me £10,000 from Mic^s to Lady Day 1825 you shall have all that time to make your calculations and shall have your option to receive your money with interest of the 6 months, or let it remain as part of the purchase at that time. I have other securities which by that time I can call in, but I have immediate payments to make here which cannot be deferred and therefore I must beg to know your mind. If you accept the first proposal I will send immediate directions to Hurns & Edge; if not, there is no occasion to mention it to them and it might be injurious to some other arrangement to make it known in vain. If you accept the second offer there is time enough, and all that would be requisite would be to send me a bond for signature and a letter of credit from your London banker on Lafitte[1] or any other house of credit at Paris. It would be sufficient for my purpose if a London banker would accept my bills at 3 months date from 7th. October when I am to make my payments and can easily do so in that form if more convenient to you to pay the money at Xmas.

This, my dear friend, is all I have to say on *business*. I have written it with my own hand to shew you that *I can write.* I beg you neither to scold or flatter me. I give you the opportunity either of suiting yourself or of serving me, and all I require is that decision and promptitude to which you are competent and which my personal circumstances require.

By attention to your kind injunctions my health has been preserved and my ministerial labours rendered light and easy. Mr. Noel preached every evening and there is some hope of his return, and so many clergy pass through Paris that I shall never be without help.

1 Jacques Laffitte (1767–1844) the wealthy Paris banker and governor of the Bank of France.

I saw the partial remains of James II. deposited *by order of H.B.M. George IV* (as appeared on a tablet on the wall) in a church at St. Germain en attendant the re-edification of a church.[1] The service was decently performed according to the Catholic rites. A Scotch Bishop made an oration in which he favored the French tongue with the importation of some phrases brought from beyond the Tweed, such as "les honneurs que nous *payons*" etc. Paris is now engaged in *paying* honor to Louis and court to Charles.[2] I paid mine to both yesterday by a sermon on Isaiah C. vi. v. 1. I only add God save King George and make you His Majesty's faithful servant and my sincere friend as I am [etc.].

1177 GEORGE CANNING *to the* KING

Foreign Office, Oct. 14th 1824.

MR. CANNING has lost no time in investigating, (in obedience to your Majesty's commands), the case and claims of Mr. Lacroix, holding the appointment of Vice Consul at Nice. Mr. Lacroix was appointed to that situation by your Majesty's Consul at Genoa, and approved (as is usual in the cases of Vice Consuls), by the Foreign Office. But although Mr. Lacroix's nomination has been thus in the usual course, the duties which he has had to discharge are of such a nature and the manner in which he has discharged them is, by the testimony of many of your Majesty's subjects, shown to have been so meritorious, that Mr. Canning has no difficulty in humbly recommending to your Majesty that your Majesty's Minister at Turin should be instructed to pay to Mr. Lacroix an allowance of £250 a year; the same to date from January *last* in order to cover any expences which he may have incurred and not brought to account.

Mr. Canning will humbly submit to your Majesty tomorrow a draft to this effect, to Mr. Hill who is still at Turin and who is fully sensible of Mr. Lacroix's merits.

1 The remains of James II were discovered by the workmen employed in digging the foundation of the new Church at St Germains on the site of the old Church, which was beyond repair. On 9 September, in accordance with the wishes of George IV expressed to the French Government, the body was removed in great state and deposited beneath the altar until the new Church was completed.

2 Louis XVIII died on 16 September and was succeeded by his brother Charles X.

F. O., Oct. 14th 1824.

MR. CANNING humbly takes the liberty of laying before your Majesty a letter which he has this day received from Sir Benjamin Bloomfield, by his son; whom Mr. Canning has recalled from Stockholm for the purpose of sending him as paid attaché to the embassy at Lisbon.

1179 SIR BENJAMIN BLOOMFIELD *to* SIR WILLIAM KNIGHTON

Stockholm, 20th October, 1824.

THE last Gazette announces several diplomatic changes and leaving the Secretaryship of Turin vacant. I persuade myself that you will engage Mr. Canning to take my son into his favorable consideration. It wd be cheering to his poor father to obtain his promotion and, to be placed with the new Minister there (Mr. Foster), a particular comfort. Mr. F. took a very great fancy to John at Copenhagen and my own intimacy with Foster would ensure the young diplomat a large share of favor. See then how many prizes I shd draw if this was achieved. I'll not add another word, for I know that your good wishes for this dear boy need no stimulus. Were His Majesty to deign his interference the next Gazette would assuredly announce his nomination.

You'll be sorry to hear that the severity of the cold has affected my bowels. I have now been suffering for 3 weeks and am this day as ailing as ever. The season has set in much earlier than usual, and infinitely colder than last year.

I trust that the King's health is as good as it is possible. Every letter I receive speaks of its excellence. God bless you.

[P.S.] The Peerage question is within a month of being disposed of. I have no reason to doubt the Government's good faith.[1]

1180 SIR WALTER SCOTT *to* SIR WILLIAM KNIGHTON

Abbotsford, Melrose, 21 October [? 1824].

I WAS applied to some time since by Moore who is now busy with a life of Byron to obtain such letters as I had from his Lordship, and in the courtesy of literature was well disposed to oblige him.[2] I have very few,

1 His peerage was not gazetted until 14 May 1825.
2 Thomas Moore (1779–1852), published his *Life* of his friend Byron in 1830.

but one of them is on a peculiar subject, being Byron's account of an interview with His Majesty when Prince Regent, which is expressed as you will see by the enclosed copy, with the high sense of His Majesty's talents and taste unless in so far as it may be a depreciation from either that the Prince Regent condescended to express some flattering partiality for a living author. I feel it a duty of the [possessor not to] permit this very interesting document to pass out of possession untill I know whether it would be agreeable to His Majesty that it should be made publick. On the one hand there may be some satisfaction in showing the publick that Lord Byron rendered the same justice to the engaging qualities of His Majesty which must be common to all who approach his person. On the other there may be reasons some of which I can guess and others unknown to me which might make it more desirable that the letter should remain private. It must be for you, my dear Sir William, to decide whether I shall part with it or not. If so you can send the copy of the letter to Lockhart[1] with your *imprimatur* and he will give it to Murray[2] who publishes the book.

The republication of the Waverley Novels has met with uninterrupted success to a very uncommon extent. I hope they have regularly been laid on His Majesty's table according to his obliging permission. I expect Wilkie and his sister here tomorrow. Your acquaintance Mrs Lockhart is still my guest, indisposed with a bad fit of rheumatism. Lockhart has been obliged to return to the Regents Park. I am dear Sir William [etc.].

1181 CHARLES WATKIN WILLIAMS WYNN *to the* KING

Newtown, Montgomeryshire,
28th Oct. 1824.

MR. WILLIAMS WYNN has this day been honoured with your Majesty's note of the 25th. respecting the Chief Justiceship of Calcutta.

No communication of the death of Sir Christopher Puller[3] has yet been received except that contained in the Bombay newspapers, and it was Mr. Williams Wynn's wish to defer laying before your Majesty any recommendation of a successor until he had an opportunity of consulting the Lord Chancellor, and was enabled to state his Lordship's opinion also upon the appointment.

1 John Gibson Lockhart (1794–1854), Scott's son-in-law; afterwards editor of the *Quarterly Review*.
2 John Murray (1778–1843). Lockhart was one of his chief literary advisers.
3 Chief Justice of Calcutta since 1823. [1774–1824.]

Mr. Williams Wynn understood your Majesty on a former occasion to refer, not to the Chief Justiceship of the vacancy of which there then appeared to be no probability, but to a Puisne Justiceship of Calcutta which was the office Sir Charles Grey[1] had himself sollicited, and to which he was accordingly appointed in the month of July last.

The character of Sir Charles Grey stands so deservedly high as amply to justify that promotion, but Mr. Williams Wynn trusts that your Majesty will pardon his expressing a doubt whether it may be expedient, so soon, to give him a second step, and that to the highest judicial situation in India, if there should be candidates of superior professional rank and experience.

The Chief Justice of Calcutta, though possessing no jurisdiction beyond the limits of his own Court, is universally looked up to as the first legal authority in India. His sanction is necessary to give validity to the regulations of Government within the capital. To his opinion the Governor General and the Judges of the other Presidencies usually refer in cases of difficulty. Under these circumstances it is not only important that he should be fully competent to discharge the duties of his office but that his opinion and decisions should carry with them the greatest weight in the judgement of others.

It has been intimated to Mr. Williams Wynn that there are at present, even among your Majesty's English Judges, more than one who are desirous of obtaining this appointment, and it will be for your Majesty's consideration whether, in this event, the selection of a person who has previously sate upon the English bench will not confer additional respectability and authority upon the office abroad.

Mr. Williams Wynn has ventured humbly to offer this suggestion, but as soon as he has obtained more information he will take the earliest opportunity of again bringing the subject before your Majesty.

1182 THE EARL OF ELDON *to the* KING

November 4th 1824.

THE CHANCELLOR was honoured yesterday with your Majesty's most gracious letter, not marked private.

He had received at Encombe a letter from Sir John Stanley announcing the death of a Puisne Judge in India, but he had had no official account of the death of the Chief Justice. Mr. Wynne, however, mentioned it very

---

1 Sir Charles Edward Grey (1785–1865). Judge of the Madras Supreme Court since 1820; succeeded Sir Christopher Puller at Calcutta.

lately in a letter to the Chancellor, and that he had done himself the honor of writing to your Majesty on the subject, and proposed again to write to your Majesty upon the Chancellor's return to town. The Chancellor has not heard further from him and supposes that Mr. Wynne is not yet in town.

The Chancellor has heard rumours importing that some of your Majesty's Judges were desirous to go to India as Chief Justices. Those whom rumour named were Mr. Justice Bailey [1] and Mr. Justice Holroyd. [2] To the Chancellor no Judge of Westminster Hall has given the slightest intimation upon the subject. Mr. J. Bailey was desirous to remove into the Court of Exchequer and your Majesty may recollect that he had obtained your gracious permission so to remove. He declined, however, at that time to avail himself of it, but the Chancellor has lately had reason, though not from Mr. Justice Bailey himself, to believe that he again wishes to go into the Court of Exchequer. Mr. Justice Holroyd has never intimated any wish to the Chancellor to change his situation.

The Chancellor humbly takes leave to state that, in his judgement, the judicial seats in Westminster Hall ought to be made, in point of emolument, such that a Puisne Judge of those Courts could have no temptation to cease to be such, unless by promotion to the offices of Chief Justices there. Whether such a most desireable improvement does or does not take place it is a matter to which the most serious consideration should be given, before a precedent should be made, which would induce gentlemen in the profession to accept Puisne Judgeship in your Majesty's Courts in Westminster Hall; not with a view of retaining their judicial seats there but in order the more readily to pave the way to their becoming Chiefs in India.

The Chancellor most deeply regrets if it has happened thro' any negligence on his part that the warrant for appointing Mr. Puller was laid before your Majesty before your Majesty's pleasure had been taken upon the subject of the appointment. He trusts, at least, that this must have happened in consequence of some misunderstanding occasioned by the very different part which is assigned to the Chancellor as to the recommendations of persons to judicial seats in Westminster Hall, and as to the recommendations of persons to be Indian, Scotch or Welsh Judges.

The Chancellor feels, most gratefully, your Majesty's most kind expressions respecting his health. Nothing could give him more cordial delight than to learn that your Majesty's health is perfectly re-established. Mr. Justice Bailey was upon the Continent only nine days.

1 Sir John Bayley (1763–1841). Judge of the King's Bench since 1808. Baronet, 1834.
2 Sir George Sowley Holroyd (1758–1831). Judge of the King's Bench, 1816–28.

[n. d.]

IT had certainly occurred to me, before I received your letter of the date 3rd. July, that if I was consulted upon the question who should succeed the Chief Justice of India I should strongly recommend that Sir Charles Grey should be his successor. The matter however rests with the President of the Board of Control and not with the Chancellor, and whether I may or may not be asked my opinion upon the subject I cannot say. Having not, as yet, been asked that opinion appears to lead to a conclusion that I may not be consulted.

The Duke of Wellington to Sir William Knighton, 6 November 1824. (*W.N.D.* II, 332–33, where the name "English" is omitted.)

1184 THE EARL OF LIVERPOOL *to the* KING

Coombe Wood, Novr. 29 1824.

LORD LIVERPOOL has the honour of sending to your Majesty a letter which he has received from Viscount Sidmouth.

Lord Liverpool very much regrets the loss of Lord Sidmouth's assistance but he is not surprised at his determination, as during the last Spring and Summer (for the reasons stated in his letter) he had become a very irregular attendant at the Cabinets, and though there always must exist more or less objection to any person being a member of your Majesty's Cabinet without holding a Cabinet office, the inconvenience is greatly increased if the individual is not a constant attendant and cannot devote a sufficient portion of his time to reading the papers and correspondence which, in obedience to your Majesty's commands are circulated amongst your Majesty's confidential servants.

1185 VISCOUNT SIDMOUTH *to the* EARL OF LIVERPOOL

White Lodge, Richmond Park,
Novr, ye 26th 1824.

I BEG the favor of you to lay before His Majesty my humble request that he will be graciously pleased to dispense with my future attendance at the Cabinet, which in consequence of my residing almost constantly in the country, would necessarily be irregular and uncertain. On this account I am very desirous of His Majesty's permission to retire from a situation which, as I cannot remain in it, consistently with my sense of duty to His Majesty, I can no longer hold with honor and satisfaction to myself.

I particularly regret that it was not in my power to attend the Council on Wednesday or Saturday last, as, on either occasion an audience, which I should have presumed to solicit, might probably have been granted without material inconvenience to His Majesty, and, in that case, the trouble which I am giving you would have been prevented.[1]

1186 THE KING *to the* EARL OF LIVERPOOL

(*c.* 30 November 1824.)

THE KING has given his serious attention to the communications which Lord Liverpool made to him yesterday.

That part which relates to the propos'd retirement of Lord Sidmouth is most painful to the King. The King is, however, deeply impress'd that if it must be so (merely from motives of his own high personal regard, not from those which he has reason to know were so strongly felt for many years by his late revered father, for Lord Sidmouth) of the heighth of impropriety there would be in suffering that most excellent servant of the Crown and of the public, after his long and distinguish'd services, to retire from office for the rest of his life without some substantial testimonial of the approbation of his Sovereign, and to which by his long and distinguish'd services he is so justly entitled. The King therefore desires Ld. Ll. to make an offer on the part of the King to Ld Sidmouth, accompanied with the strongest expression of the King's feelings of regret.

[Another draft]

If however it must be so, the King cannot consent to the retirement of this distinguished servant of the Crown and of the public, without such remuneration as shall mark to the public the great regard and estimation in which he was held, not only by the late but by the *present* King, and to which his long and meritorious services have so justly entitled him.

1 Eldon deeply regretted Sidmouth's decision as a step calculated to weaken the High Tory opposition in the Cabinet to Canning's foreign policy. He wrote to him [Thursday morning] (? 2 December 1824): "Upon going into the Cabinet room yesterday noon Lord L. showed me your note. I confess I was much disturbed by it, though I kept silence upon it; a mass of most important matter being mentioned to be brought forward, and a loss to the Cabinet of the benefit of your principles. I cannot say that the reason of your not having mentioned it is as obvious to me, as you, my dear Lord, suppose it would be. That I should have done what I could to prevent the step I admit. I fear it has paralysed the endeavours of those who remain, as to some most important matters. It may, however, relieve them from the labours consequential upon a notion that if they can't do good, they might, in some small measure, prevent evil...." (*Sidmouth MSS.*)

[1824.]

THE KING very much regrets that his Cabinet should have thought it necessary, to enter upon the consideration of a Commercial Treaty with yᵉ inhabitants of Buenos Ayres, at the present moment.

The King fears that this arrangement will carry with it, the appearance & promise, of an early recognition to the different insurrectionary States of South America.

The King cannot but feel that the whole proceedings relative to this question are premature.

It is impossible to suppose that the great Allied Powers, can view the policy of this country, as regards South America, with indifference; & sooner or later this policy will endanger the peace of Europe.

The commercial advantages are obvious; but the calamitous consequences of a renewal of war, cannot be so easily calculated on.

However, the King will not oppose, what he supposes to be the unanimous opinion of his Cabinet, & if it be thought fit to adopt a Commercial Treaty, with the inhabitants of Buenos Ayeres [*sic*], why let it be so.

When the Prince of Wales undertook the Regency of this Kingdom, during the indisposition of his revered father, the Prince abandoned all those friends, with whom he had lived in terms of the most unqualified friendship during the best years of his life; because the Prince, as Regent, thought their liberal & anti-Monarchical sentiments, unfavorable to the good government of his father's dominions; but the King now finds, that the opinions of the Opposition & liberals are uniformly acted upon.

The King cannot be supposed to be blind, to this state of things.[1]

1188

London, 13th January 1825.

GEORGE R.

IT is our pleasure to declare, that we have this day received from Sir William Knighton Bart Keeper of our Privy Purse, the sum of twenty thousand pounds, which is directed to be placed to our secret account at Messrs. Coutts & Co. G.R.

---

1 The Cabinet's Minute, dated 23 July 1824, recommending that Mr Parish, the British Consul-General at Buenos Aires, should be empowered to negotiate a Commercial Treaty, is in *Stapleton*, pp. 397–400. "Such a Treaty, *when ratified by your Majesty*, would amount to a diplomatic recognition of the State with which it had been concluded." Buenos Aires had ceased to acknowledge the sovereignty of Ferdinand VII of Spain in 1816.

[27 January 1825.]

THE KING desires that Lord Liverpool will transmit the draft of the speech, which it is proposed should be delivered on the opening of the approaching Session of Parliament, a week or ten days, previous to the third of February, that the King may have an opportunity of well considering what it may be deem'd proper or necessary to be said, on the subject of the recognition of the independance of the South American Provinces.[1]

The line of policy pursued by the King's Government under the King's direction at the close of the late war, which terminated under such happy circumstances, was *unanimity* of co-operation with the great Continental Powers, not only for the purpose of putting an end to the then existing hostilities, but for preserving the future tranquillity & peace of Europe.

The late Lord Londonderry, in conjunction with the Duke of Wellington, so effectually accomplished this desirable & great object, that this country took a position, in relation to her continental policy, that she had never before held.

The King supposes, it will not be denied, that the anarchy produced throughout the world by the French Revolution has left a record, so instructive, that the Councils of the British Government should never fail to be regulated by the wholesome remembrance of that terrible event!

That we should therefore regard, with the most anxious suspicion every attempt to revive the example of British America which unhappily for Great Britain ended in a seperation from the mother country. France treacherously assisted that successful enterprize & by her fatal policy, gave the first impulse to y^t revolution, which entailed, for a quarter of a century, such complicated misery, on the whole of Europe.

The revolutionary spirit of those days, altho' lulled & suspended, is by no means extinguished; & it would be wisdom to look to the ultimate consequences which the result of our recognition of the independence of the South American Provinces may probably produce on the evil & discontented, who are even at y^s moment control'd with difficulty, by the established power of regular Governments.

Let us even look at home, & observe the dangerous attempts which

1 On 3 February the Session was opened by commission. The King's Speech declared: "In conformity with the declarations which have been repeatedly made by His Majesty, His Majesty has taken measures for confirming by treaties the commercial relations already subsisting between this kingdom and those countries of America which appear to have established their separation from Spain." For the struggle between the Cabinet and the King over this question of recognition, see Prof. Temperley's *Foreign Policy of Canning*, pp. 145–7.

the active firebrands of Ireland are at this time pursuing, under the deceptive cloak of Catholic emancipation.

The organized schemes now so actively pursued in that unhappy country, is only a part of the same system, promoted by the same evil spirit, which gave rise to the calamities of the French Revolution.

The liberalism now adopted by the King's Government, appears to the King, to be a substantial part of that creed, which was hailed in the House of Commons in those revolutionary days, when it required all the talent & firmness of Mr. Pitt to put it down; & the support which that great statesman received, from the King's revered & excellent father, gave him the opportunity of using his great ability with such effect, as enabled him successfully to resist, the desolating storm.

The King has been long aware, that the principles of the King's early friends, were at that time the bane that threatened the destruction of our happy Constitution & the peace of the world, & if the King abandoned those early friends on his coming to the power of the Regency, for the good of the country, can the present Government suppose that the King will permit any individuals now to force upon him, measures of which he entirely disapproves; more especially when many members of the King's present Cabinet hold the same opinions with the King himself respecting the new political liberalism.[1] [& which is entirely opposed to those wise principles, that the King's Govern^t have acted upon— up to the death of the late Lord London-[derry]].

No such thing—if the present line of policy is to be *further* pursued, the King will feel himself justified in taking such measures as the Government will be ye least prepared to expect.

The King would wish to ask Lord Liverpool whether he supposes, the great abettors of this Spanish American question, (connected with the Opposition,) give their support to a recognition of the Spanish Provinces in relation to the great mercantile advantages which this measure may offer to this country, or from their love of democracy, in opposition to a monarchical aristocracy.

The King has no difficulty in answering this question; & let but the opportunity arise, the same rule of conduct would be as promptly applied, by these gentlemen, to the emancipation of our eastern possessions or to any other of the remote settlements, at present under the dominion of the British Crown.

The King cannot but be aware, that this, as well as every other Kingdom, must have its latent sources of wealth & power peculiar to itself, the cultivation of which, must be essential to the maintenance of its individual prosperity. But the King desires to observe that the policy

1 Especially Wellington (who had threatened to resign if Canning's proposal to recognize the rebellious Spanish-American colonies was accepted), Bathurst, Eldon, and Westmorland.

which is to balance the interests of Kingdoms is not to be found in hasty decision or petulant sarcasm.

The King hopes, under the Providence of the Almighty, that from the commencement of the Regency, much was done in laying the foundation of that peace which was at length happily attained; & nothing shall induce the King, for any consideration of speculative advantages, to run the risk of again disturbing the tranquillity of Europe, & involving this country in a disastrous & ruinous war.[1]

1190 THE EARL OF LIVERPOOL *to the* KING

Jany 27th 1825.

LORD LIVERPOOL had the honour of receiving your Majesty's letter,[2] together with the sealed paper,[3] which your Majesty was pleased to direct should be communicated to your Majesty's confidential servants.

This paper has been read to your Majesty's confidential servants in obedience to your Majesty[s] commands, and they have agreed to assemble tomorrow morning in order that they may deliberate upon it.

Cabinet Minute, 29 January 1825. (Stapleton, pp. 419–21; *W.N.D.* ii, 402–4.)
The King to the Earl of Liverpool [30 January 1825]. (Stapleton, p. 421.)

1191 THE KING *to the* EARL OF LIVERPOOL

[Between 1 and 7 February 1825.]

THE KING sends his kind regards to Lord Liverpool.

The King trusts that Lord Liverpool did not fail to explain to Mr. Canning the King's displeasure at Mr. Canning's note of the date of the first of February.[4]

As the King must give Mr. Canning an audience on Wednesday next, in consequence of the presentation of the Spanish Ambassador, the King desires that Mr. Canning may distinctly understand that the King will not suffer any verbal explanation on the subject of Mr. Canning's note, but if he has anything further to say on that head the King desires that it may be in writing.

1 This is the draft in Sir William Knighton's handwriting of the Memorandum which appears in Stapleton, pp. 416–19. The two documents are by no means identical.
2 *W.N.D.* ii, 401.   3 No. 1189.
4 Stapleton, pp. 422–6. This was Canning's individual reply to the King's letter of 30 January. "I certainly do not see the *necessity* of this letter", Liverpool told Canning, "but I see nothing whatever to object to the reasoning." (Stapleton, p. 422.)

Fife House, Feby 8, 1825.

LORD LIVERPOOL begs to be permitted to inform your Majesty that Lord Liverpool did not fail to express to Mr. Canning the displeasure and dissatisfaction which your Majesty had felt at his note of the first instant.

Lord Liverpool is convinced from what passed upon the occasion, that nothing was further from Mr. Canning's intention than to give your Majesty any offence, his object was merely to justify his own conduct.

Lord Liverpool will obey your Majesty's commands by making to Mr. Canning the communication your Majesty is pleased to desire respecting his audience of tomorrow.

1193 SIR BENJAMIN BLOOMFIELD *to* SIR WILLIAM KNIGHTON

Stockholm, 12th February, 1825.

MY last mails have announced your return and the melancholy event in Lord Conyngham's family.[1] You know how much I regarded Lord Mount Charles and will therefore give me credit for a sincere feeling of sorrow upon this distressing occasion. But my dear friend why have you not given me one line yourself? Surely a few moments might be snatched from your occupations to say, though only one sentence, to a poor devil frozen up in this remote corner. Our friend Mr. Davis has not written either for a long time.

Assuredly you have been apprized of a communication made to me by the Duke of Wellington upon the Peerage question.[2] As his Grace stated his recollection of the engagement and that he had made a note of it at the time, which was then before him, there was nothing left for me but the expression of my thanks to the Government, and to entreat his Grace, if it were not improper in the present stage of the question, to lay me at His Majesty's feet with the assurance of my gratitude for this fresh and high mark of his Royal favor. Let me beg you my kind friend to serve me upon this point by representing those feelings in your own amiable manner, and at the moment when it may be unintrusive.

John seems very happy at Lisbon, nevertheless I beg you to draw Mr. Canning's favourable recollection towards him. Mr. Canning saw John

1 Lord Mountcharles, the eldest son of the Marquis Conyngham, died at Nice in December 1824.

2 Bloomfield's Irish peerage was gazetted on 14 May 1825.

when passing through London and was particularly kind to him. Have you ever heard why they buffetted him about so much? A double outfit and unpaid journeys have made a deep hole in the poor fellow's pocket.

I have the pleasure to tell you that my public acts are approved and that my residence continues to be marked by the most particular distinction. I however begin to sigh for home, though upon the score of health I have no reason to regret my position. I have actively conquered my complaint which I ascribe rather to early hours and very moderate habits than to climate, certainly not to medecine.

Would I could hear well of His Majesty's health. The papers prepare us for a fit of the gout and inability to open Parliament. How much this is to be regretted, both the cause and the effect, for never was there a moment when the Monarch had such a mass of prosperity to develop to his subjects.

God bless you my dearest Knighton, [etc.].

[P.S.] I shall never forget the share you have had in the adjustment of the object now disposed of.

1194 THE DUKE OF CAMBRIDGE *to the* KING

Hanover, Feby. 15th 1825.

THE reports which you will have received by the two last mails from hence will have fully informed you of the dreadful calamity with which it has pleased Divine Providence to afflict this country.[1]

I am well aware how much this melancholy news will have affected you, and have therefore hitherto abstained from writing to you as I could not give you any additional information.

The distress of these two unfortunate Provinces of Bremen, and Eastfriesland is dreadful, but I am happy at being able at the same time to assure you that the general sympathy felt by all ranks on this awful occasion is such as it should be, and I have no doubt that the country will be ready to make every possible exertion, and sacrifice which will undoubtedly be required to relieve the unfortunate sufferers, most of whom have been driven from their homes in the middle of the night without saving an article of clothing.

The first object therefore is to provide them with provisions and clothes, and subscriptions are making at this moment all over the

1 Extraordinarily high tides caused widespread ruin by flooding, along the north German coast, and, the dykes being everywhere destroyed, huge areas were inundated.

country for this purpose, and a general committee has been formed here at the head of which I am, to receive them, and distribute them to the suffering districts.

I have every reason to believe that the amount of these subscriptions will be considerable, but the distress is so great and there are so many to be provided for, that any extra assistance in money which can be procured will be most acceptable.

You will I am sure, my dearest brother, find it very natural that I should have turned my thoughts towards England where charity is always at home, and I have in consequence written to Frederick requesting him to put himself at the head of a subscription for the relief of these unfortunate districts. He will of course speak to you on the subject, and I have no doubt that you will protect and countenance any thing which can be done towards the relief of these two unfortunate Provinces in your Hanoverian dominions which have been reduced in a few hours to an absolute state of beggary by a calamity which it is not in the power of man to have prevented.

I need not I trust assure you that every exertion will be made by the Government and myself to alleviate as much as possible this tremendous blow upon the welfare and prosperity of the country, and it will be one of the happiest moments of my life when I am able to report to you that our endeavours have been crowned with success.

I will now not detain you any longer, than to add the assurance of my ever remaining, my dearest brother, [etc.].

Sir Walter Scott to Sir William Knighton. 22 February [1825]. (*Grierson*, IX, 13–14.)
The Earl of Liverpool to the King. 25 February 1825. (*W.N.D.* II, 418.)

1195 THE KING *to* [SIR WILLIAM KNIGHTON]

King's Lodge,
Tues.ʸ n.ᵗ March 15th 1825.

I T is now so very late, that I shall only write you a few lines to thank you for your letter & its inclosure, which I receiv'd this morning. You say in your epistle that you intend being in town, *next Wednesday*, which I conclude therefore means *tomorrow*; this being the state of the case notwithstanding what I did say to you, in my former letter, I must entreat of you to come here, *as soon as you can*, after you shall have settled your present business in London, be it but for a day, before your return into Hampshire, for several little matters have arisen since my last writing to you, of various natures, pecuniary as well as domestick, which make me very desirous of seeing you, in order to talk them over, & to settle & to arrange them with you.

The accounts of my health which you mention as having receiv'd from a *certain quarter*, are certainly a *good deal* exaggerated, but upon the whole, it is certainly improv'd, & I hope (if matters continue to go on, as they have in great measure done, for the last ten days) that it will continue still progressively improving; but neither my appetite nor my sleep, are as yet, by any means what they ought to be, my spirits however, are certainly mended. You are so thoroughly acquainted with the whole carte du pâys, that it makes it quite unnecessary for me to say one word more, for I am sure that you will understand everything, by that, however little, which I have already written. Reserving therefore the entire contents of my budget, till we meet, I shall only add, God bless you d[ea]r friend, & believe me always, [etc.].

P.S. I have really much to tell you. I forgot to say that Sr H.^y Halford, intended to see you, & to give you the improved account of me, as well as what he proposes further to recommend.

1196 FREDERICK JOHN ROBINSON *to the* KING

Downing Street, March 26, 1825.

M R. ROBINSON presents his humble duty to your Majesty, and begs leave to submit to your Majesty's gracious approbation the accompanying draft of a Treasury Minute.

It relates to certain mines in Nova Scotia, the lease and working of which, it is conceived, would be highly beneficial to your Majesty's subjects generally, and would in all probability ultimately relieve this country from the expence of maintaining the Civil Government of that Province.

Mr. Robinson would not have presumed to trouble your Majesty upon this matter, had it not been for the circumstance that it is proposed in the Minute to grant a lease of these mines (upon such terms as are usual in the leasing of minerals) to His Royal Highness the Duke of York.

The draft of the Minute explains the grounds upon which it appears, that, under the peculiar circumstances of the case, His Royal Highness may be said to have an equitable claim to become the lessee of the mines in question; and Mr. Robinson has not ventured to submit the matter to your Majesty's gracious consideration, without having endeavoured to satisfy himself by every search for information which was within his power, as to the original intention of His late Majesty to direct such a lease to be made out.

Mr. Robinson will be ready to give your Majesty any further explanation upon the subject, should it be your Majesty's pleasure to require it; and Mr. Robinson will only presume to add, that it is proposed that the lease, if it should be your Majesty's pleasure to grant it to His Royal Highness, should be in all respects the same as to terms, as it would have been if granted to any other of your Majesty's subjects.

[*Enclosure.*]

1197   *Treasury Minute. (Draft.) March* 1825.

Various applications having been made to their Lordships since the termination of the war in 1815 for grants of mines in Nova Scotia, New Brunswick, & Cape Breton, and amongst others an application from Mr. Adam on behalf of His Royal Highness the Duke of York in the year 1815, founded upon an intention of His Majesty's Government in the year 1788 to make such a grant to His Royal Highness, but which was never perfected. In consequence of these applications the attention of their Lordships has been directed to this subject, with a view of considering in what mode such mines, if any shall exist, may be rendered most productive in aid of those services in these colonies to which resources of this description have, by law or usage, been rendered applicable.

In the result of the enquiries which their Lordships have directed to be made upon this subject it appears to be clearly established not only by original communications addressed to His Royal Highness the Duke of York in the year 1788 which have been laid before their Lordships, but also by the draft of an intended grant of mines in Nova Scotia which was submitted for the approval of His late Majesty's Attorney General[1] in the year 1792, and which has been found deposited in the Patent Office, that it was His late Majesty's gracious intention at that period, that a grant should be made of certain mines in the Province of Nova Scotia to His Royal Highness for his life, and for 21 years after his decease under certain reservations and limitations specified in the said draft.

The Chancellor of the Exchequer states to the Board that he has communicated with Sir Charles Long who was one of the Secretaries of the

1 Sir Archibald Macdonald (1747–1826).

Treasury at the time when the said draft of the intended grant to His Royal Highness the Duke of York appears to have been under the consideration of His late Majesty's then Attorney General; and that Sir Charles has a distinct and perfect recollection that such a grant was then intended to be made to His Royal Highness.

Under these circumstances my Lords are of opinion that His late Majesty's gracious intentions in regard to the grant of these mines in favor of His Royal Highness the Duke of York must be considered as clearly established. And the Chancellor of the Exchequer having represented to the Board, that His Royal Highness has lately applied to the Earl of Liverpool—Earl Bathurst & himself for the fulfillment of His late Majesty's gracious intentions in His Royal Highness's favor, my Lords request that the Earl of Liverpool & himself will submit to His Majesty their humble recommendation that His late Majesty's gracious intentions may now be carried into effect, with such reservations as to rent or produce as may be usual in leases of minerals.

1198 THE KING *to* FREDERICK JOHN ROBINSON

King's Lodge,
Sat.ʸ Nᵗ March 26th 1825.

THE KING sends his kind regards to Mr. Robinson, & acquaints him, that the King feels that he can in *no wise* give his *immediate* & *unconditional* consent to the grant relative to mines in Nova Scotia &c. &c. &c. as propos'd by Mr. Robinson in the box which the King has just receiv'd. The King thinks it right here to observe, that although the object in part, is not *entirely new* to him, yet, that this is the *very first intimation,* which the King has ever receiv'd of such a project having been even in contemplation, notwithstanding which the matter itself, as is now submitted to the King, for his approbation & consent, appears to be one already completely digested & arrang'd & offer'd to the King as a circumstance of most common place business.

The King justly feels (without meaning to convey the smallest censure upon Mr. Robinson,) that this is neither the delicate nor the proper manner in which the King should be approach'd upon *this*, or upon any other matter of business which may concern any branch of his family.

Mr. Robinson, however, may rely that although it is years & years, since the King has heard any thing upon this subject, that the King will lose no time in devoting his particular attention to it, & that so soon as the King shall have completely inform'd himself, & made up his mind he will acquaint Mr. Robinson with his pleasure. The King hopes, that this *necessary* delay, will not in any way impede the progress of the remaining public business, through the House of Commons.[1]

1199 FREDERICK JOHN ROBINSON *to the* KING

Downing Street, March 26,[2] 1825.

MR. ROBINSON offers his humble duty to your Majesty. He is grieved beyond measure that in the manner of laying before your Majesty the matter contained in the paper transmitted yesterday, he should have incurred (he fears justly) your Majesty's displeasure. But Mr. Robinson entreats your Majesty to believe that he had no *intention* to act in a way which might appear to your Majesty inconsistent with that respect, which it is no less his wish than his duty to shew to your Majesty upon all occasions.

Mr. Robinson however humbly solicits your Majesty's permission to state, that his only reason for throwing the communication into the form of a *proposed* Minute, was in order to render the matter more intelligible than he thought it might be, if the whole substance were contained in his accompanying letter. The Treasury itself has at present no cognizance of the business, or of the draft.

The whole question arose long before your Majesty was graciously pleased to confer upon Mr. Robinson his present office; and when it came under Mr. Robinson's notice, *some* decision upon [it] was required in consequence of the various applications which had been made to Lord Bathurst and to the Treasury for a lease of the mines in Nova Scotia. Lord Liverpool, Lord Bathurst, and Mr. Robinson were thus under the necessity of considering what it might be adviseable for your Majesty to determine respecting it; and Mr. Robinson begs leave humbly to assure

1 According to Captain Gronow, Hamlet, the wealthy London jeweller, advanced money to the Duke of York and received as security "property in Nova Scotia, consisting chiefly of mines, which, when he began to work them, turned out valueless, after entailing enormous expense. Loss upon loss succeeded, and in the end bankruptcy." (*Reminiscences*, I, 135.) Robinson wrote to the Duke of York on 19 April: "I am happy to acquaint your Royal Highness by command of His Majesty that His Majesty has been graciously pleased to accede to the proposal which I presumed to submit to His Majesty, for granting to your Royal Highness a lease of certain mines in the Province of Nova Scotia. I will in conformity with this signification of the King's pleasure, take care that the necessary measures are taken for arranging the details of the proposed grant, and for preparing the necessary documents for such signatures as may be required for its completion." (Add. MS. 40862, fo. 134.)
2 A slip for 27?

your Majesty, that if he has erred in not bringing the matter before your Majesty at an earlier stage, he acted under an impression that he could not presume to approach your Majesty upon the subject, until he had ascertained as far as possible, both by personal communication with His Royal Highness the Duke of York, and by an examination of such documents as existed respecting it, how the facts of the case stood.

Mr. Robinson humbly hopes that your Majesty will be graciously pleased to pardon him for having ventured to trouble your Majesty with this explanation: he throws himself upon your Majesty's goodness, and awaits with every deference your Majesty's pleasure. He will only add, that he does not apprehend that the decision of the question, in whatever way it should be your Majesty's pleasure to decide it, would require the sanction of Parliament, or that any length of consideration which your Majesty might think fit to give to it, would impede the progress of business in the House of Commons.

1200 THE EARL OF CLANWILLIAM[1] *to* SIR WILLIAM KNIGHTON

Berlin, June 23, 1825.

As I set off tomorrow for Tœplitz, I went this morning to the iron foundry, where I found the statue and pedestal of Blucher's monument at Breslau in great forwardness; and from the great pains which have been taken, I have much hope that the King will approve of this specimen of art from a place where, au reste, the arts neither flourish as indigenous plants or as exotics. The case will be sent off by water in a fortnight, and may reach London in about a month more—say the beginning of September. In the larger case you will find a box in which are your belongings, marked W.K.

10	Luther's monument and statue,
17	4 bracelets (two pair)
6	busts of the King of Prussia,
3	and of Napoleon
36	

I could only find those bracelets, which were good taste, and I would not send you any others. There is no small bust of the Emperor Alexander. You did not say whether it is the statue only of Luther which you wanted,

---

1 At this time Minister at Berlin.

or the monument besides, but I send both at all events, as the latter is of itself very pretty, and will always make a pretty present. Your debt is 36 dollars = £5 – 10, which you may have paid to me at Drummonds. Tell me whether you would like me to send you any more bracelets or chains: I shall be back here in a month or 6 weeks, and will with the greatest pleasure do your commissions.

I should be very glad if you would, at any opportunity, lay me at His Majesty's feet; I can never forget his gracious kindness to me, at the most trying and painful moment in my life, and I have sometimes a fear lest he should ever think I could be ungrateful.

Goodbye, my dear K. I hope and trust to see you next winter, and should be very glad in the mean time occasionally to hear from you, though you great people never find time for scribbling to exiles. Ever, dear K affect^{ly} yrs.

1201 GEORGE CANNING *to the* KING

Foreign Office, July 13, 1825.

ALTHOUGH your Majesty was graciously pleased to say that your Majesty did not require any report of the execution of your Majesty's commands with respect to the corps diplomatique, Mr. Canning thinks it his duty humbly to acquaint your Majesty with the substance of what passed yesterday, in consequence of those commands, between Count Lieven & Mr. Canning.

Count Lieven expressed the sincerest regret that he should have done anything, and (as he must confess was the case) been in some degree the cause of what was done by others, displeasing to your Majesty. He added that when he saw in the newspapers of the following day, what had been the sort of supper provided for the Ball of Monday, it struck him that he ought to have been more careful in his inquiries, before he determined to come away. But he begged me most respectfully to assure your Majesty, on his behalf, that in taking that determination, he had acted in the manner which he supposed to be most consonant to your Majesty's wishes. There was not (he says) any expectation of a supper of any kind. None had ever (in his memory) taken place at Carlton House. The first notice that he had of it on this occasion, was the seeing your Majesty & your Royal family rise, & proceed to another apartment. He then made the best efforts, that he could, to obtain information: but being pressed to decide on the instant, (not so much for himself, as for the Marchioness of Palmella[1] who, with the rest of his colleagues of the corps diplomatique applied to him for advice) he thought it safer *not* to follow your Majesty, conceiving that your Majesty had retired for the night; & that it might probably be your Majesty's pleasure that none but your My's own family should follow your Majesty into your private apartments.

Count Lieven begged me to assure your Majesty that he was anxiously looking out for some opportunity of conveying these explanations, & the expression of his sentiments thereupon to your Majesty; & to tender to your Majesty his most grateful acknowledgements for having kindly afforded him such an opportunity.

1202 MISS MARY SEYMOUR *to the* KING

Tilney St, Wednesday morning,
July the thirteenth 1825.

I FEEL how very great a liberty, I am guilty of, in intruding upon your Majesty's time but yet more so when I am led to do so, by the desire I have of expressing feelings which I have reason to fear may be displeasing to your Majesty, towards whom from my peculiar position I am more bound than *any other human being* by the very strongest ties of gratitude, respect & attachment. Your Majesty's great goodness & parental conduct which commenced with my earliest years & has been graciously extended to me to this present moment, only increases the pain & embarassment I feel in beginning upon a subject which may meet with the disapprobation of your Majesty, & I can only *implore* you to look with indulgence upon a letter written in the most trying moment of my life, when I stand most in need of all my strength of mind & possess so little; & feeling as I do how inadequate are my powers to describe the contending emotions I labour under & how impossible it is for me to write upon such a subject with all the deference & respect due to your Majesty. Your Majesty was I am aware, made acquainted five years since with an attachment that had then existed for some time between Colonel Dawson & myself & when your Majesty was applied to, justly concurred in the opinion that was felt upon the subject, by my own family, but more particularly *by her*[2] to whom I have ever owed more than a daughter's feelings of gratitude & affection. After a period of three

1 Palmella was the Portuguese Ambassador.
2 Mrs Fitzherbert.

years during which interval my judgement has been unbiassed, & I have been at perfect liberty to decide upon the nature of my own feelings, I must make the confession to your Majesty that they are but confirmed in the preference I have alluded to, though I have made every effort to conquer them, alive as I have been, to all the disadvantages which have presented themselves, but still more so from knowing them, to be in opposition to the wishes of those I most love & value: It would be disingenuous in me were I to attempt to conceal from your Majesty that time has not reconciled mama or my brothers to the step upon which my future happiness depends, though it may have made them withdraw the opposition every consideration allied with their interest for me had made them so long continue.

I dare not entreat that your Majesty should so far condescend as to add so important a favor to the innumerable ones you have already lavished upon me by affording that sanction & support on a subject (which with all my decided feelings upon) I know that your Majesty must condemn, though could I do so I should throw myself at your Majesty's feet & supplicate you not to withdraw that countenance & protection from one whose earliest impressions have been those of the warmest filial gratitude & affection & are distinct from those which I must ever retain as your Majesty's most devoted [etc.].

[P.S.] I must again entreat your Majesty's forgiveness for having addressed him but which I trust will be granted me when he feels how impossible it is for me to allow what I have expressed to be communicated to your Majesty through a less direct channel. I do not presume to ask for an answer from your Majesty but implore him to recollect how much my happiness or misery are in his hands & how predominant will the latter feeling be should I meet with a cessation of all the affection condescension & kindness that have so gratefully been experienced by me for so long a series of years, & which so independently of your Majesty's exalted situation could NEVER be made up to me under any circumstance.[1]

1 On 20 August 1825 Miss Seymour married Colonel George Lionel Dawson, the third son of John Dawson, first Earl of Portarlington. In 1827 he took the additional surname of Damer.

R.ℓ Lℊe, W.ʳ
Fri.ᵈʸ M.ℊ July 15th 1825.

AFTER the conversation I had with you yesterday, & the perfect union of sentiment between you & me, which was the result, upon the very painful subject you was desir'd to communicate, it should seem needless for me to trouble you with any thing further upon that subject. But, from the very sincere love & affection I have for so many years cherish'd for Minny Seymour, & the very lively interest I do, & must ever feel not only for her happiness, but for her future wellfare & prosperity in life, I deem it, an indispensible duty, which I owe to her, to myself, to her family, & to all parties, to state now *distinctly* to you, (for you to communicate) that which I am afraid I was able, only imperfectly to do yesterday.

From what you stated to me yesterday, I take for granted that Minney Seymour has completely made up her mind to marry Mr. Dawson. It therefore appears *decidedly* to me, that having determin'd upon this step, attended as it is, now, & indeed as it has been unfortunately for such a length of time, with so many painful & unpleasant circumstances, her *first consideration* should be & I *maintain*, that it is *positively* her *first duty now* to endeavour to place the man of her choice, in the most *respectable point of view she can*, in the eyes of the world, as the *best palliative*, or *justification* in some degree, for her sad imprudence. I do not mean to cast the smallest reflexion upon Mr. Dawson, but I have heard, & I do know, from my long experience & knowledge of the world, (what you probably may have also heard) but what you can not fail to know as well as me, that the world has not only talk'd already a great deal upon this matter & *most unpleasantly* but that the world, so long as it lasts, & is a world, will continue to talk, & to form its own opinions, & to express its sentiments upon *this*, as well as upon every other matter. The only chance therefore of accomplishing the first of these objects & of meeting the other, must depend entirely upon Minney Seymour's *own* conduct at this *present* moment. I therefore do call upon her, & enjoin her, now, as one of those who can not help feeling themselves by far the best priviledg'd, & justified, from all that purity & sincerity of affection & love which she knows that from her very birth, I have borne her, to take care, *that the whole of her fortune should be plac'd in trustees hands, & settled entirely, solely, & only upon her, & upon any children which she may probably have* hereafter. When she has done this, she will completely exonerate Mr. Dawson from every possible imputation of having been actuated upon by any principle or motive of *self interest*; it is also the best means she can adopt, in some measure to soften the just & natural feelings of her best & truest friends & relations, & may possibly tend to reconcile them more hereafter to this step, which *we do, & must all of us* so deeply lament; there is also, this last good that will arise, out of this line of conduct (but which I fear at this moment will weigh but little with her,) which is, that she will thus have secured herself & her children against every possibility of want, for the rest of her life.

I must now dearest Frederick, give you an additional trouble; in the beginning of this letter, I told you that you was at liberty to communicate its contents, but it is *now my anxious wish,* that you should read the whole of it, *in extenso,* both to Mrs. Fitzherbert, as well as to Minney Seymour, the *first moment* you can obtain an interview with them; after which, I must desire you to send for that most excellent & worthy man, & I may add valuable friend of mine, Minney Seymour's trustee, Mr. John Forster [*sic*], of Lincoln's inn, that you will then tell him that it was by *my desire* you had sent for him, you will then shew him & read him this letter, & also desire him in consequence, *immediately* to prepare & draw up, such documents & settlements as may be necessary, for the *entirely securing* to Minney Seymour *alone,* & to her children hereafter, the whole of her present property & fortune, & of vesting it entirely in the hands of *himself* & of other proper trustees, to be executed, sign'd, seal'd & deliver'd, *previous* to the marriage ceremony's taking place.

I shall now release you, & hasten to inhale as much as I can, of the pure air of this delightful spot; though I arriv'd but at eleven o'clock last night, I already fancy myself the better for it. God bless you, & believe me ever, [etc.].

P.S. Pray do not destroy this letter.

1204 THE DUKE OF WELLINGTON *to the* KING

London, July 16th 1825.

HIS ROYAL HIGHNESS has sent me by command of your Majesty the enclosed petition & memorial from Lt. Ward of the Royal artillery to your Majesty, regarding a second pension which had been granted to him; upon which I should have ventured to submit my opinion to your Majesty, if Lt. Ward had transmitted his memorial in the channel pointed out by your Majesty's regulations.

Lt. Ward received two wounds during the war in the Peninsula. He was wounded in the left thigh; and afterwards lost his right leg. For the latter wound he became entitled to and received a pension under your Majesty's regulations in the year 1814.

In the year 1816 a second pension was granted to Lt. Ward upon his application for the wound first received.

Your Majesty is aware that in consequence of the abuses in the grant of pensions for wounds the pension lists were revised; and several officers were allowed to hold their pensions for a limited period of time, while others were deprived of them altogether. Lt. Ward is one of the latter; and he was deprived of the second pension which had been granted to him for the wound first received; that wound having been reported to be not of a description to entitle Lt. Ward to a second pension under your Majesty's regulations.

Lt. Ward states that this pension was granted to him not for a wound alone but for his good services. This fact does not appear in the letters or Minutes of the late Master General; who on the contrary states distinctly in his order to grant the pension that it was granted on account of the wound. But I beg leave to recall to your Majesty's recollection that a pension for good services could not be granted excepting in consequence of your Majesty's pleasure having been taken upon the subject; which was not done.

Upon the whole then I entertain no doubt upon this case; and that your Majesty cannot interfere in it without establishing a precedent, and giving ground for the claims of others which could not be unattended to without injustice, and could not be attended to without great public inconvenience.

All which is submitted by your Majesty's most devoted subject and servant.

1205 THE DUKE OF YORK *to the* KING

South Audley Street, July 19th 1825.

I HAVE delayed making my report to your Majesty of the result of my interview with Mrs. Fitzherbert and Miss Seymour, which took place last Saturday, when I, in obedience to your commands, communicated your letter which I had the honor to receive from your Majesty to them, till I could at the same time state what had passed between Mr Foster [*sic*] and me.

Both the ladies appeared most affected by the extreme kindness of your letter, and after Miss Seymour, who was so nervous as to be hardly able to speak, had retired, Mrs Fitzherbert expressed herself in most feeling terms of acknowledgement for your goodness. She at the same time told me that she had already had an interview with Mr. Foster upon the subject of settlements, and that she had anticipated your Majesty's wishes upon that head—that Lieutenant Colonel Damer had in the course of last week applied to Lady Caroline Damer from whom he had received for answer that she was too much affected at present by the death of Mrs. Lionel Damer to be able to enter into business, but that she thought it right to acquaint him, that she had in her Will bequeathed to him the Came estate.

I yesterday saw Mr. Foster, to whom I communicated also the contents of your Majesty's letter and who desired me most dutifully to assure your Majesty, that he will pay every attention to your directions. He added also, that he was to have an interview this morning with Lieutenant Colonel Dawson, when he was determined to ascertain correctly the state of his affairs, and that he would not fail to inform your Majesty through me with the result of his information.

1206   THE KING *to* SIR WILLIAM KNIGHTON

Royal Lodge,
July 23ᵈ ½ pt 1. 1825.

I HASTEN to return to you, the packet of papers, which I have just now receiv'd from you.

As to Mr. Hoey's note respecting my signature to be affix'd to the matters upon New South Wales sent in an accompanying box, you will perceive that no such box was sent, & consequently no paper has reach'd me. I conclude that this must have arisen from this circumstance, Mr. Hoey's letter to you I perceive is dated the 21st the day before yesterday, & therefore I presume that as your letter is dated yesterday, that the box was forwarded to me with others (all of which were sign'd by me yesterday forenoon) on the 21st in the evening, whilst the note address'd to you, awaited your arrival in London.

As to Lord Hastings's letter with its contents (concerning which I neither knew, nor ever have heard any thing previous to the present moment) I must desire you to carry it, & shew it *yourself* to Mr. Peel, & to make such enquiries respecting it, as may be necessary for elucidating the matter, for I again repeat, it is one of which I have not the smallest cognizance, & therefore I can not, in the present state, as laid before me, form any opinion. However, I must just add this, that having the precedent as stated, of my father before me, it is but natural both in respect to his memory, as well as in due attention to my friend, the Marquis of Hastings that I am desirous of pursuing the same line which my father had prescrib'd, unless there should have arisen any thing *very extraordinary indeed*, which should imperiously call for a change of routine in the line of conduct, hitherto prescrib'd by the King my father, for the Constable of the Tower of London.

1207 THE KING *to* SIR WILLIAM KNIGHTON

R! L^{ge}*., July 29th 1825.*

I RETURN you the Duke of Wellington's paper sign'd, which I thought had already been approv'd & sign'd. I also send you every pardon sign'd that has reach'd Windsor since I dispatch'd all the last batch of boxes. A letter from Mr. Peel receiv'd late yesterday evening tells me, that I must some day in the course of the next week hold a Council in London, with a Recorder's report. Is not this most extraordinary after what has already pass'd on this subject.[1]

1208 THE KING *to* SIR WILLIAM KNIGHTON

R! L^{ge}*, Sun*.^{y} ¾ pt 2 p.m.
July 31st 1825.

YOU did every thing that was right respecting the Council, & I am only sorry, as it turn'd out, that you had so much unnecessary trouble. The fact was really neither more nor less, than this, that after I had written to you, in no very pleasant tone of feeling towards Mr. Peel, for this second appeal for a Council, I thought it was best upon reconsideration, to get rid of the business at once, & without any further hesitation or delay therefore to get the business over, for I felt, that it would be a continual matter of annoyance & irritation to me, until I had got it off my shoulders. To tell you the truth, that as the matter now stands I am not very sorry that it has turn'd out, as it has, for I think that it will put Mr. Peel, to some inconvenience, which I hope may tend towards its

---

1 "I am directed by the King to see you," Knighton wrote to Peel that day, "and I propose to wait on you for that purpose tomorrow at twelve—if that hour should not be inconvenient to you." (Add. MS. 40300, fo. 77.)

being a useful lesson to him for the future.[1] The papers & boxes shall be attended to, as you desire. Canning has this moment only left me, I have had much conversation with him, but which I shall keep in reserve until I have the pleasure of seeing you in London on Tuesday. Adieu my dear friend.

1209 THE EARL OF ELDON's *Private Minute respecting the Coronation Oath*[2] [? 1825]

An Act for establishing the Coronation oath.

1. Wm & Mary c. 6. s. 3.

"Will you *to the utmost of your power* maintain the laws of God, the true profession of the Gospel, and the *Protestant Reformed religion* established by law?

And will you preserve unto the Bishops and clergy of this Realm, and to the Churches committed to their charge, all such rights and privileges as by law do, or shall appertain unto them, or any of them?"

The King is a constituent part of the supreme legislative power, and as such, has the prerogative of rejecting such provisions in Parliament as he judges improper to be passed.

1. Bl[ackstone's] Com[mentarie]s 261.

1 To what inconvenience the King put Peel and others by suddenly altering the date fixed for the Council meeting, appears from the following letters. On the 29th Peel wrote to Hobhouse, the Under-Secretary of State: "Monday, 8 August, is the day fixed for the Council and Recorder's Report. It may be summoned for one. I shall of course return for it...I shall leave town tomorrow morning...." (Add. MS. 40380, fo. 293.) Lord Conyngham wrote to Peel on the 30th: "I am commanded by His Majesty to inform you that His Majesty will hold the Recorder's Report on Tuesday next the 2^d of August at one o'clock at Carlton House." (*Ibid.*, fo. 296.) Hobhouse wrote to Peel the same day: "...I have summoned the Council for 1 p.m. on Monday, 8 Augt." (*Ibid.*, fo. 300.) Knighton wrote to Peel that evening: "The King, for some reason or other, had determined previous to the receipt of my letter, to hold the Recorder's Report on Tuesday next. I am afraid that this will be very inconvenient to you. I have written to Mr. Hobhouse acquainting him of this alteration." (Add. MS. 40300, fo. 79.) Hobhouse wrote to Peel that evening: "I will give all the directions necessary in consequence of this sudden change of purpose on the part of H.M....." (Add. MS. 40380, fo. 302.) Peel replied from Kingsgate, near Margate, on the 31st: "I shall be in town early on Tuesday morning...Greville wrote to me on Friday that he was confined to his bed by the gout, and that Buller was in Devonshire. Still I suppose the absence of a Clerk of the Council would not prevent a Council being holden. At any rate the Recorder could make his Report on Tuesday. I wrote to Greville, Lord Liverpool, and the Chancellor stating that the Council would be on Monday 8th. I have no doubt they have subsequently heard from you that it will be on Tuesday. I shall not I think leave this until tomorrow evening—and shall travel all night. I presume the King will now adhere to Tuesday. If he should have changed his mind, pray let me know." (*Ibid.*, fo. 309.) "Greville will attend the Council," Hobhouse informed Peel on 1 August. (*Ibid.*, fo. 331.)
2 In 1825 Burdett's Catholic Relief Bill passed the Commons, but the House of Lords threw it out on 17 May, the Duke of York's speech, in which he declared that whatever position he might one day occupy, he would always consider the King bound by his coronation oath to defend the Established Church, being the deciding factor.

1. Bl. Coms 250.

I shall not I trust be considered as an advocate for arbitrary power when I lay it down as a principle that in the exertion of lawful prerogative, the King is, and ought to be absolute; that there is no legal authority that can either delay or resist him. He may reject what Bills, make what Treaties, coin what money, create what Peers, pardon what offences he pleases, unless where the Constitution hath expressly, or by evident consequence laid down some exception or boundary declaring that thus far the prerogative shall go, and no farther;

1. Bl. Coms 251.

For otherwise the power of the Crown would indeed be but a name and a shadow, insufficient for the ends of Government, if where its jurisdiction is clearly established and allowed, any man, or body of men, were permitted to disobey it in the ordinary course of law.

1. Bl. Coms 251. 2.

Yet if the consequence of the exertion of the King's prerogative be manifestly to the grievance or dishonour of the Kingdom, the Parliament will call his advisers to a just and severe account.

For prerogative consisting (as Mr. Locke[1] has well defined it) in the discretionary power of acting for the public good where the positive laws are silent, if the discretionary power be abused to the public detriment, such prerogative is exerted in an unconstitutional manner, (instances a pernicious Treaty and Ministers impeached for it.)

1. Bl. Coms 244.

As the King cannot misuse his power without the advice of evil counsellors, and the assistance of wicked Ministers, these men may be examined and punished, (by indictment and Parliamentary impeachment.)

The King is not only incapable of doing wrong, but even of thinking wrong.

Ibid. 251.

Resistance is justifiable to the person of the King, when the being of the State is endangered, and the public voice proclaims such resistance necessary.—And when King Charles's deluded brother attempted to enslave the nation, he found it was beyond his power; the people both could and did resist him, and in consequence of such resistance, obliged him to quit his enterprise and his throne together.

26. Hen. 8. c. 1. 1. Eliz. c. 1.

The King shall be reputed the only Supreme Head in earth of the Church of England, and shall have annexed to the Imperial Crown of this Realm, as well the title and style thereof, as all jurisdiction, authorities, and commodities to the said dignity of Supreme Head of the Church appertaining.

1 John Locke (1632–1704), the Whig philosopher.

As head of the Church, the King is the dernier resort in all ecclesi- astical causes; an appeal lying ultimately to him in Chancery from the sentence of every ecclesiastical Judge.

1. Bl. Com.ˢ 280.

It may be of some consequence to refresh the memory by the preceding extracts now when an actual attempt is made on behalf of the Roman Catholics, and an intention expressed of moving for the repeal of the Test Act: for it is well known that His late Majesty considered any general measure of concession to be inconsistent with his Coronation oath, and that he would have refused his assent to any Bill which after passing both Houses of Parliament should have been presented to him for such a purpose. That the power of doing so is legally vested in the King by the Constitution of the Realm no one can be ignorant enough or perverse enough to deny: But considering how materially though gradually the exercise of the direct legal prerogatives of the Crown has been in many instances supplanted by its influence, how expedient if not necessary, it is become to give undue, nay excessive attention to the public opinion and how easily that opinion is excited, encouraged, and perverted in this country, it will not be without interest, after alluding to the course adopted by His late Majesty in the removal of his Ministers,[1] and the dissolution of his Parliament to consider what other steps might have been taken, if the experiment of such removal and dissolution had been thought too dangerous and uncertain to be hazarded, or having been tried had failed.

Recollecting the circumstances, of unusual difficulty which attended the administration of the public affairs during the late war, and the power of the aristocratic Whigs united against the Government and assisted by the disaffected, the measure of dissolving Parliament has always appeared to me as bold as it was constitutional. There was doubt as to the disposition of the Parliament that should succeed it, and great uncertainty as to the formation of another and efficient Ministry: but "nil conscire sibi" was the happiness of the King. The mens conscia recti was rewarded and the result proved the wisdom of the measure.

It might have been otherwise; the next Parliament might have inclined towards concession; sufficient ability and influence might have been found for the general transaction of the public business by His Majesty's new Ministry, though not enough to prevent a Bill of concession from passing both Houses of Parliament. At such a crisis I am asked what steps should have been taken, and at what period in order to

1 The Grenville Ministry, in 1807.

anticipate and prevent the necessity of the Royal negative to the Bill; to avert it, or to diminish the odium which the exercise of the prerogative might have created in the minds of the disaffected and disappointed.

In every way of viewing this question, serious difficulties present themselves: the Royal name must never be used unconstitutionally or indiscreetly: In dissenting, the King should always appear to act with reluctance, and under an imperious sense of duty: the perpetual bickerings which took place between King William and his Parliaments, and the derogatory results to His Majesty should never be forgotten.

In the first place therefore the loyal should have been called upon to stand forwards and shew front: their sentiments coinciding with their King's should have been loudly proclaimed in order to create a feeling, that the King's act would be a compliance with the wishes of a large portion if not a majority of his subjects. With this view, at the supposed crisis, Addresses to the King should have been forwarded from different parts of the country praying His Majesty to arrest the approaching evil: in support of the King's right to act according to the dictates of his conscience, and in a matter in which such contrariety of opinion existed, there could have been no difficulty in procuring such Addresses; but if difficulty had been apprehended from conflict of opinion, meetings might have been convened by advertisements couched in such language as to prevent the attendance of the ill disposed. The weight or value of them would have depended on the number and respectability of the signatures. It would have been inexpedient to attempt to obtain them generally against *all* or any concession to the Roman Catholics; if so framed they might not have been reasonable or cogent enough to have influenced the Royal mind: they ought at least to have borne the appearance and to have carried with them a probability of producing such influence; but when the Bill having passed the House of Commons, had been read in the House of Lords without any expressed intention of altering it in the Committee, and still more when committed, and the proposed alterations known, the whole measure being before the public and the danger of its passing into a law being instant, not a moment should have been lost. General and vague objections might then have been reduced to particular objections, and the country called upon to come forwards with Addresses to His Majesty, entreating him to exercise his prerogative on an humble suggestion that the Bill was not consistent with the language or spirit of the Coronation oath, unless His Majesty was of opinion that no danger to the Establishment in Church or State could arise from it; and assigning specific reasons why the different clauses contained in it did not appear sufficiently to secure the Protestant Reformed religion established by law.

As soon as public notices had been given that meetings would be convened in different parts of the country to address His Majesty to this effect it would have been proper for some Peer to express his doubts in the House of Lords whether the Bill was consistent with the Coronation oath, considered as the subject matter of an Act of Parliament, and to move their Lordships to require the attendance of the Judges to assist them with their legal opinions on the comparison of the Act of K. William with the Bill then before the House. To this proposition great objections would have been made, principally on the ground that it is not their practice to apply to the Judges on a proposed alteration of the laws on a constitutional question still pending like that before them: and probably in the supposed state of Parties, the motion would have been rejected. But it would have been useful as a preparatory step; as a hint to the King, to issue an order to his Judges, requiring their opinions on the subject. To such an order I do not think that any valid objections could have been made either by the Judges themselves or by others. They are His Majesty's Council in matters of law. The interpretation of all Acts of Parliament is peculiarly within their province. The Coronation oath is the subject of an Act of Parliament. The application for their advice, would at all events have proved the anxiety with which the question had been considered, and the sincerity of His Majesty's doubts; and manifestly so far, good effects would have resulted from the order, whether complied with or declined. Difficulty might have been felt in wording the questions to be put to the Judges; but the spirit of an Act of Parliament is to be regarded as well as the words of it, and the intention of the Legislature is not to be overlooked. I think therefore that this question at least might have been proposed to the Judges; in the constitution of a statute, can alterations of circumstances or opinions occurring subsequently to the enactment be taken into consideration?

I conceive that the Judges must have answered this question, and answered it in the negative: if so, as long as any doubt remained in the mind of the King as to the possible ill effects of the measure to the interests of the State, he could not have sanctioned it, unless King William might have consented to the admission of Roman Catholics into Parliament in the very next Session after the enactment. But it is not necessary to consider whether a King who has taken this oath, *may* subsequently assent to such a measure; because all reasoning upon it must presume, as indispensible, a conscientious feeling of approbation in the Royal mind. That the conviction of the late King was deep and

The ground and cause of making a Statute explain the intent— Plowd[en's] Com.[s] 175. & 204.

sincere admits of no doubt—It is also certain that the country was divided in opinion; that every one allowed the necessity of many precautions and safeguards for the Established Church; that the efficacy of such as were proposed was denied and doubted; and that if they had been inadequate, the established religion must have suffered more or less and irretrievably, because the measure could never have been revoked without an appearance of persecution; without privation instead of simple negation of privileges and advantages; and rebellion in a distracted country.

The King thought that in consenting to a measure attended with so much uncertainty and possible danger to the State, he could not be sure that he should "to the utmost of his power maintain the Protestant Reformed religion established by law".

With that conviction so deep seated and so reasonable in itself, evinced in the manner I have suggested, and confirmed by Addresses from his subjects, the advocates for the measure would perhaps have dropped it; but if not, the reply "Le Roi s'avisera" would have created only a temporary discontent. Beyond such discontent I can hardly imagine that any consequences would have ensued: but Ministers are favorite objects of attack, and attempts might have been made to harrass them.

The King can do no wrong, and can think no wrong.

The responsibility of Ministers is of inestimable value; but some bounds must be set to it as to every thing else: the soundest theoretical principles must be applied in practice with some limits, and with caution.

An oath is of personal application to him who takes it; No other person can dive into the mind, and search the conscience: There is no appeal: the impression may yield to the arguments of others, but while it lasts, it must be obeyed: acquiescence in a measure contrary to the dictates of that conscience merely from the advice or recommendation of others, must carry with it a violation of the oath; and surely the oath directed to be taken is worse than worthless, if it is to be frittered away to an engagement by the King to act in conformity with the advice of his Parliament or his Ministers: so construed, the oath would be perfectly useless, and the security of the subject, held out by the solemnity of it, a mere delusion. It is material also to remember that a main ground of objection to the concession is the injury apprehended to the Church, of which the King is the Supreme Head, and over which it is his especial duty to keep watch.

Here therefore I contend that there is a clear instance in which the doctrine of the responsibility of Ministers could not have been applied; and unless the scruples of a King alone on the solemn matter of an oath are to be irreverently and unjustly slighted, it would have been unconstitutional to have addressed His Majesty for the removal of his Ministers on account of supposed advice to negative the Catholic Bill.

Nor could there have existed the shallowest pretence for appealing to the doctrine of justifiable resistance to the King, in a case so different from any one contemplated by our commentator Blackstone: for it would have been monstrous to assert that "the being of the State was in danger", and false to affect that "the public voice proclaimed resistance necessary". The refusal of the King would have been a simple negative —not an active exertion of power, but a determination after many boons granted to the Roman Catholics, to leave them in the improved situation in which the laws had placed them.

In the case supposed therefore, I think that attempts ought to have been made to procure Addresses to the King, and the opinions of the Judges at the times and in the manner I have mentioned: and I feel confident that His Majesty might then have refused to sign the Bill without the necessity of again, and perhaps fruitlessly dissolving his Parliament or removing his Ministers; assigning in his speech from the Throne, his reasons to be, the alarm created by the measure, and the uncertain effects of it to the establishment which he had sworn to maintain.

P.S. Whether a King, who cannot in consistency with his Coronation oath, sign a Bill of concession to the Roman Catholics, can or ought to sign a Bill to enable his successor to do so, by alteration of the terms of the oath, deserves consideration.

1210 WILLIAM RICHARD HAMILTON[1] *to* SIR CHARLES LONG

Ipswich, Aug. 12, 1825.

I HAVE at length received from the Abbate Canova his acceptance of the offer which you authorized me to make to him, of 5000 guineas for the two last works of his brother purchased by His Majesty. I cannot say that he is *perfectly* satisfied that you pay the full amount of what they are worth, or of what his brother would have expected for them, but I am persuaded he is highly flattered that these his brother's latest finished works, should be deposited in the palace of the King of Great Britain, to whom he considers himself, as his brother did during his lifetime, so mainly indebted for the halo of glory which shed fresh lustre over

1 Minister at Naples, April 1822 to January 1825.

Canova's last days, which led to the honors he received in Rome both from the Pope and from his cotemporaries, and which in fact enabled him to continue to extend his charities towards deserving artists, and more especially to bring about his magnificent project of building the church or temple at Possagno, the place of his birth. It is the anxiety to complete this monument of his brother's Christian devotion that leads the Abbate to endeavour to make the most of what his brother left to be disposed of: it is a praiseworthy motive and we cannot but respect him the more for it. There is however one proposition which you must allow me to hint before I have done with this subject, It is this—that when you write to him, or when you empower me to write to him, giving him authority to draw for the remainder of the money, the notice might be accompanied with the gift of something in the shape of a ring or box— as a further token of the King's respect for his brother's character, and of his satisfaction in being possessed of some of his most distinguished works. I think this would render him the happiest of the Romans, and would close, I hope to the satisfaction of all parties, an intercourse begun in politics, cemented in a signal act of retributive justice, and closed in a splendid and truly Royal encouragement to the Phidias of modern times.

[P.S.] We are thus far on our tour of inspection of the outposts.

Sir Thomas Lawrence to Sir William Knighton, 27 August 1825. (*Knighton*, I, 267–9.)

1211 THE KING *to* [SIR WILLIAM KNIGHTON]

> *R.^l Lodge*, Sun.^y M.^g ¼ pt 9.
> Septr. 18th 1825.

I AM awaken'd with your letter, & before I can shake off the remaining bit of a restless dog's slumber, I comply with its request, by writing you this short line, just to say, that I *hope* you will *not fail* to *come here, be it only for an hour or two.* I have *good reasons* for this, or you may depend upon it, I would not put you to the trouble of a journey, however short, unnecessarily.

1212 THE EARL OF LIVERPOOL *to the* KING

Walmer Castle, Octr 4, 1825.

LORD LIVERPOOL presents his humble duty to your Majesty, and as he understands your Majesty expects the Duke of Cumberland to come to England for a few days, he humbly conceives your Majesty may wish to be informed, of the exact state of the business, in respect to His Royal Highnesses son.[1]

The Duke of Cumberland has been informed by Lord Liverpool, that if it should be convenient to His Royal Highness, to establish himself in this country, with the Duchess, & his son, the £6,000 a year granted by Parliament[2] will be paid to His Royal Highness, and it will be for His Royal Highness to provide for the maintenance and education of his son, subject to no other controul, than the general controul, which your Majesty has by law over the education & care of all branches of the Royal family.

If on the other hand, the Duke of Cumberland continues to reside abroad, the Prince his son must be sent to this country and established here under such regulations as your Majesty may approve, in order that he may enjoy the advantages, of the grant of Parliament.

Your Majesty was pleased to put a question to Lord Liverpool, when he had last the honour of waiting upon you, whether in the event of the Duke of Cumberland being desirous of retaining his son abroad for two or three years longer, the money granted by Parliament could be received, and suffer'd to accumulate for the benefit of the Prince.

Lord Liverpool has made enquiries on this head, & he is confirmed in the opinion he then entertained, that the whole arrangement must necessarily *remain in abeyance* till the arrival and establishment of the Prince in this country, *with* or *without* his Royal parents.

Lord Liverpool has already apprised the Duke of Cumberland, that if he should think fit to send his son to this country, to be educated under your Majesty's superintendance, your Majesty might of course grant your permission to the Prince, to pay occasional visits to his parents on the Continent, such visits being subject as to time to some reasonable limitation.

1 Afterwards George V, King of Hanover (1819–1878).

2 In 1825 Parliament added £6000 a year to the income of the Duchess of Kent for the maintenance and education of her daughter, and made a similar grant to the Duke of Cumberland, provided that his son was educated in England.

1213 The Marquis Wellesley *to the* Earl of Liverpool
Copy.

Malahide Castle, Octr. 9th 1825.

ALTHOUGH it is not an official duty, nor perhaps an obligation of common friendship, I should not be happy if I did not impart to you (by the same conveyance, which acquaints my own family with my intention) that I have contracted an engagement of marriage, and that I propose to conclude it immediately.[1]

The object of my choice is an American lady, (whom you perhaps may have seen).[2] She has been in Ireland for some time; and she is worthy of my heart & hand.

I believe that you must know her name; and I am certain, that whenever I may have the pleasure of introducing her to you, you will receive her with all the respect due to her virtues, talents, & accomplishments, and with all your accustomed kindness to me.

1214 The Earl of Liverpool *to the* King

Walmer Castle, Octr 13, 1825.

LORD LIVERPOOL presents his humble duty to your Majesty, and although he has no doubt your Majesty will have heard it from other quarters, he feels it to be his duty to lose no time, in communicating to your Majesty, a copy of the letter which he has just received from Lord Wellesley, announcing his *immediate* marriage with Mrs. Patterson.

1215 Lieutenant-General Sir Herbert Taylor *to* Sir William Knighton

Horse Guards, October 15, 1825.

I HAVE received a letter from my brother in law in reply to mine respecting the representation for Windsor.[3] He naturally expresses considerable mortification upon learning that the King had expressed his

1 This "very strange and awkward event", as Liverpool described it, took place at the Vice-regal Lodge, Dublin, on 29 October, the bride being a wealthy Roman Catholic widow, Mrs Patterson. "Under any other circumstances", said Liverpool, "I am not sure it would not be for his advantage. She has no family, she would entirely govern him, but I think she has sense enough to govern him better than he governs himself." Wellesley's first wife had died in 1816. They had separated soon after his return from India.

2 "I have the pleasure of being personally acquainted with the lady", replied Liverpool, "and I may even add of some sort of connection with her, her sister having married my lamented and excellent relation and friend, Sir Felton Harvey." (*Wellesley Papers*, II, 150.)

3 [Sir] Edward Cromwell Disbrowe succeeded Taylor as M.P. for Windsor on 11 February 1823.

determination to withdraw his support from him at the ensuing election, in consequence of his vote on the Catholic question,[1] and is anxious that it should be understood that if he had been aware that such vote, as being the Court member for Windsor, could have been construed as committing His Majesty's opinion upon so important a question, he would not have given it. He considered it as the expression of his own individual sentiments upon a question which he had understood to be open to him as to all others.

He does not however presume to remonstrate, but he bows with dutiful submission to His Majesty's pleasure, humbly trusting that his conduct has not been in any other respect such as to subject him to His Majesty's disapprobation, and that his endeavors to keep up the Court interest in the borough, in which he has not been sparing of time or expence, have not been altogether useless.

He is indeed too deeply impressed with a sense of his obligations and those of his family and connexions to His Majesty to allow any other feeling than that of gratitude & devotion to influence him but this sense naturally adds to his regret that he should in any respect have incurred His Majesty's displeasure. In the situation which he now fills it has been & will continue to be his earnest study to merit His Majesty's gracious approbation, and it is his determination to devote himself zealously to the duties of his profession. Hitherto indeed it has proved more honorable than lucrative and I fear that this observation applies more particularly to the mission at Petersburg.[2]

George Canning to the King, 19 October 1825. (*Stapleton*, pp. 257–8.)

1216 THE EARL OF LIVERPOOL *to the* KING

Walmer Castle, Octr. 21, 1825.

LORD LIVERPOOL has had the honour of receiving your Majesty's letter, and will be happy to communicate with His Royal Highness the Duke of Cumberland, upon the subject to which it refers.

Lord Liverpool is only anxious for the sake of His Royal Highness, and of the Prince his son, that whilst His Royal Highness thinks it right to decline availing himself of the grant of Parliament, at the present moment, he should not do or write any thing, which should preclude his son, from having the advantage of the grant at some future time.

1 Burdett's motion, 28 February 1825.
2 He was appointed Secretary of Embassy at Petersburg in February 1825.

Your Majesty will recollect the inconvenience to which we were subject by the course taken by His Royal Highness the Duke of Clarence some years ago, and it appears to be unnecessary for the Duke of Cumberland to say more, than that "as it was not convenient to him to establish himself in England under present circumstances, and as his son was too young, to make it desireable for him to be separated from his parents, the Duke must decline availing himself of the grant at this time, considering the conditions which were understood to be annexed to it".

Robert Peel to the King, 26 November 1825. (*Parker*, 1, 387.)
George Canning to the King, 9 December 1825. (*Stapleton*, 1, 341–5.)

1217 THE BISHOP OF LONDON (DR HOWLEY) *to the* KING

Fulham Palace, Decr. 15, 1825.

AGREEABLY to the instructions given me by his Royal Highness the Duke of Cumberland, I presume to address your Majesty for the purpose of explaining the steps I have taken towards engaging a preceptor for the young Prince. Since first I was honored with your Majesty's commands I have never lost sight of this object, but have only just now been enabled to fix on a person who appears to possess all the requisite qualifications for such a charge. This gentleman's name is Jelf:[1] his connections are good, and he is nearly related to Mr. Cambridge, the highly respectable Archdeacon of Middlesex. After passing through the school at Eaton he went to Christchurch, & was subsequently elected Fellow of Oriel, of which College he is now tutor, and one of the public examining masters in the University schools.

These facts are sufficient proofs of his literary attainments, to which I may add that he is very respectable as a divine & preacher, of sound principles in religion and politics, and remarkable for correctness of conduct, good sense, good temper, and modest & pleasing manners. He is indeed two years short of the age prescribed by the Duke, being only twenty eight; but considering the character of his mind and his habits of conduct, I conceive him to be older in judgement than many who are his seniors in years.

I ought perhaps to state to your Majesty, that from his appointments in the University (exclusive of his Fellowship which may be retained

1 Richard William Jelf (1798–1871), Preceptor to Prince George, 1826–39; afterwards Principal of King's College, London.

though he should cease to reside) he desires an income of upwards of five hundred a year.

In expectation of any farther commands which your Majesty may graciously be pleased to lay upon me, & with sentiments of profound respect and gratitude, [etc.].

1218 GEORGE CANNING *to the* KING

F.O., Decr. 23, 1825.

MR. CANNING, with his most humble duty, offers his excuses to your Majesty for not having sooner executed your Majesty's commands with respect to Count Lieven.

He did not add any thing upon that subject to the despatches already prepared for Lord Strangford,[1] because one of them being necessarily a *scolding* despatch,[2] he thought the temper likely to be produced by it, equally likely to be unfavourable to the execution of a very delicate commission.

He proposes to send another messenger to Lord Strangford early next week (in order that Lord Strangford may have ample means of communication with this country); & by *that* messenger he thought it would be most advisable to convey to Ld. S. your Majesty's wishes with respect to Ct. Lieven, unmixed with any less pleasing matter.

In the mean while, however, it has occurred to Mr. Canning that it would be but considerate towards Count Lieven to afford him an opportunity of giving his opinion whether—if the step to be taken did no good —it might, possibly, do any harm.

There *may be* circumstances (with which Ct. Lieven may be acquainted) or there *may be* that in the character & feelings of the new Emperor,[3] which might make any suggestion in Ct. Lieven's favour unadvisable— or even prejudicial to Ct. Lieven.

Mr. Canning has therefore written to Ct. Lieven the letter a copy of which he humbly lays before your Majesty; & which he sends by a messenger to Brighton tonight.

Mr. Canning will take the liberty of transmitting Count Lieven's answer to your Majesty.

1 Ambassador at Petersburg, October 1825 to June 1826.
2 Contrary to instructions Strangford had recognised Russia's right to go to war with Turkey in the event of Turkey's rejection of the mediation of the Powers in the Graeco-Turkish War. He was so severely reprimanded that he sought leave of absence and never returned.
3 Nicholas I had just succeeded his brother Alexander I.

Copy.

F.O., Decr. 23d 1825.

ON the occasion of Prince Esterhazy's[1] audience of leave on Tuesday, the King, in expressing the regret which His Majesty felt at losing an Ambassador, to whom His Majesty has been so long accustomed, and whom he has distinguished with so much favour, naturally spoke of another Minister of the same rank, and towards whom His Majesty entertains the same sentiments—in short of your Excellency—with all the kindness, which you know belongs to His Majesty's nature; and with the apprehension which the late calamitous event inspires, lest he should be deprived of your Excellency, as well as of your colleague.

I have been considering whether anything can be done to ensure (or to take the chance of ensuring) His Majesty against the realization of this apprehension.

I am *quite sure* that I should receive His Majesty's commands to take any step, that might be likely to answer this purpose.

But before any such step is taken, I have thought it right to ask frankly of your Excellency, whether you see any objection to it, or would apprehend any inconvenience from it? In other words, could the declaration of His Majesty's entire satisfaction with your Excellency's conduct, during your residence in this country, of his earnest wish not to part with you, be taken amiss—& so do harm?

You will observe that I do not ask your Excellency *whether it would do good?* because it is essential to the character, as well as efficacy of such a proceeding, that it should be adopted without your participation. But it is due to your Excellency to give you an opportunity of saying whether what is intended kindly, could by possibility turn to your prejudice or discomfort.

I trust your Excellency will excuse the directness of this inquiry, in consideration of the anxiety, which I know His Majesty feels upon the subject: and I beg you to believe me ever, with the truest respect and esteem, [etc.].

P.S. I intend sending a messenger to Lord Strangford on Monday or Tuesday next, who will take charge of anything that your Excellency may have for St. Petersburgh.

1 The Austrian Ambassador at London. Metternich countermanded his recall, at George IV's request. See No. 1222 A, and also Canning's Memorandum in *Stapleton*, pp. 448–52.

F.O., Decr. 24, 1825.

MR. CANNING humbly submits for your Majesty's gracious consideration, whether it might not be advantageous, in the present state of the
world, that some fit person should be named, with as little delay as may
be, to bear your Majesty's condolances, & congratulations to the new
Emperor of Russia; and whether there be any person so fit for such a
mission (with a view to the immense political interests to which it may
be made subservient) as the Duke of Wellington.

Mr. Canning has not hinted this notion to the Duke of Wellington,
nor indeed to any one except Lord Liverpool, who concurs with Mr.
Canning in the opinion that it would be at least advisable to propose this
mission to the Duke of Wellington, although it may be doubtful whether
the state of his health would allow his Grace to undertake it.

When a similar mission was to be sent to the King of France, Mr.
Canning did not suggest the name of the Duke of Wellington, because,
however acceptable to the King of France himself the Duke of Wellington's appointment might have been, he felt a strong persuasion that the
presence of the conqueror of Waterloo at the Coronation of the successor
of Louis XVIII would have been regarded as insulting to the French
nation.[1]

But in the present instance the memory of every past political transaction appears to concur with the undisputed qualifications of the Duke
of Wellington, to recommend him, above all others, for your Majesty's
gracious selection.

1221 THE KING *to* GEORGE CANNING
Copy.

R[oyal] L[odge], Decr. 25th 1825.

THE KING sends his kind regards to Mr. Canning & returns the box
which reached the King last night at his bed-time.

The proposal of Mr. Canning respecting the Duke of Wellington's
being offered the special mission to St. Petersburgh upon the present
occasion is certainly (in many points of view) the *best & most wise suggestion.* Yet, the King must candidly avow to Mr. Canning, that after
having given the best consideration in his power to *this very important
matter, the King feels very strong objections to* it, & to many of which

1 Canning had sent his friend Lord Granville on a special mission of condolence and
congratulation on the accession of Charles X in October 1824, and the Duke of Northumberland to attend the Coronation at Rheims on 29 May 1825.

Mr. Canning has alluded in his private letter to the King. These, are, in the King's view of the matter, such very weighty & important considerations, as entirely to overbalance, from the *personal risk which the Duke must run*, whatever portion of advantage in a political point, it might reasonably be hoped, might be gained by *otherwise so desireable a nomination*.

The King is quite persuaded, that both Mr. Canning & Lord Liverpool will fully enter, & accord with these the King's sentiments, which are actuated, not only by his *personal and private feelings* for the Duke, *but*, from the *immense & incalculable importance, the preservation of such a life as that* of the Duke of Wellington, carries with it, not to *his own country alone, but to all Europe.*

The King will be glad if Mr. Canning, any morning early in the week that may suit him, will come to the Lodge about twelve o'clock; the King by no means wishes to incommode Mr. Canning or to interfere with any engagement Mr. Canning may have made for himself for the ensuing week; as that, which the King is desirous of talking over with Mr. Canning in no way presses, & a few days hence, if that should suit Mr. Canning's convenience better, will be equally agreeable to the King.[1]

The King to Sir William Knighton, 28 December 1825. (*Knighton*, 1, 286–7.)

1222 THE EARL OF LIVERPOOL *to the* KING

Coombe Wood, Decr. 28, 1825

LORD LIVERPOOL has had the honour of receiving your Majesty's letter, with the very extraordinary communication from the Duke of Buckingham, which your Majesty has been graciously pleased to transmit to him.

Lord Liverpool will not fail with as little delay as circumstances will admit at this season of the year, to communicate them to Mr. Canning & the Duke of Wellington, and he will have the honour of laying before your Majesty their humble advice, whether any, & what answer should be returned to it.

1 The King saw Canning on the 27th. (See his letter to the Duke in *W.N.D.* III, 53.) "The Duke not only accepted, but *jumped*, as I foresaw that he would, at the proposal", said Canning. "'Never better in his life', 'ready to set out in a week', and the like expressions of alertness, leave no doubt upon my mind that the selection of *another* person would have done his health more prejudice, than all the frosts or thaws of the hyperborean regions can do to it." (*Stapleton*, p. 471.)

Lord Liverpool will hardly trust himself with commenting on these papers at present, he begs only just to call to your Majesty's attention, the disingenuousness of the Duke of Buckingham's proceeding, in laying before your Majesty a copy of his letter to Lord Liverpool, without laying the letter to which it was an answer.

Lord Liverpool can assure your Majesty, that he is prepared to lay before you, every part of the correspondence which has passed upon this subject, & he trusts your Majesty will perceive by it, that he & his colleagues, have been actuated by no consideration, but a sense of what was due to your Majesty's service, & the interest of your dominions.[1]

The Duke of Wellington to the King, 29 December 1825. (*W.N.D.* III, 54–5.)

1222A GEORGE CANNING *to the* KING

Foreign Office, Janry 6, 1826. ½ p. 2 pm.

MR. CANNING presents his humble duty to your Majesty.

He has this instant seen Prince Esterhazy, who came to him, accompanied by Mr. Neumann[2] professedly to ask Mr. Canning's advice as to the course which he should take, in consequence of the communication received yesterday from Vienna.[3]

It was evident to Mr. Canning, however, that the Prince's mind and Mr. Neumann's were made up to the expediency of the Prince's *immediately setting off for his new destination.* But whether the Prince's was a *genuine* feeling of his own, or one with which Mr. Neumann (who was exceedingly strong in the expression of his opinion) had inspired him, Mr. Canning cannot confidently decide.

The advice which Mr. Canning did not hesitate to give to Prince

1 The Duke of Buckingham (the Ph[at] D[uke], as Canning contemptuously referred to him) had been angling for the Governor-Generalship of Bengal, in the belief that the Court of Directors, who were dissatisfied with Lord Amherst's conduct of the Burmese War (1824–26), would recall him. The Duke hinted to Canning that unless his wishes were gratified, the Government would lose the support of his party (eight members) in the House of Commons; and he proposed a highly discreditable bargain. In return for "the exclusive and devoted support" of his party, which should be "made over" to Canning, Canning should procure for the Duke, if not the Governor-Generalship, office at home. The proposition was of course rejected with scorn, and the Duke tried to revenge himself on Canning in March 1827. The Directors shrank from a step to which the Government was strongly opposed; as Canning said, they were "thrown upon their backs" and Amherst "remained to finish the war". (Harewood MSS.)

2 The Austrian Chargé d'Affaires in London.

3 See No. 1219. On this question of Esterhazy's countermanded recall, see Prof. Temperley's *Foreign Policy of Canning*, pp. 252–3.

Esterhazy was that he should *wait* in England the arrival of the answer to Mr. Canning's letter of the 20th ulto.

Mr. Canning represented that Prince Metternich's answer might be one of three kinds—either an unqualified assent to your Majesty's wishes, with a promise of new credentials to be presented to your Majesty—or 2^d an intimation that *having* presented his letters of recall, it was not thought right to re-accredit Prince Esterhazy to your Majesty (in the former of which cases it would be highly fortunate that Prince Esterhazy was found still in England—in the latter his departure for Paris would only have been delayed a few days)—or 3^{rdly} —the answer *might* be, like that of yesterday *conditional*, viz.—that Prince Esterhazy should be re-accredited to your Majesty "if he was still in England". Now, in this last case Mr. Canning pointed out to Prince Esterhazy that his departure for Paris, before the arrival of the expected answer to Mr. Canning's letter, would render him (the Prince Esterhazy) *personally* and *solely* responsible for the disappointment of your Majesty's wishes.

Mr Canning would fain flatter himself that his representations made some impression upon Prince Esterhazy (upon Mr. Neumann he fears, *none*). Prince Esterhazy begged time to consider of them, and promised to write to Mr. Canning tomorrow; on which day Mr. Canning intended humbly to have proposed attending your Majesty at Windsor, but, as the Prince seemed anxious to have some time for reflection, Mr. Canning consented to expect his answer only tomorrow; and will, with your Majesty's gracious permission, wait upon your Majesty on Sunday morning at the hour of your Majesty's return from Chapel.

Mr. Canning, on reading over what he has written, sees that he has not adverted to your Majesty's commands respecting the Prince Victor de Metternich.[1] He inquired of Prince Esterhazy whether the Prince Victor were not the bearer of any verbal explanations or any other than the publick despatch—a question which Mr. Canning founded on the extraordinary circumstance that the intelligence of Prince Esterhazy's protracted stay in this country had transpired *at Dover*, on the day of Prince Victor's landing; and was known in London, through the newspapers, almost as soon as Mr. Canning received Sir H. Wellesley's letter.

Both Prince Esterhazy and Mr. Neumann however positively denied that Prince Victor had any private commission, or was even acquainted with the details of the despatches which he brought—a denial of which Mr. Canning cannot help doubting the entire correctness, but which seemed to Mr. Canning to make any advance on his part towards a direct

1 Metternich's son.

communication with P. Victor, for the present, unadviseable, the rather as your Majesty will undoubtedly learn through Count Munster, more of what Prince Victor may have to say, than, warned and instructed as he would be by Mr. Neumann, Prince Victor would be likely to disclose to Mr. Canning.[1]

1223 R. PHILLIPS *to* SIR WILLIAM KNIGHTON

63 Fleet Street, Jany. 8, 1826.

I WAS well acquainted with the late ingenious Mary Robinson,[2] once the beautiful *Perditta*. I had much literary intercourse with her & as a security for a loan she put into my possession various articles of curiosity, & among others that beautiful lock of hair which His present Majesty sent to her from his box at the theatre, in an envellope on which in his own hand is written the words "To be redeemed".

I have always highly prized it as the memento of a Royal passion & as connected with an incident in the life of the most interesting woman of her age, as well as from profound respect & homage for His Majesty, but having had the misfortune to lose two considerable properties by the stoppage of bankers in London & Brighton, I am obliged to part with some available property, & it has appeared to me that such a relique might even be interesting to the King himself, & if not to him to some of his personal friends.

I may by the bye observe that my opportunities have brought me into possession of some other reliques, not unlikely to interest His Majesty. For example I possess the identical bridle which was on the horse of William Rufus when he was killed in the New Forest & it would add to the Royal collection of such curiosities. I bought it many years since of Purkis who lives in the cottage near the spot & is a descendant of the Purkis who picked up William's body & conveyed it in a cart to Winchester.

I suspect I have said enough to provoke your laughter, but I possess

1 Canning wrote on 7 January 1826:
"Mr. Canning humbly takes the liberty to request your Majesty's attention to this paper [missing], and particularly to those parts which he has marked in pencil.
"Mr Canning cannot help believing that the Prince Victor Metternich was charged with verbal instructions to urge Prince Esterhazy to hasten his departure for Paris: with orders, in case of his succeeding in that object, *not* to deliver the Emperor of Austria's letter (and that of Prince Metternich) to your Majesty, nor that of Baron Hardenburg to Count Munster *till too* late."
2 The King's mistress, *c.* 1778–80.

also the walking cane of Shakespeare which I bought of Wm. Shakspeare Hart the late proprietor of the house at Stratford on the walls of which I once saw the King's name in his own hand.

It was long a passion of mine to collect original paintings of illustrious persons & I have in this way portraits many of them worthy of a Royal palace from Chaucer, painted in the reign of Richard II down to our own age, many of them unique, & including our chief poets & men of genius.

Of MSS. original letters, &c &c I have also an extensive & curious collection.

Residing now chiefly at Brighton & not having removed most of these articles there & the circumstances alluded to having disturbed my domestic arrangements, I am constrained in opposition to my taste to convert them, or most of them into money.

My name is not unknown to His Majesty. He will remember me in connexion with the name of the Marquess of Hastings & Mr. Hayter, & for a zealous endeavour of mine, I once received an assurance from Sir John McMahon that His Majesty considered himself everlastingly obliged to me. The suitors for Royal favour are I doubt not so numerous that I never ventured to obtrude myself in any way & should not now have so presumed but I imagined the lock of hair might interest His Majesty's feelings & curiosity.

1224 ROBERT PEEL *to* SIR WILLIAM KNIGHTON

Brighton, January 13, 1826.

YOU will I am sure be glad to hear that Mrs. Peel has got rid of the cough and cold—and is I trust regaining her strength.

We shall be in London at the beginning of next week, and she will be very happy to see you on her arrival.

I had very great pleasure in reading the two articles in the Quarterly Review which you mention [1]—and before I knew that the article relating to the death of Bonaparte was written by you, and consequently when I was not prejudiced in its favour I had sent it to Lord Bathurst (who is here), and called his attention to the decisive proof which it exhibits that the cause of Bonaparte's death had been entirely mistaken by his medical attendants.

The article on the plague has quite satisfied me, that there is so much

1 *Quarterly Review*, December 1825. Art. VI, "The Last Moments of Napoleon"; Art. IX, "Plague, a contagious disease".

reason to believe that the plague is a contagious disease, that it would be unsafe to dispense with precautionary measures against its introduction.

Your position (which satisfactorily accounts for much of the contradictory evidence on the subject of the plague)—that there must be two things requisite for the spread of a contagious disorder—the contagious matter itself—and some diffused cause, like the state of the atmosphere favorable to its action, has been confirmed (if it wanted confirmation) by the state of the small pox in London in 1825.

This disorder, of which we we [*sic*] have comparatively speaking, heard so little of late, prevailed to such an extent during the last year in London, that there were more admissions of persons suffering from the small pox, into the small pox hospital—than have taken place in any one year for the last fifty years with one single exception.

1225 FREDERICK JOHN ROBINSON *to the* KING

Downing Street, Jany. 18, 1826.

MR. ROBINSON sends his humble duty to your Majesty.

It will, he trusts, be agreable to your Majesty to learn, that Mr. Robinson had yesterday, as well as to-day, a very satisfactory conversation with Sir Wm. Knighton on the different points connected with the works at Buckingham House and Windsor, as well as with those matters relating to Carlton House, to which he was commanded by your Majesty to attend.

Mr. Nash will have every facility which can be given to him for the purpose of expediting the works with which he is charged: and Mr. Nash now quite understands, and enters into, those necessary forms and regulations connected with expenditure, which are so essential, not only to the Government but to your Majesty.

The proposal of the committee for the purpose of conducting, under your Majesty's gracious commands, the furnishing of Windsor Castle, in a manner consistent with your Majesty's taste and comfort, is admirable, and Mr. Robinson enters into it with all his heart.

The estimate of those articles at Carlton House which belong to your Majesty as private property, is proceeding in; and when the time arrives will be acknowledged by the Treasury, agreably to your Majesty's commands.

Mr. Robinson can only add, that it is most gratifying to him to have an opportunity of carrying into effect your Majesty's wishes upon this and every occasion.

1226 Sir John Sinclair[1] *to* Sir William Knighton

177, *George Street, Edinburgh.*
29 January 1826.

My eldest son[2] had a most singular adventure with the Emperor Napoleon, immediately previous to the Battle of Jena; and he has been induced to draw up a short narrative of that event, (in 28 pages octave), for the purpose of supplying *"the author of Waverly"* with *"new materials"* for his intended history of that extraordinary character. Some copies of that narrative have been printed for private circulation. I beg to know, whether I may take the liberty of sending a copy of it to you, to be submitted to His Majesty's perusal. It throws some light, not only on the character of Napoleon, but on his mode of carrying on a war *"on the principles of a game of chess".*

1227 Frederick John Robinson *to the* King

Downing Street, Jany 30, 1826.

Mr. Robinson offers his humble duty to your Majesty.

He has this morning inspected with Mr. Nash all the works going on at Buckingham House, both as respects the building and the grounds; and he has the satisfaction of acquainting your Majesty, that all parts of the work appear to be proceeding with the utmost expedition, compatible with so extensive an undertaking.

Your Majesty may rely upon Mr. Robinson's attention being regularly given to these works, in order that as little delay as possible may occur in providing a town residence suitable to your Majesty's dignity and comfort.

1228 The King *to* Sir William Knighton

R! L^{ge}., Feby 1st 1826.

I have only time to write you a very short hurried line to thank you for your two letters.

With respect to the contents of *that address'd as most private & confidential* you will find that I return you the paper which it inclos'd; for the

---

1 The expert agriculturist, and President of the Board of Agriculture. [1754–1835.] Created Baronet, 1786.

2 Sir George Sinclair, second Baronet (1790–1868). In 1806 he was arrested as a spy, and brought before Napoleon, who, after examining him, ordered his release.

following reasons. In primis I find that Ld C[onyngha]m thinks it is a mark of attention & respect which he owes the Government, being one of the great officers of State, to shew himself in the House of Lords on the first day of the meeting of Parliament, & then to return here, leaving his proxy with Lord Liverpool. He therefore proposes to leave this to-morrow with Strathaven[1] as his companion, who goes for the House of Commons, & who returns on Saturday.

Secondly because, he just now inform'd me with *great glee*, that all the papers, & the marriage settlements & deeds, had *all* been return'd from Scotland *sign'd & approv'd by Lord Aboyne*. I cross examin'd him, & found that he had not even the shadow of an idea, of what you have stated to me, & therefore, of course, *not* of the contents of *that* paper which I now return you. This being the state of things at the present moment, after giving it some good consideration, & turn'd it well over in my mind, I have determin'd not to say one word upon the matter *even to Strathaven*, & the more I think it over, the more sure I am, that it is the best & wisest thing for *me* to do, & *silence* at *any rate* is the *safe* & *safest* line *here*, upon the *present occasion*; for, there is, & I do *grieve from my heart* to say so to you, no possibility for answering for *one second, what* the *bearings of the wind may be, the very next second, as it is*, & as it *has been* for the last two or three days in a *most extraordinary vascillating state*, & round & round at every point of the whole compass, three or four times in the course of each day, nay, I may without exaggeration state, three or four times *almost each hour*. You may consequently *easily judge*, of what must be, & of what is the nature of *my most painful & uncomfortible feelings*. What I further propose to do, is simply *this*, to desire Strathaven *so soon* as he shall arrive in London to call upon you; you will then, in conjunction with *our friend Dennison*,[2] be the best judges how to talk the matter over with Strathaven *first* & see what *resolve to come to*, & *afterwards should you both feel it necessary, how, whether, & how much of it, you may esteem it absolutely necessary to impart* to Ld C – m. Having said so much I must hazard further one opinion of my own but, which *I entreat of you, entirely, & only*, to deal with, as upon your better judgment you *may deem to be most expedient*, which is this, that I think if you two (I mean Mr. Dennison & yourself) should feel, that *some imperative & decisive step should, & must be taken & that you do fix what that is to be* then probably, (*even if it were not absolutely necessary*) *it would be best that*

1 Charles Gordon, eldest son of George Gordon, fifth Earl of Aboyne. On 2 March 1826 he married Lady Elizabeth Conyngham, Lord Conyngham's daughter. When, in 1836, his father succeeded the Duke of Gordon as Marquis of Huntly, Lord Strathaven took the courtesy title of Earl of Aboyne. He was Tory M.P. for East Grinstead at this time. [1792–1863.]
2 Lady Conyngham's brother.

Ld C − m being *fortunately* in town, should *be made a party himself* to whatever *measure may be determin'd upon*; by which means, then, *this measure will become the united & positive act of the father & of the uncle*. No one else can appear to be mix'd up in it, at any rate *my poor self* as I am here, & away from the scene of action, & therefore, in the event of any further discussions taking place, (which I am afraid, it is but too probable that they will) upon Ld C − m's return from town, & learning what he will have to relate, I shall be placed merely in the situation of an auditor or sort of referee, (which God knows, & alas; is not always a very pleasing thing) instead of that, which is, & would be much worse, the being tortur'd & consider'd *however unjustly*, in the light of *an active & primitive agent*. I have now concluded, & I hope you will be able to be quite master of my feelings, although from the excessive haste & hurry under which I have scribbled this, I fear that you will hardly be able to make out, & understand my scrawl. You may impart any part of this, that you like to Dennison.

As to the contents of your other letter, they are so satisfactory in general that I shall only say thank you, for them. Pray continue to write *regularly & daily* to me be it only a couple of lines, & to keep me, au fait, of all that is going on. God bless you.

P.S. Poor Mrs. Fitz[herber]t's sufferings in spite of all, I can not help deeply participating in, & commiserating.

1229 DR JOHN ROBERT HUME[1] *to* SIR WILLIAM KNIGHTON

St. Petersburg, 7th March 1826.

As you know how very little time I had to prepare for this long journey, I am sure you will forgive me for not calling upon you before leaving town. I cannot, however, refrain from writing you one line to say how very sensible I am of all your kindness; to offer you my best thanks; and to assure you that I am most grateful.

I am sure it will give you pleasure to hear that the Duke has borne this journey extremely well, and has neither suffered from fatigue, nor been in any way incommoded by the cold; but he has been more prudent & careful than I have ever seen him, and has never once pushed on beyond the stage he had fixed on in the morning, even when he had performed the

1 Wellington's Physician (1781?–1857). The Duke returned from his special Mission of condolence and congratulation early in April.

distance sooner than he expected. Our usual rate of travelling has been from 110 to 120 English miles a day, which, from the fineness of the weather, and the state of the roads, we have generally made out in 14 or 15 hours. We have slept 6 or 8 hours regularly every night, and yet we have performed a distance of nearly 2,000 miles in something less than 19 days; for, although we left London on the evening of the 8th Feby, and did not come in here till the morning of the 2d March, we halted three days in Berlin which ought not to be counted.

Excuse hurried note dear Sir William and believe me always, [etc.].

1230 GEORGE CANNING *to the* KING

F.O. March 8th 1826.

MR. CANNING, with his humble duty to your Majesty, humbly reports to your Majesty that, although there was no material business in the House of Commons to-day (being Wednesday) opportunity was taken by several members from the city to announce the appearance of returning confidence & credit; and that others acknowledged (some of them against their former opinions) the measures of your Majesty's Government to have been, upon the whole, well-considered, and successful, in a crisis of almost unexampled difficulty.

The accounts from different parts of the country to-day are also indicative of a gradual diminution of distress.[1]

1231 GEORGE CANNING *to the* KING

F.O., March 9, 1826. ½ p 11.

MR. CANNING humbly reports to your Majesty that the House of Commons has been occupied tonight with a great variety of motions; none of them of any material publick interest except one by Mr. Peel for the introduction of a Bill to consolidate the laws respecting theft, & another for a Bill to amend certain points in the practice of criminal law;[2]

1 The great commercial crisis of 1825–26 was brought about by speculation, and overproduction, and was aggravated by unsound banking methods. The Government tried to place the country banks on a more stable foundation by abolishing the clause in the Bank Charter Act which prohibited the formation of a bank with more than six partners, and by forbidding the English country banks to issue notes of a smaller denomination than £5.

2 Only this Bill was passed in 1826 (7 Geo. IV. *c.* 64: "An Act for improving the administration of Criminal Justice in England.") The other became law in 1827, whilst Peel was out of office.

which motions were prefaced by Mr. Peel with a speech of rare ability, temper, & information; & were received with unanimous approbation & applause by the House.

There was nothing else at all worthy of your Majesty's notice.

Things continue to mend in the city, & in the country.

1232 THE EARL OF MOUNTCHARLES *to* SIR WILLIAM KNIGHTON

March 13th/'26.

I REMAINED one day in Dublin on purpose to dine with the Lord Lt, he was extremely kind to me. I never saw a man so much in love in my life, the whole of the dinner he kept making downright love to his wife; she was so *sick* towards the end of the dinner that she was obliged to get up from table, I never saw a man so fussed as his Exc.ʸ was at it, he did not reappear 'till late in the evening. I saw her no more. Does not this look as if there was a young Lord Mornington forthcoming?[1]

Lord Wellesley made most particular enquiries after the King's health, I told him that H.M.ʸ had been much indisposed latterly, but I was in hopes that now he was recovering. Lord W. asked most anxiously after you & said that he was under *great obligations* to you. I told him that I knew there was no one you were so much attached to as to him, which pleased his Excʸ excessively, & I thought there was no harm in my telling him so. I never saw a man grown so deaf, worse than the D. of Wellington I think. When we meet again I will tell you what I think of the Castle establishment &c.

I hope my dear Sir William you are quite well, & that all are going on well at the Lodge.

Excuse I pray you, this scrawl, I merely write to thank you for all the *particular* kindness you have shewn me of late, & to tell you how much I feel it.

Should you have an opportunity pray have the goodness to present my humble duty to His Majesty.

1 Wellesley had no children by his second wife.

F.O., March 21, 1826. ½ p 11 p.m.

MR. CANNING humbly reports to your Majesty that the last votes of English supply were passed through their last stage tonight; & that it is now confidently hoped that the Irish votes may be finished tomorrow & Thursday.[1]

A Bill has been brought in by Mr. Arbuthnot for extending the improvements of London;[2] in the proposing of which Mr. Arbuthnot took occasion to mention (to the great satisfaction of the House) your Majesty's gracious suggestion of the improvements in Hyde Park which have so much benefitted the publick.

There was nothing else in the discussions of the evening worthy of your Majesty's particular notice.

1234 GEORGE CANNING *to the* KING

11 April 1826.

MR. CANNING with his most humble duty, begs leave to offer also his most grateful acknowledgements to your Majesty, for your Majesty's exceeding goodness in respect to the matter which, he learns from Sir William Knighton, your Majesty has been graciously pleased to consider with such singular and unhoped for favour.[3]

Mr Canning has no right to accuse Sir William Knighton of a breach of confidence in disclosing the matter to your Majesty.[4] But he does

1 Canning had written to Knighton on the 17th. "If we get through the Irish Estimates, as I hope we shall, before the holidays, Parliament will be in our power whenever dissolution may be thought advisable".

2 The Charing Cross Improvement Bill became law in 1826.

3 "The King", said Canning, "expressed himself most kindly and graciously disposed to do something that should mark His Majesty's favourable opinion of my services." Canning, however, did not want a peerage for himself, "and the circumstances of my family would not justify my accepting a peerage in the way in which alone I have ever thought of accepting one—for them—*not* in my own person". "What then remained", he added, "by which I could take fair advantage of the King's gracious disposition, but to afford His Majesty the opportunity of manifesting it—in the instance of a person who—after my own family—is the nearest to me in the world." Charles Ellis took the title of Baron Seaford.

4 Knighton had had a long conversation with Canning on the 9th, and after he had reported it to the King that evening, he wrote to Canning saying that he "could not resist the impulse of imparting" his "amiable secret relative to Mr. Ellis. I will now give you the King's own words as nearly as my memory serves me. 'I will do it for Mr. Canning with all my heart—with the greatest pleasure. I like Charles Ellis; he is a perfect gentleman. I have always (I must say so) admired his steady affection to Canning, and you know how much I appreciate grateful feelings. This is true goodness of heart in Canning and I wish you to tell him from me that I feel satisfied that the principle which prompts his wish on the present occasion, relative to Charles Ellis, will make me sure that he (Canning) will by every means in his power contribute to my peace and comfort, the few short years I have to live.'" (Harewood MSS.)

nevertheless humbly assure your Majesty that nothing could be further from his thought, when he betrayed his feelings to Sir W. Knighton, than to bring forward a request to your Majesty on the subject, at the present time.

He looked only to the possibility of preferring such a request to your Majesty at some future period, when he should have served your Majesty longer, and should have given (or endeavoured to give) more proofs of his affectionate devotion to your Majesty, and of his earnest study to contribute to your Majesty's ease and comfort.

He really cannot find words adequately to express to your Majesty his sense of your Majesty's condescending kindness in thus unexpectedly anticipating his wishes.

Mr Canning will wait your Majesty's gracious permission to mention the matter to Lord Liverpool.

He has never *hinted* it to the individual concerned: nor is it his intention to do so, till the moment—or the very eve—of its accomplishment.[1]

1235 THE EARL OF LIVERPOOL *to the* KING

Fife House, April 17, 1826.

LORD LIVERPOOL presents his humble duty to your Majesty, and as the Session of Parliament, is now approaching towards a conclusion, your Majesty may be desirous of considering, before Parliament is dissolved, whether any, and what addition shall be made to the Peerage of the United Kingdom.

The only obligation by which Lord Liverpool is in any way embarrassed, respects Lord Northland,[2] for whose elevation to the Peerage of the United Kingdom Lord Grenville made the strongest and most earnest application at the end of the year 1821 when the connection was formed between your Majesty's present servants, and the Grenville Party.

This step could not have been taken at that time, without exposing your Majesty's Government, to serious difficulties by the disappoint-

1 Canning kept the secret from him until 27 May. See No. 1243.
2 Thomas Knox, second Viscount Northland (1754–1840). Created a Peer of the United Kingdom, as Baron Ranfurly, June 1826. Reporting to Canning a conversation with the King on the 10th Knighton wrote: "H.M. renewed his objection with increased warmth, relative to Lord Northland, and said that if Lord Liverpool had committed himself to Lord Grenville, that he himself (the King) must get Lord Liverpool out of it. H.M. then added, 'that as the Grenville party was supposed to be comprehended in the person of the Duke of Buckingham, I cannot bear to do anything more for them'. I hope however when the time arrives, if Lord Liverpool stands pledged, we shall be able to get H.M. graciously to waive the objection." (Harewood MSS.)

ment which might be afforded to others: but Lord Liverpool was obliged to assure Lord Grenville that it should be most favourably consider'd, whenever any new creations in the British Peerage might take place, and Lord Liverpool was led to make this assurance, in the strongest terms, from Lord Grenville having said to him, that it was the only *personal* engagement at the close of his publick life, about which he felt a deep interest, and which really pressed upon his mind.

If your Majesty shall be pleased to carry your gracious intentions into effect, respecting Mr. Stuart Wortley,[1] Lord Liverpool humbly hopes that your Majesty will have no objection to confer the Peerage of the United Kingdom upon Mr. Duncombe.[2]

Mr. Duncombe's family, fortune, and his honourable and invariable support of your Majesty's Government, will Lord Liverpool hopes in your Majesty's judgement fairly entitle him to this distinction.

Mr. Canning is naturally anxious about his son in law, the Marquis of Clanricarde,[3] the station of Lord Clanricarde in the Irish Peerage, and the circumstance of his family having for so many years enjoy'd the Peerage of the United Kingdom, would render the revival of it in the present Lord, quite unobjectionable.

Your Majesty (as Lord Liverpool has been informed) has been made acquainted with Mr. Canning's *personal* wishes respecting Mr. Charles Ellis, and Lord Liverpool can only say that if your Majesty shall be pleased to confer a peerage upon Mr. Ellis it can not be otherwise than most agreable to Lord Liverpool.[4]

In case your Majesty should wish to make another addition from amongst the Irish Peers to the Peerage of the United Kingdom, Lord Liverpool could venture to recommend the Marquis of Thomond,[5] with whom he has no personal connection, but who is in every respect a person of fortune, character & honour, & of the highest consideration in Ireland.[6]

1 Created Baron Wharncliffe, June 1826. He was reckoned a Canningite in 1827, but he owed his peerage to the King alone.

2 Charles Duncombe (1764–1841), created Baron Feversham, June 1826. He had asked Liverpool for a peerage in May 1820.

3 Ulick John de Burgh, Marquis of Clanricarde (1802–1874) married Canning's daughter Harriet in 1825. Succeeded his father as fourteenth Earl of Clanricarde, 1808; created an Irish Marquis, 1825, and a Peer of the United Kingdom, as Baron Somerhill, June 1826. He was Under-Secretary for Foreign Affairs from January 1826 until Canning's death.

4 Liverpool was Charles Ellis's uncle.

5 William O'Brien, second Marquis of Thomond. Created Baron Tadcaster, in the British Peerage, June 1826.

6 "All I have to consider and to watch is that the BALANCE on the Protestant side in the House of Lords preponderates", declared the King, discussing with Knighton the proposed creations. (Harewood MSS.)

Dublin Castle, 19th April 1826.
½ past 11 o'Clock p.m.

The Lord Lieutenant and Lady Wellesley are just returned from the play, being the first time his Excellency has attended since the riot at the theatre.[1] When he was setting out he desired me to write you a line to night to let you know what his reception was, be it what it might. I am happy to say that it was impossible for anything to be more gratifying. Many persons declared it somewhat reminded them of the burst of loyalty which distinguished His Majesty's visit to the theatre; and the enthusiasm with which every allusion to His Majesty was caught at, seemed to connect in a gratifying manner their love for His Majesty's person, with the respect shewn to his representative.

The attention shewn to Lady Wellesley was quite overpowering. She has contrived to make herself popular with all classes to a degree that never was surpassed by any thing that can be remembered of any of her predecessors. There has not been so full or so respectable an audience since the King was here and there was not the slightest indication of party feeling.

Lord Wellesley was prevailed upon to go, by a representation of the good it would do to the poor tradespeople of Dublin. It was impossible to say that some bad spirits might not attempt a disturbance. I think therefore you will be glad to learn that the thing went off well.

Thousands of people cheered their *Exc.* all the way from the theatre to the Castle.

I rejoice to see by the papers receivd to-day that the King was well & had taken his usual airing in the Park at Windsor.

1237 The Earl of Liverpool *to the* King

Fife House, April 20, 1826.

Lord Liverpool is most truly grateful to your Majesty, for your Majesty's most kind answer to his letter.

Your Majesty's personal feelings on the subject of Lord Fife's[2] pro-

---

1 See No. 1055.

2 James Duff, fourth Earl of Fife (1776–1857), the King's "old and attached friend". Created Baron Fife in the British Peerage, April 1827. "I am quite aware of the trifling objection to some of the fooleries of his past life", wrote the King, "but who is exempt from some nonsense or other? I dismissed him from my household [in 1821], and used him *apparently* ill to please my Government and poor Lord Londonderry; but, notwithstanding this, *my friend* Fife never gave a vote against the Government afterwards, and by his loyal example when I was in Scotland did the greatest good." (*Yonge,* III, 380.)

motion to the Peerage of the United Kingdom, must operate as commands upon Lord Liverpool.

Lord Liverpool has no *personal* wish respecting Sir John Leicester,[1] and he would be obliged to your Majesty if you would allow this matter to remain in abeyance, till he has the honour of seeing your Majesty.

1238 THE KING *to* SIR WILLIAM KNIGHTON

R! L^{ge}., April 20th 1826.

IF Mr. Canning's, or his subalterns in office, patience could have lasted a few hours longer, they would have receiv'd the box you mention'd, together with another containing dispatches, *at least*, three hours *sooner* this morning than I did or could receive your letter. The fact stands thus; those two boxes I had look'd over yesterday by *twelve o'clock*, & they were taken out of my room, *as done with*, therefore they might have been plac'd in your chaise, or sent by special messenger, if their pressing nature had been stated. If for the future therefore whenever there is a box of a similar nature that requires immediate dispatch, the word *immediate* is put upon it, I shall perfectly understand what is meant, & the evil will not occur again. Nothing new, & I am immediately going out to dine.

N.B. Not a box left.

1239 SIR ROBERT WILSON *to the* KING

Regent St., May 5, 1826.

THE confidence I have invariably reposed in your Majesty's benignity and condescension induces me to take the step I am now adopting, and to flatter myself with the hope that this appeal may not be made in vain, to those generous feelings which have always been predominant in your Majesty's character and dispositions.

Nearly five years have now elapsed since I had the pain to receive a communication "that your Majesty had no longer any occasion for my services" in an army, to which I had devoted with the most ardent zeal, and many sacrifices, above twenty seven years of my life, and to which

1 Created Baron de Tabley, June 1826. See No. 255. "If you choose to let Sir John Leicester stand", wrote the King, "I have no objection." (*Yonge*, III, 380.)

I was attached, by every tie of affection, as well as of professional interest.

It would perhaps be indecorous, to trespass on your Majesty, with any detail of those transactions, which I may presume were connected with this notification, but I trust your Majesty will believe, that no act of mine, was accompanied with a motive unbecoming an officer to entertain, and, however appearances might have subjected my conduct, at the moment, to unfavorable construction, that, I was in no instance really insensible to the duties I owed your Majesty, as a Sovereign, or as a gracious benefactor to my family.

I trust, nevertheless, I may be allowed to submit to your Majesty the annexed document, as a record of those sentiments, and further to assure your Majesty, that other testimonials and facts might have been produced, if considerations of delicacy, and of propriety, had not imposed restraints on my making any use of them.

To have incurred your Majesty's displeasure, tho involuntarily, has been to me, and all with whom I am connected, the subject of the deepest regret; when, therefore, I am approaching your Majesty with an earnest solicitation, that I may be restored to your Majesty's favor and army, I am actuated by feelings which must ever be cherished by those, who are devoted to the service of your Majesty and who must regard your Majesty's approbation as its most honorable distinction.[1]

With the most profound deference and respect I have the honor to be [etc.].

1240 SIR ROBERT WILSON *to* STEPHEN LUSHINGTON

July 19th 1820.

THERE is no sacrifice I would not make, to secure a due course of justice, and give assistance to an accused party, but I do not think my interposition is indispensable, and independent of Lady W[ilson]'s state which is perilous, and anxious in the extreme, I must fairly tell you, in confidence, my position with the King.[2]

1 He was dismissed for interfering with the military at Queen Caroline's funeral, but was reinstated with the rank of Lieutenant-General in 1830. He wrote this letter under the mistaken impression that the King and the Duke of York, the Commander-in-Chief, were favourably disposed towards him. Wellington told him that it was impossible to review the case, and that none of the documents which he proposed to submit to the King for his justification could be of any use except the letter to Lushington (No. 1240), which "was calculated to make a favourable impression on the King's mind". (*W.N.D.* III, 316–22.)

2 Lushington had written to him on the 18th: "I have been informed by Mr. J. Brougham that you have expressed your determination not to proceed to Italy on the Queen's affairs. This communication has caused me the greatest regret, for I very strongly feel the very great

When I was under accusation of "Treason against all the Gov^{mts} of Europe" Lady W. without saying any thing to me, came to England, to request of the British Govt. its intervention, not by an application for mercy, or favour, but for the maintenance of the French law, which by that indictment had been violated.[1]

She saw the King, who received her most kindly and who so far from being offended at the nature of her request, sent her a letter, begging her to allow him in any event, to charge himself with the care of two of my children, a girl and a boy. This was not mentioned to me until the trial was over, and then consulting with Lord Grey, I was advised not to oppose myself to that arrangement, as it would in every point of view be unbecoming.

The King allowed 300 £ a year to Lady W. for these children, and which was paid, until I came into Parliament, when without asking any advice I wrote a letter to the King, stating, "that whilst I acknowledged, and should always bear in mind his generous conduct to Lady W., I thought it was due to him, as well as my new situation, not to allow any further trespass on his bounty".

Now, assuredly, it would not become me to put myself forward on a commission, which whatever may be said, is not exclusively an affair between the State and the Queen, but which will be regarded generally, as a question involving many personal considerations.

This is the real case, and the more I consider it, the more I am persuaded my interference in the way proposed, would be condemned.

My feeling is, that I ought to do nothing extra-judicial, but no considerations whatever, will induce me to shrink from the discharge of my judicial duties, if unfortunately, we are called upon to perform them.

I have now put you in possession of my real motives, and I think you will concur with my view of the conduct I am bound to pursue, in this distressing and embarrassing proceeding.[2]

benefit the Queen's cause would have derived from your name and exertions. . . . I know how peculiarly anxious Brougham is upon this point, and how very important he considers it to the ultimate result. Will you therefore permit me to request your re-consideration of this matter. . . ." (Add. MSS. 30109, fo. 120.)

1 In 1816 the Court of Assize of the Department of the Seine had sentenced Sir Robert Wilson and two other Englishmen to three months' imprisonment for helping Lavalette, a Bonapartist General who had been condemned to death, to escape. Wilson was also originally charged with plotting against the political system of Europe, with the particular object of changing the French Government and inciting the people to take up arms against the King's authority, but this charge was dropped for lack of evidence.

2 Lushington replied, the same day: "Most entirely do I concur in your feelings, and had I been in any degree aware of the circumstances, never should I have made the proposition to you. Excuse me for having in ignorance urged you, and attribute it to my anxiety to advance the cause I am bound to." (Add. MSS. 30109, fo. 121.)

1241 Dr Keate *to* Sir William Knighton

Eton College, May 10, 1826.

As His Majesty has on so many occasions graciously condescended to honour the Montem with his presence, and expressed his intention, the last time he so honoured us, of being present at future Montems, though he was unfortunately prevented by ill-health from being at the last, I have thought it my duty to endeavour to ascertain through you His Majesty's intentions respecting the approaching ceremony on Tuesday the 16th.

As I shall wish to make some arrangements in the event of His Majesty's being present, which would not otherwise take place, may I request you will have the kindness to give me information upon the subject, as soon as it may be convenient.

1242 Dr Keate *to* Sir William Knighton

Eton College, May 12, 1826.

I BEG leave to express my sense of His Majesty's gracious condescension, and kindness in regretting his inability to attend the approaching Montem; and also to assure you of the very sincere gratitude of the captain of the school for His Majesty's most splendid donation.

1243 George Canning *to the* King

F.O., 30 May 1826.

MR CANNING presents his most humble and affectionate duty to your Majesty, and humbly acquaints your Majesty that he has communicated to Mr. Ellis your Majesty's gracious intention to confer upon him the highest mark of your Majesty's favour and good opinion.

Mr Ellis was really overwhelmed by a communication so totally unexpected: and it was not till after four & twenty hours of reflection that he could persuade himself that he should do right in availing himself of such exceeding kindness on the part of your Majesty.

Mr Canning indeed is utterly unable to express adequately to your Majesty on this occasion, either Mr. Ellis's feelings, or his own, but he relies confidently on those of your Majesty to understand and appreciate them justly.

Dublin Castle, 6th June 1826.

I AM desired by Lord Wellesley to request your attention to an article in the New Monthly Magazine[1] for this month entitled "*The Dublin Tabinet Ball*" in which he is represented as having assumed more state than was becoming in a Vice Roy. In case the article should attract notice in England, he desired me to state the simple facts to you, and to request you to submit them in the proper quarter, if it should be necessary.

Long before his marriage Lord Wellesley had promised Lady Manners[2] to attend an annual Charity Ball to be held this year at the Rotunda under her patronage. When the time approached she suggested that if the Lord Lieutenant came in state it would attract crowds & benefit the Charity. His Excellency wished to escape the trouble of the state, as he had lately been twice at the theatre in grand costume: but he was obliged to yield for the benefit of the Charity. To heighten the effect the patronesses produced the canopy & chairs, being precisely the same as those used in St. Patrick's Hall, and at the Mansion House, when the Lord Lieutenant visits the Lord Mayor—and his Excellency went to the Rotunda exactly in the same form as he does to the Lord Mayor's dinner.

When the Tabinet ball for the distressed weavers took place the week following,[3] he was prevailed upon to go in the same manner, from similar motives. Lord Wellesley is perfectly innocent of the canopy; and indeed of the whole affair, which he tried as much as possible to avoid.

The story of Sir Harcourt Lees[4] is entirely false. I do not believe he

1 Vol. XVI, 544–51; XVII, 193–200.
2 The second wife of Lord Manners, the Lord Chancellor of Ireland.
3 On 11 May. The writer of the article alleged that though Wellesley was a man of great ability, he relied "upon the gew-gaw of a spurious Court for his importance", and was "in love with the raree-show of vice-regal honours". "A throne surmounted with a gorgeous canopy of gold and scarlet was placed at the extremity of the room for his reception, and to this seat of mock regality he advanced with his vice-queen, with a measured and stately step."
4 Rector and Vicar of Killarney. A strenuous opponent of Catholic Emancipation, he published many pamphlets in support of Protestant ascendancy. (1776–1852.) "For many years he was unknown to the public, and among his own immediate friends was regarded as a harmless and somewhat simple man who could discuss a bottle of claret much better than a homily.... What was the astonishment of all Dublin, when it was announced that this plain and unobtrusive lover of the field was the author of a pamphlet filled with the most virulent and acrimonious matter against the religion of the country, and which almost amounted to a call on the Protestant population to rise up in arms and extirpate Popery from the land!... The meeting between the Marquis Wellesley and this celebrated person at the Tabinet Ball excited all my attention. I did not perceive the latter until a certain expression of defiance, which suddenly came into the Marquis's face, directed my notice to the quarter towards which he was looking.... Seated upon the throne, with his clenched hand resting upon his thigh, and his marked and diplomatic visage protruded in all the intensity of expression for which it is remarkable, the most noble and puissant Marquis shot his fine and indignant

was present. Lord Wellesley certainly did not see him; & there always has been great civility in their intercourse.

Lady Wellesley also wished me to give you this statement of facts, but she desired me to say that she was much flattered by the commendation and not at all annoyed at the sneers with which it was mixed.

She never was at Mr. Saurins[1] house, & never concealed her religion on her arrival here.[2] She met him at Mr. Sneyd's at dinner—but nothing passed of the nature stated.

1245 THE KING *to the* DUKE OF YORK

Royal Lodge, June 12th 1826.

YOUR kind letter has just reach'd me, & deeply, as I cannot fail to feel, the disappointment of being for the present depriv'd of your long-wish'd for presence here for a few days, still more deep I do assure you, would my regret have been, had you, from any mistaken feeling of affection, or attention to me, neglected that due resignation to the advice of S.[r] Hy Halford & your other medical advisers, as well as of (*that*, to me, *the first of all considerations*) the *absolutely* necessary & requisite attention to your general health; & which here I do now state to you dearest brother is not only what you owe to yourself, but which is at the same time a positive *moral duty* by which you are holden, & bound to me, as your most affectionate of brothers, & as your Sovereign, as well as to the country, & to the very numerous circle of your friends, by all of whom you are so very justly lov'd & esteem'd. For God's sake, for my sake, & for the sake of all those to whom you are so very dear, let me enjoin you, let me implore of you now, that you have assented to adopt the line of regimen that has been present'd to you, that you will *persevere* in it, & *not suffer any other consideration on earth to induce you*, to swerve from

eyes into the soul of his antagonist, while Sir Harcourt, with a half waggish and half malevolent aspect, blending the grin of an ostler with the acrimony of a divine, encountered the lofty look of the chief governor of Ireland with a jocular disdain, and gave him to understand that a man of his theological mettle was not to be subjugated by a frown. . . ."

1 William Saurin (1757?–1839), Irish Attorney-General, 1807–22, and a strong "Protestant".

2 "She came to Ireland, accompanied by her sister, with no other object than to see the country. Having been introduced to the most fashionable circles, she did not at first disclose her religion, which might have been an obstacle to the cordiality of her reception. Her addiction to Popery was little suspected, as may be judged from her having been selected by Mr. Saurin as his political confidante. It was at a party at his house (so at least it is rumoured in Dublin) that she first revealed her leanings towards the Pope."

this, or *from any thing else* that may be deem'd best to recommend to you, until the complete re-establishment of your precious & invaluable health, & which with the blessing of God, I trust we shall very soon witness, & be enabled to return our most fervent thanks to the Almighty from the most grateful of hearts. My heart is too full, to say much more at present, except, that the very moment the company which I had invited to meet you, shall leave me, & which I could not now put off, as the greater part is to assemble to-day, I shall come to town purposely to see you, when we will settle our future places of meeting. God bless you Dst Frederick,[1] [etc.].

1246 GEORGE CANNING *to* SIR WILLIAM KNIGHTON

Brighton, June 20, 1826.

THE trees of the Pavilion garden are so full in our view, that, being the only trees within some miles of us, I cannot help wishing that, (if not against all rule) I might be allowed to take Mrs. Canning, now & then, in these sultry mornings, to walk under the shade of them.

Will you have the kindness to let me know if this may be.

Mrs. C. bore the journey better than I expected: & I think she is perceptibly better—or rather perhaps less unwell—this morning.[2]

1247 THE DUKE OF WELLINGTON *to* SIR WILLIAM KNIGHTON

London, June 27th 1826.

SINCE you spoke to me regarding a residence for His Majesty during the years 27 and 28 I have turned over in my mind the plan proposed for obtaining for the King's use the apartment in St. James' hitherto allotted to H.R.H. the Duke of Cumberland.

That residence will be very inconvenient to His Majesty. It is a single house in the centre of the town, not closed from the street, overlooked on all sides to such a degree as that every movement in the apartments can be seen by the opposite neighbours; and the avenues to it are through the most frequented parts of the town and park. I am much mistaken if His Majesty does not find that it will not answer his purpose at all.

1 The Duke was dying of dropsy.
2 Canning had bought a house in Brighton.

I should think the best expedient to be adopted would be for His Majesty to inhabit some of the apartments in Kensington Palace. His Majesty would there be in tranquility; and could see whom he pleased without being overlooked or the comments of observers. That Palace is not farther from Hyde Park Corner than Carlton House; and but little farther than St. James'; and the King's Ministers would feel no greater inconvenience in attending His Majesty there than they would at Carlton House or elsewhere.

I suggest this for your consideration. If however H.M. should determine in favour of the Duke of Cumberland's apartment the plan of proceeding which you propose would be the best.

1248 EARL BATHURST *to the* KING

August 1st 1826.

WHEN Lord Bathurst had the honor of paying his duty to your Majesty yesterday at the Royal Lodge, your Majesty made an inquiry with respect to instructions regarding Lord Cochrane.

Lord Bathurst begs most humbly to submit to your Majesty that nearly two years ago, when there was first the rumour of Lord Cochrane's intention of entering into the Greek service, Lord Bathurst sent an instruction to the Governors of Gibraltar & Malta, founded on an opinion of your Majesty's law officers, with respect to the manner & extent to which the Foreign Enlistment Bill might be enforced in that part of your Majesty's dominions. All therefore that was necessary, on hearing of Lord Cochrane's actual departure six weeks ago, was to call the attention of the two Governors to those instructions.[1]

With respect to the Ionian Islands, the Foreign Enlistment Bill is not in force there. But by the regulations of the Ionian Government, no armed vessel belonging to either of the belligerents can resort to the Ionian ports: and in the event of Lord Cochrane arriving there in an unarmed vessel, Lord Bathurst has given an instruction that his Lordship should not be allow'd to remain there.

1 Cochrane had accepted the command of Admiral of the Greek Fleet, which consisted of a steam-driven line-of-battle ship and other vessels. But his squadron accomplished little; the intervention of the Powers compelled the Turks to recognise the independence of Greece, and Cochrane returned to England.

Fife House, Sept. 6, 1826.

THE melancholy and unexpected death of Lord Gifford has render'd it necessary for the Lord Chancellor and Lord Liverpool to consider what arrangement it would be most adviseable to recommend to your Majesty for filling up the office of Master of the Rolls.

Lord Liverpool ventures therefore to submit to your Majesty, the result of their deliberation.

There can certainly now exist no difference of opinion, that there is not any person either at the *Bar,* or upon the bench, who can compete with the present Attorney Genl.[1] eventually, for the highest station and honours in the legal profession.

It would therefore be most desireable, that the Attorney Genl. should be persuaded to accept of the office of Master of the Rolls, as in addition to other advantages incident to such an appointment, it would give him practise and experience in a Court of Equity, before the time should arrive when he might be called upon to fill the first office in it.

With respect to a Peerage, Lord Liverpool would humbly submit, that it is not necessary to decide anything upon that head at present.

It may be very desireable, that the Attorney Genl. should continue in the House of Commons as Master of the Rolls, to carry through any measures which may be judged expedient in consequence of the report of the commissioners upon the Court of Chancery, more particularly as this difficult business is already in his hands, and as he would introduce it with more authority than any other person, to whom it could be entrusted. In case however, that it should so happen that his services should become necessary in the House of Lords, it would be in your Majesty's power at any time, in the course of a few days to give the House of Lords the benefit of those services.

1250 THE EARL OF LIVERPOOL *to the* KING

London, Sept. 10, 1826.

LORD LIVERPOOL has the satisfaction of informing your Majesty, that the Lord Chancellor and Lord Liverpool have just seen the Attorney Genl. who has accepted with every sentiment of gratitude towards your Majesty, the office of Master of the Rolls.

1 Sir John Copley. His appointment as Master of the Rolls was gazetted on the 13th. See Liverpool's letter to Eldon, of the 5th, where he says that Copley "should be *made* to accept the Mastership of the Rolls. He has no competitor at the Bar, at least on *our* side, nor any on the Bench, who can compete with him in the highest honours of the profession." *Twiss,* II, 575.)

Lord Liverpool has communicated with the Lord Chancellor, and Sir John Copley, respecting the *consequent* arrangements. They are all of opinion that it would be impossible to advise your Majesty to pass over the Solicitor Genl.[1] for the office of Attorney, and they agree that Mr. Tindal[2] is in every respect the most proper person now at the Bar, to be made Solicitor Genl.

Lord Liverpool humbly requests therefore your Majesty's permission, to inform Sir Ch. Wetherell and Mr. Tindal that your Majesty approves of their appointment to the offices of Attorney and Solicitor Genl.

1251 THE EARL OF ELDON *to the* KING

[*c.* 10 Sept. 1826.]

YOUR MAJESTY having been graciously pleased to permit the office of the Master of the Rolls to be offered to the Att[y] General, and that gentleman having signified his intention to avail himself of your Majesty's goodness, the Lord Chancellor has taken the liberty to direct the necessary papers, which are to receive the Royal sign manual, to be sent to your Majesty. He apologises for thus early giving your Majesty this trouble, but the vacancy of the office being attended with considerable public inconvenience, he trusts your Majesty will excuse it.

The Lord Chancellor takes leave to add that, under the influence of the most grateful feelings, which your Majesty's long continued goodness to him has excited in his breast, & which must ever continue to regulate his conduct, he could never forgive himself, if a more permanent arrangement could *now* have been made of the law offices, useful to your Majesty's interest, and grateful to your Majesty's anxious solicitude for the public welfare, and he had not been most willing, by resignation of the Great Seal, if approved by your Majesty, to have afforded every facility to such an arrangement. Under present circumstances, however, he has been induced to think that he still owes it to your Majesty to struggle somewhat longer against the difficulties which attend the execution, with competent sufficiency, of the great duties of the Chancellorship: and gratitude to your Majesty will ensure his humble, but anxious endeavours to discharge those duties to the best of his power, so long as he is entrusted to attempt to discharge them, and untill your Majesty shall be pleased to place the Seal in abler and younger hands.

1 Sir Charles Wetherell.
2 Sir Nicholas Conyngham Tindal. Solicitor-General, and knighted, 1826; Chief Justice of the Common Pleas, 1829.

The death of Lord Gifford occasions a very, very great public loss. To lose in times, like these, a person, who to an uncommon kindness of manner, an unusual sweetness of temper, a strong judgement, a vast store of professional learning, had added, as the Chancellor knows, a resolute determination to uphold, to the utmost of his power the established Constitution in Church & State, is to undergo a loss, which cannot easily be repaired even in this country, in which Providence has been pleased, from time to time, to raise up men, for public stations, of extraordinarily excellent qualities.

The Chan^r understands that the papers to be proposed to the sign manual will be sent from Mr. Peel's office.

1252 GEORGE CANNING *to the* KING

Paris, Septr. 18, 1826.

MR. CANNING presents his most humble duty to your Majesty.

He ventures to take for granted that it may not be altogether indifferent to your Majesty to learn that the rumours (which had reached England) respecting certain *arrangements* of Lord Granville's are wholly without foundation.

The husband of the lady in question had been obliged to leave Paris, to avoid imprisonment in *S[ain]t[e] Pélagie*.[1] The wife remained here, with three children, utterly destitute; & even without a lodging till she was received into the house of a tailor (Staube by name) who had married a young woman, heretofore *demoiselle de compagnie* to L^y M. In this state Ly M. addressed herself to Ld. G. for advice & assistance; & requested him to meet her in the first instance at the Princess Gallitzin's. Afterwards more than once at the tailor's; whither Lord Granville went so openly, that his curricle was often waiting at the door—& being seen in that situation by English passers-by, gave rise, no doubt, to the notion which found it's way to London.

Lord Granville had no other conversation with Ly M. than what arose out of the distressed state of her affairs: he wrote on her behalf to the Dow. Ly M. in England; & finally, upon the husband's return from England (whither he went, incognito, to obtain the means of removing his wife & children from France) Ly M. quitted Paris, (probably not without some small pecuniary advance from Lord Granville) to join her

1 For the most part political prisoners were confined in this prison, which was built in 792 and demolished in 1899.

husband in the neighbourhood of the capital, & to proceed with him to Switzerland, & afterwards to Italy.

Lady G[ranville] was perfectly apprized of every one of these interviews: and would probably have been more amused than alarmed at the colour which has been given to them in reports to England, if she had heard them, which Ld G. assures Mr. Canning she has not.

1253 GEORGE CANNING *to the* KING

Paris, Septr. 22, 1826.

MR. CANNING presents his most humble duty to your Majesty.

Mr. Canning had yesterday a private audience of H[is] M[ost] C[hristian] Majesty; some particulars of which Mr. Canning humbly ventures to presume, may be not uninteresting to your Majesty.

The King of France was unbounded in his professions of esteem & affection for your Majesty.

In speaking of the attempts which were constantly made to impute to himself & his Government a design to do away the provisions of the *Charte*,[1] & to bring things back in France to the state in which they were before 1789; H.M. said that he wished the British Govt. to be assured that no such design existed on the part of his confidential servants, that if it found a place in the heads of a few antient servants of the Court, whose *talk* did mischief, it was the mere dream of superannuation; and that for himself, he had weighed the matter well, before he set foot in France in 1814; and that he particularly remembered a long conversation with your Majesty, in which your Majesty and himself had come, by common consent, to the conclusion, that the restored family had nothing to do but to act frankly & cordially upon the institutions, which it might be found necessary to sanction; and to endeavour rather to reconcile old prejudices & feelings with an inevitable state of things, than to force that state of things back towards one now so completely destroyed, that the very elements of it could not be collected & put together.

His Majesty declared for himself that he did act cordially & sincerely in this view; and that he was much misunderstood & misrepresented if any other impression was entertained of his conduct.

The King spoke of M. Villele[2] in the highest terms. He said that M Villele was the Minister who exactly suited the crisis in which Franc was placed; that he was adroit, able, persevering, full of expedient

1 The Constitution granted by Louis XVIII at the first Restoration, 1814.
2 President of the Council in France, 1822–27.

against difficulties, & withal honest & straightforward, in the highest degree. He (M. Villele) knew that the King was determined to support him: & in that confidence went boldly forwards, without turning aside from the obstacles thrown in his way, by any party, or combination of parties. "I support him" said His Majesty "both because I think him all that I have described; & because I am persuaded that *change* is in itself a bad thing, & that a King never submits to a change of his Ministers, without losing something of his personal authority."

His Majesty went on to say something of the necessity of holding high the *religious principle*, in a State—but particularly in France. Henry the 4th (H.My said) never could have governed France, had he not conformed to the Roman Catholick religion. He would tolerate all religions, but he felt it his duty to give to the *principle* of *religion* itself all the support in his power. His Majesty evidently had in his mind in this part of his conversation the cry against the Jesuits &c but the *word* (Jesuit) was not mentioned by His Majesty.

From religion the King came, by a natural transition, to the affairs of Greece—with respect to which that which His Majesty appears to feel most strongly is the shame to Christian Powers, which results from the oppression of a Christian population. His Majesty said that he had felt a momentary displeasure & alarm at the separate understanding between Great Britain & Russia;[1] but that the explanations which had been given by both Powers separately and the communications which had since been made by them jointly had completely done away those first feelings; and that he now retained no other wish than that of co-operating with them in the most cordial & efficacious manner. "I am ready to go faster than you are ready to go", said His Majesty, "but not without you. France wants nothing for herself; & now that Russia & England have set the example of disavowing private objects, we will do the same. We want nothing, but we could not have borne to see others profit—not profiting ourselves. But when I say I am ready to go faster, I mean that I would concur in *coercing* the Porte, if she is obstinate. Russia & Austria on the one side with a couple of 100,000 men; & our naval forces on the other co-operating in the Mediterranean, we should soon bring the Turks to reason, without striking a blow. The *conscience* that we had all & each of us nothing in view but the general good, would give a *moral* effect to our intervention, beyond any force of armament. But as to armament, to show you how sincere I am in my views—send an Admiral to the

1 By the terms of the Petersburg Protocol (4 April 1826), which was the outcome of Wellington's visit to Russia, the Tsar agreed to co-operate with Great Britain in offering mediation to Turkey on the basis of a virtually independent Greece.

Mediterran[ean] of older standing than mine, & *mine shall serve under him.*"

Mr. Canning (as your Majesty may suppose) did not encourage these warlike propensities of the King of France: he contented himself with expressing the satisfaction which such declarations would (he was sure) give to your Majesty; but expressed a hope that the object in view might be attained without resort to measures of extremity.

With respect to Portugal, the King of France avowed that the arrival of Sir Charles Stuart with the Constitution at Lisbon had for a moment disquieted the French Government. His Majesty asked me whether *we* should not have felt the like disquiet at a similar appearance of a French diplomatist, with such a freight, in any other country in Europe? But he assured me that our explanations had completely & immediately satisfied His Majesty's mind; & that the subsequent deliberation of the French Govmt had only been how to co-operate with us for the settlement in Portugal, without offence & danger to Spain.[1]

Of Spain His Majesty spoke in language of great despondency; but did not appear to like to be led far into the subject. Probably the yet un-ascertained effect of His Majesty's answer to H[is] C[atholic] Majesty's letter (mentioned in Mr. Lamb's[2] last despatch) may have restrained him.

The audience was concluded, as it had been begun, by the King with expressions of his feelings towards your Majesty.

The King's health appears to be remarkably good. His Majesty had the misfortune to fall, in coming down a flight of stairs, the night before

1 John VI, King of Portugal, had died on 10 March 1826. His eldest son, Dom Pedro, Emperor of Brazil, could have accepted the throne of Portugal had he been willing to resign the imperial crown of Brazil—the Brazilian Constitution having provided that the two crowns should never be united. He preferred his American to his European dominions, and abdicated the throne of Portugal in favour of his seven-year-old daughter, Donna Maria. Before doing so he granted Portugal a constitutional charter, and, further to strengthen his daughter's position, he betrothed her to her uncle, Dom Miguel, whom his father had banished to Vienna for participating in the rebellion of 1824, and whose interests would become identified with the maintenance rather than the disturbance of the Government. Sir Charles Stuart, the British Minister who had been at Rio Janeiro negotiating the Treaty of 29 August 1825 by which Portugal recognised the independence of Brazil, brought the Constitutional Charter to Lisbon, at the Emperor's request. The Regent, the Infanta Isabella (Dom Pedro's sister), accepted the Constitution, but a portion of the Army revolted, proclaimed the reactionary Dom Miguel King, and, calculating on receiving assistance from the despotic Ferdinand VII, crossed the frontier into Spain. The Portuguese Government, fearing a Spanish invasion, urged the British General, Lord Beresford, to resume the command of its army, and appealed to England for assistance according to its treaty rights. When the Portuguese deserters invaded their country from Spain, receiving Spanish assistance, Canning, in December, sent an army under Sir William Clinton, to preserve the independence of England's oldest Ally.

2 Frederick James Lamb was Minister at Madrid, 1825–27.

last, the report of which accident had created some anxiety in Paris. But His Majesty declared that he felt no ill effect from the accident: & he certainly walked up & down his room, while conversing with Mr. Canning for upwards of an hour, without the slightest symptom of pain or weariness.

Mr. Canning did not intend that this report should extend to such a length: but he will not lengthen it by apologies to your Majesty.

1254　GEORGE CANNING *to the* KING

Paris, Sept. 29, 1826.

MR. CANNING presents his humble duty to your Majesty.

Mr. Canning had yesterday a long conversation with M. Villele, who repeated & enforced all that had been said by H.M.C. Majesty, of the anxiety of the French Government to establish & maintain a perfect confidence, & co-operation with your Majesty's Government, upon all the great questions now pending in Europe.

M. Villele began the conversation with a description of the present state of France; which he represented as highly flourishing in every thing that respected the wealth, & power, & prosperity, both agricultural & commercial, of the nation: but as sadly wanting in many of the *moral* elements of national welfare, particularly in religious feeling, in the education & intelligence of the gentry, & in any thing like an aristocracy, which might assure stability to their institutions.

M. Villele made use of one expression in this part of his discourse, which struck Mr. Canning more forcibly from it's analogy to one employed by Mr. Fox (Mr. C. thinks in the preface to his historical work[1] —which, however, M. Villele said he had never read) Mr. Fox says— speaking of Charles II^ds reign "A Restoration is the worst of Revolutions"—M. Villele said "A Restoration is the most difficult of Governments". He went on to illustrate that position by showing the constant divergency of the Court from the State; the impossibility of either reconciling the prejudices & pretensions of the returned emigrants, with the new constitutional system; or of expecting that the King should sacrifice to the necessity of union between those two bodies, his antient personal companionships & predilections.

As to the King himself, it was but justice to say that His Majesty entered most fully & cordially into the exigencies of his situation; that

---

1 *A History of the Early Part of the Reign of James the Second*, published posthumously in 1808.

he dealt with his Ministers in the fairest, & most gracious manner, that he (the King) knew that on the day on which his (M. Villele's) retirement might be necessary for His Majesty's service or comfort, he was ready to retire; but that he would stand against all difficulties, so long as he was assured of His Majesty's support.

M. Villele said that with the Chamber of Deputies he had no difficulty; and that if there were a new election tomorrow he should be sure of an improved, rather than a diminished, support of the Government in that Chamber; but that there was an evil in the absence of discussion, and a still greater one in the exceeding defect of ability & information, which pervaded the great mass of the deputies.

The House of Peers was not wanting in either of these qualities: but that it was proportionally difficult to manage. It was composed of three portions, not very unequally divided—the antient nobility, including the King's Household,—the Buonopartists, including the remnant of the *Senate*; & the Ex-Ministers of the late Reign, (almost all of whom had been made Peers)—with those whom *they* had elevated to the Peerage, during their successive Ministries. In this last class there was abundant ability, & knowledge of affairs; & of course the most active & formidable opposition of *debate*; the second class did not hold very closely together, so as to constitute a formidable *corps* of opposition; the first class (the Court & the emigrants) was of course that on which the King's Ministers had a right to reckon for support; but he verily believed that in the instances in which he had been *beaten*, it was from *that* class that the majority of black balls had been furnished. In one or two cases he had been able to *prove* to the King, by numbers, that the majority against the Government *must have been* owing to the forfeiture of promises distinctly made to His Majesty. Your Majesty is aware that the vote is by ballot, so that the actual votes of individuals cannot be positively ascertained.

However inconvenient this state of things was, M. Villele could not reconcile it to his feelings towards the King, to exact any harsh expression of H.M's displeasure towards His Majesty's habitual society. This class was dying off by time, as was indeed that of the Buonapartists; & he did not see why, in a few years, if the law of inheritance worked as well as he hoped, the House of Peers might not become a body, not indeed of the strength and consistency of the British House of Peers, but highly useful & respectable in itself, & an efficient stay both of the Monarchy & the constitutional system.

M. Villele spoke of the Oppositions *out of* the Chambers, that of the *salons* & that of the *journals*, as Oppositions that, upon the whole, he thought *not* prejudicial to the Government. The *salons*, he said, were a *puissance*, in France, of which in England we could have no adequate notion. But both they, and the newspapers were useful to him; as indicating the tendency of publick opinion, & preventing any sudden explosion of it, which might take him by surprize in the Chambers. He had not the least thoughts of interfering with the liberty of the Press: nor had the King. He flattered himself that he had *menagé* a little popularity for the King, in reserving the abolition of the censure [*sic*] for the beginning of His Majesty's reign: & he had found no reason to repent of having done so.

The King felt nothing sorely in the publick discussions, except any attack upon *religion*—which must not be confounded (he said) with attacks upon the Jesuits, or even with animadversions upon the pretensions of the clergy. So far from deprecating that *war*, if kept within due bounds, M. Villele believed that some good arose out of it. The clergy *were* disposed to encroachment. They were, generally speaking, an ill-composed body *as yet*; few men of family, or even of respectable station in life, had, *as yet*, entered into the Church. The great proportion of them, coming out of the lowest classes of society, had no connection with the enlightened classes, & no division of interest or feeling, arising from sympathy with them; & they were therefore for the most part *devoted entirely* & *exclusively* to the interests of their order, at the same time that they were ignorant of the *real* manner of promoting those interests, & intemperate in proportion to their ignorance. He thought it not unuseful that they were watched, as jealously as they were, by the publick; & he believed that this jealousy prevented many proceedings, on their part, & nipped others in the bud, with which, if suffered to grow to maturity the Government might have had the unpleasant & ungracious task of interfering.

From the internal state of France M. Villele proceeded to foreign politicks: which Mr. Canning forbears entering upon at present, lest he should intrude too long upon your Majesty's patience: but he will take the liberty of addressing your Majesty again by a messenger, whom he proposes to despatch tomorrow or Sunday.

Russell Square, Sept. the 29th 1826.

THE enclosed catalogue was conveyed to me with a letter from Mr. Brook Taylor, our Resident at Munich, informing me that the pictures are the private collection of the late King of Bavaria. He has requested me to endeavor to know whether it would be His Majesty's pleasure, that he should bid for any of them at the ensuing sale at Christmas and particularly whether it be still the King's wish to possess "the Reading of the Will" by Mr. Wilkie, as that picture will be sold with the rest of the collection.

Can you do me the favor to gain His Majesty's gracious pleasure on the subject? that I may acquaint Mr. Brook Taylor with the King's decision.

The picture as you know is one of Wilkie's finest works.[1]

Whether there is a probability that he may again paint another of so large a subject as successfully, you have better guess than I can possibly have.

I am happy to inform you that Count Munster has seen His Majesty's portrait destined for Hanover, and that it meets with his entire approbation.

It goes to Grosvenor Place in the packing case tomorrow morning.

I am just setting out for a week or ten days, on a visit to some friends, and a tour through part of Wales. My stay however will not extend beyond the time I have mentioned.

Believe me to remain with much respect [etc.].

1256 GEORGE CANNING *to the* KING

Paris, Octr. 1st 1826.

MR. CANNING presents his most humble duty to your Majesty: and takes the liberty of continuing his report of his interview with M. de Villele.

Mr. Canning thought it adviseable to put M. de Villele in possession, confidentially, of the *third* part of the communication (respecting the Protocol[2] of April) to be made to the Allies, which relates to the mode in which the Protocol is proposed to be carried into execution.

M. Villele expressed his entire willingness to co-operate for that

1 It was purchased for the National Gallery at Munich, for £1200. (Cunningham's *Life of Wilkie*, II, 404.) Wilkie had sold it for £425. (II, 32.)
2 The Petersburg Protocol. See No. 1253.

object, in the way intended to be proposed. He rejoiced that measures of force were not in contemplation. His language on this point was much less *enthusiastick* than that of H.M.C. Majesty had been: nor was there any mixture in it of that *crusading* spirit, which generally prevails among the friends of the Greeks—nor any reference whatever to Epaminondas, or Themistocles, in the other general topicks of declamation. M. Villele's view of the matter was a sober practical view (such as is taken of it by your Majesty's Government) founded on the danger, as well as disgrace to all Europe, of leaving such a war as now desolates the Archipelago to take it's course; multiplying piracies against the trade of all commercial nations, & tending to exhaust both parties to the war so effectually, that both may at any moment become an easy prey to the ambition of Russia. It is upon this last point that M. Villele feels most strongly. Fear of Russia seems to be the prevailing sentiment in his mind. The only two points in the Protocol upon which he made any objection were 1st the declaration that England could not undertake to guarantee the arrangement between Turkey & Greece: which he feared would leave the whole question in the hands of Russia. 2ndly the want, as he thought, of a sufficient security against the extension of the hostilities, which might grow out of a failure of the negotiation at Akkermann,[1] to Greece.

Upon both these points Mr. Canning had a long discussion, with M. Villele: with the detail of which he will not trouble your Majesty, especially as a short time must now decide the issue of the pending negotiation.

The discussion ended in Mr. Canning's suggestion to M. Villele that, if France thought further security against the aggrandizement of Russia indispensable, nothing could be easier than for France to propose the conversion of the Protocol into a Treaty, whereby the arrangement to be effected under the Protocol would be placed, if not formally under the *guarantee*, under the superintendence of all the parties to that arrangement, and the pledges of disinterestedness given in the Protocol by Russia to England *alone*, would become common to all the other Powers. With this suggestion M. Villele appeared well contented.

Mr. Canning had a second interview with M. Villele yesterday morning: when after some preliminary observations about the Jesuits, & the Church—subjects which are plainly very much in M. Villele's thoughts; & upon which he is singularly anxious to make it to be

---

1 On 7 October the Sultan accepted the Convention of Ackerman, which gave the two Danubian Principalities of Wallachia and Moldavia a measure of local self-government, re-established the independent rights of the Serbians, compensated Russia for losses occasioned since 1821 by the Barbary corsairs, and granted her ships the free navigation of the Black Sea.

believed that H.M.C.My has no such vehement & bigotted feeling as the newspapers, & the talk of Paris attribute to him. M. Villele himself led the way to the matter upon which Mr. Canning was most desirous of talking with him freely, that of the French army in Spain.[1] M. Villele said "If you ask me why the French army is still there, I answer frankly that I hoped that it would be by this time either withdrawn or in the act of withdrawing. I can show you my calculations of the expence of removing the garrison of Cadiz by sea. I can show you my account of arrears owing by Spain, up to September—which I trusted would be the end of the occupation. You know that we diminished the amount of force one half, last January. You shall have the account of that diminution. But in the midst of my plans & hopes, come the events of Portugal: & seeing what they are in themselves, & seeing how, in spite of all our remonstrances, Spain is disposed to deal with them—what are we to do? can we withdraw our army at this moment—at the risk of seeing a corps of royalist volunteers make an armed irruption into Portugal the next day? Would to God! we had never gone into Spain! But being there, would not Europe, would not you yourselves hold us responsible for any evil that happened, from our sudden retirement, which our continued presence there might have prevented?

Vuidons [sic] *l'affaire de Portugal*; & you shall see if we are desirous to continue a moment longer than is necessary in Spain."

M. Villele went on to say that though he thus assigned to me the true reason—that of Portugal—for his relaxing the decision to evacuate Spain this Autumn, he had not given to the Spanish Government the satisfaction of knowing that the decision had been relaxed on that ground. He had preferred appearing to yield to the importunity of the King of Spain's remonstrances & supplications; because in so doing, an opportunity had been taken of giving wholesome advice to H[is] C[atholic] M[ajesty] & of annexing conditions to the compliance.

The transaction, he said, had been this. Notice had been given some months ago to the Spanish Government to be prepared to garrison the fortresses, now occupied by the French, in the month of September; at which period it was determined to withdraw all the army; leaving only (if that were desired) a bodyguard to a small amount for the personal

1 In April 1823 the French had invaded Spain in order to overthrow the constitutional Government, and they remained encamped on Spanish soil until 1827. Canning had written in January: "It is no longer possible for me to say, with a clear conscience, that the presence of the French troops is still required to keep the Spanish factions from cutting each other's throats; or that they are continued at the entreaties of the Spanish Government, or that the threat of withdrawing them is employed from time to time for the salutary purpose of enforcing amnesties and pacifications.... The permanence of a French army in the ports of Spain, as an occupying force,...this country cannot be expected to bear." (*Stapleton,* pp. 492–3.)

service of the King. The answer to this notice was a letter from the K. of Spain to H.M.C.My, earnestly deprecating the execution of the determination announced to him; declaring that the Spanish Govt. had no troops to take possession of the fortresses, & that the whole Kingdom would be in confusion, so soon as the French troops went away. These arguments and entreaties would have availed nothing, M. Villele said, if the events in Portugal had not taken place. Those events appeared to constitute a new case. But it was thought best to take no notice of *them* in the reply to H. Cath. My's letter—which was by a letter from the King of France himself to the following effect "That it was with great pain that H.M.C.My had to declare that a compliance with the wishes of H.C.My which seemed to point to an *indefinite* continuance of the French troops in Spain, was impossible. That the burden which had been already incurred by France, by the occupation was too great, to allow of H.M.C.My's consenting to prolong it. That on the 1st of April next the French army must begin to evacuate Spain. That by that time it was hoped that H.C.M. would have put his Kingdom in better order; that absolutely nothing appeared to have been done, during the three years that the French occupation had continued, to effect that object; that discontent & misery pervaded the whole country; that there was no settled Government, no plan of conduct; & that France could not make herself responsible to the world for the continuance of such a state of things. That in the midst of the poverty & wretchedness universal among his people, & of debts unpaid & for payment of which no provision was attempted to be made, the expences of H.C.My & of his Court increased instead of diminishing." (You see, said M. de Villele, on reciting this part of the King's letter, that it was felt to be an occasion for stating the plain truth without disguise or care of offending—what follows, M. de Villele added, was I assure you the King's own *draft*—it was more than I could have ventured to suggest, though you may judge how much I approved it.) "The King of France could not take leave of H.C.My without adverting to another subject, of the most serious importance to the Spanish Monarchy. H.C.My had lost his colonies—*irrevocablement*. It might be yet time to save something from the wreck, in the way of compensation, or indemnity. But there was no time to lose. H.M.C.M. offered himself as mediator between the K. of S. & his late colonies, either singly, or jointly with any other Power, as H.C.My might please. But if Spain continued obstinately to refuse all attempts at accommodation, the time was not distant when the K. of France must think of the interests of his own subjects."[1] And thereupon it is, said M. Villele,

1 The letter (dated 23 July 1826) is in *Stapleton*, II, 120–1. (Copy at Windsor.)

that as you know, we have just issued orders for the admission of the Mexican flag into our ports.

No reply has yet been received to this letter from the King of France "à son cousin" for whom I assure you, said M. V. H.My has so little respect or regard, that were his solicitations only, & not the state of Portugal, in the way—the French garrisons would be at this moment on their route to France.

"Pour son opinion personelle" M. V. repeated that he had been as unwilling to get into Spain, as he was impatient to get out: that he should never have got in, if M. de Montmorency had not disobeyed his instructions at Verona; that those instructions were 1st not to enter into *any* discussion upon the affairs of Spain; 2d if that discussion should be forced on, to declare that France as the country, nearest to Spain, & lying between it & Europe, had the most direct interest in the tranquillity of that Kingdom, & *s'en chargerait*, but that France apprehended no danger, & that he (M. Villele) had not the slightest intention of marching an army into Spain; that M. de Montmorency had suffered himself to be *entrainé* at Verona, into engagements which he had no business to contract; but which, being contracted, greatly embarrassed M. Villele and left him no more option, in his *then position in the Cabinet*, than to change the character of the invasion of Spain from *European* (which had been given to it at Verona) to French.

Involved by M. Montmorency in a pledge that the invasion should take place, he had chosen the least of two evils, in taking the execution of it upon France alone, rather than allowing other Powers to undertake or to share it. (Russia was here, evidently in M. Villele's mind—& it is probably to the position in which he was on this occasion placed towards that Power by M. Montmorency's engagements, that the dread of Russia, which appears so predominent in M. Villele's general opinions may be referred.)

By this change (from European to French) M. Villele said that he became master of the question of evacuation, without reference to other Powers—so far as Spain & France only were concerned. The occurrences in Portugal, however, complicated that question with considerations in which other Powers had a right to share. It was *therefore*, that (he said— "Vuidons l'affaire du Portugal" and *je vous promets*, the question of evacuation, as between France & Spain, is determined.

M. Villele concluded a long exposition (which Mr. Canning indeed fears that he has made too long in the recital) with saying—that he hoped that after the explanations & assurances which he had given to Mr. Canning, Mr. C. would have no difficulty in meeting, as he had hitherto done, any motions or interrogations in the House of Commons, on the subject of the French army in Spain with the declaration of his (Mr. C's) perfect conviction that the French Govt. were sincere in their wish to withdraw it. In fact, why should we not be so? What good does it do us? What inconvenience does it not inflict upon us? *Ça nous pèse.* It discredits us too as much as it inconveniences us—for we have, as every day's experience shows us, no more influence with Spain than if our army were on this side the Pyrennees. The state of that country is as hopeless as when we entered it—and nothing do I long for so much as for the time when we may leave it to itself to *"son orgueil & sa misère"*.

Mr. Canning said that the last topicks which M. Villele had employed, made it easier for Mr. C. to answer M. Villele's question as to the House of Commons, than he should have found it, if M.V. had made no such avowals. M. Villele (Mr. C. hoped) would do him the justice to allow that he had never (since the first discussions of 1823) shown any disposition to bear hard upon France, with respect to the occupation of Spain. For three Sessions he had been able to stave off Parliamentary debate on that subject by declarations, such as those which M. Villele suggested, of perfect confidence in the intentions of the French Government; that undoubtedly such confidence was fortified by M. de V's present communication. But Mr. C. could not answer for a new House of Commons: especially for one, which, in the very first Session of it's meeting would be split into divisions, other than the usual divisions of Party, by questions in which (political) friends & foes would be strangely separated from, & mingled with each other. That such questions, it was observed by skilful judges, always created a laxity of parliamentary discipline for the remainder of the Session in which they occurred. That the Opposition, whether beaten or victorious on the side which they espoused, were apt to be led astray in their estimate of their own force, by voting either in majorities, or in minorities unusually large, that this would be especially likely to be the case in a new Parliament; & that Mr. Canning therefore would not be surprized if after the experience of a few such mixed divisions the Opposition were to be tempted to try their strength *as* Opposition, on questions of foreign politicks; from which they had for three years abstained.

That among questions of foreign politicks that of the occupation of Spain by a French army was the one upon which *an* Opposition could make the best stand. It was one upon which all English Parties & all statesmen, of all Parties, had, in the best times of our history pronounced one & the same opinion. That allowing the full force of what M. de Villele alleged respecting Portugal, the answer to it was clearly this—

that in the present state of the world, *some* new occurrence might spring up every year to justify by special circumstances the prolongation of the occupation. M. Villele would see the difficulty of replying to this answer, by new declarations of confidence. There was in truth but one effectual reply to it—& that was the one which (as Mr. C. had said) he should be unwilling to use without having given M.V. previous notice of it—namely that the occupation itself was not only not beneficial, but highly mischievous to France; & that if he wished France *ill*, he should have been glad to place her exactly in the embarrassment in which she had placed herself by that occupation.

Mr. Canning was aware that in taking up the question in this way, he should be furnishing arms to *both* the Oppositions in France; to that which had deprecated the invasion of Spain, as leading to precisely the embarrassments to which it has led; & to that which urged the invasion, with the intention of deriving advantages from it which M. Villele disclaimed; of reviving, in effect, the family compact.

M. Villele admitted, more strongly than Mr. Canning stated it, the inconvenience to which he should be exposed by such a discussion, if it took place before the evacuation. "Mais votre première ligne de défense" he said "sera toujours, n'est ce pas? in professions of confidence in our good intentions?" "Yes; but if that first line of defence is forced —as in the case supposed it will be?" "In that case" said M. Villele "il n'y a que la vérité," to fall back upon. And you cannot state that truth more strongly than I feel it."

Mr. Canning has omitted in this report all that passed on the affairs of Portugal itself: as the substance of it will come before your Majesty in drafts of despatches to Mr. Lamb & to Sir Wm. à Court.[1]

He entreats your Majesty's patience, & pardon for the length to which (that omission notwithstanding) this report has run.

1257   REAR-ADMIRAL   SIR   EDWARD   CODRINGTON[2]   *to*   SIR WILLIAM KNIGHTON

Hampton Lodge, Brighton,
2d Octr. 1826.

AT length I have received my commission as Commander in Chief in the Mediterranean, and it therefore becomes my duty as much as it is my inclination to enquire through you, my good friend, how I can most

---

1 Ambassador to Portugal, 1824–8; created Baron Heytesbury, January 1828. (1779–1860.)
2 He was in command of the allied fleet which on 20 October 1827 destroyed the Turkish Fleet at Navarino. [1770–1851.] Melville discussed his qualifications for the command in a letter to Bathurst. (*Bathurst,* pp. 613–14.)

respectfully submit to the King my desire to execute any commands which His Majesty may have for that country. You will be aware, that I do not refer to those of an official nature, which will reach me in regular course through another quarter; but to the wines, manufactures, and other productions of that part of the world. In short, you, knowing my feelings and my sense of what is due from me to my King, will put this matter in the right point of view; and I cannot leave it in better hands.

The Asia, which is destined to carry my flag, is to have long thirty-two pounders on her main as well as her lower deck, and will probably be as fine a two decker as ever went to sea. And I am sanguine in my hopes that neither she nor the flag she is to bear, will discredit the distinguished service for which they have been selected. You will believe me, that I shall readily execute any commissions of your own; which you will have sufficient time to prepare, as there is little likelihood of our leaving England before February. My colleagues of the signal committee, who have been fagging since May, and as we trust to very good purpose, gave me leave to meet my naiad son[1] at Portsmouth on Saturday; and yesterday I brought him here to his too anxious mother, whose feelings were somewhat over-excited by his having been so long c[r]uizing on that sea which bereft us of his noble-minded brother![2]

However, running into this subject reminds me that it is time to lay down my pen. I shall resume my occupation in London on Wednesday.

1258 GEORGE CANNING *to the* KING

Paris, Oct. 9, 1826.

MR. CANNING presents his humble duty to your Majesty.

Mr. Canning has been in constant intercourse with M. de Villele, & the Baron de Damas,[3] during the whole week that has elapsed since Mr. Canning last presumed to address your Majesty in this manner. The occasion of that intercourse, & the objects of it will have been brought before your Majesty in the despatches from Mr. Lamb & Sir Wm. à Court, & in the drafts of answers to those despatches, which Mr. Canning has transmitted by the last three messengers. Mr. Canning entreats your Majesty's indulgence, for that the incessant occupation of his time, during this anxious period, did not allow of his accompanying those papers with any explanatory letter to your Majesty; & for that in

1 Admiral Sir Henry John Codrington (1808–1877); entered the Navy 1823; wounded at Navarino. K.C.B., 1867.
2 Edward, a midshipman in the Royal Navy, was lost on service, 16 November 1819, at the age of 16.
3 The French Foreign Minister.

the absolute urgency of the case, which would have made the loss of a week (or less than a week) equivalent to total failure, he presumed to take upon himself without your Majesty's previous approbation, to instruct Mr. Lamb, in the event of the Spanish Government's continuing obstinate, to come away from Madrid.

Mr. Lamb's despatches of the 29th of Septr (the last submitted to your Majesty) afforded strong reason for apprehending that Mr. Lamb would be driven to the execution of that instruction. On the receipt of those despatches Mr. Canning determined to send off another messenger to Madrid, & he obtained from the French Govt., after discussion with M. Villele & M. Damas, an instruction to M. de Moustier,[1] the terms of which were so peremptory as *almost* to amount to a recall, if he failed to overcome His C. My's resistance.

Mr. Canning's messenger was in readiness—& Mr. C. was in the act of preparing corresponding instructions to Mr. Lamb, when he received from Baron Damas an extract of a telegraphick despatch from Madrid, announcing that the King of Spain had given way; & that the arms & equipments of the Portuguese deserters were ordered to be restored.

Happily therefore that cause of danger is removed: & there is a little breathing-time for endeavouring to get rid of the other causes, which lie principally in Prince Metternich's long silence, & that of the Infant Don Miguel himself, on the subject of Don Miguel's determination to take, or refuse the oath; & in the intrigues in Spain, & the alarms in Portugal, to which that silence gives rise, or encouragement.

Mr. Canning anxiously hopes that his last despatches to Sir Henry Wellesley[2] (which will also have been submitted to your Majesty) will produce an early explanation of Don Miguel's intentions, & of Prince Metternich's policy, in this respect.[3]

Mr. Canning has every reason to be satisfied with the assistance which he has received from the French Government on the late occasion. The despatches of which the telegraph has transmitted the substance, not being yet arrived, it is not known *how* the King of Spain's reconsideration of the matter of the arms has been brought about: but this point must have been accomplished (as the dates prove) before the arrival of the last instructions to Mr. Lamb. Mr. Canning has suspended the departure of his messenger, until the arrival of the despatches; which may be expected tomorrow.

Mr. Canning would have nothing farther, wherewith to trouble your

1 French Minister at Madrid.   2 Ambassador at Vienna, 1823–31.

3 Since his participation in the abortive rising against his father, John VI, in 1834, Dom Miguel had been living in exile in Vienna. He was compelled to marry his niece by proxy and to take an oath to the new Constitution.

Majesty at the present moment, but for a circumstance which occurred in one of his late interviews with M. de Villele, which it is fit that he should bring to your Majesty's knowledge, as it corrects a former statement of M. de Villele's, in a manner somewhat remarkable.

M. de Villele had promised Mr. Canning that he should *see* a copy of the King of France's letter to the King of Spain, respecting the withdrawing of the French army. Accordingly the next time that Mr. Canning went to M. Villele the latter sent to the Foreign Office for a portfolio, containing a copy of the letter—which he put into Mr. Canning's hand: requesting him (if it were not too much trouble) to read it aloud—as he, M. Villele, had not looked at it, since he saw the draft in H.M.C.My's handwriting.

Mr. Canning accordingly read it through; & found it in most parts correctly correspondent with M. Villele's description of it—in some parts even stronger & more peremptory, till he came to the last paragraph, upon which your Majesty may recollect that M. Villele particularly piqued himself, where Mr. Canning *missed* the sentence importing that if H.C.M. did not make peace with the colonies, the King of France must think of the interests of his own subjects. *"Est ce tout?"* said M. de Villele, when Mr. Canning stopped, at the end of the exhortation (sufficiently strong, & pretty nearly in the words which M. Villele had repeated to him in their former interview) *"Est ce tout?"*

Mr. Canning said that there was no more. M. Villele took the paper into his hands, & after meditating upon it said—"Eh bien! c'est comme ça—on m'a retranché une sentence dans la rédaction." Then, laughing— "il y a parmi nous, comme vous voyez, des nuances d'opinion—comme peut être chez-vous—mais n'importe—la chose est faite." And then turned to the general question of the recognition of the Sp American countries, as one which only waited time & opportunity.

Mr. Canning does not trouble your Majesty with any thing relating to the invitation to Ld B[eresfor]d to resume the command of the Portuguese army; as he has written fully upon it (again to-day) both to Ld Liverpool, & to the D. of Wellington; who has been so good as to undertake to bring it under your Majesty's consideration.[1]

The Duke of Wellington's Memorandum of the Result of Conversations with Lord Beresford. Apethorpe, 14 October 1826. (*W.N.D.* III, 423–5.)
Memorandum given by Lord Beresford to the Duke of Wellington. (*W.N.D.* III, 425–6.)
The Duke of Wellington to the Earl of Liverpool, London, 16 October 1826. (*W.N.D.* III, 422–3.)
The Duke of Wellington to the King, London, 16 October 1826. (*W.N.D.* III, 426–7.)

1 Canning's letters to Liverpool, 2 and 9 October 1826, are in *Stapleton*, II, 141–2; 145–8. See also Prof. Temperley's *Foreign Policy of Canning*, pp. 374–5.

1259 ROBERT PEEL *to the* KING

Drayton Manor, Octr. 18, 1826.

MR. PEEL presents his humble duty to your Majesty, and loses not a moment in acknowledging the honour of your Majesty's letter of the 16th instant marked "private".

Mr. Peel begs to assure your Majesty that the speeches recently made by Mr. Sheil,[1] so revolting to every feeling of common decency and humanity, have not escaped his attention. Previously to the receipt of your Majesty's commands he had made a communication upon the subject to your Majesty's servants in Ireland of the result of which he will take the earliest opportunity of apprizing your Majesty.

In the mean time Mr. Peel will also without delay consult the law officers of the Crown in this country.

1260 GEORGE CANNING *to the* KING

Paris, Octr. 20, 1826.

MR. CANNING presents his most humble duty to your Majesty; & begs leave to acknowledge, with the deepest humility & thankfulness, your Majesty's gracious letter of the 16th. Nothing can be so gratifying to Mr. Canning's feelings as your Majesty's kind acceptance of his imperfect services, & (he may venture humbly to assure your Majesty) his perfect duty & attachment.

Mr. Canning has fixed Wednesday next for the day of his leaving Paris. He is very anxious to receive here the answer—which he apprehends must already have reached Prince Lieven—to the *third* & conclusive, communication to the Court of St. Petersburgh. He *knows* as well from Count Pozzo di Borgo,[2] as through sources of information which have also been under your Majesty's observation, that the answer is every thing that could be desired, both in substance & in tone: and Mr. Canning thinks that there would be great advantage in having a conversation with M. Villele & the Bⁿ de Damas (and also with the King) after it shall have been placed, by your Majesty's & the Russian Ambassador, in their hands. Mr. Canning is the rather desirous of such an opportunity as he has seen some reason to apprehend that the King

1 Richard Lalor Sheil (1791–1851), the political agitator. Speaking in support of Catholic Association candidates at the general election, he made a violent and disgusting attack on the Duke of York, ridiculing his bodily sufferings, raking up the old Mary Anne Clarke scandal, and reading the Duke's private letters to his mistresses, in order "to put his morality into comparison with his religion". He was charged with libel, but the case was abandoned whilst Canning was Prime Minister.

2 Russian Ambassador at Paris.

was thought by his Ministers, to have gone farther with Mr. Canning, in his Majesty's conversation on Greek politicks, than they were disposed to go. It would be very desirable to know exactly on *what* we may rely.

The interval between this & Wednesday must probably also bring the confirmation, from Constantinople, of the report received yesterday by the House of Rothschild, that the Porte had consented to *all* the demands of Russia at Akkermann.[1]

Your Majesty will learn from Sir Henry Wellesley's despatches that the Infant Don Miguel, has taken the oath to the Portuguese Constitution: but that Prince Metternich has an unaccountable desire to keep the fact secret. Mr. Canning has, of course, lost no time in transmitting it to Sir Wm. à Court, to be made publick, as soon as possible, at Lisbon; & to Mr. Lamb, to be equally divulged at Madrid, *so soon as the messenger to Lisbon shall have had time to cross the frontier*.

Mr. Canning would not have deemed it necessary, or proper, to trouble your Majesty with any thing personal to himself, if it were not for the sort of interest which has been taken by the publick at Paris, in the *event*—(as it appears to be considered) of his dinner at the Tuilleries. *If* there has been (as is pretended) any struggle of parties—of State & Court—upon this *important* subject, Mr. Canning hopes he need not assure your Majesty that he has been entirely unconscious of it. He knew nothing of the intention till Monday last, when Baron Damas called upon him with a message from the King, signifying His Majesty's desire that he would dine with His Majesty on Wednesday. The invitation was next day repeated in writing from the gentleman of the Chamber; & by H.M.C. Majesty himself at the diplomatick circle on that day. No other person was present at the dinner—besides the King, the Dauphin[2] & Dauphiness, & the Dutchess of Berri.

It is said (Mr. Canning knows not how truly) that this honour has been conferred on no other individuals (not of Royal or reigning families) except the Duke of Wellington, & Prince Metternich.

The Duke of Wellington stands on grounds of his own, common to no other individual in Europe, or the world.

But Mr. Canning (—feeling nothing on his account—yet) cannot admit that the Foreign Minister of the Emperor of Austria, or any other potentate, could be entitled to a distinction, not communicable equally

1 Canning wrote to Wellington on the 20th: "Rothschild had letters yesterday from Vienna assuring him that the Porte had resolved to consent to all the demands of Russia. Your brother's [Sir Henry Wellesley's] despatches do not affirm the fact so positively, but they state that Prince Metternich expected such a result." (*W.N.D.* III, 431.)
2 The Duc d'Angoulême (1775–1844).

to the individual (however personally unworthy) who holds the same office under your Majesty. And he is satisfied that it is to this consideration solely that the determination of H.M.C. Majesty is to be ascribed.

1261 THE MARQUIS WELLESLEY *to the* KING

Dublin Castle, October 20th 1826.

MR. PEEL has been so kind as to impart to Lord Wellesley your Majesty's gracious commands of the 16th of October on the subject of the late atrocious outrage committed by a barrister [1] in Ireland against the character of His Royal Highness the Duke of York.

On this painful & most irritating question, Lord Wellesley had consulted the Attorney General of Ireland,[2] & had also received communications from Mr. Peel some time previously to the date of your Majesty's commands. The opinion of the Attorney General was of course, that the attack was libellous, but he doubted, whether a prosecution would be thought advisable by His Royal Highness's friends, as it might tend in the present moment to disturb His Royal Highness's health & repose of mind.

On this point, a letter has been written by Mr. Goulburn to Mr. Peel in a private form; the reply to which will direct the course to be pursued, under your Majesty's commands, by your Majesty's Government in Ireland; so that, if a prosecution should be deemed advisable, it may be commenced in November term.

Lord Wellesley humbly assures your Majesty, that this unparalleled crime has excited universal disgust & horror in the breasts of all your Majesty's faithful & loyal subjects in Ireland; & that all good minds would regard your Majesty's just feelings on this occasion with veneration & dutiful sympathy; and he trusts, that your Majesty will graciously receive the expression of his respectful condolence on the painful state of His Royal Highness the Duke of York's health, & on the great aggravation to your Royal feelings of sorrow, & fraternal grief, which must be occasioned by this brutal disturbance of suffering hitherto deemed sacred by the common consent of civilised society.

The crime is rendered more atrocious by the base artifice, which has involved the prosecution of the criminal in so many considerations of delicacy & difficulty; and Lord Wellesley is satisfyed, that your Majesty

1 Sheil. See No. 1259.   2 Plunket.

will deem it to be the duty of all your Majesty's servants fully to weigh all these considerations, with a view to the dignity, honor, & ease both of His Royal Highness, & of your Majesty.

1262 GEORGE CANNING *to the* KING

Paris, Octr. 23, 1826.

MR. CANNING presents his humble duty to your Majesty; and humbly lays before your Majesty a copy, (which he has obtained from the Baron de Damas), of the letter[1] from H.M.C. Majesty to the King of Spain, of which so much was said in his conferences with M. de Villele. It has been communicated to Mr. Canning in the strictest confidence; & under the understanding that no publick use shall be made of it.

1263 THE KING *to* SIR WILLIAM KNIGHTON

Royal Lodge,
Wed? Octr 24th [25th] 1826
½ pt 5 p.m.

THERE certainly seems as if there were some sort of fatality that inevitably attends upon your leaving London, be it only for a single day, for your back is no sooner turn'd than some disagreable unexpected & unforeseen *something*, is *sure almost instantly* to *start up*.

This is just the case, at the present moment, for I am sure you know me too well, to think that I would either wantonly or unnecessarily break in upon, those very few hours of family comfort & repose, of which you allow yourself occasionally to partake, & enjoy. To be as brief as possible now to the point.

Whiting[2] will deliver this with his own hand to you, & will with his own mouth detail to you all the different matter, that he has to relate, (& which he already has done to me,) better than I can possibly do, by letter, or indeed any part of it, as *that*, would both consume too much time, & take up much too much space for the contents of any letter. All I shall at present tell you is to account to you, from *whence* & *how*, Whiting is become the *principal person*, *new to us*, in this *present* matter, & to this, & this *alone* I shall *entirely confine* myself *leaving you*, after you have examin'd him, and heard *all* he has to say, *to act in every respect as may seem best to your judgment*.

1 *Stapleton*, II, 120.   2 John Whiting, Page of the Backstairs, 1822–37.

Whiting as he tells me, saw you, yesterday morning, just before you left town, for Brighton, & previous to his being under the necessity of proceeding to the Court of Justice, to attend thus upon his subpœna in the cause of young Wharton[1] against S.ʳ Richard Birnie.[2]

The cause was at length determin'd to be withdrawn, & was so, after some considerable demur. Whiting seems, (at least it appears so to me at present from the accounts I have drawn from him) to have conducted himself, *very well indeed*, & with a greater portion of *sagacity & prudence*, than I gave him credit for possessing in his nature. It seems that he had several different interviews with many of the parties & witnesses concern'd in the cause, amongst the rest, with Mr. Smith the attorney, who he (Whiting) says, is, as civil, well-meaning & loyal a man as exists; with young Wharton's sister, my housekeeper, & last of all, (& what is of most importance) with the young wretch himself, than *whom*, as Whiting I think *justly says, there can not be a greater villain existing on the face of the whole earth.*

The mass of lies & horrors which this villain has been upwards of these five years been inventing, accumulating, & putting by to make use of when it might suit his purpose, against the whole Royal establishment, every individual connected with it, & in it, as well as all my best & dearest friends, & last of all myself, is really too shocking to imagine, & as I have already said much much too great in substance & extent for me to attempt to detail. *But the main point which makes me deem it indispensibly necessary to dispatch Whiting to you, is, that this young villain has to a great extent, acknowledg'd to Whiting, his privacy to, & connexion with Harriet Wilson[3] in particular, as well as others of her hellish gang. This I consider as a matter of much too great importance, to leave you a single instant, in ignorance of. It is true the cause is withdrawn, but upon what plea, I know not, but, though it be withdrawn, yet,*

1 The *Court and City Register* describes George Wharton as second clerk in the kitchen under the Lord Steward, 1824–27.

2 The London police magistrate; knighted, 1821. (1760?–1832.)

3 Harriette Wilson, the celebrated courtesan (1786–1846), was the daughter of John Dubochet, a clockmaker in Mayfair. Her *Memoirs*, published in paper cover parts in 1825 by John Joseph Stockdale (1770–1847), went through over thirty editions in one year, and so great was the demand that a barrier had to be erected to regulate the crowd which surged round Stockdale's shop. As Sir Walter Scott declared, she "lived with half the gay world at hack and manger, and now obliges such as will not pay hush-money with a history of whatever she knows or can invent about them". (*Journal*, I, 41.) Referring to Frederick Lamb, one of her clientele, she wrote: "Had he...only opened his heart, or even purse, to have given me but a few hundreds, there would have been no book, to the infinite loss of all persons of good taste and genuine morality." (II, 655.) In the first volume she describes how she offered herself to George IV when he was Prince of Wales, who replied, through Colonel Thomas: "Miss Wilson's letter has been received by the noble individual to whom it was addressed. If Miss Wilson will come to town, she may have an interview, by directing her letter as before." (I, 7.)

having been so nearly before the publick, & such a number of persons connected with it, & collected upon the spot to hear it, as Whiting tells me there was, & learning (as you will learn also from Whiting) the rancorous & revengeful spirit & sheer villainy which alone actuates the proceedings & objects of this vile monster, I am sure you will see the absolute necessity there is, of some step, be it only of precaution, being immediately taken. Once more regretting from the bottom of my heart, the urgent reasons which have compell'd me to intrude upon your comforts even for a single moment, I hastily conclude, with the assurances of my unalterable regard & affection.

1264 FREDERICK JOHN ROBINSON *to the* KING

Blackheath, Nov. 3, 1826.

MR. ROBINSON offers his humble duty to your Majesty: and hopes that your Majesty will be graciously pleased to pardon him for intruding upon your Majesty with any matter personal to himself.

Your Majesty is perhaps aware that during the last eight months Mr. Robinson has been kept in a state of continual anxiety from the very uncertain condition of Lady Sarah's[1] health: and this circumstance has rendered doubly severe to him the heavy blow with which it has pleased God to afflict him, by the death of his only child.[2] The kindness of your Majesty's heart will readily understand how essential it may be to the comfort and consolation of the poor child's mother, that she should be enabled at a distance from the scene of her distress, to compose her mind, and seek to renovate her health; and Mr. Robinson ventures therefore to hope that your Majesty will not be displeased, if in order to accompany Lady Sarah to Norton, he requests permission to absent himself from the approaching *early* Session of Parliament. Mr. Robinson flatters himself, that as your Majesty's Government are most desirous to confine the business to be now transacted in Parlt, within the narrowest possible limits, your Majesty's service will not be embarrassed by his absence: were it otherwise, he would not have presumed to solicit your Majesty's indulgence.

Mr. Robinson knows not how he can sufficiently excuse himself to your Majesty for this intrusion: but he knows too well the goodness of your Majesty's disposition, not to feel an humble confidence that your Majesty will condescend to pardon him.

1 Robinson married the only daughter of the fourth Earl of Buckinghamshire in September 1814.

2 Eleanor, d. 31 October, aged 11.

Arlington Street, November 9, 1826.

I THINK it my bounden duty to lose no time in communicating to your
Majesty that I have felt it encumbent upon me to have a conversation
this day with Lord Liverpool on the critical situation in which this
country is at present placed.

I have sent down the heads of my conversation with him, which I have
the honor to lay before your Majesty: [1] they were drawn up hastily but
I will answer for it that they contain correct views of the present state of
affairs in the United Kingdom, which Lord Liverpool did not seem disposed to deny had become very serious.

I mentioned to him my intention of placing the paper in your Majesty's
hands which he begged me to entreat your Majesty not to discuss with
any body until he should have had an opportunity of considering the
purport and of submitting his sentiments to you upon it.

The Earl of Liverpool to the King, 10 November 1826. (*Yonge*, III, 435–6.)

1266 THE DUKE OF YORK *to the* KING

Arlington Street, November 11, 1826.

AT the risk of appearing troublesome I must give myself the satisfaction
of returning your Majesty my most heartfelt thanks for your very
gracious and affectionate letter.

I can only repeat that your Majesty does me but justice in being persuaded that my late communication to Lord Liverpool has been produced
by the strong sense I felt of the very critical situation in which this
country stands, and by my conviction that affairs can not go on any
longer in their present anomalous state, and that the decision to be
taken does not arise from any desire of change, but from absolute
necessity as every day which passes over under present circumstances
adds to the danger. This sentiment ought to guide the conduct of those
who have at all times put themselves forth as the friends of the Crown
and the supporters of the Constitution under which your Majesty and
your Royal ancestors have filled the Throne, and therefore they ought
not to be appalled by the apprehension of a struggle which however
arduous it may be at the commencement, must prove ultimately suc-

1 See *Yonge*, III, 432–5. The Duke was afraid that the Government's neutrality on the
question of Catholic emancipation was endangering the Protestant ascendancy.

cessfull, in as much as the great body of the British nation staunchly clings to the same principles, those principles in which we have gained honor and security since the year 1688.[1]

1267 GEORGE CANNING *to the* KING

F.O., Nov. 13, 1826.

MR. CANNING presents his humble duty to your Majesty; and has the great satisfaction of laying before your Majesty a despatch this instant received from Sir Wm. à Court, announcing the arrival of the messenger, whom Mr. Canning despatched from Paris on the 19th ulto with the notification of the taking of the oath by the Infant Don Miguel. The messenger arrived at Lisbon at 7 o'clock of the morning of the 30th the day fixed for the opening of the Chambers!—consequently in time for the insertion of the intelligence in the Infanta Regent's speech.

Twenty four hours later—and the Chambers would have gone into their first deliberation, under the impression that the Infant was determinedly hostile to the Constitution: the consequences of which might have been fatal to the peace of both Kingdoms of the Peninsula! Whatever were Prince Metternich's motives for wishing to expose those Kingdoms to such a trial—that object has been happily disappointed.

1268 SIR WILLIAM KNIGHTON *to the* KING

Carlton House, Saturday night,
18 November 1826.

I HAVE the honor to acquaint your Majesty, that His Royal Highness has sent me the inclosed,[2] to transmit to your Majesty.

Lord Liverpool's letter has been returned to me, by His Royal Highness.

I have seen the Duke of Wellington, & delivered your Majesty's

1 Even the anti-Catholic members of the Cabinet disapproved of the Duke's communication to Lord Liverpool. "You will have done great good in preventing our master beginning the affray", Bathurst wrote to Wellington on the 21st, "and I trust that this inconsiderate act of the Duke of York will, by your means, soon be buried in oblivion." (*W.N.D.* III, 464.) On the 16th Peel reported to Bathurst a conversation with the Duke of York the previous day. "Although he said he was not ashamed of it, I could perceive that he was sorry that he had interfered. He could not but see that my impression was that it would have been better if he had abstained from any interference whatever." (*Bathurst*, p. 616.)

2 No. 1269.

gracious message; Lord Liverpool had already shewn his Grace the Duke of York's paper, as well as the letter which his Lordship had written to your Majesty.

The Duke of Wellington's opinion seems quite to coincide with Lord Liverpool's view of the subject; namely, that the true policy is, to be quiet, & *not to force a crisis*. This I believe is exactly in unison with your Majesty's feelings! I do therefore hope, that at present, at any rate, your Majesty will be troubled no further, on this anxious & painful subject.

The Duke of York, seem'd I thought, feeble in spirits & strength this morning; most warmly excited in *affectionate feeling* towards your Majesty.

I inclose a letter for Lady C[onyngham], which contains a message from His Royal Highness, that she will come & see him on her coming to town.

1269 THE DUKE OF YORK *to the* KING

Arlington Street, November 18, 1826.

I BEG to acknowledge the receipt of the paper addressed to your Majesty by Lord Liverpool which you were graciously pleased to direct Sir William Knighton to send to me, and which I have the honor to return; in obedience to your commands. I feel truely grateful to your Majesty for a confidential communication which I had no claim to expect, but which has proved the more satisfactory to me, as it affords to me the opportunity of setting myself right in your Majesty's opinion, and of removing any impression which may have arisen from Lord Liverpool's total misapprehension of the principle and the object of my recent communication to him, as clearly shewn by the observations he has made upon it.

I may conscientiously assure your Majesty that nothing could be further from my thoughts than to wish to produce or to hasten any crisis, embarrassing to your Majesty or to your present Government, or to suggest exclusions which the circumstances of the country, the state of affairs and your Majesty's genuine policy would not admit; still less to encourage divisions in the Cabinet which must be prejudicial to the general interests of the country, while the administration of affairs is confided to that Cabinet. I do not think that there is any thing in the paper which I put into Lord Liverpool's hands and of which I had the honor of sending to your Majesty a copy, on the 9th inst, which can be so interpreted; but to guard it against such possible construction, I indeavored to state verbally to Lord Liverpool all that appeared to me calculated to produce a different understanding of my motives.

The object I had in view was as a true and steady friend to his Administration and principles, to call Lord Liverpool's attention to the state of the country and to that of public affairs, in reference to the agitation of two questions vitally affecting its interests, its security and prosperity, and I was led to do so from a conviction of increasing evils, of impending mischief, and from an apprehension that this state of things was approaching to a crisis and threatening consequences which had not been contemplated, and which do not appear to me to be even now clearly appreciated.

I may be mistaken, and God grant I may be so, but, with this conviction on my mind, with an earnest, anxious, and affectionate solicitude for your Majesty's welfare and for the interests and the prosperity of your dominions, with feelings which I had been taught by our late revered parent to consider as inseparable from the principles which seated his family upon the Throne of these realms, and which the Sovereigns of his family have sworn to maintain, it cannot be surprizing that my apprehensions should be thus excited by a course of events, tending to undermine and to destroy those principles, and that my anxiety to avert evils which I dread, should lead me to warn others against the encroachments which have, with encreasing and frightful rapidity, been made upon the established Constitution of this country.

These reflections have never been absent from my mind, and they occurred with additional weight during a period of sickness, of protracted and painful confinement when my thoughts were alive, as ever, to the welfare of your Majesty and that of my country, although my *personal* interest in its concerns might be supposed to be drawing to a close.

In stating this, I do not do so from any idea that it is necessary to relieve myself from the imputation of being swayed by selfish motives or feelings, for I may, with truth, declare and I am convinced that your Majesty gives me credit for the assurance, that you have not, in the numerous ranks of your subjects, one more devoted to your person, one more anxiously solicitous for the preservation of your valuable life, one who prays more sincerely that he may continue your subject while his existence is prolonged.

Lord Liverpool has stated to your Majesty that it was deemed impracticable, in 1812, to constitute an Administration upon the exclusive

Protestant principle, and that it was then understood that your Majesty's servants and all persons in office, should be at liberty to take the course in Parliament upon it which they might think proper, according to their own individual opinions, and he proceeds to submit whether it would not be as impracticable at least now, as in 1812, to form an Administration upon the exclusive Protestant principle, and whether the attempt to do so must not infallibly lead to an Administration of an opposite character.

In noticing these observations of Lord Liverpool, I have no intention to impeach the policy or the wisdom, nor to question the necessity which dictated the advice given to your Majesty in 1812, however I may, upon general principles, have lamented the necessity for admitting such a system and its results, not only as they apply to what is termed the Catholic question but as having, indisputably, often produced evils and embarrassments of minor importance. On the contrary my reason for transcribing these observations, is that I may more pointedly declare to your Majesty that it is my opinion, and that which I endeavoured to impress upon Lord Liverpool's mind that, under present circumstances, any change is to be deprecated and that the object of my communication to him has been altogether mistaken, if it has produced an impression that I meant to suggest the exclusion of any individuals from your Majesty's present Councils.

1270 GEORGE CANNING *to the* KING

[November 21, 1826.]

MR. CANNING is sorry to say that he thinks he sees indications of rather a troublesome Session. But he especially fears that the subject of *Ireland* will be forced very early into discussion, (after Christmas); & that even until the time of discussion arrives, it will be made matter of daily allusion & constant intermixture with all other topicks of discussion.

Mr. Canning humbly hopes that your Majesty has not experienced any inconvenient fatigue from your Majesty's exertion of to-day.[1]

1 When he delivered the Speech from the Throne at the opening of the Session.

F.O., Nov. 21, 1826.
¾ p 11 p.m.

MR. CANNING with his humble duty to your Majesty, humbly reports to your Majesty that the proceedings of this evening in the House of Commons have been unusually tedious and disagreeable. Upwards of twenty members have spoken; of whom no less than eight (including the mover & seconder) were new members. The topicks of debate were numerous & desultory in the like proportion.

The Address was moved by Mr. Liddell[1] in a speech of considerable ability, & great promise: and was very respectably seconded by Mr. Winn[2]—whom Mr. Canning (when Mr. W. was recommended to him as a seconder) believed to be a young gentleman of Mr. Liddell's standing, but who turns out to be a man of a certain age, heretofore a lawyer, & now a County Magistrate.

Mr. Brougham followed, with a general attack upon the Address, but without moving any amendment: Mr. Canning replied to Mr. Brougham & the debate was considered as at an end—when to the great disappointment & dismay of the House, Mr. Hume presented himself, & moved an amendment twice as long as the speech & Address together; upon which a discussion arose, which branched into all imaginable subjects. Mr. Hume's amendment, which recommended all kinds of reforms, including that of the House of Commons, was seconded by Mr. Marshall, the new member for Yorkshire; who proves to be no great accession to the County representation. The other speakers *upon* it, were

   × Mr. Maberly[3]
   × Mr. Dawson (the new member for Co. Louth)
   o Mr. Western,[4]   o Mr. Waithman   o Mr. Brogden
   o Mr. Fergusson[5] (the new member for Kirkudbright)
   o Sir Robert Wilson
   × Mr. Grattan junr[6] (the new member for Dublin)
   o Mr. Moore—the other new member for Dn
   o Sir Joseph Yorke[7]   o Mr. Calcraft

1 Henry Thomas Liddell (1797–1878), M.P. for Northumberland, and a Canningite. He succeeded his father as second Baron Ravensworth in 1855, and was created Earl of Ravensworth in 1874.

2 George Mark Arthur Way Allanson Winn (1785–1827), second son of the first Baron Headley.

3 John Maberly (Abingdon).

4 Charles Callis Western, Baron Western (1767–1844), the expert agriculturist. Peerage, 1833.

5 Robert Cutlar Fergusson (1768–1838). Judge-Advocate-General, 1834.

6 The son of the famous orator.

7 The Admiral, and son of Charles Yorke, the Lord Chancellor. He was a Lord of the Admiralty, 1810–18. [1768–1831.]

× Mr. Martin (Galway)   o Mr. Benett[1]
× Sir Ronald Ferguson,   × Alderman Wood,
o Mr. Robinson (new member for Worcester)

It would be difficult to say who *spoke for*, or *against* the amendment—but those marked o *voted* against it—those × for it.

The numbers on the division were

$$\begin{array}{lr} \text{For Mr. Hume's amendmt---} & 24 \\ \text{Against it} & 170 \\ \hline & 146 \\ \hline \end{array}$$

Mr. Brougham and the Whigs being in the majority—Sir F. Burdett &c in the minority.

After this division another amendmt was moved by Mr. Grattan (Dublin) pledging the House to retrenchment, & to inquiry into the state of Ireland—on which the numbers were

$$\begin{array}{lr} \text{Ayes} & 58 \\ \text{Noes} & 135 \\ \hline & 77 \\ \hline \end{array}$$

the Whigs voting in the minority.

1272 EARL BATHURST *to the* KING

Downing Street,
Decr. 14th. 9 P.M. 1826.

I HAVE humbly to submit to your Majesty the inclosed melancholy intelligence, which I have (late in the day) receiv'd from the Admiralty.

By the death of the Marquess of Hastings, your Majesty has lost as gallant a soldier, and as attach'd a servant as any Monarch ever possessed.

By his death the Government of Malta has become vacant.

At the time, when I humbly submitted to your Majesty that the situation of Lord High Commissioner of the Ionian Islands, and the Government of Malta should be divided, I was fully aware that by such a division, either the Government of Malta, or the office of Lord High Commissioner became more than what your Majesty's service required in the Mediterranean.

No doubt could be entertain'd that of the two situations that of the

1 Whig M.P. for Wiltshire.

Ionian Islands required to be the most upheld, and nothing therefore could have induc'd me to have submitted to your Majesty that the Government of Malta should be continued on the same high establishment as that of Gibraltar but the consideration that in submitting such an establishment to your Majesty, I was enabled to bring under your Majesty's most gracious consideration an individual highly distinguished by birth, whose public services were of no common magnitude, whose liberality was known to have involved him in such insuperable difficulties, as not to allow him to live in England, and whose long devotion to your Majesty imperiously demanded that I should if possible secure for him an honourable retreat.

With his death the obligation of maintaining Malta as a Government of the first class is at an end, and even if the pressing exigencies of your Majesty's service did not make reductions at the present moment prudent, the relative situations of Gibraltar, Malta & the Ionian Islands would require a change.

I beg therefore humbly to submit to your Majesty that the Government of Malta should be reduc'd to that of a Lieutenant Government.

And now, Sir, having humbly submitted to your Majesty the very alter'd character of the Government of Malta, may I be permitted with all possible humility to submit to your Majesty the name of M. General Ponsonby[1] for the situation of Lt. Governor.

If I were not convinc'd that his military services made him worthy of your Majesty's countenance & protection no personal feelings would induce him to submit his name to your Majesty: but when in addition to this I beg most humbly to state, that not only the interests of a dear daughter are at stake, but that such an appointment will come so much within the range of personal intercourse that Lady Bathurst & myself may feel that his professional pursuits will not altogether estrange our daughter from us, and that even with Lady Bathurst's health she may be able occasionally to visit them, I am embolden'd to hope that your Majesty will be graciously pleas'd to signify your Majesty's approbation of this, my humble recommendation.

Bounden as I shall ever feel myself to be by the many signal instances of your Majesty's gracious disposition towards me, I shall consider it as a most marked instance of your Majesty's continued favor & indulgent acceptance of my poor services if your Majesty should be pleas'd to approve of this appointment.[2]

1 Major-General Sir Frederick Cavendish Ponsonby (1783–1837), grandson of second Earl of Bessborough (1704–1793). Lieutenant-Governor of Malta, 1826–35. G.C.M.G., 1828. He married Lord Bathurst's younger daughter.

2 The appointment was gazetted on the 22nd.

Fife House, Decr. 15, 1826.

YOUR MAJESTY will have heard the account of the melancholy death of the Marquis of Hastings.

By this sad event, another Blue Ribbon becomes vacant, and Lord Liverpool will be obliged to your Majesty to inform him, whether it would be agreable to your Majesty's pleasure, that the Duke of Devonshire should be recommended to your Majesty for it.

If this mark of distinction is ever to be confer'd on his Grace, whilst he is in opposition to your Majesty's Government, there appears to be less objection to give it to him upon the present occasion, when it will be in some degree connected with his return from his mission to Russia,[1] and when it need not be confer'd *singly*, but upon him, in conjunction with the Duke of Leeds.[2]

1274 CHARLES ARBUTHNOT *to* SIR WILLIAM KNIGHTON

Whitehall Place, Friday night.
15 Dec. 1826.

I WILL briefly tell you all that has passed.

When upon leaving you I went in to Ld Liverpool he spoke to me of the two Blue Ribbons; he told me that as the D. of Leeds was to have one, he had named the D. of Devonshire for the other to the King; that he had done this because he was aware of the King's regard for the Duke; but that he himself was indifferent upon the subject. He was desirous however that the D. of Wellington shd be told of what he had done; & he therefore should be obliged to me if I wd name it. I was to add however to the D. of Wellington that he (Ld. Liverpool) had no personal wish respecting it; but that if the King was desirous of doing it, the having sent the D. of Devonshire to Russia wd be a sufficient reason for it to the world.

I found the Duke at the Ordnance, & I deliver'd my message. Towards the D. of Devonshire our Duke has every personal good feeling; but he considers it as most important to the King that the great Tory families shd not be displeased; that already they were on many accounts out of humour; & he therefore shd think it far better to give that Ribbon to

1 He had officially represented the British Government at the coronation of the Emperor Nicholas I at Moscow on 3 September 1826.
2 The honour was conferred on both of them in May 1827.

some great Peer of our own Party. He named Ld Powis,[1] the Duke of Richmond,[2] & Ld Excter.[3] He seem'd to lean the most to Ld Exeter.

All this I am to state to Ld Liverpool; but I am to add that if unfortunately the Ribbon shd have been given away from our own Party, he (the Duke) will in talking about it make the best of it he can, & will defend the measure as much as he is able. The Duke's great object is to keep our Tory Party as strong for the King as he possibly can.

The Duke of York had told Sir Herbert Taylor to mention the *Tower* to the Duke, & to express his wish that he shd have it instead of Plymouth.[4]

The D. of Wellington was, as he had desired me to tell you, indifferent about it; but he immediately assented to the D. of York's wish, & indeed the more readily as it was intimated to him, that for the good of the service it was desireable that the *Ordnance* & the *Tower* shd be in the same hands.

I think I have told you every thing. I think the question of the Ribbon very important. I shall tomorrow morning write & inform Ld Liverpool of what has passed between me & the Duke respecting it.

I leave London tomorrow. Shd I have occasion to write I will.

[P.S.] I called on you, but you were gone out.

1275 THE EARL OF LIVERPOOL *to the* DUKE OF DEVONSHIRE
Copy.

[*c.* 16 Dec. 1826.]

KNOWING the particular pleasure, and satisfaction, which it would afford the King to have an opportunity of conferring upon you the Order of the Garter, I have availed myself of the unfortunate death of poor Lord Hastings, to recommend you to His Majesty for this distinction.

His Majesty has commanded me to express to you the gratification which he shall receive from giving effect to this recommendation.

I need not assure you how personally agreable, it must be to my feelings on every account, to be the instrument of accomplishing His Majesty's wishes under circumstances which so properly admit of it.

1 Edward Clive, first Earl of Powis (1754–1839), eldest son of Clive of Plassey.
2 Charles Gordon-Lennox, fifth Duke of Richmond (1791–1860). Postmaster-General in the Reform Ministry, 1830–34.
3 Brownlow Cecil, second Marquis of Exeter (1795–1867).
4 Wellington's appointment as Constable of the Tower of London was gazetted on 29 December. He resigned the Governorship of Plymouth which he had held since 1819. (*W.N.D.* III, 496–9.)

Decr. 17th 1826.

I HAVE this day received your Majesty's letter announcing to me the distinguished honor which it is your gracious intention to confer on me. The possession of the decoration of the Garter is certainly what beyond all other distinctions I should have preferred and wished for, but it is impossible for me to find words to express my feelings of the tenfold value which it acquires when accompanied as it has been by the expressions made use of by your Majesty towards my parents and to myself.

Recollections of unvaried constant goodness to me, of honors conferred and of happiness increased, might almost become oppressive did I not feel that if ever attachment was heartfelt and gratitude sincere, those feelings are what are experienced by Your Majesty's most faithful [etc.].

The Duke of Wellington to the King, 18 December 1826. (*W.N.D.* III, 496–7.)

1277 The Earl of Liverpool *to the* King

Coombe Wood, Decr. 19, 1826.

LORD LIVERPOOL has this moment received your Majesty's most gracious communication and begs to be allowed to express his entire satisfaction at your Majesty's determination to confer upon the Duke of Wellington the Gov! of the Tower, and to allow him to hold together with it the Gov! of Plymouth. Lord Liverpool will immediately write to the Duke of Wellington upon the subject.

Whatever Lord Liverpool['s] feelings and opinions may be respecting the conduct of the individual to whom your Majesty refers in your gracious communication, it was never Lord Liverpool['s] intention to make any objection to his appointment to the vacant Government, if it should have been your Majesty's disposition to confer it upon him. Lord Liverpool is however most deeply sensible of your Majesty's kind consideration of his feelings upon the present occasion.

Montreal,[2] *Seven Oaks*, 22 Decr. 1826.

I have explained the plan fully to Lord Liverpool.

He entirely concurs with all of us, who had previously seen it, in admiring the whole of the proposed arrangement; and he is prepared to give the official sanction for carrying all of it into execution, except with respect to that part which embraces the site of St. James Palace.

He is strongly of opinion that the buildings on the north side of the Park should not at present be made to extend beyond the limits of Marlborough Gardens, westward. He thinks there would be a strong public feeling against the demolition of the State Rooms so recently completed at a considerable expence: &, what is of more importance, he feels that until the King is completely established in His Majesty's new residence, & until His Majesty shall have had some experience of the fitness of that new building for the purposes of State as well as for his domestic comfort, it would be both unwise & unbecoming to deprive His Majesty of the only apartments in which he can at present hold his Court in London.

He therefore recommends most decidedly, that the plan of building upon the garden of St. James's Palace be postponed for the present.

I apprehend therefore that the next step now to be taken is to desire Mr. Nash to prepare a new plan in which St. James Palace & it's garden shall remain unaltered; and if His Majesty should be graciously pleased to approve of the same I would upon being made acquainted with his pleasure, prepare a Minute of Treasury for the sanction of Lord Liverpool, under which the Woods & Forests would be authorized to proceed without farther delay in the execution of it.

The Duke of Wellington to the King, Sudbourne, 23 December 1826. (*W.N.D.* iii, 503.)

1279 George Canning *to the* King

F.O., Decr. 26, 1826.

Mr. Canning presents his humble duty to your Majesty: & takes the liberty of mentioning to your Majesty, that he has at his disposal the place of a *foreign messenger*: which, if your Majesty should happen to have any one for whom your Majesty would wish such an appointment, Mr. Canning will be most happy to fill up according to your Majesty's nomination.

1 Joint Secretary of the Treasury since February 1823. (1778–1855.)
2 Lord Amherst's seat. Herries rented it during Amherst's absence in India as Governor-General.

The individual must, (according to the rules of the office) be a *subject* of your Majesty; & not more than 35 years of age; he must understand at least *one* foreign language; & (what has greatly contributed of late to the improved despatch of your Majesty's foreign service—as for instance in the conveyance of the intelligence of Don Miguel's oath from Paris to Lisbon) must be capable of performing journeys on horseback.

1280 SIR HERNY HALFORD *to* SIR WILLIAM KNIGHTON

3 o'clock—Tuesday, Dec. 26, 1826.

ONE line to say that we proceed from bad to worse, tho' *slowly*—but decidedly de pis en pis. More nourishment has been taken, tho' liquids only, in the last 48 hours, and there has been a sufficiency of sleep—but the sores are miserably worse than ever—fresh sloughs and those deeper than ever—and more extensive.

The D[uke of York] made his Will this morning, and sign'd it with great composure and with a firm hand.

My language to the K. has been that matters are worse but NOT YET those signs which precede immediately the awful crisis; but that they may occur at any time.

P.S. The Duke is to receive the sacrament on Thursday from the hands of the Bishop of London.

Sir Henry Halford to Sir William Knighton, 28 December 1826. (*Knighton*, I, 357.)

1281 THE MARQUIS OF ANGLESEY *to the* KING

Beaudesert, Decr. 31st 1826.

THE MARQUIS OF ANGLESEY has the honor to present his humble duty to the King, and to represent to His Majesty, that in the event of the situation of Master General of the Ordnance becoming vacant, he has the ambition, (and he trusts it may not be thought other than a laudable one,) of aspiring to fill that important office.[1]

The Marquis of Anglesey has reason to know that his appointment to

1 Wellington succeeded the Duke of York, who died on 5 January 1827, as Commander-in-Chief, and, at the King's request, retained the office of Master General of the Ordnance.

it, would not be disagreeable to the distinguished corps he would have the honor to command.

If he is diffident of his ability to do the fullest justice to that most important branch of service, he can yield to no man in zeal and anxious solicitude for the honor of the King and the prosperity of His Majesty's Government.

The Marquis of Anglesey has not applied, nor will he apply to any of His Majesty's Ministers upon this subject.

He does not presume to press the consideration of it upon His Majesty.

He is content to make known to the King, this, his anxious desire, and whatever may be His Majesty's decision, the Marquis of Anglesey will be fully satisfied of it's justice and its wisdom.

1282 THE DUKE OF CUMBERLAND *to* SIR WILLIAM KNIGHTON

Berlin, Jany. 3d. 1827.

I RECEIVED this morning yours of the 20th and return you my best thanks for its contents. Alas my fears have not been falsified, and I never deceived myself from the moment I knew that my poor brother was attacked by that vile disorder though certainly never were there such contradictory reports spread of any one's state than have been about him and even till within the very last mail, I can assure you that the accounts my sisters wrote to me, as also those my brother the Duke of Cambridge gave me, were all of his amendment, but at the same time saying he complained of his legs. Strange and ridiculous as it may sound that I, who am no phisician and totally ignorant of anatomy, still my common sense would not permit me to swallow all those reports, and I feared that the malady or the consequences of it had fallen thus and that sooner or later a mortification would be the consequence; the few words you say in your letter proves to me too clearly that if perhaps not correct in all I state, still the conclusion is right; and all hope is over. His loss is a grievous one both for his family and friends, and I may add a national loss, for certainly he has done prodigeous service to his country, and the army owes every thing to him; my dear brother the King will never get such a Commander in Chief for his army, one who acted more fairly and honourably than he has ever done; whenever his end arrives I feel, no I cannot tell you, all I feel for the dear King brought up, and educated with him; I own to you my heart bleeds at all this and I can think of nothing else. I fear the worry & hurry of the last fortnight must have been too much for a frame already so inervated [*sic*] from disease & confinement.

I wish I could talk of more agreeable subjects, but alas there seems to be a general gloom every where, and in every thing, and you can form to yourself no idea the sensation which has been produced by that very eloquent and yet ill-judged speech of Mr. Canning, which from his want of circumspection has violently offended every foreign Cabinet, and I must say, in one part he certainly did not shew that respect he owed my brother, who is his master and his King, when he braggs publicly that *he* Mr. C. did every thing.[1] I must own my loyal, as well as brotherly feelings were not a little enraged and irritated at this part of his speech, and I should think several of his colleagues cannot be well pleased at all this.

I am happy to learn the Chancellor is recovering. His loss is a precious one for my brother, as he is a perfect *honest* man. Poor Liverpool I hear from all sides is breaking, and though perhaps he may hold out a little longer, it is supposed he has an organic complaint.

With my best & kindest love to my brother, believe me, [etc.].

P.S. I perceive my son is improving under Jelf, who is *every thing* I can wish.

1283 HENRY BURGESS *to* THOMAS MOORE[2]
(*Copy.*)

Curzon Street, 24th January 1827.

I WAS favored with your letter of the 14th. by Mr. Orme, but a press of business prevented me from writing to you ere now. I lent the letter you allude to, respecting the generous gift of the Prince Regent, to a gentleman from whom it will be impossible to get it back in less than a fortnight—probably longer. I regret that before I parted with it I was not apprized of your intention to publish another edition of the life of Mr. Sheridan.[3]

I am not certain whether the sum was £4000 or £3000, but it was given unasked for, in the most gracious manner by the Royal personage as soon as he knew that it would be of essential service to Mr. Sheridan;

1 Canning's famous speech, 12 December 1826, in which he boasted that he had "called the New World into existence to redress the balance of the Old".
2 See No. 159.   3 The first was published in 1825.

and the highly distinguished nobleman (who was the warm friend and admirer of the latter), to whom the disposal of the money was entrusted, placed it in the hands of a person who with another gentleman professed that they had the means, with that sum, to effect the purpose for which it was intended; but after it had been lodged in the person's hands it was, under unwarrantable pretences, detained until it was too late to render the assistance so kindly meant, and the letter I mentioned to Mr. Orme was written by the nobleman to Mr. Sheridan intimating that as the purpose for which it had been given could not be effected, he had per-emptorily insisted that it should be delivered to Mr. S.

This gracious donation, but for the unjust detention of it, would have relieved Mr. Sheridan from the difficulties that harrassed him at that time and prevented the pungent distress which so pressed upon him in the Spring of 1814 and which, in the irritation of the moment, produced the letter he wrote from the spunging house to Mr. Whitbread;—but here in justice to the memory of Mr. Whitbread and to his family I deem it incumbent upon me to say that that letter ought not to have been given to you for publication, unless accompanied with the reasons why the sum mentioned in it had been withheld; particularly as Mr. Sheridan or his family never would have received a shilling from the theatre but for the perseverence of Mr. Whitbread in his promise to rebuild the theatre, and to which he applied so much of his time and mind. In that letter Mr. Sheridan says that if Mr. Whitbread had not forcibly withheld from him the £12,000 in consequence of a threatening letter from a "miserable swindler" he should at least have been out of the "reach of *this* state of miserable insult".

The fact is that Mr. Whitbread confided in a list or statement de-livered to him by the treasurer of the theatre and myself of the bonâ fide debts due from that concern and he made his arrangements with the creditors and proprietors accordingly; and whatever was due to Mr. Sheridan would have been paid to him upon the faith of the list so de-livered—but Taylor of the Opera House claimed from Mr. Whitbread the payment of upwards of £20,000 which he pretended to be due to him from the proprietors of the late theatre and threatened to file a Bill in Chancery to obtain an injunction to restrain the expenditure of the sub-scription money until he was paid. Such an unexpected claim alarmed Mr. Whitbread who was advised by counsel not to pay the proprietors any money until it was disposed of; and which, after a most strict in-vestigation, turned out to be nothing but an impudent attempt to obtain a large sum of money altho' not a shilling was due: but not the slightest blame ought to be imputed to Mr. Whitbread on this account,—he and the committee were by the Act of Parliament responsible for the distribution of the subscription money to the creditors of the theatre, according to the list delivered; and if Taylor's claim had been proved, the committee of which he was chairman would have been liable for the money they might have paid to Mr. Sheridan after the notice of that claim.[1]

Messrs. Longman & Co. did me the favor to send me the Edinburgh Review published for the last month and I was sorry to observe that in page 42 the writer, in his remarks upon your Memoirs of the life of Mr. Sheridan, in that part which treats of the ministry of Lord Grenville, says, "but it was not till the year after[2] that he (Mr. S.) consummated his *perfidy* to the Party". If this accusation was made from the part Mr. Sheridan took respecting that short lived Administration, it was from a perfect conviction that the answer they had prepared to the Address of the two Houses was unfit to be sent forth to the world either as the sentiments or the diction of the Heir Apparent who, at that time, was the representative of his Sovereign; and especially as that answer would be considered as the first official act of his Government and that, if the answer had been adopted, it would have compromised the Prince Regent with the opinions and principles of that Administration,—or, if the accusation of "perfidy" was for withholding the intended resignation of the Household from the knowledge of the Commons, it was that such resignation would be on the supposition that the Grenville Ministry would be continued, but which Mr. Sheridan foresaw (and which every unbiassed mind, accustomed to view affairs of this kind as they really were, must have seen) that it was impossible such a Ministry, with such opinions and principles, could have the confidence and esteem of their Royal master or of the nation and, therefore, that their speedy dismissal was certain; and on referring to the letter[3] I shewed you and of which I refused to give you a copy (mentioned in a note, page 648), I think that the conduct of Mr. Sheridan did not in the slightest manner deserve the harsh imputation of perfidy.

I write this in haste and it will give me much pleasure if it will in any manner assist you; but I ought to apologize for taking up your time respecting Mr. Sheridan's conduct towards the Grenville Ministry. As a matter of course *my opinion* is not to be mentioned.

[P.S.] I do not think you ever saw the picture of St. Caecilia painted by Sir Joshua Reynolds for Mr. Sheridan. If you have not and will call here

---

1 The King's version of these incidents, as reported by Croker, is in *Croker Papers*, I, 305–9. 2 I.e. in 1812.

3 The Prince of Wales's well-known letter to Moira, 30 March 1807. (Colchester's *Diary*, II, 115.)

when you are in town I doubt not that you will prefer it to that at Knowles. The celebrity of Miss Linley,[1] (as also of Mr. Sheridan), induced Sir Joshua to make it one of his best finished pictures, and I have been told by Sir Wm Beechey that he took more pains in painting the face than in any other picture he ever painted; and the beauty, and I may say, almost celestial softness of her countenance (so happily depicted by that eminent artist) excels almost everything of the kind.

Sir Herbert Taylor's Memorandum respecting the Duke of York's last illness, 9 June 1826 to 5 January 1827. (*Annual Register*, 1827, pp. 442–60.)
The Duke of Wellington to the Earl of Liverpool, 8 January 1827. (*W.N.D.* III, 534.)
The Duke of Wellington to the King, 8 January 1827. (*W.N.D.* III, 534–5); 24 January 1827. (*Ibid.* III, 564.)

1284 THE EARL OF LIVERPOOL *to the* KING

Bath, Jany 30, 1827.

LORD LIVERPOOL has the honour to transmit to your Majesty, a letter with its enclosures which he has just received from Lord Beresford.

Your Majesty will perceive by it, that Lord Beresford's return to this country may be daily expected. It is much to be regretted that the Portuguese Govt. would not give to Lord Beresford the powers and authority necessary for rendering his command of the army efficient, but Lord Liverpool is satisfied that the continuance of Lord Beresford in Portugal, would be an unmixed evil, if he had either no duty to perform, or if he was not allowed to perform the duty entrusted to him, in a manner that might be advantageous to the general cause.

1285 THE DUKE OF WELLINGTON *to* SIR WILLIAM KNIGHTON

London, Febry 7th 1827.

THE question of the poor Duke's debts[2] was this day taken into consideration, but I think it is universally felt that it will be impossible to prevail upon Parlt. to pay them without referring them to the

1 Elizabeth Ann Linley, Sheridan's first wife. (1754–1792.) Referring to Sheridan's progress in winning her affection, Moore wrote: "Like that Saint by whose name she was always called, she had long welcomed to her soul a secret visitant, whose gifts were of a higher and more radiant kind than the more wealthy and lordly of this world can proffer."
2 The Duke of York's debts amounted, it was said, to £200,000. Lord Londonderry suggested that the officers in the Army should raise a subscription for the payment of these debts, but Wellington said that such a project would create more distress than it would

consideration of a committee, and generally felt in the Cabinet that the proposition itself would be ill received and occasion very unpleasant discussion upon the principle of paying debts of that description. I don't think it probable after what passed, that the Govt. can come forward upon this subject.

I shall be much obliged if you will mention this to His Majesty.

There is another subject upon which the King spoke to me yesterday that is the return of their Royal Highnesses the Dukes of Cumberland and Cambridge to this country in order to take their seats in the House of Lords,[1] which upon consideration I think had better be avoided. Strength is not wanted in that House; and I confess that I am more apprehensive of the evil which might result from any jealousy which the presence (on a sudden) of these Princes might occasion than I am of any evil which might result from their absence.

It is a great object for the King to keep himself quiet and without discussion with any body on this question. I think he will not avoid discussion if his brothers come over by his desire.

1286 THE EARL OF LIVERPOOL *to the* KING

London, Feby 8, 1827.

LORD LIVERPOOL has the honour to inform your Majesty, that your Majesty's confidential servants have had under their consideration the propriety of making an addition under present circumstances[2] to the income of their Royal Highnesses, the Duke and Duchess of Clarence.

By the decease of His Royal Highness the Duke of York, twenty six thousand a year falls in to the publick.

Your Majesty's servants would humbly propose to your Majesty, to recommend to Parliament, to make an addition to the income of His Royal Highness the Duke of Clarence, of eight thousand a year, and to

relieve. The Duke's doctors thought that his illness was aggravated by worry about his financial position, and in August 1826 Peel had suggested that the King might be willing to co-operate with the Treasury in overcoming the financial difficulties. (Add. MSS. 38195, fo. 186.) A few days after the Duke's death the Government agreed to make a special grant of £6440 from the Droits of the Crown for the payment of his servants' wages and of debts incurred by them on his account, but, said Liverpool, "it is not to furnish a precedent for any further demands, for I cannot admit, and I am sure Parliament will not admit, that the Duke of York or any Prince of the Blood has any better claim upon the public for the payment of his debts than the First Lord of the Treasury or the Chancellor of the Exchequer". (Add. MSS. 38302, fo. 179.)

1 And to vote against the Catholic Relief Bill.
2 The Duke of York's death had made the Duke of Clarence heir-presumptive.

grant to the Duchess of Clarence four thousand a year. Her Royal Highness has at present no separate income of any sort. The allowance thus granted to the Duke of Clarence would make his income equivalent to that of the Duke of York with the exception of the late Duke's professional income & the income which he derived from Germany, neither of which could properly be taken into the account.

From the respect which your Majesty's servants all feel towards the memory of your Majesty's beloved and lamented brother, they would not think it fitting that any communication should be made to Parliament upon the subject till after the Address of condolence of the two Houses to your Majesty.[1]

The Duke of Wellington to the King, 20 February 1827. (*W.N.D.* III, 597–9.)

1287 FREDERICK JOHN ROBINSON *to* SIR WILLIAM KNIGHTON

Downing Street, Feby 26th 1827.

I AM much obliged to you for your letter: and I hope you will take a proper opportunity of assuring His Majesty how sensible I am of His Majesty's goodness in expressing his gracious approbation of my humble endeavours to contribute to his personal comfort in any matter in which my official situation may enable me to do so.

Since I had the pleasure of seeing you, I have seen the Duke of Montrose with the view of ascertaining how far some portion of the *immediate* demands upon us for the *more ordinary* furnishing of portions of Windsor Castle (such as papering & servants rooms) can be undertaken by the Lord Chamberlain's department. The Duke was very anxious to assist me in any way that could be devised; and I trust that upon beating the matter out, we shall be able to get some help in this way, and be thereby enabled to facilitate the important object of getting the Castle ready for His Majesty's reception at the earliest possible period. I can truly say that I am most anxious to make every practicable exertion for this purpose.

You did not mention His Majesty's health. I earnestly hope that it is re-established; and that His Majesty is no longer troubled with any severe gout.

1 The Royal message was presented to both Houses of Parliament on the 15th, and on the following day the Government moved a resolution whereby the sum of £3000 (not £8000) was to be added to the Duke's income, and £6000 a year to be granted to the Duchess.

Treas[ury] Chamb[ers], 27 Feb. 1827.

I AM greatly obliged to you for your letter which I received yesterday.

Your account of the King's health is most satisfactory. You can scarcely imagine how much solicitude has been expressed on that point by all persons here who felt how much the calamity which has befallen Lord Liverpool might possibly affect the feelings of His Majesty.[1]

The accounts at Fife House are given out as being favorable to the hopes of a gradual recovery: but I really do not rely upon them. The few who could speak with the most knowledge & with the greatest authority upon the subject either decline to speak at all, or use very guarded language. It does not appear to me that Sir H. Halford has a sanguine or even a favorable view of the case.

We remain in all material respects, just as you left us. The most absurd rumours & conjectures are afloat. Every man has a project for the reconstruction of the Government; and I have found not a few who have been kind enough to communicate to me, in the strictest confidence, the arrangements which have been decided upon! Most of these are such as I happen to know to be quite impracticable.

In the meantime I am pursuing my own laborious vocation without looking to the right hand or to the left. I am not in the following of any Party. My business is with the public interests & my duty to promote the King's service wherever I am employed.

I do not quite like what you say of your own health. I hope the next account from you will be better.

[P.S.] There are two warrants to which we should be glad to have the King's signature. One of them is for the appointment of a new Commission of Customs—another for a new Commissioner of Audit. I beg leave to recommend these to your attention upon the usual understanding that I must not be supposed to wish that you should press for the signature with the least chance of giving trouble.

1 On 16 February the Prime Minister moved an Address to the King on the subject of the grant to the Duke and Duchess of Clarence. The House of Lords never saw him again. On the following day he had a seizure, from which he never recovered. He survived until December 1828, but the stroke put an end to his political life.

Jany[1] 27th 1827.

I AM still a cripple, & even hobling to the end of my terrace with a stick retards my progress towards recovery. I hear you are gone to Brighton. I should have written to you yesterday, but the petitions in the H. of C. lasted till past six o clock, & as my ancle is so much worse, from sitting with my leg down for three or four hours yesterday, I shall not venture there to-day.

We think we are very strong on the Catholic question & as far as we can judge of a new house, those who have examined the lists (at least our friends) think a majority is sure, but we have still a little suspicion the question may be postponed.

The King could render the loyal Protestants an effectual support, if he would allow you or some one to speak to Fife & Lord Graves. It would confirm the interest he takes upon this vital question. It is more for their example than their votes, that their support is so wanting. Genl. Duff,[2] Lord Fife's brother is a good Protestant & votes with us, & says as the factions in Dublin abused the Duke of York, who gave him a regiment, that nothing shall induce him to vote for them.

The election petitions have hitherto turned out fortunately & to the advantage of the Protestants & the Govt. Lord Darlington has lost two for Ilchester, & some one observed, he was like an old man who had lost his *hat* & *wig, Conversation Sharp*[3] was a hatter, & John Williams a Whig, the latter being deposed we shall be relieved from some long speeches on the Chancery business.[4]

I am about to relate not to argue, but I hear many wise men, who know the extent of the D. of Wellington's capacity, the soundness of his judgement & his intuitive perception into all matters of business, not-withstanding the arguments agst him, think him, at the present time, the fittest man for the First Minister. The Duke & Peel are looked upon as the props & support of the old established principles by which the country has been governed, & if they act as subordinates, it will unhinge all the confidence of the greater part of the people of property in the country, who abhor some of these *new vagarys*, & the feeling agst them will be shown in the course of the Session.

1 Evidently a slip for February. Parliament met, after the Adjournment, on 8 February.

2 Sir Alexander Duff, M.P. for the Elgin group of Burghs, and Colonel of the 92nd Regiment of Foot. He voted against the Catholic Relief Bill in 1829. Lord Fife, who was elected for Banff-shire on 29 June 1826, was unseated on a petition, 2 April 1827.

3 Richard Sharp (1759–1835). He was well known in the literary world, and was a successful business man, amassing a fortune of nearly a quarter of a million.

4 Their return was amended by the House of Commons, 22 February, in favour of Lionel Talmash and Felix Thomas Talmash.

It was said at the Jacoben booksellers—Ridgway on Saturday, & who has lately assumed a high tone from the publication of a certain speech, that nothing was to be decided for a fortnight or three weeks & they had it from authority.

The Corn proposition,[1] as intended to be proposed, has been so diluted, that it is supposed the country gentlemen will have little cause to cavil. However it will probably occupy us till Easter.

[P.S.] Burdett told a *Whig* last night, he should not decide upon the mode he should shape his motion untill he had consulted Mr. Canning.[2]

1290 THE DUKE OF WELLINGTON *to* SIR WILLIAM KNIGHTON

London, March 2, 1827.

I WAS about to write to you when I received your note[3] of yesterday. I am very sorry indeed to find that you have had a relapse.

I can receive the Judges and the principal gentlemen of the County of Hants at S[trathfield] Saye on Sunday; and I attend the Assizes at Winchester on Tuesday as Lord Lieutenant of the County; and I shall not be back till Tuesday or Wednesday.

I really know nothing which should give occasion for my troubling His Majesty. But I shall be ready to attend H.M.'s commands whenever H.M. may express a wish to see me.

1 On 1 March Canning moved the resolutions which were subsequently embodied in the Corn Bill. The measure was designed to put an end to extraordinary price fluctuations, to give reasonable protection to the farmer when prices were low, and reasonable protection to the consumer when prices were high. With every rise of one shilling above sixty shillings in the price of corn in England, the duty on imported corn was to be reduced by two shillings, and with every fall of one shilling the duty was to be increased by two shillings, the duty being twenty shillings when the price was sixty shillings (Winchester measure). The Bill excited the indignation of the landed interest, but it passed the Commons on 12 April.
2 Canning advised Burdett to bring the Catholic question before the new House of Commons in the shape of a general resolution, and not by Bill.
3 See *W.N.D.* III, 603.

Whitehall Place,
Monday night 2nd [5th] March [1827].

THE DUKE has this moment left me, meaning to beg to see you to-morrow morning.

The time was when you always wished to communicate with me. Whether you still wish it or not I don't so well know; but as the Duke feels that you are his best ally, & as in every detail he gives me he invariably points out how invaluable at each step yr aid has been, I cannot resist telling you that if the Duke is to be saved to the King & the country it will be mainly yr doing. You will see what is now written to the King. I am sure that if you do not back what is written by yr personal presence & efforts, the Government will be broken up by the fatal arrival of one single man.[1] Great as the Duke's character is it wd go like chaff before the wind if he were to be in the King's Councils one moment after a refusal to the measure which has been prepared; & turn our eyes wch way we will, there is no one to replace him, & much less is there one to fill a single Cabinet office in the House of Commons.

It is for the King & for the country that I now tremble.

As for office I personally care not a straw, or rather it wd be a comfort to me to be in private life. But I am alarmed at the frightful danger which threatens us; & I am sure it cannot but gratify you to know that the Duke lauds you daily to me, & that now his hope of mastering this infamous intrigue[2] arises mainly from what he is sure will be yr efforts.

[P.S.] You know I am always glad to see you when it suits you to call, & I could tell you all the Duke feels.

George Canning to Sir William Knighton, F.O. 3 March 1827. [*Knighton*, I, 371.]

1 Canning, having recovered from his illness, returned to London from Brighton on 27 February. He and the Duke, his chief rival for the premiership, had been on bad terms since 1824. Wellington disapproved his liberal foreign policy and had secretly intrigued to bring about his dismissal. Canning's skilful management of the King, and the popularity of his foreign policy, won for him the King's favour, but George IV was opposed to him on the Catholic question. So Canning and the Duke were at loggerheads in 1827, and there was no prospect of either serving in a Ministry of which the other was head.

2 At a later time Arbuthnot asserted, quite unjustifiably, that Canning had been intriguing for the premiership and negotiating with the Opposition even before Liverpool fell ill on 17 February. As early as 10 March Arbuthnot said that the Duke could not divest himself of the view that, directly or indirectly, there had been an understanding with some of the Opposition leaders. The Whigs had discussed the situation at a party meeting as early as 19 or 20 February and had agreed to support Canning in the event of his becoming Prime Minister. They gave an account of their deliberations to Canning's friend E. J. Littleton, who passed on the information.

F.O., March 3d 1827.

L E T me call your attention to the *moral* of Thursday night's proceedings.[1] Your two Treasury friends,[2] but Herries especially, drew so gloomy a picture of the H. of C. to me on Thursday morning, as, if I had been a very nervous person (which luckily I am not) might well have daunted me for the day. The great land holders had all got together. They were determined upon *prohibition*,[3] no compromise would appease them. The Lords were more violent even than the Commons, & they were all pledged to each other—Rutlands—Beauforts[4]—Clives, Lauderdale &c &c.

Well. Under these impressions I rose, about $\frac{1}{2}$ p 6—and when I sat down a little before 8—the bumpkins were running about the House in knots of three & four—& no three of them agreeing on what point, or in what direction to attempt to muster an opposition. One only, a thorough malignant, & furious *ultra* in politicks, as well as upon corn, attempted a feeble cry about free trade.[5] It fell flat: & before he is six days older, he shall rue the attempt, if he gives me (as I trust he will) the opportunity.

Now, my dear Sir, the other buggaboo[6] is not really more formidable than was this of corn. That is to say, there are means of settling it by compromise—*if my hands are free.* Your Lushingtons & Herrieses are, I verily believe, as much mistaken about this matter, as about the other. *But*, if *absolute prohibition* is insisted upon—be assured that before two years are over your head, you will have *unlimited importation* of Catholicks.[7]

[P.S.] Above all things, do not, I entreat you (for his own sake) let Copley be the Sir E. Knatchbull of Monday.[8]

1 1 March, when Canning introduced the Government's Corn Resolutions.

2 The two Secretaries of the Treasury, Herries and Lushington. The functions of the Joint Secretaries were not so well defined a century ago as they are now, and there is evidence that both the Parliamentary Secretary and the Financial Secretary (as they are now styled) were then responsible for House of Commons' management.

3 Upon a new Corn Bill, that is, similar in principle to the 1815 Act which prohibited the importation of foreign corn so long as the home price was less than eighty shillings per quarter.

4 Henry Charles Somerset, sixth Duke of Beaufort (1766–1835).

5 Sir Edward Knatchbull, ninth Baronet (1781–1849), M.P. for Kent. The term *malignant*, first applied to Ultra Tories who were opposed to Catholic emancipation, was soon to be applied to all who opposed the Canning Ministry, Whigs as well as Tories. Knatchbull misrepresented, or misunderstood, Canning's views on free trade.

6 The Catholic question, which Burdett brought forward in the Commons on the 5th.

7 A most accurate prediction!

8 Sir John Copley, the Master of the Rolls, spoke against Burdett's motion, on the second night of the debate, and Canning made a violent attack upon him in reply. The motion was unexpectedly defeated (276 *v.* 272).

1293 Frederick John Robinson *to* Sir William Knighton

Downing Street, March 13, 1827.

Mr. Chantrey[1] has sent home the bust which His Majesty was so graciously pleased to command him to execute for me; and altho' I am unwilling to trouble the King with any letter to His Majesty upon the occasion, I should not do justice to my own feelings and my sense of His Majesty's goodness to me if I did not request you to take an opportunity of saying to His Majesty, that I trust I shall always prize so gracious a gift as I ought, and that whatever branch of my family it may descend to, will find recorded upon its pedestal a charge to preserve it with a lasting sense of its value in my eyes.

The Windsor estimate is now presented. I have raised it from £50,000 to £100,000; and I flatter myself that by the aid of the Lord Chamberlain's department, which I mentioned to you in a former letter, *that* addition to the vote originally intended will enable us to give every necessary facility towards expediting the completion of what will be necessary for his Majesty's comfort.

1294 Lord Bloomfield *to* Sir William Knighton

Stockholm, 17th March 1827.

Since the date of your very kind & affectionate letter what a political calamity has befallen us! Thus distant from the scene we can but imperfectly estimate the consequences that must follow poor Lord Liverpool's retirement from publick life.

In any view of them they are most deeply embarrassing. However; in looking back we find consolation & safety in the wisdom with which the King's decisions have been taken in similar perplexities & danger. The retrospect drives from us all apprehension, and we feel only anxious that His Majesty's own health may not suffer.

A million of thanks for the interest you take in John. He is still delicate and I fear greatly that this winter has been too severe for him. He however came here an invalid & therefore we can not yet fairly judge. He says he wrote from Stutgardt the very post after he received his appointment to this mission, to thank you & to express his acknowledgements for the desirable change. He is an excellent young man of business & delightful to live with.

I can not chime in with the grumbling about the Duke of Wellington's appointment to the hd of the army & his having so much. If he is no

---

1 Sir Francis Legatt Chantrey (1781–1841), the sculptor. Knighted, 1835.

to be favored; who, in God's name, since William the Conqueror's time, is?

Our friend Keppel's nomination to the Govt of Portsmouth delighted me.[1] He wrote in great spirits about it & full of right feeling on the occasion. I trust he may live long to enjoy the "loaves & fishes" it will help to furnish.

Lady B[loomfield] is very much obliged by your kind recollection of her & charges me with her best compliments. She has borne the severe winter better than any of us. Only fancy, the quick-silver below zero 20 degrees of Fahrenheit; even within these last few days it has been at 4 & 6. We are however looking to a break-up on the first change of wind.

I have not yet had an answer from Mr. Canning, but do not anticipate any opposition to my application for leave.[2] I shall be long in reaching England as my medical advisers continue to insist on the necessity of the waters at Aix la Chapelle. The delay is the most cruel privation to both myself & my poor invalid at home. In my last of the 9th ult, I explained how severely I had been attacked.

God bless you my dear friend [etc.].

P.S. Many diplomatick changes are named to me. Indeed some must be. I therefore entreat you to be my vigilant friend in case an opening, to which I might be considered eligible, should offer.

1295 THE KING *to the* EARL OF LIVERPOOL

Royal Lodge, Saty. March 24, 1827.

I TAKE up my pen in a great hurry, just to acknowledge your two letters[3] & to return you the papers which you desired to have sent back. I am truly happy that you feel yourself so much recover'd as to think of coming on Monday, when *we* shall all of us be truly rejoic'd at seeing you, yet, at the same time, I think it right to inform you, that I am expecting a large party on *Tuesday next*, to stay till *Thursday*, therefore, as you are not even now I fear, quite stout, should *you prefer* remaining with your family till Thursday pray do. What little business *I* have to impart to you there is no hurry about, & will therefore keep very well till that time.

1 The King's friend, General Sir William Keppel, G.C.B., was gazetted Governor of Portsmouth, 1 January 1827.
2 Bloomfield was on leave from 28 April 1827 to 8 October 1828, and his son was Chargé d'affaires during this period.
3 Unimportant, in his own handwriting.

Downing Street, 26 March 1827.

SINCE I sent the hurried letter which I wrote on Saturday at the moment
of my gallopping off for Brighton, where I knew that my excellent wife
was anxiously waiting for me, I have had a little time to reflect upon the
present posture of affairs.

I wish that my reflexions could bring more of comfort to my own
mind, to the parties who now compose the Government, and to the
country. But though unused as my sanguine temperament is to look at
any but the rosy side of any state of human life, I see nothing but great
mischief and disappointment from the operations which are now going
on, unless they are immediately stopp'd.[2]

No course could be more kind than the determination taken by Mr.
Canning & Mr. Peel when at Brighton[3] of advising the King to do that
which His Majesty's own gracious disposition towards an able & faithful
Minister would have suggested—to give ample time for any change
which by God's mercy might be made in Lord Liverpool's condition. It
appeared also that the opportunity which a short interval would afford
of virtually disposing both of the Catholic and the Corn questions, would
materially facilitate the organization of the Government. Of the rejection of the Catholic claims I felt the fullest confidence,[4] and that there
would then be no immediate conflict in the Cabinet; whilst the plan for
altering the Corn Laws seemed so manifestly advantageous to the landed
interest, without pressing unjustly upon other classes of the community,
that I contemplated no feelings but those of restored contentment and
satisfaction towards Mr. Canning on the part of the landed interest. To
him I looked as the person who would be selected by the King as Lord

1 What is evidently the draft of this letter is in Parker's *Peel*, I, 454, where it is dated
"Treasury Chambers: March 1827". The two are so dissimilar that the Windsor copy,
which is the letter as sent, is here given.

2 Many Tory Peers, including two "Catholics" (the Marquis of Londonderry, and the
Duke of Buckingham, who had quarrelled with Canning because he had declined to support
the Duke's claims to the Governor-Generalship of India or to Cabinet office at home), had
been intriguing to deprive Canning of the premiership which Liverpool had recognised to
be his rightful inheritance, and to induce the King to form a "balanced Government"—i.e. a
Government consisting of both "Catholics" and "Protestants"—"without Mr. Canning's
assistance". (*W.N.D.* III, 611.) Wellington declined to lend himself to such intrigues.

3 Canning was ill in bed at Brighton on 17 February when Liverpool was disabled. Peel
set off for Brighton that afternoon and saw Canning next morning, and they agreed to advise
the King to treat the Prime Minister's illness as a temporary indisposition: "If Lord Liverpool
should ever come to himself sufficiently to learn what had passed, it would be gratifying to
all parties that no steps had been taken, or even mooted, for the disposal of his succession."

4 As one of the Government Whips he had exceptional opportunities of forming an accurate
estimate. But it was generally expected that the "Catholics" would have a majority, and
their minority of four is to be attributed to accidental circumstances.

Liverpool's successor & every act and every thought of mine has had this object in view.[1] I sincerely felt that in so acting and thinking I best discharged that duty which, with me is paramount to all others—that of gratitude and affection to the King and to Lord Liverpool.

With this purpose I have vigilantly watched, and I think frequently counteracted the efforts that have been made to extinguish Lord Liverpool [and place the D. of W. in his situation].[2]

I thought and still conscientiously think, that a course more dangerous to the happiness and honor of the D. of W[ellington] than making him the Minister could not be taken, and that the unrivalled fame of his Grace, shining with higher lustre than ever in the great duties of Commander in Chief, ought not to be put to hazard by placing him at the head of an *ultra* Civil Government, whose motions would be watched throughout the country, with all the jealousy of a military despotism, and whose legitimate acts of authority and vigour his Grace would be incapable of explaining in his own House with the eloquence and force which the dignity and safety of the Crown require in the First Minister.

But other thoughts have filled the heads and actuated the conduct of some of his Grace's adherents. They have made and are still making efforts (I am persuaded) against his Grace's better judgement, to induce certain Dukes and ultra Protestants to address the King for the election of his Grace and the exclusion of Mr. Canning.[2] This unjust and short-sighted scheme is now actively at work. I know from accident that one of the most loyal and sincere friends of the Ministry and the country has been invited to be a party to it, and that he comes to town this day [with the view of seeing the King on the subject].[4]

No time therefore is to be lost in counteracting this mischief [and in bringing the King's mind to a right decision].[4] The Crown has an unqualified choice, and the present posture of our affairs [when a meddling junta of the aristocracy, instigated by a foolish female,[5] are trying to force the King into an odious choice][4] illustrates the wisdom of our forefathers, in leaving the appointment absolutely to the King. Happily it cannot be in more patriotic hands. For George IV has in all the great measures of

---

1 It is worth noting that Lushington was an anti-Catholic.

2 These words were erased but are just visible.

3 An allusion to the famous "aristocratic Round Robin". See note 2, p. 207. Wellington returned the Duke of Buckingham's letter of the 20th containing promises of Tory support, and told him to consider it *non avenue*. (*W.N.D.* iii, 611.) A few days later the Tory Peers made another attempt to induce Wellington to take the premiership, but they were again rebuffed. The Duke of Newcastle, one of the leading anti-Catholic Peers, saw the King on the 24th or 25th, and threatened to withdraw his support from the Government if Canning became Prime Minister.

4 These words are erased.   5 Mrs Arbuthnot.

his Government followed with encreased benefit to England and to the world the glorious career of his august father, and Gt. Britain stands at this moment renowned above all the nations of the earth. In contemplating this great consummation the King gives, graciously gives, to his Minister and friend Lord Liverpool his full share of praise, and must, I conclude, desire to continue in the same course of moderation and wisdom. The first expectation that any man would form from these premises would be to see as Lord Liverpool's successor the person most confided in by him, most capable of following & explaining the principles of his Ministry. In this respect there are only two persons in the Government about whom there can be a doubt—Mr. Canning & Mr. Peel.

That Lord L. had the highest regard and respect for both, I know beyond all doubt from his own expressions of admiration of their great powers; but Mr. Canning from priority of age, long experience, and eloquence of the highest quality was regarded by him as the best claimant of the two; always however predicting that nothing but a Radical Whig triumph could ultimately keep the Government out of Mr. Peel's able hands.

It is because I think that I see the dawn of this triumph in the intrigues that are now going on, that I am anxious to draw the most prompt consideration to the subject.

Lord L's real state has been explained to me, with much feeling, by Lady Liverpool,[1] and it is quite clear that for some time to come he can be competent to no public business, and that the hope of his ultimate recovery depends upon his being rigidly kept from it. That there is a pressure on the brain is unquestionable. Occasionally it subsides & reason resumes a limited power—but after a short respite Lord L. feels the pressure returning—puts his hand to his forehead—and in a state of pain & forgetfulness, says "I am but a child", and in sorrow sheds most plenteous tears. The time that has now elapsed, and his present state shew how much more is necessary to render him of any use as a member of the Government and therefore no reproach can be cast upon his colleagues [although they are one and all of his creation][2] for submitting to His Majesty the expediency of an immediate re-organization of his Government. I humbly conceive there are three courses for His Majesty's choice.

1st. To command Mr. Canning to form a Government precisely upon the principles of Lord Liverpool, retaining with him all those who will

1 Lord Liverpool's second wife (d. 1846). She was the daughter of Charles Chester, the first Lord Bagot's brother, and was married in 1822.
2 These words are erased.

give him their cordial support and co-operation, leaving to him the selection of new persons in the place of those who decline. This I suspect will give him some fund for personal friends and followers, which will gratify and strengthen him in his Ministry, without giving reasonable ground of offence to any & without causing trouble to the King or perplexity in his Councils.

2nd To desire Mr. Peel to form an exclusive Protestant Government.

I will not say that this is impracticable IF OTHER EFFORTS SHOULD FAIL, but I am sure it would be a most distressing CHOICE to make; and I firmly believe that Mr. Peel has too much patriotism to encourage or attempt it; and if he would not do it for himself certainly not as secondary to the D. of W—— for independent of the personal objections to the Duke, the time is come when it is essential to the Crown's proper influence in the State, that its First Minister should be in the House of Commons.

But as the head of an *ultra* Government what would be Mr. Peel's position?

He would have, besides the whole body of Whigs, the influence and the talents of Mr. Canning to contend against; and I have not the shadow of a doubt that the Catholic question would be revived in some shape and I now *know* that it would be carried. This would open a conflict between the two Houses, and drive into the arms of the Radical Whigs, one of the most powerful instruments of good or evil by which the institutions and the aristocracy of this country can either be protected or destroyed. [That Mr. Canning's mind is already half prepared for this course I know perfectly well, and it will require the King's wisdom and skill to avert it.][1]

The 3rd course
Is a mixed Government of Whigs and Tories, beginning by a concession of the Catholic claims, contrary to the feelings of the country and the wishes of the King. May God protect us from it. Ever affectionately yrs.

[P.S.] I have written this currente calamo: but I think you will be able to make it out.

1 These words are erased.

Royal Lodge,
Monday night, March 26th 1827.

I WAS actually on the point, (quite undress'd) of stepping into bed, when the inclos'd reach'd me. As I of course concluded, that, on the one hand, it might contain papers that might require my *immediate* signature & to which you do not like delay, & on the other *certainly* no *political* or *private* papers that you could *either wish or intend to conceal from me*, I did not hesitate to open the dispatch, & I have now order'd the messenger to leave THIS, *not* until *five in the morning in order*, that (in your state of health) *he* may not interrupt your night's repose. Upon the merits & the different points contain'd in *this paper*, (however *well*, & *privately possibly* intended for *your eye*) & after the *very long* & *interesting* conversation which, so *lately*, as this *very morning* took place between you & me, & the *conclusive result* to which, *as it appear'd to me*, that we *then* came, *it does seem to me*, that *it would be time thrown away to dissect this paper, & to reargue* it, (as we already have in our interview of today) *seriatim*. There is one point, or rather one position laid down in it, which *even* according to *your own feelings in unison with mine*, you must know *must be put quite out of the question*. All that good temper, all that conciliation, all that *the strictest sense of honor & liberality* can dictate, *I am ready & prepar'd to act upon & to meet* with even the very essence of that spirit. But, let the stake be *what it may*, & the risk be *however great, I must not, I can not, & more I will not tolerate, even the possibility of the most trivial breath of inconsistency, or of duplicity* being affix'd *upon me, or my character. I know, I may repose myself in perfect confidence in your hands* & that, (however difficult the chrysis may be) *you will exert yourself in this cause*, upon *the same principles of conscientious rectitude, which alone actuate me.*

I am too much fatigued & worn out, to add a word more, except that I am always, [etc.].

Royal Lodge, Sat.ʸ March 30th [31] 1827.

ONE line, only to tell you that I am *most anxious* to see you for a few moments *at any rate*, & as early *tomorrow morning*, as you can make it *convenient to yourself*. I have much to tell you, & *much too much* to be able to write it. It is in general, very comforting, & far more satisfactory &

pleasing, that even my most sanguine hopes could have led me to expect upon the appearance of things in general, during the last few days.[1]

1299   GEORGE CANNING *to the* KING

F.O., 30 March 1827.

MR. CANNING humbly reports to your Majesty, that, upon the bringing up of the resolution for the vote of supply (procured by Mr Robinson a few evenings ago) Mr. Tierney proposed to defer any farther proceeding thereupon until the 1st of May, in order that the grant might be made to a known and responsible Administration.

Mr Canning replied to Mr. Tierney, in the sense which your Majesty was graciously pleased to approve yesterday,[2] and apparently so much to the general satisfaction of the House that Mr. Tierney consented not to press his motion to a division. Unluckily however in expressing this consent, Mr. Tierney thought proper to assume, as a *condition* of it, that the new Administration was to be *declared* before the adjournment of the House for the holidays. This condition Mr. Canning did not feel himself authorized to adopt, and Mr. Tierney therefore (at the instigation of some persons around him) revoked his determination not to divide— although many members had left the House in consequence of that declared determination. The numbers upon the division were therefore small, in comparison with the fulness of the House at the early period of the evening.

The Opposition were	80,
The majority ———	153
	73

1 On the 28th the King saw both Wellington and Canning. He told the Duke that he wanted a "Protestant" Prime Minister, but did not ask him to form a Government. Subsequently he told Canning that he wished to reconstruct the Ministry on the principles of the Liverpool Administration by appointing a "Protestant" Peer to fill Liverpool's place. Canning advised the King to form a Ministry which should represent the King's opinions on the Catholic question, and offered to resign the Foreign Secretaryship in order that the attempt might be made. The King would not accept his resignation. Canning therefore felt that if a No Popery Government was not to be formed—if the Liverpool Ministry was to be reconstructed on the old principle of allowing the Catholic question to be an open one—he would not be justified in consenting to be excluded from the premiership solely on account of his opinions on that question. So he plainly told the King that "the substantive power of First Minister he must have", otherwise he should resign. Neither Wellington nor Peel would serve under Canning, nor would Canning serve under any anti-Catholic. To avoid the difficulty of choosing a new Prime Minister, the King suggested to Canning on the 29th that the matter should be decided by the Cabinet, but he abandoned the proposal after both Canning and Peel had advised against its adoption.

2 Canning said that the King had expressed his intention of filling up the vacancy in the Government, all reasonable hopes of Liverpool's recovery having been dissipated.

Several Opposition members—(Mr. Calcraft, Sir R. Wilson and others) either voted with the Government or went away—evidently thinking the division, after what had passed, unfair.

But although the temper of the House was upon the whole as good as could be expected or desired, Mr. Canning thinks it his duty not to disguise from your Majesty the impression of himself and his colleagues (Mr. Peel and Mr. Robinson) that it is highly expedient that no time should be lost in making the necessary arrangements; that it is probable that other opportunities (on the remaining stages of the Corn Bill for instance) will be taken to renew the subject of this evening's discussion; and that as the adjournment *cannot* now take place before the beginning of the week after next (perhaps not more than a day or two before the usual time of adjournment for the Easter holidays) it would be very desirable both for the tranquillizing of the impatience in and out of Parlt and for the carrying on of your Majesty's service after the recess, that whatever writs may be necessary to be moved in the House of Commons (in consequence of new arrangements) should be moved before the adjournment.

George Canning to the King, 31 March 1827. (*Stapleton*, pp. 586–7.)
Robert Peel to the King, 31 March 1827. [*Parker*, I, 457, where the following paragraph—the last—is omitted: "Mr. Peel trusts to your Majesty's usual goodness to excuse him for adding, that it appears to Mr. Peel to be of very great importance that your Majesty's arrival in London should not if possible, be deferred beyond the day on which Mr. Peel understood it to be your Majesty's intention to be in town—namely Wednesday next."]

1300 GEORGE CANNING *to the* KING

F.O., April 2d 1827.

MR. CANNING presents his humble duty to your Majesty: and has the satisfaction to lay before your Majesty an official note this day received from the Spanish Minister, Ct. de Alcudia, proposing arrangements for the settlement of all difficulties between Spain & Portugal, & for the general tranquillization of the Peninsula.

The King of Spain proposes 1st To reduce his army—on condition 2dly that Portugal shall discontinue her armaments—3dly that the *French* shall withdraw their army from Spain & 4th England hers from Lisbon simultaneously.

This is the very consummation to which Mr. Canning has always ventured to look forward, as the *proof of the sum*, in respect to the interference in behalf of Portugal. But Mr. Canning confesses that it is beyond his hopes that the *proposal* of it should come from Madrid.

India Board, 3 April 1827.

MR. WILLIAMS WYNN presents his duty to your Majesty and humbly submits for your Majesty's consideration the appointment of the Reverend J. T. James, A.M. of Christ Church, Oxford, to the Bishopric of Calcutta.[1]

Since the arrival of the intelligence in September last, of the heavy loss which India had sustained in the person of the late lamented and excellent Bishop, Mr. Williams Wynn has been assiduously engaged in the endeavor to procure a proper sucessor to a post of so much importance, and he has received much valuable advice and assistance from the Archbishop of Canterbury and the Bishop of London. It has however been found that the deaths of the two late Bishops[2] and of other high public functionaries have created an impression of the hazard attending a residence in India which has deterred several of those who appeared most eligible, from accepting this situation.

After the difficulty which Mr. Williams Wynn has experienced in this respect, he considers himself fortunate in being at length enabled to submit to your Majesty the name of a gentleman whose character and attainments justify the hope that he may discharge the duties of the episcopal office, to the advantage of India, and who seems particularly fitted to pursue the steps of Bishop Heber by the conciliation and mildness of his temper.

Mr. Williams Wynn feels it his duty to entreat your Majesty's pardon for bringing this appointment forward at a period when your Majesty is engaged in business of more importance, but the advanced time of the season renders it highly desirable that the future Bishop should make his preparations for leaving England with as little delay as possible.

1302 ROBERT PEEL *to the* KING

Whitehall, April 3, 1827.

MR. PEEL presents his humble duty to your Majesty and has the honour to submit for your Majesty's consideration a letter which has been addressed to Mr. Peel by Lord Melville on the subject of the distinction of the Green Ribbon.

1 Dr John Thomas James (1786–1828) was appointed. He landed at Calcutta in January 1828 and died seven months later.
2 Dr Thomas Fanshaw Middleton (1769–1822), Bishop of Calcutta, 1814–22; and Bishop Heber (1783–1826).

Admiralty, 2d April 1827.

I RECEIVED a few days ago a letter from Lord Aboyne by which I find that he has been apprized of the King's intention to confer on him the Green Ribbon. I think it right to communicate this circumstance to you as in all probability you may not be aware of it. His Majesty mentioned the matter to me at Brighton, but I do not know whether Lord Liverpool had also been apprized of it.

There can be no question that Lord Aboyne is a person on whom the Order of the Thistle may with propriety be conferred; but I did not understand that His Majesty proposed to carry the intention into effect immediately, or until at least one other vacancy had occurred which, by the bye, is likely soon to happen in the person of Lord Morton.[1]

The establishment of the Order from its first institution by King James 5th. has been the Sovereign and twelve Knights, in allusion (as tradition has handed down) to the twelve Apostles, and the Scotch Peers are not a little jealous in adhering to that number, as I found at the period of the Coronation when His Majesty announced the intention of creating four extra Knights, myself being one of them. The sensation was so strong among the existing Knights that if *my* humbly soliciting to decline the honor at that time, though most graciously conferred, could have had the effect of preventing the measure, and thereby allaying the sort of feeling which I observed to prevail among them, I should most willingly have renounced it. On that occasion however it was intimated by His Majesty's authority that there was no intention of permanently keeping up more than the ancient number, and accordingly the two last vacancies have not been filled up. When I saw the King at Brighton he stated his opinion that it might be reasonable still to keep up (as I understood His Majesty) two supernumerary Knights on the ground that for many years past, and I believe ever since the Union with Scotland, two of the Knights have been English Peers wholly unconnected with Scotland. I am by no means sure however that I correctly understood His Majesty on this last point.

1304 CHARLES ARBUTHNOT *to* SIR WILLIAM KNIGHTON

Whitehall Place, 3d April 1827.

I WENT back to the Foreign Office with a most satisfactory reply from the Duke; & it was arranged (upon the suggestion of Huskisson) that the first meeting shd be, not between Peel and Canning, but between

1 George Douglas, Earl of Morton. He died in July.

Canning & the Duke. To this the Duke (whom I again saw) most cordially agreed; & the Duke was to be appointed to go to the Foreign Office to-day at one o'clock.

I afterwards detailed to Peel all that had passed, & pleased him very much by thus letting him know that all misunderstanding was removed.

As it seems to me of essential consequence that there should be some talk with the Duke before he goes to Canning, I have arranged with him that he should call on me at twelve; & I intend that Peel shd be here at the same time.

I will take care that you shall know the results. It is unlucky that I must go to the House before 4 to-day to ballot for a committee to prevent being taken into custody; but the very moment that I learn what has passed the whole shall be communicated to you.

I had fully resolved to abstain from all interference, as I saw not how I could do good; & I was aware that under circumstances like the present, the best motives were often ill appreciated.

I have however by chance been brought forward, & I shall rejoice if I can at all aid in relieving the King from all his trouble & embarrassment.

I have burnt y[ou]r note.[1]

Henry Brougham to Sir William Knighton. York, 4 April 1827. [*Knighton*, I, 373–5, line 9, for "formed" read "founded"; line 15, after "who" insert "never". P. 374, lines 9, 10, "in your capacity of a man of science" should be in italics.]

1305 GEORGE CANNING *to the* KING

F.O., April 9, 1827.

MR. CANNING presents his most humble & affectionate duty to your Majesty. He has seen Mr. Peel, according to your Majesty's gracious command; & has learnt from him the name of the individual[2] whose

1 At this interview Canning explained what had passed at his audience with the King at Windsor, and he thus described the interview to Knighton: "Everything that was in doubt between us has been cleared up satisfactorily, and we parted, as you would have wished, all being left well." (*Stapleton*, p. 588.) He again saw both Wellington and Peel on the 5th, but without result. "My belief is", Canning wrote to Knighton, "that he (the Duke), and perhaps P. too, hoped the explanation between me and the D. would end in *my* begging *him* to take the Government. I mention this, because it is contrary to the *belief* which I had before stated to you, that the D. never thought of himself for that post. Further light has changed that belief entirely. Of this be assured, that we shall never advance one step till the K. fixes, and is known to have fixed, his choice...." (*Stapleton*, p. 589.)

2 Wellington. This was the last attempt to exclude Canning from the Premiership. No Government could be formed without his co-operation, and he refused to serve under Wellington or Peel.

appointment Mr. Peel conceived to be likely to solve all difficulty. But Mr. Canning is obliged, in frankness & honesty to say that it does not, in *his* mind, afford any such solution. Mr. Peel wished, & Mr. Canning agreed that the name should not be stated in writing: but it will of course be disclosed to your Majesty by either of them, when they wait upon your Majesty tomorrow. *No* other name, more calculated to answer the purpose occurred to either.

Mr. Peel will wait your Majesty's commands as to the time at which he should wait upon your Majesty.

1306 THE EARL OF ELDON *to the* KING

Monday, April 9 [1827].

THE LORD CHANCELLOR sends to your Majesty the letter he read when he had the honor of waiting upon your Majesty this morning, together with an additional paper[1] from Mr. Peel to the Chancellor.

He trusts these papers fully justify what passed in conversation this morning with your Majesty before he had received either paper, as they undoubtedly very accurately represent what Mr. P. had stated to the Chancellor.

He humbly adds an expression of anxiety that these papers may be returned to him.

1307 THE EARL OF ELDON *to the* KING

Tuesday Morning [10 April 1827].

THE LORD CHANCELLOR has received His Majesty's message to wait upon him at eleven o'clock: he regrets that he is unable to obey the commands, with which he has been honored, in consequence of being compelled, by the standing orders of the House of Lords, to be upon the Woolsack this day, hearing causes from ten o'clock till the evening, when the ordinary business of the House begins, and, there being at present no Deputy Speaker, he cannot leave the House.[2]

1 Peel's two letters to Eldon, 9 April, are in *Twiss*, II, 589–92.
2 The King saw Peel that afternoon. The interview failing to produce an arrangement, the King sent for Canning and commissioned him "to prepare with as little delay as possible a plan for the reconstruction of the Administration". The phrasing was ambiguous, but Canning took it to mean that he was to be Prime Minister.

1308 THE EARL OF ELDON *to the* KING

[11th April 1827.]

THE LORD CHANCELLOR offers his humble duty to your Majesty. He found it impracticable to wait upon your Majesty yesterday at the hour your Majesty mentioned. In obedience to your commands he has called at a very early hour this morning—in his way to the Court, the business of which, necessary to be finished to-day & to-morrow, obliges him to be there *very early,* and he humbly awaits your Majesty's commands.

1309 VISCOUNT MELVILLE *to the* KING

Admiralty, 12th April 1827.

LORD MELVILLE has the honor humbly to solicit that your Majesty will be graciously pleased to allow of his retirement from the situation which he now holds at the Admiralty. He would not venture to intrude that request if he could flatter himself that his longer continuance in office, under present circumstances, would be attended with advantage to your Majesty's service. Lord Melville however most earnestly beseeches your Majesty to beleive that he can never forget the unvaried favor & gracious kindness with which your Majesty has been pleased on all occasions to accept his humble endeavours to promote your Majesty's service, & to anticipate, as far as might be in his power, your Majesty's wishes & commands.[1]

1310 THE MARQUIS OF LONDONDERRY *to the* MARQUIS CONYNGHAM

Holdernesse House, April 12th 1827.

IN obedience to your Lordship's communication I waited again this day at St. James's when I was inform'd His Majesty could not see me, but that he would be graciously pleas'd to send for me tomorrow or as soon as convenient.

My object in addressing your Lordship is to request of your Lordship to remind His Majesty of his kind intention of granting me an audience,

1 On the 7th Melville had told Arbuthnot, who passed on the information to Peel and Wellington, that, although he supported Catholic emancipation, he never would belong to any Government in which his anti-Catholic colleagues were not included. The resignation of all the anti-Catholics in the Cabinet (Wellington, Peel, Westmorland, Bathurst, Eldon, and Bexley, who subsequently withdrew his resignation) therefore caused Melville too to retire.

as I feel at this moment it is particularly important to me to see His Majesty as connected with the situation in which I am placed.[1]

The Duke of Wellington to the King, 12 April 1827. (*W.N.D.* iii, 630–1.)
The King to the Duke of Wellington, 13 April 1827. (*W.N.D.* iii, 631.)
The Marquis of Londonderry to the King, 13 April 1827. (*W.N.D.* iii, 635, where it is dated the 12th. The MS. shows the date corrected from the 12th to the 13th.)

1311 ROBERT PEEL *to the* KING

Whitehall, April 13, 1827.

MR. PEEL presents his humble duty to your Majesty and has the honour respectfully to solicit your Majesty's commands with respect to the mode in which it may be most agreeable to your Majesty that Mr. Peel should deliver up the seals of the Home Department. Mr. Peel trusts that he may be permitted humbly to assure your Majesty that he retires from your Majesty's service with deep regret, and with a very grateful recollection of the kindness and confidence with which your Majesty has uniformly treated him.

If it shall be deemed of the slightest advantage to your Majesty's service that Mr. Peel shall continue to conduct the current business of the Home Department until your Majesty's commands with respect to his successor shall be signified, his humble services are entirely at your Majesty's disposal.

Every information and assistance which Mr. Peel may be enabled to give to his successor in respect to the pending business of the office, shall be given by him with the greatest cheerfulness.

1312 THE DUKE OF MONTROSE *to the* KING

London, April Fourteen 1827.

YOUR MAJESTY having been graciously pleased to fix on your Majesty's humble & dutiful servant for the head of your Majesty's Household it appears to me, that I ought not to take any measure of consequence, without first imparting my intention to your Majesty.

The Lord Chancellor Eldon, the Duke of Wellington, Earl Bathurst and Mr. Peel, not venturing to continue their services to your Majesty, under the present selection of your Majesty's chief Minister, it becomes

1 Londonderry now threw up his Household post of Lord of the Bedchamber.

me to state to your Majesty, that it is my intention to resign to your Majesty's Minister, the situation of Lord Chamberlain of your Majesty's Household, as the great officers of your Majesty's Household ought to be firm supporters of the measures of your Majesty's Minister.

Your Majesty's gracious favor so often shown to the Duke of Montrose must have left a grateful impression on the mind of your Majesty's dutiful subject & servant, but he proudly claims upon higher principles, a devoted attachment to your Majesty's person and Royal family.

1313 THE MARQUIS OF GRAHAM *to the* KING

London, April 14th 1827.

YOUR MAJESTY having been most graciously pleased yourself to appoint your Majesty's humble & dutiful servant one of your Majesty's Household, I feel it particularly incumbent upon me previous to my offering to your Majesty's Minister my resignation of that situation, to inform your Majesty of that determination.

Conceiving that the officers of your Majesty's Household, ought to give a firm & decided support to the measures of your Majesty's Government, I think it necessary though with deep regret, to offer my resignation of the situation I now hold, as I look upon it as absolutely impossible for me, to hold out to myself, any expectation, of being able to give that support, to the measures which probably will be put in execution by the Minister whom your Majesty has been pleased to select.

1314 THE DUKE OF DORSET *to the* KING

[*c*. 14 April 1827.]

IT is with feelings of deep and unfeigned regret that I approach your Majesty on this occasion. A strong sense of gratitude for the many favors your Majesty has been graciously pleased to bestow upon me, and the warmest attachment (if I may be so allowed to express myself) to your Majesty's person, render the step I find myself compelled to take, unusually painful; but as I have the misfortune to differ on some momentous questions, with the person whom your Majesty has thought proper to place at the head of your Government, I feel that I might in some degree embarrass his Administration were I to retain a place, which on constitutional as well as on other grounds ought to be filled by one fully prepared to support it. I must therefore humbly request that your Majesty will be graciously pleased to accept my resignation of the office which I have had the honor to fill in your Majesty's Household.[1]

1315 MAJOR-GENERAL VIVIAN *to* SIR WILLIAM KNIGHTON

St. James Palace, 10 o'Clock a.m.
15 Ap! 1827.

I CALLED thus early in the hope of communicating to you the result of my mission.

I returned at one o'clock this morn^g with Lord A[nglesey]: ALL WELL. He had a fortnight since in reply to a letter from Lord Londonderry *declined* joining the Party then forming against Mr. Canning—so that he is quite at liberty and quite prepared to do every thing to support His Majesty (for whose kindness he feels most gratefull) & His Majesty's Government. He feels some alarm at the thoughts of being obliged to speak in the House, & he is not quite at ease on the Corn question on which his opinions differ from the late Administration in some measure, but His Majesty will no doubt hear all this from himself. I mention it to you in order that you may if you think proper hint it to the King. Lord A's dread of being called on to speak is so great that he seems to think he might do better in Ireland than at the Ordnance. Of course you will not in any way notice to him my having touched on these subjects, but I think it is right that these feelings should be known in order as I said before that His Majesty may be prepared on them.[2]

I see by the papers this mor^g that some of His Majesty's Household are going. Should an opportunity offer of giving Lord Uxbridge[3] the appointment of Lord of the Bed Chamber or something of that sort, I think it would be most gratefully received & be very acceptable for Lord U. is very poor. I wish you fully to understand I mention this entirely from myself, Lord Anglesey never breathed a syllable on the subject.

1 "The King", said Greville on 17 June, "was very civil to the Duke of Dorset, and repeatedly told him that what had passed would make no difference in their private friendship."

2 Lord Anglesey's appointment as Master General of the Ordnance was gazetted on the 30th. "Whether Lord Anglesey is to be in the Cabinet is doubtful", wrote Stapleton (Canning's private secretary) on the 27th. "It just depends on his vote on Corn, on which he entertains some doubts." The Corn Bill had not yet been introduced into the House of Lords. (*Stapleton*, II, 309.)

3 Henry Paget, second Marquis of Anglesey (1797–1869); succeeded his father, 1854.

[April 1827.]

WOULD the King be pleased to mention to the Archbishop of Canterbury the infinite importance of *Lord Manners's* continuing another six months at least in Ireland, & to induce his Grace to write in that sense, (simultaneously with His Majesty) to Lord Manners?[1]

1317 LORD MANNERS *to the* ARCHBISHOP OF CANTERBURY

Dublin, April 18th 1827.

HIS MAJESTY's sentiments on the Roman Catholick question, so unreservedly declared to you & the Bishop of London, are most satisfactory & gratifying; and perfectly consistent with all I have ever heard His Majesty express on that subject. I think it very important that those sentiments shd be known here, not only to remove the doubts upon the minds of some of the Protestant supporters of the King's Government, but to obviate the expectation that has been erroneously raised & circulated, of this change in the Cabinet, having arisen from an alteration in His Majesty's opinion on that most important subject.

With respect to His Majesty's wish that I should continue in office for another year, and which I am bound to consider as a command, I hope that I shall appear as complying with that command substantially, and in such manner as to accomplish every object the King has in view, by not resigning the Great Seal sooner than the end of October or beginning of November; (i.e.) not until the end of this Session, and the Summer following—this arrangement, I hope, will afford abundant opportunity to His Majesty to decide upon my successor, without inconvenience or embarrassment.

Engaged as His Majesty must be upon matters of the highest importance, I think it wd be less interruption, and more convenient to the King, that you shd make this communication, than that I should trouble His Majesty with a letter; and therefore (if you see nothing disrespectful in it) I would be greatly obliged to you, to present my humble duty to

1 The King and Liverpool, it was believed, had arranged that the Lord Lieutenant and the Lord Chancellor of Ireland should be changed at the end of the 1827 parliamentary Session. Lord Manners, the Archbishop's brother, had, indeed, wished to retire whilst Liverpool was Prime Minister, and his determination to do so was strengthened when Canning kissed hands. The King, said Canning, "wrote to Lord Manners not to resign in a hurry, because His Majesty apprehended that he might otherwise be instigated to strike with the rest of the Ultras, and so anticipate the natural time of his removal, and give to the renovation of the Irish Government the air of an angry breaking-up, which of all things the King wished to avoid." (*Wellesley Papers*, II, 162.)

His Majesty and express in the strongest terms, how much I am impressed by His Majesty's kindness to me, and the confidence he has reposed in me; and that I most anxiously hope, that what I have suggested will meet His Majesty's approbation.

Sir Herbert Taylor to the King, 18 April 1827. (*W.N.D.* III, 647–9.)

1318 GEORGE CANNING *to the* KING

F.O., Apr. 24. 1827. 11 p.m.

MR. CANNING presents his humble & affectionate duty to your Majesty.

He has appointed the Duke of Devonshire to attend your Majesty tomorrow at *two* o'clock; unless his Grace should receive a summons for an earlier hour. The Duke of Devonshire is heart-broken at the prospect of *not* entering into your Majesty's service: but Mr. Canning fears, nevertheless, that the Duke will not venture to act without Lord Lansdowne—unless your Majesty's authority should overbear his present apprehensions.

Mr. Canning ventures to flatter himself that your Majesty will be not displeased to hear that, if the negotiation with Lord Lansdowne goes off (as Mr. Canning conceives it will) Mr Wm. Lamb will not refuse to undertake the office of Home Secretary of State. The Cabinet is therefore, in any event, completed.[1]

1 The resignation of half the Cabinet compelled Canning to seek assistance from the Whigs. They reluctantly waived their demand that Catholic emancipation should be taken up as a Cabinet question, but stood out for a "Catholic" government in Ireland, which the King would not in principle concede. Their negotiations with Canning resulted in a provisional agreement on the 27th. The Catholic question was to remain, as in Liverpool's time, an open question; as it was impossible to find an anti-Catholic to take Goulburn's place as Irish Secretary, the King was obliged to agree to the appointment of the "Catholic" William Lamb. One or two Whigs were consequently enabled to take office immediately, the Duke of Devonshire becoming Lord Chamberlain and Scarlett Attorney-General; and it was arranged that as soon as the difficulty about the other Irish appointments was surmounted, Lansdowne and Carlisle should enter the Cabinet, and Tierney be given office. The "Catholic" Wellesley remained in Dublin for the time being.

F.O., Apr. 26. 1827. ½ p.m. [*sic*].

MR. CANNING with his most humble duty to your Majesty humbly lays before your Majesty the answer which he has received from Lord Lansdowne to the letter which Mr. Canning addressed to his Lordship at Bowood the day before yesterday.[1]

Mr. Canning does not venture to give a positive construction to this letter, until he shall have seen Lord Lansdowne, & the Duke of Devonshire; who have announced their intention of calling upon him this morning.

They are this instant arrived.

1320   GEORGE CANNING *to the* KING

St. James's Palace, Apr. 26 [a slip for 25], 1827.
½ p 4 p.m.

MR. CANNING presents his most humble duty to your Majesty.

He has absolutely *no occasion* to trouble your Majesty to-day.

Having already[2] apprized your Majesty of *Mr. Scarlett's* acceptance of the Attorney Generalship, *independently* of Lord Lansdowne's determination, (whatever that may be) he has now only to add that he has obtained *Mr. Wm. Lamb's* promise to take the Home Secretaryship, if Lord Lansdowne shall finally refuse it.

Lord Lansdowne is expected in town tonight.

Mr. Canning ardently wishes your Majesty success in the work in which your Majesty is now engaged. He has reason to believe that the

1 In his letter of the 24th Canning explained to Lansdowne why he could not accept the stipulation that the Irish Secretary should be a pro-Catholic. "After the confiding and generous manner in which the King has sanctioned the proposed distribution of Cabinet offices [ten 'Catholics' to two 'Protestants'] I could not bring myself to submit to His Majesty any limitation of his royal discretion upon a point (and the only one) which his Majesty has specially reserved." Canning expressed a hope that though Lansdowne himself had declined the office of Home Secretary, his self-denial need not extend to his friends, and that the Duke of Devonshire and Scarlett would be willing to accept the posts of Lord Chamberlain and Attorney-General. Replying next day from Bowood, Lansdowne said that if the proposed appointment of William Lamb as Irish Secretary were considered as a permanent appointment, the difficulty he felt "on this branch of the subject" would be in a great degree removed. The suggestion that some of his friends should take office involved "mixed considerations of too delicate a nature to be committed to paper" and he reserved this question for oral discussion. (Harewood MSS.)

2 In a letter to Sir William Knighton, dated 11.45 a.m., 25 April. Canning said in another letter of the 25th that Lord Fitzwilliam approved of Scarlett's acceptance and would return him again for Peterborough. (Harewood MSS.)

Duke of Devonshire, if he does not yield to-day to your Majesty's wishes, will at least not give a *final answer* in the negative.

Mr. Canning has just seen Lord Fife, & persuaded him to take his Peerage at once—leaving the disputed point to be settled hereafter.[1]

1321 GEORGE CANNING *to the* KING

F.O., April 27, 1827.

MR. CANNING presents his most humble duty to your Majesty; and has the satisfaction of acquainting your Majesty that Lord Lansdowne has not only released the Duke of Devonshire but has earnestly exhorted his Grace to obey, without further delay, your Majesty's commands.

Lord Lansdowne went from Mr. Canning to call upon the Duke; but as Mr. Canning just learns by a note from Ld. L.— did not find him at home.

Mr. Canning writes to the Duke, to desire his Grace to wait upon your Majesty as soon as he has seen Lord Lansdowne.

1322 GEORGE CANNING *to the* KING

Downing Street, May 1, 1827. 10 P.M.

MR. CANNING humbly reports to your Majesty, that upon the motion for a new writ for Mr. Sturges Bourne,[2] Mr. Peel took the opportunity of making a vindication of his retirement; which was upon the whole very satisfactory as to himself, and perfectly respectful towards your Majesty. For his colleagues he was generally thought to be not quite so successful.

Mr. Peel was followed by Mr. Duncombe, the member for Yorkshire, by Sir Thomas Lethbridge[3] & by Mr. Dawson;[4] who pronounced panegyricks upon Mr. Peel & endeavoured to raise an apprehension in the House that the Catholick question would be made a Cabinet question & forced forward upon the country. This apprehension was combated (not very judiciously) by Sir Francis Burdett—but with good effect by Mr. Brougham (who declared that he afforded *his* support to the Government, with the perfect knowledge that the Catholick question was *not to*

---

1 The Earl of Fife was now given a Barony in the peerage of the United Kingdom, and was reappointed a Lord of the Bedchamber later in the year.
2 William Sturges-Bourne (1769–1845), who succeeded Peel as Home Secretary. He was one of Canning's closest friends, but disliked office and accepted the seals of the Home Department only at Canning's earnest request and as a temporary appointment.
3 Tory M.P. for Somersetshire.
4 George Robert Dawson, Tory M.P. for Londonderry County, and Under-Home Secretary from January 1822 to April 1827. He married Peel's sister Mary in 1816.

be a Cabinet question)—and Mr. Canning humbly hopes that it was effectually removed by his own speech (which closed the debate) & in which Mr. Canning took occasion to read to the House the *written compact* of the Cabinet on this subject; & to declare his determination to respect the feelings of your Majesty, & not to agitate those of the people of England upon it—a declaration which Mr. Canning flatters himself was received with confidence as well as approbation by the House.

1323 GEORGE CANNING *to the* KING

Downing Street, May 3, 1827.
½ p 10 p.m.

MR. CANNING humbly reports to your Majesty, that the time of the House of Commons has been wasted this evening in an unprofitable debate raised by Mr. Dawson (brother in law of Mr. Peel) upon a question put by him to Mr. Canning, as to the filling up of the offices still vacant. Mr. Canning to the question whether the arrangement for filling up of those offices was in progress, answered "Yes"; but declined any further explanation. Whereupon Mr. Dawson launched forth into a violent attack upon the Administration, and upon the Opposition for coming to their support—concluding with a motion for the "patent constituting the Judge Advocate"[1]—as a cover for the debate which his speech was evidently intended to provoke.

Mr. Dawson was answered by Mr. Brougham in a speech of more than ordinary force; and one as remarkable for the prudence with which it steered clear of all inconvenient topicks, as for the clearness with which it expressed his determination to support the Government. After Mr. Brougham's speech Mr. Canning interfered to endeavour to bring the House back to the real business of the day (a motion for a committee on the shipping trade) which Mr. Dawson's factious motion had interrupted. Mr. Peel rose, avowedly to support this proposition of Mr. Canning's but instead of confining his speech to that object, suffered himself to be drawn on into a violent attack upon the new supporters of the Ministry, in which he certainly threw away all the moderation which he had professed & to a great degree preserved on the first night of the meeting; & which produced from Sir Francis Burdett a speech full of *Tory* sentiments, delivered with the greatest animation & effect.

It was highly amusing & edifying to observe this transformation of character.

1 James Abercromby's appointment as Judge-Advocate-General was gazetted on the 17th.

After Sir Francis Burdett, Sir Edward Knatchbull indulged in a furious declamation against both the Government *and* it's supporters; which Mr. Canning felt it absolutely necessary to notice with some part of the severity which it deserved—and to declare that *the standard of Opposition is now openly raised.* "Better this than a continuance of hollow pretences of unreal neutrality."

The House received this declaration in a manner which leaves no apprehension of the want of zealous support. The night has decided many wavering Tories.

Lord John Russell followed Mr. Canning—disclaiming Parliamentary Reform to which Mr. Canning had taken an opportunity of announcing his unaltered & uncompromising opposition, as well as to the motion for the repeal of the Test Act.

Sir George Warrender[1] concluded the debate with an expression of his determination to give a constant attendance in Parl[t] until the factious spirit of the new Opposition should be put down—a sentiment only important from the manner in which it was generally received.

This unexpected debate having now lasted till $\frac{1}{2}$ p 9—it was felt to be too late to begin upon the business of the day—which is therefore deferred till Monday.

Mr. Canning learnt in the House from what appears good authority, that the Roman Cath. Association in Ireland has adjourned itself *sine die*.

1324 GEORGE CANNING *to the* KING

Downing Street, May 4, 1827.

MR. CANNING humbly reports to your Majesty that, there being no publick business in the House of Commons to-day, he thought it better to keep himself out of the way of impertinent questions by not going down to the House.

He learns that the only occurrences of the evening were a foolish & furious ebullition from Sir Th. Lethbridge; which produced nothing but laughter; and a very violent little speech from Lord Castlereagh,[2] which had no effect whatever.

Mr. Canning's object & wish is to force the *new* Opposition to come to a regular attack (such as he understands has been announced in the House of Lords) when he shall be able to meet them on a fair field; & (he hopes) to give a good account of them to your Majesty.

1 M.P. for Westbury, a Commissioner of the India Board since 1822, and a Canningite. Succeeded his father as fourth Baronet in 1799. (1782–1849.)

2 Frederick William Robert Stewart, son of the third Marquis of Londonderry, and M.P. for Downshire. (1805–1872.) Succeeded as fourth Marquis, 1854.

St. James's Palace, May 4th 1827.

I WISH you to read that part in the report of the newspapers which is said to be the speech of the Earl of Mansfield[1] the other night, which I have mark'd with my pen, & which implies a *direct calumny* upon *my Protestant faith, & upon my honour*. *This, I* do not *choose* to pass unnotic'd, & your Grace, *is my best* testimony, that I do not deserve as King of this country, this wicked attempt to misrepresent & falsify both my principles & conduct to my Protestant subjects. Your Grace will make Lord Mansfield acquainted with these truths, in any manner that you may think proper.

1326 GEORGE CANNING *to the* KING

Downing Street, May 5, 1827.

MR. CANNING presents his most humble & affectionate duty to your Majesty, and, having reflected, since he left your Majesty's presence, on the admirable letter to the Archbishop of Canterbury, which your Majesty was graciously pleased to communicate to him, he ventures humbly to submit to your Majesty whether, if the Archbishop should not already have read, or shewn that letter to the nobleman, for whose admonition it is intended, it might not be adviseable that such admonition should be conveyed rather by the Archbishop himself—*verbally* stating what your Majesty's feelings were, as expressed to *him* the Archbishop.

Mr. Canning suggests this from the apprehension that the actual communication of a letter from the Sovereign to a Peer of Parliament touching his Parliamentary conduct, (however justly & *personally* offensive to the Sovereign) might, possibly, be represented in Parliament as an interference with the freedom of Parliamentary debate.

Mr. Canning humbly trusts that your Majesty will not mistake the motives of the suggestion, which he presumes to offer to your Majesty; nor doubt of his readiness to *stand* by your Majesty, if any such attack shall be *made*.

George Canning to the Duke of Wellington, 5 May 1827. (*W.N.D.* IV, 16–20.)
The Duke of Wellington to George Canning, 6 May 1827. (*W.N.D.* IV, 20–6.)

1 William Murray, third Earl of Mansfield (1777–1840). In his speech in the House of Lords on 2 May he implied that had George III then been on the throne he would, as a staunch "Protestant", never have consented to the formation of a Cabinet in which "Catholics" were in an overwhelming majority. And he pointed out that George IV had consented to these appointments after he had assured the Archbishop of Canterbury of his "determination to exclude from a preponderance in his councils those who supported a measure which he could not conscientiously approve". (*Parl. Deb.* N.S. XVII, 470.)

Downing Street, May 8, 1827. 12 p.m.

MR. CANNING humbly reports to your Majesty, that the House of Commons has been chiefly occupied tonight in discussing the Report of a Committee on the Penrhyn election:[1] the debate, though it has lasted so long, contained nothing worthy of your Majesty's particular notice.

There was no previous battle to-day; though one of the brothers of Mr. Peel,—Jonathan[2]—has not yet spoken. But there seems to be a pretty clear understanding in both Houses that there is to be no more violence, at least for the present. It has only done good to the Government, & harm to the assailants.

1328 GEORGE CANNING *to the* KING

Downing Street, May 11, 1827.
½ p 11 p.m.

MR. CANNING humbly reports to your Majesty that the business of the House of Commons, (which was to vote estimates in a Committee of Supply) was preceded this evening, as usual by a preliminary discussion on the state of the Administration; begun (nearly as usual) by Sir Thomas Lethbridge.

In the course of this discussion several persons declared their support of the Administration, who had not spoken before; among them Sir John Sebright,[3] Mr. Wodehouse[4] (M.P. for Norfolk) Lord Tavistock (with some little qualification) Sir Joseph Yorke,[5] Lord Clifton.[6] No *new* persons declared against it, and the tone of the new Opposition was greatly moderated—particularly that of Mr. Peel himself, who disclaimed hostility, and denied concert with *any* Opposition. It is evident that some admonitions have reached the seceders from their friends out of doors & in the country; which lead them to believe that the disgusting violence with which they set out does harm only to themselves.

Notice of a motion on the Administration was given by Mr. Beaumont[7] (heretofore member for Northumberland) ; which Mr. Canning

1 See No. 1337.   2 M.P. for Norwich. [1799–1879.]

3 M.P. for Hertfordshire, and an independent country gentleman. (1767–1846.)

4 Edmond Wodehouse, an independent member.

5 Tory M.P. for Reigate and an anti-Catholic. (1768–1831.)

6 Whig M.P. for Canterbury. Succeeded his father as fifth Earl of Darnley in 1831. (1795–1835.)

7 Thomas Wentworth Beaumont, M.P. for Stafford in the Parliament of 1826–30; formerly a Tory, at this time a Whig, and later a Radical. (1792–1848.)

hailed with gratitude, declaring that he would henceforth answer *no* questions, in preliminary debates; but would reserve himself entirely for the day of Mr. Beaumont's motion.

Mr. Canning abstained (though he must confess not without great difficulty) from any allusion to what had passed in the House of Lords.[1]

After this discussion, the House proceeded to the estimates, in which considerable progress has been made—*including* the vote for Windsor Castle.

1329 FRANCIS LEGATT CHANTREY *to* SIR WILLIAM KNIGHTON

Belgrave Place, 14 May 1827.

THE dilemma in which I am placed respecting His Majesty's statue and my anxiety to do that which is right must be my excuse for thus addressing you.

I am under an engagement with the committee at Brighton to complete the statue of His Majesty in bronze by the 12th of August and fearing that His Majesty may desire to see the model, I have on that account delayed to proceed with the mould. You will feel that I cannot delay it much longer if I am to complete my engagement within the time.

As there is no possibility of placing the statue in St. James's Palace for His Majesty's examination without doing my work the greatest injustice; may I request you will ascertain if His Majesty will be graciously pleased to allow me to place it in the Grand Staircase in Windsor Castle for inspection, after I have made the mould for casting the bronze.

This arrangement will enable me to fulfil my engagement with the committee—if no unforeseen accident occur—and also afford me the advantage of exhibiting my model in a light equally favorable with that of my own studio, and surrounded by architecture of proper dimensions to enable me to determine a most material point—the size.

1330 SIR HENRY TORRENS *to the* KING

Horse Guards, 18th May 1827.

THE ADJUTANT GENERAL humbly submits to His Majesty a return of the recruiting of the army for the year 1826—which amounts to 17,210 men; and also a return of the casualties for the same year, which

1 Lord Grey, the leader of a small group of anti-coalition Whigs, made a violent attack on Canning in the House of Lords on the 10th, and denounced the Coalition as unprincipled.

amounts to 12,300 men. The number of men recruited beyond what appears necessary to fill up the casualties, have been applied to fill up the establishments to the last augmentation, and may also be applied to casualties supposed to have taken place during the last four months of the year in the East Indies, of which the details have not been received.

The Adjutant General is now directing the exertions of the recruiting districts to an average scale of 1000 men per month, so as to provide 12,000 men for the current year, which it is calculated, will be sufficient to supply the numbers at present wanting to complete certain regiments, and the *probable* number of casualties of the present year, as shewn by the accompanying memorandum.

Abstract of the Casualties of the Army in the Year 1826

	Deaths	Discharges	Desertions	Total
Cavalry	284	633	151	1068
Foot Guards	138	411	70	619
Infantry	3651	3875	2320	9846
Total	4073	4919	2541	11533
R¹ African Colonial Corps	289	126	32	447
West India Regts. Cape and Ceylon Corps Malta Fencibles, and Newfoundland Veteran Companies.	91	211	18	320
Total Colonial Corps	380	337	50	767
General Total	4453	5256	2591	12300

Adjutant General's Office,
3rd May 1827.

Downing Street, May 19, 1827.

MR. CANNING presents his most humble duty to your Majesty; & humbly lays before your Majesty a list of the persons who are to be introduced to your Majesty before the Council tomorrow, on acceptance of office, or promotion.

Lord Lansdowne—a seat in the Cabinet.[1]

Lord Carlisle[2]—1st Comm[issione]r of Woods & Forests. ⎫
Mr. Tierney[3]—the Mint. ⎬ With seats in the Cabinet.
⎭

Mr. Abercrombie[4]—Judge Advocate.

Sir James Macdonald[5]—Comm[r] of the India Board.

Lord Lansdowne requests a few minutes audience of your Majesty. Mr. Abercrombie is to be sworne of the Privy Council: as is (with your Majesty's gracious permission) Mr Wilmot Horton, Under Secrety in Lord Goderich's department; the peculiarity of whose situation in the House of Commons, as doing all the business of that department, in the absence of his principal, distinguishes him from other Under Secretaries of State; & who had moreover a positive promise of promotion to a Privy Counsellor's *office*; which the late changes have made it impossible to fulfil; & in lieu of the fulfilment of which he is content to accept this honour & to remain where he is.

1332 VISCOUNT GODERICH *to the* KING

Downing Street, May 21, 1827.

LORD GODERICH offers his humble duty to your Majesty, and begs leave to report to your Majesty what has passed this evening in the House of Lords.

Lord Harewood[6] put a question to the Bishop of London touching

1 It was arranged that he should succeed Sturges Bourne as Home Secretary at the close of the Session.

2 George Howard, sixth Earl of Carlisle (1773–1848). He was one of Canning's earliest friends, but a member of the Whig Party.

3 He had just refused the Governor-Generalship of Bengal.

4 James Abercromby, first Baron Dunfermline (1776–1858), the son of Sir Ralph Abercromby. He was a prominent member of the Lansdowne section of the Whig Party, and was Speaker of the House of Commons, 1835–39.

5 M.P. for Calne, one of Lansdowne's pocket boroughs. He succeeded his father as second Baronet in 1826. (1784–1832.)

6 Henry Lascelles, second Earl of Harewood (1767–1841); succeeded his father in 1820.

certain statements which had appeared in some of the newspapers, and which represented the Bishop to have communicated to the clergy of his diocese certain communications which had passed between your Majesty and his Lordship. The Bishop was called upon to state whether that account was accurate, and if accurate, whether he had any authority to make the statement in question.

The Bishop of London replied that the account published was substantially correct, and was proceeding to answer the second part of the question, when he was interrupted by Lord Spencer, who questioned the propriety of asking or of answering any such interrogatives. Lord Eldon then objected to any reference to your Majesty's name & opinions. Lord Lansdowne also protested against such a course, and insisted upon the obvious impropriety of making use of your Majesty's name in that manner. He was followed by Lord Grey, who whilst he concurred in the objections which were urged against the putting and answering such questions, suggested that the whole matter was of a nature to justify a specific motion in the House.

Lord Harrowby argued against the reasoning of those who considered that the House ought to take up the question at all, and he very forcibly put the impropriety of introducing your Majesty's name in debate.

Lord Rolle[1] gave a contingent notice of a motion upon the subject: but nothing definitive was fixed.

Lord Goderich humbly asks your Majesty's pardon for troubling your Majesty with this detail: but he has thought himself bound in duty to your Majesty to communicate what has passed.[2]

The Duke of Wellington to Sir Herbert Taylor, 21 May 1827. (*W.N.D.* IV, 34–5.)
The King to the Duke of Wellington, 21 May 1827. (*W.N.D.* IV, 35.)
George Canning to the Duke of Wellington, 10 p.m. 21 May 1827. (*W.N.D.* IV, 35; *Stapleton*, pp. 596–7. Two letters.)
The Duke of Wellington to George Canning, 22 May 1827. (*W.N.D.* IV, 36.)
The Duke of Wellington to the King, 22 May 1827. (*W.N.D.* IV, 36–7.)

1 John, Baron Rolle (1750–1842), a zealous Pittite in his House of Commons' days. Peerage, 1796.

2 At a public dinner of the clergy of London on 8 May the Bishop of London declared that whilst the ministerial changes were in progress the King sent for him and the Archbishop of Canterbury and stated to them that his opinions on the Catholic question were still those of his late revered father; that he took precisely the same view of the Coronation Oath which his father and the Duke of York had taken, and that nothing could shake or alter his opinions on that momentous question.

Downing Street, May 22, 1827.

MR. CANNING presents his humble duty to your Majesty: & humbly lays before your Majesty a letter which he has received this day from Lord Wellesley, reporting the progress of the negotiation for Lord Norbury's retirement from the Chief Justiceship of the Common Pleas in Ireland.

It is obvious that Lord Norbury knows the full value of that retirement, & is resolved to make the best market of it that he can.

Mr. Canning was at first somewhat startled at Lord Norbury's proposition: but upon more dispassionate reflection, and after consultation with the Lord Chancellor, he feels it his duty not to withhold from your Majesty his humble opinion that, under the peculiar circumstances of the case, there are perhaps sufficient grounds for taking it into consideration.

1st. It is of immense importance that Lord Plunket should be established in the Common Pleas, before the vacancy occurs in the Chancellorship of Ireland.[1] His existence out of office would greatly embarrass that arrangement.

2dly. Lord Norbury, old as he is, is in robust health; & may yet set the Government at defiance for many years—unless the Government were prepared to do, what *ought* perhaps, in flagrant instances of judicial incapacity, to be done (but what the feelings of every man would revolt at doing)—to bring forward that incapacity, in Parliament, as a reason for removing Lord Norbury *by Address*. This proceeding has never yet been resorted to—in any instance—though sometimes threatened; & it might lead from one instance to another—to that of poor Ld Stowell, for example—who is, Mr. Canning believes, older than Lord Norbury; & in point of physical strength much more impaired.

3dly. Lord Norbury's incapacity is of that doubtful & desultory sort, which it would be very difficult to establish by satisfactory proof—to his prejudice—in any inquiry that must precede a Bill: while on the other hand it is such as exposes, by his continuance on the Bench, the administration of publick justice in Ireland to ridicule & contempt.

4thly. The *remainder* to Lord Norbury's second son appeared at first sight to Mr. Canning a *strong* proposal: but as the peerage must *otherwise* descend to the *eldest* son, without any special grant; & as the eldest son is represented to be an idiot, & as it appears to Mr. Canning (after

1 In April Plunket had been raised to the peerage and offered the office of Master of the Rolls, but the opposition of the English Bar to the appointment of an Irish lawyer was so strong that he resigned almost immediately, Sir John Leach succeeding him. Plunket was appointed Chief Justice of the Common Pleas in Ireland. See No. 1343.

some recent exhibitions in the House of Lords) peculiarly desirable to avoid encreasing, among their Lordships, the number of specimens of irregular understanding, in another generation, perhaps the trans-mission of the Peerage (if granted) to the younger son of Lord Norbury, would be as much an escape from a difficulty, as an extension of a favour.

Under all these circumstances, & with a view to all these considera-tions of publick advantage on the one side, & publick inconvenience on the other, Mr. Canning (with the concurrence of the Lord Chancellor) ventures humbly to submit to your Majesty an opinion (not made up without anxious deliberation) that it might be expedient to authorize Lord Wellesley to close with Lord Norbury's terms, if (after a new trial) he finds it impracticable to obtain the resignation by an advance in the *Irish* Peerage.[1]

It cannot be necessary to state to your Majesty that Lord Norbury is *Protestantissimus*.

George Canning to the King, 25 May 1827 (two letters). [*Stapleton*, II, 314–15.]

1334 LORD LYNDHURST *to* SIR WILLIAM KNIGHTON

[May 1827.]

I FORGOT to tell you that I mentioned to Brougham a few days since at the Bar of the H. of Lds that I shd probably have a communication to make to him in a short time.[2] He understood my meaning and *then* said

1 Lord Norbury accepted an Irish Earldom, with remainder to his second son, Hector John Graham Toler (1781–1839), the elder son Daniel (d. 1832) succeeding to the Barony.

2 Brougham received a patent of precedency on Thursday, 31 May, and appeared in his silk gown before the Privy Council. (*The Times*, 2 June 1827.) He had talked the matter over with Canning at Gloucester Lodge on 26 May and wrote to him at great length next day, making a strong appeal for promotion on behalf of the other "hero of 1820", his friend Denman. "Probably", he said, "you are imperfectly acquainted with our professional etiquettes and feelings on the matter of rank. From accidental circumstances it had long ceased to be of any importance whatever to me, and nothing could have so well agreed with my individual interests as the Chancellor leaving things in their present condition—that is—making no promotion at all. My request has uniformly been, therefore, that he would promote nobody, as if he did, I should run a risk of competition on the Northern Circuit which I am now wholly free from—and as I saw that I might be forced to take rank if others did, in self defence—a step to be avoided both for public and private reasons, he felt unable to comply with this, and I then was desirous that he should leave out our circuit, in which case I might run the risk of letting men of other circuits go over my head. This too was found impossible, and *their* remonstrances to me at length drove me from that ground. I should in the opinion of some be seriously injured if not ruined on the Circuit which I now lead, were I to stand still and let others be promoted. My own opinion is different, but a risk undeniably there would be. . . ." (Harewood MSS.)

that which he repeated yesterday "I really wish for no change: I wish things to remain just as they are on the Northern Circuit &c &c." Nothing was then said about the INTRODUCTION. The objection on *this ground* is therefore a *pretence*.

In the course of the conversation which I had with him yesterday I observed that if he were appointed *alone* it would be too much like a *political* affair. He said it would be *so* considered if he were appointed with *others*. He appeared to wish for postponement. I collect from the whole of the conversation that he fears lest his political course should be supposed to have been influenced by his wish for professional promotion. He will *boast* therefore of the *refusal* &c. I think this will be his game and you must, if you can, prevent it. If he can persuade the two other candidates Pollock[1] and John Williams to consent that the promotion on their circuit should be deferred till the eve of the Assizes, or till next year, we can have no objection to such an arrangement. This may effect the object which he *appears* to have in view, viz. to free himself from ye imputation of being influenced by interested motives.

Pray burn this.

Insist that the waver of the *introduction* was never meant as a *condition*; it was merely a suggestion of what it was supposed might be not *unpleasant* to all parties. I had better see him again on this point.

1335 LORD LYNDHURST *to the* KING

[May 1827.]

THE LORD CHANCELLOR, offering his very humble duty to your Majesty, feels it incumbent upon him to be himself the first person to communicate to your Majesty what the Chancellor will not deny has been the effect of indiscretion and imprudence, which he will not represent, or presume to represent, as excused by what he considers as a breach of confidence by another person.

Dining a few days ago at Lord Londonderry's a conversation took place after dinner upon public matters between him & Mr. Littleton[2] the

1 Sir Jonathan Frederick Pollock, first Baronet (1783–1870), afterwards Chief Baron of the Exchequer. He took Silk in 1827.
2 Edward John Littleton, first Baron Hatherton (1791–1863). Irish Secretary, 1833–34; Peerage, 1835.

member for Staffordshire, &, among other matters, upon the language which Mr. Brougham & others had often held in the House of Commons respecting the Chancellor & silk gowns. In the course of that conversation the Chancellor was so imprudent, as to have mentioned to Mr. L., conceiving himself, and expressing himself to be conversing in perfect confidence (and indeed, whether that had been expressed or not, it should seem to him that no gentleman could, otherwise, understand, than that it belonged to such a conversation to be consider'd as confidential) that, whatever might be said or thought of the Chancellor, he did not object to Mr. B⁸ having a silk gown, if your Majesty thought proper to bestow it, and the Chancellor did state, in confidence, the terms, in which, upon one occasion, when Mr. B. had used very strong language about the Chancellor in the House of Commons, your Majesty had, when the Chancellor afterwards had the honor of seeing you, called his attention to what the newspaper had represented Mr. B. to have said in the House, and adverted to the conversation, which the Chancellor, on the preceding Sunday, had addressed to your Majesty respecting his having a silk gown, as affecting both him & other gentlemen at the Bar with respect to that subject. To the surprise of the Chancellor & to his regret, he, with great pain, learns from Lord Lauderdale, this morning, that Mr. L. has not thought himself bound to consider this as confidential, but has communicated it to Mr. Brougham: and the Chancellor has little reason to hope that Mr. B. will make a proper use of that communication with respect to the Chancellor, but (and that most deeply grieves him) with respect even to your Majesty.

The Chancellor regrets that he has not acted with the discretion, which ought to have governed him—nor will he, upon reflection, pretend that any reliance upon a confidence, called for & received, would form a sufficient apology for the indiscretion.

He has, therefore, deemed it to be his duty to inform your Majesty, (himself) of what has thus happened—to express his extreme & painful concern on account of it—and to throw himself upon your Majesty's goodness to determine whether that can induce your Majesty to overlook what the Chancellor himself feels on his part so incorrect, tho' nothing wrong was intended.

If any public notice is taken of this, the Chancellor proposes to say no more than that he will not open his lips as to any thing, that passed with any person, on such a subject, & that he leaves it to such a person to consider for himself what his conduct ought to be.

Berlin, May 25, 1827.

I TRUST that you have not misconstrued my long silence, which has not been caused either by neglect or forgetfulness, for God knows I have not ceased thinking of you day and night, knowing all the worry and anxiety of mind you must be labouring under, and I wish that I could persuade myself that it was at an end, but I fear there is still much to be done, at least so one must suppose from all that one reads in the newspapers, and knowing how much your time must be taken up, and having really nothing to write worth mentioning I determined to postpone addressing you untill I could write myself, not choosing, the little I had to say, to trust to another person, and *this* is the first essay I make.

I do most sincerely hope not only for the sake of England but I may say for all Europe that your health may not suffer from all you are going through, and as far as I can learn from Mary I hear that you are now in remarkably good health. It is impossible for any one who is not on the spot, or who is not perfectly informed of all that has passed to form a ripe judgement on the present state of things and therefore I shall abstain from saying any thing except, that I never was more aghast than upon hearing the first accounts which just arrived here while I was so very seriously ill,[1] and the Duchess, knowing how deeply interested I was upon all that was passing, kept back all the English newspapers and letters for upwards of five days. You can easily conceive what was my astonishment on hearing the first account and I need not say to you that every one here from highest to lowest was equally surprized. Certainly there never was a period in my opinion so critical for all Europe as the present one, for since the occurrences in Spain, Portugal and France the democrats are raising their hopes again.

You have been informed through Baron Reden, for I directed him to give you an account, of the most extraordinary visit we have had here of the Duke of Brunswick[2] and the most charitable thing one can say of him

---

1 He had undergone an operation for cataract.

2 Charles, Duke of Brunswick (1804–1873), elder son of Frederick William, the Duke who fell at Quatre Bras. By the will which he made shortly before his death, Frederick William appointed the Prince Regent guardian of his two sons. The character of the elder boy was so frivolous that George IV delayed putting the government of Brunswick into his hands until 1823—more than a year after he had attained the age of a Prince's majority. The Duke then issued a Proclamation containing a preposterous attack upon the King and Count Münster, to whom the administration of the Duchy had more particularly been confided. He charged them with attempting to prolong his minority beyond the legal age, with perverting his education, and with malversation in the government. He declared that as the last year of the minority had been illegal, the decrees and ordinances issued during that period were null and void, unless ratified by himself; and in particular he declined to recognise the decree granting the people of Brunswick constitutional government. Münster replied to these

is that he is *mad*, at least from beginning to end, his conduct, his manners, and even his dress were such that every one could form no other idea of him but that. Nota bene he did not know, when he was here that Schmidt Phiseldeck had gone to Hannover, and I understand from Frederica who sat next him at table at the King's Palace, that his language was so extraordinary and so indecorous respecting the treatment he had met with during his *minority*, that it came to high words between them, so much so that she told him she could not sit and hear all he said against you, but what can one expect from any one who has *no* religion, and who does not even believe in a future life, and turns every thing serious into ridicule. I for my part had not two words with him, having refused his visit and consequently never went to him; the more I can learn, I seriously now begin to believe that he is mad, and understand that his phisician is very much alarmed about him, as he has lost all sleep, and he is recommended now to go to Carlsbad. I had a long conversation a few days ago with the King here respecting him who is as much shocked as I am at his conduct. I am wicked enough to say that for the sake of his country, and his excellent subjects, I wish that he did something so outrageous that steps could be taken to confine him, for it is lamentable to see a Prince descended from such an antient House expose himself in the manner he does, not only by his language but by his conduct. His ill treatment to [*sic*] this unfortunate Schmidt Phiseldeck I can only consider as an insult to you and what makes the thing a thousand times worse is his base ingratitude, as certainly through you[r] good management during his minority not only the finances of the country, but his own private fortune as well as his brothers have been prodigiously encreased; it is a luck for him that I did *not* know while he

allegations in an outspoken pamphlet, "A Refutation of the calumnious charges hazarded by the Duke of Brunswick against his august guardian", which so infuriated the Duke that he sent Münster a challenge. It was calmly ignored. Schmidt Phiseldeck, one of the Brunswick Privy Councillors during the minority, was driven out of the Duchy by threats, and a reward was offered for his arrest. The Hanoverian Government took him into its service and refused to surrender him. George IV, as King of Hanover, applied to the German Diet to compel the Duke to make satisfaction for the insults which he had heaped upon him, and the Estates of the Duchy urged the Diet to recognise the Constitution which the King had given them. The Courts of Vienna and Berlin interposed their mediation to prevent the necessity of the Diet pronouncing a public sentence, but the Duke would listen to no mediation, and in 1829 the Diet decided every part of the cause against him. He was required to apologise to George IV and to recognise the new Constitution of April 1820. When he refused to obey the Diet's decree, the King of Saxony was ordered to occupy the Duchy with his troops; the Duke then gave way, but a few weeks later, in September 1830, his misconduct drove his subjects to rebellion. His brother William (1806–1884) was appointed to rule in his stead, at first as Regent, but in 1831, after Charles's formal deposition by the German Diet, as sovereign Duke. Most of the Duke of Cumberland's subsequent letters contain references to this quarrel between the Duke and his uncle.

was here, the conversation he had with the Duchess or else I should have had no hesitation in giving him as complete a dressing, as ever one gave another, and that too in the presence of all the R. family, who I am certain would have joined me. The younger brother I hardly ever see, in the beginning of his stay he used to call upon me, but after an explanation I had with him respecting the impropriety of his conduct in his military duties,[1] he has thought proper to withdraw himself from my house; the loss is *his* and not *mine*, for at least he was sure when here, of meeting nothing but *good* company. I have had *no* quarrel with him, and therefore only invite him on those occasions, when I cannot help it, I am told that he and his elder brother are at daggers drawn and the elder treated him devilishly ill and most unbrotherly when he went to Brunswick last summer, since which time a very great coolness has existed between them.

Today I am going to Charlottenburg to a family dinner, when the bride of Charles is to arrive;[2] tomorrow evening the marriage ceremony takes place, but I have excused myself with the King from attending the night fêtes, as I think it more prudent to avoid the danger of catching cold which I might be liable to in driving back from Charlottenburg at night which is good 4 English miles from hence, where naturally from the concourse of people the heat will be intense; this privation does not cost me much, but I own it required great resolution on my part to resist the attending the two days manœuvres of the 21st and 22d but I was afraid of the dust and heat which by all accounts must have been tremendous, so much so that I am sorry to say that *four* if not five men of the 1st and 2d Foot Guards died litterally from the heat, and many are now lying in the hospital in consequence of it, as yet I have not heard all the particulars as none of the Princes have been in Berlin since the manœuvres, but I hear the King is excessively angry and has issued very *strong* orders of enquiry into the causes of these melancholy events. I attended on Friday last the grand parade, and on Saturday the exercise of the corps and have the satisfaction to say that I could see every line of the different corps with my naked eye, as well as any other officer could, for I am become longsighted and at a distance can see every thing, but when reading or writing I must use preserving glasses. The Duchess desires her kindest regards and love.

George Canning to the King, 28 May 1827, 3 p.m. (*Stapleton*, pp. 599–600.)

1 He was in the Prussian Army.
2 Prince Frederick Charles Alexander (b. 1801), the third son of Frederick William III, married Princess Marie Louise Alexandrine (b. 1808), daughter of the Grand Duke Charles Frederick of Saxe-Weimar.

Downing Street, May 28, 1827.
$\frac{3}{4}$ p 11 p.m.

MR. CANNING humbly reports to your Majesty, that the House of Commons has been occupied tonight chiefly with a debate on the borough of Penrhyn; against which an election committee had reported a charge of bribery & corruption at the late election.

Mr. Legh Keck,[1] the chairman of the committee, brought in a Bill for throwing the borough open to the neighbouring hundreds; that is— admitting the inhabitants of those hundreds to vote, concurrently with the burgesses of Penrhyn.

To this proposition Lord John Russell moved an amendment for entirely disfranchising the borough, with the view of transferring the two members to some large unrepresented town—Manchester is the one in contemplation.

Mr. Canning, who thought the evidence sufficiently strong to justify the measure of punishment proposed by Mr. Legh Keck; but *not* to warrant total disfranchisement, supported Mr. *Keck's* Bill, but the House was in a much more *reforming* temper than Mr. Canning; & after a long & desultory debate, the total disfranchisement was carried on a division by 123 to 69—54.

The speakers in the debate were

× Mr. Legh Keck	o Lord Sandon[6]
o Lord John Russell[2]	o Mr. C. Wood[7]
× Mr. Barclay senior[3]	o Mr. Marshall
o Lord Milton	× Mr. W. Lamb
o Mr. Phillips[4]	o Mr. Ald. Wood
o Lord Althorp	o Lord Rancliffe[8]
o Mr. Warburton[5]	o Sir J. Newport
× Mr. Canning	o Mr. Brougham
o Mr. Hobhouse	o Mr. Cresset Pelham[9]
× Mr. W. W. Wynn	× Mr. Sturges Bourne.

1 M.P. for Leicestershire, and an independent country gentleman.
2 Afterwards Prime Minister and first Earl Russell (1792–1878).
3 David Barclay, one of the members for Penryn.
4 George Philips, M.P. for Wootton Bassett.
5 Henry Warburton, Radical member for Bridport (1784?–1858).
6 Dudley Ryder, second Earl of Harrowby (1798–1882). Canningite M.P. for Tiverton. Succeeded his father, 1847.
7 Charles Wood, M.P. for Grimsby.
8 George Augustus Henry Anne Parkyns, second Baron Rancliffe (1785–1850). Whig M.P. for Nottingham.
9 John Cresset Pelham, Tory M.P. for Shropshire.

London, May 29th 1827.

BEFORE I would take charge of the inclosed paper [1] I was made certain that there was no mode by which the unfortunate person to whom it related could bring it under His Majesty's notice, unless I could interest you in her favour; and I did not think it proper that I should know of the circumstances therein stated without at least giving you the option of laying them before the King, knowing as I do His Majesty's affection for his late brother and how keenly he feels everything that can affect his reputation and honour.

I shall have done my duty in sending you this paper; and I leave it to you to lay it before His Majesty or not. Whatever you may decide, or whatever may be His Majesty's determination in regard to the person to whom it relates it is not necessary that I should know what your decision or that of His Majesty is; and you may rely upon it that I shall never enquire from any other quarter.

1339 SIR WILLIAM KNIGHTON *to the* DUKE OF WELLINGTON

Hanover Square, 30 May 1827.

I HAVE thought it better to acknowledge your letter, by writing to you quite confidentially, on the subject of the enclosure.

This document I had already seen, for it was brought to me by Mr. George Colman; I refused to receive it, & stated that I thought, as Sir Herbert Taylor was the Duke of York's confidential friend & executor, it should pass through him, provided it was thought a case for His Majesty's gracious consideration.[2]...

I shall wind up this account to your Grace, by stating what I believe is only known to two individuals besides myself, (one of whom is George Harrison, who assisted me in the transaction) that about a year previous to the Duke of York's beginning the unprincipled foolery of his house, His Royal Highness, as you may remember, was in a state of the greatest money distress. His Majesty was brought acquainted with this, & with that gracious affection, & superior goodness of heart, which belong so entirely to himself, directed me to borrow, by any means, the sum of

1 The enclosure is missing. It was evidently an application for relief from a woman with whom the Duke of York had formed a connexion.

2 Sir William Knighton then enumerates certain similar claims upon the Duke of York's estate in addition to a number of outstanding debts, and points out the embarrassment of the situation thereby created for the King.

fifty thousand pounds. This I effected, & carried it in bank notes with my own hands, to the Duke of York, as a present from His Majesty, the receipt of which I have in the Duke's own hand, in a letter to the King his brother. The last five thousand pounds of this loan, I paid off about two months since. This secret transaction will explain to your Grace, why His Majesty did not appear to take that intense interest that Mr. Peel & others appeared to exercise with a view to relieving the Duke of York, relative to the building of his house, in the last weeks of his life.[1]

As I have written so much & so confidentially to your Grace, I think it right to add to the number of facts, I have stated, one more, to shew the high & exalted principles of our present gracious King.

When I came to the care of His Majesty's Privy Purse, your Grace pretty well knows, the great embarrassment of His Majesty's private affairs; but with that upright principle of character, which I may say regulates every transaction of his life, so conscientious & so determined was His Majesty to do his duty relative to his debts, *that for three years & nine months*, His Majesty only drew for a solitary three thousand pounds. Twice in this interval His Majesty assisted his poor sister the Princess Elizabeth with small sums; ten thousand pounds His Majesty last year gave the Duke of Clarence, & as you know, his private benevolence stands unrivalled!

I feel & I believe, how much & how sincerely your Grace loves the King; & to you, whom His Majesty has always felt as to a brother, by placing the domestic affections of his life—in your bosom, I know that I am not doing wrong, in giving you this interesting detail; every word of which I have put down with scrupulous accuracy, as if I was writing the record of an affidavit for a Court of Justice.

1340 THE DUKE OF WELLINGTON *to* SIR WILLIAM KNIGHTON

London, May 31, 1827.

As you will have seen by my note of the 29th I did not expect or wish for any answer; and although I am much flattered by the confidence with which you have written to me I think it best that such a document as your letter should not exist particularly in your handwriting. I therefore send it back to you to be destroyed.

I will tell the person who gave me the paper which I enclosed to you that Mr. Coleman has already been informed of the channel through which application ought to be made.

1 See No. 1285 n. 1.

Downing Street, May 31, 1827. 11 p.m.

MR. CANNING humbly reports to your Majesty, that the principal business in the House of Commons this evening has been a motion of Mr. Hume's, for the repeal of an Act imposing a stamp on small publications, for the purpose of repressing blasphemous & seditious writings; one of the Six Acts passed in the year 1819, & intended to be permanent.

Mr. Hume's speech was answered by the Attorney General in one of great clearness & force.

The object of Mr. Hume's motion was to distress the new Whig allies of your Majesty's Government who had voted *against* the Six Acts at the time of their enactment.

Mr. Peel followed Sir James Scarlett; & Lord Milton Mr. Peel; Mr. Peel of course opposing the motion; Lord Milton *half* supporting it.

The other speakers in the debate were

Mr. Lennard [1]	against the motion.
Sir Robert Wilson	do
Mr. Canning	do
Lord Howick [2]	for it
Mr. Batley [3]	against it
Sir J. Newport	do
Mr. Warburton	for it
Lord Wm. Russell [4] (sen^r)	against it

The numbers upon the division were   Ayes   10

Noes   120

110

Downing Street, June 2, 1827.

MR. CANNING presents his humble duty to your Majesty.

Mr. Canning is humbly of opinion that the measure of severity recommended to be exercised towards this gentleman *is* absolutely necessary, for the maintenance of the character of the Indian administration.

1 Thomas Barrett Lennard, Canningite M.P. for Maldon (1788–1856).
2 Son of the second Earl Grey. Whig M.P. for Winchelsea. Succeeded to the earldom, 1845. (1802–1894.)
3 Charles Harrison Batley, Tory M.P. for Beverley.
4 The Duke of Bedford's brother. Lord George William Russell and Lord John Russell were his nephews. He was M.P. for the family borough of Tavistock. (1767–1840.)

Downing Street, June 4, 1827.

MR. CANNING presents his humble duty to your Majesty; & has the satisfaction to acquaint your Majesty that Lord Wellesley has succeeded in prevailing with Lord Norbury, (after a hard fight) to accept the *Irish* Earldom for himself & his second son, and to surrender the Common Pleas to Lord Plunket.[1]

1344 COLONEL MEYRICK SHAWE *to* SIR WILLIAM KNIGHTON

Dublin Castle, 5th June 1827.

YOU will have heard from other quarters what answer was given to the letter of which I was the bearer. I did not write to you because I know you do not wish to be unnecessarily mixed up in matters of this nature though always ready to be of use to your friends when you can with propriety.

I also feared that I might fail to give a correct idea of the sentiments of another. It is best to let men speak for themselves.

I felt it to be my duty on arriving here to give the impression I had received myself in England that nothing unkind or unfriendly was intended by the proposed change in this country and that it was Mr. C's wish to secure the best thing in his power for Ld W[ellesley] on his retirement from hence. I was so far successful as to prevent any disturbance of temper—and having put the case fairly before Lord W. I left his own mind to deliberate on the subject.

It is unluckily that circumstances should require a change before six months hence when he would have expected it naturally. But he now apprehends that there exists some reason which either is founded on, or may be construed by the public into, a disapprobation of his conduct here which has created a desire *somewhere* to call him away from hence hastily, & to send him to a distance.

I suggested the obvious motives, viz. of his natural time having approached nearly, and the difficulty of serving him except at a distance. Without entirely denying that these last might be the sole motives—and without any warmth of temper he seems to have written with a view to ascertain the truth as to the cause of the change here and he wished to

1 See No. 1333.

reserve his decision on the proposals made to him until he is informed upon that point. His inclination is to remain in England after leaving this and he thinks that by great economy he may be able to do so.

Under these circumstances I can do no more than to recommend calmness & prudence and I must in justice admit that he appears to be disposed to consult both in his conduct.

I have spoken fully to him on the subject of Mr. T...ns supposed influence when he has pressed me to mention any ground of dissatisfaction with him. But he is not inclined to admit this to be a sufficient cause.

1345 SIR FREDERICK BEILBY WATSON[1] *to* SIR WILLIAM KNIGHTON

auth^{zd} G.R.

Royal Lodge, Windsor, 6th June 1827.

THE KING desires that you will make a serious representation to the Government, of the extreme neglectfulness and the inefficient execution of the works here under the *superintendence of the Office of Works in London*—pointing out particularly the great inconvenience which His Majesty is now exposed to by the non-completion of the bath adjoining His Majesty's own apartments, which was expressly directed to be completed during His Majesty's late absence in London—that a bridge which was lately constructed upon a floating principle has actually sunk in the water, and in all respects His Majesty is so dissatisfied with the manner in which the duties of that department are fulfilled, that His Majesty desires that you will call upon the Government to inquire into the organization of that department, and to suggest such improvements as may render it more efficient.

Some immediate censure should be sent to the Board preliminary to its re-formation.

1 He had recently been knighted and appointed Master of the Household.

1346 THE EARL OF ERROLL[1] *to the* KING

London, June 7th 1827.

WITH the deepest regret and most profound respect I feel it my duty to lay at your Majesty's feet, my resignation as one of your Majesty's Lords of the Bed Chamber.

I humbly trust to the great kindness and condescension I have so frequently experienced from your Majesty that your Majesty will not for a moment believe that I have acted in the present instance without the most mature consideration, and that nothing but the feelings of conscience could prompt me to have taken the part I have on the present occasion. I beg most respectfully to state to your Majesty that although I have felt it my duty to vote against your Majesty's Ministers on this important question that it is by no means my intention in future to oppose your Majesty's Government.[2]

With every sentiment of gratitude and devotion to your Majesty,[3] [etc.].

1347 THE EARL OF MACCLESFIELD[4] *to the* KING

8th June 1827.

I HAD hoped that the very few remaining years of my life would be added to the forty seven already past in honorable service near the person of my Sovereign.

But having in conformity to my often avowed opinion and the sentiments so generally expressed by the agricultural interests in my neighbourhood, been induced to vote for what appeared to be an improvement

1 William George Hay, eighteenth Earl of Erroll (1801–1846).
2 The Government's Corn Bill substituted duties upon the sliding-scale principle for the downright prohibition of imports, when the home price was under eighty shillings, under the Acts of 1815 and 1822. It was wrecked by a member of the Liverpool Cabinet which had been responsible for its introduction, for on 1 June Wellington carried an amendment in Committee, that no foreign corn which should be placed in bond after the passing of the Act, should be taken out for home consumption until the average price should have reached sixty-six shillings. By continuing the system of prohibition the amendment destroyed the principle of the Bill.
3 At Lord Erroll's particular request, his letter was forwarded to the King by the Duke of Clarence, who wrote to his brother (7 June): "I have to remark that however reluctantly Lord Erroll conceives himself as a *Scotch* Peer obliged in *principle* to oppose the Corn Bill which is made a measure of Cabinet, His Lordship in every other point will invariably support your Majesty's Government." (Windsor Archives.) Lord Erroll had married Elizabeth FitzClarence, one of the Duke of Clarence's daughters, in 1820.
4 George Parker, fourth Earl of Macclesfield (1755–1842). In December 1780 he was appointed a Lord of the Bedchamber to the Prince of Wales and subsequently filled various Household posts.

in the provisions of the Corn Bill of which I had supported the principles, I regret to find that my doing so, while in the Household, may possibly be thought liable to constructions injurious to your Majesty, as well as inconvenient to your Ministers, and that it is therefore incumbent upon me to tender to your Majesty the resignation of my office whenever your Majesty shall be pleased to accept the same, and to receive again that badge of distinction which by the gracious favor of your Majesty, and that of your late august father I have for so many years held with increased sentiments of veneration and attachment.[1]

1348 GEORGE CANNING *to the* KING

Downing Street, June 8, 1827. 11 p.m.

MR. CANNING humbly reports to your Majesty that the vote of credit for Portugal passed this evening in the House of Commons, after a short discussion in which Mr. Bankes & Mr. Hume opposed the grant, and Sir James Mackintosh (who has been prevented from attending the House, during the Session, by severe illness) made a splendid speech in favour of it.

This vote closes the Committee of Supply & of Ways & Means.

1349 THE BISHOP OF SALISBURY (DR BURGESS) *to the* BISHOP OF ST DAVID'S[2]

Tuesday morning [12th June 1827].

I HAVE had opportunities of hearing so much on the subject of the *Corn Laws* since I have been in London, in favour of the Duke of Wellington's amendment; & I find so many of Lord Liverpool's friends concurring with that amendment; that I shall vote *for* the Bill so amended, unless

1 He made it clear to Canning that there was no political feeling in his vote—"nothing but a strong country gentleman opinion on the warehousing". "He had no idea that he was risking the final passing of the Act." "After Lord Macclesfield's explanation", wrote Canning on the 7th, "his staying away on the Report would be quite satisfactory to me, and I assure you, a thousand times more so than his resignation, either now or after a vote in opposition." (Harewood MSS.) He voted with the Government on the 12th.

2 John Banks Jenkinson (1781–1840), nephew of Charles Jenkinson, first Earl of Liverpool. Dean of Worcester, 1817–25; Bishop of St David's, 1825–40.

I shall hear to night (which I do not expect) sufficient reasons for voting *against* it. I mention this in consequence of our conversation on the subject last week.[1]

1350 VISCOUNT GODERICH *to the* KING

Downing Street, June 12, 1827. 11 p.m.

LORD GODERICH presents his humble duty to your Majesty, and begs leave to report to your Majesty, that the amendment introduced by the Duke of Wellington into the Corn Bill upon a former night, has this night been confirmed by a majority of 133 to 122. Of Peers present 85 voted in favor of the Duke's amendment and 78 against it, the difference being made up by proxies.

The effect of this vote is so important as regards the principle of the Bill, and the amendment itself is, in Lord Goderich's humble opinion, so prejudicial to the landed interest and to the aristocracy of the country, and so calculated to produce consequences the very reverse of those with a view to which it was professedly proposed and supported, that it will be incumbent upon your Majesty's servants to consider very seriously how the Bill should be dealt with, whenever it may be sent back to the House of Commons.

---

1 Canning submitted to the King the following votes of the Bishops on the 12th:

For the Duke of Wellington's Amendment:

Present	*Proxies*
Bishop of Salisbury	Bishop of Ely
Bishop of Bath and Wells	Bishop of Carlisle
Archbishop of Cashel	One proxy
4 Bishop of Killaloe	4
	3
	—
	7

For the Bill

Present	*Proxies*
Archbishop of York	Bishop of Lincoln
Bishop of London	Norwich
——— Gloucester	Peterborough
——— St. David's	Bangor
——— Chester	Chichester
——— Llandaff	Litchfield
——— Bristol	7
	6
	—
	13

Downing Street, June 12, 1827.

MR. CANNING presents his most humble duty to your Majesty and humbly submits to your Majesty that Mr. Sturges Bourne has communicated to him the first application from the city of London, for an audience of your Majesty in order to present an Address, voted to your Majesty by the city.

Mr. Canning ventures most humbly to represent to your Majesty that it has been the invariable usage to receive such Addresses, in the manner proposed; and (what is certainly more annoying) to receive, in the first instance, the Sheriffs, for the purpose of learning your Majesty's pleasure as to the time of receiving the Address.

The Sheriffs have for this purpose occasionally gone to Windsor, in former times even to Weymouth.

If your Majesty could so far comply with this usage (without personal inconvenience) as to allow the Sheriffs to wait upon your Majesty at Windsor, this, or early next, week, the reception of the Address might then be conveniently fixed upon for the day on which your Majesty (if your Majesty should so think fit) might come up to town for the Council on the speech: and your Majesty would thus get rid at once of a plague which may otherwise be hanging over, and may be perpetually renewed during the summer.

Mr. Canning humbly entreats your Majesty's pardon for presuming to intrude upon your Majesty with these suggestions: which he assures your Majesty he would not have done if he did not think your Majesty's comfort interested in the decision.

1352 WILLIAM STURGES-BOURNE *to the* KING

Whitehall, 12th June 1827.

MR. STURGES BOURNE presents his humble duty to your Majesty and regrets to trouble your Majesty again on the subject of the city Address, but an enquiry having been repeated by the city Remembrancer respecting the time at which your Majesty might be pleased to receive the Sheriffs, and subsequently the Address of the Common Council, Mr. Sturges Bourne thinks it his duty to apprize your Majesty of this renewed application; and he takes the further liberty of adding, with a view of saving your Majesty unnecessary trouble, that it has not been unusual for the Sheriffs to proceed to Windsor to learn the Royal pleasure.

Downing Street, June 13, 1827.

MR. CANNING presents his humble duty to your Majesty; and has the satisfaction to acquaint your Majesty that he has at length succeeded in bringing to a favourable issue his communications respecting the Deanery of Canterbury, and the promotions in the Cathedral at Durham.

The Dean of Canterbury[1] has made his option to take the Bishoprick of Rochester, resigning his Deanery; rather than to wait another turn.

The Bishop of Durham[2] consented on Tuesday, to the *double move* in his Lordship's Cathedral; against which he had exhibited for some time manifest symptoms of reluctance; conceiving (not quite correctly) that he was thus giving away *two* pieces of preferment instead of one.

However, Mr. Canning has now written to Mr. Sumner,[3] and he has this morning seen Dr. Wellesley,[4] who accepts the transfer from St. Paul's to Durham: which cannot be completed in less than six weeks from this time.

Mr. Canning will lose no time in acquainting the Bishop of Chichester, with your Majesty's gracious intentions in his favour.

Mr. Canning humbly lays before your Majesty a correspondence which he has lately had, respecting a living which lapsed to your Majesty's gift, in consequence of a decision of the House of Lords, annulling a bond of resignation, which Lord Sondes,[5] the patron of the living had taken from the incumbent (whom Ld. Sondes presented to the living) in favour of his (Ld. S's) brother.[6]

The decision in this case being one of peculiar hardship, Mr. Canning did not think it becoming to take advantage of it, on the part of the Crown.

He sends *all* the papers: but perhaps your Majesty will be sufficiently informed of the merits of the case, by perusal of the letters (which are very short) without the enclosures, to judge of the propriety of the draft of the letter to Ld. S. which Mr. Canning humbly submits for your Majesty's approbation.

1 Dr Hugh Percy (1784–1856), the third son of the first Earl of Beverley. He married the Archbishop of Canterbury's daughter and became Dean of Canterbury in 1825. In the summer of 1827 he was consecrated Bishop of Rochester, and was translated to Carlisle before the end of the year.

2 Van Mildert, formerly Bishop of Llandaff.

3 John Bird Sumner (1780–1862), afterwards Archbishop of Canterbury. From 1827 to 1848 he held the second stall in Durham Cathedral. In 1827 he declined the offer of the See of Sodor and Man; in the following year he became Bishop of Chester. He was Dr C. R. Sumner's brother.

4 Gerald Valerian Wellesley (1770–1848), Lord Wellesley's brother. He was now made a Prebendary of Durham.

5 Lewis Richard Monson, third Baron Sondes (1792–1836).

6 The Rev. Henry Monson.

Phœnix Park, 13th June 1827.

LORD WELLESLEY is now writing to Mr. Canning and will state his feelings regarding his retirement from Ireland fully & freely.[1]

Of course he will conform to His Majesty's wishes readily & cheerfully. But if his departure from hence should be immediate it will be painful to him and have a more injurious effect upon his interests and honor in his view of the case, and in fact, than probably is contemplated on your side of the water. It is perhaps natural enough for any one at a distance to say—"If Ld W. is to come away soon, of what importance can a few months sooner or later be"?

This was the view I took of it on leaving London.

Although I was not told so, I could perceive that there was a wish that Lord W. should quit this country as early as July or August. Deeming that point inevitable (tho' I had no authority for *saying* so) I endeavoured to prepare his mind for it; and I also endeavoured to lead him to reflect maturely before he gave up India or a foreign mission.

He has reflected deeply & calmly on these points and upon a view of his own happiness & honor he has decided against foreign employment at present. No one can appreciate his reasons but himself for declining to go abroad.

His reasons for wishing to remain in Ireland until Xmas next are these

1. The delay would avoid all appearance of a recall.
2. He could complete some plans of public benefit.
3. He could reward two or three persons of high honor who have been most useful to him in the public service, & whom he has not had an opportunity of requiting. These are debts of a public & most honorable kind.
4. He would not owe a shilling on returning to England; and in the interim by resuming his hospitable habits on Lady W's return he would put the people of Dublin in good humour. His private means would pay his remaining encumbrances leaving almost all his salary to be expended here.

If he leaves this sooner, there will be a little remnant of debt, that must always annoy him; and which he will not have the power to discharge from his private income.

In January next he would return to England happy, contented & unembarrassed. Now it would be the reverse.[2]

1 Wellesley's letter is in *Wellesley Papers*, II, 199–200.
2 The day after Canning kissed hands as Prime Minister he set on foot plans to remove Wellesley from Ireland, presumably in order to meet the King's wishes that the Government

Horse Guards, June 16, 1827.

I RETURN poor ensign Souter's letter and sincerely regret the failure of his mother's application which I assure you I urged as far as I could more than once but the War Office regulations are *very imperative*. I have seen the son repeatedly & I give him great credit for his affectionate solicitude for his mother who will, I am persuaded, receive your proposed gift of £50 most gratefully, for, by her son's account, she is in extreme distress, and you are doing one of your usual kind acts.

I wrote lately to Sir Edmund Williams and as there are, I think, two or three Lieut. Colonels upon the move, I trust that the opportunity of placing him on full pay will soon offer, nor have I lost sight of the object. I had heard of the melancholy event in poor Sir M. Seymour's family & I sincerely condole with you & him on the loss of his son.[1] Your observation on the miseries & perils of this life is unfortunately too just and perhaps no one has more opportunities of learning & witnessing the distress they occasion than I have *almost daily*, & altho' a merciful Providence has hitherto conferred upon myself blessings & advantages which greatly preponderate in the scale, I trust this does not weaken my feeling for others, on the contrary when I compare my lot with that of thousands who communicate their affliction & distress to me, it encreases my desire to attend to their cases.

Lord Palmerston told me on Tuesday last that Mr. Canning retains the Chancellorship of the Exchequer and that he is to continue in his present office for an indefinite period.[2] I consider the Duke of Wellington's return to the H.Gds to be, under all circumstances, out of the question & no other Comm[r] in Chief appears to be thought of. I have therefore proposed to Lord Palmerston, subject of course to the King's gracious approval, that I should work on here as at present until Michaelmas next and that I should endeavor to get M.Genl. Sir John Colborne[3] to replace me as his Lp's deputy and if he should accept & come at Michaelmas I will readily assist and work on *under him* for a month or six weeks until he has got well into harness.

of Ireland should be in anti-Catholic hands. But Wellesley refused the Governor-Generalship of Bengal and also the Embassy to Vienna, which could have been opened for him—Wellesley's brother Henry being ready to succeed Lord Amherst at Calcutta. "I have always felt and expressed a most cordial desire to serve in your confidence and under your directions", Wellesley wrote to Canning on the 11th, "but I should prefer that service either here or in England, at least for the present." (*Wellesley Papers*, ii, 198.)

1 James, a captain in the 38th Regiment. He died at Cawnpur.

2 Canning's original intention was to hand over the Chancellorship of the Exchequer to Palmerston at the close of the Session, and to relieve Lord Dudley of the Foreign Secretaryship.

3 Afterwards Lieutenant Governor of Upper Canada; created Baron Seaton, 1839. [1778–1863.]

I have written privately to ascertain the wishes of Sir John Colborne who is one of the most valuable & distinguished officers in the service and a very efficient man in all respects, generally beloved, very unassuming and most correct & respectable in his private conduct.

I have told him that my retirement & his acceptance are subject to His Majesty's pleasure and I anxiously hope that His Majesty will be pleased to sanction this arrangement which will be beneficial & satisfactory to the army. I am certain that I may appeal to your friendly aid on this occasion and I do not hesitate to say that the comfort of my future existence depends upon my being released from the course of confinement & painful drudgery I have so long undergone, and which has during the last 6 months been so harassing to mind & body that I could not have borne it, if I had not indulged the hope of emancipation. The business has however not suffered from this feeling; there is no arrear, except in my private correspondence which I have not been able to keep down altho I sit up night after night (it is now near two a.m.) and every thing has gone on smoothly & satisfactorily; the interests of the service and of individuals have not, in a single instance, been neglected.

I wish it to be clearly understood, my dear Sir William, that I am not disposed to urge any thing for myself beyond retirement from official duties. I am perfectly satisfied with what I have and the provision which I owe to His Majesty's protection & bounty & the marks of his approbation so kindly shewn during years past & more recently have amply rewarded me. I do not wish to embarrass the Government by dwelling upon any expectations which may have been held out of the Government of the Cape. If it should be at their disposal, there should be no other candidate whom it may be right or convenient to prefer, and His M. should think fit to approve of my being sent there, I shall be happy to obey His My's commands;[1] but I shall not feel either mortified or disappointed if this should not prove the case, and His Majesty's gracious permission to go in the ensuing Spring to the Continent for a couple of years will be received with equal gratitude, and will in many respects suit my purpose & inclinations quite as well.

Pray forgive my troubling you with this long story about myself & believe me [etc.].

1 Sir Galbraith Lowry Cole (1772–1842) was appointed Governor of Cape Colony in January 1828.

Downing Street, June 17, 1827.

MR. CANNING presents his humble & affectionate duty to your Majesty: and humbly acquaints your Majesty that, upon a full consideration of the circumstances in which the Corn Bill is left by the late extraordinary proceedings in the House of Lords; & of the alarm very generally excited by those proceedings, your Majesty's servants have come to the opinion that it would not be advisable that Parliament should separate without *something* being done to quiet that alarm, & to guard against a part at least of the dangers to which the country may be exposed in consequence of it's secret disappointment.

If the Government itself were not to do any thing, it would have to combat a hundred crude & wild propositions, from other quarters, friends as well as foes: for the uneasiness is so general[1] that all the world is devising measures for the occasion.

All that your Majesty's servants propose to do, however, is to bring in a Bill for allowing the quantity of corn now in bond,[2] in this country, & the small quantity expected from Canada, to come into consumption, under the rules & conditions laid down in the Bill which has failed. This will be sufficient to meet any difficulty which might arise from high prices, growing out of the present state of things, before the harvest. If the harvest is as abundant as it promises, there will be no necessity for doing any thing more, until after the next meeting of Parliament. If otherwise, Parliament must be called—at an inconvenient time: but it will be a consolation to your Majesty's servants that it is no fault of theirs that the country is exposed to such an inconvenience.

In bringing forward this new measure, it will be Mr. Canning's object to steer as clear as possible of any angry allusions to what has been passing in the House of Lords, unless the discussion is forced upon him: satisfied, that, however just a ground your Majesty's Government in general, & himself in particular may have for retaliation, it would be unseemly to mix any thing of a personal nature with a subject so deeply interesting to the country as that of the subsistence of the people. He trusts, however, that he shall still find a fit opportunity for the sort of exposition which he humbly took the liberty of mentioning to your Majesty yesterday.

The new Bill, even if not pertinaciously opposed, must, Mr. Canning fears, protract the Session till towards the end of next week.

1 Since the prospects of a good harvest were not favourable and the price of corn had been steadily rising—from 55s. 1d. in January to 59s. 10d. in June.
2 About 600,000 quarters.

Mr. Canning has learnt from authority which he believes fully entitled to credit, that Lord Grey has been elected chief of the combined Tory & Whig Oppositions in the House of Lords; and has at least *not declined* the post to which he has been thus invited.[1]

The King to Sir William Knighton. Royal Lodge, June 18th 1827. [*Knighton*, I, 375, where, however, the following portions of the letter are omitted:

"I yesterday received yr. letter for which I return you many thanks.

"Our parties of the last week appear to have answered completely, as *every one*, at least, seems, & *expresses themselves* highly pleased with them, & I do most sincerely pray & hope that the feeling of satisfaction may *continue*, both from the impression of what has already taken place, at the same time that it will furnish a reasonable encouragement & expectation that the same gratification & satisfaction will again occur, whenever a repetition may be desired, by any fresh attempt at the enlargement of our society, thro' the invitation of any other parties through the course of the year.

"On Saturday morning last previous to his leaving the Lodge, I had a long political conversation with C——g, upon many heads, the particulars of which would carry me into a far more extensive field of detail than I have now either time, or than it would be practicable for me to compress within the compass of any letter, & therefore shall reserve what I have to narrate until I shall *next* have the pleasure of seeing [you] & which I do not conceive & hope, cannot *now* be very remote. I had flattered myself that this would not have been later than Saturday next or this day sen'night at the very furthest, (& that I should have had to summonze you at that period) from what passed between C——g & me last Saturday until I last night received the inclosed from C——g, which will explain to you everything, as well, the change of (?) vacation on the part of *Govt.* as, the necessary delay of a few days which this will in consequence occasion. What the effect of this intended measure of the Govt. may be, God alone knows, for I can not presume to calculate, or indeed to form any idea to myself of the results.

"Canning's arrangement on Saturday last with me was that I was to come to London on Saturday or Monday next, for the speech, when I was to have taken also the City Address, thus killing two birds with one stone, & afterwards to have returned immediately & quietly here. By C——g's inclosed letter to me, it appears as if the plan now must be postponed now at any rate for some few days longer, as the speech cannot be finally drawn up until the fate of this new measure in Parliament shall be known. This however (& notwithstanding my earnest desire of giving you as long a spell of relaxation as possible with your family) makes *me anxiously desirous* of seeing you *at the latest, here* on *Saturday next*, in order to *go* through *everything, everything* with you *previous* to my being called up to town, as well as to afford *you* the necessary time & opportunity of seeing C——g before the final drawing up of the speech, & besides, for the quiet digestion of many other understandings, arrangements & settlings, which otherwise will be, & would be, hurried over, without that special care, with which they ought *invariably* to be weighed & watched, & in many instances perhaps be entirely slurred over, if not completely neglected & forgotten.

"We are all of us, thank God, going on very comfortably, & in general in good health & spirits. Dearest Eliz^{th} is certainly improved, & I think visibly improved & improving for the last two days, since our party broke up. Nevertheless I think *she* also I think is very desirous, at least if I am to judge from the many questions she put me yesterday, respecting the day upon which your arrival here might be looked for & depended upon. As to my poor self...."]

1 There was no truth in this report.

Downing Street, June 18, 1827.
¾ p. 11. p.m.

MR. CANNING has great satisfaction in humbly reporting to your Majesty that the resolutions moved by Mr. Canning this evening, preparatory to a temporary Bill (such as Mr. Canning took the liberty of describing to your Majesty yesterday) have been adopted, after a very useful discussion, by a majority of 238 to 52 = 186.

The speakers in the debate were

× Mr. Western (who brought forward a proposition for rev[iv]ing the Corn Bill of 1822,¹ to which proposition Mr. Canning's resolutions were moved as an amendment)
o Mr. Canning
o Mr. Peel
o Mr. Whitmore²
× Colonel Wood³
× Mr Benett (Wilts)
o Sir John Newport
× Sir E. Knatchbull
o Mr. Baring⁴
o Mr. Huskisson
o Lord Morpeth,⁵ who spoke with great ability
o Mr Otway Cave⁶

It is never quite safe to prophecy results, upon a first night's debate & division: but there is every appearance of a probability that the Bill will go through all it's stages rapidly, & without any serious opposition.

---

1 That is, by repealing the clause in the 1822 Act which suspended the operation of the provisions of the Act until the average price should have reached eighty shillings per quarter: a price which had never been attained since 1822.
2 William Wolryche Whitmore, M.P. for Bridgnorth. Thomas Whitmore was the other member.
3 Thomas Wood, M.P. for Breconshire; an ultra-Tory.
4 Alexander Baring, first Baron Ashburton (1774–1848), the financier.
5 Canningite M.P. for Morpeth; succeeded his father as seventh Earl of Carlisle in 1848. (1802–1864.)
6 Whig M.P. for Leicester.

Admiralty, June 18th 1827.

Lord Erroll has the Bedchamber to give up and has beyond a doubt a claim on the country as his Lordship is the *only* Scotch Peer whose property has *not* been restored since forfeited in 1745. Add to which his Lordship's great grandfather the Earl of Balmerino[1] was most *unjustly* beheaded owing to a private animosity from another Peer. By the death *this* morning of the Duke of Gordon[2] the situation of the Keeper of the Great Seal in Scotland is now vacant and is I believe worth *more* than the Bedchamber. Under this impression I venture most strongly to recommend the Earl of Erroll to fill this present vacancy and ever remain, [etc.].

1359 George Canning *to the* King

Downing Street, June 19th 1827.

Mr. Canning presents his humble duty to your Majesty: and deems it right to acquaint your Majesty that he yesterday saw the Dean of Canterbury; &, in consequence of the vote of the Duke of Northumberland, & of the absence of the Archbishop of Canterbury (who neither appeared in the House of Lords nor sent his proxy) on Tuesday last, took the opportunity of asking the Dean what were his (the Dean's) dispositions & intentions as to the support of your Majesty's Government in the House of Lords.

The Dean appeared to Mr. Canning to be somewhat taken by surprize: but acknowledged in the most unequivocal terms the right, & even the duty of Mr. Canning to make the inquiry. The Dean declared unequivocally for himself that he conceived any man who accepted such a favour from the Crown, to be bound in honour, and as a general rule, (subject of course to occasional variations in cases of conscience or feeling) to give a steady & sincere support to the Administration. But he added, that, peculiarly circumstanced as he was, he thought himself obliged to consult his near connexions, before he should return a definitive answer to Mr. Canning's question; and required a few days for that purpose. Mr. Canning readily acquiesced in this proposal. He expects to see the Dean again tomorrow or Thursday morning.

1 Arthur Elphinstone, sixth Baron Balmerino (1688–1746).
2 Alexander, fourth Duke of Gordon (1743–1827).

Downing Street, June 19, 1827.

MR. CANNING, with his humble duty, returns to your Majesty two letters addressed to your Majesty, which he presumes your Majesty may wish to keep.

Mr Canning has executed your Majesty's commands with Lord Macclesfield, Lord Errol and Lord Delaware.[1]

Lord Macclesfield expressed himself deeply sensible of your Majesty's great goodness. The other Lords professed and appeared to be equally sensible of it: but they each frankly owned that they must reserve a right to vote, as they had been voting, on any question connected with the Corn question.

Mr. Canning did not think himself either authorized or warranted to consent to such a *compromise* between your Majesty and your Government on the one hand, and two officers of your Majesty's Household on the other. He therefore desired to *defer* the final signification of your Majesty's pleasure, *until the Corn Bill and all that may follow it shall have been disposed of*: in which he trusts he shall not have acted otherwise than in conformity to your Majesty's wish & opinion.[2]

Downing Street, June 19th 1827.

MR. CANNING presents his humble duty to your Majesty: and has humbly to acquaint your Majesty that by the death of the Duke of Gordon (which took place yesterday) a Green Ribbon, and the high office of Keeper of the Great Seal of Scotland, are become vacant.[3]

The disposal of these honours is a matter of some difficulty, in consideration of the present unprecedented state of the Scotch Representative Peerage.

Of the 16 Scotch Peers, no fewer (Mr. Canning is sorry to say) than

---

1 George John Sackville West, fifth Earl De la Warr (1791–1869).

2 "His Majesty", wrote Canning to his friend Lord Binning on the 17th, "has authorized me to assure Lord Macclesfield through you that he should be grieved to lose the service of so old and attached a friend of his family." (Harewood MSS.)

3 The Duke of Gordon was invested with the Order of the Thistle in 1774, and at the time of his death was the second Knight in seniority, the Duke of Clarence being the first. He was Keeper of the Great Seal of Scotland, 1794–1806, 1807–27.

eleven, voted on Friday last, in the majority on the D. of Wellington's amendment viz.

The Marquesses of { Queensberry [1]
{ Tweeddale [2]

The Earls of { Kellie &
{ Errol (by pairing off)

Viscounts { Arbuthnot [3]
{ Strathallan [4]

Barons { Saltoun [5]
{ Napier [6]
{ Sinclair [7]
{ Gray [8]
{ Belhaven [9] 11

Lord Forbes,[10] who has been within these few weeks appointed your Majesty's Commissioner of the Assembly of the Church of Scotland, went away from the House, without voting. — 12

Lord Elgin [11] has not taken his seat. 13

The only three who voted with your Majesty's Government were Lord Roseberry,[12] & Lord Colville [13] (present) & Lord Home [14] (by proxy).

Mr. Canning has received from H.R.H. The Duke of Clarence the inclosed letter, recommending Lord Errol for the office of Keeper of the Great Seal. He thinks it his duty not to withhold this letter from your Majesty's perusal: although he humbly conceives that after what has so recently past, your Majesty would hardly think it expedient, not merely

1 Sir Charles Douglas, fifth Marquess of Queensberry (1777–1837).
2 George Hay, eighth Marquis of Tweeddale (1787–1876), afterwards Governor of Madras.
3 John, eighth Viscount Arbuthnott (1778–1860).
4 James Andrew John Lawrence Charles Drummond, Viscount Strathallan (1767–1851).
5 Alexander George Fraser, sixteenth Baron Saltoun (1785–1853), a Lord of the Bedchamber.
6 William John, eighth Baron Napier (1786–1834).
7 Charles St Clair, thirteenth Baron Sinclair (1768–1863).
8 Francis, fourteenth Baron Gray (1765–1842).
9 Robert Montgomery Hamilton, eighth Baron Belhaven and Stenton (1793–1868).
10 James Ochoncar Forbes, seventeenth Baron Forbes (1765–1843).
11 Thomas Bruce, seventh Earl of Elgin (1766–1841). He sold the "Elgin marbles" to the nation in 1816.
12 Sir Archibald John Primrose, fourth Earl of Rosebery and sixth Baronet (1783–1868), the grandfather of the Prime Minister. He was given a Barony of the United Kingdom in January 1828.
13 John, ninth Baron Colville (1768–1849).
14 Alexander, tenth Earl of Home (1769–1841). In 1798 he married Elizabeth, the second daughter of Henry Scott, third Duke of Buccleuch and Queensberry (1746–1812), and sister of Charles William Henry Scott, fourth Duke (1772–1819).

to retain Lord Errol in your Majesty's family; but to distinguish him with so signal a mark of your Majesty's Royal approbation.

Lord Melville has caused it to be intimated to Mr. Canning that Lord Liverpool intended the Great Seal (when it should be disposable) for Lord Home: who is married to a sister of the late Duke of Buccleuch. This, however, was when the whole interest of that great family went cordially with your Majesty's Government. Lord Montagu,[1] who now represents that interest, has voted in opposition. Still, however, as Lord Home has himself voted right, in the midst of so general a defection of his colleagues, & especially as he is very poor, it might perhaps be not unadvisable that your Majesty's choice should fall on Lord Home, if his character in other respects should be such as to befit him for the dignity of the station.[2] Mr. Canning states this qualification, because he has a vague notion of having heard something to the disparagement of Lord Home's habits of life, which he would make it his business to clear up, before he ventured finally to recommend him to your Majesty's consideration.

With respect to the Green Ribbon Mr. Canning ventures humbly to submit to your Majesty that the prompt bestowing of it upon some Scotch Peer who has supported your Majesty's Govt. at this crisis, could not but have a beneficial effect, as counteracting in some degree the threats & promises, which Mr. Canning has reason to believe, have been prodigally held out by Lord Lauderdale & Lord Melville to all their brethren of the Scotch Peerage; and as appears by the result, too successfully.

The Ribbon would be no object to Lord Home; whose circumstances would render it rather a burden to him than a distinction.

Lord Roseberry, from his rank & station in Scotland, would perhaps be the natural choice: but Mr. Canning does not think it right to mention his name to your Majesty, without stating at the same time that he knows Lord Roseberry's views to be directed to a British Peerage; to which (at a proper time) Mr. Canning is humbly of opinion that his large fortune, & high place in the Scotch Peerage may perhaps be considered as entitling him to aspire. In that case, the previous grant of the minor honour would be, in some sort, thrown away.

Lord Colville is, as Mr. Canning understands, in very straitened circumstances; & is so far liable to the same objection as Lord Home, in respect to a reward purely honorary: but, on the other hand, Lord Col-

1 Henry James Montagu Scott, second Baron Montagu; third son of the third Duke of Buccleuch and Queensberry. (1776–1845.)
2 The Duke of Argyll was appointed. See No. 1365.

ville, being an Admiral, & *not* having received the Red Ribbon (which his younger brother Genl. Sir C. Colville has)[1] it is probable that the honour of the Green Ribbon would be more sensibly felt by him, than by most other members of the Scotch peerage; among whom the antiquity of his family, joined to his professional character, would tend to make the selection as uninvidious as any that could be made.

Lord Colville is one of those, to whom, (according to Mr. Canning's information) the menaces to which he referred have been unsparingly applied: but in his instance (almost alone) without effect.

A signal mark of your Majesty's approbation, could not perhaps therefore be more justly or usefully bestowed, than on Lord Colville.

Mr. Canning humbly assures your Majesty, in conclusion, that he has no personal acquaintance, with either of the three Lords, of whom he has spoken favourably to your Majesty—& consequently takes no *personal* interest in what may befall them:—but he deems it his duty humbly, but earnestly, to represent to your Majesty the absolute necessity of countervailing the factious canvassings, by which the late majority in the House of Peers has been procured, by conferring the favours of the Crown on persons who are zealous in supporting your Majesty's Government.

The *only* other Scotch Peer (not of the 16) who appears to have voted with the Ministry, is Lord Moray:[2] an individual perfectly unexceptionable, & whom (from family connexion) Mr. Canning would very naturally be glad to suggest to your Majesty for the vacant Ribbon, if your Majesty should not approve of Lord Colville. But Ld. Moray is of such retired habits, that he would never seek such a distinction: & he is at this moment abroad for the ensuing summer & winter.

1362 GEORGE CANNING *to the* KING

Downing Street, June 20, 1827.

MR. CANNING presents his humble duty to your Majesty.

Since the sending off of his letter of yesterday, Mr Canning has learnt that *the Duke of Argyll*[3] is to be added to the Scotch Peers, who voted with your Majesty's Government against the Duke of Wellington's amendment.

1 Sir Charles Colville (1770–1843), Commander-in-Chief at Bombay, 1819–25; Governor of Mauritius, 1828–34.

2 Francis Stuart, tenth Earl of Moray (1771–1848). His first wife, Lucy, who died in 1798, was the second daughter of General John Scott, and was therefore Mrs Canning's sister.

3 George William Campbell, sixth Duke of Argyll (1766–1839); a Whig.

The Duke of Argyll *paired off* (with Lord Orford):[1] his name therefore was not in the first list of presents & proxies.

Mr. Canning has received the inclosed letter from his Grace which he thinks it his duty to lay before your Majesty.

There are matters connected with the Great Seal of Scotland, upon which Mr. Canning wishes to obtain information, before he submits any distinct proposition to your Majesty. He has, as he fears, already wearied your Majesty with written communications upon this & other subjects within these few days; and therefore, if your Majesty would graciously permit him to avail himself of your Majesty's kind permission, he would wait upon your Majesty on Saturday morning, at any hour that may be agreeable to your Majesty.

Mr. Canning is to see the Bishop of Chichester tomorrow.

1363 THE DUKE OF ARGYLL *to the* KING

Tuesday, June 26th 1827.

THE various acts of kindness which I have experienced from your Majesty, for so many years, and the gracious manner, in which you have always attended to such requests as I have ventured to make to your Majesty, embolden me on the present occasion, to express my wish, that your Majesty would have the goodness to allow me to hold the office of Keeper of the Great Seal of Scotland vacant by the death of the Duke of Gordon.

If I should be fortunate enough to obtain the object I seek, I feel confident that your Majesty is sufficiently well acquainted with my character, to be convinced that I am not a person likely to swerve from that personal attachment which I have always had for your Majesty, or from those political principles, on which I have felt empowered to ask Mr. Canning to support my pretension to this office.

1 Horatio Walpole, third Earl of Orford (1783–1858).

Berlin, June 28th 1827.

I RECEIVED about a quarter of an hour ago, a long letter from the Brigadier, written by your order, & I return you many thanks for all contained in it; not only the expressions of friendship and kindness towards myself and family, but also for the short explanation of *all* that has of late taken place. You may depend upon it, no one has felt more deeply than I have for the dreadful and painful situation in which you have unfortunately been placed, and I was ever sure that you would never lose sight of that great question[1] on which the safety and wellfare of the British Monarch and Empire must stand or fall, and by your having appointed brother William to the high situation he now holds,[2] and our friend Anglesey to the Ordnance, you have shewn publicly, the purity and *staunchness* of your sentiments upon the *great* question. William's speech at that public meeting, must also have done great good.[3] It is impossible by letter to enter fully into a business of such consequence as that which has taken place, and to pretend to offer an opinion, without being master of the whole subject, and therefore I shall abstain from saying more now, than that from the bottom of my heart, I do wish that you may find that all may go on quietly and not be worried more. The prorogation of Parliament, which probably will take place in three days, will I hope tend to quiet that fermentation which now seems to predominate throughout the country, and which must ruin all society: I own I thank my stars that I was absent, and therefore have less of those feelings which seem to fill every mind. Times may come, when I trust I shall have the comfort of seeing you once again, and then we can talk quietly over all that has passed, and I may learn then the truth, for as you may suppose, such unaccountable histories are propagated and even augmented by the time they reach us, that one is aghast! And such extraordinary things and changes have occurred, such an extraordinary junction has taken place, of persons so totally differing for years in opinions and sentiments, that it will require some time before one can make up ones mind to give credit

1 The Catholic question.

2 The office of Lord High Admiral was revived for the Duke of Clarence, and he was assisted by a Council composed chiefly of those members of the former Board of Admiralty who had not resigned. Unlike former First Lords of the Admiralty the Duke was excluded from the Cabinet.

3 At the Anniversary Dinner of the Society for the Promotion of Christian Knowledge (22 May), the Duke, who was in the chair, said: "Whether the declaration I am about to make be popular or unpopular, I think it right, in reference to the peculiar character of this meeting, to assert, at this time, that to the sound and strict principles of the Church of England, I am unalterably attached—and that it will be at all times and under all circumstances my first desire and duty to maintain those principles."

to it all; at times the whole appears to me as a dream, and I may add a *bad one*, which makes me start again. Lamentable it must ever be to see so many old and staunch friends, *even that one has been accustomed to see for the last 30 years supporting the Crown, and its interests, now gone, and such a change of actors on the seats in Parliament*, must to one who has been absent, appear quite extraordinary. I only say, that I never felt so deeply interested in any public occurrence as I have done on the present, and that I did not believe, that I had still so much feeling left in me for public affairs as I now find I have; for every mind has been totally engrossed with all that has been going on. I have always been of opinion that the King of England is no enviable situation, from all I witnessed during the life of our late revered father, bad as the times were then, yet I must own now [? never] was he placed in so trying or difficult situation as you are dearest brother, but Providence will stand by you, as he did by him, and I trust you will still live to see many many happy years. To me it is inexplicable, how any man that has means to live out of office, can wish to be in it, in a country like England, when every blackguard newspaper can at once ruin the character of a man, and hold up that person who has been for many years an object of respect to be attack'd, abhorred and detested, and ill used by his countrymen. Excuse the length of my letter, but being alas too far to enjoy a comfortable chat, has induced me now that I am writing, to prose a little, and as the post goes out tomorrow, and I shall be at Potsdam with the King, I shall hardly have time to write tomorrow, therefore I took up my pen, and wrote to you immediately.

P.S. I forgot to say that the King of Prussia has dismissed Beckendorff (Mrs. B's son) one of the cleverest men I ever met with, who was at the head of all the public institutions for learning, as also of the University here, for having renounced the Protestant faith, and embraced the Catholic. I have been for a year doing my utmost to prevent his taking this mad resolution, for I can only term it thus, as he has ruined himself and family, having had a salary of near 7,000 dollars, about £1,000 a year, but the priests are like the devil, they never let loose their prey. The King could do no other than what he has done, after the decided line he had taken about his sister the Duchess of Köthen. His connection with Adam Müller[1] has been his ruin who likewise is supposed to have been chiefly instrumental in the conversation of the Köthens.

The Marquis Wellesley to the King, 28 June 1827. (*Wellesley Papers*, II, 200–2.)

1 Austrian Consul-General at Leipzig.

July 2^d 1827.

YOUR MAJESTY will permit me, I hope, to express my thanks for the honor your Majesty has conferred upon me, in appointing me to the office of Keeper of the Great Seal of Scotland. I beg your Majesty to believe, that I feel much more than I venture to express with respect to your Majesty's kindness on this occasion.

1366 THE DUKE OF CUMBERLAND *to* SIR WILLIAM KNIGHTON

Chateau de Schönehausen, July 3^d 1827.

IT must appear most extraordinary to you as it does to me that *I* this day the 3^d July have *received only* the 2 letters you wrote to me on the 24th & 27th of last Jany, the former communicating to me by my brother's direction the intelligence of his gracious intention of naming me as Colonel of the Blues,[1] and also a printed copy of the order to the British army announcing the Duke of Wellington as Commander in Chief. I do hope *you* will make the necessary enquiries at the Foreign Office how such a gross neglect can have taken place, for certainly one should think a letter with your name on the outside of the cover must have struck those belonging to the Office of the necessity of instantly forwarding it. This explanation on my part was necessary to prove to you that *no blame* can attach itself to me for not having sooner replied to your two letters, & I own now fairly to you I could in no way explain to myself the cause of your long and continued silence, especially as in the first place I had in a letter to you requested you to let me know how my brother was after than great shock his health and spirits must have suffered after the death of our late dear brother Frederick.

What extraordinary things have occurred since that period, never do I remember in my life such awful times. Many extraordinary & irksome political scenes & changes have I witnessed during my late father's reign, but surely never was any one of those to be compared to what has lately taken place in England. Knowing the sincerity of my affection for my brother and attachment to all that regards him, you may easily conceive all the anxiety of mind I have gone through about him, knowing full well all the worry of mind he must [have] suffered during that momentous time. As far as I can learn I am happy to hear he enjoys perfect health, and now that Parliament is prorogued, I hope things may become

1 The Duke's appointment as Colonel of the Royal Regiment of Horse Guards, *vice* Wellington, was gazetted on 23 January.

tranquil again, and political fever become less violent, which I understand rages mightily now, so as to make every sort of society disagreeable. I shall write a few lines to my brother to explain to him my apparent neglect in not having at the time he ought to have expected it, written *officially* to him to thank him, though I did it from myself as soon as I received the 1st report from the regt of the Horse Guards, for recollect *to-day* I receive that intelligence I ought to have had 6 months back. I hope soon to hear from you again.

1367 THE DUCHESS OF KENT *to the* KING

Kensington Palace, 4th July 1827.

I AM most exceedingly thankful to your Majesty for your advice; and I therefore avail myself of a *most favorable* subject to vaccinate our dear little girl[1] on Monday next.

I shall therefore be ready to obey your Majesty's gracious desire to receive me, and my children whenever you please after the 18th of this month.

I cannot close this note, without again thanking your Majesty, for so kindly and affectionately entering into my feelings: I have great comfort in thinking, I can have the benifit of your advice, and that you will not think me troublesome in seeking it, when I may feel the want, or propriety of having it.

Victoria and Feodora[2] are most grateful for your message, and share with me, in the pleasure we shall have in so soon seeing you.

Ever believe me, with great respect and attachment, Sir, [etc.].

The King to the Marquis Wellesley [10 July 1827]. (*Wellesley Papers*, II, 203–4. The MS. is an undated draft, in Knighton's handwriting, with a few verbal differences from the printed letter.)

1368 GEORGE CANNING *to the* KING

Downing Street, July 12, 1827.

MR. CANNING presents his humble duty to your Majesty; & humbly submits for your Majesty's gracious approbation, & signature (if approved) three warrants for pensions, under the Act of Parliament "for

1 The future Queen Victoria.
2 The Duchess of Kent's daughter by her first husband, the Prince of Leiningen. In February 1828 she married Ernest Christian Charles, Prince of Hohenlohe-Langenburg. [1807–1872.]

rewarding civil services"; to Mr. Huskisson, Mr. Planta, & Mr. Hobhouse.[1]

The state of Mr. Huskisson's health is such, that, although Mr Canning entertains a sanguine hope that a relaxation from business for a couple of months may restore it, it is impossible nevertheless not to look forward to the danger of his being obliged to suspend his official labours for a much longer time, or even to discontinue them.

In such case, it will (Mr. Canning ventures to hope) be your Majesty's gracious wish that Mr. Huskisson should be relieved from anxiety respecting the security of his retirement. The pension to which Mr. Huskisson is entitled (subject to your Majesty's pleasure) is £3,000 a year. He surrenders into your Majesty's hands a claim to one for £1,200, which he has held since he was Under Secretary of State in 1800[2]—but which of course has been dormant while he has held an efficient office.

The other two warrants are for pensions to Mr. Hobhouse, Under Secretary in the Home Department, whose term of service entitles him to it, independently of the consideration of his eminent qualifications, & (Mr. Canning is sorry to add) broken health; & to Mr. Planta, who has completed his term of service in the Foreign Office, & is now transferred to the more precarious situation of Secretary to the Treasury.[3] These two pensions are, under the Act of Parliament, of £1,000 each.

The Duke of Wellington to Lord Maryborough, 14 July 1827. (*W.N.D.* IV, 63.)

1369 THE MARQUIS WELLESLEY *to the* KING

Phœnix Park, July 15th 1827.

YOUR MAJESTY'S most gracious acceptance of Lord Wellesley's humble tribute of affection and duty demands from him the most cordial expression of gratitude.

Lord Wellesley is deeply sensible of your Majesty's condescension & goodness in signifying to him your Majesty's kind disposition to meet his wishes; & in the favor & indulgence, with which your Majesty is pleased to consider him.

1 Henry Hobhouse (1776–1854), Permanent Under-Secretary of State since June 1817. He now became Keeper of the State Papers, and superintended the editing of the *State Papers of Henry VIII*.

2 Huskisson was appointed Under-Secretary of State for War in 1795 and retired with Pitt in 1801.

3 He succeeded Lushington (who became Governor of Madras) on 19 April.

Lord Wellesley has received a letter from his kind & warm friend Mr. Canning, to which he has returned an answer, requesting that your Majesty will be pleased to relieve Lord Wellesley from the Government of Ireland, by sending a successor to take charge of it in the beginning of the month of January 1828.

Lord Wellesley receives with every sentiment, which they are calculated to inspire, your Majesty's most benignant assurances of kind regard for Lord Wellesley's future happiness; which must ever be connected with your Majesty's service, with the honor of your Majesty's Government, & with the glory, peace, & prosperity of your Majesty's reign.

Lady Wellesley returns her most dutiful & grateful acknowlegements, for your Majesty's gracious & kind remembrances.

1370 CHARLES ARBUTHNOT *to* SIR WILLIAM KNIGHTON

Stratfieldsaye, Monday 16th July 1827.

As I saw how great your anxiety was that the Duke of Wellington should again be in habits of intercourse with the King, & as in consequence of y^r absence from the Royal Lodge you may not be acquainted with what has very recently passed upon this subject, I will write a few lines to apprise you of a communication made to the Duke by Lord Maryborough.

It appears that the King had mentioned the Duke with great kindness to Lord Maryborough: that Lady Conyngham had done the same, as from the King, in speaking to Lady Maryborough: and that an intimation had been made that the Duke, if he went to Fern Hill, might ride to the Royal Lodge for the purpose of enquiring after His Majesty's health. This, it was said, might at once give the ready means to the King of sending for the Duke, & of thus putting an end entirely to the separation which so unfortunately has taken place between them.

The Duke came to me as soon as the communication had been made to him by his brother.

I have no hesitation in owning that I caught eagerly at the idea; & laying aside all other considerations, it was my advice to the Duke that he should avail himself of the opening thus offered. The Duke was impressed with the same feelings that I was; & his first impulse was to present himself at the Royal Lodge at the earliest moment that he could. Upon reflection however it occurred to him that by acting in this manner,

& by availing himself of an *intimation* which had not at all the character of a *command*, he shd render himself liable to the most serious imputations equally affecting his public and his private character. It could not, he thought, fail to be said by the Minister that he had gone to the King without being sent for; & as in point of fact this could not be denied, it would not be in his power to make it evident to the world that he had received full authority for the step which he had taken.

The question then was how, & in what terms, a reply shd be made to Lord Maryborough's suggestion. It would not be possible for me to relate in detail what the Duke wrote to his brother,[1] but it will be sufficient for me to assure you that the King must, I am confident, be highly pleased with every sentiment wch has been expressed in the letter. The Duke says that without a command he has no right to intrude upon the King's privacy—that were he to present himself without receiving the command he should subject himself to misrepresentations which he never could explain; but that if His Majesty should deign to order his attendance, he should fly to his presence at any time—and from any distance—with the greatest joy & alacrity.

This is the purport of the letter, & in part I have given the very words. It rejoices me to feel that the opening is now made; & trusting as I do that ere long it will be well followed up, I have now the earnest hope that the King and the Duke, who ought never to have been parted, will if possible be more firmly united than ever. United I mean for the good of both.

The Government it is true has now taken a shape which must sever the Duke—as long as the present Party is in power—from the King's Councils; but it is a consolation to feel that if the hour of danger & of trouble shd arise, there will be close to the King's side a man who has passed his life in affronting danger for the Throne's sake, & who was chosen by the Sovereign now on the Throne as the one to whom his honour—his comfort—and his safety were for ever to be exclusively confided.

It is in the recollection of the sentiments uttered by the King—when the loss of Lord Londonderry was to be supplied—that I express myself as I have done. In taking leave of my official house I had the irksome task of arranging & destroying papers; but those papers I would not destroy which contained the warm effusions of the King's heart towards the Duke—though in truth it nearly broke my heart to consider how great & melancholy the change has been. Between the King & the Duke a meeting alone can be required. To his Sovereign there is from the

1 The letter, dated 14 July, is in *W.N.D.* iv, 63.

Duke the same unbounded attachment that you used to observe; and surely the King has not driven from his mind that reliance upon the Duke, & that fondness for him, which I as well as yourself have with pleasure so often witnessed.

Between the Duke & the King's Minister the case is widely different. It would be useless—nay worse than useless—to say a word as to the cause of their disunion; but the Duke never c^d forget that he it was who had conciliated for the Minister the favour of the King which is now enjoyed;[1] and putting aside all other subjects of difference, it must for the duration of his life be borne in mind that the service then rendered has since been ill requited.

Of all this however I will say no more. I will not even ask you to let me know that you have received my letter; & indeed it may be better to give an answer to it. I have written it because I am confident that it will rejoice you—as in truth it will me—when the King & the Duke can again meet; & the account wch I have given you of the Duke's letter to his brother will show that a command from the King will be received with the utmost joy & will be obeyed with the utmost speed.

George Canning to the King, 20 July 1827. (*Stapleton*, pp. 600–1.)

1371 GEORGE CANNING *to the* KING

Chiswick, July 22, 1827.

MR. CANNING presents his humble duty to your Majesty; and humbly lays before your Majesty a letter which he received yesterday from Lord Melville, on the subject of the Lieutenancy of the County of Edinburgh, vacant by the death of Lord Moreton.[2]

Whatever may be the present state of the Duke of Buccleuch's[3] interest, Mr. Canning humbly apprehends, that considering his Grace's minority, and other circumstances stated in Lord Melville's letter, your Majesty may probably deem it right that the arrangement, which has been so long understood to be provisionally determined on, should be carried into effect, by the appointment of the Duke of Buccleuch to the Lieutenancy, so soon as his Grace shall be of age.

1 That is, in September 1822.
2 The Earl of Morton.
3 Walter Francis Montagu Scott Douglas, fifth Duke of Buccleugh (1806–1884).

Chiswick, July 24, 1827.

MR. CANNING presents his humble duty to your Majesty; & is most happy to be enabled, by the accompanying letter from Sir Charles Bagot, inclosing one from Lord Bagot[1] to his brother, humbly to recommend to your Majesty the filling up of the vacant Deanery of Canterbury in the manner which he hopes will be most agreeable to your Majesty's feelings.

If your Majesty shall be graciously pleased to approve of Mr. Richard Bagot's[2] appointment to that dignity, your Majesty will, perhaps, have the goodness to let Mr. Canning know, where he can learn the particulars of Mr. Markham's present situation, in order that *his* succession to Mr. Bagot's canonry of Windsor may be forwarded at the same time.

Mr. Canning humbly takes the liberty of laying before your Majesty a letter from the Solicitor General of Scotland;[3] announcing, by desire of Lord Hopetoun, his Lordship's intention to give his support to your Majesty's Government.

The Duke of Wellington's Memorandum on the Proposed Reduction of the Army, 4 August 1827. (*W.N.D.* IV, 106–18.)

1373 THE DUKE OF CUMBERLAND *to the* KING

Schönehausen, Augst 6th 1827.

As unfortunately I cannot offer you on the 12th my sincere congratulations on the day,[4] accept them in writing, and believe me they are dictated by a heart which is most faithfully attached to you. God grant this year may prove a less stormy one for your feelings than the last has been, and that the horizon may clear up, and that all the heavy clouds that now overwhelm us may be dispersed. I was most happy to see by the newspapers that our friend Wellington had paid you his respects on the 19th, as I feel sure that no one is more faithfully attached to you than he is, and the time may yet come when he may be of great service to you. Believe me dearest brother that my thoughts are incessantly occupied with you and that though I do not choose to trouble you with long

1 William Bagot, second Baron Bagot (1773–1856).
2 Dean of Canterbury, 1827–45; Bishop of Oxford, 1829–45. [1782–1854.] He, Sir Charles, and Lord Bagot were brothers. Lord Bagot had voted against the Corn Bill, and Canning refused to nominate his brother Richard until he had received a satisfactory explanation of that vote.
3 John Hope (1794–1858), Solicitor-General for Scotland, 1822–30; Lord Justice Clerk, 1841–58. He was related to the Earl of Hopetoun (1803–43).
4 The King's birthday.

epistles yet my heart is always with you, and should ever an opportunity offer itself, and I find myself de novo in your presence I trust we may have a comfortable chat like of old, of all that has taken place. I write this day, as I propose tomorrow going for a fortnight to Strelitz, not having been from home now, since last Octr. and wishing to pass the 12th, which is also my brother in law's birthday, with him. The K. of Prussia returns back from Töplitz the 25th when the camp of the 3ᵈ corps d'armee is to be formed, and on the 9th of Septr the grand Autumnal manœvres commence, which are to last till the 22ᵈ. We shall have about 35,000 men together assembled.

I received a letter from Hertford from Warsaw who informs me that previously to his coming here he proposes going to Crackow & from thence to Vienna, and if he still can manage it, he will come to Dresden & Berlin; I should feel very sorry at not seeing him.¹ His nephew the son of George Seymour² of the navy, & Captain Meynell³ arrived at Berlin yesterday, I met them at dinner and they dine here this day with me, and another English gentleman recommended by Lothian⁴ who told me he saw you at Ascott Races looking remarkably well. I forget his name but I think it is Malby, I dined in company with them at Temple's:⁵ Capo d'Istria you have probably heard has taken & received his dismission from the Emperor of Russia, he is expected here in three days, and is going forthwith to Paris & London to see how matters stand previous to his deciding whether or not he will accept the situation of *Protector* offered him by the Greeks. I had a few lines from Adolphus yesterday, he had not written during the whole time of his stay at Pyrmont from whence he had just returned, and was to set out the following day for Rumpenheim, the estate of Landgrave Frederick's.⁶ His visit there will probably not be of very long duration, as I understand the old gentleman proposes coming to Strelitz the beginning of Septr. I hope therefore my brother may be induced to come & assist here the manœvres. I went on Friday last the 3ᵈ to Sans Souci pour faire ma cour to the Pr. Royal⁷ & rest of the Royal family there, it being the King's birthday, and I thought of you, how highly interested you would

1 In the summer of 1827 the Marquis of Hertford was sent on a special mission to Petersburg to invest the Emperor with the Garter. The ceremony took place on 9 July.
2 Admiral Sir George Francis Seymour (1787–1870), the eldest son of Vice-Admiral Lord Hugh Seymour (1759–1801). 3 Lord Hertford's cousin.
4 John William Robert Kerr, seventh Marquess of Lothian (1794–1841).
5 Sir William Temple (1788–1856), Palmerston's brother, and Chargé d'Affaires at Berlin, July 1827 to February 1828.
6 Brother of William IX, Elector of Hesse-Cassel, and the Duke of Cambridge's father-in-law.
7 Afterwards Frederick William IV of Prussia.

be to see that delightful spot, where the great Frederick lived so many years. I went & paid my annual visit to the Kings chambers, I feel a particular sensation when I enter that apartment, where are still all the marbles that he used, as also the little eye glasses & lorgnette he always carried in his waistcoat pocket. The Pr. Royal inhabits contiguous apartment[s] also remarkable in their way, as they are the rooms which Voltaire used to inhabit. They are on the ground floor leading to the terrace, at the end of which is the ground, where all his favourite grey hounds are buried, & there are little stones over each of them bearing the name of the dog. This séjour is the favourite one of the Pr. Royal and he always asks the King's permission to reside there while H.M. is at Toplitz. Now God bless you dearest brother, may every blessing & happiness, that this world can afford, attend you, is the sincere wish of [etc.].

1374 HENRY BROUGHAM *to* SIR WILLIAM KNIGHTON

York, Tuesday night [7 August 1827].

Y o u will easily beleive how dreadful this sad event,[1] already of course over—proves to me & not the less so because at a distance from every one I desire to communicate with.

The general damp & even dismay—cannot be described. The popularity of the Govt. was greater in this County even than in London, and all men of any sense or reflexion & many who have but little of either are now in the greatest alarm at the thoughts of being once more delivered over to the domination of Londonderry, Ellenbor'[2] & Co. Our trust is in this, that the King & the country are compleatly in the same boat, and that we shall be saved now as before by his firmness, from the worst of fates.

I certainly speak only as one of the country for *my trade* keeps me above all temptation of political offices—but I am the less biassed on this account in my judg^t and speak my wishes & opinions with the less scruple, because disinterested.

Pray be good enough to keep always in your mind that the same offer

1 Canning died next morning at Chiswick.
2 Edward Law, first Earl of Ellenborough (1790–1871), afterwards Governor-General of India. He had repeatedly criticised the Government's foreign policy whilst Canning was Foreign Secretary, and in 1827 he was acting with Lord Grey in opposition to Canning's Ministry. In 1828 he became Lord Privy Seal in Wellington's Ministry.

& pledge I gave C. last Spring, I deem to continue now with increased force & zeal. I am quite aware of certain objections to me in a certain high quarter—they are not unnatural & I blame them not—but I am still as anxious as ever to lend my very utmost and in all ways in my power *wholly out of office*, to save that quarter from the odious thraldom preparing for it as well as for the country. I will in any way most desireable serve *under* Huskisson (or whoever else is to lead us in the Commons) even more actively & submissively & chearfully than under C. because it will be more wanted—& I can answer for others as for myself to the uttermost.

1375 THE KING'S *Memorandum*
Copy.
Royal Lodge, Aug. 8, 1827.

THE KING recommends the Cabinet to reorganise the Government.[1]

The King has no desire to dissolve the present Government, provided they can agree in those principles of governing the country upon which the King has acted from the time the King undertook the Regency, up to the period of the King's coming to the Crown, and from that hour to the present.

The King distinctly stated to poor Mr. Canning (on his becoming Minister) that the King had no desire of forming what is termed, an exclusive Tory Government, as in that case it would have deprived the King of the distinguished talents of many members of the present Cabinet. Nevertheless there was a distinct understanding between the King and his late lamented Minister (Mr. Canning) on many very important points.

The King will begin, for example, by mentioning the question of Parliamentary Reform. The King joined with Mr. Canning, in giving his decided negative to that destructive project.

The King could not of course require of Mr. Canning to abjure his strong and settled opinions upon the subject of Catholic emancipation: but there was a distinct understanding that the King's conscientious feelings should not be disturbed upon that painful question, upon which the King's opinions are unalterably fixed: and moreover if at any time this question was to be forced upon Mr. Canning, from that moment the Cabinet was to be considered as dissolved.

1 Upon hearing of Canning's death the King at once sent for Goderich and Sturges-Bourne, making a conditional offer of the Premiership to the former, and vainly urging the latter to take the Chancellorship of the Exchequer.

If the present Government therefore chose to proceed upon the basis, thus framed by Mr. Canning, the King would then place Lord Goderich at the head of the Treasury.

The King desires to have the decision of the Cabinet with as little delay as the pressing circumstances of the case will admit of.

1376 VISCOUNT GODERICH *to the* KING

Downing Street, Aug. 9, 1827.

LORD GODERICH offers his humble duty to your Majesty, and beg[s] leave to transmit to your Majesty, th[e] assurance of your Majesty's confidential servants that they will not fail to take your Majesty's gracious communication into their immediate and serious consideration.

1377 VISCOUNT GODERICH *to the* KING

Downing Street, Aug. 9th 1827.

LORD GODERICH transmits to your Majesty, with his humble duty and grateful acknowledgements for your Majesty's kindness to him (of which he cannot but feel himself unworthy) the answer of your Majesty's Cabinet upon the memorandum which by your Majesty's commands Lord Goderich laid before his colleagues.

Lord Goderich and Mr. Sturgess Bourne will be ready to attend your Majesty whenever it shall please your Majesty to lay your Majesty's commands to do so.

1378 THE CABINET *to the* KING[1]

Downing Street, Aug. 9th 1827.

YOUR MAJESTY's confidential servants humbly beg leave to tender to your Majesty their dutiful acknowledgements for the gracious expression of your Majesty's wish to retain them in your Majesty's service, into which they entered with the most earnest desire to promote the honor and dignity of your Majesty, and the well-being of your

1 In Goderich's handwriting.

Majesty's subjects. Your Majesty's servants are sensible that they were honored with your Majesty's confidence upon principles which were calculated to promote these great objects; and by these principles they are entirely prepared to abide.

Your Majesty is pleased to call to their particular attention the two great questions of Parliamentary Reform and of Catholic emancipation, as subjects upon which your Majesty refers to a distinct understanding between your Majesty and Mr. Canning.

Upon the first question, that of Parliamentary Reform, your Majesty's servants have at no time entertained the thought of bringing forward or supporting it as a measure of Government.

Upon the subject of Catholic emancipation, your Majesty's servants beg permission humbly to observe that it was stated in a Minute by Mr. Canning, upon the formation of the present Government, that "the Catholic question was to remain, as in Lord Liverpool's Government, an open question, upon which each member of the Cabinet should be at liberty to exercise his own judgement, either in supporting that question if brought forward by others, or in propounding it either in the Cabinet or to Parliament; but if any member of the Cabinet should deem it an indispensable duty to bring forward individually the Catholic question in Parl^t, he was distinctly to state that he did so in his individual capacity". None of your Majesty's confidential servants hesitate in declaring their adherence to the terms of that Minute; and feeling the deepest anxiety to avoid disturbing your Majesty's feelings upon a question of so much delicacy and importance, none of them consider themselves called upon, at any time, to propound that question in the Cabinet, without a conviction of the most urgent necessity.

If, whilst Mr. Canning was at the head of your Majesty's Councils, any other Member of the Government had felt himself compelled to propound that question to his colleagues, and if it had been carried by a majority of the Cabinet against the declared objection and resistance of Mr. Canning, who was your Majesty's First Minister, such a decision contrary to Mr. Canning's opinion, would obviously have forced the question upon him in such a manner as to have led to the dissolution of the Government of which he was at the head. But your Majesty's confidential servants beg leave humbly to state to your Majesty, that they did not understand that such a decision, supposing Mr. Canning to be a party to it, would from that moment have dissolved the Government, although it would have been of your Majesty's prerogative to determine, under such circumstances, whether the Government so deciding, should continue to possess your Majesty's confidence.

Your Majesty's servants having thus presumed humbly to submit to your Majesty their sentiments and feelings upon the two important points to which your Majesty has been graciously pleased to direct their special attention, as preliminaries to the reorganisation of the Government, have only in conclusion to repeat to your Majesty the assurance of their devoted attachment to your Majesty's person, and of their earnest and cordial desire to render, upon every occasion, the conscientious discharge of their duty to your Majesty, compatible with your Majesty's wishes, feelings and comfort.

1379 THE MARQUIS WELLESLEY *to* SIR WILLIAM KNIGHTON

Phœnix Park, August 9th 1827.

You can properly estimate the affliction by which I am overwhelmed in receiving the dreadful intelligence of my dear friend Canning's alarming condition of health. The last account affords a gleam of hope. As I find that you have had the kindness to visit him on his bed of sickness & anguish, perhaps you will extend your goodness to me, & inform me, whether I must prepare my heart for his irreparable loss.

I must also trespass still further on your friendship, & must request you to give me some consolation respecting the result of this severe visitation on our beloved Royal master; it will require all his fortitude to relieve the tenderness of his generous heart under such affliction. If the sympathy of one of His Majesty's oldest & most devoted servants can be acceptable, I trust, that you will assure His Majesty of my most unfeigned participation in the just sorrow, by which his great mind is so severely affected.

You will confer a great obligation on me by an early answer to this letter.

If you should see Canning, pray assure him of my warmest & most anxious affection; I cannot abandon the hope of his recovery.

Lady Wellesley desires me to add her best compliments to you.

[P.S.] I am most happy to hear so good an account of your son, my godson; I wish you would tell me, what classical author, Greek or Latin, is his favourite, in order that I may send him one of my best editions

1380 THE KING *to* VISCOUNT GODERICH

Copy.

Royal Lodge, August 10th 1827.

THE KING sends his very kind regards to Lord Goderich.

As the King is very desirous of preserving the present Government, the King will accept the note transmitted to the King by Lord Goderich from the Cabinet, without entering into further detail: the Cabinet being fully in possession of the King's conscientious feelings & sentiments upon the Catholic question.

The King desires that Lord Goderich will send back a copy of the King's last note to the Cabinet.

1381 THE KING *to* VISCOUNT GODERICH

Copy.

Royal Lodge, 10 August 1827.

THE KING proceeds to suggest to Lord Goderich (a point exclusively between the King and Lord Goderich as First Minister) the best & safest mode of filling up the different offices.

It is impossible with any degree of security to the stability of the present Government, to admit any further Whig member in the present Cabinet, without its being at once designated a *Whig Administration*, & hence would be the continuance of weakness in the House of Lords, as in that case the Govt. would be deprived of all accession of Tory support, which is an object highly desirable to the King's feelings.

Lord Lansdowne should now take the Colonial Office which removes him from the embarrassment of Ireland. The King urgently hopes that Mr. Sturges Bourne will be prevailed upon to resume the office of Home Secretary of State; an appointment particularly agreeable to the King's feelings, & highly satisfactory to the country.[1]

To get possession of the Lonsdale interest the King would strongly recommend that the office of Woods & Forests should be pressed upon Lord Lowther, (but of course without a seat in the Cabinet). Should this arrangement however unfortunately not take place, the King desires Lord Goderich will leave the nomination of this office open, until the King shall have had the opportunity of conferring with him upon the subject; this being an office very much connected with the King's personal comforts.

1 Sturges-Bourne refused not only to return to the Home Office, but also to take either the Chancellorship of the Exchequer, or the Colonial Secretaryship with the "lead" of the House of Commons, and insisted on retaining the minor office of First Commissioner of Woods and Forests. See No. 1386.

The King would wish to urge in the *strongest manner* the propriety of the Duke of Portland taking the office of President of the Council: the Duke's near connexion with the late Mr. Canning renders this *necessary even* if it should be *temporary*; & it need not interfere with his intention of going upon the Continent.[1]

One word respecting Lord Dudley & Ward:[2] Lord Goderich may acquaint him that the King will carry into effect his friend Mr. Canning's intention of recommending him to the King for a rise in the Peerage. The King is not quite certain from what passed between Mr. Canning & the King in a late interview, as to what Ld. Dudley's final intentions are, relative to the holding office. If he should retire, the King strongly recommends that the Marquis of Wellesley should be looked to as his successor, in as much as it would be satisfactory to Europe, & to the corp deplomatique, very important considerations at this particular moment.[3]

Finally the King is of opinion that since Mr. Sturges Bourne declines the office of Chancellor of the Exchequer that Mr. Herries is by far the most proper person to fill that important situation:[4] the King hopes that Lord Goderich's sentiments will be in unison with the King's relative to these proposed arrangements.

1382 VISCOUNT GODERICH *to the* KING

Downing Street, Aug. 10, 1827.

LORD GODERICH begs leave to acknowledge with dutiful respect your Majesty's most gracious communication.

He is fearful that it may be found impossible to complete the arrangements so speedily as to have them all made public tomorrow: but your

---

1 The Duke of Portland, Mrs Canning's brother-in-law, succeeded Lord Harrowby (who retired because of his advanced age) as Lord President of the Council.

2 John William Ward, fourth Viscount Dudley and Ward, and (September 1827) Earl of Dudley (1781–1833), Foreign Secretary, 1827–28.

3 Dudley was anxious to resign the Foreign Secretaryship in favour of Lansdowne, but was dissuaded by Goderich, who was fully aware of the King's disinclination to strengthen the Whig element in the Cabinet. Wellesley had hoped to succeed Canning as Prime Minister, and would also have liked the Foreign Secretaryship. (*Wellesley Papers*, II, 207–8.)

4 On 3 July Herries had written to Canning, resigning his office of Financial Secretary to the Treasury on account of ill-health, but expressing his readiness to take some easier office which might be at his disposal. At Canning's earnest request, however, he agreed "to give him a little time to look for a proper successor". Herries, therefore, was not at all anxious to become Chancellor of the Exchequer, and on the 10th strongly urged Goderich to appoint Huskisson. (*Herries*, I, 131–6, 152, 154–5.)

Majesty may rely upon Lord Goderich's doing all in his power to accelerate the settlement of a matter of such importance to your Majesty.

Lord Goderich cannot but feel how unworthy he is of the confidence which your Majesty is pleased to place in him: but if he should fail in fulfilling your Majesty's expectations, he humbly throws himself upon your Majesty's goodness, and presumes (for which he solicits your Majesty's pardon) to hope that your Majesty will impute it to his own deficiencies, and not to any want of feeling for all that belongs to your Majesty's happiness and honor.

1383 VISCOUNT GODERICH *to the* KING

Downing Street, Augt. 10, 1827.

LORD GODERICH with his humble duty to your Majesty, transmits to your Majesty a copy of the memorandum which your Majesty commanded him to communicate to the Cabinet.

Lord Goderich has a thousand apologies to make to your Majesty for having omitted to send it in conformity with your Majesty's commands, with his former note of this evening.

1384 AUGUSTUS GRANVILLE STAPLETON[1] *to* SIR WILLIAM KNIGHTON

Charles St., Augst 11, 1827.

I COMMUNICATED to Mrs. Canning the kind inquiries which you told me the King had made concerning her, & she desired me to tell you how deeply she felt His Majesty's kindness. She added that the only consolation which she found in her present desolate condition, was derived from all that she understood that the King had said and done in proof of his regard & esteem for her lost husband's memory.

1385 AUGUSTUS GRANVILLE STAPLETON *to* SIR WILLIAM KNIGHTON

Downing St., Augst 11, 1827.

I PRAY you to lay my humble duty at His Majesty's feet, and to express to him the deep sense of gratitude which I entertain for the great kindness which he has manifested towards me.

1 An illegitimate son of Canning's friend, the first Earl of Morley, and Canning's private secretary, 1824–7. [1800–1880.]

Had His Majesty thought proper simply to signify his pleasure that I should be appointed to the Commissionership of Customs, I should have been at a loss to find words to thank him for such a signal mark of his Royal favour—but the peculiarly kind way in which he has conferred it has increased the weight of my obligation to him a hundred fold. It is indeed gratifying to my feelings, and my greatest consolation for my loss, that His Majesty should have recorded his opinion that the conferring a grace & favour on me, is also a mark of respect for the glorious and never-dying memory of him, whose confidence & protection it was the boast and happiness of my life to enjoy.[1]

1386 WILLIAM STURGES-BOURNE *to the* KING

Whitehall Place, 11 August 1827.

MR. STURGES BOURNE presents his humble duty to your Majesty; & as Lord Goderich, in pursuance of your Majesty's command, is proceeding to reorganise your Majesty's Government, he feels it to be his immediate duty to express to your Majesty his most grateful sense of your Majesty's gracious intentions towards him, as expressed to him by your Majesty on the 8th instant. And to assure your Majesty that no personal considerations should induce him to pray your Majesty to allow him to decline any office with which your Majesty might be pleased to honor him, if he could entertain a reasonable hope of being able to discharge its duties to your Majesty's satisfaction, and with credit and advantage to your Majesty's Government. He knows the indulgence with which your Majesty is pleased to regard the services of your Majesty's Minister, and feels that he should therefore be guilty of the greater injustice to your Majesty if he were to presume to undertake the discharge of the duties of an office most arduous in itself, and the difficulties of which would be incalculably enhanced by being connected, as it was proposed to be by your Majesty, with the conduct of your Majesty's service in the House of Commons. His entire and certain conviction of his own inability either to undertake the administration of the finances of the Kingdom, or to maintain with effect that station in the House of Commons to which he has alluded, makes it incumbent upon him to implore your Majesty to relieve him from that degree of anxiety

1 Stapleton was appointed a Commissioner of Customs on 31 August, *vice* Sir Frederick Watson, who had become Master of the Household.

which would in his case be inseparable from so distinguished a situation in your Majesty's Government.

Mr Sturges Bourne begs further to add that it would have been his first wish to have been allowed under that severe loss which reaches even your Majesty, to relinquish that less prominent station in your Majesty's Government with which he was favoured, for the temporary purpose of preventing an arrangement which Mr. Canning apprehended would be less acceptable to your Majesty. But he is so anxious to testify to your Majesty practically how sensibly he feels your Majesty's generous disposition towards him, and how entirely he also feels it to be his duty to undertake, at your Majesty's bidding, any task that it is within his competence to perform, that if your Majesty should on any account deem it useful to your Majesty's service that he should retain his present situation as one of your Majesty's confidential servants, he shall bow to your Majesty's commands, only hoping for a continuance of that indulgence which he has already received at your Majesty's hands.

1387 John Wilson Croker *to* Sir William Knighton

Adm[iralt]y, Aug. 11th 1827.

I A M penetrated with the King's goodness to me and have endeavour[ed] to express some part of what I feel in a letter which on the occasion of his birth day, I might with the less presumption venture to address to His Majesty. I enclosed you the letter & a copy of it which I would beg of you to read & if in your opinion there is no impropriety in it I would beg of you to cause the letter itself to be deliver'd to His Majesty tomorrow—the very peculiar circumstances under which this favor has been done makes it so much of a personal favor from the King himself that I think I cannot do wrong in acknowledging it as such, though I must be ever grateful to Mr. Canning's memory who in so liberal & kind & I must add *unexpected* a manner recollected, what was really, on my part, rather a hint than a request; & that hint itself was founded on some *denunciations* of vengeance against *me*, made, as was reported to us, by some persons who had been my friends, whose *mistaken* & *unjust* prejudice will, I am satisfied in good time, subside if not vanish altogether.

And now let me also unburden my heart of part of *our* debt of gratitude to *you*, for this & for so many other proofs of consideration & friendship. *We* know the *value* of your kindness, tho' we do not attempt to express either *it*, or the extent of what we feel for it.

Royal Lodge, 12 August 1827.

THE KING sends his very kind regards to Ld Godrich [*sic*].

The King has been disappointed in not seeing Ld Goderich to-day & hopes, that he will come really prepared for the purpose of settling the different offices of the Govt tomorrow.

The King has quite *made up his mind not* to extend the Cabinet with any more members belonging to the Whig Party.

The King has no personal objections to Lord Holland, but, the King has the very strongest objections, to run any risk, that the present Govt should bear either the name, or even the semblance of a Whig Administration.[1] It would be fatal to its stability, & what is more of consequence, in direct opposition to the King's principles, for Lord Godrich must remember what the King's conduct has been in governing this country—from the year '11 up to the present hour.

At the age of 65, the King is not to put this aside, to satisfy the crotchets of individuals. These observations arise from what pass'd in conversation with Ld Anglesey on Tuesday night.

1389 THE DUCHESS OF KENT *to the* KING

Turnbridge Wells, 12th August 1827.

THERE is no one, who has more reason to wish your Majesty, many, many, happy returns of this day, than my child and myself: we do so most earnestly—most warmly: we feel we have your Majesty's support and protection.

Victoria writes herself—and only regrets, she cannot send your Majesty some pretty flowers.

The only offering, I could think of making on this day, is the resemblance of our little angel: it will bring her to your Majesty's feelings, as, in all the innocency of her character, she appeared before you lately.

Feodora and Charles[2] have every sentiment on this day, they so gratefully owe your Majesty, for your graciousness to them.

With every feeling of attachment and respect Sir, [etc.].

1 Lord Dudley was ready to resign the Foreign Secretaryship in favour of Lord Holland.
2 The Duchess's son by her first husband. (1804–1856.)

Copy.   *Royal Lodge,* 13th August 1827.

THE KING desires distinctly to state, that the King has no personal objection to Lord Holland; on the contrary, the King has every kind feeling towards him.

The King cannot at present however consent to re-organize the Government, except with persons already filling offices.

The King has a settled opinion that this is the only mode of giving stability to the Government.

Whenever the time shall arrive which can only be determined by experience, the King will have no objection to consider the wishes of Lord Holland's friends.

1391 JOHN CHARLES HERRIES *to* SIR WILLIAM KNIGHTON

Great George Street, 14 August 1827.

I RECEIVED last night from Lord Goderich a message from the King which has quite over whelmed me. His Majesty's condescension & goodness are such that I cannot attempt to *express* my gratitude for them.

The way in which I must *prove* it, must be [by] exerting myself, to the utmost of my poor abilities, wherever I can do so with any hope of advantage to his service.

In the present instance his gracious proposal that I should undertake the office of Chancellor of the Exchequer comes to me at a most unfortunate time for me; when I am literally incapable, by reason of my impaired & precarious health, to discharge the duties of it, so as to have any hope of effectually promoting His Majesty's service.

I am about to write to Lord Goderich to state to him the painful necessity under which I am placed of soliciting the King's permission to decline the office under these circumstances: but I should nevertheless have gone myself to Windsor this morning to have apprised you of this intention, if a sudden & violent attack of illness in the night had not put me in a situation to render it improper for me to leave the House this morning.

I send this to you by a messenger because I know you expected me between eleven & twelve o'clock.[1]

John Charles Herries to Sir William Knighton, 15 August 1827. (*Herries*, I, 183–4.)

The King to the Duke of Wellington [15 August 1827]. (*W.N.D.* IV, 96.)

1 "I felt myself", he said, "placed in a very embarrassing situation by this sudden call to an office which had been at no time an object of my thoughts or wishes, and which, in the present condition of my health and strength, I could not contemplate without dismay." (*Herries*, I, 156.) His letter of the 14th to Goderich is in *Herries*, I, 181.

Downing Street, Aug. 15th 1827.

LORD GODERICH presents his humble duty to your Majesty. After repeated communications with Mr. Herries, who feels as a good subject ought to feel your Majesty's gracious intentions towards him, Lord Goderich regrets to state that considerations affecting his health which is greatly deranged and requires immediate and lengthened absence from all business, compel him to entreat your Majesty's pardon for declining to accept the office of Chancellor of the Exchequer.

Lord Goderich ventures therefore humbly to submit to your Majesty that your Majesty's service will be best promoted by placing in that situation Lord Palmerston, whose appointment would have the advantage of not adding any new member to the Cabinet in the person of the Chancellor of the Exchequer. If Lord Palmerston should become Chancellor of the Exchequer Lord Goderich would humbly solicit from your Majesty permission to offer to Mr. Herries the office of Secretary at War without a seat in the Cabinet.[1]

Lord Goderich is conscious that it is upon your Majesty's goodness and indulgence alone that he can rely to pardon him for not having literally executed your Majesty's commands in this matter. But your Majesty may be assured that let who will be in the post of Chancellor of the Exchequer Lord Goderich will consider it to be his own especial duty to consult in all departmental Treasury business your Majesty's ease and comfort. Lord Goderich begs to add that he will execute your Majesty's commands in respect to the vacant Bishoprick of Carlisle, and that he enters fully into the opinions so forcibly expressed by your Majesty as to the Episcopal Bench.

---

1 Herries was not informed of this offer to Palmerston, and, having received a message from the King, had reconsidered his refusal. He wrote on the 15th. "I felt myself compelled to declare that I would do my best to meet His Majesty's wishes", but later in the day he told Goderich that he "should be most happy if he appointed some other person to the office." (*Herries*, I, 158–60.) The King replied to Goderich's letter stating that though he would be very happy to do anything that might be agreeable to Palmerston, he still wished Herries to be Chancellor of the Exchequer. Herries then decided that he had "no choice but to go to Windsor to accept the Seals". The Whigs raised objections to the appointment of an ultra Tory, and the Government was threatened with dissolution.

Limmers Hotel, Conduit Street,
15th August 1827.

I ARRIVED in town yesterday, and I deem it proper to acquaint you that I shall be here for a few days upon my private affairs; and I hope I may have a chance of seeing you before my return to Ireland.

My business here is to endeavour to vindicate the D. of Wellington against a most unjust & unfounded insinuation in Mr. Long Wellesley's[1] late pamphlet that his Grace interfered to prevent a reconciliation with his father. This insinuation is founded upon his own misconstruction of a letter from me, which he ought to have construed in a directly contrary sense; but I am bound to do justice to the Duke whose conduct & intentions were most kind towards his ungrateful nephew on that occasion.

I had obtained Lord Wellesley's leave to come over for this purpose before we heard of Mr. Canning's danger. Lord Wellesley then stopped me; and for obvious reasons he would not allow me to visit London until after he heard that Lord Goodrich had received His Majesty's commands to fill up the vacancy in the Cabinet. He was afraid that it might be supposed that he had sent me here, if I appeared in London before matters were settled. The intelligence of Lord Goodrich's commission gave great satisfaction in Ireland.

Lord Wellesley told me he had written to you and it is therefore unnecessary for me to say how deeply he has felt the death of Mr. Canning. I am persuaded no one can have felt it more sincerely and I assure you that the inconvenience this sad event must have occasioned to His Majesty was one of the first reflections he made, and was often repeated.

Humble an individual as I am, I feel the loss of I might almost presume to say a friend—who always treated me with a degree of kindness & condescension which I never can forget.

I am happy to inform you that I left Lord Wellesley in the enjoyment of perfect health and in a more vigorous state of mind and body & more happy than I have known him for years. His circumstances are greatly

1 William Pole Tylney Long-Wellesley, fourth Earl of Mornington and second Baron Maryborough (1788–1857), son of William Wellesley-Pole, third Earl of Mornington. In 1812 he married the daughter of Sir James Tylney-Long and subsequently squandered her vast fortune and lived a profligate life. Early in 1827, on account of his having committed adultery, the Court of Chancery deprived him of the custody of his children, and, their mother having died in 1825, the Duke of Wellington, Long-Wellesley's uncle, was appointed their guardian. Long-Wellesley threatened "most scandalous expositions of family secrets" unless his parental rights were restored, and Wellington consequently declined to bring about a reconciliation between Lord Maryborough and his son until the threat was recalled. The correspondence is printed at great length in the pamphlet, and was widely copied by the newspapers.

improved and although he has lately declined situations of great emolument, he is content & satisfied with his determination. He has satisfied his own feelings and he is in good humour & in charity with all mankind. Late events have interested him very much and he feels inclined to take an active part in whatever is passing on his return to England.

I never saw two men better suited to each other that [*sic*] Mr. Lamb & Lord Wellesley. Mr. Lamb is a man of great moderation & good sense as well as liberality, which last is tempered with great discretion.

It is my intention to return to Ireland as soon as possible after I have settled how I may do justice to the D. of Wellington in the tiresome affair with his nephew.

So long an intrusion upon your time demands every apology. But I hope you will excuse me. Lord W. desired I would give you his best regards and so did Lady Wellesley who is wonderfully recovered. I cannot conclude with [out] saying that Ld. W's mind is become quite right on the subject of Mr. Johnstone.

The King to the Duke of Wellington, 17 August 1827. (*W.N.D.* IV, 96.)

1394 MRS CANNING *to the* KING

Harcourt House, August 20th 1827.

I CANNOT sufficiently express to your Majesty the grateful feelings of my heart overwhelmed as I am with the deepest sorrow at the severe & irreparable loss I have sustained.

If any alleviation can be felt under my present dreadful and hopeless affliction, it can only be from the assurance that your Majesty has so truly estimated the talents, the virtues, and the singleness of qualities possessed by him whom I deplore.

Your Majesty's gracious proposition relative to the Peerage becomes an honorable record to my dear husband's fame under a Monarch whose enlighten'd and benevolent mind stamped an increase of character upon the individual whom he selected for his confidential servant.

Under these circumstances your Majesty may suppose that I must hesitate before I can decline such a gracious and public mark of your Majesty's favor. But there are some considerations connected with this distinction which I hope your Majesty will allow to be explained rather than stated on paper.[1]

With the sincerest prayer for the continuance of your Majesty's health & prosperity, I am, [etc.].

1 See No. 1395.

1395 THE KING *to* WILLIAM HUSKISSON

Copy.

[August 1827.]

THE KING sends his very kind regards to Mr. Huskisson.

The King was already in possession of the state in which poor Mr. Canning's private affairs were left, before the King received Mr. Huskisson's communication.

The King felt desirous on the afflicting event of Mr. Canning's death, to give some testimony of the King's public and private feelings towards his memory, and hence the offer of the Peerage to Mrs. Canning. But the King was not then aware of the existing difficulties in regard to income.

Under such circumstances the King quite approves of the conduct of Mrs. Canning in hesitating to receive this distinction, until some opinion shall have been formed as to the prudence of the proposed measure; by which the King means from the necessary consequences that must follow; for the Peerage (thus circumstanced) could not be conferred, without a Parliamentary grant to sustain it, and that must of course become a matter for much consideration.

Mrs. Canning will however have the satisfaction and comfort of knowing that whatever it may be thought right to recommend, her husband's fame will alone be thought of; inasmuch as the King's confidential advisers on this subject happily embrace the late Mr. Canning's public and private friends.

1396 THE KING *to* SIR WILLIAM KNIGHTON

Royal Lodge, Th.ʸ n.ᵗ Augt 23ᵈ 1827.

A LETTER which I have receiv'd late this eve.ᵍ from Lord Goderich, respecting some unforeseen difficulties respecting the Bishopricks & which requires almost an immediate answer, has decided me to desire you to make me, *a very early* visit *tomorrow morning. See you I must*, & if your business requires it, you may return to London (after having seen me) as soon as you please. It is impossible to calculate, (especially at the present juncture) *what* may arise, from one moment to another; & it is also, next to impossible to tell how matters, (*even the most trifling*) may, in consequence become of the utmost importance. It is therefore I want, & *that I do call for your immediate attendance & presence.*

Till I see you, I shall add no more, than that I am always, [etc.].

1397 VISCOUNT GODERICH *to the* KING

Downing Street, Augt. 23, 1827.

LORD GODERICH presents his humble duty to your Majesty, and begs leave to enclose to your Majesty a letter which he has this morning received from Dr. Pett,[1] stating grounds upon which he considers himself called upon, by his age and infirmities, to decline the elevation to the Bench for which your Majesty had been graciously pleased to designate him.

Perhaps your Majesty may think it proper that Lord Goderich should endeavour to remove Dr. Pett's scruples.

Information has just been received from Paris, stating that Mr. Huskisson arrived there on the 20th inst: he was greatly shocked at the intelligence which reached him upon his arrived [*sic*], and was much fatigued and agitated with his very hurried journey.[2] The couriers, which conveyed to him the intelligence of Mr. Canning's death, had missed him on the road: and he had set off on his return as soon as he heard from Lord Granville of the alarming nature of Mr. Canning's illness.

He will doubtless be in England in a few days.

1398 VISCOUNT DUDLEY AND WARD *to the* KING

August 23, 1827.

LORD DUDLEY with his humble duty to your Majesty humbly acknowledges the receipt of your Majesty's letter of this day's date. Lord Dudley humbly assures your Majesty that he will not fail strictly to obey your Majesty's commands both in receiving Sir W. Knighton and in observing that secrecy which your Majesty enjoins.

1399 VISCOUNT GODERICH *to the* KING

Downing Street, Aug. 28, 1827.

LORD GODERICH presents his humble duty to your Majesty, and begs leave to acquaint your Majesty that Mr. Huskisson is just arrived in London, and awaits your Majesty's commands, whenever it may please your Majesty to convey them to him.[3]

1 The Rev. Phineas Pett (? 1755–1830). He had been Canning's tutor.
2 Huskisson had been seriously ill for six months and was at this time recruiting his health on the Continent.
3 The Whigs had threatened to withdraw from the Ministry if the King insisted on the appointment of Herries as Chancellor of the Exchequer, but on the 21st it was decided to shelve the whole question until Huskisson, the leading Minister in the House of Commons, returned from the Continent.

Knighton's draft.

[August 1827.]

THE KING desires Lord Goderich will acquaint Lord Lansdowne that the King has heard with deep concern that objections are made by some members of the Cabinet to the proposed appointment of Mr. Herries as Chancellor of the Exchequ.

The King desires distinctly to state that on the death of poor Mr. Canning, the first object & desire of the King was to preserve the fabric which the King's lamented Minister Mr. Canning had raised; & raised be it remember'd at the expence of his valuable life.

When Mr. Canning died the King at once placed himself in Mr. Canning's situation & bethought what Mr. Canning would have done could his superior spirit have still directed the miserable affairs of our present existence.

The King's first act was to send for Ld Goderich whom the King knew Mr. Canning intended at one time[1] to place at the head of the Treasury. The King next proposed to Mr. Sturges Bourne to fill the office of Chancellor of the Exchequer because the King knew Mr. Canning had at first proposed that office to him—but on finding Mr. Sturges Bourne's feelings to [be] averse to that or indeed to any office, Mr. Canning next thought of Mr. Herries. The King has it, or had it, in Mr. C's own hand. Mr. C. was at the same time alive to some difficulties arising out of the feelings of other individuals—& he dealt with them accordingly; but until Mr. C. had made up his mind to quit the Foreign Office Mr. Herries was the person he had decided on to take the seals of ye Chanc^r. During the three last interviews the King had with Mr. Canning, Mr. Herries's name was constantly brought before the King in consequence of ye intended retrenchments. Mr. Canning even made use of Mr. Herries's name to the King as the instrument to shew the necessity of these intentions—& added, he is the only man I can rely on for the actual knowledge of the great question respecting finance.

One of the many agreeable qualities Mr. Canning possess'd, as the King's First Minister was—that Mr. Canning never kept any thing back from the King. There were no minor secrets, & Mr. Canning even imparted to the King a Treasury Minute[2] which Mr. C. said Mr. Herries had drawn relative to the reduction necessary. Is it then surprising that Mr. Herries's name & great qualifications should have press'd upon the King's mind upon the death of Mr. Canning, as the fittest person to fill the office of Chancellor of the Excheq.

1 In April, when forming his Ministry. Stapleton says that Canning was "always in doubt" about giving up the Foreign Secretaryship. 2 See *Herries*, I, 139–44.

The King naturally thought y^t in nominating this gentleman the King was not only adding a most agreable person to the Cabinet but giving strength (which is the fact) to the Govt.

The King desires therefore to know what this objection means—as to the infamous disgusting attacks in the newspapers the King treats them with the contempt that such disgraceful conduct deserves.[1] As to the suddenness of the rise—the King would be glad to know if the services of this gentleman are to be lost to the country untill he shall have pass'd through certain offices, because he happens to be at this moment the fittest man in the Kingdom for this particular situation. The King has the authority of the late Mr. C. on that point—& of Lord Farnbo^{gh} of whom the King made a particular point of enquiring. Finally only yesterday Mr. Huskisson's had concurrence [*sic*] that Mr. Herries was the fittest man. The King supposes Ld. G. must be sensible also of his having reap'd so largely from his services. Is the King therefore to be debarred from fulfilling a duty to the country because it does not suit the fancy or the temper of particular individuals. The King is satisfied that this does not rest with Ld Lansdown because he has fill'd the office of Chancellor of the Excheq^r[2] & knows the difficulties.

The office requires ability & not aristocracy—but those who fill it well confer the benefit of aristocracy on their country. The late Mr. Perceval one day held his brief—& the next fill'd the office of Chanc^r of the Exqu^r & finally was Minister of the Kingdom. This gentleman was his present secretary—his aid—his every thing.

The most valuable among you—Mr. Huskisson was Secretary to the Treasury.[3]

The King's excellent & valued friend Ld Farnb^{gh} whom the King has lately made a Peer was Secretary to the Treasury.[4]

The King will have those that are proper for their business & if there be room after this—the Cabinet may if they please look out for ornaments.

1 He was accused of selling to his friend Rothschild, the banker, valuable information which his official position had enabled him to acquire.
2 In the Grenville Ministry, 1806–7.   3 1804–6; 1807–9.   4 1791–1801.

Downing Street, Sept. 1, 1827.

LORD GODERICH offers his humble duty to your Majesty.

From all that Lord Goderich can learn, the feelings of Lord Lansdowne and his friends are materially softened, and he is convinced that your Majesty's gracious message to Lord Lansdowne to attend your Majesty at Windsor this day, has had a most beneficial effect; and he is most sanguine in his expectation that the kindness and condescension with which your Majesty treats all those whom your Majesty invites to approach your Majesty, will lead to a satisfactory result of this harrassing business.

Lord Goderich humbly hopes that your Majesty will pardon him for taking the liberty of making this communication to your Majesty, vague as it is: but he is so anxious that the final arrangement of your Majesty's Government should be such as to relieve your Majesty from any farther trouble & anxiety, that he has presumed to intrude upon your Majesty with the substance of what has reached him as to the present disposition of Lord Lansdowne & his friends.[1]

1402 VISCOUNT GODERICH *to the* KING

Downing Street, Sept. 1, 1827.

LORD GODERICH cannot refrain from expressing to your Majesty, with his dutiful acknowledgements for your Majesty's gracious letter, the joy which he experiences at the termination of the recent difficulties in a manner so satisfactory to your Majesty's feelings, honor and comfort. But if he were to attempt to express what he feels as to the part which your Majesty has yourself taken in these transactions, he is conscious that he could convey but an imperfect idea of the sentiments which such conduct must excite in every well constituted mind.

He fears that in saying this, he has gone beyond due bounds: but he humbly hopes that your Majesty's goodness will pardon his presumption on account of the motive which has dictated it.

The Council is appointed for Monday, agreable to your Majesty's commands.

1 The attacks on Herries in the Whig press made it impossible for him honourably to withdraw his claims to the Chancellorship of the Exchequer. He might however, have agreed to the appointment of Sturges-Bourne or Huskisson, but neither would take that office and the Whig members of the Government decided to resign if Herries became Chancellor. At Huskisson's request Goderich wrote to the King urging him to give Lansdowne a cordial reception that afternoon (1 September), when he was to be asked whether he would resign or remain. Lansdowne, however, tendered his resignation but was in the end persuaded to stay.

Downing Street, Sept. 12, 1827.

LORD GODERICH begs leave, with his humble duty to your Majesty, to trouble your Majesty upon the subject of the vacant Bishoprick.

He saw Dr. Pett this morning, who still feels so strongly the force of those reasons which in the first instance induced him to decline the gracious offer which your Majesty was pleased to make to him, that his acceptance of a seat on the Bench is now out of the question.

It appears by what had passed between Mr. Canning and the present Bishop of Rochester,[1] that an expectation, if not a positive promise, of early promotion, was held out to his Lordship when he accepted the See of Rochester; and in furtherance of that expectation, Lord Goderich would humbly submit to your Majesty that he might be promoted to the Bishoprick of Carlisle.

With respect to the Bishoprick of Rochester, which would in that case become vacant, Lord Goderich has had much communication with the Bishop of London; and three individuals have occurred to them as persons, whom your Majesty might be advised to grant that Bishoprick.

1st. Dr. Coplestone,[2] whose name was formerly submitted to your Majesty by Lord Liverpool.

2. The present Bishop of Sodor and Man (Dr. Murray,[3] nephew to the Duke of Athol)[4]

& 3. Dr. Davison of Oxford, well known in that University as a man of great learning, and distinguished by some published lectures which are highly esteemed.

With respect to Dr. Coplestone, it is needless for Lord Goderich to trouble your Majesty with any remarks, as his character is doubtless well known to your Majesty.

The elevation of the Bishop of Sodor and Man to the See of Rochester would vacate his present Bishoprick, the presentation to which is now vested in the Crown: and it appears that some time ago Lord Liverpool had given a favorable consideration to his case.

As to Dr. Davison, Lord Goderich has every reason to believe that as a clergyman of the Established Church, and of high reputation in Oxford, he would be a very fit person to place upon the Bench; but he thinks it right to state to your Majesty that it is by no means clear that his

1 Dr Percy.

2 Edward Copleston (1776–1849), Dean of Chester since 1826; Bishop of Llandaff and Dean of St Paul's, 1828–49.

3 George Murray (1784–1860), Bishop of Sodor and Man since 1814; Bishop of Rochester, 1827–54.   4 John Murray, fourth Duke of Atholl (1755–1830).

opinions upon the Catholic question are in conformity with those who are adverse to it.

Lord Goderich has a thousand apologies to make for troubling your Majesty with so long a letter: but having to submit so many as three names for your Majesty's consideration, he could not avoid that trespass; and he was unwilling to intrude upon your Majesty at the Royal Lodge, unless your Majesty should command his attendance for the purpose of giving to your Majesty any explanation upon these matters.

1404 THE KING *to* VISCOUNT GODERICH

Copy.   *Royal Lodge*, Sept. 13, 1827.

THE KING sends his very kind regards to Lord Goderich, and thanks him for his letter.

The King regrets much that Dr. Pett declines the being raised to the Bench.

As to the other names which have been submitted by Lord Goderich to the King in consequence, two, out of the three, are perfectly known to the King, & have frequently occurred in the different conversations which the King has held from time to time with Lord Liverpool respecting the promotion to the Bench.

Allowing the full & just tribute to Dr. Copplestone's talents, & abilities which they are entitled to, it was nevertheless (for reasons well weighed & discussed over between the King & Lord Liverpool) then finally determined that Dr. Copplestone's name was not again to be brought forward.

This being the state of the case, the King highly approves in consequence of Mr. Canning's engagement to the Bishop of Rochester of speedy translation to another Bishoprick, that it should now take place, and that Lord Goderich should offer him the See now vacant at Carlisle, subject to such further arrangements respecting his other preferments as may be proper; & that then the Bishoprick of Rochester should be offered to the Duke of Athol's nephew, the Bishop of Sodor & Man.

The King highly approves of the communication which has taken place upon this head between Lord Goderich and that excellent prelate & man, the Bishop of London.

The King thinks that Lord Goderich cannot be surprized, after the strong sentiments which the King has expressed to Lord Goderich respecting the promotions to the Bench in general, & after the very fair & candid statement of Lord Goderich respecting Dr. Davison, if the King states that he could not listen to such a nomination for a single moment.

Ramsgate, 14th September 1827.

I AM embarrassed and at a loss how I can express, *as I feel*, the deep sense I entertain of your Majesty's graciousness: I am most sensible of the favor you have shown Miss Lehzen;[1] who is, all gratitude!

I am very glad your Majesty approves of my coming to the sea: I am *delighted* at your kindness in thinking of us, as you do.

Victoria thinks a great deal, of your message; and ask's many questions how you are—and is most particular in knowing, if I have yet sent back, her best love and duty, to her "dear uncle King".

Feodora is quite flattered with your Majesty's constant recollection of her.

Believe me, with every sentiment of grateful attachment, Sir, [etc.].

1406 COLONEL MEYRICK SHAWE *to* SIR WILLIAM KNIGHTON

London, 18th September 1827.

I SEND you a copy of the hasty sketch of some of the measures of Lord W[ellesley]'s administration in Ireland. I am sorry I have not been able to make it more fit to be seen. But I wrote under many interruptions and I had a bad copyist. The mem.ᵐ I sent you the other day relative to the Catholic Association joins on to the first part of the sketch. I also send a mem.ᵐ on the Tithe Composition Act and I hope to send you from Ireland a mem.ᵐ upon the police establishment and perhaps one or two other points of importance to the internal tranquility of Ireland.

You may depend upon my not having stated anything that I do not sincerely believe to be true, and I hope I have not made any mistakes although I had nothing to refer to but my memory.

P.S. I annex a short note separately relative to the means by which the Press in Ireland has been employed to thwart Lord W. It is but one instance of many that might be produced. I have put it separately because it points so closely to particular persons. Lord W. is not aware of the particulars of this transaction.

---

1 Queen Victoria's governess since 1824. The King now conferred on her the rank of a Hanoverian Baroness. (d. 1870.)

Copy.

THE principal scope of Lord Wellesley's instructions upon his going to Ireland at the end of the month of December 1821 and the main objects of his policy were to administer the existing laws in a spirit of mildness and impartiality, which might give to the different religious sects and political Parties of that country a confidence in the equal and unbiassed dispensation of justice: to correct the notion which has long unhappily prevailed in Ireland, that there was one law for the rich and another for the poor—one law for the Protestant and another for the Catholic; and by removing the real or imaginary causes of distrust in the impartial administration of justice to induce the people to confide in the protection of the law, and to yield it a willing obedience. It was also his object to discover if possible the causes of the continual appearances of discontent and the frequent recurrence of disturbance in Ireland and to suggest the proper remedies: and it was a farther object to conciliate all Parties and sects in Ireland, by shewing an equal degree of personal civility, and of attention to individuals of every persuasion, with a view to reconcile them to each other and to the actual system of the Government. For this purpose Lord Wellesley was not only permitted, but enjoined to admit Catholics to the enjoyment of a certain portion of the patronage of Government, by occasionally appointing duly qualified persons of that religion to such legal and other offices as *by the existing laws they were permitted to hold*, but to which none had yet been appointed, although for many years past they had been eligible by law to hold them.

This discretionary power has been exercised very sparingly, and with great caution by Lord Wellesley. It has only been extended to a certain proportion of the Chief Constables, under the Police Act; and, in a few instances, to the office of Assistant Barrister of Counties. There is an Assistant Barrister in each of the 32 Counties of Ireland. Ten vacancies have occurred since Lord Wellesley went to Ireland; and he has made of course but ten appointments of which *three* were Catholics, Messrs Farrell, Cruise, and Howley. They are men of high character at the Bar, of moderate principles and strongly recommended by the law officers of the Crown. Although these appointments have been but few, they have mitigated the sense of exclusion hitherto felt by the Catholics at the Bar; and they have had a tranquillizing effect. The lower order of Catholics have been encouraged by seeing a Catholic lawyer preside at Quarter Sessions, and the example it has afforded of Catholic barristers administering the law in the same spirit as their Protestant brethren on the

Bench, has inspired a more general confidence in the impartiality of the law.

Lord Wellesley has been equally cautious in the personal attention he has shewn to Catholic gentlemen of rank who are received at the Castle. It has been confined to Catholics of the first rank, and to men of moderate conduct: and in no instance has particular courtesy been shewn to any agitator or demagogue; though all who present themselves are of course received with civility.

Lord Wellesley took an early opportunity after his arrival to state publicly with reference to the Catholics that "he came to administer the laws not to alter them", and he has rigidly adhered to that principle. He has also carefully abstained from encouraging hopes of any change of system, beyond the conciliatory intentions of His Majesty's Ministers above alluded to, which had been fully discussed and agreed upon between Lord Liverpool, Lord Sidmouth, Lord Londonderry and Lord Wellesley before Lord Wellesley left England. It was not unreasonable to hope that views so moderate and beneficial might have been carried into effect without giving offence or exciting the opposition of any political Party in either Kingdom. Moderate however as these views were, they could not be acted upon without indirectly limiting the influence of a Party in Ireland who were jealous of a monopoly they had long enjoyed, not only of a principal part of the patronage, but also of the *ear* of the Irish Government. Their long possession of the exclusive confidence of Government had enabled them to keep all other Parties aloof from the Castle, and to represent themselves and their friends as the only persons who could safely be employed in places of trust and emolument, or who could be relied upon for correct information regarding the state of the country. Every avenue to the Castle and every office immediately connected with Government was filled with their friends and adherents, and it was scarcely possible for the voice of any other Party to reach the Lord Lieutenant for the time being or his Secretary. The underlings in office who are all indebted to this Party for their situations were devoted to its interests and were constantly on the alert to watch and impede any change of system, and Lord Wellesley has uniformly experienced their secret and unremitting opposition and counteraction in every department. It was chiefly by their means that the Press was turned against him. Of two newspapers in the pay of Government one espoused Lord Wellesley['s] policy upon his arrival in Ireland and it was immediately rejected by every individual connected with that Party. The advertizements of all the departments under Government were withdrawn from it, and the consequence has been ruinous to the proprietor.

A new paper called the Dublin Evening Mail was established by this Party for the professed object of defending the Protestant ascendancy, but really for the purpose of writing down Lord Wellesley's Government, and not a single number of that paper has been published without a personal attack upon his private or public conduct.

Lord Wellesley has always considered the prevailing notion that it is necessary to govern Ireland through a Party, to be wrong in principle and mischievous in practice. Whilst Ireland had a Parliament, it might have been necessary to a certain extent. The Kings Ministers in England must rely upon a Party to carry their measures in Parliament, which is the proper field for Party spirit, and where its action is legitimate & wholesome; but the Executive Government of England does not employ the aid of a Party to carry the laws into effect. The Government of Ireland since the Union being purely executive the system of governing through a party ought to have been discontinued.

The aid of a Party for such a purpose could only be purchased by conferring upon it the enjoyment of exclusive privileges which must render it an object of jealousy and hatred to the great majority of the nation, and in order to retain this monopoly, it is the interest of such a Party to accuse all others of turbulence and disaffection. It would be difficult to imagine a system better calculated to keep alive the discontented spirit of the Irish, and as long as it continues it is in vain to look for union or tranquility amongst the people of that country.

The system adopted by Lord Wellesley under the sanction of His Majesty's Ministers of admitting Catholics to a certain share in the places of emolument under Government, and of receiving information from re[s]pectable and well disposed persons of every persuasion without distinction was viewed by the exclusive loyalists as an invasion of their inherent rights and as an impeachment of their veracity.

Lord Wellesley was not at first aware of the extent to which they carried these high pretensions. He had no intention to hurt their feelings and spared no pains to conciliate a Party who from their rank fortune superior information and professed attachment to British connexion were entitled to every degree of consideration. But for some months before Lord Wellesley's arrival in Ireland that Party had taken a groundless alarm that some great alteration of system was in contemplation. The sudden and unexpected change in the Government of Ireland and the appointment of Mr. Plunket (whom they supposed to be hostile to them) to the office of Attorney General seemed to have increased their fears and they manifested a jealous and hostile disposition towards his Government from the instant of its commencement without waiting until the course of Lord Wellesley's measures could have convinced them of the moderation and impartiality of his views. A similar instance of hasty prejudgement has recently been exhibited by the Corporation of Dublin when the freedom of that city (which has heretofore invariably been granted to every Chief Secretary on his appointment) was withheld from Mr. Lamb on his arrival in Ireland, and before he could have given offence to any party. Lord Wellesley was nearly three years in Ireland before he made a Catholic appointment beyond that of a Chief Constable.

Before entering upon an enumeration of the principal measures of Lord Wellesley's administration in Ireland it will be proper to advert shortly to the state in which he found that country upon his arrival in Dublin on the 29th of December 1821, and to some of the difficulties he had to contend with.

A general insurrection prevailed in the South of Ireland where the civil power had ceased to have any authority, and was incapable of affording protection: the movements of the insurgents had assumed so serious an aspect that it was deemed prudent to concentrate the troops, to call in small detachments, and to withdraw safeguards from the houses of the gentry, and most persons who could afford to quit their homes had fled to the towns for safety. It is proper to remark that these disturbances had no connexion with political or religious causes. The acts of violence then committed were confined to a lawless resistance to the payment of rents or tithes, to attacks upon the houses of the gentry for the purpose of seizing arms, and sometimes of robbery and also to vindictive outrages against any person who ventured to occupy a farm, from which a tenant had been ejected for nonpayment of rent. The insurgents consisted of the peasantry and lower class of farmers who were reduc'd to great distress by the fall of prices after the war. The landlords of Ireland under an expectation very generally entertained at that period, of an early return to high prices had not had the prudence to make timely abatements of rent. Their tenantry had become universally discontented and some local acts of oppression by an agent on Lord Courtnays[1] estates occasion'd an explosion which soon spread throughout the South. The insurgents conceived the wild project of scaring the gentry from the country by terror and occupying the lands rent free. The resistance to payments of every sort was general. Even the priests dues were withheld. The Catholic clergy on this occasion took an active part in support of the laws, but without avail; and it is a remarkable circumstance contrasted with events at the late general election, that Lord Wellesley was informed upon his arrival in Ireland, that the *worst feature* of the disturbances in the South

1 William, third Viscount Courtenay, afterwards Earl of Devon (1768–1835).

was, that the *Roman Catholic priests had lost all influence with the people.*

It of course was Lord Wellesley's primary duty to put down this insurrection, and it was completely effected in a few weeks by a proper application of military force & by the immediate appointment of Judicial Commissioners, before whom the offenders were speedily brought to trial, and the sentence of the law carried into immediate effect. Convicts sentenced for transportation were marched from the dock to the place of embarkation, and this promptitude had the best effect. Occasional outrages have since then been committed; but no serious disturbance has appeared in the South of Ireland since that period.

Upon his arrival in Dublin Lord Wellesley found the Irish Government in the greatest possible state of alarm from other causes. The several entrances of the city of Dublin were fortified with pallisades & cannon. The gates of the Castle were shut, and the guards were doubled, stones were carried to the roofs of the house of the Commander of the Forces, and of other public buildings in order to be rolled down upon the assailants, and Dublin appeared in a state of siege. The cause of alarm proceeded from exaggerated reports of the objects and hostile intentions of illegal and nightly meetings held in Dublin and the neighbouring Counties as well by Ribbon as by Orange Societies; and it was confidently believed that an attack upon the capital was meditated by the Ribbon men. Such meetings certainly took place, and no doubt they were just objects of vigilance on the part of the Government. But that their intentions against Government were hostile, or that they had any design upon the capital was a pure invention of interested informers whose tales were too readily credited in a moment of panic. Lord Wellesley immediately directed his attention to ascertain the real object of these meetings, and as his enquiries were not confined to any Party, he speedily arrived at the truth, and he was convinced that no violence was ever intended, and that the object of the meetings was defensive on both sides against an imaginary danger. Two days after his arrival he ordered the gates of the Castle to be left open as usual, the guards to be reduced, and the barriers to be taken down, and from that day no guard has been reinforced or centinel doubled in Dublin, although some attempts were made to get up an alarm more than once in the early part of Lord Wellesley's administration.

The history of these secret meetings is shortly this. The Orange Party in Dublin took it into their heads soon after the Kings visit to Ireland that a change of system adverse to their interests was intended, and in order to avert the supposed impending danger and to muster and recruit their forces they directed the Orange Lodges throughout Ireland to assemble and renew their oaths of allegiance and also the Orange oaths. This general movement amongst the Orange men naturally produced corresponding movements amongst the Ribbon men who assembled for similar purposes, and took an oath to be true to each other and to be ready to turn out whenever called upon. Whether these orders proceeded from any leading committee in Dublin or by what authority the Ribbon men were to be called upon to turn out has never been clearly ascertained. But it has since been ascertained beyond a doubt that neither party meditated aggression. The alarm was kept up by trading informers who introduced themselves into the meetings of both Parties and who carried false and terrifying reports, of the hostile intentions of one Party against the other, in order to keep up a state of disquiet which they found extremely profitable. At one time Lord O'Neil[1] was represented to be on his march from the North at the head of 100,000 Orange men to put down the Catholics, and tales equally absurd were invented of the opposite Party. If the Castle had been thrown open to all Parties willing to give information as it has ever since been, the alarm would never have been felt to such an extent or have produc'd the effects it did.

If Lord Wel[le]sley had not render'd any other service than to detect and expose this mischievous system of false alarms his Government would not have existed in vain. Several attempts were made in the early part of his administration to counteract his policy by creating alarms for the purpose of excluding the Catholics from favour by rendering them objects of suspicion and terror. The last great effort of this sort was at the close of 1825, the period when Pastorini's prophecy[2] was expected to be fulfilled. A plan was then laid for terrifying the Government which probably would have succeeded with any Lord Lieutenant who was not a native of Ireland and thoroughly acquainted with the people. Several persons of the highest rank & respectability (many of whom no doubt were themselves sincerely alarmed) agreed to endeavor by simultaneous representations of danger from various parts of the country to impart their fears to the Government, and induce it to adopt some extraordinary measures of defence. They declared that their lives & property were in danger, they called for the protection of a military force, and asked for assistance to arm their tenantry and to fortify their houses. Had the Protestants been permitted to arm themselves, the Catholics of course would have done the same in self defence, and the Parties would soon

1 Charles Henry St John O'Neill, second Viscount and first Earl O'Neill (1779–1841), Grand Master of the Orangemen in Ireland.
2 For this, see Parker, *Peel*, I, 342.

have come to blows. But Lord Wellesley had early intelligence of the plan for spreading alarm, and at the same time he had information on which he could rely which convinced him that there was not the slightest ground for apprehension. He therefore remained unmoved and the people who had been for many weeks in a state of terror, dismissed their fears when they saw that the Government did not share in the alarm. That Winter, which was looked forward to with so much dread, passed away without a single outrage. The attempt has never since been renewed, and the trade of informer is nearly abandoned.

Lord Wellesley has never acted upon the ex parte information of any person or Party (however respectable) regarding the state of the country without enquiry. Wherever any secret information of insurrectionary movements, or reports from individuals of cases of disturbances or riots have reached Lord Wellesley, he has sometimes, in cases of minor importance, sought for information from some respectable unprejudiced person in the vicinity, but in general he has sent some barrister of rank and reputation, usually a Kings Counsel to institute a regular inquiry into the circumstances upon the spot. The effect of this practise has been useful in a twofold degree; it has discouraged hasty and designing representations on the one hand; and on the other hand it has satisfied the people that they would not be condemned unheard. Representations of this nature have often proceeded from ill temper, and from petty disputes between local factions, and not unfrequently from designing persons with a view to cause their corps of yeomanry to be called out upon pay, or to create for themselves or friends the office of a local Stipendiary Magistrate. The new police establishment has afforded additional means of checking false alarms and interested reports. On such occasions the Inspector General of Police for the district is directed to proceed and enquire upon the spot; and by the means of his officers and men who are spread in all directions, no deception can escape detection. The result has been that the race of informers is nearly extinct and that the alarms have disappeared with them.

It is evident from this short view of the leading features of Lord Wellesley's policy, that however well adapted to the welfare of Ireland under the circumstances in which he was placed, it was very ill calculated to gain popularity. It was naturally disagreeable to that Party in Ireland which had always given a bias to the feelings and language of the fashionable world regarding the Government of the day, because it was calculated to abridge their privileges; whilst, at the same time, it fell very short of the extravagant hopes, and expectations of the opposite Party. Both Parties had a direct interest in depreciating the value of

Lord Wellesley's measures. The ascendancy Party were naturally disposed to traduce a system which was calculated to admit the Catholics to a share of the patronage, whilst the Catholics for whose benefit this moderate alteration was intended, were unwilling to allow or acknowledge any improvement of their condition, lest it should be said that they ought to be contented.

Mr. O'Connell stated the case quite fairly and without disguise in a late speech at the Catholic Association. He "denounced Lord Wellesley as the worst enemy of Ireland, because his measures were calculated to cajole, and tranquilize the Catholic population by a partial redress of their grievances and thus to render them indifferent to the great object of unqualified emancipation." All Parties were thus united in withholding from Lord Wellesley the credit which was due to his services.

Amongst the difficulties which Lord Wellesley has had to contend with, the proceedings of the Roman Catholic Association hold a prominent rank. The leaders in that assembly have not only opposed occasional impediments to Lord Wellesley's efforts to tranquilize the country, but they have frequently endeavoured to underrate the benefits he has been able to confer upon the Catholics of Ireland. Lord Wellesley was quite aware when the Association was first formed, of the embarrassments it was likely to occasion, and he lost no time in considering the means of checking its proceedings, or of dissolving it if necessary. A considerable difference of opinion arose upon that subject. Lord Manners conceived that the existing laws were sufficient for that purpose. The Attorney and Solicitor General of Ireland were of a different opinion, and the law officers of the Crown, in England concurred with them. The draft of a Bill was accordingly prepared in Ireland for the purpose of controuling the Association: but it was considerably softened down in England, in order to ensure its favorable reception in Parliament. Upon hearing that such a law was in contemplation, Mr. O'Connell boasted that it was impossible to frame a law, which could prevent the Association from meeting and acting in some shape or other.—He said it had only to accomodate its form to the Act of Parliament; and as soon as the Bill was passed he suggested the necessary alterations in the form of the Association, so as to evade the provisions of the Act. As it was found impossible to dissolve the assembly in its new form, the Government of Ireland could do no more than watch its proceedings—a reporter employed by Government attended all its meetings. His reports of their proceedings were constantly perused without delay by the Lord Lieutenant, and whenever any seditious or libellous matter appeared, it was invariably submitted to the law officers for their opinion, as to its liability to prosecution. Mr. O'Connells speech in which he expressed his hope. "that a Bolivar would arise to avenge the wrongs of the Irish people" afforded the first opportunity for the interposition of the law, and Lord Wellesley did not hesitate to cause Mr. O'Connell to be arrested and bills of indictment to be prefered against him; but the bills were thrown out by a Protestant Grand Jury of the city of Dublin, who affected to doubt the illegality of the speech, although the legal authorities were clear as to the seditious tendency of the words spoken by him. The Jury were supposed to have been actuated by the unjust and inveterate hostility of that party, towards Mr. Plunket, whom they hoped to expell from the office of Attorney General, by shewing that the Government had no chance of obtaining justice in any cause brought before the Courts by him.—That spirit has shewn itself towards Mr. Plunket on so many occasions, that it is impossible to doubt its existence.—The degree of public attention which was attracted by this transaction, was supposed to have raised the importance of the Association, and a strong disposition appeared on both sides of the water to doubt the wisdom of noticing Mr. O'Connell's speech. These doubts were said to have been expressed by some high legal authorities connected with the Government of England—when Mr. Plunket was attacked in the House of Commons, not one voice was raised in his defence. He was however able to vindicate himself; but what he then experienced taught him caution for the future. The vigilance of the Lord Lieutenant, nevertheless, was not relaxed; and every instance of libellous or seditious language or of apparent illegality in the proceedings of the Association, was invariably submitted to the law officers of Ireland—several occasions occured in which the Attorney and Solicitor General of Ireland gave a decided opinion that the proceedings were illegal, but they always declined giving any opinion, upon the expediency of a prosecution; and they usually expressed a doubt, whether a conviction could be obtained from any Jury, before which a trial was likely to take place. On these occasions the case and opinion of the Irish lawyers was always referred by the Lord Lieutenant to His Majesty's Ministers; who, with the advice of the law officers in England decided that it was inexpedient to prosecute, in every case that was submitted to them, except in that of Mr. Shiel.—A prosecution was commenced against Mr. Shiel with the approbation of the Government and law authorities of both countries—but although his conduct had excited a very general feeling of disgust and disapprobation, yet a doubt of the wisdom of the prosecution very soon began to prevail; and the law officers have thought it prudent to let the prosecution drop. Mr. Peel a few days before he went out of office, declared in the House of Commons in the most manly and unqualified manner, that His Majesty's Ministers had entirely approved of the conduct of the Irish Government towards the Catholic Association, and he took his full share in the responsibility of their forbearance.—Although these attempts to bring the great offenders to justice were not successful, they were useful in checking the intemperance of the demagogues, and in preventing the mischief their violent speeches were calculated to produce in the country; but on the other hand, they no doubt tended to encrease the importance of the Association, and many well informed persons are apprehensive that any further attempts of the Legislature to put down the Association would not be attended with better success. Persons of this way of thinking, are inclined to hope, that if the Association is unnoticed its spirit will die away in time. The Association is however a monstrous evil; and it has usurped so many of the functions of the legitimate Government, that the co-existence of such conflicting authorities, would appear to be almost incompatible. At the same time it cannot be denied that some advantages have resulted from its operation as a safety valve. The feelings of discontent which find vent in violent speeches, might otherwise be employed in plots and conspiracies; and scarcely anything like secresy can be maintained, whilst such an arena exists for the public discussion of grievances. The extensive power and authority which this unauthorized and self constituted assembly now possesses over the Catholic population of Ireland is however a natural object of apprehension and jealousy.— It has sometimes acted beneficially in discouraging outrages when it has suited their own purposes, but that such a body should possess the means of agitating or tranquilizing so large a proportion of the population of Ireland, is in itself a source of danger. The means by which that power has been acquired, and the manner in which it is exercised by the Association are supposed to be equally simple and effectual. During the two first years of its existence the Association setting [*sic*] in Dublin, did not appear to have much communication with the country; and it was imputed to the leaders of that assembly, that there was no sympathy between them and the people, and that they were more intent, upon their own views of personal ambition, than upon the professed object of obtaining some general advantages for the Catholics. Mr. O'Connell noticed these reproaches in his speeches at that time; he said that as the people of England doubted whether the mass of the Catholic population of Ireland felt any interest in the objects so eagerly pressed by the Association, he would take care that Addresses to that effect should be presented from every parish in Ireland. The Association immediately began to court the Catholic clergy: praising them in the most glaring terms, and declaring a determination not to accept any restoration of civil rights unless accompanied with a suitable provision for their clergy. Until then, the Catholic clergy did not appear to take much interest in the proceedings of the Association; but a close union was henceforth established between them; and the Association became at once possessed of the readiest and most effectual means of communicating with the people, and of giving them any impression they pleased. Great pains were now taken to give the lower class of Catholics a high idea of the advantages from which they are excluded on account of their religion. Arguments of this nature addressed to their vanity as well as to their worldly interest, were eagerly listened to. The priests resumed all their influence over the people; who had shown but little respect for it in the disturbances of 1822 when it was exerted in favour of landlords and Government, in opposition to the lawless views of the peasantry. The collectors of the Catholic rent, are also of a class of persons through whom the Association may readily communicate with the people. By the active application of these means they certainly have succeeded in making the Catholic peasant as anxious for emancipation as the demagogue. It is a great mistake to ascribe the eagerness of the Catholics for emancipation to religious feelings alone. Their anxiety to participate in the honors and emoluments of the state, and to be released from disabilities which they consider degrading, is a still stronger motive with them for persevering in their demands. It would be uncandid to deny that this anxiety is now felt by the lowest as well as by the highest class of Catholics. Their opponents conceive that nothing short of a restoration of all that they possessed before the Reformation would satisfy them; but many of the best informed men in Ireland believe that if a safe mode could be found of admitting the Catholic laity, to a fair participation in the places and employments under Government, and of confering a moderate provision upon the clergy, the whole body of the Catholics would be content. The Catholic laity certainly do not desire to see their clergy possessed of wealth.

What Lord Wellesley's opinion may be at present upon the question of Catholic emancipation is not known to any one but himself. It may no doubt have been affected by the experience he has acquired during his residence in Ireland; but he has not lately expressed his sentiments on the subject. He has however been heard to say that nothing he has seen in Ireland has materially altered the opinions he expressed in the House of Lords in his speech on Lord Fitzwilliams[1] motion on the 31st Jany.

1 William Wentworth Fitzwilliam, second Earl Fitzwilliam (1748–1833), the Whig statesman.

1812. The only good report of that speech is to be found in Cobbetts Parliamentary Reports, volume 21. page 431.

TITHE COMPOSITION ACT.

It has generally been admitted that the unequal pressure of the tithes upon the poor in Ireland, and the oppressive manner of collecting them were amongst the principal causes of the discontents in that country. The inequality complained of was created by a resolution of the Irish House of Commons in the early part of the last century, which deprived the Church of the tithes of agistment. By that resolution grass lands became exempt from tithes, and the maintenance of the parochial clergy was thrown exclusively upon tillage.

Many evils are ascribed to this unjust spoliation of the Church property, and the prevalence of Popery amongst the peasantry of Ireland has been partly attributed to that cause.

The tillage of Ireland was at that period so scanty, that in order to produce a sufficient income for a Protestant clergyman it became necessary to unite several parishes. These "unions" as they are called were so extensive, that it was quite impossible for the Protestant pastor to have communication with more than a small part of his flock, and the Roman Catholic priest naturally took possession of the void space—

The agricultural pursuits of the resident gentry, and gentlemen farmers, was chiefly confined to grazing and they seldom grew corn sufficient for their own consumption. The tillage of Ireland was therefore in the hands of the poorer class of farmers, and of the peasantry, and they alone paid tithes—

Thus, in the Catholic provinces of Ireland, the income of the Protestant rector was derived from the poorest class of his parishioners; who, with very few exceptions were all Catholics.

The collection of tithes under such circumstances was a painful operation although the Protestant clergy were very moderate in their demands; and it became their uniform practise, to employ proctors or tithe farmers for that purpose.—The Protestant rector having quietly submitted to the loss of the tithe of agistment and never demanding small tithes, was content to receive little more than half what he was entitled to by law. But his proctor with whom he had contracted for a fixed annual income contrived to wring a great deal more from the cultivator of the soil, whose crops he had the power of viewing and valueing very much according to his interest, or caprice—This gave rise to constant litigation and to frequent riots, and violent resistance to what the peasant conceived to be exorbitant demands.

It was reported to the Lord Lieutenant about four years ago that there were six hundred tithe causes for tryal in one parish in the South of Ireland. The inconvenience of this system had long been acknowledged and several persons of the greatest ability had endeavoured to form plans for altering it, but they were all abandoned upon meeting some obstacle that was deemed insurmountable, and a very general opinion began to prevail that the evil was without remedy.

When Lord Wellesley went to Ireland, Lord Liverpool requested him to endeavour to correct the tithe system; and as it happened fortunately that Lord Wellesley had some time before considered the subject very fully with a view to bring it before Parliament, he was prepared to undertake the task with advantage. He had satisfied himself that the mode of collection was capable of improvement, without any encroachment upon the property of the Church, or medling in any degree with the principles of tithe property. In this view of the subject the task could not have been confided to safer hands; for no man living can entertain a higher respect for the Established Church, nor a more sacred regard for its property than Lord Wellesley.

As soon as he had collected the local information which was necessary to enable him to consult and protect the various interests connected with the subject, he sent his plan privately to Lord Liverpool who submitted it to the Cabinet by whom it was unanimously approved.

Lord Wellesley procured the practical information he required by means of personal communication with individuals in Ireland and by the aid of his private friends. The Chief Secretary at that period was too much occupied to spare time for it; and the despair of effecting any good deterred others from undertaking it.

Lord Wellesley found that a change of system was anxiously desired by the parochial clergy, and by the great majority of the landed proprietors, and also by the peasantry universally. On the other hand the Bishops, with scarcely any other exception than the Arch Bishop of Cashel,[1] were decidedly adverse to it; as were also some great landlords, and the whole body of grazing farmers. The Bishops wrote a strong remonstrance against any change of system: but it is much to their credit that they have since acknowledged their error, and that every one of them have declared, either by letter to Lord Wellesley, or in Parliament, that the measure has been highly beneficial to the Church.

When the plan proposed by Lord Wellesley was approved by the Cabinet and returned to him by Lord Liverpool he delivered it to Mr. Goulburn who drew the Bill destined to give it effect with great ability

1 Richard Lawrence, Archbishop from 1822 to 1838 (1760–1838).

and dispatch, and he afterwards watched its progress with great zeal and diligence. As the Bill was drawn by Mr. Goulburn without any communication with the Attorney General (who did not see it until it was printed) or with any Irish lawyer, some few practical defects were discovered in the Bill which have since been remedied by Mr. Goulburn.

The principle of the plan was very simple. As it was allowed by all that the amount of income actually received by the parochial clergy was not too great, it was evident that if that amount could be assessed in an equitable manner, and collected without exposing the parishioners to the extortions and vexatious proceedings of the tithe proctor, the evils of the system would be remedied and the object in view would be attained.

The principal impediment to any such arrangement proceeded from the exemption of grass lands from the tithe of agistment, by which the whole burden of the tithes was thrown upon tillage. An Act was passed in the Irish Parliament immediately before the Union confirming the resolution of the Irish House of Commons before alluded to, by which the tithe of agistment had been withheld from the Church for nearly a century; and as it was not advisable to attempt the repeal of that Act, Lord Wellesley proposed that the landed proprietors should make a voluntary surrender of that right of exemption for a certain term of years, and agree that the rectors income should be assessed equally upon every acre in the parish whether under grass or in tillage, according to its value—the assessment to be made by persons appointed by the rector and by the parishioners. The rectors income to be settled by the average of his receipts, and of the price of corn, for the seven years preceeding the agreement. It is highly to the credit of the land owners, that they readily and with few exceptions have agreed to the sacrifice required of them. The average rate of tithe for an acre of wheat before the Tithe Composition Act was from ten to twelve shillings an acre. All other sorts of corn paid in proportion. Under the Tithe Composition Act the average rate of tithe is from $1/6^{s\,d}$ to two shillings p. acre. When it is considered that the greater part of the tillage in Ireland is in the hands of the poor, and that every peasant and poor farmer, is relieved by the composition not only from the heavy and uncertain rate of tithe he had hitherto paid, but also from the annual valuations of his crops and other vexatious proceedings of the rector, some idea may be formed of the degree of comfort & satisfaction this arrangement has given to the poor, and of the wide extent of its operation. The Act is not compulsory; but it has been voluntarily adopted by a very great proportion of Ireland, and it is spreading over the country, at the rate of two or three parishes a week. In no instance has it failed to give satisfaction. The advantages of the arrangement are manifold and important. The income of the rector has in many instances been somewhat increased, and it has been greatly enhanced in value by the regularity of payment. It is collected either by the vestry or by a receiver appointed by the rector as may be agreed upon between them. It is paid cheerfully and all cause of dispute or ill will between the clergyman and his parishioners is removed. The landlord scarcely feels the sacrifice he has made, and he is fully compensated by the encreased comfort and contentment of his tenantry. The small farmer and the peasant is relieved from a heavy rate of tithe which is now converted into a moderate land tax equitably and mildly assessed and levied. But perhaps the Established Church is the principal gainer by this arrangement, inasmuch as it has put an end to the hostility which the Catholic peasant may be supposed to have felt against it when the Protestant rector was chiefly supported by a heavy tax upon his tillage, whilst the Protestant landlord paid no tithe for his extensive park and pleasure grounds.

The Dublin Evening Mail was set up for the express purpose of writing down Lord Wellesleys Government.

Yet this paper is supported by the Church and by every department under Government[1] by [several words obliterated]. Chief Constables appointed by Lord Wellesley upon applying for their commissions have been required to subscribe to the Evening Mail in order that they might be edifyed by daily libels upon their benefactor, and it appeared in a late trial in the Court of Kings Bench, that a gentleman appointed by Lord Wellesley to a seat at one of the Public Boards in Dublin, at the recommendation of a highly respectable and liberal nobleman friendly to Lord Wellesley's Government (who would be shocked if he knew it) became security for the proprietor of the Evening Mail, a week after his appointment, in order to sustain that paper then sinking under pecuniary embarrassments, and it further appeared, that he has ever since applied the patronage of his office which is very considerable to the object of maintaining that paper.

The Party who support the Evening Mail have had the address, to prevent the publication of this trial in any Dublin newspaper. The Patriot which is supposed to be Lord Wellesley's paper received an order from some secret enemy in the Castle not to publish it. The silence

1 [Marginal note in pencil] "This is quite correct in point of fact. But as it points to particular persons it is only meant for your own information. Many similar cases could be stated."

of the other papers must have been purchased. It has however been printed and circulated by the plaintiff in the trial.

These instances are mentioned to shew the species of opposition which every attempt to correct abuses in Ireland has uniformly met with. A history of the counteraction Lord Wellesley has experienced would be amusing and instructive, and it is wonderful that he has been able to effect any good under the difficulties he has had to contend with.

1408 WILLIAM HUSKISSON *to the* KING

Eartham, 21st September 1827.

MR. HUSKISSON presents his humble duty to your Majesty, and begs leave to acknowledge, with every feeling of gratitude, the exceeding kindness of your Majesty in condescending to take an interest in the re-establishment of Mr. Huskisson's health. He trusts, notwithstanding some slight interruptions, that, upon the whole, he has not lost ground since he had the honour of paying his respects to your Majesty.

Mr. Huskisson regrets extremely that your Majesty's considerate goodness should have prevented your Majesty from ordering Mr. Huskisson to attend at the Royal Lodge to receive your Majesty's commands.

Mr. Huskisson hopes that it is unnecessary for him to assure your Majesty that, in the discharge of those high publick duties which your Majesty has graciously confided to him, he can have nothing more at heart than to pay the most implicit deference to every wish in which your Majesty's personal feelings and comfort are concerned. In this disposition Mr. Huskisson will communicate with Lord Goderich on the arrangements which your Majesty is desirous should take place, in consequence of the Government of Jamaica being now vacant. Until they can consider the subject Mr. Huskisson is confident that your Majesty will forgive him, if he asks your Majesty's leave to abstain from submitting any advice to your Majesty, upon a matter of so much importance as the appointment, under present circumstances, of a successor to the Duke of Manchester.[1]

Mr. Huskisson feels that he should be wanting in duty to your Majesty if he omitted to take this opportunity of humbly stating to your

---

1 William Montagu, fifth Duke of Manchester (1768–1843). Governor of Jamaica, 1808–27; Postmaster-General, 1827–30. Huskisson referred to him as a "coarse, vulgar, stupid Duke", a "Jamaica-polished Grandee".

Majesty that, in accepting the Colonial seals, he considered the very intricate and delicate questions which, in consequence of the resolutions of Parliament[1] in 1823, have grown up, and are now pending, between this country and Jamaica, as involving the most formidable part of the labours which he was about to undertake. The attention which he has since devoted to this subject has convinced him that he did not overrate either its magnitude, or the difficulties with which it is beset; and that the greatest care and circumspection will be requisite to ward off the dangers which might arise both to this country, and to the most valuable foreign possession of your Majesty's Crown, from a continued misunderstanding upon points in respect to which the Legislatures of Great Britain and Jamaica are now unfortunately at issue.

Mr. Huskisson entreats your Majesty's indulgence for the liberty he has taken in presuming to trouble your Majesty with these observations. They pressed the more forcibly upon him, at the moment when he received your Majesty's letter, from his having been engaged yesterday in preparing a long dispatch to the acting Lieutenant Governor of Jamaica,[2] explanatory of the reasons which will impose upon your Majesty's servants the painful duty of submitting to your Majesty, at the next Council, an Order for disallowing the Slave Law Consolidation Act passed, in the last Session of the Jamaica Legislature:[3] this Act being the only return which that Legislature has made to the resolutions so strongly urged upon them in your Majesty's name, and in furtherance of the unanimous votes of Parliament.

The too probable consequence of this state of things, Mr. Huskisson apprehends, may be the revival, next Session, in the House of Commons, with increased difficulties, and feelings exasperated on both sides, of all those topicks of irritation connected with the state of the West India population, which it has been the anxious endeavour of your Majesty's Government to set at rest.

With these apprehensions of increasing perplexity (which Mr. Huskisson well knows were entertained by Mr. Canning) Mr. Huskisson

1 On 15 May 1823 the House of Commons had passed Resolutions declaring the expediency of adopting effectual measures to ameliorate the condition of the slave population in the Colonies.

2 Major-General Sir John Keane, first Baron Keane (1781–1844). K.C.B., 1815; Peerage, 1839.

3 "An Act to alter and amend the Slave Laws of this Island" (December 1826). The Act was disallowed because it forbade slaves to act as religious teachers, prohibited meetings for religious worship between sunset and sunrise, threatened with punishment persons collecting money from slaves for charitable or religious purposes, and contained a multitude of other objectionable clauses. Huskisson's Despatch is dated 22 September. The Jamaica House of Assembly declined to pass an amended Bill, alleging that its independence would be destroyed and the safety of the island endangered. (December 1827.)

feels that every thing connected with the management of your Majesty's affairs in Jamaica will require the most serious deliberation.

Mr. Huskisson returns to town on Tuesday next, and will wait your Majesty's commands to attend your Majesty on this subject. Your Majesty will perhaps allow him to mention that Thursday is fixed for a meeting of your Majesty's confidential servants on the not less intricate affair of Greece.

1409 THE DUKE OF CUMBERLAND *to the* KING

Schönhausen, Sept. 29th 1827.

MY last letter which our friend Sir William will deliver to you contained nearly all that had reference to the business in question, and God knows with my most anxious desire of not being too prolix I could not make it shorter than I did, and yet I fear it was much too long. I shall in this one therefore give you in the first place an account of *all* I have heard and think on the Brunswick business[1] on which I have had confidential communications *here*, and then give you a short resumé of our military manœuvres which I think may interest you.

According to my humble opinion the Brunswick business which was so judiciously submitted by you to the mediation of the Emperor of Austria, and the King of Prussia has been most disgracefully, not to make use of a stronger expression, mismanaged, by Pr. Metternich; Count Münster who writes me word, he had shewn you all my letters on this subject, does me justice in his last letter by saying "I had proved myself a true prophet in saying that Metternich would marr the whole business by undertaking himself to bring the Duke to reason, a thing as impossible as the removal of St. Paul's Cathedral. The only hopes I had of this mediation of Austria and Prussia was, that perhaps these two Monarchs might in some measure command respect and deference in him; the fact is Prince Metternich has since a long time had a dirty political plan of his own, which he never loses sight of, and which I think it highly necessary you should *privately and confidentially* be made acquainted with, namely that of gaining over to the interest of Austria all the minor Princes of Germany. That this is self evident I need not say; examine only how Austria does act at the Bundstag; and I strongly suspect that this said plan of his was the cause of his wishing, before Prussia acted, to have a conversation with the Duke. Nay I know from the most *undoubted*

1 See No. 1336.

authority that Metternich, after he had failed in his undertaking, made use of the following expression "that in *form* the Duke had failed towards you, as his guardian and uncle, but that in the *fact* he was *right*". Now you may be assured that he has spoken in this manner to the Duke, and I cannot but express my surprize how such a consummate politician, as the Prince is, can have been so much off his guard, to have expressed *such* an opinion to the person he did, and who repeated it to me yesterday with the utmost indignation. In fact *here* at Berlin there is but one opinion that reigns throughout all the Royal family, namely, that the Duke's conduct is not merely highly indecorous, but most ungrateful and infamous towards you. Your own character demands the fullest atonement, and that too in the eyes of all Europe. To obtain this there are but two means; the one by the mediation of the Emperor of Austria and the King of Prussia the two first Powers in Germany, and that failing, then 2dly by having recourse to a much more objectionable means, but alas! the only one remaining, by forcing him. God knows I am the last person to recommend strong measures, when less objectionable ones will succeed, but alas! here there is no medium, you must have justice done you, you try what fair means will do, failing in that, then you have no choice left; and the minor Princes must be taught they cannot insult on every occasion the higher Powers. I still hope that you will insist on the two Sovereigns trying *what* they can effect *acting together*, and you may rely on Prussia's feeling *all* that is right. Nothing ever raised my indignation more, than the impudence of the proposal of Pr. Metternich, that you, the King of Great Britain, should consent to plead your cause before a Commission composed of Monsieur Münch de Billinghausen, a Hannoverian Commissioner, and one from Brunswick, why everyone can foresee, that the result would have been that the Austrian and Brunswick Commissioners would outvote the Hannoverian one, and when I heard of this mad proposal, I could not help exclaiming, why the proposal is a *fresh insult* to my brother. Excuse my talking thus warmly on the subject, but it is more than flesh and blood can bear, it is more than a gentleman even in private life could endure. It is high time that something should be done to put the smaller Powers again in their proper places; and no time should be lost to remodell the Bundstag which is a *farce*, and a very expensive one too there is no denying. If you choose to read that part of my letter respecting Brunswick to Munster you may, but I will write to him fully on the subject and probably he will lay it before you.

Our manœuvres this year were upon a very grand scale the two corps d'armées, that of the Guards, and the 3d when joined which they were from the 7th gave us 35,000 men in the field; the 3d armée corps entered the camp the 25th of Augt. that is to say all the infantry of that corps consisting of the 8th, 12th, 20th and 24th regiments of the line, with their Landwehr regiments bearing the same numbers, each three bat^n strong so that there were 24 battalions of infantry forming two divisions, and each Div: composed of two brigades, each regt. of the line and its Landwehr regt. forming one brigade of 6 battalions, about 600 men strong each, so that each Division was about 7000 strong. The first week they were exercised in detail, on the 31st. the cavalry of the 3d armée corps joined the camp, namely the 4 regular the 6th Cuirassier, the 3d Lancers, my Regt. of Hussars, and Prince William's (King's brother's) Dragoons; and the 12 squadrons of Landwehr cavalry. The whole army corps of the 3d being united we exercised in a body the whole week, and on the 7th Duke Charles took ye command of the whole being the senior General. The 9th was grand Church parade and the two army corps were marched up in 3 lines the infantry in the first, the cavalry in the 2d, and the artillery in the 3d. After the King had passed the lines, they marched by the infantry in close columns of batt^{ns}, the cavalry in $\frac{1}{2}$ squadrons, and then the artillery after passing, we marched to our different stations, where the altars were placed, and each Division had its altar and service performed, it lasted from 9 in the morn^g till past 1 at noon. The two following days the troops exercised near Berlin then we had one resting day and on Thursday and Friday we again had manœuvres in the vicinity of Berlin. On the Saturday the troops all marched to Nauen and environs where they were divided into 2 corps the one commanded by D. Charles, the other by Pr. William. The King had given out his ideas as to the object of the manœuvres and these two Generals were ordered to execute them. Certainly D. Charles shewed the greatest skill and completely beat Pr. William, and there were all sorts of ruses de guerre executed by both sides. The whole succeeded to the King's full approbation, and when I say this, it is a clear proof that it went off well, as H.M. understands the profession most masterly and requires a great deal. The appearance of the troops was magnificent, and we had hardly any accident, one artillery man had his hand injured by his own negligence in cleaning the gun. I trust this will find you in perfect health. The Dss desires her kindest love, she is better and hopes to be able to write by next post. Believe me ever Dearest brother [etc.].

Huntly Lodge, Octr 15th 1827.

YOUR MAJESTY'S gracious message communicated by Mr. Huskisson added to the strongest attachment for your Majesty's person so forcibly impels me to the expression of my feelings, that I cannot refrain from entreating your Majesty to believe that if I consider myself at present incapable of serving your Majesty as I could wish, it is with the warmest gratitude, and sentiments of loyalty which form part of my very being, that I presume to lay myself at the feet of your Majesty, as your most faithful & devoted servant.[2]

1411 WILLIAM HUSKISSON *to the* KING

Somerset Place, 21st Octo. 1827, 11 p.m.

MR. HUSKISSON, with his humble duty to your Majesty begs to acknowledge your Majesty's condescension in sending, for his perusal, the letter which your Majesty has received from the Duke of Gordon, and which he now returns.

As your Majesty is graciously pleased to require Mr. Huskisson's sentiments in respect to the meaning of the Duke of Gordon's letter, he takes the liberty of observing to your Majesty, that the Duke of Gordon does not appear to place any part of his unwillingness to accept the particular situation offered to him by your Majesty's command, upon any special circumstances attaching to that situation. Upon the whole, therefore, although the wording of the Duke of Gordon's letter is not very clear, Mr. Huskisson feels himself bound (with whatever regret he has

1 George Gordon, fifth Duke of Gordon (1770–1836). In February 1828 he succeeded his father as Keeper of the Great Seal of Scotland. An attempt had already been made to secure his support. Arbuthnot wrote on 15 July: "The Duke of Gordon went to the Royal Lodge by command. The King was very civil to him, and said that he should have preferred him for India, but that Jamaica was open, and he might have that government. The Duke replied that he was going to Scotland, and that in the present state of things he preferred not being in office. Nothing could be more staunch than the Duke is to us." (*Bathurst,* p. 639.)

2 Huskisson inadvertently offered the Duke the post of Lieutenant-Governor of Canada without a previous communication with the Commander-in-Chief of the Army. Wellington had the right to take the King's pleasure with respect to the military part of the arrangement. (*Huskisson Papers,* pp. 254–5.)

The Duke of Gordon wrote to the Duke of Wellington on the 14th: "There is no one whose friendship and kindness towards me have been more uniform than yours. I therefore was not surprized altho very much flattered and gratified by your letter which I received last night, and as we have been friends above 40 years, I trust we shall continue so through life as firmly as the old rock which supports the Castle where you have so handsomely appointed me [i.e. the Governorship of Edinburgh Castle]. When you have an opportunity pray say what is proper from me to His Majesty." (Wellington MSS.)

come to that conclusion) to state to your Majesty his apprehension that it cannot but be considered as implying an indisposition on the part of the Duke of Gordon, to engage in any connexion of office with your Majesty's present Government.

Mr. Huskisson begs leave to inclose to your Majesty the answer, of the same date with the letter to your Majesty, which Mr. Huskisson has received from the Duke of Gordon, and which, owing to its having been addressed to Eartham, Mr. Huskisson did not receive in town till this evening.

If Mr. Huskisson had not had the opportunity of comparing with that answer the letter to your Majesty, he might have felt something more of hesitation in forming an opinion in respect to the Duke of Gordon's meaning.

Mr. Huskisson has thought it right to communicate the correspondence to Lord Goderich, who entertains the same view of it as Mr. Huskisson.

It does not appear to Lord Goderich, or to Mr. Huskisson, that the disappointment of not being able to obtain the benefit of the Duke of Gordon's services in Canada need make any alteration in the other arrangements mentioned to your Majesty by Mr. Huskisson, with Lord Goderich's concurrence, and of which your Majesty has been graciously pleased to approve.

Mr. Huskisson asks your Majesty's permission to be allowed to postpone the submitting of any new proposal, in respect to the Government of Canada, until he shall have given the subject further consideration.

All the intelligence from that part of your Majesty's dominions confirms Mr. Huskisson in the opinion, that it will be essential to select, for that important station, some person uniting, if possible, rank with habits of business, and powers of conciliation.[1]

1412   VISCOUNT GODERICH *to the* KING

Downing Street, Octr. 27, 1827.

LORD GODERICH presents his humble duty to your Majesty, and craves your Majesty's pardon for expressing his grateful sense of the kind interest which your Majesty has been graciously pleased to take in the event which has just occurred in his family.[2] No one can value such marks of your Majesty's goodness more highly than Lord Goderich.

1 Lord Dalhousie was appointed in 1828.
2 Lady Goderich gave birth to a son and heir on the 24th.

By the death of Lord Pembroke, the Garter and the Lord Lieutenancy of Wilts have become vacant. Upon the subject of the former honor Lord Goderich will presume to trouble your Majesty in a few days: but with respect to the Lord Lieutenancy of Wilts, Lord Goderich would venture humbly to submit to your Majesty, that Lord Lansdowne's rank, station and property in that County, appear to point him out as a person upon whom it might be proper to confer that situation; and whilst, considering the cordial & effective support which Lord Lansdowne gave to Lord Goderich in the House of Lords, (when Lord Goderich stood much in need of it), it would be personally very agreable to Lord G. to be authorised by your Majesty to offer it to Lord Lansdowne, he thinks at the same time that such an arrangement would be of general utility to your Majesty's service.

1413 VISCOUNT GODERICH *to* SIR WILLIAM KNIGHTON

Downing Street, Oct. 27, 1827.

SINCE I saw you, I have recollected that Lord Pembroke's death not only vacates the Garter, but also the Lord Lieutenancy of Wiltshire. Now this is Lord Lansdowne's County: and I confess it strikes me, that under all the circumstances of the case, it would be very difficult to avoid making him the offer of either the Blue Ribband or the Lord Lieutenancy. If the former were offered to him, the latter might very properly be offered to Lord Aylesbury:[1] but the most *natural* thing to do, would be to offer the Lord Lieutenancy to Lord Lansdowne, to which his residence & property in the County gives him a reasonable claim. I think, I confess, that with *two* things vacant, to which he might fairly aspire, he would justly consider himself as neglected by me, if *neither* were offered to him: and I cannot but feel that he has, individually, some personal claims upon me for such marks of attention. His consenting to act under me in the House of Lords, when he joined Canning, was owing entirely to *personal* sentiments towards me, and very contrary to the wishes of some of his more eager friends, who thought it lowered him.

Pray let me hear how you think this idea would be taken: because if agreed to, the sooner the offer be made, the better: "bis dat, qui cito dat".

1 Charles Brudenell Bruce, second Earl and first Marquess of Ailesbury (1773–1856).

London, October 27th 1827.

I HAVE the honor to report to your Majesty the death of General the Earl of Pembroke, Colonel of the 6th Dragoons and Governor of Guernsey.

I request your Majesty will signify your pleasure whether I may recommend Lt. General Sir William Lumley, K.C.B. to your Majesty to succeed the Earl of Pembroke as Colonel of the 6th Dragoons. He is a Lt. General of the year 1814, has suffered in your Majesty's service, served creditably during the late war, and commanded the British cavalry in the Battle of Albuhera to the satisfaction of Lord Beresford.[1]

His Royal Highness the Duke of Gloucester mentioned to me some time ago that, after the return of the expedition to the Helder[2] it had been intended by the late King to appoint him to one of the principal military Governments, that this intention had been dismissed at different periods, and that he wished that His Royal Highness' claim should be taken into consideration whenever an opportunity should offer. He at that time particularly mentioned the Gov.t of Guernsey; and since the death of the Earl of Pembroke I have again received from His Royal Highness an intimation of his wish that his claim should be considered.[3]

There may be an advantage, and on the other hand it might by some be considered inconvenient that a member of your Majesty's Royal family should be appointed Governor of Guernsey. If this last should be the case and your Majesty should be disposed to consider of the claim of His Royal Highness the Duke of Gloucester to one of the great Governments I would beg leave to submit to your Majesty that Field Marshall the Earl of Harcourt[4] should be removed to Guernsey; and that His Royal Highness the Duke of Gloucester should be appointed Governor of Plymouth.

If however your Majesty should think it proper that the Duke of Gloucester (whose claim as stated to me by His Royal Highness I have considered it my duty to submit to your Majesty upon the first opportunity) ought not to be appointed to a military Govermnent, I would

1 His appointment was gazetted, 9 November.

2 In 1799. This joint Anglo-Russian expedition was under the command of the Duke of York, and captured the Dutch fleet in the Texel, but had to evacuate Holland after an unsuccessful attack on Bergen.

3 The King's friend, General Sir William Keppel, was gazetted Governor of Guernsey, and the Duke of Gloucester Governor of Portsmouth on 8 November.

4 William Harcourt, third Earl Harcourt (1743–1830).

then beg leave to submit to your Majesty's pleasure that I might be permitted to recommend to your Majesty that General Lord Hill[1] should be appointed Governor of Guernsey; and that General Lord Lynedoch[2] should be appointed Governor of Hull vice Lord Hill.

All of which is humbly submitted to your Majesty by your Majesty's most devoted subject and servant.

1415 THE DUKE OF WELLINGTON *to the* KING

Novr. 2nd 1827.

I HAVE just received your Majesty's most gracious letter of the 1st inst.

I must do His Royal Highness the Duke of Gloucester the justice to tell your Majesty that when he spoke to me upon the subject of a military Government in February last, I begged him not to mention the subject to any body; but to leave it in my hands.

The reason for my making this request was that I was already in possession of your Majesty's opinion respecting the Duke being appointed to a Government, which your Majesty will recollect that you stated to me in conversation upon the Tower in the preceding month of Decr.

I did not inform His Royal Highness of your Majesty's opinion, and I discouraged him from making an application to your Majesty by which he would learn it, because I know how much your Majesty's comfort and happiness depend upon the society of your sister Her Royal Highness the Duchess; and I did not wish to expose that intercourse to be interrupted by any little irritation which the Duke might feel upon the subject; and I confess that I hoped that I might be able to persuade your Majesty to comply with the Duke's anxious wishes.

I submitted the case to your Majesty entirely as that of one of your Majesty's Royal family; and I am really anxious that your Majesty would be graciously pleased yourself to inform His Royal Highness of this favour done to him; as being the mode best calculated to insure all the advantages to be derived from this arrangement.

I am very grateful to your Majesty for your gracious kindness to Lord Hill.[3]

1 Rowland Hill, first Viscount Hill (1772–1842). Barony 1814; Viscounty 1842.
2 Thomas Graham, Baron Lynedoch (1748–1843).
3 The King promised to appoint him to the next military Government that should fall vacant. (*W.N.D.* IV, 146.) In 1828 he succeeded Wellington as Commander-in-Chief of the Army, with the title of Senior General upon the Staff.

I delay to transmit the official recommendations respecting this arrangement till I shall receive your Majesty's commands consequent upon this letter.

All of which is submitted to your Majesty by your Majesty's most grateful and devoted subject and servant.[1]

1416 THE EARL OF DUDLEY *to the* KING

Foreign Office, November 5, 1827.

LORD DUDLEY with his humble duty to your Majesty, humbly submits to your Majesty the name of Sir William à Court now your Majesty's Ambassador at Lisbon as a fit person to be employed as your Majesty's Ambassador at S. Petersburgh. In case this appointment should meet with your Majesty's gracious approbation, Lord Dudley would also submit to your Majesty the propriety of raising Sir William à Court to the Peerage at the first suitable opportunity.

Descended from an ancient and honourable family, engaged from his youth in the publick service, zealous in his attachment to your Majesty's person and Government, employing excellent abilities guided by sound discretion with unwearied industry in performing the duties of the various and trying stations which he has successively filled during a long course of years, Sir William à Court seems to have a reasonable claim upon your Majesty's favour. Lord Dudley ventures also humbly to submit to your Majesty that this splendid reward conferred by your Majesty upon a man as irreproachable in his private as he is meritorious in his publick life, and who in an arduous career has so often gained the praise and never once incurred the censure of his official superiors, would operate as a salutary example to your Majesty's diplomatic servants and encourage them to display the same skill and fidelity in a profession to which must often be entrusted the interests and honour of your Majesty's Crown.[2]

Should this proposal meet with your Majesty's gracious approbation, Lord Dudley would then humbly submit to your Majesty the name of

1 The King wrote to the Duke of Wellington on 2 November: "I heard from the Duke of Gloucester on the same evening I wrote to you, a most proper letter, in every sense of the word. I yesterday gave him Portsmouth. He immediately came over from Bagshot to kiss hands, & to thank me; he is quite delighted. I told him he would hear from you officially. You will therefore be so good as to write to the Duke, & acquaint Keppell that he is remov'd to Guernsey." (Wellington MSS.)

2 He was raised to the peerage, as Baron Heytesbury, in January 1828, and appointed Ambassador to Russia the following June.

Mr. Frederic Lamb now your Majesty's Minister at the Court of Madrid as a gentleman eminently qualified by his abilities and knowledge of the affairs of the peninsula to succeed Sir William à Court in the honour of representing your Majesty at the Court of Lisbon.[1]

1417 THE DUKE OF CUMBERLAND *to the* KING

Berlin, Novr. 10th 1827.

I AM rejoiced to hear by letters I received yesterday from England that you are now perfectly recovered from your late attack of gout, & trust & hope from the bottom of my heart that you are free from this evil for the winter; here it has begun very early, for we have had pretty hard frost already, so much so that there has been ice, but naturally this is of no duration, and in the next 24 hours we have rain again. I am most happy to have had it in my power to ascertain and prove that the assertion, which Pr. Metternich made Merveldt, of his having, in a conversation with the King of Prussia, brought him round to his view of the subject respecting the Brunswick business, *to be perfectly false*, for I have since I wrote last week to Münster seen Major Genl. Witzleben who was present at Toplitz when the King saw Metternich, & he solemnly declares no such thing ever took place, on the *contrary* when Metternich broached the subject, H.M. stopped his mouth by saying, "What, you don't mean to defend the Duke's conduct towards the King of England." Count Bernstorff who dined with us the day before yesterday also shrugged up his shoulders & *hinted* that really Metternich's faculties begun to fail him, & one could clearly remark this by his whole conduct of late. Now I do not pretend to say this, for though I can easily believe that his strength & perspicuity of viewing objects, from his hard working, added to his debauchery, may have been weakened, still on this occasion I firmly believe there is a great deal of *craft* on one hand, and also a good deal of *spleen* that induces him thus to act now. My reason for saying this is, that his great object has been constantly to gain over the lesser Princes of Germany to the Austrian interest, & then his vanity is such that it flatters him to be consulted by them on all occasions, thus he paid his court in the first instance to the D. of B. when at Vienna, & now he has completely got this deluded young man into his hands, & I am sure that that ridiculous & I must add insulting proposal of submitting the whole business to a Commission under Monsieur de Munch

1 This appointment was made in December 1827.

originated solely in Metternich, but how he could be so mad to suppose that you would ever accept such a proposal is to me inconceivable. Thus much to explain his *craft*, and now for his *spleen* I assume this is produced from the Greek affairs which he has and will indubatably constantly try to work against. Unfortunately I hear, he has such a complete empire over the mind of the Emperor that he can do whatever he chooses with him. It is for this reason I wrote last week so strongly to Münster to beg that he would press you to insist *on no step* being taken in this business unless *jointly* with the *two Sovereigns* of Austria & Prussia, and you may rely on what I say to you, that the *latter* is as fully impressed with the *gross misconduct* of the D. of B. as anyone of us can be. I expect the return of William of Brunswick from his brothers the day after tomorrow, as his leave of absence expires that day, and I know he was anxious to be back here for the 13th the birthday of his cousin the Pss Royal. I shall make a point of seeing him, and will inform you if I learn any thing worth reporting. Till now I believe you have found perfectly correct all I have informed you. The last conferences of Merveldt with Metternich, I have not yet been able to see, but have directed Reden to write to Hannover for a copy, as it is absolutely necessary for us to know all that passes in order that we may know how we are to act. There has been strange work going on on the part of Bavaria towards the Grand Duke of Baden[1] and a publication has appeared on the part of the latter Sovereign, I have only received it yesterday, but have not yet had time to read it. All this really requires serious attention, and it strikes me that some measure ought to be taken if possible to put a stop to all this scandale by a full understanding amongst all the Houses of the Princes of Germany as to the House Verträge. I mean by this to ascertain the laws in each of their respecting family compacts, the regulations of minorities, and guardianships. That this is very difficult to do I am fully aware of, but still I believe no one will deny if such an object could be obtained, it would be most desirable & would prevent many difficulties which sooner or later I fear will arise.

By the papers arrived yesterday I see Hart[2] is finally appointed Chancellor in Ireland, and as I understand that the Catholic meeting orators are so indignant at his appointment, I must suppose his Lordship's principles are not in harmony with theirs. I have been indignant of late in reading so many hints that there was an idea that that vagabond Mr. Brougham should be appointed to a high official situation, this I

1 Louis I (1763–1830) succeeded his nephew Charles V in 1818.
2 Sir Anthony Hart (1754?–1831), Vice-Chancellor of England, April 1827; succeeded Lord Manners as Lord Chancellor of Ireland in October.

cannot for a moment believe that any Minister, whatever his private opinions, or feelings may be, could so far forget that respect and duty to his Sovereign and master, as to offer him such a gross insult to propose the nomination to any situation under Government a man who has insulted on all occasions personally his Sovereign.

The death of the reigning Queen of Saxony at Liepzig the 6th was very sudden at last, her loss will be severely felt as she was universally beloved at Dresden.

We received last Tuesday the melancholy news that the Dss of Dessau [1] our eldest daughter was prematurely brought to bed the 3^d of a Prince, who died a few hours afterwards, this is the 2^d time that she has been disappointed in her hopes, and as she has as yet no son, the loss is the heavier. Thank God the accounts of the mother are very good, and by our not having had any letters since I trust all is going on well, but naturally Frédérica [2] is very uneasy. I hope however this day's post will bring us good news. Now God bless you, the Dss and George desire their best love & regards, [etc.].

1418 THE MARQUIS OF LANSDOWNE *to the* KING

Whitehall, Novr. 12th 1827.

LORD LANSDOWNE presents his dutifull respects to your Majesty and proposes to avail himself of your Majesty's kind permission to wait upon you at Windsor on some business connected with this department on Wednesday next. To save your Majesty the trouble of writing again, he proposes being at the Lodge at one o'clock on that day, if he is not in the mean time informed, that any other hour will suit your Majesty better.

Lord Lansdowne incloses a letter he has received from Lord Wellesley, as your Majesty may like to be acquainted with his Lordship's intentions with respect to leaving Ireland, & also with the important circumstance that by the precautions directed to be taken the 4th of November [3] has passed over with very little of the usual ebullition of Party feeling.

1 Frederica, daughter of the Duchess of Cumberland and Prince Frederic Louis Charles of Prussia, married Leopold, Grand Duke of Anhalt Dessau.
2 The Duchess of Cumberland.
3 The anniversary both of the birth and of the marriage of William III.

Berlin, Novr. 13th 1827.

I PROMISED you in my last letter which I sent off on Saturday, and which I hope you have received, to write again this day if I heard anything new from William of Brunswick who was to return here yesterday. He called upon me and I will state to you now, all he told me. "He said his brother was greatly agitated, so much so, that he had hardly any rest, he neither eat nor slept, and talked of nothing else but of Münster's refutation, that the person (an attorney I believe) through whom he had sent his challenge to Münster, had refused to deliver it, that now he had sent a fresh one and this by 5 different hands, in order that he might be sure of their arriving safe. That *he* William had done all in his power to prove to his brother the folly and impropriety of his conduct, and had told him *all* that *I* had said to him previous to his departure, but that his brother was as obstinate and wrongheaded as ever; that his brother had written himself *now* to Prince Metternich to *consult him* how he was to act in consequence of this manouver of Münster, that in the meantime he was preparing a counter refutation which was to be wrote by Friske. This is a précis of what he told me of the present state of things at Brunswick. There are still two curious anecdotes he mentioned in the course of the conversation, which I drew from him, namely first, that Metternich has *never* written him one line, or has any communication passed between the Duke and Metternich, since they saw each other last summer at Vienna; nothing can prove more clearly than *this* how extremely inconsistent Metternich's conduct is at present, that *he* who has so completely got possession of the Duke, who gives him complete protection by declaring that he is perfectly right in the whole business, that notwithstanding all this, he should never have written him one line in consequence of this refutation of Münster's that has appeared in all of the conversations he has had with Merveld, all this shews a levity on the part of Metternich which is inconceivable.

2dly. He told me that previous to any step taken, Hurlebusch disapproved of the Steck Brief against Schmidt Phiseldeck and when the Duke ordered him to draw up those statements and libels he did, that he stated to the Duke that by doing it he would *get deep into the mud*. I think the German expression William used was "dass er wurde sich ein hübschen bouillon machen" [*sic*]. It appears that *he*, the Duke himself, collects all the materials, and then makes them draw up the papers. As I have not time to write today to Münster, perhaps you will have the goodness to send him this letter to read, that he may know all that I can learn respecting this business. I am going the day after tomorrow for a few days to a grande chasse at Strelitz to my brother-in-law, where the Prince Royal as well as Pr. William the King's son are also going.

We received on Sunday the grand news of the victory gained by the Allied fleets over the Turkish & Egyptian fleets, which has caused universal joy here.[1]

Frederica desires her kindest love and believe me [etc.].

The Duke of Wellington to the King, 13 November 1827. (*W.N.D.* IV, 158.) There is no copy of the King's reply in the Windsor archives, but the original, dated Royal Lodge, 14 November 1827, is among the Wellington MSS. at Apsley House. "I receiv'd your letter yesterday mark'd *confidential*, I shall *strictly* consider it, as *such*. On the same evening that I had the pleasure of seeing you, the Lord High Admiral sent me for my signature the document conferring upon S[i]r E^d Coddrington the G.C.B. which I immediately return'd with my signature. I mention this, only to shew you, that the measure was already settled."

1420 VISCOUNT GODERICH *to the* KING

Downing Street, Novr. 16, 1827.

LORD GODERICH cannot acknowledge your Majesty's letter of yesterday, without expressing, with his humble duty to your Majesty, his grateful sense of the condescending kindness with which your Majesty has been graciously pleased to convey to him your Majesty's sentiments upon the two points, to which your Majesty's letter refers. Nothing can be more agreable to Lord Goderich's feelings, than such a testimony of your Majesty's favor, except its being in his power to shew, in the humble discharge of his duty to your Majesty, how highly he values such condescension.

Lord Goderich entirely and cordially concurs in your Majesty's desire to translate the Bishop of Llandaff[2] to the See of Winchester; a choice not more gratifying to your Majesty's personal feelings, than proper in all respects as regards the individual. The necessary steps shall immediately be taken for carrying your Majesty's intentions into effect.

With respect to the sucession to the Bishoprick of Llandaff, Lord Goderich cannot hesitate to admit the entire fitness of Dr. Coplestone for the honor which your Majesty proposes to confer upon him; and in order that his sentiments may be clearly understood upon the point to which your Majesty refers, Lord Goderich has requested Dr. Coplestone to come to town, conceiving that that point can be most satisfactorily ascertained by a personal interview, at least in the first instance.

1 The Battle of Navarino, 20 October.   2   Dr Sumner.

Lord Goderich will now, with your Majesty's permission, state for your Majesty's consideration, what occurs to him upon the subject of the preferment which these arrangements *would* vacate.

The Bishoprick of Llandaff is so small in itself that Lord Goderich humbly presumes that your Majesty would not wish it to be disunited from the Deanery of St. Pauls with the assistance of which it is a very eligible piece of preferment. But there are some similar considerations connected with another Bishoprick, which Lord Goderich humbly begs leave to bring under your Majesty's consideration with respect to the disposal of the Deanery of Chester. He alludes to the Bishoprick of Rochester of which the income does not exceed £800 per ann: and the only piece of preferment, which Lord Goderich was enabled to offer to the new Bishop, was the living of Bishopsbourne, previously held by the present Bishop of Carlisle;[1] the real value of this living is not more than £1100 per ann:, so that the total income of the Bishop is under £2000; and Lord Goderich was so strongly impressed with the manifest inadequacy of that income, that he could not avoid assuring the Bishop that he should feel it to be his duty to take the earliest opportunity of recommending to your Majesty to take his case into your Majesty's gracious consideration. It appears to Lord Goderich therefore that the Deanery of Chester which Dr. Coplestone's elevation to the Bench would vacate, would furnish an opportunity of effecting this object, which Lord Goderich humbly begs leave to state to your Majesty to be of real importance to the dignity of the episcopal station, under the present circumstances of the Bishoprick of Rochester. Altho' therefore this is a different arrangement from that pointed out in your Majesty's letter, yet if your Majesty should be graciously pleased to approve of this proposition (which appears to arise naturally out of the state in which the preferment at the disposal of the Crown now happens to be placed) Lord Goderich cannot but flatter himself that your Majesty will feel it to be consistent with those views respecting Church preferment, which he knows to influence your Majesty's opinion upon such subjects.

There is now vacant also a stall at Westminster, from the recent death of Dr. Fynes Clinton, which Lord Goderich thinks might, with your Majesty's approbation, be conferred upon Mr. Manners Sutton,[2] late chaplain to the House of Commons, in whose favor Addresses have been presented to your Majesty by that House of Parlt. The means of providing for such persons are limited; and as a considerable time has

1 Dr Hugh Percy.
2 The Rev. Thomas Manners-Sutton (? 1795–1844), the Archbishop of Canterbury's nephew.

elapsed since Mr. Manners Sutton ceased to be chaplain to the House of Commons, perhaps your Majesty will be graciously pleased to approve of what Lord Goderich has ventured to suggest with respect to that gentleman.

Lord Goderich humbly entreats your Majesty's pardon, if after having troubled your Majesty with so long a letter upon these subjects, he postpones the other topics of your Majesty's letter till tomorrow.

Lord Goderich craves your Majesty's indulgence upon this point, because the extreme pressure of the business under the consideration of the Cabinet, added to much anxiety with which he has no business to trouble your Majesty, has hardly left him a moment to turn that matter in his mind.

1421 THE DUKE OF CUMBERLAND *to* SIR WILLIAM KNIGHTON

Strelitz, Novr. 18th 1827.

I RECEIVED here yesterday your letter announcing to me your having delivered my letter to my brother, & that he approved of all I had stated therein to him. I trust & hope he is convinced that no brother, or anyone else can be more faithfully attached to him, to his interests, or honour than I am, and that it is my constant prayer that every thing may go to his perfect satisfaction.

Since I have seen you, I have had communication with some of my old political friends, and am happy to say that they perfectly coincide in opinion with me respecting the D. of Wellington's having accepted the gracious offer of my brother and renewing the command of the army.[1] This is a very great satisfaction to me, & I hope now that all will go on smooth; but it seems to me (at least at this distance) hardly possible to form any distinct notion as to the present state of the feelings and sentiments of the servants of H.M. and *this* will only shew itself whenever Parliament meets. It seems to me to rest simply on this, whether Lord Goodrich has nerve enough to stand against the extravagant demands of the Whig Party of his colleagues; but as my brother has shewn so much character and determination on the late occasions, Ld Goodrich must I should think see that he will be supported by my brother, and that ought to give him strength of mind to face these gentlemen. Mind if my brother has at any time any thing he wishes to communicate to me, write me but two lines & every due attention shall be paid to it. Give him my best & kindest love and believe me, [etc.].

1 In August, after Canning's death. (*W.N.D.* IV, 96.)

Royal Lodge,
Fri.ʸ n.ᵗ ½ pt 12. [? 16 November] 1827.

ACCORDING to my promise, & altho^h quite knock'd up, I write this short line, accompanying Ld Goderich's list of Baronets,¹ upon which I have put my remarks & queries, which I wish to be answer'd satisfactorily, before I send my final fiat. One man, Mr. Williams, if it is the Mr. Williams, who has lately dispos'd of Moor Park to Lord Grosvenor,² I believe him to be not unworthy of such a mark of distinction. But there has been two Mr. Williams, cousins to each other both members of Parliament; one a most respectable loyal man, & always supporting the King's Government. The other one of the very worst of Radicals, invariably opposing the King & his Government in every instance, in short one of the staunchest, bitterest & very worst of Whigs, a friend of Hunt's &c &c &c, and I rather believe he was member for Dorchester, but I am not quite sure of this. All I mean is this, that a thorough enquiry should *first* be made, because, if it should turn out to be Williams the late or present Radical, (for once a Radical, always a Radical) he *shall not be made a Baronet.*³

God bless you, I am much too fatigued to say more, than to desire you to carry Lord Goderich's paper back to him, with my remarks upon it.

1423 VISCOUNT GODERICH *to the* KING

Downing Street, Nov. 19, 1827.

LORD GODERICH presents his humble duty to your Majesty, and now begs permission to lay before your Majesty what has occurred to him upon the latter point adverted to in your Majesty's letter of the 16th.

If the two Peerages to Lord Roseberry and Mr. Lambton⁴ (amounting however to only *one addition* during the present Parlt)⁵ had not been

---

1 "I gave [the King] a list of a dozen baronets whom I proposed to make", Goderich wrote to Huskisson on the 6th. "He took it and said he would look it over; and I do not think he will object to any, at least not *pertinaciously*, although there were one or two whom he did not seem to relish very much." (*Huskisson Papers*, p. 257.)

2 Robert, second Earl Grosvenor, afterwards Marquis of Westminster (1767–1845). Moor Park is in Herts.

3 Owen Williams and Thomas Peers Williams, who shared the representation of Great Marlow, voted with the Whigs, but Robert Williams, the member for Dorchester, was an anti-Catholic.

4 John George Lambton, Lord Grey's son-in-law. Created Baron Durham, January 1828; Earldom, 1833. (1792–1840.) With Lambton in the Lords, said Goderich, Grey's influence would be diminished. "I am sure it will strengthen the Government." (Add. MSS. 38752, fo. 17.)   5 The Earl of Rosebery being a Scottish Representative Peer.

brought into question, until your Majesty was graciously pleased to call Lord Goderich to his present post, he might probably have felt less of difficulty in postponing them for a limited period: but the embarrassment to which he fears the postponement would expose him in the conduct of your Majesty's service, arises from the very peculiar situation in which Mr. Canning found himself, when compelled to seek for strength in new quarters. At this crisis the two individuals in question were amongst the foremost in declaring their unqualified support of your Majesty's Government; and their wishes as to the Peerage were urged upon him, not certainly as *conditions* of support from others, but as objects to which their friends looked as being of the greatest importance in rendering that support efficacious. If under these circumstances, their wishes were now to be complied with, it would be rather the completion of an arrangement originally contemplated by Mr. Canning, than a new act on the part of Lord Goderich; and it ought not therefore to excite any uneasy feelings in the minds of those who may be now more favorably disposed towards your Majesty's Government than they were some months ago. It appears also to Lord Goderich that the arrangements already carried into effect, & now in contemplation with respect to the Church, as well as your Majesty's disposition to offer the blue ribband to Lord Powis, would tend still further to allay such uneasiness if it should exist.

Upon the whole, Lord Goderich would presume humbly to submit to your Majesty's gracious consideration whether under all the circumstances of the case, your Majesty's service would not be best promoted by allowing the proposed Peerages so far to take their course, as to admit of their being announced by the time Parliament meets. Upon the question of time, it may also be necessary to bear in mind your Majesty's gracious offer to confer a Peerage upon the family of Mr. Canning. Lord Goderich understands that Mrs. Canning intends to avail herself of this distinguished proof of your Majesty's kindness in marking your Majesty's feelings towards the memory of her husband, should be [*sic*] circumstances in which her family finds itself, in any degree admit of it. From the date of that offer, as well as from the peculiar character of this Peerage, your Majesty will probably think that it should precede, were it but for a few days, those to which Lord Goderich has now adverted.

Upon the subject of the Baronetcies, with respect to some of which your Majesty required explanation, Lord Goderich has to state that Cap^n Ricketts[1] is a naval officer of much acknowledged merit and

1 Vice-Admiral Sir Robert Tristram Ricketts (1772–1842). Baronetcy, December 1827.

service: he is a man of competent fortune, and a relation of Mrs. Lawrence of Studley, who feels a strong interest in his favor.

Mr. Wakeman[1] is much recommended by one of the members for the County of Worcester, and Lord Goderich understands him to be a man of large fortune & highly respectable.

With respect to Mr. R. Williams, Lord Goderich has been unable to ascertain as yet any thing precise: and therefore he humbly submits to your Majesty that his elevation may at all events wait.[2]

Lord G. has written to Mr. Horne Elphinstone[3] to acquaint him with your Majesty['s] gracious intentions, & will communicate to all the others, whenever he knows your Majesty's decision respecting the two gentlemen above refered to.

1424 THE EARL OF DUDLEY *to the* KING

F.O., Nov. 21, 1827.

LORD DUDLEY with his humble duty to your Majesty acknowledges the letter of yesterday's date which he had the honour to receive from your Majesty last night.

Lord Dudley humbly acquaints your Majesty that there is at present no vacancy in this office, but Lord Dudley will take care that in obedience to your Majesty's commands the first that occurs shall be considered as reserved for Sir Walter Scott's son.[4] In the mean time Lord Dudley will not fail to make Sir Walter acquainted with your Majesty's gracious intentions towards his family, and Lord Dudley reckons himself fortunate in being made the channel through which your Majesty's favour is to be conveyed to the most distinguished man, with whose acquaintance Lord Dudley has been honoured near thirty years.

The diplomatic appointments mentioned by your Majesty as agreeable to your Majesty all appear at a first view, such as it would be proper to recommend to your Majesty, but Lord Dudley would humbly request of your Majesty to be allowed a day or two to turn the subject in his mind, in order that he may be able to offer to your Majesty any such remarks as further consideration may suggest to him, and as may seem to him likely to lead to the benefit of your Majesty's service.

1 Sir Henry Wakeman (1753–1831). Baronetcy, December 1827.
2 He was not made a Baronet.
3 Sir Robert Dalrymple Horn Elphinstone (1766–1848).
4 The novelist's second son, Charles, was appointed to a clerkship in the Foreign Office shortly afterwards. (1805–1841.) See Scott's letter to Knighton, 15 November. (*Knighton,* I, 387–9. Copy at Windsor.)

Downing Street, Nov. 21, 1827.

LORD GODERICH presents his humble duty to your Majesty, and begs permission to acquaint your Majesty that Mr Denison,[1] one of His Royal Highness the Lord High Admiral's Council, is about to accompany Lord William Bentinck[2] to India.

Lord Goderich would humbly recommend to your Majesty that the seat in the Council, thus vacated, should be offered to Lord Sandon, the eldest son of Lord Harrowby, whose introduction into official employment Lord Goderich conceives would be very useful to your Majesty's service.[3]

1426 VISCOUNT GODERICH *to the* KING

Downing Street, Nov. 22, 1827.

LORD GODERICH presents his humble duty to your Majesty, and begs leave to acquaint your Majesty that he has had an interview with Dr. Coplestone.

Nothing could exceed the frankness and fairness with which Dr. Coplestone expressed his sentiments upon the important point to which the conversation referred, or could more tend to raise his character as a man of the highest honor and the strictest integrity.

The opinions which he stated himself to entertain, were such as would lead to the belief that however he might think that under certain circumstances he might think some modification of the laws now in force with respect to the Roman Catholics, might not be unadviseable, yet that the present moment would not be a fit one for such a measure: and whilst he cannot profess an undeviating hostility to all and every part of that question, yet upon some of the points with respect to which relief is sought by the Roman Catholics, he objects to concession.

Lord Goderich has thus, in obedience to your Majesty's commands, held this communication with Dr. Coplestone, fully impressed indeed with the extreme delicacy of its nature, and by no means unapprehensive

1 John Evelyn Denison, first Viscount Ossington (1800–1873), Speaker of the House of Commons, 1857–72. Appointed a member of the Lord High Admiral's Council, 2 May 1827. The state of his wife's health prevented him from going to India as Lord William Bentinck's private secretary.

2 Appointed Governor-General of Bengal in succession to Lord Amherst, June 1827; sailed, January 1828.

3 Lord Sandon's appointment had not been gazetted when the Goderich Ministry collapsed.

of the embarrassment which a knowledge of it by others might entail upon Lord Goderich. He felt it therefore to be his duty to state to Dr. Coplestone in the outset that all which was about to pass between them, was strictly confidential and secret; and Lord Goderich feels most deeply impressed with the infinite importance of that secrecy being maintained.

Under these circumstances it will be for your Majesty to consider, whether Dr. Coplestone's opinions as thus explained constitute an insuperable bar, both now and at any future period, to the elevation to the Bench of one so eminently qualified for that distinction in all that respects individual abilities, character & reputation.

If however it should not be your Majesty's pleasure to view the case in that light, Lord Goderich would *humbly*, but *most earnestly* entreat your Majesty to allow the new Bishop to be chosen from persons educated at Cambridge.

1427 THE KING *to* VISCOUNT GODERICH

Royal Lodge, Novr. 23d 1827.

THE KING desires, that Lord Goderich will see the Bishop of London, shew him, first, Lord Goderich's note to the King, (which the King incloses for that purpose) & then, let the Bishop of London, see the King's answer. This note of the King's, may also be shewn to Dr. Coplestone, but *in confidence*.

Lord Goderich may as well remember, that Mr. Canning, in one of his speeches made at Liverpool, years ago, publicly declar'd, that he thought it a *principle of duty, not to disturb the King's mind*, (the late King being then living) during the life time, of his *then* Sovereign.[1] At the age of sixty five, the King would ask Lord Goderich, why this dutiful respect, is not to be extended, to himself. If however Dr. Coplestone does not give way, the King remembers, that Lord Liverpool mention'd two Cambridge men to be thought of, one, Dr. Chafey[2] a few years ago Vice-Chancellor, the other, the King does not immediately recollect, but perhaps the Bishop of London, may. There is another very excellent Cambridge man, the Honble. Mr. Cust.[3]

1 This speech is not given in Therry's edition of Canning's *Speeches*.
2 The Rev. William Chafy (1779–1843), Master of Sidney Sussex College, 1813–43, and twice Vice-Chancellor.
3 The first Baron Brownlow had two sons in holy orders, Henry Cockayne (1780–1861) and Richard (1785–1864).

1428 Dr Copleston *to* Viscount Goderich

Copy.

Chester, Nov. 24, 1827.

In the late interview with which your Lordship favored me, I was so little prepared for the subject of the conversation, that I feel some anxiety lest I should not have conveyed with sufficient accuracy the impressions of my mind upon the main point of your Lordship's inquiry; and I trust it will not be thought presuming too far upon your goodness if I submit to your consideration, a brief, but a deliberate statement of the opinions I then intended to express.

I have always openly avowed myself adverse to unqualified emancipation—and if called upon to vote upon the question of admissibility to Parliament, my conviction has hitherto been against it. But having witnessed the progressive relaxation of the laws against the Catholics without danger or inconvenience to the Established Church, I have never felt so sure that *nothing* further can with safety be granted, as to join in the petitions and addresses which express that sentiment—nor do I think I could conscienciously think that I could give an absolute pledge to that effect.

The advocates however of the Roman Catholics have hitherto always seemed to me to aim at so much more than appear'd consistent with true policy that I have no apprehension of being induced to support their measures. And it is only in compliance with a feeling which I hope is neither arrogant nor unreasonably scrupulous, that I shrink from a declaration the full extent of which my judgement does not approve.

I was obliged to leave London for Chester immediately after my interview with your Lordship, and am now about to return to Oxford. I mention this to account for the delay in making this communication— a step which I venture upon trusting to your Lordship's kindness & candour for given [*sic*] it a favorable construction, altho' I by no means wish to impose the trouble of any further notice.

1429 The King *to* Viscount Goderich

Copy.

Royal Lodge, Nov: 27, 1827.

The King sends his very kind regards to Lord Goderich.

The King has read with very great attention Dr. Copleston's letter to Lord Goderich, on the subject of Catholic concessions. If the King understands the version of Dr. Copleston's letter *correctly*, the sentiments there utter'd, are nothing more than the echo of the opinions of those who support the established Protestant Constitution in Church & State in Parliament.

Under these circumstances it may be convenient to elevate a man of so much learning & acknowledged ability, to the Bench. The King therefore desires that Dr. Copleston may be acquainted with his being appointed Bishop of Llandaff and Dean of St. Pauls.

Dr. Ward,[1] Lord Goderich's old tutor, has been mentioned to the King. It will give the King great pleasure to approve of any proposition relative to that gentleman, and as Dr. Philpot,[2] it seems, cannot be thought of at *present*, perhaps Dr. Ward might be appointed to the Deanery of Chester. The King fears that it is not very valuable, but being so appointed, he may be transferred to a better when the opportunity [?occurs].

1430 VISCOUNT GODERICH *to the* KING

Downing Street, Nov. 28th 1827.

LORD GODERICH with his humble duty to your Majesty, begs leave to offer to your Majesty his warmest and most grateful acknowledgement for the very gracious manner in which your Majesty was pleased to write to him yesterday.

Lord Goderich has in consequence written to Dr. Coplestone to-day to offer him the Bishoprick of Llandaff and the Deanery of St. Pauls: and will not fail to acquaint your Majesty with his answer as soon as it is received. There can scarcely be a doubt that he will accept it, & consider it, as he ought, the strongest proof of the high opinion which your Majesty is pleased to entertain of him.

Nothing that your Majesty could have done towards Lord Goderich personally, could be more gratifying to his feelings that [*sic*] your Majesty's kindness about Dr. Ward, for whom Lord Goderich thinks a very satisfactory opening may be made thro' the medium of the Bishopric of Sodor & Man. That Bishoprick might, Lord Goderich humbly submits to your Majesty, be very beneficially disposed of, by offering it to Dr. Rice,[3] the Dean of Gloucester, brother to Lord Dynevor: he is a very

---

1 William Ward, Bishop of Sodor and Man, 1827–38. (d. 1838.)

2 Henry Phillpotts (1778–1869). Dean of Chester, March 1828; Bishop of Exeter, 1830–69. He vehemently opposed Catholic emancipation until the surrender of the Wellington Ministry in 1829.

3 Dr Edward Rice (1779–1862), Dean of Gloucester. He was the younger brother of George Talbot Rice, third Baron Dynevor. (1765–1852.)

worthy man, and has a large family, and Lord Goderich thinks that the Bishoprick of Sodor and Man might be very acceptable to him. Should this arrangement be agreable to your Majesty, and should Dr. Rice agree to it, the Deanery of Gloucester might then be given to Dr. Ward, and the Deanery of Chester to the Bishop of Rochester.

Sir Geo. Rose declines the Baronetcy which Lord Goderich was authorised by your Majesty to offer to him: but Lord G. finds (what he was not before aware of) that a Baronetcy was some time ago all but made out for Mr. Chamberlain,[1] who has been for a considerable [time] chargé d'affaires at Rio Janeiro. He may therefore, if your Majesty pleases, be the substitute for Sir Geo. Rose. Lord Goderich has reason also to believe that Lord Wellesley would wish to recommend one or two Irish gentlemen for that honor, upon which Lord G. will hereafter take your Majesty's pleasure.

Lord Clive[2] has returned an answer in a very *friendly tone*: he will be in town tonight to see Lord Powis, & Ld G. expects to see him to-morrow. He will communicate the result to your Majesty.

According to what Lord G. understood to be your Majesty's pleasure, he returns his letter of the 22nd, together with the paper marked secret which accompanied yr Majesty's letter to Lord Goderich of the 23rd.

1431   MRS CANNING *to* WILLIAM HUSKISSON
Copy.

Woresley Park, Novr. 28, 1827.

THE message which I have received from you, stating the necessity of my immediate decision on the subject of the Peerage, not being accompanied with a notification that it was the intention of the Government to propose any means of obviating the difficulties which induced me in the first instance to hesitate in accepting His Majesty's most gracious offer, I am led to conclude that no such intention exists. I have therefore no new grounds upon which to form my decision, and as, after the most painful & anxious deliberation, I have come to a determination which may appear in some degree inconsistent with my former opinions on the subject, I must trespass on your time & patience in order to explain the motives upon which I have formed my present decision.

1 Henry Chamberlain, Consul-General and Chargé d'Affaires at Rio Janeiro, 1815–19. Created a Baronet, December 1827. (d. 1829.)
2 He succeeded his father as second Earl of Powis in 1839. (1785–1848.) See No. 1433.

The gracious intention expressed by H. My of shewing *through me* the opinion His My really entertained of the splendid talents which had been devoted to his service, conveyed to me in the most feeling & condescending manner a very few days after the deplorable event—excited naturally in my mind the warmest feelings of unbounded gratitude, and the first impulse of my heart was to accept immediately & without hesitation so public & explicit a testimony to that worth & those talents, of which the Sovereign was at once the best & the most unquestionable judge. Upon further consideration, however, I felt that I should not be justified in accepting such a distinction contrary to the generally acknowledged rule of the inexpediency on national grounds of raising to the Peerage any one who had not the means of supporting the dignity with independence, without in the first instance asking leave to state to H.M^y how I was situated in that respect. Upon this communication H.M^y was graciously pleased to allow the offer to remain in abeyance, as some means might be found in the interval tending to obviate these difficulties.

I am free to confess that the objection on that score remains in full force, and when therefore I decide, as I now do, to waive all further hesitation & to accept H.My's most gracious offer, it is from the conviction that such a public and unequivocal testimony of H.My's sentiments, *invaluable* as it *always* was in my estimation, becomes in a manner *essential* to that fame & memory (which is the nearest & dearest object of my care & solicitude, *if* it is to be the *only* tribute to its excellence. I must likewise observe that, as I think, I can clearly prove that my children have the strongest claim upon every principle of justice & equity to that portion of my private fortune which was successively employed in aid of the salary of office & which if replaced would enable me to provide, if not splendidly, at least independently for the successor to the Peerage. If this claim when fairly stated the country refuses to acknowledge, I shall consider myself as fully exonerated from all responsibility on the ground of public expediency, and if a Peerage so earned & so granted remains destitute of sufficient support, the disgrace (if any there be) cannot surely rest on the possessor.

To you who are acquainted with official life, I need hardly observe that the salaries attached to most of the high official departments of the State, are very inadequate to the claims upon them for expenditure, & I believe I shall be borne out in my assertion that since those salaries were fixed at the commencement of Mr. Pitt's Administration, there is scarcely an instance of any individual filling those offices, who had not at the same time a large sinecure in aid of the official salary. Mr. Pitt, who while he filled the highest office of the State had likewise the sinecure of the Cinque Ports & was therefore in the annual receipt of 12,000 of the public money, died leaving debts to the amount of 40,000. Mr. Perceval held the same offices together with the Chancellorship of the Duchy of Lancaster: Lord Liverpool enjoyed the same sinecure which Mr. Pitt held—while in the instance in question the two departments in the Government which necessarily entail the greatest expenditure as well as the greatest labour, namely the Foreign Office & the House of Commons, were held together for nearly 5 years upon the salary of 6,000 a year attached to the Foreign Office. No aid could be derived, from the Alienation Office as the *whole* salary was given up to the deputy. The result was obvious. I may add that these offices were undertaken at the call of his King & country, not only with a perfect foresight of the embarassments in which he would thereby involve his private property, but at the sacrifice of an appointment [1] which while it gave the certainty of providing fully for his family, afforded an ample & honorable field for the exercise of that immense grasp of intellect with which he was endowed.

How true & sincere the regret was at being called upon to sacrifice this favorite destination you can bear witness. I can most solemnly assert that this regret continued to the latest hour of existence, but being persuaded that he could not refuse such a call consistently with his duty to his King & country, the sacrifice was made at once *unconditionally* & with that generous & noble disregard of all private pecuniary considerations which pervaded every action of his life—even the expenses incurred (to the amount of £2000) in preparations for India were never mentioned.

Of the extent or the merits of the services which this sacrifice enabled him to perform for his country it is not for me to speak. They have now become matter of history—to the nation and to the world. I fearlessly & proudly leave the task of pronouncing judgement on them. The loss of life consequent upon the immense bodily & mental fatigue endured—while it renders all earthly compensation to me & to his family impossible—places the consideration of the subject on much too high & sacred ground to allow of being polluted or measured with reference to any pecuniary matters. I have therefore purposely endeavoured to confine the statement of my case to the simple detail of facts as they would bear upon the claims of any private individual before a Court of Equity—as such alone I wish them to be considered. That a British Parliament will refuse to listen to such a claim I cannot allow myself to think.

You who know me will easily believe that it has not been without a

1 The Governor-Generalship of Bengal.

severe conflict of feelings nor until after much anxious deliberation that I have determined to use every endeavour to obtain the decision of Parliament upon the subject. To have either my name or my private affairs brought under public notice is on every account so repugnant to my feelings and so contrary to all my principles—that I should certainly have much preferred any personal inconvenience to such an alternative had my own interests alone been concerned. But I have no right to give up without a struggle the claims of my children.

In stating to you thus fully my views & intentions—I beg to be distinctly understood as neither claiming nor asking any assistance from H.My's Government.

Constituted as that Government is I am bound to believe that if they do not voluntarily come forward in support of H.My's gracious intentions, it must be from some very strong & cogent reasons of inexpediency.

I have now nothing more to add to this already long detail—except to express my regret at being forced to trespass so much upon your time.[1]

1432 THE KING *to* [SIR WILLIAM KNIGHTON]

Royal Lodge, Novr. 29th 1827. 4 o'cl^k p.m.

YOUR letter came safely to me this morning, & I can never sufficiently thank you for the contents, which indeed are most satisfactory on every head, but some of which I must talk over with you the first opportunity I shall have, of a few minutes private conversation with you, for, much more can be convey'd, understood & done, in such a private & tête a tête communication, than can be effected, by volumes of correspondance with the pen. Pray therefore come to me here, *be it only for an hour*, *early* tomorrow morning *if possible*, but if that *can not absolutely* be, then, at the next very earliest moment you can appropriate to this object.

Ld Goderich has likewise written to me & return'd me my last note,

1 The matter was brought before the House of Commons by the Wellington Ministry in May 1828, and a Bill was introduced to amend the Act of 1817 which had empowered the King to grant pensions, not exceeding £40,000 in all, to the holders of public offices who should have filled their offices for not less than two years. Canning would have been entitled to one of these pensions had he lived, but the Act contained no provision for granting it to his family on his death. The amending Bill therefore authorised the Crown to grant to one of Canning's sons the pension to which the Prime Minister would have been entitled. As the elder was in the navy and his life consequently exposed to more than the average risk, the pension (£3000 a year) was granted for the life of the second son, afterwards Governor-General of India; his brother was drowned whilst bathing at Madeira in October 1828.

but has neither sent me copies of my first letter to him, nor of Dr. Copleston's last letter to him, which I think it is very important *to me*, & *for me*, to be in possession of. There are, also, one or two matters of a less important nature in his letter, but which I should wish to talk over with you with as little delay as may be, for, I must do so, before I send an answer, & which I think ought not to be delay'd beyond the afternoon of tomorrow.

Although I feel quite certain that you must both have heard of, & in all probability have seen the advertisement in the Morning Post of this day (for nothing escapes your vigilance) yet, I feel (after what you shortly told me, in part of our last interview,) fully justified by my feelings towards you, in forwarding to you, the paper, with its advertisement.[1] Now God bless you [etc.].

P.S. Pray send a word in answer, whether you can come tomorrow, & at what hour I may be expecting you if you do.

1433 VISCOUNT GODERICH *to the* KING

Downing Street, Nov. 30th 1827.

LORD GODERICH, with his humble duty, begs leave to acquaint your Majesty that he has seen Lord Clive upon the subject of the Garter. Lord Clive's language, both with respect to his own sentiments and to those of Lord Powis, was quite friendly towards your Majesty's Government: but he stated that upon full consideration Lord Powis felt himself obliged to decline the honor which he was aware your Majesty would have been much pleased to confer upon him. Lord Clive represented that his father had entertained the same feeling with respect to the Garter many years ago when Mr. Pitt offered it to him as a result of his accepting the Lord Lieutenancy of Ireland;[2] and he added that, altho' Lord Powis had no sort of hostile feeling towards the Government, yet he was not prepared to pledge himself to that uniform support which the ac-

1 "HARRIETTE WILSON'S NEW VOLUMES, Parts XVII and XVIII, price 5*s*., are now ready, including the Rescued Suicide, Eliza Elliott, Charles Tyrrell, Esq., and distinguished City characters, with the Beauties and Deformities of the Author's Prime Favourites.
"Also, Plates, Part XII, containing 10 full lengths, coloured, 2*s*. 6*d*.
"Stockdale's Budget, 4to., 6*s*. 6*d*.
"Paris Lions and London Tigers, [by Harriette Wilson] 12 plates, 7*s*. 9*d*....."
"J. J. Stockdale, 20, Coventry Street, St. James's."
2 The appointment was gazetted on 21 November 1805, but Pitt died two months later, and the appointment never took effect.

ceptance of such an honor would necessarily have implied. Lord Goderich cannot but regret that your Majesty's wishes upon this subject should be thus disappointed, but he thinks that *the offer* has not been without its good effect, particularly as Lord Clive stated that his father was much pleased notwithstanding his resolution to decline accepting it.

Lord Goderich begs to acquaint your Majesty that Lord Stafford has resigned the Custos rotulorum of the County of Stafford. This office was never disjoined from the Lord Lieutenancy till Lord Stafford some years ago resigned the one [1] and retained the other. Perhaps your Majesty will think that it would be expedient to reunite the two offices, and thus to put them again upon the footing which universally prevails in England. In Wales they are not unfrequently separated, but in England very rarely. Lord Talbot is Lord Lieutenant of the County of Stafford. [2]

1434 MRS ANNA CREWE[3] *to the* KING

At Mrs. Moor's, Castle Gate, Scarborough,
December 3d 1827.

MAY it please your most gracious Majesty,

That you will so far condescend as to read a few lines from an old female friend; one to whom your most gracious Majesty, has repeatedly given *most substantial proof's* of your *former* friendship and good wishes.

In my youth, the idea of *old age*, with all it's attendant evils never for a moment obtruded it's self upon my MERRY and *thoughtless* heart! If I had enough for *to day*—*tomorrow* was never thought of: and notwithstanding all the advice and good council I repeatedly received from *an old friend*—a person whom your Majesty will *well* remember—and who used to give me the following lecture almost every morning—"Oh! Pitt'a, Pitt'a, you will never take my advice, "*bean why?* You will be always as poor as a rat; their is Finch'a, & Wyndham, they will be riding in their coaches when they are old: but you,—you will die in a workhouse for you will never take care of the main chance."

My answer to this, *her daily* lecture, was invariably the same: no *Dolly*, if I live to be *old*, which I very much doubt—my old friends will never see me in *want*. They will remember that I never took advantage

---

1 "In some evil hour of irritation", said Huskisson. (*Huskisson Papers*, p. 253.)

2 "I know nothing of Lord Talbot's politics", Huskisson wrote to Goderich, "and should rather fear that they are not friendly." Yet, because of the customary union of the two offices, "it would be a great slight upon Lord Talbot to pass him by". (*Ibid.*)

3 The Drury Lane actress.

of their partiality for me, by getting them to give me settlements, and bonds, which in their cooler moments—they would, if not curse—at least despise me for a mercenary and sordid wretch. This was an answer, *she, poor soul*, never liked. But it has ever been my greatest *comfort*: notwithstanding all the poverty and privations I have suffered.

I have however, not unfrequently been *rewarded* for my confidence in my friends: witness your most gracious Majesty's repeated acts of munificence towards me. But to the point:

My FIRST *friend*, the present Lord River's,[1] has been most kind to me, on MANY occasions—and has *recently* sunk in my name *one hundred* and *fifty pounds*: which has purchased for me a small Government annuity of thirteen pounds eighteen shillings per annum. This small annuity together with my *pension* of forty pounds a year as the *widow* of a *Lieutenant*, would be *fifty* three pounds eighteen shillings per annum. This sum however would not more than enable me to pay for my board and lodging in some decent family: but would leave me nothing for *cloaths, washing*, and *medical attendance*: and when *death* put a period to my troubles, *the parish* would be compelled to give me a coffin.

I am now, please your most gracious Majesty, *very near* THREE SCORE years of age—and now feel the want of many little comforts, which my age, and infirmities require. For upwards of eighteen years, I never made the least application to any of my old friends: untill the Almighty was pleased to deprive me of the means of getting an honest livelihood *on the stage*: In that situation, I personated EVERY QUEEN *in the drama*: and by that circumstance went by the name of, *the Queen of Bath*. Now I am sure your most gracious Majesty, will think with me, that *Her poor Majesty*, ought not to want those little comforts, in her old age, which *many* of her late *theatrical subjects* enjoy in great profusion.

I have for the last three years been most dreadfully afflicted with the *sciatic* in my left hip: and the rheumatism in all my limbs; and notwithstanding every advice, and an expensive journey to *Brighton*, in order to try the effects of *Mahomet's—Champooing* Medicated Vapour Baths— (and which I used for *three months*)—I am still a cripple, and must ever remain so. Could I therefore ADD a little to the small annuity just purchased for me, it would releive my mind from all uneasiness, and I could then look forward to *old age* with the comfortable idea that I should not *die in want*!

I even flatter myself, that your most gracious Majesty's amiable con-

---

1 George Pitt, second Baron Rivers (1751–1828). He figures in Harriette Wilson's Memoirs. He "has not only often permitted me to apply to him for money, but once, when I named a certain sum to him, he liberally doubled it".

descension will experience some degree of *pleasure* in the opportunity of adding *a last token* of your friendship, in AID of so desirable an object; in order to enable me to sit in the chimney corner for the remainder of a troublesome life, in some degree of warmth and comfort, in this *cold* region of *the north*: the place indeed, in which I past my days of inocence & youth.

And I shall ever, as I have for many years done, never close my eyes to sleep, before I have implored of the Almighty, to bless, protect, and prosper your most gracious Majesty, both in this world and that which is to come!

1435 THE KING *to* SIR WILLIAM KNIGHTON

Royal Lodge, Sun.^y N.^t Decr 9th 1827.

I WRITE one short line, by a messenger, that is going to summons Dudley to be with me, at ½ pt 12 tomorrow, in consequence of matter contain'd in the submitted draft of an intended dispatch to Lord Granville, relative to the Greek question, which would be not only most *imprudent* but *positive perdition*, if allow'd to go. Perhaps it may be as well, that this should happen during your absence from this place, as the members of the Govt. will see, that I have *fix'd principles*, & that *I can*, & *that I do*, when it is *necessary act entirely from myself, & by myself*.

I think if you would like it, or, have nothing to do tomorrow, in particular, to prevent it, you might manage by an early visit to Dudley, to apprize him of your knowing that I had sent for him here. You might then come here & return with him after his interview with me, & which would enable you to *see me*, judge how *very correct I am*, in all my *views*, & which after, on your road to London, you will be quite capable of canvassing & discussing over with him.

1436 VISCOUNT GODERICH *to the* KING

Downing Street, Decr. 11, 1827.

LORD GODERICH presents his humble duty to your Majesty.

Lord Goderich has considered with the most anxious attention all that your Majesty was graciously pleased to state to him on Saturday last, upon the subject of the representation which Lord Goderich felt it to be his duty to lay before your Majesty, in regard to his power of continuing to conduct your Majesty's service in a manner satisfactory to your Majesty['s] feelings, and conducive to the honor and dignity of your Majesty's Crown.

But the more Lord Goderich has reflected upon the important subject of that representation the more he is convinced, that the present state of things, as it affects the Government, makes an attempt to strengthen it before the meeting of Parliament, indispensible.

The Government requires under the present circumstances of the country, some more solid and united support, upon which it can confidently rely, than is to be found amongst the conflicting elements of which its supporters are now composed.

Some of the most powerful and influential of both Parties in the State, who have so long been opposed to each other, are now united in a determined opposition to the Government; and there are many others on both sides, who whilst they profess no hostility, openly avow that their support will depend upon the more or less degree in which the measures and general character of the Government may tend towards the respective principles and opinions which they entertain.

The existence of this qualified support, and the reasons for it become necessarily mixed up in the discussion of every measure which the Government have to decide upon; and Lord Goderich in conducting its affairs, is thus compelled, from the very necessity of the case, to look not (as his public duty would require) exclusively to the intrinsic fitness and utility of its measures, but (in the most inconvenient degree) to the extent to which they are likely to be supported or opposed.

Lord Goderich cannot but feel that such a state of things places the Government in a condition of inevitable weakness; and when he considers all that is passing around us, the unsettled state of Europe, and the magnitude of many domestic questions, he is convinced that a Cabinet, necessarily weak (not from its own deficiencies but from external causes beyond its controul) cannot do justice to your Majesty's service, or avoid exposing your Majesty to embarrassments and difficulties of the most serious nature.

If then the Government be thus weak, the necessity of additional strength is manifest. That strength cannot be obtained from one side only, for such an attempt would infallibly cause the immediate dissolution of the Administration: and no resource seems to be left, but the endeavour to procure it from both sides in a manner which would ensure a more extensive, and above all a more decided adhesion and support on the part of those who are now unsettled.

It was from these considerations that Lord Goderich presumed humbly to submit to your Majesty his opinion that the beneficial consequences above detailed would result from placing the Ordnance in the hands of the Duke of Wellington or of Lord Hill, from making Lord Wellesley, [in] the place of the Duke of Portland, who is most anxious to retire, President of the Council, and introducing Lord Holland into the Cabinet; and Lord Goderich still feels himself compelled by a sense of duty to your Majesty, to tender to your Majesty his humble advice that that arrangement can alone enable him to conduct your Majesty's affairs as he ought, and as your Majesty has a right to expect.

Should your Majesty feel that this arrangement would not produce the anticipated benefits, or should your Majesty deem it, upon any grounds, altogether inadmissible, Lord Goderich must beg leave humbly to tender to your Majesty his resignation of the post to which your Majesty was graciously pleased to call him.

Altho' Lord Goderich has not presumed to submit these views to your Majesty without having first consulted some of the most influential members of the Cabinet, he has not thought it right to communicate with all of them: in order that in any event as little embarrassment as possible may be caused to your Majesty, and that as the considerations applying to the present state of things, refer more particularly & personally to himself, your Majesty might be the better enabled to retain as many of your Majesty's present servants, as it might be agreable to your Majesty to continue in your Majesty's service.

Lord Goderich cannot conclude this statement without venturing to add, how deeply he feels his own inadequacy to discharge the great duties of the situation to which your Majesty's far too favorable opinion called him. His own natural infirmities have been aggravated by a protracted state of anxiety during the two last years; his health is enfeebled, and above all he fears that the health of one dependent upon him for support and strength, is still in a state of such feebleness and uncertainty as to keep alive that anxiety to a degree not easily compatible with the due discharge of duties which require the exertion of all the energies of the strongest mind.[1]

1 Early in November the King had suggested to Goderich that Wellesley, who was succeeded as Lord-Lieutenant by Anglesey, should take the Duke of Portland's place as President of the Council. But Lansdowne would have resigned had Wellesley alone been admitted to the Cabinet, for when on 1 September he had withdrawn his resignation he had extracted from the King a promise that Lord Holland should be given the first Cabinet vacancy. This difficulty caused the proposal to be dropped for the moment, but when, early in December, the King again pressed Goderich to strengthen the Ministry by bringing Wellesley into the Cabinet, Goderich, who was "quite unnerved and in a most pitiful state", was persuaded by Huskisson to make a stand on this question of Holland's claims, and to send the King an

1437 THE KING'S *Note respecting* LORD GODERICH'S *letter of resignation*

Wed.ᵞ m.ᵍ, Dec.ʳ 12th 1827.

LET the Chancellor & Mr. Herries see this, but they are to keep the contents quite confidential.

1438 THE KING *to* VISCOUNT GODERICH

Copy.   [12 December 1827.]

THE KING has received Lord Goderich's note, submitting to the King, the tenour of Lord Goderich's resignation if certain arrangements are not entered into with the view of what is termed strengthening the Government.

The King understands the representations submitted in Lord Goderich's note to be made in consort with some of the most influential members of the Cabinet, but that most of the Cabinet are ignorant of Lord Goderich's views.

Can Lord Goderich satisfy the King's mind, that the Duke of Wellington will accept a seat in the Cabinet with the present members. This is a fact of which Lord Goderich had better satisfy himself. The King can have no difficulty in placing the Ordnance in the Duke's hands.

The King can only regret that Lord Goderich's domestic calamities unfit him for his present situation, but over this the King unhappily has no control.[1]

ultimatum on the 11th. Unknown, however, to Huskisson and Lansdowne, who had seen and approved the draft of the letter, and to their utter astonishment when the fact became known, Goderich added another paragraph, which gave the King an excuse for getting rid of him. On the 14th the King sent for Lord Harrowby, but when he was granted an audience three days later, Harrowby firmly declined to return to active politics.

1 "The King", said Huskisson, referring to this reply, "has looked only to the postscript, and has confined himself to replying that he is very sorry Goderich finds himself unfit for his situation and for the domestic misfortune which has led to it, but that over that misfortune he has no control. A very natural answer—but a very pretty kettle of fish must be the result." (Add. MSS. 38752, fo. 240.) Goderich decided that it did not amount to an absolute rejection of his ultimatum, "but that it adds as a *condition*, the introduction of the Duke into the Cabinet as a more effective pendant to Holland. If I refuse to try it, he will then be able to say that I refused to try what would have reconciled him to the rest of the proposition. If I try it and fail, then he will be able to say that it is not his fault, for that the introduction of Holland was deemed by me to require a 'pendant' and that if such a pendant cannot be got, he is fairly entitled to say that upon my own showing, the other part of the arrangement would not do, and ought not *now* at all events to be persisted in." (*Ibid.* fo. 210.) Huskisson wrote to Goderich, in the evening of the 13th, after seeing the King: "He spoke very kindly of you... but at the same time without committing himself to anything, though I should say that his apprehension, rather implied than expressed, seemed to be that he must find another Minister—and where, he said, can I find one? He rather gave me to understand that he had explained himself to the Chancellor and desired him to confer with Dudley, but whether in the way of proposing anything, or merely for consultation, I could not make out....He said that he had ordered the Chancellor to attend him tomorrow." (*Ibid.* fo. 223.)

Downing Street, Dec.ʳ 12, 1827.

Lord Goderich presents his humble duty to your Majesty; and begs leave to acknowledge with every respect your Majesty's gracious communication of this day.

Lord Goderich will not presume to trespass further upon your Majesty at the present moment; but he ventures humbly to hope that your Majesty will be graciously pleased to grant him an audience when your Majesty comes to London tomorrow.

1440 The Earl of Dudley *to* Sir William Knighton

F.O., Decr. 13, 1827.

At my request Mr. Canning promised [to] mention to the King the name of Capt. Drummond[1] of Hawthornden to be made a Baronet. After his death I reminded Lord Goderich of the same thing—but owing to my neglect in not furnishing him with a written memorandum Capt. D's name has been omitted in the lists. I am a good deal concerned at this accident the blame of which falls almost exclusively upon myself. It is the more awkward because the "batch" was to be in the Gazette tomorrow.

Lord G. promised me at the Council to-day to speak of it to H.M. if he had an opportunity—but that opportunity may not occur, and I must confess that I should be a good deal mortified and placed with respect to some of my friends in a most embarassing situation if the mistake were to turn out irreparable.

If in the course of the evening you should have an opportunity to aid in extricating me from this unexpected difficulty, I should really be obliged to you—and you may, if you think fit, on my part humbly represent to H.M. that I should consider his consent to Capt. D's being inserted in the list as a valuable mark of condescension and favor in addition to those by which he has already bound me to his person and service.

It is right to add that Capt. D. is a person whose pretensions to the honour he aspires to are quite unexceptionable on the side of character, family, & fortune.

1 John Forbes Drummond, Commander R.N.; Baronet, 22 December 1827; died, May 1829.

1441 JOHN CHARLES HERRIES *to* SIR WILLIAM KNIGHTON

Downing Street, 13 Decr. 1827.

I TAKE it for granted that the political objects which have been lately pressed upon the King will at least be suspended under the present circumstances.

William Huskisson to the King, 14 December 1827. (*Huskisson Papers*, p. 259.)

1442 VISCOUNT GODERICH *to the* KING

Downing Street, Dec.ʳ 14, 1827.

LORD GODERICH presents his humble duty to your Majesty.

Altho' under present circumstances, he feels that he can hardly presume to approach your Majesty with a request, he yet humbly relies upon your Majesty's goodness to pardon him if he mentions to your Majesty that amongst the list of gentlemen whom it was proposed to create Baronets, one name was omitted, viz: that of Mr. Drummond of Hawthornden, about whom Lord Dudley is very anxious, and whom Lord Dudley informs Lord Goderich, Mr. Canning certainly intended to recommend to your Majesty for that honor.

Lord Goderich humbly submits this to your Majesty, in case your Majesty should be graciously pleased to think it proper to create Mr. Drummond a Baronet. He is a man of considerable fortune, and a very respectable gentleman.

When Lord Goderich first spoke to your Majesty upon the subject of Baronetcies, he was not aware of Mr. Drummond's name having been in contemplation.

1443 THE EARL OF HARROWBY *to the* KING

Sandon, 4 p.m.
Saturday [15 December 1827].

LORD HARROWBY has just receiv'd your Majesty's commands to attend him at Windsor Lodge, and in his way thither to pass through London to see Mr. Huskisson. He will have the honour of obeying them with as little loss of time as possible—but, as it would not be possible for him to reach London tomorrow, so as to wait upon His Majesty at

Windsor Lodge in the course of that day, after seeing Mr. Huskisson, without travelling all night, to which he does not feel himself equal, he proposes to pay his duty to your Majesty early in the afternoon of Monday.

The condescending interest which your Majesty was graciously pleased to express in the marriage of his daughter Georgiana with Mr. Wortley[1] induces me to take the liberty of mentioning that she has within these three hours brought him a son.[2]

1444 WILLIAM HUSKISSON *to the* KING

Somerset Place, 16th Dec. 1827.

MR. HUSKISSON presents his humble duty to your Majesty, and has the honour to transmit the answer from Lord Harrowby to your Majesty's letter, which Mr. Huskisson has just received under cover with the inclosed note to himself.

Perhaps your Majesty will be pleased to signify to Mr. Huskisson your commands, whether Lord Harrowby should attend your Majesty tomorrow at one o'clock, or as soon after as he can reach the Royal Lodge.

Mr. Huskisson begs to offer his humble acknowledgments to your Majesty for acceding to his request to be permitted to communicate with Lord Goderich.[3] The Lord Chancellor entirely concurred.

1445 THE KING *to* SIR WILLIAM KNIGHTON

Royal Lodge, Mon.[y] ¾ pt 7 p.m.
Decr. 16th[4] 1827.

I HAVE only time to write a very short line, it being now past seven o'clock, & Huskisson having left me, only a few minutes ago.

I did not write before, as till now I had nothing [to] tell. Lord Harrowby who you know was sent for, has been here, & came before Huskisson, having had [an] interview with him in London, previous to his coming here. Harrowby from fair reasons of downright declining health, does not accept office, at the same time saying, that he had long

1 John Stuart-Wortley (1801–1855), succeeded his father as second Baron Wharncliffe, 1845. In 1825 he married Lady Georgiana Elizabeth Ryder, Lord Harrowby's third daughter.

2 Edward, afterwards third Baron, and (1876) first Earl of Wharncliffe (1827–1899).

3 To inform him that Harrowby was to be offered the Premiership; "and in the event of his accepting, that the King will quickly press you to take the Presidency of the Council". (*Huskisson Papers*, p. 260.)   4 A slip for 17th.

wish'd & had determin'd to retire from all political career, before he sent in his resignation, & that he had often press'd it upon poor Canning, & therefore, he had only remain'd in office so long as he had, out of personal feeling towards Canning. That his affections & wishes, were with this Government, were just the same as ever, & as if he was still a member of it. That I must not suffer the Govt. to be dissolv'd, or to dissolve itself, that Goderich, must be compell'd to stay at any rate at present & till the close of the Sessions if possible. That it would be right, when, (& perhaps at an early moment,) but not till some time after the opening of the Session to look for additional strength in the official situation in the House of [Lords] to Ld H[ollan]d in the first place, & perhaps also to Ld W[ellesley].[1] With every part of this, upon talking it over with H[uskisson]—he seems to agree with Ld H[arrowb]y & in general, as the least evil, as it appears to me, it is less disagreable & painful to my feelings, than any other alternative which could be propos'd under existing circumstances.[2]

I have sent H[uskisso]n to the Chancellor referring the whole to his better judgment & with my conditional approbation in case it should meet with his. Huskisson is very properly desirous that I should see the Chancellor & Dudley tomorrow after he shall have seen them, & in order not to make the Chancellor break up his Court at an unusual early hour, I have authoriz'd him to appoint them to be here at five o'clock, to stay [to] dinner, & afterwards to sleep here or return to town, just as they may find it necessary. Perhaps you had better see the Chancellor, who will tell you all this in detail, & more at length, than I am at present able to do. I do not say to you, *come down*, because I leave that to you to judge for yourself, for I never know what may make it absolutely necessary for you to be upon the spot, at the moment, but I hope you will come when you like & perhaps tomorrow may be something of an interesting day. In haste adieu.

1 Huskisson thus referred to his conversation with the King: "I had much talk with him about Holland and he gives way for Easter, or, if wished, a week or two sooner, so that point, I think, may be settled to Lord Lansdowne's satisfaction. About Wellesley, he says, he is indifferent, but he must not come in before Holland, if he comes in at all." (*Huskisson Papers*, p. 262.)

2 In deciding to retain Goderich in the Premiership the King was greatly influenced by a rumour that Grey had formally coalesced with the ex-Tory Ministers with the object of defeating the Government at the beginning of the Session, and of forcing the King to take them back. "This," remarked Lansdowne, "when it comes to be explained at Windsor, will be *rather* more disagreeable than Holland in the Cabinet." (Add. MSS. 38752, fo. 237.) The King told Huskisson that he would not submit "to have a Government of Ultra Tories, formed upon the Whig principle of being forced upon him by this sort of combination, but not compensating, as the Whigs did, or affected to do, for this principle, by holding popular doctrines—on the contrary, setting public opinion at defiance". (*Ibid.* fo. 303.)

Whitehall, Decr. 17th 1827.

LORD LANSDOWNE presents his humble duty to your Majesty & thinks it right not to delay till he has the honor of seeing you again, acquainting your Majesty that Mr. Fynes Clinton[1] & Mr. Henry Ellis[2] have been reported by the Archbishop of Canterbury, the Chancellor & the Speaker, as two persons qualified to succeed the late Mr. Planta[3] as head Librarian of the British Museum.

From the peculiar nature of the situation, and under the circumstances of the moment Lord Lansdowne feels it his duty to ask your Majesty's attention to the subject, before he directs the appointment to be made out in favor of either of those gentlemen according to the form prescribed. He begs to suggest however to your Majesty that tho' he understands both to be possessed of great industry & literary attainments, the last named Mr. Ellis appears to him to have some claim to preference from twenty years of faithful service in the Museum, & from having given great satisfaction as Keeper of the Manuscripts.

Lord Lansdowne has been requested by the committee of the Thames Tunnell Company to present to your Majesty, a small but beautifull model of that singular work, which he sends by the messenger.[4]

1447 LORD LYNDHURST *to* SIR WILLIAM KNIGHTON

George St., Thursd^y [? 20 December 1827].

I HAVE seen Herries to-day & from what he stated to me I have reason to think it very probable that he and Bexley may at no distant period ask permission to retire from the Government. The ground is the arrangement respecting Lord H[olland].

They are to see Goderich tomorrow. I think it right that the King should be prepared for this. I mentioned to His Majesty when His

1 Henry Fynes Clinton, M.P. for Aldborough, 1806–26. (1781–1852.)

2 Sir Henry Ellis (1777–1869). Keeper of the printed books in the British Museum, 1806–27; Principal Librarian, December 1827.

3 Joseph Planta (1744–1827). Succeeded his father as Assistant Librarian, 1773; appointed Keeper of the MSS., 1776; and Principal Librarian, 1799. Joseph Planta, the politician, was his son.

4 In 1824 a company was formed to carry out Brunel's design of a tunnel under the Thames from Rotherhithe to Wapping, near the east end of the London Docks. Brunel was appointed engineer at a salary of £1000 a year. Work was begun in 1825 but the enormous difficulties that were encountered delayed the completion of the tunnel until 1842. The river broke into the workings on several occasions between 1827 and 1838.

Majesty was so kind as to receive Lord D and myself at Windsor[1] that I thought this possible if not probable as respected *Herries*. Should they determine to adopt this course my situation will be most *painful*. I shall be left, with the exception of Ld. Anglesea, alone in the Cabinet as to questions connected with the support of the Church and the Protestant interest. Try if possible to prevent this desertion, the effect of which it is impossible to calculate.

I write this with my usual freedom and in my accustomed tone of confidence.

It is so essential that the King should not be taken by surprize upon so material a point that I have thought it right to send a special messenger to you at Winds.

William Huskisson to the King, 29 December 1827. (*Huskisson Papers*, p. 275, where the important endorsement is omitted: "This letter was not sent, but the original was delivered to His Majesty at an audience at the Royal Lodge on the 21st of February 1828." It was a letter resigning office. Add. MSS. 38753, fo. 138.)

1448 VISCOUNT GODERICH *to the* KING

Downing Street, Dec. 29, 1827.

LORD GODERICH presents his humble duty to your Majesty.

He takes the liberty of enclosing letters which he has received from Mr. Lambton, Lord Rosebery and Mr. Bootle Wilbraham, expressive of their sense of your Majesty's gracious condescension towards them in conferring upon them the honor of the Peerage.

The title by which Lord Rosebery wishes to be created a Peer of the United Kingdom is that of Baron Rosebery. Mr Bootle Wilbraham mentions his in the enclosed letter. Mr. Lambton begs permission to take the title of Baron D'Arcy, of Harraton & Herrington; but Lord Goderich thinks it right to state to your Majesty that the Duke of Leeds feels some difficulty as to the title of D'Arcy being conferred upon one of the *younger* branches of that antient family, from which Mr. Lambton as well as his Grace is descended. There are however some circumstances connected with that title, which shew that the antient title of D'Arcy (which is now extinct) has at various times been borne by *different* branches of that family, and that it has not been either solely or uniformly confined to the elder branch.

1 On the 18th. (Add. MSS. 38752, fo. 304.)

Lord Goderich has represented this to the Duke of Leeds, who perhaps may in consequence wave any further objection. If however the title, desired by Mr. Lambton, should prove to be objectionable (which Lord Goderich hopes it will not) Mr. Lambton would then humbly solicit your Majesty's permission to take the title of Durham, in which County the greater part of his property is situated.[1]

Lord Goderich humbly requests your Majesty to be graciously pleased to return him the accompanying letters.

Lord Goderich begs permission to add, that Mrs. Canning has finally resolved to accept the Peerage, independent of the question of fortune. She is anxious for the rank of Viscountess, partly because the dignity of Viscount was given to Lord Sidmouth and to Lord Melville upon their first creation, and partly because the rank of Baron would leave Mr. Canning's descendants, being the elder branch of the family, below Lord Garvah,[2] who is the son of the younger branch.

If your Majesty sees no objection, Lord Goderich thinks that her wishes in this respect might be complied [with] upon the grounds which she alledges.

1449 VISCOUNT GODERICH *to the* KING

Downing Street, Decr. 30, 1827.

LORD GODERICH presents his humble duty to your Majesty; and beg[s] permission to enclose to your Majesty a letter[3] which [he] has this day received from Lord Hill. Lord Goderich regrets to find that his Lordship declines the appointment of Master General of the Ordnance; upon the same grounds as those which some years ago induced him to decline the offer of being Lieut: Genl. of the Ordnance.[4]

Lord Goderich begs leave humbly to acquaint your Majesty that Lord Wellesley arrived in London last night. As Lord Lansdowne is out of town, Lord Wellesley has requested Lord Goderich to make his arrival known to your Majesty, and to solicit on his (Lord Wellesley's) part from your Majesty the honor of the usual audience, whenever it may please your Majesty to command his attendance.

1 See No. 1453.
2 Colonel George Canning, created Baron Garvagh, 1818. (1778–1840.) He and the Prime Minister were cousins.
3 *W.N.D.* IV, 173.
4 "...Namely, that I had never been accustomed to office duty, that I feared I should ill perform the services required of me, and that a permanent residence in town would most materially affect my health...."

Royal Lodge, [Sunday,] Dec. 30, 1827.

I WRITE a short line, merely for the purpose of wishing you and yours from my heart a happy New Year, and many returns of the same. I shall trouble you with but little on the present occasion, though I have *much, and that too of great importance,* [*as well publicly as privately, and as it relates to myself,*] *which I must with the shortest lapse of time possible discuss and talk over with you; and therefore I rely upon your affection for me that you will not disappoint me,* but that *you will be punctual*[*ly*] *with me at the Lodge by noon, and not later than on Wednesday* [*next*] *the 2nd,* by which time I trust the old mansion will be completely restored to its wonted tranquillity and quiet. But *see you I must on that day.*

It was fully my intention to have written you a few lines on Christmas Day, but I was then, and had been confined ever since this day sennight, to my room with a general cold and feverish attack, attended with great tightness and oppression upon the chest, and for which, by Sir Henry's[2] advice, we were obliged to have recourse to the lancet, which produced the expected relief, but not such entire relief as to set me free from my chamber, but from which, thank God, I am to emerge this day, by going down[stairs] to dinner for the first time [since last Saturday sennight. I cannot likewise disguise from you that I have also had different causes of the most poignant and distressing nature to tear my poor feelings almost to shreds and to drive me for a time almost distracted; to you, and to you alone, dr. fd. it is that I can and that I do look therefore for my relief, *as it is you and you alone who can and who I am sure will (from your real affection and attachment to me) entirely put an end to them, and by your powerful exertions and means, crush and put the extinguisher upon that host of vipers and hornets, which seems in particular at this moment, to have congregated itself together and purposely, to sting me personally, as well as through all those that are dearer to*...].[3]

My affection for you made me feel that, however I might be suffering myself, it would be both cruel and unjust in me, knowing how very little time you ever allow [to] yourself to pass in comfort with your family, (especially at this season of the year,) were I to write *that* to you *which*, from your affection to me, might have induced you generously to break up your domestic board by coming away to me suddenly, or at any rate (have)[4] cast a damper over those happy, cheerful, and enviable hours,

---

1 A much mutilated version of this letter is printed in *Knighton*, I, 340–2. There the letter is wrongly dated 1826, and no italicised passages appear. The portions of the letter which are enclosed in square brackets are not in *Knighton*.
2 Sir Henry Halford.
3 A whole sheet is here missing.   — 4 Not in the MS. but in *Knighton*.

which [when undisturbed] you cannot fail to enjoy when surrounded by your happy domestic circle; and that long may this be your case, dr. fd., my best prayers are, and ever will be offered up.

Now good-bye to you. I look forward[s] with impatience *to Wednesday next, the 2nd, [that is not to be expressed,] when I rely and depend upon seeing you.* Till then, God bless you!

[P.S. If you should by chance receive this tomorrow in London pray write to me in the course of the day.]

1451 JOHN CHARLES HERRIES *to* SIR WILLIAM KNIGHTON

Montreal, 31 Decr. 1827.

I AM here for a day or two chiefly for the purpose of being out of the way of some other people until I have had another conversation with you.

Pray send me a messenger to let me know of your arrival in London as soon as it takes place.

The Chancellor I know wants also much to see you. We see matters quite in the same light.

1452 LORD LYNDHURST *to* SIR WILLIAM KNIGHTON

Geo. St., Monday, [? 31 December 1827].

I EXPECTED that you wd be in town about this time and I wrote in that expectation. I wished to see you, because I felt it my duty in some way to communicate to the King that I was convinced the Government could not go on in its present form. Such is my firm belief and I think upon such a point the King must not be taken by surprise. This is confidential and entirely for yourself.

Downing Street, January 2nd 1828.

LORD GODERICH presents his humble duty to your Majesty. By a letter which he has received today from the Duke of Leeds his Grace does not desire to press any objection against the title desired by Mr. Lambton: but the Duke expresses a strong wish that the Barony of D'Arcy Nevill that expired with the last Lord Holderness should be revived in his person.[1]

Upon this point Lord Goderich will take an opportunity of speaking to your Majesty.[2]

He humbly begs your Majesty to be graciously pleased to return him the letter with which he presumed to trouble your Majesty on Saturday, as he has no memorandum of Mr. Bootle Wilbraham's proposed title except what was in Mr. W's letter that he transmitted to your Majesty on that day.[3]

1 Amelia, daughter of Robert D'Arcy, fourth (and last) Earl of Holderness (1718–1778), married in 1773 Francis Godolphin, then Marquis of Carmarthen, afterwards fifth Duke of Leeds.

2 Lambton was created Baron Durham of the City of Durham and of Lambton Castle by letters patent dated 29 January 1828—three weeks after the collapse of the Goderich Ministry. The other peerages which had been promised were also conferred notwithstanding the change of Government. Lambton told Grey that he did not consider the peerage "a favour received from the Administration". "I consider it a matter of right which had been long withheld from my family, and which my consenting to receive was more a favour conferred on them than one granted to myself." (New, *Durham*, p. 94.) His grandfather had been offered a peerage when the Duke of Portland joined Pitt's Ministry, and had refused it because of his political attachment to Fox. (Reid, *Durham*, I, 178.)

3 The following letters throw additional light on the subject of the peerages:

Viscount Goderich to the Duke of Wellington. Downing Street, 17 January 1828.

I am much obliged to you for your letter.

I send you some papers (all I have) upon the subject of Mr. Bootle Wilbraham's peerage. His answer to mine of Decr 22, is with the King: it contains an unqualified acceptance of the honor. His letter of the 6th of Jany refers to certain changes in the Government which he thought probable (not those which have just occurred) and which he thought would give so different a character to the Government as to render it impossible that he should give it his support: and upon that supposition he declined it. This I mentioned to the King on Tuesday the 8th, when I last saw His Majesty.

The enclosed letter from Sir H. Taylor I received last night, and it arose out of a conversation which I had with him in the morning, whereby it appeared that the reasons which led Mr. B. Wilbraham to decline the peerage on the 6th are not deemed by him to be any longer in existence. A warrant for this peerage is before the King, in consequence of a note from His Majesty to Lord Lansdowne, of Tuesday last, which referred to it.

With respect to Mr. Lambton's title, I know it would be much more agreable to him to have the title of Durham than that of Wearmouth: but the warrant sent down to the King on *Tuesday* night contained Wearmouth. I was not at that time aware that the objection to Durham was removed, and Wearmouth was then chosen in order to avoid delay: and if the adoption of Durham now, should cause any delay, I am sure that Mr. Lambton would prefer, in that case, to abide by Wearmouth.

[P.S.] I should mention that the warrant for Mr. Lambton's peerage was originally sent down (with the rest) on *Monday* night: but the *title* was left blank, to await His Majesty's

Spring Gardens, Jany. 6th 1828.

THERE is much talk of changes in the Ministry. Certain indications prove that these reports are not entirely without foundation. It is understood that on Friday last Lord Goderich would have again resigned had not Lord Grantham[1] arrived just in time to persuade him differently. From what I see and hear I think the King will find that he must decide in forming a Ministry either exclusively Tory or exclusively Whig. The majority of the *John Bulls* like a plain downright straightforward course, and are already quite nauseated with the twistings and patchings of the middle Party. They perceive that there is no force or energy in the

decision. If the King felt no objection to Durham, *that* title would have been inserted: if it was objected to, the blank was to be filled up with Wearmouth. That warrant, with the title blank, is still before the King, as well as the second warrant which was sent down on *Tuesday* night, with the title of Wearmouth, so that His Majesty may sign whichever he pleases.

[Enclosures]

Viscount Goderich to E. Bootle Wilbraham. Downing Street, 22 December 1827. *Copy.*

I trust you will forgive me if I take the liberty of making a proposition to you without having any certain knowledge how far it may be agreable to you to accede to it; but it is one which I could not make to you, if I did not flatter myself that you would consider it at all events as a mark of my personal esteem for you, and respect for your family and connections.

I have often heard it mentioned that a peerage was an object to which you might naturally aspire, and that it had been in contemplation to offer [one] to you, and no doubt can be entertained that in your case such an honor would be most worthily bestowed.

I have communicated my feelings upon this subject to the King, and I have received His Majesty's commands to tender this proposition to you, in the hope that there may not exist in your mind any considerations which would induce you to decline it. . . .

E. Bootle Wilbraham to Viscount Goderich. Latham House, Ormskirk. 6 January 1828. *Copy.*

I have to apologize to your Lordship for intruding upon your time in consequence of reports having just reached me, which appear to be credited, that there is reason to apprehend a change in the Administration.

This change, those who feel as I do, a full confidence in your Lordship, must lament and deprecate, above all if they tend to the Whig Party taking the lead in the Administration, as well as to the predominance of those principles which I have uniformly resisted and am unable to support, however cordial my attachment to His Majesty, and however great my desire to continue to his Government that support which (with a very short interval) I have given to it for upwards of 32 years.

The recent gracious communication which you so kindly made to me has imposed upon me the necessity of troubling your Lordship, and I hope that you will acquit me of indiscretion or indelicacy in alluding to reports which concern either your Lordship or the arrangements of the Government when you consider that I owe it not less to His Majesty or to your Lordship than to my own character to decline taking advantage of an offer, the acceptance of which might be construed into pledging me to the adoption of principles & the support of measures which might be inconsistent with the line of conduct to which I have always adhered and which I shall continue to maintain. (Wellington MSS.)

1 Thomas Philip Robinson, third Baron Grantham (1781–1859), Goderich's brother. He succeeded his father in 1786, and his maternal aunt, the Countess De Grey, as Earl De Grey, in 1833.

Government and that all their plans are weakened and drivelled away by the necessity of compromise and accommodation to conflicting opinions.

The King may postpone the evil day when he must undertake the unpleasant task of acting vigorously, but should not this take place within one month or two it must before three or four, and delay will only increase the difficulty.

His Majesty wished to try a mixed Government in 1812 and it failed. The singular combinations of Mr. Canning's character enabled him on a late occasion to amalgamate Parties into a phalanx of some strength, but now they are deprived of his energy and peculiar talents it must fall to pieces from the discordant nature of its own material.

Various reports are brought to me daily of the strong language used in political coteries by those of both Parties who dislike half measures. Of these I shall speak to you when you come to town.

1455 VISCOUNT GODERICH *to* SIR WILLIAM KNIGHTON

Downing Street, Jany 7th 1828. 4 p.m.

I AM very sorry that I was so unfortunate as to miss you yesterday when you called in Downing Street, but I had been trying to breathe a little fresh air for two or three days.

I regret it the more because, from your last account of His Majesty, I have felt very uncomfortable about his health, and from not having [heard] from you upon that subject since Saturday I am very anxious about it.

I am sorry however (as you may easily believe) to say that it is of *especial importance* that I should be permitted to see the King tomorrow, and I propose therefore to be at the Royal Lodge at two o'clock. I would on no account have ventured to intrude upon the King at this moment, but the urgency of the case is such that I cannot in duty to His Majesty avoid soliciting an audience.[1]

1 Goderich went to Windsor on the 8th to inform the King that his Government was about to break up. Herries and Huskisson had quarrelled over the proposal to nominate Lord Althorp chairman of the Finance Committee of the House of Commons that was to be appointed at the beginning of the Session. Goderich found he had to choose between losing his Chancellor of the Exchequer and losing his Colonial Secretary, and the resignation of either meant the dissolution of the Ministry. After making his report to the King Goderich was merely requested to send for Lyndhurst, who in turn was ordered to send for Wellington. Next day the Duke was asked to form a Government.

S. Audley St., Jany. 8th 1828.

M A Y I request your attention to me? My exertions to forward my colossal group have been unceasing, and my expenses in consequence so great that I am compelled to ask your further assistance.

My desire is if possible to arrange my work that I may commence the erection at Windsor in the following Spring; indeed I am afraid from the frequent enquiries of His Majesty that I have already trespassed on his kind forbearance to urge me to its completion.

I see on looking over my papers that in the 10 years nearly that I have had the honor to be employed on His Majesty's works that I have rec^d only 6500£ st., consequently my ballance will be heavy, indeed I assure you I have the last year that I might not often plague you sold 1500£ stock. I hope therefore you will do as much for me as you possibly can.

If I could only prevail upon you to do me the honor to look at my work, its magnitude and process would at once declare the necessity of great means to accomplish it.

1457 SIR WILLIAM KNIGHTON *to* ?

Royal Lodge, 9 January 1828.

Y O U will be so good as to call on Mr. Westmacott and give him the draft for one thousand pounds, and you may acquaint him that throughout this year he shall have a thousand pounds a quarter.

You will at the same time acquaint him that I understood the amount of the equestrian statue to have been ten thousand pounds—the base five thousand—Will you desire him to let you know if this be correct. I ought to have some rule to go by, or I shall not know what is before me. You may tell him that he may rely on a thousand pounds a *quarter* provided my version of this expence be correct. Call upon Lady Stepney[1] with her half year. Take it in a little bag of gold, and make her sign the receipt. Take the inclosed draft to Mr. Kirwan—he lives in Pall Mall—make him sign the receipt—with my compliments.

I am anxious—if it be possible to get that twenty thousand out of the Duchy of Lancaster by the twentieth of this month.

Tell Mr. Dickie not to make up my books *entirely*, until he hears from

---

1 Catherine, Lady Stepney (d. 1845). She married Sir Thomas Stepney in 1813, and published several romances. See *Knighton*, I, 419–21.

me—I am anxious to have as little money in my own hands, when my account is settled, as possible.

P.S. You will acquaint Mr. Westmacott that my payments have been made very relugarly [*sic*] to him; that if I had been made acquainted with any conditions, I should have endeavored to have fulfilled them. But do ascertain what the amount is to be.

[*Endorsement.*] 10th Janry. I called at Mr. Kirwan's as desired, but learnt that Mr. K. was in Italy.

1458 THE EARL OF MOUNTCHARLES *to* SIR WILLIAM KNIGHTON

Arlington St, 9th Jany 1828.

As soon as I received your letter this morning I went to the Infante,[1] and told him that His Majesty had been graciously pleased to command me, to offer to His Royal Highness the black horse upon which he rode to cover when at Windsor. The Infante appeared extremely pleased at this mark of His Majesty's condescension and kindness, and desired me to endeavour to express to the King "how grateful he felt for this additional proof of His Majesty's kindness, a kindness of which he is every day the more and more sensible, and which he never can or will forget".

Don Miguel intends quitting London on Sunday next for Stratfieldsaye; His Royal Highness is most anxious to arrive as speedily as possible at Lisbon; at the same time however he says that he quits London with more regret than any capital he has as yet visited, and with feelings deeply impressed with the kindness and attention which he has received from every one during His Royal Highness' stay here.

The Infante desires me if possible to lay these expressions at His Majesty's feet.

I shall in submission to His Majesty's commands attend His Royal Highness to Plymouth.

John Charles Herries' Memorandum concerning the Finance Committee of the House of Commons, with correspondence. (*Life of Herries*, II, 12 *sqq.*)

1 Dom Miguel, who visited England on his way back to Lisbon from Vienna.

1459 THE DUKE OF WELLINGTON *to the* KING

London, Jany 10th 1828.

As your Majesty will be anxious to hear from me at the close of this day, I write to report that Mr. Peel having come to town this day I have just come from a discussion with the Lord Chancellor and him, which as far as it has gone has been as satisfactory as I could have expected.[1]

Which is humbly submitted to your Majesty by your Majesty's most dutiful and devoted subject and servant.

1460 THE DUKE OF CLARENCE *to* SIR WILLIAM KNIGHTON

Admiralty, Jany. 10th 1828. 5 p.m.

I AM this instant favoured with your letter of today and sincerely rejoice you are enabled to write under all the present circumstances such continued favourable reports of the King.[2]

You may assure His Majesty that whatever you *write* or *say* to me shall be disclosed to no man or woman living. All I can wish and desire is that the Monarch of this country may have a *permanent* and *useful* Cabinet agreeable to the wishes of my brother and possessing the confidence of his subjects. I am truly happy to add the reception of Don Miguel in London has gone off without a single drawback and I am convinced this Prince will leave the metropolis with gratitude and well disposed towards our gracious and excellent Sovereign.

1461 LORD LYNDHURST *to* SIR WILLIAM KNIGHTON

George Street, 11 Jany. [1828]. 6½ o clock p.m.

WHEN yr messenger arrived here I was at the D of W[ellington]'s, where I have been detained till this moment. In obed[ien]ce to His Majesty's commands communicated in yr note, I have to state the following particulars as to the actual position of affairs.

Peel and Bathurst and Huskisson and Goulburn have consented to serve under the Duke. Dudley *will* accept, and he and Wm Lambe are proposed by *Huskisson,* and to this proposition no objection has been

1 Peel's views as to the composition and character of the new Government are in *Parker,* II, 28.

2 His letter of the 7th, inquiring about his brother's health, is in *Knighton,* I, 400–1.

made. The main point to be decided is as to Lansdowne and the Whigs. When *that* is fairly settled, the whole affair may be, at once, completed. Huskisson is convinced that Lansdowne will not accept.[1] Some discussion has arisen upon this part of the subject, and it is felt, and perhaps with justice, that the offer to Lansdowne would cool the zeal if not weaken the support of our Tory friends, who are at present very warm and active in favour of the embryo Government. It would be a poor compliment, it is said, to offer to an able and tried friend an office which had been refused by Lansdowne. It is also considered that to give Lansdowne the opportunity of refusing place, might have the effect of setting him up again with his ultra Whig friends and render his future opposition more effective than it might otherwise prove. On the other hand if Lansdowne should consent to remain in office it must of course be in connection with S[pring-]Rice, Macdonald and perhaps Abercrombie etc. which would be offensive to our friends and very troublesome to the Government, exposing us to perpetual annoyance by communicating our counsels, views etc. etc. These reasonings have prevailed. As the Duke is on the road, perhaps this sketch will be considered a sufficient compliance with H.M.'s wishes. But in fact there is nothing further at present to communicate.

[P.S.] Pray present to His Majesty my humble duty and earnest wishes for the restoration of his health.

1462 THE EARL OF MOUNTCHARLES *to* SIR WILLIAM KNIGHTON

Saturday [12 January 1828].

ONE line I must write you to thank you for yr approval of my conduct with the Infante, & one line more with respect to the *snub* that accompanied it also. I have latterly been so *entirely* occupied with Don Miguel that I have not *once* gone into any club or society where politicks have been discussed since the Prince has been in the country, & at this moment I give you my word, I know nothing save that Goderich is out, & that the D. of Wellington is forming or helping to form a Govt. but

1 Lansdowne told Peel that he could not serve under an anti-Catholic Prime Minister. (*Parl. Deb.* N.S., XVIII, 299.) Wellington, in conversation with the Duke of Devonshire, said that in view of his and Peel's opinions on the Catholic question, it would be as little advisable to make an offer to Lansdowne as for Lansdowne to accept one.

how or of what materials I have *not the most* distant conception; but I suppose that upon my return to town I shall hear of the whole affair being finally settled: of one thing you may be assured, whether I resign my Lordship of the Treasury or not,[1] I shall never give up, without His Majesty's *positive commands*, my situation in his family,[2] after the King's *constant amazing kindness* to me, I shd indeed be *more than ungrateful*, were I to quit his service, or to pledge my vote in any manner in opposition to His Majesty's wishes. I have spoken to no one on the subject, & you *may depend* I shall *pledge myself* to no one. Forgive my dear Sir William all this talking of self, but I wanted to explain my feelings to you least you might hear any thing to the contrary.

P.S. Am I to write for the road to go, Dudley[3] has given me no directions *whatvr.*

1463 LORD LYNDHURST *to* SIR WILLIAM KNIGHTON

One o'clock—Sunday morng.
[13 January 1828].

I CONTINUE to obey H. Majesty's commands. It is proposed to include Westmorland in the new arrangements. I think the appointment will damage us *much* in public opinion and I have so stated it to the Duke, but it is thought he has *claims*. *I* would disregard them. I cannot tell you how much, in my opinion, this nomination will injure us with the world. I think our gracious master has expressed himself to me in such terms upon diff[eren]t occasions with respect to Westmd. that he will not be disposed to approve the appointment. His Majesty's will, however, which to me will always be a law, must decide. I think the question one of very great importance and have therefore sent a special messenger with this note.[4] I think we are *popular* with the *King's* support, and

1 He remained in office, but resigned early in 1830.
2 He was First Groom of the Bedchamber and Master of the Robes.
3 The Foreign Secretary.
4 On the 12th Wellington suggested to the King that Westmorland should again fill the office of Lord Privy Seal if Lord Carlisle, to whom the offer was first made, declined it. (*W.N.D.* IV, 187.) Wellington told Westmorland on the 18th why he was to be left out altogether. He had "found in all quarters the difficulties and objections insurmountable; and I have no doubt that if I had persisted I must have resigned the commission". (*W.N.D.* IV, 201.) Two other ultra Tory stalwarts, Eldon and Bexley, were, in Croker's phrase, "put in the dirty clothes-basket".

public opinion in our favour, we may feel confidence as to the success of our Ministry.

Herries the Duchy of Lanr.[1] Goulburn Chr. of Exchr. Qn as to this? Bexley a pension. The rest is free from objection.

1464 LORD LYNDHURST *to* SIR WILLIAM KNIGHTON

George St., Monday [14 or 21 January 1828].

WERE you so good as to mention to the King what I told you about Sydney Smith?[2] You know the promise I was obliged to make him, in conseq.ce of the mixed character of the former Administration. The vacant stall at Bristol would *acquit me*, and it would be desirable that this affair should be disposed of before the new Governm.t is formed. These are points which I wished you to submit on my behalf to the King, and which I would have stated myself when His Majesty was so kind as to honor me with an audience, had they not at the moment escaped my recollection.

1465 THE KING *to* [*the* DUKE OF DEVONSHIRE]

R[oya]l L[od]ge, 14 January 1828.

I WRITE to you from my sick bed. You must have heard what has happened in the Government; and my object in writing to you is to express my sincere hopes that you will remain as you now are, in my family, and about my person, and that my friend Carlisle will decide to continue in the Cabinet. I look upon you both as personal and attached friends.

I desire to add, that to the Marquis of Lansdowne I have nothing but the kindest feelings.[3]

Ever your sincere friend.

1 The circumstances of the break-up of the Goderich Ministry made it necessary for the Duke to remove Herries from the Exchequer. He was appointed Master of the Mint, and Lord Aberdeen Chancellor of the Duchy of Lancaster. (*W.N.D.* IV, 187, 215.)

2 The famous clerical wit (1771–1845). He was now given a prebendary stall at Bristol Cathedral. See *Mem. of Sydney Smith* (1855), II, 285.

3 Carlisle intimated that he could not join the Government unless Lansdowne was also included. The Duke of Devonshire told the King that he had taken office in April 1827 only with the view of facilitating the union of the Whigs with Canning, and that he could not retain it under Canning's enemies. The King told him that his resigning would "break his heart and drive him out of his senses". For these negotiations see my Article in *Engl. Hist. Review*, October 1935, p. 639 *et seq.*

Downing Street, Jany 14, 1828.

LORD GODERICH presents his humble duty to your Majesty, and solicits your Majesty's pardon for presuming to lay before your Majesty the case of Mr. Wynne for a grant of the Parliamentary pension which it is competent to your Majesty to give under the regulations of the Act of Parliament to the President of the Board of Controul.

Mr. Wynne has held that office for six years, and your Majesty is probably not unaware that he has a large family and very slender means of providing for them: and Lord Goderich ventures to add that he feels something of a personal interest in this matter from the great kindness and confidence which for some years past he has experienced from Lord Grenville and the different branches of Mr. Wynne's family.

He feels at the same time that in now mentioning this case to your Majesty he is taking a step in which he fears he is not warranted under present circumstances, but he humbly trusts that your Majesty will be graciously pleased to pardon him on account of the motives which have induced him to lay the matter before your Majesty.

The Duke of Wellington to the King, 14 January 1828. (*W.N.D.* IV, 190–1.)
The Duke of Wellington to the King, 16 January 1828. (*W.N.D.* IV, 196–7.)

1467 THE DUKE OF CLARENCE *to* SIR WILLIAM KNIGHTON

Admiralty, Jany. 15th 1828. 5 p.m.

HAVING been out at dinner yesterday I could not answer immediately yours of 14th instant of the morning and have delayed till now thinking I might have had another line before my return into the country. I [am] now setting out and unless sent for shall not be in town before 17th instant.

I hope in God the King is *permanently* recovering as it is *slowly*. I wish His Majesty had *not* been in *bed*. But I am glad my brother did see Don Miguel because I really believe this Prince leaves England with the *most* favourable impressions.

I augur *well* of the *new* Government from the *utter* silence of the whole. It proves things advance *prosperously* and that *ability* is used.

I am anxious to see the King at ease and the Ministers enjoying the confidence of the country.

Royal Lodge, Jany. 16th 1828.
¾ past 12 p.m.

I WRITE as you may suppose out of my bed and I am vex'd today
(I suppose from having been overdone yesterday)[1] after a very disturbed
and restless night and with a fresh accession of gout this morning, though
not violent yet sufficient to be very irritating and painful.

The box with the whole of its enclosures reached me late last night
(and which I desire that *you* will carry and shew our Duke *yourself*) as *he*
I believe *at present* is in possession of the key of the box of any other
office than that of the Commander in Chief, and settle *then* with him
when and *what* sort of answer should be sent to Lord Lansdowne, for
I would not forward *any* until I had heard from the Duke. Indeed, from
what we know of the two notes written in my own hand *but yesterday
morning* & the *purport* of them both to Ld Lansdowne, as well as to
Ld Goderich, *this box* (I mean its contents) appears to me to be a most
extraordinary, if not *impudent*, proceeding towards myself & *speaks
volumes for itself*. I am wholly unable now to state the particulars of all
the different points of view which it brings before *me*, but I am sure they
will not escape either yours or the vigilant, quick and scrutinizing eye
of the Duke.

In much pain dr. fd., [etc.].

1469 LORD LYNDHURST *to* SIR WILLIAM KNIGHTON

George Street, Thursday [17 January 1828].

I AM in a difficulty about Lord Carlisle. The King desired me to see him
again and to *press* him to continue. H. Majesty at the same time authorized the Duke to make offers of appointments to different persons, and
the letters were written at Windsor and immediately forwarded. Upon
the return of the Duke the next morning to London, it was found that if
the offers so made were accepted and Huskisson and his friends continued in the Government, all the places would be filled. I was therefore
placed in a very difficult situation in consequence of the command I had
received from H. Majesty. It became *impossible* to receive *Carlisle* unless
the Duke could be prevailed upon (which was also impossible) to recede
from the offers which he had made. Will you have the kindness, when
a fit opportunity presents itself, to explain this affair to H. Majesty.[2]

1 When there was a Privy Council meeting.
2 For the negotiations with Carlisle, see *W.N.D.* IV, 187, 190, 196, 200, 209.

Admiralty, Jany. 19th 1828. 5 p.m.

IN answer to yours of this morning I must lament the *slow* recovery of the King. But the weather thank God appearing to be inclined to take up I trust His Majesty will now soon be as well as you and I wish him.

I have seen the Duke of Wellington and of course his Grace has informed me of *the* Government being *nearly* formed. I can only say the *honour* and *comfort* of *my brother* and the *security* of *his* Realms are what I look to. I know the *greatness of mind of the Duke* and I am aware by experience that *a* Minister *with* the *King* and the *Treasury* can do a great deal. *Huskisson* being *secured* I should think *the* Minister *must* have the House of Commons and *the* Duke is *sure of the Lords.*

I shall be in town next week Tuesday Thursday and Saturday from ten till five and on 28th instant I settle at the Admiralty till Easter. I shall ever be ready and happy to receive you.

I do not like to trouble the King with unnecessary letters and consequently have not written. But I must request you will express to His Majesty my anxious concern for his health and welfare.

1471 THE KING *to* SIR WILLIAM KNIGHTON

Royal Lodge, Saty. ½ pt. 6.
Jany. 19th 1828.

I HAVE delayed writing to you till I had tried how far my strength would allow me to sit up, and to be moved to the next room; but alas; the Wilson [? business][1] of yesterday has entirely knock'd me up & destroy'd almost all the little amount of strength I had, & this too I am sorry to add, without having answer'd as hitherto, our expectations of complete relief. I therefore can not hold a Council till Tuesday next when you may, at a venture if you please appoint it at three o'ck. I am much oblig'd to you for your kind letter, & do *most sincerely* hope that the Duke of Wellington may succeed in persuading the Duke of Devonshire to remain in *my family.*

1 Alluding, presumably, to the blackmailing activities of Harriette Wilson and her "hellish gang".

Royal Lodge, Saty. Nt. ½ pt. 9.
Jany. 19th. 1828.

I HAVE signed your warrant and warrants.

At the same time I have received the inclos'd which does affect my private feelings deeply. The letter is so very and truly gentlemanlike and liberal that I regret that Lord Lansdowne was not communicated with [at the same time] as Lord Carlisle [was, and] as you know that it was my wish and opinion that he should have been. You will acquaint the Duke of Wellington with this and shew him *this* and Ld. Lansdowne's letter as soon as possible as I must reply to it in the course of tomorrow.

I know the Duke of Wellington, as *my friend,* will enter into *my* feelings, and therefore I wish to see him tomorrow morning as early as he can. I write this out of my bed, *what a precious anodyne* for my night.[1]

1473 THE MARQUESS OF LANSDOWNE *to the* KING

Whitehall, Saturday, Jany 19th [1828].

LORD LANSDOWNE presents his respectfull duty to your Majesty and trusts he may be permitted to state that nothing but an apprehension of intruding upon your Majesty at a time when he has been deeply concerned to learn you had been suffering from indisposition has prevented him from soliciting an audience this week, humbly to represent to your Majesty the embarrassing situation in which he has found himself placed since the virtual dissolution, as he was informed, of Lord Goderich's Administration by continuing to exercise the duties of an office which the forms of the Constitution have made the most responsible of any, by connecting it with almost every act of authority, and without having received any intimation that could justify him in holding communication with any person now in your Majesty's confidence.

In humbly submitting this statement of his present feelings, Lord Lansdowne is most anxious not to be understood as asking from your Majesty any disclosure of your sentiments or intentions which it might be in the slightest degree inconvenient to make, but only as expressing a hope that with the same condescending kindness and attention he has invariably experienced from His Majesty he may be early informed of

1 The addition of the words enclosed in brackets explains the faulty grammar.

any determination which ought to affect his publick conduct, and that in the meantime he is best consulting your Majesty's wishes and interests by continuing to the best of his ability to transact all business that is indispensably necessary for the ordinary course of your Majesty's Government, but abstaining at the same time from making himself responsible for more important acts.

1474 THE DUKE OF WELLINGTON *to* SIR WILLIAM KNIGHTON

19 January 1828.

THE DUKE OF DEVONSHIRE called upon me less than a quarter of an hour after you left me. He had been early to Chiswick and had not heard of my wish to see him, or of my visits till he returned.

I began by telling him that I was quite convinced that the subject on which I was about to speak to him gave him as much pain as it did to me, viz. this separation from the King; and that I had been anxious to converse with him upon the subject in order to endeavour to discover some mode by which that painful separation might be avoided.

The Duke said that he had been to Windsor and had suffered much in his conversation with the King, and in taking leave of him; but that the truth was that he and his friends had taken office and had joined Mr. Canning's Govt and had remained in office under that of Lord Goderich with Lord Lansdowne and his friends; and that if Lord Lansdowne did not remain in office, it was impossible for him to do so.

I answered that the King had expressed to me the greatest satisfaction with the services of Lord Lansdowne, and that I could have no prejudice against Lord Lansdowne for whom I entertained the highest respect. But that employed as I was in this delicate commission by His Majesty it was my duty to suggest what I conscientiously believed would tend to form an Administration for His Majesty most capable of conducting his affairs; and that I could not think it was advisable to incur the risk of Lord Lansdowne's refusal of office, while I was certain that his acceptance of an offer of office made to him would reduce the Govt to the same difficulties as had been experienced by Lord Goderich. I begged the Duke to reflect upon what I had just said to him; to be assured that the Govt now to be established, although in the hands of different men, would be found on all subjects equally enlightened and just and much stronger than those with which he had been connected; and I entreated him to consider whether he could not devise the means by which he could continue in office; and I told him that I would readily consider any plan which he should suggest.

The Duke repeated that nothing but the acceptance of office by Lord Lansdowne could induce him to remain.

He then told me that he was much gratified by my communication to him and to Lord Carlisle, and after some conversation about the state of the King's health he went away. This is in a great degree the detail of what passed.

1475 THE KING *to the* MARQUIS OF LANSDOWNE

Copy.

[20 January 1828.]

THE KING sends his very kind regards to the Marquis of Lansdowne.

The King is most truly sensible of the concern and kind consideration manifested by Lord Lansdowne at the King's indisposition. The King desires to acknowledge this dutiful attention on the part of Lord Lansdowne with every sentiment of kind feeling.

The King hopes to have it in his power to receive Lord Lansdowne at the Royal Lodge on Tuesday next at three o'clock, for the purpose of relieving Lord Lansdowne from that official responsibility to which Lord Lansdowne's note particularly refers.

The King naturally concludes that Lord Goderich acquainted Lord Lansdowne in detail of all that passed at Lord Goderich's last audience with the King, the result, the consequence, of necessity speaks for itself. But the King desires in conclusion distinctly to state that Lord Lansdowne has not been called upon to execute any one responsible act since Lord Goderich declared the Government to be virtually dissolved, but what had been already settled by the King with Lord Goderich, as the King's responsible adviser.

1476 VISCOUNTESS CANNING *to the* KING

Harcourt House, January 20th 1828.

I HOPE that I shall not be considered too presumptuous if I venture to address directly to your Majesty the expression of my humble and grateful acknowledgments on the completion of the spontaneous mark of your Majesty's favour so graciously conveyed to me some months ago.

The honour which your Majesty has deigned to confer on me, as the representative of the individual who had the happiness to enjoy your Majesty's confidence, is most valuable and gratifying to my feelings as a testimony of your Majesty's favourable opinion and approbation of the services of a faithful and devoted servant: and the kindness and condescension with which your Majesty's gracious intentions were communicated to me must for ever excite in my breast sentiments of the most unbounded gratitude and devotion.

With the most profound reverence, duty, and attachment, I am, [etc.].

1477 VISCOUNT GODERICH *to the* KING

Downing Street, Jany 21st 1828.

LORD GODERICH presents his humble duty to your Majesty. Understanding that the Duke of Wellington is about to kiss hands upon being appointed First Lord of the Treasury, Lord Goderich trusts that your Majesty will be graciously pleased to pardon him if he presumes to offer to your Majesty his dutiful and respectful acknowledgments for the great kindness which upon so many occasions during the many years that he has been in your Majesty's service it has been his pride and happiness to experience from your Majesty.

For ten years he has been one of your Majesty's confidential servants in high and important offices, of which he has always endeavoured to discharge the duties with zeal and fidelity with a devoted attachment to your Majesty's person and Government, and he trusts he may without presumption add, not without advantage to your Majesty's service.

Under circumstances of no ordinary difficulty he has recently found himself unable to carry on your Majesty's service as the head of the Government conformably to your Majesty's intention in the formation of that Government. But altho' this has placed him in the painful situation of now quitting your Majesty's service, he never can forget your Majesty's kindness towards him during the time that he occupied that eminent station; and whilst he is conscious that he undertook that task from no other motive than a paramount sense of duty to your Majesty, he humbly presumes to hope that your Majesty does not ascribe his ultimate want of success to any deficiency in an earnest desire to serve your Majesty to the best of his abilities, but to occurences which at the moment were beyond controul.

If during the eighteen years of his past official life his services have in any degree obtained your Majesty's gracious approbation, there is no subject in your Majesty's dominions who could more warmly appreciate the expression of such approbation, or who could more sincerely feel how many motives he has for endeavouring at all times to deserve its continuance, by a faithful discharge of those public duties that still remain to him to fulfill.

Lord Goderich has thus presumed to trouble your Majesty with the expression of his humble acknowledgments for all your Majesty's favours; and it would be no ordinary source of gratification to him personally to assure your Majesty (whenever it might please your Majesty to permit it), of his faithful and loyal attachment and of his unceasing anxiety to promote your Majesty's happiness and honor whenever and wherever it may be in his power to do so.

1478 THE EARL OF ROSSLYN *to the* DUKE OF WELLINGTON
Copy.

Woburn Abbey, Jany. 23rd 1828.

I HAD the honour to receive your two letters of the 15th.[1] & 21st. on my arrival at this house yesterday, having been detained by the snow, and I cannot adequately express how much I am flattered by the honor your Grace has conferred upon me, or my gratitude for your kind partiality in recommending me to His Majesty's notice and proposing me for an office[2] of such high distinction, and one which has always been the greatest object of my ambition.

It is with great regret I add that under all existing circumstances I feel that I cannot with propriety avail myself of this mark of favor which His Majesty has been graciously pleased to confer upon a person so undeserving.

I must entreat your Grace to have the goodness to lay at His Majesty's feet my most humble and dutiful acknowledgment of the deep sense I entertain of His Majesty's gracious condescension, and the concern I feel that my sincere and dutiful regard to the interests of His Majesty's service and the credit of your Grace's Administration, compell me to beg to be excused from obeying His Majesty's commands.

My long connection in politics with some few friends and my concurrence with them in political principles and opinions, to which I stand

1 *W.N.D.* IV, 193–4.
2 Master General of the Ordnance, with a seat in the Cabinet.

pledged and which I cannot abandon or compromise without such a loss of character as would render me but little useful to those I might be permitted to join, together with my apprehension that differences of opinion still continue between many of those who will fill high stations in the Government and myself upon subjects of importance that must necessarily come forward immediately, form great obstacles to an engagement with the Administration from which, if once entered into, I cannot with honor recede.

I cannot conclude without assuring your Grace that the consideration that you are to be at the head of the new Government would weigh powerfully with me as an inducement to accept your Grace's proposition if I felt that I could do so with credit to myself and advantage to your Grace's Administration, and that in declining it I must desire not to be held as one about to engage in any general or systematic opposition.[1]

I have the honor to be, [etc.].

1479   THE DUKE OF DEVONSHIRE *to the* KING

London, Jany. 23d 1828.

YOUR MAJESTY's letter and the permission to wear the Order of St. Andrew have given me the greatest pleasure, as much as I am capable of feeling at a time like the present when it has been necessary for me to act against the dearest wishes of my heart and to deprive myself of what was my greatest happiness and pride. The Emperor's letter is most kind and valuable to me from the expressions it contains relating to your Majesty and the assurances of his continued regard towards myself.[2]

With the strongest feelings of attachment and gratitude I have the honor to be [etc.].

1480   THE KING *to* SIR WILLIAM KNIGHTON

R! L^{ge}, Wed^y ½ pt 12 p.m.
Jany 23^d 1827 [1828].

As the carte du pays is somewhat chang'd, to what you expected, since you left me, & as, in all probability you may deem it adviseable, therefore to change, in consequence, your plans of returning here, I will endeavour, as briefly as possible to give you a short sketch. To begin,

1 Lord Rosslyn joined the Wellington Ministry as Lord Privy Seal in June 1829. Ellenborough says that this letter was communicated to the Cabinet on the 24th. (*Diary*, I, 6.)
2 The Tsar conferred this honour upon the Duke at the King's request. (*W.N.D.* IV, 256.)

In the first place, God knows owing to whose, or to what neglect, lo & behold, upon, & when they were all assembled, there was no Clerk of the Council forthcoming, consequently, no Council could be held, no business could be done, & no one could be sworn.[1] The result of this, is, that another Council is to be assembled here at three o'clock, *next Saturday*, (instead of the following Monday, as was previously fix'd) when the whole body is to be sworn in, *& when the speech is also to be read*; *pray take notice of this*, & endeavour, that the speech should be sent for my consideration, on *Friday* evening, or at the *very latest*, as *early* as *possible* on Saturday morning *when I depend upon having you with me*, although, you were immediately afterwards to depart again for London.

I was, as you may easily believe most dreadfully fatigu'd & done over, but, to the best of my judgment, every thing went off, with every one of them, to perfection, in their different way, & I understand, both from what they said to me, as well as, from the manner in which they express'd themselves to others upon leaving me, there is not one of them, that was not *highly pleas'd*, with the audiences which I gave them. Some of the audiences were necessarily very long, particularly, those of *Lansdowne*, *Carlisle*, & *Peel*, to whom (as I told the Duke afterwards) I had given a very strong lecture respecting his conduct both as to the past, as well as to the future, & which *he* (the Duke) not only *highly* approv'd of, but to use his own expression, said, that it would do, "a monstrous deal of good, & much more so, than I could have any idea of", in short, he was delighted at it.

Upon the whole I feel quite satisfied with myself, only, that I am suffering sadly from the exertions & fatigues of yesterday, this morning, after having pass'd a very bad & restless night. I shall therefore say no more at present but keep all particular details till we meet; however I must express my desire that you will write as soon as possible all you know, & hear, & tell me what will be the change in your intentions of your next visit here, in consequence of what I have now written.

The Duke of Wellington to the King, 24 January 1828 (three letters). [*W.N.D.* IV, 213–15.]

---

1 There is no reference to this accident on the 22nd in Greville's *Diary*, but Ellenborough said that Greville had not been apprised of the intention to hold a Council. The new Ministers, who were to take the oaths of office, were kept waiting at the Royal Lodge for three hours before they were admitted to the King. (*Ellenborough's Diary*, I, 1.)

London, January 25th 1828.

HAVING considered it my duty to your Majesty to submit for the consideration of your Majesty's servants the question whether it was expedient that I should remain in command of your Majesty's army while filling the situation of First Lord of the Treasury; and having withdrawn myself from the room while the Cabinet were discussing this question, they agreed unanimously in an opinion as stated in the Minute which I now inclose to your Majesty.

I cannot express to your Majesty the pain which this decision has given me; and feeling as I do my own incompetency to fill the arduous situation to which your Majesty's gracious favour and confidence have raised me, I would earnestly intreat your Majesty to relieve me from it, and to allow me to serve your Majesty in my profession if I could point out to your Majesty at this moment any person likely to give satisfaction to your Majesty who could be placed at the head of your Govt.[1]

I assure your Majesty that no preference of mine shall impede your service; and in conformity with the opinion contained in the Minute of Cabinet I hereby tender my resignation of the office of Commander-in-Chief.[2]

I intend of course to continue to the best of my abilities to perform the duties of Commander-in-Chief till your Majesty will appoint some person to that office.

All of which is submitted to your Majesty by your Majesty's most dutiful and devoted subject and servant.

---

1 The previous letter shows that Peel would have been unacceptable to the King, and, too, Wellington was aware that some of the Tory rank-and-file in the House of Commons would have been reluctant to support a Government of which Peel was the head: his views, except on the Catholic question, were too progressive. Lady Shelley, for example, writing to her friend the Duke, said: "[Sir John, her husband] Shelley for the future intends to be guided entirely by you. As for me, I need not trouble myself about politics any longer! This confidence we could neither of us have felt if Peel had become Premier. I am happy to know that this sentiment is very general among the members of our Party—and this in spite not only of our high opinion of Peel's talents, but also of our liking for him personally." (*Diary of Frances, Lady Shelley*, II, 172.)

2 "I certainly did not contemplate this necessity as being paramount when I undertook for his Majesty the service of forming his Government", he wrote to Lord Hill. "But even if I had, I don't think that I could have declined endeavouring to perform the service, and it is useless to regret that I did not make the retention of my office a condition without which I would not serve his Majesty as he desired I should." (*W.N.D.* IV, 253.)

1482   *Minute of the Cabinet, Foreign Office, Jany. 25th 1828.*

[Enclosed in the above.]

THE Cabinet most deeply regret the great personal sacrifice which their opinion will impose upon the Duke of Wellington.

Their unanimous opinion is that it is of great importance, with reference to the impressions in Parliament and the country generally, and to the stability of the Government, that the Duke of Wellington on accepting the office of First Lord of the Treasury should resign that of Commander-in-Chief.

The Duke of Wellington to the Duke of Argyll, 27 January 1828. (*W.N.D.* IV, 215.)

1483   THE MARQUIS OF LANSDOWNE *to* SIR WILLIAM KNIGHTON

January 27th 1828.

THE inclosed letter which I have lately received relates to a private transaction respecting pictures, upon which by His Majesty's desire I made some time since a communication to Mr. West.[1] I was unwilling to trouble His Majesty with it during the last fortnight when his attention has been so differently engaged, but it is proper that he should be made acquainted with the contents, which perhaps you will have the kindness to do when a fit occasion presents itself.

I am informed that in what is called the Court Circular the day after that on which some of His Majesty's late Ministers attended at the Lodge for the purpose of resigning the seals of office, it was stated that His Majesty was prevented from holding a Council on that day by a neglect in the Home Office.[2] I am desirous of stating that the assertion is quite unfounded, and as I believe the Circular upon such occasions is either sent from or corrected at Windsor, and as I should be sorry that either I or any person in the office over which I lately presided should appear to have been the cause of disappointment to His Majesty, on so important an occasion, I will beg the favor of you to direct that the error may be corrected thro' the same channel in which it originated.

1 Raphael Lamar West (1769–1850), the eldest son of Benjamin West.
2 See No. 1480.

Newman Street, January 7th 1828.

IN reply to the letter which I had the honor of receiving from your Lordship on the 21st. of last month, I beg permission to say I never have considered any balance was due to me on account of the pictures painted by my late father for His late Majesty.

According to my father's book of accompts the first picture he painted by command of His late Majesty was in the year 1769 and the last in 1810.

In the intervening space of time (forty one years) he executed 56 pictures for His late Majesty, and received on that account £34,162 – 15 – 0, which sum covering the prices marked against the pictures, no balance can be due to me or any of my family.

Although the sum received appears to be considerable, yet, when taken in the aggregate, it is evidently not more than would be necessary for moderately carrying on the expences of my father's family during so long a period as forty one years.

I here take the opportunity of mentioning what I have repeatedly heard my father say—that it never was intended the £1000 per annum (which he received for many years by quarterly instalments and which is included in the before mentioned amount of his receipts), should be a final remuneration to him for the long devotion of his time and talent to His late Majesty, but only meant for enabling him to go on with the domestic expences of his family until the great work he was engaged on for the Royal Chapel in Windsor Castle should be finished, when, I understood it was intended by His late Majesty to have further rewarded my father and honored him on the completion of his labours.

This great work, intended as an illustration of revealed religion, not having been finished before the death of my father, added to my not yet having been able to dispose of the large collection of his works left by him at his death to my brother and me, are the principal causes, as I have stated in my memorial, of the misfortunes which are now visited upon me—and I have mentioned what I have understood were the intentions of His late Majesty towards my late father, not with the view of bringing forward any claim on the Royal family, but that a knowledge of those intentions might reflect honor on the memory of my father's beneficent benefactor.

I will now offer to your Lordship my most grateful acknowledgments for your condescension and goodness in having presented my memorial (containing a representation of the distress into which I am reduced) to His present Majesty. I at the same time, in conjunction with my brother, respectfully request of your Lordship to express to His Majesty our humble but deep sense of duty and gratitude for his gracious intention of restoring to us, for our benefit, those pictures which were finished and designed by our father and intended as part of the before mentioned work for the Royal Chapel in Windsor Castle.

As this letter is a private communication I will venture to express to your Lordship in confidence that these pictures I fear will not be to me of that assistance which I am so much in need of at this moment—because they can be considered when given as part of the security for redeeming the mortgage which is on our property, and therefore cannot be available for relieving my immediate distresses—and as we have not disposed of the body of my father's works already in our possession it is natural to suppose we shall have the same difficulty with the additional pictures— but the intention of His Majesty is nevertheless most benevolent and munificent and whenever these pictures can favourably be disposed of I should hope they would prove, as His Majesty graciously intends, a benefit to the family—which intention will ever be remembered by me with the profoundest feeling of duty and devotion.

I can assure your Lordship my necessities are such at this moment that if I were not to be an intruder at the table of my relatives I know not how I should be able to sustain myself, and when I consider that all the labour of my father's arduous life has proved in vain for leaving a support for his family, and that the prime of my life has passed away endeavouring to assist him in the subordinate but necessary part of all the great works he was engaged in for His late Majesty—whereby I lost the opportunity of acquiring a knowledge of some profession that might now have enabled me to provide for myself, my wife, and my daughter, I must confess I cannot help feeling that my situation is most adverse and unfortunate, not having the smallest degree of derivable income.

[P.S.] Your Lordship has mentioned in your letter that His Majesty proposes to reserve one, out of the number of pictures he graciously intends to restore, for our benefit. If the picture could be named to me I would particularly attend that special care should be taken of it.

1485 Sir William Knighton *to the* Marquis of Lansdowne

Copy.

Hanover Square, 28th Jany. 1828.

I HAVE the honour to acknowledge your Lordship's letter which was sent up to me from Windsor this morning.

I will not fail to lay before His Majesty, the first opportunity, Mr. West's private letter to your Lordship.

With respect to the newspaper report mentioned by your Lordship, I suppose it can hardly be necessary for me to say that I know nothing. During the last week I have not had it in my power to be at Windsor but for a short time, and on the afternoon of your Lordship's audience I was not there. I never heard that a Council was intended to be held on that day, either previously or since, and was quite unacquainted with the unfounded assertion you allude to until I had the pleasure of receiving your Lordship's letter.

The proper mode of contradicting this mis-statement (if it be worth while), would appear to be by directing the Council Office to do so. As to what is called in the newspapers "the Court Circular" I am told that it is well known at most of the public offices that some one man has during the last five and twenty years been permitted, (perhaps as a necessary evil) to collect and to communicate what relates to Councils, Recorders Reports, Levees, Drawing Rooms &c. but it would be no easy matter, I apprehend, to trace how such communications are made when the Court is not held in London.

I can however, should it be your Lordship's pleasure, approach His Majesty for the purpose of giving me permission to examine the servants of the establishment whether the misrepresentation in question originated from any *of them.*

I am sure I know enough of your Lordship's honorable mind to excuse me for expressing my indignation at any supposition (if such there be), that I have directly or indirectly any communication with the agents of newspapers, or newspaper paragraphs.

1486 The Marquis of Lansdowne *to* Sir William Knighton

Berkeley Square, Jany. 28th 1828.

I TROUBLE you with a few lines merely to acknowledge the favor of your letter and to request you will give yourself no further trouble on the subject I had adverted to in mine of a misrepresentation in what is called the Court Circular.

I had certainly conceived that statement of occurrences on Court days to be issued with authority, or something like authority, from the Royal Palace, and I therefore took the liberty of calling your attention to the imputation of neglect of duty thus cast, if not upon me, upon those whom up to that day I was bound to protect; but if it is not an authorized communication it is quite unworthy of any further notice—nor could I have supposed it originated in any case from wilful error in the person appointed to collect the information permitted to be given.

1487 THE KING *to* SIR WILLIAM KNIGHTON

Royal Lodge, Jany. 28th 1828.

AS your letter to me of this day was very brief, so will my answer be equally so, as I have nothing new either to tell or to state, except that I have received this morning a most amazing handsome letter from the poor Duke of Argyll, in consequence of his unforeseen dismissal from his office, which I have forwarded to the Duke of Wellington, for I can in no way submit to the Duke of Argyll's supposing that I either was the promoter or had the least share in his dismissal, and I have stated that, if this can not *now* be remedied, a thorough & clear explanation of this must be made to the Duke of Argyll in justice to myself. Pray come whenever you like for you know I am always glad to see you.[1]

1488 THE DUKE OF WELLINGTON *to the* KING

London, January 29th 1828.

I BEG leave to submit to your Majesty the usual reports.

The debate upon the Address was short; turning principally on Lord Holland's objection to the term "Antient Ally" applied to the Porte; and the epithet "untoward" applied to the Battle of Navarin. The debate was certainly in favour of the Govt.

All of which is submitted to your Majesty by [etc.].

The Duke of Wellington to the King. 29 January 1828. (*W.N.D.* IV, 219–20, subject to the following corrections:

p. 219. l. 1. Substitute the following: "I received your Majesty's letter of 7 p.m. yesterday, in the night, and I now lay before your Majesty. . . ."

p. 220. l. 10. After "Majesty" add "does".

p. 220. l. 11. After "but" substitute the following: "the arrangement could not have been avoided, and I confess that I see no remedy for it."

p. 220. l. 13. After "is" add "humbly" and delete "for your Majesty's pleasure".)

1 See the King's letter of this date to Wellington, in *W.N.D.* IV, 219.

Thury evg 7 o clk Jany 31st. 1828.

I THANK you for your very interesting letter, and I do most highly approve of the whole of its contents.

In the last conversation I had with the D[uke] of W[ellingto]n, upon Scarlett's resignation, he stated to me that he was entirely of opinion that Scarlett should continue to be employed by me in all my affairs.[1] Now, surely, if that cannot be under present circumstances, can you not through the means of the Chancellor and by means of a confidential communication with him from me, see if it be not possible to persuade Mr. Ser[jean]t Cross[2] to resign his Att[orne]y Gen[era]l[shi]p to the Duchy of Lancaster, or even dismiss him in order to replace Scarlett, the Chancellor promising Ser[jean]t Cross any one of the first and best situations which may fall vacant, and which he is capable of holding; at any rate assuring him [the rest is missing].

1490 THE DUKE OF CUMBERLAND *to* SIR WILLIAM KNIGHTON

Berlin, Feby 2d 1828.

DEAR SIR,[3]

Young Seymour[4] brought me yesterday your letter of the 22d, and I have written to my brother, which I have now not done for near 6 weeks, feeling it more delicate not to obtrude myself upon him, during a time of so much worry & bustle.

I need not say, I feel rejoiced at the last Govt. being broke up, and hope from the bottom of my soul that the D. of W[ellington] may meet with *that* support that his noble conduct has a right to demand from every loyal Briton. That the Session will be very stormy I have no doubt of, and I have no doubt very extraordinary scenes will take place, as I under-

1 Scarlett was invited to remain Attorney-General, but, on the advice of Lord Fitzwilliam and Lord Milton, he resigned. [*W.N.D.* IV, 216; *Life of Lord Abinger*, p. 110 *et seq.*] "He cannot stay", said his son-in-law, the lawyer Campbell, "without a rupture with Lord Fitzwilliam [who provided him with a seat in the Commons] and the whole of the Whig party.... All that could be said is that Scarlett was not put in by Lansdowne and the Whigs, but by Canning, and that he is therefore justified in acting with Canning's friends." (Hardcastle, *Campbell*, I, 452.)

2 Sir John Cross (1766–1842). King's Serjeant, 1827; Attorney-General of the Duchy of Lancaster, 1827; Knighted, 1831, and appointed Judge of the Bankruptcy Court.

3 The Duke's subsequent letters are addressed "Dear Knighton".

4 Sir George Hamilton Seymour (1797–1880), the diplomatist. Secretary of Legation at Berlin, 1828–29, and Chargé d'Affaires, 2–26 February 1828, during Lord Clanwilliam's absence.

stand Party runs very high. However, as before said, I hope every thing will go on well. I await with anxiety a letter from the Duke which I hope may explain the inclusion of some names, & *exclusion* of others,[1] which I own have *astonished* me not a *little*. Still I am one of those who feel it a *duty* not to *cavell* or *find fault*, but to be impressed with the fullest confidence in him, that he has *done all he could do* & I believe him to be so perfectly honourable and so truely attached to my brother that I feel easy on his subject. How will Herries & Huskisson go on? I depend on my brother's giving me timely notice if the Catholic question comes on, which I feel confident they will force on the House to embarrass Government, and according to my calculation the numbers pro and con are equal in the Cabinet.[2] You say Rosslynne has *accepted*,[3] I own I am surprized at *his* doing it, having always looked upon him as totally and exclusively belonging to Lord Grey.

Excuse this scrawl, but I have had a multiplicity of letters to write, and have written a very long letter to my brother. Thank God you give a good acct of his amendment, and now that he has *all* this off his mind I trust he will be soon entirely off the sick list. We are all *well* here. I am daily expecting to hear from Vienna.

1491　THE DUKE OF WELLINGTON *to the* KING

London, February 7th 1828.

THE LORD CHANCELLOR informed me that he had reported to your Majesty the details of the interview which his Lordship and I had with Sir Charles Wetherall on Tuesday last, with a view to prevail upon him to leave in the hands of Sir James Scarlett the management of certain causes of your Majesty regarding the Dukes of Cornwall and Lancaster which will shortly come under trial in the Court of King's Bench. I did not make any report to your Majesty upon the subject because I intended to see Lord Eldon again yesterday morning in order to request him to use his influence with Sir Charles Wetherall to induce him to comply with the request which I had made. I must do Lord Eldon the justice to say that he has assisted me as far as is in his power, but hitherto without

1 Eldon, Bexley and Westmorland.
2 The "Catholics" were Aberdeen, Dudley, Ellenborough, Grant, Huskisson, Melville and Palmerston; the "Protestants"—Bathurst, Goulburn, Herries, Lyndhurst, Peel and Wellington.
3 See No. 1478.

effect; but I have seen his Lordship again this afternoon and he is to see Sir Charles Wetherall in the morning.

I am very apprehensive however that there is so much of professional etiquette bound up with this affair that it will be impossible to attain your Majesty's object. The regular course is that in a trial at Bar in which your Majesty's interests are involved it is the duty of the Attorney and Sollicitor General to attend to and lead the cause on the part of your Majesty, and there is no instance to the contrary, excepting a trial in the Court of Exchequer in the time of Sir Wm Garrow which is not considered a precedent. If Sir Charles Wetherall had not himself as Attorney General acted in the cause and obtained a decision in your Majesty's favour with which your Majesty had expressed your satisfaction, and if the cause was likely to come on in a few days, it might be possible to authorize Sir James Scarlett to carry it on; but under existing circumstances it is thought that the ordinary rules of the profesion would prevent Sir Charles Wetherall and the Sollicitor General from giving up their claim to perform your Majesty's business.

Although, as I before stated to your Majesty, Lord Eldon is to see Sir Charles Wetherall tomorrow, I think it possible he will not produce any alteration; and as I told the Lord Chancellor that I would write to your Majesty this night I have thought it best to let your Majesty know how the case stands.

All of which is submitted to your Majesty by your Majesty's most devoted subject and servant.

1492 THE DUKE OF MONTROSE *to the* KING

London, Feb. 7th 1828.

YOUR MAJESTY'S communication yesterday, by Sir William Knighton has been received by your Majesty's humble and attached servant with sentiments the most grateful.

To have the honor of re-entering your Majesty's household[1] after the painful circumstances which acted upon the Duke of Montrose last year is easier felt than expressed.

Many may not give credit to the motives of your Majesty's humble servant, but his conduct was dictated by principles which your Majesty will, he flatters himself, approve.

1 As Lord Chamberlain. See No. 1312.

Your Majesty's humble servant did not feel that he possessed importance enough, in your Majesty's consideration, to presume to give uncalled for advice though he conceived, by depriving himself of the honour, gratification, and advantage of serving your Majesty, he, in the most honest and forcible manner, evinced the alarm he felt on your Majesty's account.

That your Majesty's humble servant might not be mistaken is not to be presumed by him; but he anxiously solicits that your Majesty will have the goodness to attribute his conduct to the dictates of conviction, and the alarm for your Majesty's best interests.

It remains only to assure your Majesty of the duty and attachment of your Majesty's devoted subject and servant, and that he will, as soon as his health will permit, have the honour of presenting himself to your Majesty at Windsor, if that should be agreeable to your Majesty.

1493 THE EARL OF DUDLEY *to the* KING

Foreign Office, February 7, 1828.

LORD DUDLEY with his humble duty to your Majesty submits to your Majesty a paper exhibiting at one view some reductions and some appointments which Lord Dudley will propose to your Majesty in the Foreign department.

Your Majesty will at once perceive that the reductions, besides that of Buenos Ayres of which your Majesty has already approved, are not very considerable, and that they do not affect any person that has enjoyed a larger salary for the same functions. Lord Dudley is induced to propose them to your Majesty both because he is persuaded that they may take place without detriment to your Majesty's service, and because they may serve to anticipate criticisms that might otherwise be made in Parliament, and to allay that jealousy that would be excited by maintaining undiminished the expenditure of the department. A comparatively small sacrifice may therefore be adviseable on the score of prudence as well as of œconomy.

Under the head of appointments your Majesty will observe the name of Mr. Henry Fox[1] to whom in case he should prefer remaining in

---

1 Henry Stephen Fox (1791–1846), son of General Henry Edward Fox, and grandson of Henry Fox, first Lord Holland. He was Secretary of Legation at Turin, 1824–26, and Secretary of Legation at Naples, 1826–28. In July 1830 he was appointed Envoy Extraordinary and Minister Plenipotentiary at Buenos Aires.

Europe with an inferior rank, Lord Dudley would wish to be able to propose to be Secretary of Embassy at Vienna. His *name* may perhaps not appear to suit that post, but Lord Dudley has good reason to believe that he is uninfluenced by the other branch of his family, and disconnected with their politicks. His abilities certainly render him fit to serve your Majesty on a more active scene than Naples.

The removal of Mr. Fox either to Vienna or Buenos Ayres would allow him to be replaced by Mr. Strangways,[1] and open Florence to Lord Albert Conyngham.[2] They may be all gazetted as soon as your Majesty's pleasure is signified.

Lord Dudley cannot conclude without offering to Y.M. his humble thanks for those expressions of continued kindness and favour which your Majesty is graciously pleased to employ towards him in the letter he received from your Majesty last night. Lord Dudley hopes he may be permitted to say that the countenance and favour that have been shown to him by your Majesty ever since he had the honor to serve your Majesty, have added the sentiments of profound gratitude and unalterable attachment to your Majesty to that duty and respect that he owes to your Majesty in common with all your Majesty's subjects.

1494 THE DUKE OF WELLINGTON *to the* KING

London, February 8th 1828.

I HAVE to report to your Majesty that I have heard from Lord Eldon again this evening, but I am sorry to say that Sir Charles Wetherall still is of opinion that he could not refrain from appearing in the Court of King's Bench in your Majesty's cause, without a total loss of professional honour.

1 William Thomas Horner Fox-Strangways (1795–1865), son of the second Earl of Ilchester; succeeded as fourth Earl in 1858.

2 The youngest son of the Marquis Conyngham (1805–1860). He was created Baron Londesborough in 1850. See No. 1576.

[February 1828.]

THE CHANCELLOR with his humble duty to your Majesty, begs permission to express to your Majesty the grateful sense he entertains of your Majesty's kindness and condescension in the confidential letter which he has received from your Majesty.

The Chancellor communicated your Majesty's official letter last evening to the Duke of Wellington, agreeably to your Majesty's commands. It appears that Sir C[harles] Wetherell has consulted with Lord Eldon since the meeting at Apsley House and the Duke of Wellington is to see Lord Eldon by appointment, in the course of this morning, for the purpose of again talking over the subject.

The Chancellor, as soon as he learns the result, will communicate it to your Majesty. If Sir C. Wetherell talks of this affair and makes it a point of honor, it may be difficult for him to recede; but if he had at once said, which the Chancellor humbly thinks he might have done, that he would *give directions* that Sir J. Scarlett should *go on* with the cause, the Chancellor cannot feel that, as far as he, Sir C. Wetherell, is concerned, there would have been any difficulty in it. There might be some delicacy with reference to the Solicitor General, who practices in the Court of King's Bench, but the Chancellor would have endeavoured to surmount it.

The Chancellor feels most sensibly the extent of the sacrifice which the unyielding temper of Sir C. Wetherell may occasion to your Majesty.

1496 THE KING *to* SIR WILLIAM KNIGHTON

Royal Lodge, Feby. 8th 1828.

MANY thanks for your kind letter. You will find in the box several letters added to those which you were desirous should be returned and some of which, I think, should be preserved, and therefore I have taken this opportunity of sending them to you. You will perceive, amongst the rest, one private one from the Chancellor and two from the Duke of Wellington, all relating to and explaining how the matter stands respecting Wetherall and Scarlett, with which I am sure that you must be already thoroughly acquainted; however, I consider it as most adviseable at any rate to forward them to you. As dinner is waiting, I shall only add that I am always, [etc.].

P.S. All here unite in kindest regards to you.

The Duke of Wellington to the King, 8 February 1828 (two letters). [*W.N.D.* IV, 258–9.]

London, Feby. 9th 1828.

THE CHANCELLOR, with his humble duty to your Majesty, begs leave to state to your Majesty, which he does with much regret, that the conferences between the Duke of Wellington and Lord Eldon have *not* been attended with a successful result and that Sir Charles Wetherell has not receded from his first decision.

The Chancellor will, with your Majesty's permission, pay his duty to your Majesty on Wednesday at the Council at Windsor, when the Chancellor will inform your Majesty of the result of his inquiries respecting the Recorder's Report, if it shall so please your Majesty.

The Chancellor has enclosed the warrant for the appointment of the Attorney General that it may be ready for your Majesty's signing if your Majesty should think proper to allow it to proceed.

The Chancellor begs permission to express his grateful devotion to your Majesty's service.

1498 THE DUKE OF WELLINGTON *to the* KING

London, February 10th 1828.

I WRITE to Mr. Wynne according to your Majesty's commands to inform him that your Majesty will receive him on the first Council day. Since I have been in office Lord Goderich has spoken to me three or four times respecting the application which his Lordship has made to your Majesty after the dissolution of his Government, that your Majesty would be graciously pleased to grant a pension to Mr. Wynne; and I had an interview with his Lordship on that subject three days ago in which Lord Goderich pressed me to compleat the arrangement as being one commenced by him, but left incompleat in consequence of the change of the Administration. My answer to Lord Goderich was this.

I must consider this arrangement as one compleat by His Majesty having given his consent to it during the period of his Lordship being in office, and such consent having been conveyed to Mr. Wynne; or incompleat in consequence of His Majesty not having given his consent to the arrangement, notwithstanding that His Majesty did not disapprove of the application in favour of Mr. Wynne. That I could not talk to his Lordship on other grounds.

That in the first case, that of your Majesty having given your consent and the consent having been conveyed to Mr. Wynne previous to the dissolution of the Administration, I had nothing to say to the arrangement. That in the last case, that of the arrangement having been proposed subsequent to the dissolution of the Govt and not having been consented to by your Majesty, it would be my duty to take your Majesty's pleasure upon it if anything was to be done; and that it could not be expected from me that I should take your Majesty's pleasure upon this arrangement solely because his Lordship had; or because he felt an interest for Mr. Wynne.

Lord Goderich was not much pleased with this answer, but I believe it is strictly correct in principle.

All of which is humbly submitted to your Majesty by your Majesty's most dutiful and devoted subject and servant.

The Duke of Wellington to the King, 11 February 1828. (*W.N.D.* IV, 262.)

1499 THE DUKE OF WELLINGTON *to the* KING

London, February 11th 1828.

I HAVE had the honor of receiving your Majesty's letter of this day's date. I thought it probable that your Majesty would be spoken to by Lord Goderich or Mr. Wynne or by both on the subject of the pension proposed by the former to be granted to the latter; and I wished that your Majesty should be made acquainted exactly with what passed between Lord Goderich and me upon the subject, as your Majesty has been almost in the exact words that passed.

I have had no other communication with Lord Goderich, and none whatever with Mr. Wynne. And your Majesty may rely upon it that neither upon this nor upon any other subject will I do more than that which I cannot avoid, viz. receive the application of an individual before I shall consult your Majesty's wishes and pleasure.

I earnestly recommend to your Majesty to sign Sir Charles Wetherall's patent. I certainly never made a greater exertion than I did to prevail upon Sir Charles Wetherall to consent to forego his claim as your Majesty's Attorney General to lead in your cause in the Court of King's Bench. I think that Sir Charles Wetherall refused to comply with my earnest entreaties from a sense, however erroneous, that a point of professional honour was involved in his compliance with this request; and his conduct will be so understood by the profession and represented to the public. It would not be adviseable that it should appear that your Majesty had not granted him this office because he had refused to comply with my wishes on this subject; an act which would be called professional degradation. Such delusion might injure even your Majesty's cause, and I would earnestly recommend to your Majesty to sign his patent and send it to London without delay.

All of which is submitted to your Majesty by your Majesty's most dutiful and devoted subject and servant.

1500   THE KING *to the* DUKE OF WELLINGTON
Copy.

Royal Lodge, Feby. 12th 1828.

WHEN you tell me that this gentleman, Sir Charles Wetherall, does not yield to his Sovereign's commands, under your representation, because professional dishonor to him would be the consequence, I have nothing more to say; I have no right to dishonor any man! If my Minister or my Chancellor, or both, entail upon me a man quite incompetent for the purposes I require, the King I suppose must resign himself to the political motives that induced the appointment. I have a desire however to satisfy my own consistency; I would therefore wish that this letter should be shewn to the Lord Chancellor for the purpose of having it legally represented to me that this man would be exposed to professional dishonor by the course that his Sovereign desired him to pursue. I only hope it will not happen in another matter.

I desire you to believe, my friend, that I am not acting from temper in this matter (although reason enough), but I do think I have great cause of complaint against Lord Eldon and Mr. Peel by whom this gentleman must have been originally recommended for the situation of Attorney General.[1]

1 The King's suspicions were justified. Eldon wrote: "I found it likely that they were not going to restore Wetherell to the Attorney-Generalship, which he resigned nobly when we resigned [in April 1827], and by which step he has lost the Vice-Chancellorship. The D. has sent me word that as he understood that I wished that Wetherell should be restored to that office, he is re-appointed."

Whitehall Gardens, Feby. 15, 1828.

MR. PEEL with his humble duty to your Majesty begs leave to report to your Majesty the proceedings of the House of Commons of this evening.

Mr. Peel proposed the appointment of the Finance Committee. The House was exceedingly full—and there was an universal expectation that explanations would be required on the subject of the dissolution of your Majesty's late Administration.

Mr. Peel was followed in debate by Mr. Hume who confined himself entirely to the question before the House, the appointment of a Finance Committee.

Mr. Goulburn said a few words in reply to the observations of Mr. Hume.

The names of the members of the Committee were then read and agreed to. Mr. Huskisson's name had been omitted by his own desire. Mr. Alexander Baring and Mr. Brougham requested him to serve—and he said a few words—expressing his readiness to service, if it was the general sense of the House that he should be upon the Committee.

The Speaker then proposed his name—and it was placed upon the Committee without objection or remark of any kind.

There being no more business before the House Mr. Peel moved that the House should adjourn—and the House accordingly did adjourn, to the great surprize of the members generally, who had expected a discussion of a different nature.

Mr. Peel begs leave humbly to add that he has not learnt on what account the intention of calling upon Mr. Huskisson for explanations was abandoned. The prevailing impression appeared to be—that the abrupt termination of the debate was not intentional—that the Speaker put the question of adjournment before it was expected—although at the regular time—and that the member who proposed to commence the political part of the discussion was taken by surprize.

1502 SIR WILLIAM KNIGHTON *to the* KING

Sunday night, 17 February, 1828.

I THINK it *right* to have the honor of writing a few lines to your Majesty previous to my departure, which will be in an hour or two, expressive of my *affectionate*, my *dutiful*, and my *devoted* attachment! Having said this much, I shall proceed to state that I have this morning seen the Duke of

Wellington and had a very agreeable and satisfactory conversation with him. Your Majesty may rely that he will act up to the letter; namely one hundred and fifty thousand this year for Windsor, one hundred thousand this year for the King's Palace, and the same sum next year,—and a sum will be put aside from the Board of Works to carry into effect the different items in the Parks—Mrs. Broadwood's is to be bought at twenty one thousand pounds.

There may be some little boggle about the estimate of the fixtures of Carlton House, but if anything be said, be pleased to put it aside until my return and I PLEDGE myself to take care of it.[1]

I have seen Lord Dudley this morning who lives entirely under the influence of real duty and affection towards your Majesty.

I sent for Mr. Freeling[2] and I have seen him. It is impossible for any man to be impressed with more grateful feelings towards your Majesty. He is quite delighted! If your Majesty should not have happened to have signed the Baronets warrants today perhaps you would be gracious enough now to do so, as that would bring them into Tuesday's Gazette. They are in the little H.D. Box in the anti-room. Mr. Nash I have not been enabled to see but he has received his directions to make his estimate, and the proposed alterations in the front elevation are all to be acted upon without a moment's delay.

I hope and believe that everything is left quite straight for your Majesty, and that my absence will not impose any inconvenience on your Majesty relative to the concerns of the public buildings &c. Mr. George Harrison has been with me today for some time, and I am now satisfied, if I succeed in the object of this journey and which I feel satisfied I shall, it will give a stability and security to your Majesty's *private affairs* and public character not to be questioned.[3]

God bless and preserve your Majesty! is the prayer of your Majesty's most affectionate and devoted subject & servant.

1 See, on this point, Wellington's letter to the King, 21 February. (*W.N.D.* IV, 269.)

2 Sir Francis Freeling (1764–1836). Secretary to the General Post Office; created Baronet, February 1828.

3 Knighton was frequently employed on confidential missions for the King, and in 1828 he was sent to Paris to buy up the bonds which the Prince's agents had issued in 1788 as security for a huge loan. A sum of £350,000 was raised on the Continent through persons named John James de Beaume, Vaucher, and two Dutch bankers, Abraham and Simeon Boas. The transaction ruined the lenders, and the Boas brothers committed suicide. See Nos. 1511, 1518. When in 1792 the bonds at maturity were presented for payment, the Prince's agents repudiated their liability; the unfortunate French holders of the bonds were expelled the kingdom under the Alien Act, and many of them, it is said, were guillotined on their arrival in France.

Whitehall, February 18, 1828.

YOUR MAJESTY's commands shall be obeyed, and the name of Captain FitzGerald submitted to the Lord Lieutenant upon the first opportunity; but it is my duty to apprise your Majesty, that it may be a considerable time, before any such opportunity may occur. The local Magistrates of police it is not intended to fill up, when they become vacant; as their functions are superseded by the establishment of the constabulary force. There are only four Inspectors General of Police, one for each province. They are officers of the utmost importance, as upon their skill, vigilance and ability depend the efficiency, the character, and the ultimate success of that measure, which has already done so much towards repressing disorder, and maintaining the public peace in Ireland. An enquiry is now pending into the conduct of one of them, Major Powell, which may possibly terminate in his dismissal, but unless such should be the event, your Majesty will perceive, that there is no probability of the Lord Lieutenant's having it in his power at an early period to place Captain Fitz-Gerald in that situation.

With feelings of the utmost respect and the warmest attachment I beg leave humbly to lay myself at your Majesty's feet and to subscribe myself [etc.].

1504 ROBERT PEEL *to the* KING

Whitehall Gardens, Tuesday morning.
3 o'clock a.m. [19 February 1828].

MR. PEEL presents his humble duty to your Majesty and begs leave to submit to your Majesty an account of the proceedings in the House of Commons this evening.

The discussion was commenced by Lord Normanby[1] who referred to the disappointment which had been caused on Friday last by the debate having passed off on that evening without the expected explanations from Mr. Huskisson and Mr. Herries, and called upon those gentlemen to enter into explanations on this evening respecting the causes of dissolution of the last Administration.

Lord Normanby was followed by Mr. Huskisson and Mr. Huskisson

1 Constantine Henry Phipps, afterwards second Earl of Mulgrave and first Marquis of Normanby (1797-1863). In 1827 he was a Canningite, but he soon joined the Whigs and became one of their leading statesmen.

by Mr. Herries. Each of those gentlemen entered into very detailed explanations as to the differences that had arisen upon Lord Althorpe's proposed nomination to the Chair of the Finance Committee. Mr. Herries read all the letters which had passed upon that subject between Lord Goderich and himself, and expressed his conviction that the difference about Lord Althorpe was the ostensible rather than the real cause of the breaking up of your Majesty's late Government. Mr. Tierney explained the part which he had taken with reference to Lord Althorpe's nomination.

The enclosed paper contains a list of the speakers. The debate did not close until $\frac{1}{2}$ past two o'clock.

Mr. Peel humbly begs leave to assure your Majesty that throughout the discussion your Majesty's conduct throughout the whole of the proceedings which preceded the dissolution of Lord Goderich's Administration was spoken of in terms of the most dutiful respect. Mr. Peel thought it desirable to state to the House that your Majesty in calling upon the Duke of Wellington to form a new Administration had explicitly informed his Grace that the Government of Lord Goderich had dissolved itself—that your Majesty had given it a cordial support and would have continued to do so if it had not been dissolved by its own internal dissentions.

The Duke of Wellington to the King, 21 February 1828. (*W.N.D.* IV, 269–70.)
The Duke of Wellington to the King, 23 February 1828. (*Ibid.* IV, 273.)

1505 THE DUKE OF WELLINGTON *to the* KING

London, February 23rd 1828.

I BEG leave humbly to submit to your Majesty a letter from the Lord High Admiral and a memorial from Vice Admiral Lord Viscount Torrington,[1] of the latter of which a copy has been sent to me.

It is my duty to submit to your Majesty that your Majesty cannot now listen to an application from Lord Torrington for a reward for services rendered by his ancestor[2] one hundred years ago, without rendering your Majesty liable to similar applications from other families; more particularly considering the opulence which has been enjoyed by this family and is still enjoyed by some of its branches.

1 George Byng, sixth Viscount Torrington (1768–1831).
2 George Byng, first Viscount Torrington (1663–1733). He commanded in the Mediterranean during the War of the Spanish Succession, destroyed the Spanish Fleet off Cape Passaro in 1718, and was First Lord of the Admiralty, 1727–33.

But in writing to your Majesty upon this subject I am under the necessity of drawing your Majesty's attention to the state of the pensioners upon the 4½ per cent fund. The fund for the payment of their pensions is nearly exhausted; and it will be absolutely necessary to remove those to the Civil Lists of England Ireland and Scotland whose pensions will exceed the produce of the 4½ per cent revenue. There is now no other mode of providing for the payment of these pensions.

But it is obvious that this arrangement, however just and necessary in relation to the claims of the pensioners on the 4½ per cent fund, will prevent your Majesty and your Government from making any grant for any pensions whatever for the next three or four years.[1]

All of which is submitted to your Majesty by your Majesty's most dutiful and devoted subject and servant.

1506 VISCOUNT GODERICH *to the* KING

Downing Street, Feby. 23rd 1828.

WHEN your Majesty was graciously pleased to admit me on the 13th. inst. to an audience, the emotions which naturally arose in my mind upon that occasion precluded me from executing a purpose which was nevertheless very prominent in my mind when I solicited the honor of being permitted to attend your Majesty. This purpose was humbly to bring under your Majesty's consideration a request which on the 14th. of January I had presumed to submit to your Majesty upon the subject of the grant of one of the Parliamentary pensions to Mr. Wynne; and as it was a matter affecting the future prospects of another and not of myself, I the more regret having then omitted to speak to your Majesty upon the subject.

In my letter to your Majesty of the 14th. of January, I presumed to lay before your Majesty the grounds upon which I thought your Majesty might properly be advised to give a gracious and favorable consideration to the case, and I will not trouble your Majesty with a repetition of those reasons. I would however, with all submission, solicit your Majesty's permission to state the great interest which upon many accounts I feel in the result of this humble representation to your Majesty: and as your

1 The revenue derived from the four and a half per cent duties on the produce of certain West Indian Islands, including Barbados, Antigua, Montserrat, Nevis and St Kitts, together with the *droits* of the Crown and Admiralty, which arose out of captures in war, remained entirely at the Crown's disposal until the accession of William IV, when it was surrendered to the public.

Majesty was graciously pleased, in answer to my letter, to intimate to me that your Majesty did not disapprove of my application, but that it must then remain open for future consideration, I hope I shall be pardoned for again bringing the matter under your Majesty's notice.

I am fully aware that any directions which your Majesty might be graciously pleased to give in this matter must proceed thro' the Duke of Wellington; and I have thought it my duty to apprize his Grace that I have taken the liberty of thus renewing my former humble application to your Majesty. Feelings of delicacy in a matter personal to himself may naturally prevent Mr. Wynne from submitting his own case to the Duke; and the Duke on the other hand may feel a difficulty in taking any step without some formal application from Mr. Wynne to himself. Having however originally laid the request at your Majesty's feet, and being deeply sensible of the gracious manner in which it pleased your Majesty to receive it, I have presumed with all deference to hope that your Majesty's condescension and goodness might incline your Majesty to express to the Duke of Wellington that your Majesty's impressions were not unfavourable to a compliance with what I had ventured to solicit in my letter of the 14th. of January.

If in taking the great liberty of addressing your Majesty upon this occasion I have gone beyond the strict line of duty, I have humbly to entreat your Majesty's pardon. Nothing would have induced me to do so but a strong interest in the future welfare of a former colleague and an unbounded reliance upon that goodness and indulgence which have led your Majesty to treat me upon so many occasions with a favour and kindness of which I shall ever retain the most grateful sense, [etc.].

1507 THE DUKE OF WELLINGTON *to the* KING

London, 11 a.m.
February 24th 1828.

I THINK it proper to inclose to your Majesty a letter which I have just received from Lord Goderich.

I understood your Majesty's answer to Lord Goderich as conveying that your [Majesty] did not disapprove of his Lordship's application notwithstanding that it was made after his Lordship had intimated to your Majesty that the Govt of which he had been the head was dissolved; but that "it must remain for future consideration;" that is, that the subject of the application, a pension for Mr. Wynne, must remain for future consideration.

It appears to me that every subject for future consideration must be intended to be considered in the usual manner.

I request your Majesty to send me back the inclosed letters, as after receiving your Majesty's commands I must reply to them.

All of which is humbly submitted to your Majesty by your Majesty's most dutiful and devoted subject and servant.

1508 VISCOUNT GRANVILLE *to the* KING

Paris, February 25th 1828.

LORD GRANVILLE has received from the hands of Sir William Knighton your Majesty's most gracious letter; he feels with the deepest gratitude the condescending kindness of your Majesty and is always most anxious to mark his sense of it by an unbounded zeal in obeying your Majesty's commands.

He humbly begs leave to state that to his knowledge the Duke of Devonshire quitted with the sincerest regret and pain a situation in the service of your Majesty which placed him so near your Majesty's person.

Both he and his sisters[1] have an heartfelt sense of your Majesty's unvarying kindness to them, and are most devotedly and affectionately attached to your Majesty.

1509 THE KING *to the* DUKE OF WELLINGTON
Copy.

Royal Lodge, 25th Feb. 1828.

I RECEIVED three boxes from you in the course of yesterday, to the contents of all of which I am now about to reply: but as the most pressing subject (as it appears to me) is respecting Lord Goderich's application and letters, both to you and to me, in favor of Mr. Wynn's pension; and altho' that came in the last box which I received from you I shall for this reason proceed to touch upon it first.

I have no copies of any of the letters now by me which I can lay my hand upon to refresh my recollection. I therefore do write entirely from

1 Lady Granville and Lady Carlisle.

memory; however I am confident that you will find that my statement is as nearly correct as possible.

Two days after Lord Goderich had been with me to acquaint me with the blowing up of his Administration, and the *very morning subsequent* to my first interview with *you* and the *Chancellor*, I received a letter[1] from Lord Goderich asking (and I think I may almost say) claiming a pension for Mr. Wynn on his retiring from office. To this letter I replied "that as it was a matter of notoriety that his Administration had been defunct for some days, I could then return no other answer than that it must remain for further consideration at a future time".

I rather think I either sent Lord Goderich's letter by, or at any rate desired Sir Wm. Knighton to mention it to you, and which I know he did, and that I approved much of what he stated to me you said upon that subject, that drew from me a short letter to you in which I think, (as nearly as I can trust my recollection) I expressed myself, if not in the very words, at least to this effect: "That I could not see why it was to be considered an invariable practice & consequence that every man, (and probably only to serve some political or Party object at the moment), who (either with or without talents to recommend him), happened to have the good luck to find himself placed in a seat in the Cabinet, that such a man & under such circumstances in which I consider Mr. Wynn precisely to stand, is to expect or to conceive that if the Administration of which he has been a member is dissolved, or if he chooses to retire of himself, in either of these cases that he is to be immediately entitled to a pension from Parliament".

These I am pretty sure, if not in the very words themselves, are the sentiments which I then expressed to you and I cannot say that as yet, nor even from what is alledged in Lord Goderich's letter (which I received thro' Mr. Peel yesterday evening), that I do see the most distant reason to countenance me in any change of those sentiments.

Now here this matter, at least so far as I am concerned, must rest; for I can say no more than I already have done upon it, and I must leave it therefore entirely in your hands as *my Minister* to act upon it as you may think best.

With respect to the Lord High Admiral's application in favor of Lord Torrington for a pension and his Lordship's memorial for that purpose to me, no other answer can be given I think but this: "That for the present such a grant is quite impossible", because (as you have stated to me) the funds from which such pensions are drawn are limited to a certain extent, and that they are already stretched to their utmost possible

1 No. 1466.

extent. My sentiments upon this head when generally considered unite entirely with those which you have expressed in your letter to me, that no further pension should now be promised, or even thought of, until such time as by the contingencics such as deaths &c. which will in the course of nature not unfrequently occur, the pension fund may again be adequate to admit of fresh names being placed upon its list without the possibility of its exceeding its limits, and thus run the risk of any encroachment upon the Civil List (and which God knows is already scanty and pitiful enough), but which ought never to be applied to any other purpose but to itself alone.

The last topic my dear friend which I mean to touch upon arises *necessarily* out of the last [? first] paragraph in your letter in which you acquaint me that it is Mr. Dawson the brother of Mr. George Dawson (the Secretary to the Treasury) who is recommended to succeed to the Deanery of St. Patrick (and in whose appointment I readily acquiesce), you following this up by submitting to me or rather reminding me, "That the question (meaning the Catholic question), being a neutral one in the Cabinet, it must be equally so among the friends and supporters of the Government, and that the merits pretentions and claims of individuals must be considered *without reference to opinions upon the question*". You afterwards in corroboration of this principle quote the cases of Dr. Kaye[1] and the more recent one of Dr. Coppleston.

In all the common matters of general patronage I am ready to admit the fairness of this principle, but *I never have* and *I never can* subscribe to it with respect to the Church, especially where *dignified* Church preferment is the question.

P.S. According to your desire I return in the box all the papers you inclosed.

1510 THE DUKE OF WELLINGTON *to the* KING

London, February 26th 1828.

I AM much concerned that I should have so entirely misunderstood your Majesty's intentions as it appears I have done.

Understanding the Roman Catholic question to be a neutral question in the Cabinet, I naturally took for granted that as usual it was to be so considered in relation to the claims and pretensions of all your Majesty's

---

1 John Kaye (1783–1853), Bishop of Bristol, 1820–27; of Lincoln, 1827–53.

subjects who were to be considered for appointments to office, promotion and preferment in relation solely to their services and merits, and not in reference to their opinions upon that question; and I so explained myself to those of your Majesty's servants who made enquiries from me on this subject.

I made no exception in these explanations in respect to the clergy; nor do I think that I should have done justice to your Majesty if I had hesitated to state this principle without exception, considering the practice of the several Administrations of which Lord Liverpool, Mr. Canning and Lord Goderich have been the head.

However the error and the mistake are irretrievable. It is impossible to stand committed to your Majesty's servants upon one principle, and to your Majesty upon an opposite one; and I most deeply lament that so insurmountable a difficulty should have arisen in the performance of the duties of the office to which your Majesty has been graciously pleased to elevate me; and to fill which I have made so many personal sacrifices in hopes that I might be able to render some service to your Majesty.

I have communicated with no one upon the subject to which this letter refers; and I would conclude by assuring your Majesty that I could have no interest in this question nor in any recommendation which it might have been my duty to submit to your Majesty, excepting the honour of your Majesty's Government, the benefit of your service and to give your Majesty satisfaction. All of which is submitted to your Majesty [etc.].

1511 THE DUKE OF WELLINGTON *to the* KING

London, April 2nd 1828.

SIR WILLIAM KNIGHTON informed me this morning, by your Majesty's command, of the fraud practiced upon your Majesty about forty years ago, and of the securities in existence in consequence of that fraud; of which securities I had heard when I was your Majesty's Ambassador at Paris in the year 1814.[1]

I earnestly recommend to your Majesty to allow these securities to be sought for and bought up. However iniquitous the transaction may have been on the part of those who practiced this fraud upon your Majesty it is very desirable that it should not become the subject of discussion in a Court of Law. Yet this would be the probable consequence of leaving

1 See No. 1502.

these securities in the hands of their holders. It must likewise be observed that at this distance of time all those who had any knowledge of the transaction being probably dead, and as it would be impossible for your Majesty to give your testimony upon it, the result of such discussion would be very uncertain; and the establishment of one of these bonds would establish the claims of the holders of all, with interest for nearly forty years.

I therefore earnestly intreat your Majesty to allow that they may be bought up without loss of time, as I understand they can be without difficulty.

All of which is submitted to your Majesty by your Majesty's most dutiful and devoted subject and servant.

1512 THE DUKE OF WELLINGTON *to the* KING

London, April 24th 1828.

I BEG leave to submit to your Majesty the report of an amendment in the House of Lords this evening moved by Lord Eldon upon the report of the committee on the Sacramental Test Bill.[1]

I moved to adjourn the further consideration of the report till tomorrow; and I beg leave to submit to your Majesty that it is very desirable that the Lords of your Majesty's Household should attend the House.

All of which is submitted to your Majesty by your Majesty's most dutiful and devoted subject and servant.

The King to the Duke of Wellington, 25 April 1828. (*W.N.D.* IV, 405–6.)

1 On 26 February Lord John Russell carried a motion for the repeal of the Test and Corporation Acts by 237 to 193 and the Government abandoned its opposition to the repeal Bill which was subsequently introduced and passed.

London, April 25th 1828.

I SUBMIT to your Majesty the report of the proceedings in the House of Lords this evening.

The Lord Chancellor made an admirable speech on the principle stated in conversation with your Majesty this day. Neither Lord Eldon nor Lord Redesdale could make any reply to his argument upon the Test Act.

I beg to report to your Majesty that none of the Lords of your Majesty's Household were present excepting Lord Roden,[1] who voted against the Govt, and Lord Maryborough.[2]

All of which is submitted to your Majesty by your Majesty's most dutiful and devoted subject and servant.

1514 THE KING *to* SIR WILLIAM KNIGHTON

St. James's Palace, April 29th 1828.

As you seemed desirous to have a line from me and as I think you specified this day in particular as probably the latest opportunity by which any letter could reach you previous to your return, I now take up my pen and send you a few lines.

If you have not already settled the object of your present expedition to your satisfaction I do most sincerely hope that you will very shortly and return almost *immediately*, for I assure you that your presence and exertions are much wanted here.

You will hardly credit what I say when I tell you that since your departure, and the perfect conviction with and in which you left me, that orders would be instantly issued for the proceeding with our works, up to yesterday no one single step has been taken to carry this into effect and that Wyatville,[3] in consequence, not having been able after various repeated and unsuccessful applications to procure any sort of direction or order, or even *encouragement*, was brought to a standstill, having nearly, within a trifle, completed all that part of the work for which he had engaged himself and for which he had received any directions from the

1 A Lord of the Bedchamber since the previous March.
2 Master of the King's Buckhounds.
3 Sir Jeffry Wyatville, the architect, who designed extensive alterations and additions to Windsor Castle after 1824.

Govt and the Commissioners: and was on the very point of dismissing and discharging from the necessity of the case, (having neither money to pay with, nor expectation to hold out) the greater part of that immense body of workmen, in the different branches, which have been and I hope *still* are in his employ at the Castle; and which, if he were now to send about their business he, Wyatville says, it would be next to impossible but, at any rate, a very considerable length of time before he could collect them again together, or any as able, and well instructed workmen in their different lines, when called upon, *de novo*, to recommence and complete the whole or any part of those works [which] were unfinished, with the *same degree* of *perfection* and *solidity* with which the present existing part is done and which speaks for itself; not to mention the great loss of time and the very great increase of expense that must of necessity occur were he now to desist, or not now to proceed immediately.

However, I am in some hopes that Wyattville, at last, will not be brought to this disgraceful and really abominable dilemma, for I stated the matter *strongly* to the Duke yesterday and he *positively promised me* that he would *immediately* give Wyattville *written orders* to *proceed with all speed*.

Poor little Nash is almost in the same state and therefore I need not tell you the same tale over again about him.

Of politics I shall say nothing as our papers will convey all that passes *outwardly here* as completely as I could but, *quand à l'intérieur*, I shall keep that for your return. All I shall however remark is this, that these are strange times, and that we have very queer and odd people to deal with.

Now then, I shall say no more, except, keep up your health and spirits, finish your business as speedily as you can, and *return as soon as possible*.

1515 THE DUKE OF WELLINGTON *to* SIR WILLIAM KNIGHTON

London, May 2nd 1828.

I ENCLOSE you another paper which I have received since I came to the Treasury.

It was settled that the whole revenue of the Woods and Forests this year should be applicable to finish the London Parks; which is all that it can do, and that next year it should be applicable solely to Buckingham Palace.

This is an application for £1000 in advance for planting at Windsor.

I assure you that we have not a shilling. Every farthing of money that can be scraped together has been applied to H.M's. purposes; and if we don't adhere strictly to what has been settled respecting the future application of the money coming in, H.M. will be disappointed in that which must be more important than a few additional plantations in Windsor Park.

1516 THE DUKE OF CUMBERLAND *to* SIR WILLIAM KNIGHTON

St. James Palace, May 17th 1828.

I HAVE considered over with very serious attention our conversation of the other day, and think it *best* and *wisest* to explain to you my feelings on the subject without disguise, leaving it for you to make what use you may choose of this paper.

You intimated to me, if I understood you right, "that my presence here was a *comfort* to my brother, and that he liked and doated on my son and that he wished very much that the Duchess and myself should come & pass sometime here, that as my son was here, I was entitled to the annuity granted to H.M. to give me for the maintenance of my son". I think as far as I can recollect this is in a few words the main set of our conversation. To this my reply is that not only inclination, but the very sincere & devoted attachment I have for my brother would induce me to do all in my power to gratify his wishes, & further the views and prospects of my son. I mean a point which we all wish for most anxiously but I think it most prudent in order to bring it to bear that neither one of the parties concerned should at their present age dream of, as I am convinced, was that done, it would rather prevent than forward our fervid wishes.

My services are always at my brother's commands and there is no *personal* sacrifice that I am not ready to make at any time to be of the smallest use to him, for I am not vain or arrogant enough to imagine that I possess talents enough to be of great use to him, but one quality I do not yield to any one however great his talents may be, that is love, affection and devotion to him, and therefore on whatever subject he may talk to me, he may depend upon my giving him an *honest* & conscientous opinion. I make use of the word *"personal"* that is to make the distinction of sacrificing what I may deem the comforts & happiness of my *wife* & *child* these, as a man of honour I am bound to consider and not to play with. You know and I need not enter into all the treatment I have had to experience for the last 14 years, namely that to this hour I have not received, or my wife, one additional shilling from what Government thought it fit to allow me as a Prince, when a batchelor, I found I could not live in this country, I bid it farewell having passed the 3 first years of my marriage, when I found myself daily involving myself more and more. To do this I was forced to borrow of Mr. Coutts ten thousand pounds to get away, this loan thank God with its interest is *now* paid off within I believe two or three hundred pounds which by Xmas is done so that I may say that is settled. The other debts I had are also gradually paying off. I established myself at Berlin where I have been rec.^d with open arms, enj[oyi]ng full comfort & happiness, can live as well as *all* the Princes there, and have not *one single shilling debt* there. My house is excellent and bien monté. *Here* I have litterally *nothing*, and if I am to come here must monter myself afresh. Now from the situation in which Providence has placed my son to the Crown of Hannover I must keep up his & my interest there & it is necessary I should for his and my sake keep my eye there, therefore I cannot settle entirely in this country without visiting Hannover at times & cannot break up my establishment there, but if the Government and the country really wish my son to be *educated* here they must put the father and mother of that child in a state that they can live here. As before said the Dss has never *had* a shilling, now if she comes here, I cannot give *her* less than three thousand pr an. for her own expenses, ergo only 3000 would remain for me. Do you pretend to tell me that I could with that sum in addition to what I now have live *here*? as the King's brother? Lord knows I am not *envious*, and am the last man to make unnecessary difficulties, but I must be just to myself.

What a difference of income have not *all* my brothers and above all one person who in fact is a stranger, I mean Prince Coburg. How this is to be done I know not nor do I pretend to dictate for as I feel comfortable and happy where I am, and find I can live there I can go back and live there, again, always ready to come when my brother wants me, but never will I separate my child from myself or his mother, that no one can expect or demand of me. The nation must see that his parents have done their duty by him, and therefore upon that point all their lies are amply refuted.

I should like to have a line from you in reply to this, and trust that I have been sufficiently fair & explicit in *all* I have stated.

1517 William Huskisson *to the* King

Downing Street,
5 p.m. 20th May 1828.

Mr. Huskisson, with his humble duty to your Majesty, takes the liberty of soliciting permission to wait upon your Majesty at any time that your Majesty may do him the honour to appoint.[1]

William Huskisson to the Duke of Wellington, 20 May 1828. (*W.N.D.* iv, 449.)
The Duke of Wellington to William Huskisson, 20 May 1828. (*Ibid.*)
The Duke of Wellington to the King, 20 May 1828. (*W.N.D.* iv, 450–1.)
The Duke of Wellington to William Huskisson, 21 May 1828. (*W.N.D.* iv, 457–8.)
The Duke of Wellington to the King, 23 May 1828. (*W.N.D.* iv, 458.)

1518 Lord Lyndhurst *to* Sir William Knighton

May 23rd 1828.

It is my decided opinion that the fraudulent bonds issued by De Beaune [*sic*] in the year 1790 and 1791, or in the succeeding years, should be got possession of provided it can be effected on moderate terms, say four or five pounds each.

1519 *Warrant by the* King *to* Sir William Knighton

Our Royal will and pleasure is that you, our trusty and well beloved Sir William Knighton, Baronet, the Keeper of our Privy Purse, do proceed to Paris for the purpose of buying up certain fraudulent obligations issued at Paris in the years 1790 and 1791, or in the succeeding years, by a person of the name Jean Jacques de Beaune; provided such obligations can be purchased for a sum not exceeding, upon an average, five pounds for each obligation.

Given under our Royal sign manual this   day of May 1828.

Prepared for your Majesty's Royal sign manual in obedience to your Majesty's gracious commands.

Geo. Harrison
23 May 1828.

The Duke of Wellington to the King, 25 May 1828. (*W.N.D.* iv, 462–3.)
The Duke of Wellington to the King, 27 May 1828. (*W.N.D.* iv, 470.)

1 On the 19th Huskisson and Palmerston voted against their colleagues on the question whether the members for the corrupt borough of East Retford, which was to be disfranchised, should be transferred to a large unrepresented town (Birmingham). Huskisson at once wrote to the Duke, offering to resign. Wellington too hastily accepted this offer as an actual resignation, and all the Canningites in the Cabinet (Charles Grant, Lord Dudley and Palmerston) and some who held non-Cabinet posts, followed Huskisson out of office.

OLD M.— appears by the books that have been referred to, first to have done business with Cox & Merle in the years 1792 & 3. At that time no address stands against his name. In 1795–6, and a part of /97, he does more business with them and his address then was Tower Royal. The party who gave me this information has often been to this address. He says it was a miserable lodging, he thinks a green grocers where old M. was only occasionally to be found. All his transactions with Cox's were changing away French money for English, but upon what terms does not appear from the memorandum books the party in question now has access to.

[P.S.] Old M. was at that time a man of about thirty five.[1]

1521   *A Memorandum, by a Secret Agent*

MERLE's father was called at Brighton Captain M. from his commanding a small smuggling vessel, which service he was actively engaged in for many years. His wife at that time (fifteen years ago) kept a lodging house in Black Lion Street, Brighton, which was at once a brothel, a hell, and a receptacle for smuggled goods. The father used to propose to his lodgers to deliver smuggled goods for them in London or elsewhere and the son (the present Gibbons Merle) should the parties accede to the father's proposal was then ready to lay an information against them. The mother is dead. Old Merle from being a Frenchman was very much in league in early life with some of the low instruments of the Revolution and was always ready at their call to do any work of infamy they might propose. He was at that time a good deal at Dieppe and one of his daily occupations was entrapping emigrants on board a vessel he owned there; taking their money under the pretence of bringing them to England and then landing them at some other French port in the midst of their enemies.

When the establishment at Brighton was broken up all the family was in the greatest distress until the son tricked Lord Sidmouth, and afterwards Lord Kenyon,[2] which brought him in connection with the London Press. The old man has, ever since the finish of the Brighton establishment, been living at hide and seek. Although I cannot say so positively

1 His son, Gibbons Merle, was at this time the editor of the *Globe and Traveller*, a Whig-Radical evening newspaper.
2 George, second Baron Kenyon (1776–1855), son of the Lord Chief Justice.

I have every reason to believe the old man's name is *Charles*. These people have no relationship or connection whatever with *Count Merle*. Their connections are very extensive in France, most of them of the lowest and most abandoned class. They know some respectable persons as, for instance, Galignani[1] who is an old acquaintance of their's. Gibbon's wife was the daughter of a harlequin. Her name I cannot learn.

1522 *A Memorandum, by a Secret Agent*

MERLE went to Paris in April and returned in May or early in June. I saw him at the Globe and Traveller office the morning after his return. He almost immediately remarked to me, as if it were uppermost in his mind "What an extraordinary thing it is the constant passing through Dover of Sir Wm. Knighton incog. to and from Paris. He travels in the suite of his courier who is a Captain Carr or some such name. He walks out of Dover ordering his carriage to follow. Large boxes are continually arriving from France for Sir Wm. and they are forwarded without examination at the Custom House. I am puzzled as to his object. He cannot be smuggling although the boxes look like it. I am told he is negotiating a marriage for the King with some Catholic Princess and that he is endeavouring to obtain a *Concordat* from the Pope. Whatever it is however I shall know it, for Sir William's agent at Dover is a particular friend of mine and he has promised to tell me all his movements at Dover and has referred me to a house in Paris where I shall always know them there. I am also acquainted with Sir Wm's agent at Boulogne, but that is not important, the house at Paris is the place for information".

The next day he received a letter from Dover, upon which he remarked "I fear my Dover friend's information will be so important that he will get frightened at divulging it". A few days after he said to me at the office, he must either go or send a confidential agent to Paris, and implied a wish that I would go, adding that this would be a second White Dwarf (explained afterwards) to him and as valuable, and if he succeeded with his information, whenever it might be, he should take it to the Times which would pay liberally for it. I did not take the hint and on the following day Merle came to my house and particularly pressed me to go

---

1 In 1814 Giovanni Antonio Galignani (1752–1821), an Italian residing in London, went to Paris and began to publish an English daily newspaper, *Galignani's Messenger*. After his death the paper was conducted by his two sons, Jean Antoine (1796–1873) and Guillaume (1798–1882), and publication ceased only in 1904.

to Paris which I declined. I saw him the next day when he said he could not get leave of the proprietors of the Globe to go himself and that night he should send a person. (This must be about 10th. June). That person he said was an Irishman. On the following morning he told me the Irishman (who was under great obligations to him) had a brother in Paris and to him he had written instead of sending specially. When I next saw Merle to speak upon this subject he appeared disappointed and said Sir William had not gone to places which would have enabled the persons he (M) was referred to in Paris to know his movements.

About a week after this he read an extract from a letter which he said he had received from his Irishman in Paris (who it seems according to Merle's statement was teaching English there), in which he says that among his scholars was the son of one of the Ministers and he was himself in office under his father. He proposed to send to Merle all political information he obtained for 2000 francs a year, in which information would be included the movements of Sir William Knighton and his agents. He told me subsequently he had arranged for 1600 francs and afterwards stated that Sir William's frequent visits to France related to some money transactions and other business of the King's when he was Prince of Wales. It was at this period thought desirable to get if possible at the name of this Irishman and I proposed to write to Merle to the effect that a friend of mine having been robbed by a man when in Paris, whither he was going in pursuit, wished for the assistance of someone well acquainted there and that it had occurred to me that it would be putting some money in his Irish friend's pocket if he would give my friend a letter to him. The letter I wrote I placed in the hands of a confidential friend who took it to Merle. He gave him letters to M. Marie at Galignani's, Rue Vivienne No. 18, and to M. Petit Rue de l'Odeon No. 29. Merle did not notice the Irishman, upon which my friend reminded him, and he then gave a letter for M. Fitzhenry who he said was to be heard of at Galignani's. (I shall have some intelligence in a few days about these individuals).

Merle, in a conversation since the writing of these letters, expressed himself dissatisfied with the Irishman, adding at the same time that his arrangements are complete and that he does not now require the Irishman's services.

The following is a sketch of Merle's family history as detailed to me by a confidential person employed by Lord Liverpool to trace it out, several years since, in consequence of their having come under the *surveillance* of the Government.

Merle's father was called at Brighton Captain Merle from his commanding a small smuggling vessel, which service he was actively engaged in for many years. About 15 years since they kept a lodging house in Black Lion Street which was at once *a brothel a hell* and *a receptacle for smuggled goods* (these were the words used by my informant). Old Merle from being a Frenchman was much in league in early life with some of the low instruments of the Revolution. He was at that time chiefly at Dieppe and one of his occupations was entrapping emigrants on board a vessel he owned there, taking their money on pretence of bringing them to England, and then landing them at some French port. When the establishment at Brighton was broken up, the family was in great distress until the son (Gibbons Merle) tricked Lord Sidmouth and afterwards Lord Kenyon, which brought him in connection with the London Press. The introduction to these noblemen arose from the following circumstance. Wooller's[1] *Black Dwarf* was then making a great noise, and Merle proposed to commence a paper called the *White Dwarf*. Lord Sidmouth was drawn into a confidential correspondence with Merle who threatened to publish it on the supplies of money for his publication failing. Lord Kenyon was then induced to commence the True Briton[2] evening paper to keep Merle quiet, he being promised the management. Old Merle has been since the close of the Brighton establishment living at hide & seek. I believe his Christian name is Charles. Their connections are very extensive in France but few of them respectable.

It was stated to me that old Merle in the early part of the Revolution probably had lived in *St. Thomas Apostle* in the city, and was engaged as a money changer and then became a good deal connected with the emigrants who had escaped to this country in converting their jewels and French coin into money circulating here. It was thought desirable to get at this fact, but after a long and rather extensive enquiry the only trace of this I can meet with is through an old clerk of Cox & *Merle's* in Little Britain (*no connection or relation whatever of these people*) who tells me that in the years 1792 & 3, a French Jew by the name of Merle used to come to their house (they were gold refiners and bankers), and according to the books he has referred to did some trifling business with

1 Thomas Jonathan Wooler, the Radical journalist, was editor and proprietor of the *Black Dwarf*, 1817–24.

2 The *White Dwarf*, edited by Gibbons Merle, lasted from 1817 to 1818; the *True Briton* from July 1820 to November 1822, when it was incorporated with the *Traveller*. See *Westminster Review*, January 1829, p. 221. The *True Briton* was "at one time respectable by its able opposition to the Bill of Pains and Penalties". "Lord Kenyon is supposed to have lost in two years more than £7000 by the *True Briton*", which "commenced as a furious Orange paper. In three months it became liberal, and under new management reached a good circulation. It then assumed Orange colours again; and, under another manager, the circulation fell away almost to nothing."

them in changing foreign coins and plate. In 1795, 6 and a part of 1797 he did more business with Cox & Merle and his address was then in *Tower Royal, the next street to St. Thomas Apostle*; but the individual in question whether the old Merle we are speaking of or not only lived there occasionally according to the old clerk's information. This was a man at that period of about 35.

Captain Spencer to Sir George Cockburn, 12 July 1828. (*W.N.D.* iv, 525.)
The Duke of Wellington to the King, 14 July 1828. (*W.N.D.* iv, 528.)
The Duke of Wellington to the Duke of Clarence, 14 July 1828. (*W.N.D.* iv, 529.)
The King to the Duke of Clarence, 15 July 1828. (*W.N.D.* iv, 531.)

1523 THE KING *to* [SIR WILLIAM KNIGHTON]

Royal Lodge, July 13th.
2 o'clk. p.m. 1828.

I RECEIVED your letter yesterday and therefore shall expect to see you & Lowther tomorrow. The inclosed applications I have just received, and I authorize you without delay to order the appointment of Sergeant Surgeon to me, to be made out at the Lord Chamberlain's office, in favour of Sir Astley Cooper.[1] I am afraid that my poor brother William has bamboozled himself and bothered himself into a sad dilemma, and entirely from the folly and wicked misstatements of others, particularly of *his Secretary*.[2]

Lord Melville (who I have just now *again* seen) is entirely of this opinion. I therefore do much wish that you, (as you know so much of the matter) would continue to see my brother, and the D. of Wellington, with as little loss of time, as may be, and see, if with your usual intellect, you can bring about an amicable and creditable adjustment of this very unpleasant affair.

N.B. *As yet*, there has passed nothing unpleasant between William and the Duke.

1 The appointment was gazetted on 11 August. He had been created a Baronet in 1821. [1768–1841.]

2 The Duke of Clarence had involved himself in a quarrel with his Council over their respective jurisdictions, and on 11 August the King accepted his resignation of the office of Lord High Admiral. The lengthy correspondence on the subject is in *W.N.D.* iv, 513–665. The great seal was again put in commission, and Lord Melville again became First Lord of the Admiralty. Croker and Barrow were the two (public) Secretaries at this time.

St. James's Sqre,
July 21st 1828, Monday.

SIR RICHARD HUNTER, (whom you recommended to me for the *sine-cure* of my medical adviser) has remained with me for many years with great attention, affection, integrity and fidelity. I conferred the honour of Knighthood upon him in Ireland; and, if any valuable medical station had opened, I would have appointed him to it, with perfect confidence in his capacity to discharge its duties.

I am now very anxious to promote him in his profession; and it would afford me great satisfaction, if he could succeed to the station of Serjeant Surgeon now vacant. If you could assist him in this object, I should be much gratified. A person wholly out of power, insulted, and exiled, can scarcely expect even ordinary notice from those, who owe their very existence to his former kindness and indulgence. But although wounded, I am not yet destroyed; it will be painful to you to announce, that I never enjoyed so good health; and still more to assure my enemies, (whom I *know*) that I never was more equal to that bold and determined effort, which is now become equally necessary for my honor, and for that of the King, as well as for the safety of the country. I am most anxious to vindicate myself, and to bring my secret, base, cowardly enemies to open battle; and with the blessing of truth, reason, and justice, I entertain no doubt of complete victory, on my very first public movement, which cannot long be delayed.

[P.S.] Sir Richard Hunter is the bearer of this.

The Duke of Wellington to the King, 21 July 1828. (*W.N.D.* IV, 549–50.)

1525 VISCOUNT MELVILLE *to the* DUKE OF CLARENCE
Copy.

India Board, 21st July, 1828.

THE gracious kindness and condescension with which your Royal Highness has been pleased to receive such communications as I have felt it my duty, and have ventured to submit to your Royal Highness on matters connected with the naval department, embolden me again to intrude on your Royal Highness with reference to some correspondence which has recently taken place with your Royal Highness and which has been communicated to me by His Majesty and the Duke of Wellington.

I can assure your Royal Highness most truly and sincerely that I have perused that correspondence with great regret; but it is evident to me that it has arisen entirely from misapprehension. On the one hand your Royal Highness must naturally and properly feel extremely jealous of any appearance, however unintentional, of an attempt to encroach upon the legitimate functions of your high office; and on the other hand the members of your Council must and ought to feel that they have an important duty to fulfil, not only to your Royal Highness but also to His Majesty and the public.

Your Royal Highness is aware that I have spent fifteen years at the Admiralty and, as far as relates to the ordinary business of the office, your Royal Highness will probably be of opinion that I must necessarily have acquired some experience and knowledge of the mode in which that business ought to be conducted.

I have no difficulty therefore in assuring your Royal Highness, and in earnestly entreating you to believe, that unless you adopt as a positive rule from which you will on no account and under no circumstances deviate, that all official orders and instructions of every description which your Royal Highness may be pleased to issue shall pass through the regular channel of your Council and public Secretary, great confusion and great detriment to His Majesty's service must ensue. Any other course would not only produce those effects but it would be directly at variance with the practice in former times when the office of Lord High Admiral was not in commission, and it would also be positively at variance with the declarations publicly made in Parliament by His Majesty's Ministers at the period of your Royal Highness's appointment to the office of Lord High Admiral.

I have frequently heard in conversation many erroneous notions promulgated as to the duties and functions of a Lord High Admiral or First Lord of the Admiralty, and as to the supposed professional knowledge requisite for those situations. I am persuaded that with the official experience which your Royal Highness must have acquired it is unnecessary for me to remind you that nine-tenths, or probably a much larger proportion, of the business in the Admiralty office is more of a civil than of a strictly naval character, and that the official course of proceeding in regard to it ought accordingly to be in conformity to what prevails at the War Office, or the Ordnance Office or any other department where the business is of a similar description with what is transacted at the Admiralty. In those departments everything is conducted in the most regular method, and your Royal Highness may be assured that without such a system the business could not be properly transacted.

It perhaps may have occurred to your Royal Highness at the period of your entering on the duties of your present office that they were in most respects similar to those which belonged to the office of Commander in Chief of the Army, as discharged by His late Royal Highness the Duke of York. I am persuaded however that your Royal Highness must now be aware that the two situations are totally different in their character and functions. The Commander in Chief had no Council assigned to him by law; but in fact his powers were infinitely more circumscribed than those of your Royal Highness with your Council. The Commander in Chief's functions were strictly limited to promotions and discipline; he could not order the smallest expenditure without the previous official sanction of the Secretary at War in all cases, and generally of the Treasury; and in all matters relating to the distribution of the forces at home and abroad, and even as to discipline, he had again to resort to the sanction of the Secretaries of State for the Home or Colonial Departments and to the Judge Advocate General. But that is not all; for though he had no regular Council I can assure your Royal Highness of my own personal knowledge that from the day on which the Duke of York entered on his office in 1795, (His Royal Highness not being a member of the Cabinet) the Adjutant and Quarter Master General, and most frequently the public Military Secretary, were in constant communication with His Majesty's Government, and I think I can also venture to add that His Royal Highness on no occasion issued any order of the slightest importance without the knowledge of those officers, or even against their opinion, especially if they had been previously apprized of the sentiments of His Majesty's Government.

In the naval department however all those various checks and functions are centered in the Admiralty Office, and it is absolutely impossible that any person whatever, even with all your Royal Highness's zeal and exertions, can discharge those duties with satisfaction to the public except through the medium of your regular official instruments. No man's physical health and strength are equal to it and any attempt at a different course of proceeding must be most injurious to the public service.

I should with all humility make the same observation in regard to various details, as to mustering ship's companies, inspecting marine and other corps, examining into sundry matters in the dock yards, &c. which your Royal Highness feels it your duty to go through. There can be no question as to the utility of such proceedings but your Royal Highness has various other and most important duties to perform and the whole naval department to superintend; and if the performance of those separate duties shall either be injurious to your health, which is of the highest public importance, independently of anything relating to the Navy, or if it shall interfere with your Royal Highness's general supervision of the department, which it must do, I can confidently assure your Royal Highness that both the public and the Navy will be much better pleased with your Royal Highness's undertaking no more than what necessarily belongs to such general superintendence than by any exertions which your Royal Highness can make in regard to those other, though by no means unimportant, details.

I have now performed an irksome duty, and I can assure your Royal Highness that if I had not invariably experienced your gracious favor I should not have ventured to obtrude my opinions or to encroach on your Royal Highness's time. I have the consolation however to hope and believe that your Royal Highness will do justice to the motives which have induced me to address you on the present occasion.

Circumstances have recently occurred at the Admiralty which gave me great concern and I honestly, though I hope not disrespectfully, declare to your Royal Highness that I should accuse myself of ingratitude, and of requiting most unworthily the kindness with which your Royal Highness has been pleased to honor me, if I withheld from your Royal Highness the expression of the sentiments and opinions which I have ventured to submit to your favourable and indulgent consideration.

1526 THOMAS DENMAN'S *Memorial to the* KING

The humble Memorial of Thomas Denman of Lincoln's Inn, Esquire,
Barrister at Law,
Humbly sheweth,

That your memorialist has practised at the English Bar more than twenty years with some degree of reputation, and without any charge whatever having been preferred against him.

That in the course of last year his respectful application for precedency was rejected while very numerous promotions of much younger men were made to his disparagement and serious injury.

A circumstance was assigned by rumour as the cause of his exclusion the existence of which he never could have believed if it had not afterwards been affirmed to him by the Lord Chancellor, and to which he could not have been justified in adverting if it had been brought to his knowledge by any inferior authority.

Your memorialist heard, with extreme sorrow but with still greater astonishment, that a speech delivered by him in the discharge of his duty as an advocate, in the House of Lords in October 1820, had been perverted to a sense wholly foreign to his intention and most abhorrent to his feelings—a passage quoted from a Greek historian for an entirely different purpose having been construed into an insinuation of a revolting nature against your Majesty.[1]

He had the mortification to learn that your Majesty had been led to think him capable of giving utterance to such an insinuation.

Your memorialist sincerely declares that the misfortune of lying under this suspicion is heavier and more intolerable to him than any consequences to himself that can result from it.

He is particularly desirous of assuring your Majesty that from the first moment when he had authentic information that such a stigma was affixed to his character he made every exertion in his power to remove it, having then and repeatedly since that time importuned the Lord Chancellor to lay before your Majesty his solemn disavowal of the offence imputed to him.

And he earnestly prays your Majesty to believe his declaration that no such insinuation was ever made by him; that the idea of it never entered his mind; and that he is utterly at a loss to conceive how it ever came to be suspected, or could even be thought possible.

Your Majesty's dutiful subject and most humble servant.[2]

London. July 24th 1828.

The Duke of Wellington to the King, 30 July 1828. (*W.N.D.* IV, 559.)
Dr Sumner to the Duke of Wellington, 30 July 1828. (*W.N.D.* IV, 559–60.)
The Duke of Wellington to the King, 1 August 1828. (*W.N.D.* IV, 564–5.)
The Duke of Wellington's Memorandum for the King upon the state of Ireland, 1 August 1828. (*W.N.D.* IV, 565–70.)

1 Denman had recently learned from Lyndhurst that the real cause of the King's abiding resentment was his firm conviction that Denman's Greek quotation from Dion Cassius (*Parl. Deb.* N.S. III, 1090) had been deliberately intended to convey a personal imputation against the King of being guilty of a practice of revolting depravity. The "honest chambermaid's Greek" had in reality been applied to such witnesses as Rastelli and Sacchi who came forward with perjured evidence to betray their former mistress.

2 This is enclosed in the Duke of Wellington's letter to Sir William Knighton, 8 October 1828. (*W.N.D.* V, 116–17.) A portion of this Memorial is printed in the *Life of Denman*, I, 287.

Hannover, Friday, Augst 22d 1828.

I ARRIVED here yesterday morning at 9 o'clock having stopped at Neudorff for an hour to speak with Minister Ompteda who is there drinking the waters, and I felt anxious to learn from him if any thing had come to his knowledge respecting the Brunswick business. He read me a letter he had received the day before from hence from his colleague Minister Meding (?) who informed him, that the Duke had hit upon the following plan, namely to throw off as much as he could *all* suspicion that *he* had actuated Monsieur de Praun to attack Münster, he has formally issued an order to *all* his loving subjects "forbidding them under pain of his Sovereign displeasure from *molesting* any Hannoverian subject, or interfering in this concern". This is on one side artfull enough but at the same time will not and cannot blind sensible persons as to the real truth. However I feel it necessary previous to my leaving *this place* to be fully master of the subject, and therefore have desired to have a meeting with your *three Ministers* this day in order to learn from them *all* the proofs they have in their hands, and with them to read over in succession all the papers that they have on the subject; I think this the more necessary as then I shall be better able to speak with Minister Bernstorff and Major Gen. de Witzleben, and the King of Prussia. I found this the more necessary, as unfortunately poor Minister v. Bremer is very far from being well, and I really fear you will very soon lose him, as he had last Sunday something resembling an *apoplectic attack* which I fear from his constitution will be his end, as he is very fat and short necked, and this is the 2d. attack he has had in two years, I must say, a greater loss you cannot have, than when this man dies, for a more faithful servant no Sovereign ever had, or one, who knows the country better than he does, or is more beloved or respected. I called upon him, as he wrote me word he was not able to come to me, I talked to him a little on the subject, but I perceived that it fatigued him, and therefore proposed adjourning the further consideration of the subject till this morning at *ten*, when I have appointed both Minister Meding and Stralenheim to meet me at Walmoden's Garden where he is now residing by your kind permission.

I trust and hope you will approve of this, especially as then I shall hear what each has to say on the subject and I must add that I never met men more anxious or fully penetrated with the necessity of now following up the business to the bottom. The appointment you chose to make of Stralenheim to be Minister has given *universal satisfaction throughout the country* and certainly he is *now* of double utility as he is an excellent lawyer, and therefore his advice is of very great weight. I hope to be able to end this business here this day and in that case I shall leave this *tomorrow* morning for Berlin, where by travelling all night I hope to arrive Sunday to dinner which naturally I am most anxious to do, especially as I must I believe leave home again the 30th or 31st as I hear the King of Prussia means to pass the review of the 5th army corps the 2d of Septr. at Liegnitz; but you may depend upon it that I shall willingly sacrifice my own private wishes if I can be of any service to your interests, and therefore if I find I cannot get through the whole this day I shall remain here still tomorrow. I fear this letter may be long and perhaps prolix, but I shall add after my conference with the Ministers the result of all that passes. There is but one opinion here upon the subject, and a general feeling of indignation towards the Duke, and also that the inveteracy of the Duke's is such towards Münster, that it would certainly be very imprudent in him to risk coming over here, for a man capable, as he is of such malice, would certainly by dint of money get some one to destroy him, if he could get at him. I was told yesterday that the reason, he had pitched upon this Praun to challenge Münster, was, that he was so famous a pistol shot, an amusement the Duke is constantly practising, and thus saw how well he shot. I also heard that the Duke of Lucca had done all in his power to persuade this wrong headed man to follow the advice given him not only by the K. of Prussia but by most of the other Sovereign Princes to whom he had sent his papers, and I understand none wrote more strongly to this effect than my brother-in-law the Grand Duke of Mecklenburgh Strelitz, and the two Grand Dukes of Darmstadt[1] and Baden. It is also asserted that the D. of Lucca went so far as to say, that *he himself* would willingly go over to England and be the bearer of such a letter. This I heard here, and I give it you as it has been told to me.

3 o'clock

I attended the meeting as mentioned in the former part of my letter, and the three Ministers Bremer, Meding and Strahlenheim were present as well as the two Cabinet secretaries Hoppenstedt and Rose; we went through every paper from the period, that the Duke had consented to send over a person with a letter to apologize to you for his conduct, up to the present moment, and this took us from ten o'clock till near two, as we had to read all the dispatches from Minister Reden, Merveldt, and Strahlenheim, likewise the correspondence with Major Gen. Arnscheldt; during the meeting, Minister Bremer received a dispatch from Merveldt from Vienna in which he tells us that Metternich had received a courier

1 Lewis I, Grand Duke of Hesse-Darmstadt (1753–1830).

from the D. of B. disavowing entirely any cognizance of Praun's business, which Metternich thinks it right to give credit to; that *this* has been done at his suggestion I have no doubt, and therefore he thinks it necessary to declare his full belief as to the innocency of the D. of B. Upon this occasion however I must say that I think Merveldt has conducted himself *well*, and I am happy to be able to do so, having totally disapproved his conduct on former occasions. It appears to me however perfectly necessary on *our* side that we do not allow ourselves to be thrown off our guard, or even to accede to any accomodation, without ample satisfaction being made you on *all* points, and a certainty of no further insult being made. Never has a man shewn the cloven foot more clearly than Metternich in his whole conduct and especially now by having the baseness after knowing so well, and having had so many proofs of the Duke's duplicity and lying to declare, that he was perfectly satisfied as to the innocence of the Duke, this he does for two reasons 1st to pay his court to the Empress the Duke's cousin german, and 2nd for a much ignobler reason, one which I have learnt since I have been here, namely that he had received a present of 60,000 dollars about 10,000 pounds from the Duke, at least this report is publickly stated as I hear by inhabitants of Brunswick.

Major Genl. Arnscheldt's declaration as far as it goes is very good, but the main object for us must be to get the declaration of Oberforstmeister von Volkheim, if we can get this, which I hope then we may risk any thing but this cannot be done 'till he has got his wife and children away from Brunswick, for *there* he can never return, and some arrangement must be made for him. I also understand there are papers of de Witt's publication in the booksellers hands at Hamburgh where there are *notes* written under the Duke's own hand *these* I have strongly recommended the Ministry here to press their Consul Monsieur de Duve to get a sight of and to *protest* their being returned back to the Duke, he having claimed the assistance of the magistracy there to procure them for him. I trust *this* will meet your approval; I have now I am afraid bored you a great deal too much, but I have God knows tried to be as concise as I could, and yet I feel horrified, when I see I am at my fifth sheet. Upon mature reflection I beg and pray do not send any immediate answer to Merveldt, but let us first wait and hear whether the two mediating Powers wish to have the business referred to the Bundstag, for it strikes me that if this be ultimately necessary, it will be infinitely more for our advantage that this be done by them, as if it came from us, for if we do it, it will appear that we are dissatisfied with them, whereas if they do it, they must having once done so support it themselves and Metternich can play us no further trick.

I am sorry to add I find poor Bremer very very far from being well, and today even less well than yesterday, I again repeat *his* loss will be a very great one; I wish from the bottom of my soul I may be wrong, but I own I fear he will not last long, Replace him, I know no one, but the only man now here who from his character and abilities seems to me to be a fair candidate for the situation of Minister is *Grote* who is now the head of the Chancellery of War, the same I spoke to you about before. Excuse my mentioning this subject to you again, but I know full well you will be worried again with the name of two persons who certainly though not deficient in talents, still from character do not stand high in the public estimation. I shall try to see Bernstorff as soon as I get to Berlin.

God bless you [etc.].

PS. Having now done all the weighty business, I shall before I leave this tomorrow visit the stables.

You need *not shew* my letter to Münster, as I have written to him myself, on account of *what* I have said respecting *Grote*, as that militates against his two nephews *Scheele* and *Schulte*, and when I say this it is not that I wish to conceal from him my opinion for these two *individuals*, for I would tell him the same in person *but* why at a distance *hurt* his feelings; my opinion is from my *personal* [? knowledge] of their characters and their conduct during the time of Jerome Buonaparte, which has made them *hated* by the whole country. My feelings are not personal towards them as individuals, but from love for the country and its *valuable* inhabitants.

1528 THE DUKE OF CUMBERLAND *to the* KING

Chateau Schönhausen, Augt. 26th 1828.

I ARRIVED at Berlin on Sunday last the 24th at 4 in the afternoon in perfect health and without the slightest accident, I travelled all Saturday night, having left George and his suite at Halberstadt the evening before. I had intended taking the road straight from Hannover to Halberstadt, but was informed by *all* that I risked breaking my carriage, if not my nut, I therefore having taken that road in the spring, did not desire to encounter the same disaster as I had then, and determined to take the straight road, but at the same time, in order to avoid all I could, I ordered my post horses to meet me outside of the town of Brunswick, and thus drive round the town and not pass through it, *this* I did and thus saw no one.

On my arrival at Berlin, I heard Frederica meant to come to town to take leave of the Pss Royal[1] who was to leave Berlin as yesterday and go to Munich to her mother's, where she is to remain for three months untill the Pr. Royal returns from his tour to Italy, where he goes as soon as the reviews are all over. I then wrote my wife two lines to announce my safe arrival and desire her to come to me during which time I dressed myself in order to go and pay my respects to the King, but learning from my brother-in-law, that he was unwell with a bad cold and swelled face and that he had been unable to appear at a dinner he had given that day to the Duke of Lucca, I postponed my visit to His Majesty till yesterday morning for which purpose I rode over from hence. I found him *better* and he received me as he always does most kindly, expressed himself in the strongest manner respecting you and the Brunswick business and said that no Monarch ever had had more difficulties of all sorts to encounter than you had had during the last year; he said he admired beyond measure your resolution and determined conduct on the great question that seemed now to agitate all minds in England and he added all Europe, for he said "Les Catholiques veulent se pousser partout". I assured him you were as firm and as decided in your Protestant principles as he himself was, et *cela dit tout*. I hope and wish that you would take an opportunity of seeing and speaking yourself very firmly and decidedly with the new Archbishop,[2] when he comes and pays hommage, which I suppose he must *now* do, in order to be able to enter into his official duties; he certainly when I saw him last the 8th of this month spoke to me in the most clear and unequivocal way that he considered if ever the Catholics were allowed to sit in Parl! that the Established Church would be in the greatest danger, and consequently the State, and I am sure your talking with him will be of the greatest possible use.

I wanted to see Minister Bernstorff yesterday, but was told he was too unwell to receive me, I am going up to town this morning to meet Major Genl de Witzleben and shall have some conversation with him which, though I shall not be able to report *this* day by the post I fear, I shall not fail to forward you by Saturday's mail. Though I have not yet been 48 hours here, I have already set about your commissions and hope very soon to have every thing ready for you, the *sash* is ordered, the prints also, and the Dss will lose no time and see Monsieur Rosenstirn the head of the porcelaine manufactory to give him *your* plate to get it copied. I mean also to send you the regulation *sabre* as now worne by all the officers of light infantry, chasseurs as well as fusiliers, and I think you

1 Elizabeth, daughter of the King of Bavaria, and wife of Frederick William IV of Prussia.
2 Dr Howley, Bishop of London, succeeded Dr Manners-Sutton, who died in July.

will find *this* infinitely more appropriate than *those* now worne by those in the Hannoverian officers of light infantry, which they wear like *Hussar* officers and are dangling about their legs, the most *absurd* thing for men who are to be running through woods hedges, and terrain coupé. I have also ordered you a pr. of silver epaulettes similar to *those* worne here by the General Officers on their frock uniforms only *what* we have in *black* I have ordered to be made in yellow, and you can not imagine, how very *brilliant* they look on a *plain* blue coat with a *red collar*. Besides as now all over Germany the *epaulette* is considered equally as the sword knot and hat tassel to be the colours of the country so ought the Hannoverians to do the same, and in my humble opinion the *different ranks* can be made out the same *there* as *here*, if you wish it, and will only direct *Taylor* or *Watson* to let me know I will have a *modell* of each made and send it equally to you. *If you will let me know your pleasure by return of post*, I will try to get all *ready* for you and send it at the beginning of Oct.ʳ by the quarterly messenger. I leave *this* again on Saturday next the 30th with my brother-in-law and we shall arrive the 31 at Liegnitz, the King sets off the 31st and arrives there the 1st on the 2d the review of the 5th corps d'armée begins. I have not yet the papers, but shall be able to forward *all* that to you by Saturday's post.

With very deep and sincere regret have I read in an English paper, the only one I have seen since I left England, that William has been wrongheaded enough to *resign*, I own, I had still hoped when I left England, that he would have seen his error and upon reflection have seen that he had but one thing to do, namely to have acknowledged his mistake. Today we expect an English mail and I hope to receive letters, and I trust very good accounts of you whose health and happiness I have so much at heart. Frederica writes herself, as also *all the boys*, and all I shall say is that they feel deeply your infinite kindness to them all, for which accept my most grateful thanks. George is constantly talking of *you* and all your kindness for him, as also of Lady C[onyngham]'s and her dear daughters, to whom I beg to be remembered most kindly. I hear the Warwicks[1] were *here*, but they never announced themselves to the Dss, and thus she had not an opportunity of shewing them those civilities, she otherwise would certainly have done. I hear that the negotiations are still going on about the *Electress*, and Lt. General de Natzum left this on Saturday last and is gone to her to Bonn, where she is now residing, *what* the plan is, I have been too short a time here to learn, if I hear any thing you shall be informed. Now God bless you [etc.].

1 The Earl and Countess of Warwick.

Schneehausen, Augt. 28th 1828.

THOUGH I have been every morning to town, I have not been able to see Bernstorff as yet, so very ill he is at present, and this illness I hear is much increased by the constant expectation of the news of the death of a brother-in-law of his a Ct. de Reventlow the Danish Minister at this Court; but I hope this day to see *Ancillon* who acts for him, but whether *he* is concerned with the Brunswick business or not I am not perfectly sure. However I had the day before yesterday a very *long* and *confidential* conversation with M. Gen de Witzleben, as I mentioned to you I was to have in my last letter. He assured me the King was *determined* to bring this *scandale*, as he termed it, to an end, and that he had laid his *most positive injunctions* on Bernstorff to declare *there* his sentiments to the Court of Austria; at the same time that the D. of Brunswick had been urged to make the most ample apology *not* in the sense as Metternich had originally *wished* and *proposed*, but taking in *all* the original 4 points as proposed by Prussia, and also for his *last* infamous and *atrocious* conduct, which the King considers as having been offered to you in the person of a servant of yours; "assuring him at the same time, if he did not now come to terms, that he might rely on it, if H.M. the King of Hannover should deem it necessary to take the matter into his own hands, he would know what he had to do, and that in that case he, the K. of Prussia should certainly not interfere; by this he meant if you felt yourself forced to march troops and occupy the Brunswick country, that he *would not* by any means prevent it". But I hope from the bottom of my soul, that it will not be necessary to proceed to such extremities, and that the two mediating Powers will bring this business to a speedy conclusion; I have written to Baron de Reden your Minister to inform him, that I thought his presence more necessary *here* now than at Dresden, and I expect him daily here, as he must press *this* matter with Bernstorff. I shall add *all* that passes between Ancillon and myself in another part of my letter, which I shall leave open for that purpose.

I enclose you a letter of thanks from my son *Charles* which by the stupidity of my servant, he omitted putting up in my Tuesday's packet for you, also a letter which Frederica had written the 5th and sent off that day to George which he was to have presented to you on your birthday but it arrived in England after my departure and was therefore returned here; and only reached me yesterday. As I have had *no* private letter from England since my departure except one from Adolphus and one from Thornton neither of which touch upon William's business I am at a loss to make out *how* the matter has finally ended, what I mean is, that when I left England, I had flattered myself that the conversation he either had on the Tuesday with Lord Lyndhurst, or was to have with him the ensuing day, would have brought him to his senses, certain it is a great pity that *he* has allowed himself to be led on by the advice of others, and though *perhaps* there may have been *blame* on the side of his Council in some degree, still, he suspecting that, (this I put hypothetically) ought to have acted then with *double* caution and prudence, and not have exposed himself by an overt act against the laws to place himself so perfectly in the wrong as he seems to me, from all I know, to have done. Any man may commit an error, may be led to act wrong, but if he will but give himself time to reflect, he then surely would have acted much wiser, by saying he acknowledged he had overstretched his powers and begged your pardon for it. Thus the whole business might have been amicably concluded. I cannot describe to you, how very very deeply I feel this, first knowing how all *this* must more or less worry you, and 2dly knowing how uncommonly well William did his business, and how *popular* he was with all the navy; and of what vital consequence in these days it is for the Sovereign that his navy and army should have at their head (if it is feasable) a Prince of the Blood Royal, for certainly the Sovereign ought to be able to put his whole confidence in his brothers, who ought to have no interest dearer to their hearts than those of their brother and such a one as you are; at least this is my creed.

The King here is so much better that he went yesterday to Paritz, a small estate he has about 20 English miles from hence, he returns I believe to Charlottenburg today after dinner; on Saturday he sees the whole corps d'armée of the Guards at Zehlendorff, after that there is an early dinner at a shooting lodge in the Gruben Wald in honour of Princess Liegnitz's [1] birthday where we shall all go; and that evening my brother-in-law Charles and I set off for Liegnitz where we shall arrive the Sunday evening, and be ready to receive the King, who leaves Berlin the Sunday morn^g and arrives then the Monday at Liegnitz. I enclose you the projet of *all* the days.

29th Friday

I had a long conference yesterday as I had promised with Ancillon as I found Bernstorff utterly unable to see me and he was so very very unwell yesterday, that he was forced even to put off Ancillon. We had however a very full and long conversation on *all* that had taken place and he told me, that as far as he knew, Metternich had up to this time not sent any reply to the proposals made immediately by Bernstorff on the reception

1 Frederick William III's second wife. This morganatic marriage took place in 1824.

of the papers. I, it was, who told him of the D. of B. having firmly and seriously *denied* having any cognizance *even* of Praun's intentions, "Ah! said Ancillon, est-il possible qu'aucune personne peut croire une telle assertion? la chose n'est que trop claire en elle-même". I fear from the state of Bernstorff's health, I shall not be able to see him ere I leave this place which I do tomorrow evening, but Ancillon has promised me to try to see the Minister if possible *this* day and then communicate to me, what he learns. However I am perfectly content here with all I *find* here and plainly perceive that Prussia is determined to bring this business to a conclusion and that too a speedy one. Reden will arrive here in three days from Dresden, and I shall leave him my strong injunctions to push on the Minister.

I have received last night a few lines from Mary, but though she enters unfortunately into no details, still I am happy to learn that William and Sir G. Cockburn have *met*, have had an explanation, and have shaken hands, this gives me thus some hope that *all* may be still comfortably arranged, which no one wishes more anxiously or firmly than I do. She also assures me you are recovered from your cold, and have dined again at that enchanting spot the Virginia Water, where I assure you both father and son have enjoyed most happy and pleasant hours, and we talk very often of them. George talks a great deal of his friend Whiting. Yesterday evening as it rained and it was impossible to go out, he amused himself by putting on his check shirt, and straw hat to please his mother. Tomorrow being the Pss. Liegnitz birthday, I have desired Frederica to carry him with her to the Gruben Wald, where the dejeuner dinatoire at *12* is to be, and there he shall pay his respects to the King in his Hussar uniform.

Your prints are all ready, and with your permission I shall bind them up in a set of *albums* just as the Duchess has hers, which you can then have lay on your table, and at times amuse yourself by looking at them. The Princess Charles and Pss Liegnitz are to meet the King the 7th at Koppesdorff I think, attend the two days when the 2 army corps manœuvre against each other, and then accompany him to Breslau. I fear I shall not be able to write again 'till after my return from Silesia which will be the 14th or 15th. My best regards to all the dear ladies, tell Lady C. that I often think of our *ecarté* parties, and look forward with pleasure to their renewal next spring. Now God bless you and believe me [etc.].

PS. Pray has Lord Lyndhurst sent you the warrant to sign? Do remind him of that.

R[oyal] L[odge], Friday 29th A[ugust 1828].

You desired me to write to Paris, but I am fearful you may have changed your plans on account of having landed at Calais—however I venture to tell you a little how we are going on. H.M. has attended the Egham races two days & is quite well. Jane[1] & Francis are here—he was very successful at Brighton, but here *not* so. The K. *won* both days—we went *quietly* to see Sir George Warrender's &c which is the most lovely place I almost ever saw—it reminded me of Switzerland. Added to this excursion, I have been to Denbies for two days to see my sister[2] who is returning to Italy.

Much has been said & done about the return of the D. of Clarence to the Admiralty. The Rl. family (with the K. at their head) are very anxious for his return. Sir George Colburne[3] has explained his conduct most satisfactorily, & the D. of Clarence & he are the greatest friends. However the D. of W[ellington] takes no notice of this, & now the D. of Clarence gives as a reason for his leaving the Admiralty, the patent restricting him so much he can be of no use to the K. or the country.

Sr H. Taylor is delighted with his situation of Adjutant Genl.[4] Poor Torren's death was most sudden & awful.

Lord Grey's brother[5] being promoted to the living of Bishopgate makes a great sensation—Lady Jersey[6] takes the credit or rather the merit of it.

The Lievens are staying at *Lord Sefton's*[7] near this—they took us to Sr George Warrender's yesterday, when every soul in the house was gone to the races, except E[tt] Maria & myself. The Duke of W[ellington] returns from Cheltenham tomorrow & is to be here in a day or two.

I have done all I cou'd to keep every thing quiet here respecting the

---

1 The daughter of the Marquis of Anglesey. She married Lord Francis Conyngham in 1824. Both died in 1876.

2 Lady Conyngham and her sister, Maria, who married Sir Robert Lawley, first Baron Wenlock, in 1793, were the sisters of William Joseph Denison (1770–1849), the millionaire banker.

3 Admiral Sir George Cockburn (1772–1853), a Lord of the Admiralty 1818–30.

4 Lieutenant-General Sir Herbert Taylor succeeded Sir Henry Torrens as Adjutant-General to His Majesty's Forces (gazetted, 25 August).

5 The Rev. Edward Grey (1782–1837), Bishop of Hereford, 1832–37.

6 Sarah Sophia, eldest daughter of John, tenth Earl of Westmorland, married George Child Villiers, fifth Earl of Jersey (1773–1859), in 1804. (1785–1867.) "Lady Jersey", said Greville, "affects to be entirely in the Duke's confidence. . . . She contrives to make the Duke see a great deal of her, for he calls on her, and writes to her perpetually." (*Greville*, 13 February 1829.)

7 William Philip Molyneux, second Earl of Sefton (1772–1838), a notable Whig member of the House of Commons and a racing enthusiast. He was created a Baron of the United Kingdom in 1831.

Admiralty, but I have found some difficulty in persuading the K. not in any way to be a party in the business, but to let his brother & the D. act for themselves, & I must do the D. of Clarence the justice to own, that he has been most anxious to keep his brother from interfering.

We have nothing new here, the *ups* & *downs* go on as usual. I shall not ask for a box to send this letter, but enclose it to Lord Stuart.[1]

Lord C[onyngham] desires his kind remembrance to you. Adieu my dear Sir Wm.

The Duke of Wellington to the King, 4 September 1828. (*W.N.D.* v, 14.)

1531 THE DUKE OF CUMBERLAND *to* SIR WILLIAM KNIGHTON

Breslow, Septr. 11th 1828.

BY this time I take it for granted you are safely settled again in old England and *I* not yet at the end of my peregrination. Our journey to Berlin went off very well, I was obliged to remain 2 days at Hannover to make myself master of how our matters stood respecting the Brunswick business, for which purpose I thought it most adviseable to have a conference in pleno in order that I might learn the *opinion* of each Minister and not be afterwards told *this* I did, or did not say; and I am happy to say that the last Minister which my brother appointed about 3 months ago seems to me to be a most *excellent* choice, a man of sound sense, & what is at this moment of great weight an excellent lawyer, which from his having filled the situation of President of the *highest* Court of Justice he must be. Since that I had very satisfactory conferences with the Ministry of Foreign Affairs, and also with the King himself *who* says that he will prove to my brother that he has as much his honour at heart as if he was acting for himself, but Metternich is playing his old, his crooked tricks, and as they are at Berlin as fully aware of this as we are, there is no danger.

What an extraordinary speech is that of Mr. Dawson,[2] is he grown

---

1 Lord Granville resigned the Paris Embassy when the Huskissonites left the Ministry, and Sir Charles Stuart, who had been raised to the peerage as Baron Stuart De Rothesay in January, succeeded him.

2 Speaking at a public dinner at Londonderry on 12 August, the King's birthday and the anniversary of the siege, George Dawson, Peel's brother-in-law, declared that the peace of Ireland depended not upon the King's Government but upon the dictation of the Catholic Association, and plainly intimated that if a rebellion was to be avoided the Catholic claims would have to be conceded.

mad? or has he done [it] to secure a seat,[1] any how he has disgraced himself in my humble opinion in the grossest way, and I should think must hurt his brother in law. The appointment of Taylor,[2] which I have only seen in the papers here, an extract out of the English, I do look upon as a most excellent one. I felt very much shocked at reading the acct of poor Torrens' death. I gave particular directions that my *English letters* should *not* be forwarded to me, as I have been living in villages, and as I only get home on Saturday, the day the English post leaves Berlin, I write this beforehand for fear of arriving there too late to read & answer, but should any thing from you be arrived, I shall answer you the Tuesday the *16th.* I have no direct accounts from England since the 22d of last month & therefor you can easily imagine my anxiety to get my letters. The weather was dreadfull the *first day* and I do not remember ever to have been wetter, but thank God fine weather succeded and our manœvres have gone off to perfection, but had the rain returned, we must have given up all idea of manœvre, for the rivers had begun to overflow, so much so that in going to the our [*sic*] quarters, the water passed through the carriages. Mind to fullfill your promise; and let me hear from you soon.

The Hannoverian messenger shall bring over to my brother the things he commissioned me to get.

1532 SIR THOMAS LAWRENCE *to the* MARCHIONESS CONYNGHAM

Russell Square, Sept^{ber} the 12th 1828.

I KNOW not how to frame a petition, which I fear must appear so unreasonable to you, from its subject having been of too frequent recurrence. Yet I must venture to present it, from my strong wish that the near completion of the fine engraving from the portrait of His Majesty may be finally corrected in the resemblance of the countenance from the original picture; and from the equally anxious desire & earnest solicitation of the engraver; who informs me of the strong necessity that exists for re-inspection of the face, now that every other part of the plate is wrought up to its full form and calls therefore for increas'd power, in the great essential effort of the work.

If Madam, your Ladyship, with His Majesty's gracious sanction, can

1 Dawson was M.P. for Londonderry and Joint Secretary of the Treasury in the Wellington Ministry.
2 Sir Herbert Taylor. See No. 1530.

give me authority to remove the picture to the engravers for exactly one month and no more you will confer on me a very great obligation, and most materially assist in the successful completion of, what (I must believe from the devoted affection of His Majesty's subjects,) is an object of national importance.

I take the liberty of offering my respects to the Marquess, and have the honor to remain, [etc.].

1533 THE DUKE OF CUMBERLAND *to* SIR WILLIAM KNIGHTON

Schoenhausen, Sept. 15th 1828.

I READ in the papers that you had landed in England via Ostend, therefore flatter myself I shall perhaps already by next mail receive a letter *from you*, especially as I am grieved to learn my brother has had the night of the 4th to the 5th a fresh attack of his spasms. Knowing him, as I do, I feel fully convinced, that they are produced by worry of mind, & what that is I can easily imagine especially as the newspapers are all at work respecting the great question.[1] Any thing more extraordinary, or more uncalled for than Mr. Dawson's speech[2] I never have read; but coming from him, and considering his very near connexion with Mr. Peel, it certainly *must* strike *every Protestant* and I fear must create much agitation and irritation *both* of *which* ought to be *most studiously avoided* at this moment, when a single spark may set all in a blaze. Clear it is from what has passed of late, that the Protestants in Ireland are all alive now to their situation, better late than never, but what a pity that the present spirit had not existed some years back, much & great mischief might have been spared. During my late tour in Silesia, I have been living in the heart as it were of Catholicism, for there are great numbers still in that province, and I learnt there how extremely *busy* the Bishop of Breslau is trying to make converts there, and was not the King in this country in a very different situation from that of a King of England, there would be soon serious work in that province, but the Bishop is paralyzed by that.[3] I trust I shall have all my *brother's* commissions finished to be enabled to send them over by the *next* Hannoverian messenger.

1 The Catholic question.   2 See No. 1531.
3 The population of Silesia was then about two millions, of whom about half were Catholics. In some of the villages of the circle of Liegnitz the Protestants had been distributing Bibles to the Catholics. The Prince Bishop of Breslau, M. von Schimonsky, ordered the Catholics to surrender their Bibles; when they hesitated to obey he claimed the assistance of the civil power, but this was not forthcoming.

Chateau Schönhausen, Sept. 15th 1828.

BELIEVE me it was with great concern and deep regret I learnt upon my arrival *here* the day before yesterday, that you was so unwell the 5th, of which I was informed by Frederica who had just received a letter from Lady C. I hope to God you are again now recovered, but I own to you I hate these attacks of spasms, being well aware that though finally caused by catching cold, still their origin is produced from *worry* of *mind*, and I fear you have had much to do that of late; for though I have no *private* letters of any certain *dates* or *accounts* still I have had some that do not much relieve my anxiety upon *certain* things, however I am still persuaded if we are *but true* to ourselves we shall parry the storm. I see by a paper that our friend Knighton is returned to England, and therefore I hope to get soon a letter from him, and learn a little *what* is going on; for suspense is a dreadful state to remain in, and I know *this* is the *period* that *much was* to go on.

I arrived here on Saturday last at 12 o'clock that is to say at Berlin, having made the journey from Breslau there in about 27 hours, after cleaning myself and read my English letters, I got on my horse and rode here, which will prove to you that I was not much tired, though I had been 27 hours constantly in an open carriage. I had the satisfaction of finding Frederica remarkably well, but poor dear George suffering from a feverish cold, but I am happy to say it is of no consequence and he was yesterday much better and in *high* spirits, complaining only of the hardship of being obliged to keep his bed; this however I think the doctor perfectly right in insisting upon, as it is the sole manner of keeping him quiet, and preserving him that moisture of skin necessary to carry off the cold he is labouring under. He shewed me the two very kind letters he had received from Lady C— and Maria and knowing the carte du pays as I do, Maria's interested me very much, as she gives so full an account of all the improvements and alterations going on in that lovely spot the Park. I got up very early this morn^g in order to have a few hours partridge shooting, and I am now expecting the keeper to let me know where the covies lay; this will be probably the only day, I shall have for partridge shooting, as the day after tomorrow the garrison of Berlin march for the camp at Potsdam, where I shall go. The King is expected back this evening from Silesia having passed two days at his brother's Prince William, I found Clanwilliam here on Saturday, he had reached Berlin two days previous to my return, he looks uncommonly well and seems to have enjoyed very much the tour in Norway; Lothian who had accompanied him has returned home by Hamburg. The Gowers were to arrive at Potsdam on Saturday last and at Berlin *this* day. I have written to invite them and the rest of my countrymen to dinner for *tomorrow*. Of Adolphus I have not heard a word since he left England, and therefore am totally ignorant where he is, or when he comes to Hannover; by the newspapers I see old Royal was to be at Francfort, therefore suppose as long as she is there, he will not leave that part of the world. I shall write to you again as soon as I have any thing worth mentioning, and shall not fail to send you all your commissions executed, by the quarterly messenger as soon as I arrive at Hannover, which will be the 1st or 2d Oct.ʳ Now God bless you, and grant that the next letters from England may bring me good accounts of you. My best regards to all the ladies, Frederica desires her *kindest love* and George est à vos pieds.

PS. One thing I forgot to mention the misalliance that Max[imilian] Taxis[1] has made by marrying a Mlle de Dörenberg at Ratisbon, the father as well as the whole family was informed by the late Prince (father to the present one) that he never would consent to this union, and no sooner had the Prince closed his eyes than the son of Monsieur de Dörenberg set at him and never lost sight of him 'till the thing has been accomplished. He has had the impudence to announce his marriage formally to *all* his relations, but I believe they have *all* determined not to take the least notice of it or give him the slightest answer, this I know is the case *here* with Prussia, and Mecklenburgh, and I should suppose you will not consider this young lady as a fit person to be the niece of the King of Great Britain and Hannover.

16th

I received yesterday via Hannover a letter from Munster dated the 2d. he seems not to agree with his colleagues at Hannover and myself as to our presenting the Brunswick business to the Diet at Francfort; the fact is this that I as well as the Ministry at Hannover are of opinion that it should be presented there not *by us* but by the *two mediating Courts* themselves, who will then be *bound* to *support* what they themselves present, and I rather believe, at least if I have *not* misunderstood what Reden told me, and what Witzleben also said, that the *Court* of Prussia has *actually* taken steps to that effect, however, I mean to ride into town this morning to try to have an interview with Ct. Bernstorff, and through him ascertain the actual state of things, I should not have failed to have done it yesterday, but know Monday is his busiest day and *this* would have put

1 The elder son of Prince Charles Alexander and Princess Theresa of Tour and Taxis. He was therefore the Duchess of Cumberland's nephew.

him out. Have I anything worth adding I shall not fail to do it and therefore shall carry my letter to town unsealed.

Berlin ½ past 2 o'clock

I have called at Bernstorff's, but he is so very ill that he let me know, he was utterly unable to transact any business, thank God I have just received a letter of the 8th giving a much better account of you dearest brother, and I trust as the weather is I hear so fine, that you will be enabled to profit of it, and get your daily drives. Ben Bloomfield has just announced himself, he arrived this morning early from Dresden, I have invited him to come and dine with us at Schönhausen. God bless you and believe me ever [etc.].

1535 THE DUKE OF CUMBERLAND *to* SIR WILLIAM KNIGHTON

Schoenhausen, Septr. 19th 1828.

YOUR letter of the 10th reached me yesterday afternoon, and as the post leaves this again tomorrow I will not omit directly acknowledging it. Probably ere you receive this, you will have had a 2d epistle from me in consequence of my having heard of my dear brother's being severely indisposed, but *that* he has been in a constant state of suffering for the last month, I had not been aware of. I am no phisician & perhaps am talking or I should rather say writing like an ignoramus, but nevertheless I cannot help thinking that these *attacks* in the bladder are neither more nor less than the effect of a malady very common in *these* climates which is the *blind piles* and if at times *leaches* are not applied to the *arms*, to draw off the blood from those parts, which is as it were stagnated, they cause violent cholicks, and spasms in the bladder, which may become very fatal. Excuse my mentioning *this*, but having lived so many years in a climate, where I may say 99 persons in a 100 are more or less tormented with piles, I own I cannot help thinking that those *pains* my brother complained of in his loins, and which he *called* rheumatic were nothing else but the complaint of this climate, and when one considers the sedentary life he has now for so many years habituated himself to one cannot be surprized at it. Taking it in all, the 4 months I had the happiness & pleasure of passing near him, I really think he appeared to me to be remarkably well, except that one *bout*, but that he had in great part drawn upon himself by innaction.

Only use your endeavour to get his apartments ready for him at the Castle, that he may get established there previous to the very damp weather; then I hope he may, when once recovered from this fit of the gout get through the winter comfortably.

You surprize me by saying you had found *all* in politicks in *statu quo*, I have received *no* letters whatever of any consequence, since my departure from England, & therefore, naturally, all I know is merely from the newspapers and from what others tell me who have their correspondents in England; but it appears to me, as if the irritation on *both sides* of the question seems to encrease daily, and even much more so since I have left old England, for I see they are forming Brunswick Constitutional Clubs[1] every where in Ireland. I own my curiosity is great to learn *what* they mean to do, and believe me that often & often do I feel myself as it were in a wilderness, when I turn over this great question in my mind, seeing danger round me every way I consider the question. To me it is self-evident that sooner or later it must come to a crash and therefore we must be constantly on our guard.

I heard a curious anecdote that passed here at Berlin immediately after the last division of the House of Lords. A person expressed in society his regret that the question had been lost, & talked the old hackneyed language of the cruelty and unfairness of keeping so many subjects from enjoying the same privileges that their brethren did. Upon this a very sensible & clever man, a Catholic, took up the word and said "You will be perhaps surprized at hearing *me* who from being a Catholic ought to bewail this defeat, but having studied as I have done the Constitution & history of England, I solemnly declare that was I an Englishman I should certainly never give my vote for the emancipation". This is a fact you may depend upon and must prove *how* very dangerous it would be ever to *allow* R. Catholics to sit or vote in Parlt. any thing short of that, perhaps I might be not so tenacious about, but their having political influence I cannot accede to.

Tomorrow morning I start for Potsdam, where the reviews take place this year, and they are to last till the 27th inclusive, and on the following day all the troops will probably have a resting day & the 29th march back to their respective quarters. I shall for my person come back here for 24 hours & then proceed to Hannover to assist the manouvers there which last till the 12th, then take a few days shooting in our woods there & get back here by the end of the month Octr when we shall settle in our town mansion. But as I have before said to you, if at any moment my

1 Protestant Associations established on the model of the Catholic Association, with the object of resisting the Catholic claims.

brother feels *anxious* for me to come to him, *he* has only to communicate to me his wishes & I will forthwith set out to join him; mind when I say this my good friend, do not think that I am VAIN enough to think I can be of *much* use to him, but this I affirm that he has *no one* who is more faithfully or zealously attached to him than I am and am ready to serve him at any time or moment he thinks I may be of the slightest *use* or *comfort* to *him*. I am most happy to say the Dss I find remarkably well for her, and our dear boy is now quite recovered from a feverish cold he had for about a week, he went out again yesterday for the first time. By this time I suppose you have had enough of me, but as I had this morning some time to myself I have indulged myself in a quiet cose with you.

I shall not write to my brother by this post having nothing material to write to him, for Minister Bernstorff lays so ill in his bed, that he can see no one upon business.

P.S. The Dss desires to be remembered to you very particularly & thanks you for *all your kindness* for our dear boy, who also sends you his kindest regards. Pray favour me very soon with a letter again as you may easily conceive my anxiety respecting my brother.

1536 THE DUKE OF WELLINGTON *to* SIR WILLIAM KNIGHTON

London, Sept. 26th 1828.

I AM very much obliged to you for your letter. I hope that I shall hear from you again tomorrow.

I beg that you will tell the King that I do not trouble His Majesty with a letter, but that the Cabinet having met this day unanimously agreed upon a Proclamation to be issued by the Lord Lieutenant of Ireland to prohibit the illegal assemblages of people which have lately taken place in Ireland, to warn all men of their illegality, and to call upon all Magistrates &c. to prevent if possible these assemblages and to put them down.[1]

Orders have been sent to the Lord Lieutenant to issue this Proclamation, and to be prepared to carry it into execution.

I will send you a copy of it in the morning for H.M's information and I think it will do him good.

1 For this Proclamation see *Ann. Reg.*, 1828, *History of Europe*, p. 143; and *W.N.D.* v, 85 *et seq.*

1537 CHARLES ARBUTHNOT *to* SIR WILLIAM KNIGHTON

Woodford, 26 Sepr. 1828.

HAVING been at Lord Westmorland's there was some delay in my receiving the packet franked by you, and wch. I now send back to Mr. Danvers, or I shd. have sooner acknowledged the *line* in the inside of yr. frank of the 22nd inst.

I write one line to thank you for your line, and to say that it has been most gratifying to me to see how our friend the Premier relies on you. When you were absent some affairs went on not pleasantly, and he said to me it is all owing to *your* being away.

He waited anxiously for yr. return; and I am sure you will like as I like to see the open, frank, and unbounded confidence wch. he places in you. I need not intreat you to aid him all you can. He has but the one object of doing good, but he is surrounded with terrible difficulties, and those who love and revere him must do for him all they can. I am sure you will. Ever affly yrs.

[P.S.] We have been very uneasy about the King, but I trust he is really getting better.

If you shd. write again do let me know how he is, for his life is most essential, putting aside all private considerations.

The Duke of Wellington to Sir William Knighton, 27 September 1828. (*W.N.D.* v, 85–6.)

1538 THE EARL OF ABERDEEN *to* SIR WILLIAM KNIGHTON

Foreign Office, Octr. 4, 1828.

I HAVE seen Mr. Seguier[1] respecting the pictures which are in the apartment of the Society of Antiquaries, and which His Majesty is desirous of having transferred to Windsor Castle. His Majesty shall most certainly be obeyed; but it would relieve me from some difficulty, if the removal of the pictures might be delayed for a short time. The fact is, that a notion exists in the Society that the pictures in question were presented to the Society by His late Majesty; and as the Society is not at present assembled, I should have to exercise the authority of President in a very unusual manner by ordering the pictures to be moved at once.

1 William Seguier (1771–1843), conservator of the royal picture galleries under George IV, William IV and Queen Victoria.

The Society resumes its meetings in the course of next month; and if there should be no objection to this delay, I would then immediately state the matter to the Council, and the pictures should be delivered forthwith to Mr. Seguier.

It was my intention to have submitted this, most humbly to His Majesty, the next time that I attended His Majesty; and I also should have perhaps ventured, humbly to suggest, whether His Majesty might not have been graciously pleased to convey some mark of his Royal favour to the Society on the occasion.

Will you, my dear Sir William, take a seasonable opportunity of explaining the cause of my humble request for this short delay; and above all things, make it abundantly clear, that I am most anxious implicitly to obey the King's commands. Should there be any objection to this delay, pray have the kindness to inform me of it, and I will take measures to carry the business into effect directly.

Although His Majesty was graciously pleased to speak to me himself upon this subject, I have thought it better not to trouble His Majesty with a matter of such small importance. Being also certain that you will have the kindness to say for me what I wish.

Believe me, Dear Sir William [etc.].

The Duke of Wellington to Sir William Knighton, 5 October 1828. (*W.N.D.* v, 112.)

1539 THE DUKE OF CLARENCE *to the* KING

Bushy House, Octr. 6th 1828.

I TRUST in God your sad and long confinement is now over and that we may all look forward to your restoration of health for a very considerable time. Under this persuasion which I like to cherish I venture to throw myself before my best and oldest friend on a point which as a father I must have nearest my heart. My daughters thanks to your kindness are in that situation that I have but one unmarried and she is so young that in all human probability she will be settled well in life.[1] They five therefore are off my mind. My four sons are in a different situation and claim

1 Amelia FitzClarence (d. 1858) married Lucius, tenth Viscount Falkland, in 1830. Her sister Sophia (d. 1837) married Lord De L'Isle and Dudley in 1825; Mary (d. 1864) married Lieutenant-Colonel Charles Fox, of the Grenadier Guards; Elizabeth married William George, Earl of Erroll; and Augusta married (1) in 1827, John Kennedy Erskine, second son of the Marquis of Ailsa (d. 1831), and (2) in 1836 Lord John Frederick Gordon.

my consideration. The three eldest are honourably and fairly following their profession and the youngest in a short time will be in the Church.[1] But they have not any positive provision beyond their professions. It is not for me to urge my Sovereign who is the best and kindest of brothers to place himself in a situation with the Minister of difficulty and therefore beyond the desire of permanent provision for my sons I cannot and will not press. But I will venture to suggest that my utmost desire would be to see my sons possessing the same permanent allowance as has been most graciously and kindly bestowed on my daughters. I state this wish with the more confidence as I have not the most distant desire to apply for any thing on my own account and must and do again repeat beyond the wish I venture not to go for fear of placing my affectionate and tried brother and friend in difficulty with the Minister.

Having now done my duty as a father to my sons I have only to repeat my sincere and unalterable regard and affection for yourself and am convinced the goodness of your excellent and feeling heart will do me the justice to see that my natural and just desire to provide for my children was the sole cause of thus writing.

The Duke of Wellington to Sir William Knighton, 8 October 1828. (*W.N.D.* v, 116–17.)

1540 THE DUKE OF CUMBERLAND *to* SIR WILLIAM KNIGHTON

III

Hannover, Octr 11th 1828.

I HAVE received the day before yesterday your letter No 2. dated Septr. 29th, and I have followed your example by numbering mine, this is the 3d I have written to you since your return home. Your letters are at all times most acceptable to me, but never more so than this time, for I had heard, *the* very evening previous to the receipt of your letter, from the D. of Cambridge that my dear brother had had a violent attack of an

2 The Duke had four surviving sons:

i.   George Augustus Frederick FitzClarence, Earl of Munster (1794–1842), married Lady Mary Wyndham, daughter of George, Earl of Egremont.

ii. Frederick (1799–1854), married Lady Augusta Boyle, daughter of George, Earl of Glasgow.

iii. Adolphus (1802–1856), Rear-Admiral; died unmarried.

iv. Augustus (1805–1854), rector of Mapledurham; married Sarah, daughter of Lord Henry Gordon.

inflammatory nature and that in consequence thereof Halford had ordered *bleedings*. Now the very word simply used would already have alarmed me, as I always understood when *gout* shewed itself, one was very averse to using the launcet, but I cannot deny that *bleedings* in the *plural* number did alarm me dreadfully and therefore your letter was a real godsend to me. Your letter alas confirms the assertion and plainly shews me that he must have caused you *all* a dreadfull alarm. Christ what a loss he would be to us all, and I may say to all Europe! for every day, nay every hour I plainly see that the salvation of England depends, and though God knows I am no political coward & have still pretty strong nerves, still I cannot feel *easy* 'till I hear again from you my dear friend & trust that you will have the kindness to give me a line, as I have the fullest persuasion & confidence that you will exactly tell me how *matters* stand [*sic*]. Never was any man's life more necessary than *his* at this extraordinary crisis in which our wretched country is placed, for to judge from all that appears in the public papers, the moment is nigh at hand, that a Civil War is ready to break out in Ireland, when it has not already. To be sure every thing at a distance appears worse than when on the spot and therefore my view may be wrong, but I judge merely from *all* I read in the public prints. The situation of my valuable friend the Duke of Wellington is very difficult, and I trust he will act with *prudence* and yet if necessary with *decision*. He wrote to me a most friendly and *confidential* letter, which I received the 6th & immediately on the 7th replied to, in which I gave him most honestly and fairly my opinion.[1] That madman Mr. Dawson has *done* the Govermt and the Duke in particular the *greatest mischief*, for it has shaken very much the opinion of the Protestants, as to the purity of his intentions. Now I, *who* have the most IMPLICIT FAITH in his honour & in all he says, am not in the least shaken in my opinion as to him; however we must take men as they are, & only lament that they are so ready to give way to believe what any mischievous person may set about respecting another, and therefore it appears to me after the most serious consideration I can give to the present state of things, that it will be necessary for the Duke of W. to *strengthen* himself and his Cabinet with some person whose *Protestant principles* are *decidedly* known and who will carry weight and influence with him; *this* is a moment most decisive for him, in my *most humble* but most honest opinion, it strikes me that in the new arrangement *which* is making in the Cabinet by the removal of Melville to the Admiralty, & Ellenborough to the Board of Controul, that he should try to get that great pillar of Protestantism Lord Eldon to *join* him with *heart* and soul,

1 See *W.N.D.* v, 114–16.

why then not make Bathurst *Privy Seal* and directly make Eldon Pres^t of the Council,[1] *this* could at *once* knock up all *doubts* where they exist, & he has a most able *debater* not only on this *important & vital question*, but a man *who* would attend the law causes in the H. of Lords, and be of great assistance to Lord Lyndhurst. This is my honest opinion & I give you my sacred word of honour uninfluenced for I have *not* had *one single line* from Eldon since I left England, which rather surprizes and makes me believe that *he* is out of *humour* & therefore does *not write*; whether this is the case or not, I know not, but his silence at this particular crisis makes me believe it.

I have this moment received the melancholy account of my sister the Dow^r Queen of Wurtemburg's death, I hope this may not shock my brother as he must feel still weak from his late confinement. I have not seen her since June 1797, consequently 31 years ago and have hardly any recollection of her. Her decease will be severely felt at Studtgardt as she was with justice very much beloved and respected there. From the letter I have received it appears though ill for the last three days, they did not expect her death so soon, the King had been with her a few minutes be-fore, she went herself to her [*sic*] when it appears she died of what they term here a paralatic stroke of the brain. The D. of Cambridge who saw her about a month ago at Francfort told me previous to our being aware even of her late illness, that he found her dreadfully altered the last time he saw her & that he thought she could not last long, as he imagined she had water on her chest, but from all I can learn it appears this was not her malady.

I have given my brother pretty detailed accounts of the state of our troops here and must say that as far as it is possible in the present state of things, I must own that I am perfectly *satisfied* & cannot sufficiently praise the zeal and attention of officers & men. *All* the *interior* is good and what fails may be perfectly attained in a *month* by being assembled together and being put on the *present system* of tactics & manœuvring of which they know nothing, but this can be easily obtained whenever the Sovereign issues his order, that they should adopt it; for the officers and men are so zealous that they would soon get into it. The great mis-fortune here is that all comes from the *civil* and not from *military*

1 This had been suggested by the King on 10 October, but Wellington was against it. Eldon, he said, was "very little disposed to take upon himself the lead of, and responsibility for, the measures of the Government for which he is so highly qualified; and he is as little disposed to support in public the decision to which the majority may have come.... To call Lord Eldon to your Councils just at present would be considered by the public as an indication of a remarkable change in them, which could not fail to be injurious to your service". (*W.N.D.* v, 133–6.)

authority, which may do very well in England but will not do *here* on the Continent where we have not the safe guard of *sea* to protect us.

Let me hear from you soon and believe me [etc.].

[P.S.] My best regards to the ladeis; who is to be the new Irish Representative Peer, a Protestant or Catholic?

1541 THE DUKE OF CUMBERLAND *to the* KING

Hannover, Oct^{er} 13th 1828.

LITTLE did I think when writing to you last, that I should receive in a few hours after I had sent off my letter the melancholy account of the demise of our poor sister, however thank God from a letter Adolphus received yesterday from the King of Wurtemberg it appears her end was easy and she was herself to her last gasp. Adolphus told me when I first saw him, therefore previous to either of us knowing she was so ill, that he was very much struck at the alteration he found in her since last year, that she had a most extraordinary sort of lethargic affection, that she at times fell asleep while conversing, and could then continue some hours in that state. As I have never seen her since June 3^d 1797[1] upwards of 31 years ago, I have hardly a recollection of her, however one cannot help feeling deeply when one branch of the old tree drops off. Adolphus who has frequently seen her and been in constant correspondence with her naturally feels her loss much more than I do, as really I can say I do not know her. Poor Elizabeth will feel it very deeply I fear, and the more so as she could not manage coming to Francfort to see her.

Never was a letter more acceptable to me than the last I received from Knighton, for I had heard from Adolphus the day before that you had had an inflammatory attack, but his letter has set me at ease, as he assures me that Halford felt perfectly *easy* and *satisfied* that the *evil* was completely removed, God grant that this *fit* of the gout, which has been hanging about you now ever since last July *more* or less, having fixed in your hand may secure you a good winter's health; but I own I do long more and more *now* to hear you are safely lodged in the Castle, which I am sure during the winter months must be more congenial to your health than the Cottage, however delightful it is; as in wet weather it must be damp; and you can equally enjoy your drives from the Castle as you have now a drive straight from the Castle through the little Park,

1 The date of her departure from England, after her marriage.

which is as private as the Lodge, and you have the opportunity even in bad weather when unable to get your drive, to walk about that beautiful Gallery. Our manouvers ended last Saturday & without any one accident occurring the whole time, upon the whole the weather was very *favourable* it is true we had rain, but it only did so after the troops had got into their camp & the cavalry into their cantonments. I never saw horses stand their work better, for though they certainly had hard work, especialy the last 4 days, the country being a very fat rich soil consequently very deep & heavy yet they did not look at all pulled, & I am sure they were never under 10 *hours* being in constant exercise. On Thursday last, it being a resting day, I took the opportunity of riding over to Memsin (?) which is about five English miles from Hage to see the stud there. The buildings are very *bad*, & not worth repairing, especially as the paddocks, if one may term them so, or rather I ought to say the fields are separated from the stables by the Weser which generally overflows in autumn, and this makes the distance from the fields to the stables I should think upwards of *ten* English miles and at times it is impossible to move the horses the roads being utterly *impassable* from the water. In my humble opinion the Chamber should try to purchase an estate which is perfectly contiguous to the fields being on the same side of the river and only between two and three miles from them, it would not be necessary to purchase the whole estate, but merely that part which is so contiguous & lies so convenient, I am told by those who know the estate that it is perfectly adapted for it; and I believe it may be had for 30,000 dollars about 6000 £ English, and *what* was not wanted might either be *let* or parted with. The stud of young horses seem to me to be very promising there are some young black and brown horses which I think will in the course of two years be good recruits for the carriage horses. The day after tomorrow I propose going to the Solingen to see the stud at Neuhause (?), where the saddle horses are; and shall not fail to make you my report of it, there I understand the buildings are capital. To prove to you how correct I am in what I stated respecting the advantage it was to the country the encouraging the breed of horses, I saw during the manouver one *Jew* horse dealer who had bought up from the *peasants* in the neighbourhood of Hage *ninety* foles fallen last spring and taking one with the other he had paid *ten* louis d'ors per head, which is no less than 900 louis d'ors *all* money coming into the country from the neighbouring countries. They give for 4 year old horses from 60 to 90 louis d'ors. He told us he had bought one young stallion for which he had given 120 louis, and unfortunately for him had sold it the next day for 150, and that had he kept it only a few days longer he might

[441]

have had 200, as it had been bought from the 2nd person for that sum to go to Vienna. I think this speaks for our breed being much improved. Now dearest brother I suppose you have had enough of me, and will wish me to Jericho for having written you so long a letter, but the pleasure of conversing with you being denied me at this distance, I feel too happy in being able per litteram scriptam to do it. Now God Almighty bless you and grant that you may very soon be restored to perfect health, this is the most sincere wish dearest brother of [etc.].

The Duke of Wellington to Sir William Knighton, 21 October 1828. (*W.N.D.* v, 153.)

1542   THE DUKE OF CUMBERLAND *to* SIR WILLIAM KNIGHTON
No. 4.

Berlin, Novr. 10th 1828.

I ARRIVED here *last* night, and found all my letters just *arrived* as I got out of my carriage.

Many many thanks for your *confidential account*, which thank God upon the *whole* is a great relief to my mind. I felt certain that I should hear *very soon* from you, and therefore though I do not deny I felt *uneasy* at the *various* & different reports flying about the state of my dear brother's health, still I felt sure they must be grossly exaggerated, as I had *no* line from you. That the evil in the bladder is always a very *serious* one, there is no denying, but from your description thank God, no very *alarming* state appears to exist at this moment, & you may *smile* when I say so, but though no medical man, & having little or no knowledge of pharmacopia, still I am *firmly* persuaded that his bladder complaint is solely produced from piles, which are naturally produced from his sedentary life, & full living. This complaint is most *general here* in the Northern climates & therefore I hear constantly of such examples. My son Prince Frederic of Prussia a young man just 30 years old suffered all last *year* from this vile complaint which also attacked his bladder so bad, that he was utterly unable to bear the motion even of a carriage, he has been *now* for two years taking the waters and using the baths at Ems, I think, which have proved most *beneficial* to him, for I hear he is now able to go out a shooting again. I do long to hear that he is safely lodged in his new appartments at the Castle, which I feel confident will be much more *wholesome* for him, than those he at present inhabits at the Cottage, however delightful they are during the summer months.

I have been 4 weeks in the country of Hannover, and am now pretty well master of *all* that is going on there. It is a beautiful, and a happy country full of resources, and if properly administer'd might be made a great deal of. What fails there is one, who has nerves to act and make them all pull together, and not allow each department to act for itself, the natural consequence of which is that each branch acts not only for itself but instead of aiding each other, they rather cause difficulties to each other, than aid each other. I do not at all feel comfortable about my brother[1] there, though certainly I have left him in better spirits than when first I joined him, but his nerves are dreadfully shaken, and he certainly requires a great deal of management, any *violent* business requiring energy would I fear be too much for him. It is a very great pity for he is of all the most angelic best tempered men I ever met with, incapable of doing harm to any one. At first I could not get him out a shooting, he had a total dislike *to all* exertion, but I never ceased urging him on, & at last succeeded in getting him to accompany me to the parties and I really think now he has been out, his spirits are become much better. I had a great deal of difficulty in persuading him to accompany me on my journey back to the environs of Hildesheim where we had a famous day's shooting, but by leaving it to him to fix *himself* the day, and making for him a place that he might unite *this* party with another at a Count Stallberg's I completely succeeded. I was very lucky for I shot myself *fourteen hares* that day. Our weather is now complete winter and we have much snow & ice, it began with the month, and I had a dreadful cold journey.

I mean to write by this same post that goes tomorrow to England to my brother, and shall then make him some further reports on the Brunswic business. I have already sent to Count Bernstorff to know when he will see me, for he is unable, I hear, still to leave his room, he has now been nearly 4 months laid up with the gout.

You surprize me *not a little*, by stating that nothing new has transpired on the great question, for I understood that the D[uke of Wellington] meant to make his 2d communication to my brother in the course of last September, and we are now fast approaching to Decr.[2] There are all sorts of reports afloat, and I am one of those who give no ear, or believe any thing till I know it officially. I depend upon your friendship to let me know how my dear brother [is] & you may depend on my keeping

1 The Duke of Cambridge.
2 The Duke's first Memorandum containing his reasons why the King should allow the Government "to take into consideration the whole state of Ireland", was dated 1st August. (*W.N.D.* IV, 565–70.) His subsequent communications to the King, 14 October and 16 November, are in *W.N.D.* V, 133–6; 252–68.

to myself all you write to me *on that* as well as on all other, as you well know that my brother has not one more truly faithfully attached to him than myself. God protect him and preserve his life for *us* all still many many years.

I found the Duchess far from being well, she has caught a violent cold, and complains of pains all over her, but George looks thank God remarkably well & I am happy to say Jelf says that he is going on famously with all his masters, which certainly speaks highly to his credit, as he certainly had enough when in England to have turned his little head, but his disposition is so angelick that I trust and hope that he will prove himself an honest, and true man, one *who* will do honour to the situation of life for which he is born, & which his parents will ever be mindful to impress on his heart & mind. His attachment to his dear uncle is great, & I hope with God's mercy that this spring when his mother will come over to England to fetch me back, that he will then be found by my brother still improved in every way.

Now God bless you, and let me hear from you *as often* as you can. Excuse this scratching out, but I was interrupted and not having read *what* I had just written I had added a few words respecting George, upon which subject I had just previously been writing.

1543 THE DUKE OF WELLINGTON *to* SIR WILLIAM KNIGHTON

London, Nov. 12th 1828.

Y OU never told me what you had done about Mr. Denman.[1] He looked very hard at me at the Lord Mayor's[2] dinner on Monday, and I think that I shall have him here in the course of this week.

1 See No. 1526, and *W.N.D.* v, 116, 153, 243.
2 Matthias Prime Lucas.

London, Nov. 12th 1828.

I ENCLOSE you a letter[1] which I wrote yesterday to Lord Anglesey which I beg you to shew to His Majesty.

It is impossible to say what his answer will be to this letter, but it has appeared to me impossible to allow him to go on any longer without a knowledge of what is thought here of his conduct.[2] Believe me, [etc.].

1545 THE DUKE OF CUMBERLAND *to* SIR WILLIAM KNIGHTON

No 6.   *Berlin*, Novr. 17th 1828.

I RECEIVED yesterday yours of the 7th and cannot tell you what bliss it was, the sight of your hand writing, for all sorts of the most infamous stock jobbing tricks are now going on between London & the Continent, the Saturday (day before yesterday) an estafette arrived here from Hamburg with the account of the King's being very ill, and that the Duke of Wellington *had* resigned. I certainly, when it was told me, declared I did not believe either the one or the other piece of news, which however gained great credit for a few hours, but I said that I was sure that if my brother was so ill, as this report made him, I should have had a special messenger, as also certainly if the D. of W. had quitted; this quieted many persons, who certainly had given credit to this report. However you can easily imagine that the idea of a *possibility* though *not* a *probability* fidgetted me somewhat, & gave me ample food for meditation; but yesterday morning at 11 o'clock when the letters were brought to me, I felt a great stone off my heart. Your account of my dear brother's health is most acceptable, and I feel *certain* if, whenever my brother feels the oppression which he complains of on his chest, he would only apply *leaches* to the *arms*, and bleed thus copiously there, it will not only relieve his head & chest, but prevent the affection of the bladder. I see you smile at my pretending to give medical advice and opinions, but as this complaint is so common here in the north of Germany & that I would almost say 99 persons out of a 100 have it more or less, I hear enough of it. *Two* things tell him from me he must most cautiously abstain from, which are, taking *all heating things*, and *catching cold*, and above all keep

1 *W.N.D.* v, 240–1.

2 The King, said Wellington, "feels that in Ireland the public peace is violated every day with impunity by those whose duty it is to preserve it; that a formidable conspiracy exists, and that the supposed principal conspirators, those whose language and conduct point them out as the avowed principal agitators of the county, are admitted to the presence of his Majesty's representative in Ireland, and equally well received with the King's most loyal subjects".

his *feet warm*. Now I suppose you have had enough of my medical discussion, and will say like Dr. Allypot in the play, "Damn phisik".

The letter of Lord Bexley, you have sent me, is in my humble opinion the *very best* I have ever read on the subject, and he has done that, which till now never was done sufficiently to please me, namely, shown the absurdity of comparing our situation to those of Prussia & the Netherlands, which are totally & entirely different. It does great credit to Bexley, who certainly is a very sensible man, and an honest man. That something must be done one way or other, I do most perfectly agree with you, but what that is, certainly is beyond the reach of my conception, for *all* you cannot, you dare not give the Catholicks, & short of all they will not accept. My faith is *great* in the D. of W. and I never shall believe that *he* will propose to Parlt any thing like *emancipation*, what I mean is that *any one Catholic* shall sit in either House of Parliament, for in my view of the subject, even the admission of one in either House would destroy the *principle*, & it is for that, I stand up and combat.

I enclose you for my brother's perusal my public and official reply to Lord Enniskillen[1] on accepting the office of Grand Master of the Orange Great Lodges in Ireland, which I trust & hope he will approve of. I have written it with great caution & in a manner which I think will meet with his approbation. Knowing so perfectly well as I do *his* sentiments and opinions on that great question, I thought when speaking of our late revered father, that I should have *failed* by *him*, if I did not say *that* which I *have done* and which was necessary to give the lie to all those infernal insinuations put about last year, as if he had *changed* his *opinion*, or was *lukewarm* to the cause. I am most curious to learn who is to be the new Privy Seal,[2] at least I have not seen a successor named as yet; whoever he may be, God grant he may be one who is a staunch Protestant.

At last my effects are arrived *here*, and the Duchess received yesterday those two beautiful *ice pails*, which the King had the great kindness to send her; they certainly are most beautiful & splendid, so that she has ordered two glass covers to be made in order to place them in the drawing room, they certainly prove how wonderfully well our silversmiths work.

I should suppose that Parliament will now not meet 'till the middle or end of Feby as the Xmas holydays follow so soon after the time the present adjournment is fixed, that it would be useless to assemble them

1 John Willoughby Cole, second Earl of Enniskillen (1768–1840), one of the Irish Representative Peers. Created Baron Grinstead (U.K.), 1815. His younger brother, Sir Lowry Cole, was Governor of Cape Colony.
2 The Earl of Rosslyn.

then, and it is a period of the year when the country gentlemen are not fond of being called from home; and I fear that the next Session will be a most boisterous one, it certainly will be a most momentous one for our country, and God grant us wisdom, that we may only conduct ourselves *prudently*, and not allow us to commit a similar folly as last year of *sacrificing our dearest interests by compromises*. I look on that repeal of the Corporation & Test Acts to have been our ruin.

The Duchess still suffers with her cold, and cough; George is in high force & is writing to his uncle.

1546 THE EARL OF MOUNTCHARLES *to* SIR WILLIAM KNIGHTON

Windsor, Novr. 24th 1828.

I WAS in hopes to have seen you here last night, but as I now hear that you will not be down at Windsor before Wednesday, on which day I must be in town for the Treasury, I venture to write to you, begging of you if you disapprove of what I am going to ask, or if you think there will be difficulty in managing it, to put this letter in the fire & not mention the circumstance to anyone. You are so kind to me that I hope you will not be vexed or think unreasonable the application.

You are aware that the "Outrangership of Windsor Park" is still vacant, the salary of which is from 5 to 600 a yr: but it vacates a seat in Parliament. Lady Bloomfield is Ranger of Hampton Park, Lady Mansfield of some other, & many of the Princesses have also Parks. Now what wd give me such pleasure wd be *if* there were no objection to it, at least if you saw none, (for in point of fact I believe none exists) that the King should give *it Jane*. I wd willingly give up my Treasury then, which wd please the D. of Wellington as it is a place that he can give to any one; & it wd give the greatest satisfaction to Jane. Do you think my dr Sir William this project is entirely out of the question, only say one word to that effect, & I will think no more of it; but it wd suit me & my plans so much better than holding the Treasury: at any rate pray forgive this long letter.

I am writing to you from the Castle, whilst the King is attending to the Recorders Report which will last most likely till past 7 o'clock. H.My got here a little after 2 o'clock, saw Mr. Peel for nearly two hours, & gave short audiences to the D. of Wellington, Lord Aberdeen & the Chancellor. The D. of Clarence was here also.

The Duke of Wellington to the King, 26 November 1828. (*W.N.D.* v, 288.)
Thomas Denman to the Duke of Wellington, 2 December 1828. (*Life of Denman*, I, 290.)

1547 THE DUKE OF WELLINGTON *to* THOMAS DENMAN

Copy.

Strathfieldsaye, Decr. 4th 1828.

I HAVE received your letter of the 2nd. instant and I shall take an opportunity of making known to the King again your anxiety that His Majesty should give credit to the assurances contained in your memorial presented to His Majesty.

It gives me great satisfaction that I should have been the channel by which your memorial was conveyed to the King and that His Majesty should have been most graciously pleased to attend to it.[1]

1548 THE DUKE OF WELLINGTON *to the* KING

Stratfield Saye, Decr. 4th 1828.
12 at midnight.

As I am sending to your Majesty the report of the death of Lord Liverpool, which I have just received, I think it proper to trouble your Majesty with a few words upon the subject of the office of Lord Warden of the Cinque Ports.

It is an office of great influence and power but without any salary or emoluments and the three last holders of it were the Ministers of His late Majesty and of your Majesty.

If any salary were attached to the office I need not say that I should humbly suggest to your Majesty that a person should be appointed to fill it who had less reason than I have to be grateful to your Majesty for your gracious acceptance and reward of his services, and less reason to be satisfied with his lot. But as the office has great influence and power and nothing else I humbly submit to your Majesty that the person who is your Minister at the time it falls vacant should be appointed to fill it.

In submitting the suggestion to your Majesty I beg leave to assure you of the gratitude with which I shall receive this fresh mark of your Majesty's favour if your Majesty should think proper to attend to it; and that nothing can impair the affection and devotion of your Majesty's most dutiful subject and servant.

1 The King accepted Denman's explanation and granted him a patent of precedence.

1549 THE DUKE OF WELLINGTON *to the* KING

Strathfield Saye, Dccr. 6th 1828.

I HAVE received your Majesty's letter and I beg leave to return your Majesty my most grateful thanks for this fresh mark of your Majesty's gracious favour, which it will continue to be my study to merit.

Which is submitted to your Majesty by your Majesty's most dutiful and most grateful subject and servant.

1550 ROBERT PEEL *to the* KING

Whitehall, Decr. 6th 1828.

MR. PEEL presents his humble duty to your Majesty and begs leave to acknowledge the receipt of your Majesty's note of yesterday in reference to the case of Joseph Hunton.

Mr. Peel has considered that it would be satisfactory to your Majesty that he should again personally confer with the Lord Chancellor and the Lord Chief Justice upon this case, and having done so he begs permission to submit to your Majesty their opinion which is in concurrence with his own.

Mr. Peel deeply regrets to be under the necessity of stating to your Majesty that that opinion is not in favour of the mitigation of the capital sentence passed upon the prisoner.

It appears to them as it does to Mr. Peel that it would be very difficult hereafter to enforce the capital sentence of the law in any case of forgery, if mercy be extended in this case.[1]

Your Majesty will no doubt bear in mind that the two last Reports of the Recorder presented three separate cases of forgery. From some doubt upon the evidence given on the trial of Peter Fenn,[2] and on account of the bad character of some of the witnesses against him, a respite has been sent for him in order that further inquiry might be made. The life of another prisoner whose name appeared in the same Report with that of Hunton was spared, his offence being of a less aggravated character than the one of which Hunton was convicted.

1 Joseph Hunton, a partner in the house of John Dixon & Co., drapers, was found guilty at the Old Bailey in October of forging and uttering a number of bills of exchange, and was hanged on 8 December. He was a Quaker with a wife and ten children, and the jury recommended him to mercy. Great efforts were made to save his life, "The whole body of Quakers were in motion", said Peel. "One petition alone had 5,000 signatures." (*Parker*, II, 42–3; *Ann. Reg.* 1828. *Chron.* pp. 143, 150, 173.)

2 He was sentenced to death at the Old Bailey in September for forging two bills of exchange, but he was reprieved. He was described as a schoolmaster, of Hyde Street, Bloomsbury. (*Ann Reg.* 1828; *Chron.* p. 118.)

Under these circumstances and taking into consideration the extent and the system of forgery committed by Hunton it appears to the Lord Chancellor, to the Chief Justice and to Mr. Peel, that the ends of public justice require that the law in this case should be allowed to take its course.

Mr. Peel at the same time feels it to be his duty to transmit to your Majesty the accompanying petitions on behalf of the prisoner. These petitions have been seen by the Lord Chancellor and the Chief Justice but do not alter their impression as above stated.

Sir William Knighton to the Duke of Wellington, 3 January 1829. (*W.N.D.* v, 418–19.)
Sir William Knighton to Sir Henry Halford, 3 January 1829. (*Ibid.* v, 419.)

1551 THE EARL OF MOUNTCHARLES *to* SIR WILLIAM KNIGHTON

London, 7th Jany. 1829.

I HAVE called repeatedly at yr house to enquire after you, & in the hopes of seeing you particularly at this moment when I really want very much to talk with you on different matters.

I think I could have gotten the D. of Wellington to have asked the King for that small place for Jane on condition of my giving up the Treasury, which I am most willing to do, & indeed which I think I shall at all events now do; but you have always been my friend, & from old & still existing habits I like doing nothing without talking the matter over with you: but this really I have had so much at heart that you know not how much you wd have obliged me by doing it.

My family I never ask for anything, it is sufficient for me to wish a thing for them to put an extinguisher upon it.

Jane is, as you may imagine, in rather an angry mood at her father's recall, which of course all her family keep up in her.[1] It certainly does appear hard; & when he was popular with all classes in Ireland, for I have letters from Lord Enniskillen &c upon it, all saying that they had gt *confidence* in him, however I always say we do not yet know the rights of the case. I could tell you a gt deal of gossip about it, but you wd vote me a bore, & desire me not to talk of things I don't understand, so I will say no more.

I hope you are quite well, & that there is nothing passing to vex you tho' I fear there always must be something going on so to do.

1 Lord Anglesey, the Lord Lieutenant, was recalled for declaring himself in favour of an immediate Catholic Relief Bill, in a letter to Dr Curtis, the titular Catholic Primate of Ireland.

Berlin, Jany. 10th 1829.

I FOUND here on my return from Magdeburg where I went the 2d on a great shooting party *three* posts arrived from England, all that very day I returned, and I had flattered myself I should have heard either from Knighton or Watson, but no letter has reached me; however Mary gives me the very best and most comfortable accounts of your health, and a most interesting detail of your reception to the little Queen.[1] I own I feel happy that you was able to shew her Windsor Castle dans toute sa gloire, for I do think it must strike every one for its good taste and magnificence; and I rejoice to hear you feel yourself so perfectly comfortable there. I long to see it now that it is occupied. I can with great satisfaction assure you, I found Adolphus *now* perfectly well, & recovered his good spirits. I passed three days with him at Magdeburg, where we had excellent sport, there were in the 4 days chasse 3,000 hares killed, but the last day the cold was so intense, that I could hardly use my fingurs and I still suffer from the frost in my fingurs. Reden read to me yesterday his last dispatch which will inform you completely of the very excellent feelings the King & his Government have in the Brunswick business, and we must now await what further steps the Austrian Chancellor will determine upon, but one thing is certain that if Metternich does not act with vigour, that Bernstorff is fully determined not to join him in his exposé. It appears to me that whenever you bring the business before the Diet, you must at the same time declare that in doing it you reserve to yourself the right, that in case the Diet does not quickly dispatch it & that too in a manner due to your honour and character, you shall take it into your own hands.[2] This declaration will soon settle the work, which, I fear, otherwise Metternich will use every means in his power to keep in suspense, as it is to me perfectly clear, that his infamous Jesuitical and double conduct is solely caused from his *personal* hatred to Münster, and thus does he sacrifice his duty as servant to the Emperor to his own private feelings. The opinions here are all most violently raised against him, and I think I never saw such a feeling as it is now.

I have expected to have had some message from you through Knighton, especially after that most curious letter[3] of the Duke of Wellington to the titular Irish Bishop.[4] As I shall probably see you ere long I shall reserve giving you my opinion upon it, but I own it does not satisfy me, and I feel positive that our position would have been truely

1 Donna Maria, Queen of Portugal, who visited England in the autumn of 1828.
2 See No. 1336.   3 *W.N.D.* v, 326. (11 December 1828.)
4 Dr Curtis, titular Archbishop of Armagh.

dreadfull had not our Brunswick Clubs been in existence, I fear we should otherwise have had a repetition of what unfortunately passed last spring regarding the Corporation & Test Acts, some vile compromise. There will be I hope plenty of petitions presented to our House for the not granting any thing more to the Catholics. If you wish me to be with you by the 5th Feby,[1] only let me know per return of post and that PRIVATELY, and I will be *there*. I think I may be of some service to you, and therefore you know there is no sacrifice I am not ready to make, except change my principles on that great question on which I sense the security of your Crown depends. This letter I reckon you will receive this letter the 16*th* or 17th and if you send me your answer directly I can have it here the 24th or 25th, and then I will be with you the 5th of Feby. Let me only find a steam vessel at Calais, and I think certainly to be in time. A messenger from Ld. Heytesbury just arrived leaves this at 8 this evening & therefor can certainly be in England the 16th. Your answer being sent off the following day will reach me the 24th at latest, and I shall depart the 26th et la chose est faite, only order Watson to have fires lighted in my rooms that I may not find them cold.

Now one word more respecting the china, I enclose you the reply of Monsieur de Rosenstein the head of the Royal manufactory, and it depends on a further order from you, if I shall order the china to be made or not. Your messenger if you choose it can bring a competence with him, I say messenger, for as the winds now are, one cannot be sure as to the arrival of the mails, via Holland or Hamburgh. Now God Almighty bless you dearest dearest brother, & may you live to see many happy returns of the season. Frederica and George desire their best love and with my best regards to all friends, believe me [etc.].

Memorandum from Robert Peel to the King on the Catholic Question [12 January 1829]. (*W.N.D.* v, 436–40.)

1553 THE DUKE OF WELLINGTON *to the* KING

London, January 18th 1829.

I HAVE the pleasure to inform your Majesty that the Duke of Northumberland has accepted the office of Lord Lieutenant of Ireland.[2] I will give directions that the usual papers should be sent down for your Majesty's signature.

Which is submitted to your Majesty by your Majesty's most dutiful and devoted subject and servant.

1 At the opening of the Parliamentary Session.
2 His letter of acceptance is in *W.N.D.* v, 453.

Foreign Office, Jany. 20th 1829.

LORD ABERDEEN, with his most humble duty, thinks it right to inform your Majesty that the Prince de Polignac has received the commands of his Sovereign to return immediately to Paris; and that his Excellency leaves London this night.

The Prince de Polignac has assured Lord Aberdeen that his sudden departure is occasioned by the desire of His Most Christian Majesty to receive his opinion and advice upon the present state of the French Ministry, but without any intention of placing him in a prominent situation in the Government.

While expressing his strong desire to return to his post as Ambassador at your Majesty's Court, the Prince de Polignac did not deny that he might possibly find himself compelled to sacrifice his inclination to a sense of duty.

1555 THE DUKE OF CUMBERLAND *to* SIR WILLIAM KNIGHTON

No. 8.   *Berlin*, Feby. 4th 1829.

YOURS of the 15th & 16th reached me only *last* night, and I return you many thanks for it. Most happy am I to have so much better accounts of my brother's health, but *I own to you easy* I am not, for alas if he continues this damnable practice of laudanum, he must not only in the end kill himself but previous to that palsy himself; and if ever mans life was valuable not only for his own family's sake, but for his country, and that of all Europe it is HIS. The same post brought me a long letter[1] from the D. of W. relating to me in the most confidential manner *all* that has led to Ld. A[nglesey']s recall, which in my humble opinion he ought to have been many months back when he received O'Connell decorated in his treasonable colours. At the same time the Duke has shewn a forbearance and coolness which does him the greatest honour. I shall just write two lines to my brother to inform him I propose being in England about the 14th or 15th for in the present moment I feel my character requires this sacrifice of my comfort, only order *good fires* in my rooms. I shall naturally drive down to Windsor directly, and shall enquire if you are there.

1 *W.N.D.* v, 442–3. (14 January 1829.) On 2 February the Duke wrote again, to inform him that a Catholic Relief Bill was to be introduced into Parliament, and, too late, strongly urging him to postpone a visit to England until the Catholic question had been finally set at rest. "There is no doubt that you will be put forward [by the 'Protestants'] as a leader in the cause, and that you will be left there, to be responsible for all the consequences of the violence of others." (*Ibid.* v, 482–3.)

1556 The Duke of Wellington *to the* King

London, February 26th 1829.

I AM convinced that your Majesty will excuse my sending you the inclosed letter which shews the effect produced by unauthorized reports of your Majesty's sentiments and opinions.

This is a letter from a clergyman to Mr. Peel. He had offered to vote for him and he now declines to carry into execution what he offered to do for the reason stated in the second page of this letter; which is submitted to your Majesty by your Majesty's most dutiful and devoted subject and servant.[1]

[Enclosure]

1556A The Rev. W. Brownlow *to* Robert Peel

Craven Court, Feby 24th 1829.

I BEG you to accept my thanks for the civility and politeness of your reply to my letter. I seem however to have had the misfortune of making myself misunderstood and from ignorance troubled you with a letter when it should have been addressed to your committee. Having lent at all times my very humble support to Government I felt willing to do it on this occasion if it could be done without charge to myself, but I think it candid to state that the declaration of His Majesty which has appeared since the date of my letter and by which it appears his sentiments are at variance with those of his Ministers and that he considers the anti-Catholick side of the question to be the side of the Constitution has tended much to determine my own doubts on the subject and brought me to the resolution of giving my vote on this momentous occasion to Sir R. Inglis.

1557 The Duke of Wellington *to* Sir William Knighton

Windsor Castle, Feby. 26th 1829.

I INCLOSE a letter which I beg that you will give to the King as soon as H.M. will be awake.

The King will recollect that I advised the King not to allow the D. of Cumberland to come over. I now tell you that, if he stays, he will do

---

1 Peel felt that he could not retain his seat, now that he was committed to a policy, for his strenuous opposition to which, the University of Oxford had elected him its representative. He offered himself for re-election, but in spite of Whig support, he was defeated by the ultra Tory, Sir Robert Inglis.

much better to recommend to the King an Administration which will carry on His Majesty's affairs to his satisfaction. If this was done at once we would all take our stations in Parlt in a becoming manner, and the new Govt would have no difficulties to contend with arising out of the mode of its formation. If it is delayed we shall all be involved in discussions and I can see nothing before me but chaos.

1558 THE BISHOP OF WINCHESTER (DR C. R. SUMNER) *to the* KING

London, March 9th 1829.

I MUST begin this letter by throwing myself at your Majesty's feet, with feelings of the most devoted gratitude, as well as of the most affectionate attachment.

In acknowledging the gracious communication which your Majesty has condescended to make to me I shall not hesitate to state to your Majesty all that I feel and think on the subject in the most unreserved manner; well knowing that your Majesty's benevolent and exalted character will be pleased to approve the liberty I take in so doing.

I consider the proposed measure as one of *political expediency*; but it does not belong to me to discuss it in this point of view.

I also consider it a measure of *religious expediency*, because it is my firm belief that without an alteration of the existing laws the Irish branch of the united Church of Great Britain and Ireland cannot long stand.

I could not however consent to support the measure even on the ground of *religious* expediency if I believed that it tended to injure the Protestant, or strengthen the Roman Catholic religion.

If, for instance, it had been proposed, by the introduction of *vetos* and *Concordats*, to acknowledge an authority which ought not to have any power in a Protestant country I should have objected to the measure as inconsistent, in this respect, with Protestant principles. Or, had it been intended to incorporate the Roman Catholic religion with the State by paying its priesthood from the public purse, or by any other mode of national recognition, direct or indirect, as a conscientious Protestant I must have opposed a measure which would have incurred the guilt of countenancing and supporting a corrupt Church.

But, in the measure actually brought forward by your Majesty's Government I can see nothing which is at variance with the true principles of Protestantism, or which will take away one real bulwark from the Established Church.

On the contrary, I believe that the settlement of the question in the way proposed will remove the chief obstacle which now impedes the conversion of the great mass of all classes of the Irish people.

The disabling statutes have unquestionably tended to prevent Roman Catholics of rank and influence from opening their eyes to the errors of their Church by the dread of appearing to forsake what they consider a persecuted cause and a party in disgrace.

The same causes, operating in a different way, place the lower ranks in Ireland under a like disadvantage. Experience proves that there is little prospect of success, on any great scale, in promoting the education or diffusing Scriptural knowledge among the people while the present irritation between the two contending parties renders every agent of Protestant benevolence an object of suspicion, and makes it a very dangerous matter to incline to the Reformed Church. The projected measures will give, for the first time, fair play to the Protestant religion in Ireland, and I can trust to its truth for its extension.

I think, therefore, that in promoting an arrangement likely to diminish the number of opponents of the Reformed Church I am doing what is most likely, at the present day, to maintain the Protestant religion, as by law established, according to the true spirit and letter of your Majesty's Coronation oath.

Your Majesty will perceive that my opinion is so settled that this is a benefit to this Protestant Church, and especially to the Irish branch of it, that, if I vote at all, my conscience will not permit me to vote against the measure.

The question therefore is, whether, considering the high station in which your Majesty has been graciously pleased to place me in the Church, I shall do justice to myself if I give no vote on the introduction of this Bill into the House of Lords. If not to myself, it is impossible that I should do justice to your Majesty's selection. It cannot be concealed that if the Bishop of Winchester takes no part in so important a discussion, even by vote, the public must know that his private opinion favors it, but that the command of his Royal patron bids him be silent. This would be alike injurious to the honour of your Majesty and to this necessary measure of your Majesty's Government.

May I venture humbly to add that it would be destructive, in the judgment of the religious world, of my own character as a Christian Bishop.

Foreign Office, March 24, 1829.

LORD ABERDEEN presents his most humble duty to your Majesty and humbly begs to inform your Majesty that the conferences, having been brought to a conclusion, His Imperial Majesty the Emperor of Russia has consented to entrust the British and French Ambassadors with full powers to negociate on the part of the Alliance. It is proposed that the two plenipotentiaries should repair to Constantinople forthwith; but although a basis of negociation has been agreed upon, according to which a proposition for defining the limits of Greece is to be made to the Porte, Lord Aberdeen humbly begs to state to your Majesty that your Majesty's servants are of opinion that every endeavour should be used to restrict the extension of the proposed frontier. In this view there is good reason to believe that the Government of His Most Christian Majesty entirely concur; and that any apparent deviation from it at the present moment is to be ascribed to the force of circumstances of a temporary nature. In order however to do justice to this view of the case it is essentially necessary that the representative of your Majesty should be fully impressed with the necessity of supporting it; and should be prepared at the proper time to take that part in determining the conduct of the French plenipotentiary which will probably be required to obtain, and to preserve, his entire acquiescence.

Lord Aberdeen humbly begs to mention to your Majesty that, for some time, Mr. Stratford Canning has felt the difficulty of his situation in this respect. From his known opinions, and from the zeal with which he cooperated to extend the frontiers of Greece in the conference at Poros, he is sensible that he should be ill qualified to urge their future restriction, with effect, when at Constantinople. Lord Aberdeen humbly lays before your Majesty extracts of a letter which he has received from Mr. Stratford Canning and which will serve to explain his own feelings upon this subject.[1]

On the whole your Majesty's servants are humbly of opinion that, from the peculiar situation of Mr. Stratford Canning, and taking into consideration the feelings which he has expressed, the probable success of the future negociation at Constantinople would be greatly increased by its being placed in other hands. It is with every sentiment of respect for the distinguished ability and valuable services of Mr. Stratford Canning that Lord Aberdeen humbly ventures to lay this suggestion before your Majesty for your Majesty's gracious consideration.

1 The greater part of these extracts is in *W.N.D.* VI, 11.

General Statement of Works executed for HIS MAJESTY *by* RICHᴰ WESTMACOTT ESQ., *and Works in progress*; *with Payments on the same.* 28th March 1829

	£			£
			P. Contra	
1819 The Waterloo Vase	4,500	1823 July 9th	By Cash Sir Wm. Knighton Bart by the hands of the Rt. Honble. Sir	
Restoration of a Statue of Venus	150		Charles Long ...	1000
Paid Braithwaite[1] for Machinery	240 – 9	1825 March	By Cash Sir Wm. Knighton Bart	2000
		1826 Janry	By Do.	1500
		June	By Do.	1000
1824 Equestrian Statue of His late Majesty now nearly completed—with allowance for old metal	18,712	Novr.	By Do.	1000
		1827 April	By Do.	1000
		July	By Do.	1000
		1828 Jany.	By Do.	1000
		Febry.	By Do.	1000
		July	By Do.	1000
		1829 Janry	By Do.	1000
	23,602 – 9			£12,500

1561 THE DUKE OF WELLINGTON *to* SIR WILLIAM KNIGHTON

London, April 20th 1829.

YOU will have been anxious to know how matters have been going on since you left town.

I was not able to go to Windsor till Wednesday. The Duke of Cumberland had arrived on that morning at nine.

I saw H.M. who immediately approved and consented to what I proposed, viz the restoration of their offices to those who had resigned them. He was not in bad humour but cold and I did not remain with him more than half an hour. I asked him whether the Peers who had had audiences had declared their intention of supporting the Govt. He said they had not. That they talked of going to their homes and of endeavouring to reconcile their neighbours to the new order of things.

I saw Lady Conyngham who was very much alarmed at the prospect of having the D of Cumberland there so long. But she told me nothing excepting that the K. was more easy since he had given the Royal Assent

1 John Braithwaite (1797–1870), the engineer.

to the Bill. I have seen different persons since who have been there. The D. of Cumberland keeps the whole house in awe, particularly the lady. The King is very much annoyed at the sort of relation between her and his favourite brother. She appears to be in perpetual alarm lest he should say something to annoy her; and the King sees the whole. Under these circumstances they say that the residence at the Castle is not the pleasantest that could be found.

The papers say that the D. of C. returns tomorrow. I understand that Lady C. proposes to stay till the last moment. When I spoke to her about her return she talked of the beginning of the week.

We have done nothing yet about our new arrangements. I wait for a few days still. I have been confined to my house by a very bad cold. But I am now better and go into Hampshire tomorrow.

Present my comp[limen]ts to Lady Knighton and believe me my dear Sir William ever yours most sincerely.

1562 THE KING *to* SIR WILLIAM KNIGHTON

St. James's Palace, June 9th 1829.

Sʳ Wᴍ. KNIGHTON to explain my great anxiety, to have the Duke of Cambridge reside in England, on account of his son's education. This anxiety is encreas'd in consequence of George of Cumberland being prevented from receiving his education in this country. It may then be explain'd to the Duke of Cambridge, those views which I entertain respecting him, himself, & his family, & which I have communicated to Sʳ Wm. Knighton in the presence of the Duke of Wellington.[1]

The King to the Duke of Wellington, 14 June 1829. (*W.N.D.* v, 616.)
The Duke of Wellington to the King, 15 June 1829. (*W.N.D.* v, 617–18.)

1 The King seems to have wished the Duke of Cambridge to resign the Government of Hanover in favour of the Duke of Cumberland, and to have sent Knighton to Hanover to communicate with Adolphus on the subject. "People disapprove of it", Wellington wrote to Knighton on the 26th, "and view it very much as I do. In his conversation with you and me upon this subject, the King certainly adopted this principle, viz. that nothing should be done to induce the Duke of Cambridge to resign, or which could afford ground for him to think that he ought to resign, or for a report that he had been obliged to resign in order to avoid being turned out.... I cannot act in this affair in any other manner than that of which the principle was adopted in the conversation with the King above referred to; and that is, that the movement should originate with the Duke of Cambridge himself.... I have every reason to be certain that the arrangement will be very unpopular there [in Hanover]...." (*W.N.D.* v, 621–2.) On 24 July the Duke told Aberdeen that the King had heard that his brother did not intend to resign his Government of Hanover. (*W.N.D.* vi, 42.) Adolphus retained his position until 1837, when the Duke of Cumberland succeeded to the throne.

London, June 16th 1829.

I INCLOSE a letter from the King and my answer regarding making Nash a Baronet. I have received no reply.

I understand that if Mr. Edwards is not an attorney at present he was one; and that his son is one in partnership with the same person with whom the father was.

To create Nash a Baronet will be attended with the greatest inconvenience at present. There are at least one hundred pressing applications from gentlemen, many with hereditary claims from officers of the army and navy and others in the Civil Depts, all of whom would be offended by this preference of Mr. Nash. All this hostility which will thus be created against Nash will only increase the difficulties which the Govt must expect to meet with in all discussions respecting Buckingham House. The King is not aware of the position in which this Govt stands, and of that in which all Governments must stand in the existing state of Parties, and how much those difficulties are increased, particularly in reference to his own objects by measures such as this creation of Mr. Nash to be a Baronet, with remainder to his nephew.

The Duke of Wellington to Sir William Knighton, 18 June 1829. (*W.N.D.* v, 620–1.)

1564 THE DUKE OF WELLINGTON *to* SIR WILLIAM KNIGHTON

London, June 20th 1829.

I AM very anxious and shall be delighted to see you before you go to Windsor. I am going there on Monday to attend a Chapter of the Order of the Garter, and the Council[1] on the speech. When one goes to Windsor no person can answer for the hour of return. I therefore think that it will be best that I should call upon you at any hour that I return after nine and before twelve.

I will certainly return on that night even if I should be invited to stay for dinner; and if I should not be able to go to you, you might possibly call upon me at six in the morning before you go. I have latterly been in the habit of rising at six, and even if I should go to bed late I could receive you at that hour.

The Duke of Wellington to Sir William Knighton, 26 June 1829. (*W.N.D.* v, 621–2.)

1 The Cabinet Council, which met formally to approve the King's Speech delivered at the close of the Session, on the 24th.

Royal Lodge, July 9th 1829.

As the D— of C[umberland] writes himself to you to inform you of the difficulties which have befallen him and that will still for some time prevent him from leaving England, I shall only scribble a few hasty lines, especially as I am sorry to add that my unfortunate eyesight is grown so much more dim ever since your departure, that I can scarcely (writing as I am now doing by candlelight) see a single letter that my pen is tracing upon the paper. Anything that may tend to curtail your journey,[1] if it is a *matter* of pleasure to you, must naturally be, a *matter* of *regret* to me, but also the sooner I see you again the more I shall rejoice, both on *publick* grounds as well as *my private* affairs. My health will undoubtedly be a subject that you will be desirous of being well inform'd upon. Bodily I am passibly [*sic*] well, but alas! as to every other symptom you left me with I grieve to say that they have increas'd, are gradually increasing & day by day getting worse & worse; & above all my unfortunate sight. I am most anxious on *every account* to learn your success in the objects of your mission, all I am sure of is that if you are not completely so, the fault will not lay with you. There are a variety of political rumours & very unpleasant ones to me, floating abroad, & some I fear bear even upon the face of them but too much appearance of truth. You know how honorably & how fairly I have conducted myself to all parties; but notwithstanding all the warmth of friendly advice I have given, everything that passes under the eye of the public proves but too much & too sensibly that is entirely disregarded & completely without weight & therefore entirely cast aside....

1566 SIR WILLIAM KNIGHTON *to the* KING

Berlin, 18 July 1829.

I HAVE the honor to acquaint your Majesty, that I arrived here yesterday morning, & last evening the Duchess of Cumberland delivered to me your Majesty's most kind & gracious letter, for which I beg leave to offer my warmest & most grateful thanks.

Your Majesty may judge of my surprize, on learning from the Duchess, that she left this, for England, on Thursday next [*sic*]; Her

---

1 Knighton left London for the Continent on 24 June. (*Memoirs*, II, 65.)

Royal Highness proceeds by Dusseldorf & Calais; a route the most desirable as she avoids the Court of Weimar &c &c.

On my way to Hanover, on Monday last, just the other side of Eine-beck I fell in with the Duke of Cambridge & his whole family. The Langravine & her lady in the first carriage, the two children[1] & the tutor in the second, & finally the Duke & Duchess of Cambridge. The poor Princess Elizabeth, was very much overcome at thus unexpectedly meeting me.[2] It was settled that I should wait on Her Royal Highness the following morning, at Rothenkirchen, whither they were all proceeding. I therefore returned to Einebeck & proceeded early in the morning.

I had a long conversation with the Duke of Cambridge, previous & after I had seen Her Royal Highness the Landgravene.

I mentioned to the Duke, your Majesty's great anxiety, that his son should be educated in England; that it was very important that the Duke & Duchess should think earnestly on this, because that Prince George of Cambridge must always be a dependant Prince on England, but that Prince George of Cumberland was *otherwise circumstanced*, in consequence of his relation to Hanover. To this the Duke of Cambridge replied, "that it was very true, that it had been long his own feelings, that this late purchase of Cholmondley House, was with that object, & that your Majesty's wishes on this & every other occasion, would always be his; that the great object of his life always had been, & ever would be, to do his best to give your Majesty satisfaction, & by every action to show his real affection & attached feelings towards your Majesty". In saying this, his Royal Highness was greatly agitated, & added, that he had lately been unhappy from an apprehension that your Majesty was not satisfied with him. I desired His Royal Highness to put such a supposition, out of his head; that your Majesty was all affection & kindness towards him!

The Duke then went on to desire me to speak to the Duchess on the subject of Prince George's going to England. Her Royal Highness is, I understand, an excellent mother, & shed tears at the thoughts of being seperated from her son. In the progress of this detail of conversation I soon discovered, that the Duke of Cambridge *never* for *a moment contemplated the quitting Hanover*, unless he was desired to do so; & it consequently occurred to me, that it was much better to leave matters to

1 George and Augusta, the Duke's children. "The young Prince George", wrote Knighton in his Diary (14 July 1829), "seems just what a child should be." (*Memoirs*, II, 71.)

2 Her husband, the Landgrave of Hesse-Homburg, had died in April. Leaving no issue, he was succeeded by his brother Louis (1770–1839).

remain *thus*, for the present, because the discussion can at any moment be renewed by me, if it should be your Majesty's pleasure, I should do so, after your being in possession of the present state of things connected with the Duke of Cambridge's feelings. I did not think it right, for reasons which I will state to your Majesty, when I have the happiness of again throwing myself at your Majesty's feet, to pursue this matter further.

The Duke of Cambridge now intends to come over to England in April next, with the Duchess; in the meantime Cholmondley House will be clean'd & furnished. I have the greatest hopes & confidence in believing that your Majesty will be graciously pleased to approve of what I have done so far in this matter.

I now come to Her Royal Highness the Landgravine. Poor soul! it is impossible to describe her affectionate feelings towards your Majesty. She is certainly a *most sensible* excellent person; full of true integrity of heart, & devoted in the strongest manner towards your Majesty.

Her Royal Highness has entered into no *written* engagement with Rothchild; but she had pledged her honor, to her late husband, & this has been extended to the present Landgrave that she would contribute six thousand pr ann towards the interest of this loan. This leaves her eight thousand pr ann. for her own use. With this she can live comfortably & liberally at Hombourgh but not so in England. In short, I could plainly perceive, that her happiness is the cultivation of that feeling which so strongly marks attachment to her late husband. It is a curious circumstance that the very day she put on her mourning for the Landgrave, that day eleven years she was a bride. I had a long string of the most interesting conversation with Her Royal Highness which I shall reserve for your Majesty. The same thing I must do, with respect to the Duke of Brunswick. I spent half a day at Brunswick & picked up a good deal of information.

In consequence of your Majesty's letter there are many objects of my journey I shall entirely put aside, & proceed at once to Paris & England.[1]

With every sentiment of the *sincerest attachment* & *devotion*, I am [etc.].

The Duke of Wellington to Sir William Knighton, 14 August 1829. (*W.N.D.* VI, 85.)

1 He describes his journey home in his Diary. (*Memoirs*, II, 72–5.)

1567 CHARLES KEMBLE[1] *to* [?]

T.R. C[ovent] Garden, 14 September 1829.

HAVING understood that His Majesty does not approve of the present situation of his private box in Covent Garden Theatre I have been endeavouring to fit one up for him on a level with the Dress Circle. In a day or two I hope to have the pleasure of shewing it to you, if you would do me the honor of naming the hour when I may expect you at the Theatre.

1568 SIR WILLIAM KNIGHTON *to* [?]

15 September 1829.

HAVE the goodness to call on Mr. C. Kemble and beg him *not* to give himself any trouble respecting a box, for this year at least.

1569 FRANCIS LEGATT CHANTREY *to* SIR WILLIAM KNIGHTON

Belgrave Place, 6th Oct. 1829.

MR. CHANTREY presents his respects to Sir William Knighton and has the honour to send him the bust of His Majesty which was in the Exhibition last year and which is the one particularly named by Sir Charles Long.

Mr. Chantrey was anxious to have seen Sir William Knighton for the purpose of consulting with him on the propriety of placing a few words on the back of the bust to mark it as the one on which Mr. C. worked with more satisfaction to himself than can be expected he should feel in finishing those that have been done when he had not the means of correcting them from His Majesty and Mr. C. hopes that Sir William Knighton will accept this explanation as his apology for not having sent the bust sooner to Hanover Square where he called twice without having met Sir William at home.

The Duke of Wellington to Sir William Knighton, 10 November 1829. (*W.N.D.* VI, 293–4.)

1 The actor (1775–1854).

Paris, November 14th 1829.

LORD STEWART [*sic*] acquainted me this evening with some new practices resorted to by Harriet Wilson to extort money, & I am afraid I must conclude from the tone & manner of His Lordship's conversation that she has had some success with him. As I am so intimately concerned in much of the matter I hope I shall not be thought impertinent if I speak my sentiments upon it with all possible freedom. You are acquainted with the conduct I pursued when in the year 1825 or 6 she tried to intimidate those who she imagined would not resist, into a compliance with her demands. You know that I then gave formal (*I believe legal*) notice to Stockdale (her publisher) of my determination to prosecute him, both by way of indictment & of action, for a libel, & so as to wrest from him the pretence of being prevented by the technicallities of law from substantiating by proof the truth of the charges he might bring before the world against me. You will also recollect that whilst I was at Buenos Aires, & in consequence of being informed of the renewal of the woman's menaces, I wrote to you expressing my resolution to prosecute her or her publisher & strenuously objected to the practice of any *concession* to her *demands.* You will not therefore be surprized that I now feel the greatest pain from the suspicion I entertain that money may have been given to procure the silence of the calumniator, although solely given by Lord Steuart. To do so is not only wholly useless as a cure for the evil but it must encourage the woman's desire for plunder and shew her the certain means of gratifying it, and, what is worse, it places those who are innocent in the position of the guilty and gives the greatest possible facilities to the slanderer for throwing over her lies the colour of truth. I confess it galls me, it cuts me to the soul, to be obliged to submit to being defamed in such a manner and to be not only restricted from defending myself publickly, but further to be exposed to plausible suspicions that hush-money has been applied to silence my assailants.

Nothing but my entire respect for Lady Conyngham could force me

1 John, second Baron and first Viscount Ponsonby (? 1770–1855). He held many diplomatic appointments between 1826 and 1850. He was Envoy Extraordinary and Minister Plenipotentiary at Buenos Aires from September 1826 to July 1828. Harriette Wilson became his mistress in 1806 and the story of their intimacy is recounted at great length in her *Memoirs.* She alleged that he had been engaged to Lady Conyngham, and that he had broken the engagement a few days before the marriage was to have taken place, because his father withheld his consent. "She adored him beyond all that could be imagined of love and devotion....For many years her sufferings were severe; her parents trembled for her reason. No one was permitted to name her former lover in her presence." (*Memoirs,* I, 78.) Harriette Wilson evidently suppressed that portion of her Memoirs in which Lord Stuart figured: she merely referred to the fact that this "good-natured, obliging Ambassador" [at Paris, 1815–24, 1828–31] kindly forwarded her "valuable *Memoirs*" to Stockdale in London.

to abstain from instituting a prosecution against Mrs. Wilson for attempting by letters menacing to bring false & foul charges against me, to extort money from me to buy her silence, and I avow myself to be unable to comprehend why her Ladyship should submit, for one moment, to bear with the villainies of that woman. What can Lady Conyngham have to apprehend? She has her perfect innocence to support her, and, *if the accusations could be substantiated they go only to establish my infamy.* I alone could be branded.

I have said that my unbounded respect for what I conceive to be Lady Conyngham's wishes *has* power to prevent me from prosecuting Mrs. Wilson for her threatenings &c. &c. &c. but I must guard against being understood to consent to remain passive if those threatenings shall be carried into execution by her or by her agents. The contrary is the fact and I have prepared everything & directed Counsel to be retained for prosecution in that case. If innocent people shrink from facing slanderers they will never enjoy tranquillity and the morbid delicacy that induces them to do so will be the chief instrument in the hands of their persecutors wherewith to inflict renewed pains and deeper sufferings. I cannot conceive any case in which it can be necessary or wise to act so. My grief and indignation at being made the *means* by which this abandoned woman is able in her pursuit of gain to lacerate the feelings of a person whom I have known so well, and known only to respect the more, the more I did know her, is almost beyond my powers of endurance.[1]

I have the honor to be, [etc.].

P.S. It may be advisable to mention that amongst the preparations made for a prosecution, and which are now in the hands of my attorney, there is a letter from Harriet Wilson to me in which she admits the injustice of what she had alledged against me and expresses her sorrow for what she had done.

1 Greville wrote on 31 July 1831: "Not very long after [1823] Canning got into favour, and in this way:—Harriet Wilson at the time of her connexion with Lord Ponsonby got hold of some of Lady Conyngham's letters to him, and she wrote to Ponsonby, threatening, unless he gave her a large sum, to come to England and publish everything she could. This produced dismay among all the parties, and they wanted to get Ponsonby away and to silence the woman. In this dilemma Knighton advised the King to have recourse to Canning, who saw the opening to favour, jumped at it, and instantly offered to provide for Ponsonby and do anything which could relieve the King from trouble. Ponsonby was sent to Buenos Aires forthwith, and the letters were bought up. From this time Canning grew in favour, and shortly gained complete ascendancy over the King." Canning, however, had won over the King to his side as early as April 1825; Ponsonby's appointment to Buenos Aires was settled seven months later.

1571 John Wilson Croker *to* Sir William Knighton

Admy. 17th Novr. 1829.

I am amusing myself, and hope to amuse others, with a new edition of Boswell's life of Doctor Johnson. Among the hints which I have received for my work a learned gentleman acquaints me that there is in that portion of the late King's library, which His Majesty has reserved, a M.S. common place book of Doctor Johnson's.

Do you think that I might venture to solicit a sight of this book? His late Majesty condescended to afford Mr. Boswell some information for the first edition: perhaps His present Majesty may be equally gracious towards *me*.

If you think so, and that you can find a fit occasion of laying my grateful duty and humble request at His Majesty's feet, you will confer an additional obligation on [etc.].

1572 The King *to* Sir William Knighton

W^r C^{tle}, Sat^y n^t ½ pt 11.
Decr 26th 1829.

Though blind as a beetle I endeavour to scribble a few lines. The enclos'd will speak volumes for itself, & therefore renders it unnecessary for me to say a word upon the subject till I see you. All at present is buried in my own breast & *communicated alone* to you. The consequent distress & agitation of my mind, as to how I am, & how I ought to proceed & to act under all the existing circumstances, wh are well known to you, you may easily imagine. Not a word shall transpire from me, until I see you which I hope will *be at latest*, at a *very early hour on Tuesday morning*, when we will concert the best & most eligible mode of proceeding. My main object is to arrange everything with you, & to ensure quiet & comfort, before any alarm however absurd can be given rise to, from any cause, but most especially before either any vague report, or article copied from the foreign papers, may reach us here. When you come you can easily state that you had [been] *unexpectedly* call'd up to London, upon some important Duchy business, which indispensibly requir'd your presence there on Wednesday, & that as that was the case, your *natural* feelings had render'd unavoidable for you, not to take Windsor in your way, to satisfy yourself that *all was well*. Thank God, we do continue so at present, & therefore you will easily conceive *my dread*, that any thing should occur, that might, (or indeed that I think would at least risk, if not inevitably overthrow) interfere with our at present bless'd prospects of tranquillity. I have also one or two other

[467]

matters, of less importance which I should like to talk over with you. God bless you.

Robert Peel to Sir William Knighton, 8 January 1830. (*Knighton*, II, 94–5.)

1573 THE KING *to the* DUKE OF WELLINGTON

Copy.

Windsor Castle, Jany. 19th 1830.

THE KING cannot but *deeply regret* the selection made by France and Russia of Prince Leopold as the Prince to be placed at the head of the Greek Kingdom.

Without entering into a detail of reasoning, the King considers Prince Leopold *not qualified* for this peculiar station.

Nevertheless the two Great Powers, France and Russia, having conjointly named Prince Leopold to be placed at the head of the Greek Kingdom, the King, in deference to the desire of the two Great Powers, gives his assent.

The Earl of Mountcharles to the Duke of Wellington, 24 January 1830. (*W.N.D.* VI, 436.)
The Duke of Wellington to the King, 25 January 1830. (*W.N.D.* VI, 439–40.)

1574 SIR WILLIAM KNIGHTON'S *Diary*

1st February 1830.

I SAW the Duke of Wellington at half past nine in the morning; he had recommended Mr. Jelf as canon of Ch: Ch: in the room of Dr. Hay. The Arch-Bishop of Canterbury recommended Dr. Bull (Howley the Arch-Bishop) having advised Archdeacon Cambridge to advise Jelf to apply for a canon of Ch: Ch: But this Howley did when he was Bishop of London. The Duke of W. had written a letter[1] to the King complaining of the misconduct of the Duke of Cumberland towards the Govt. That his Grace did not complain of a fair opposition—but H.R.Hss's was unfair, inasmuch as he misrepresented facts to His Majesty & told stories of the Governmt that were untrue. The Times newspaper abuses the King for not paying the Duke of York's debts; H.R.Hss says, that the Times is the Duke of Wellington's paper. This is a lie! This one instance out of many.[2]

1 *W.N.D.* VI, 455–6 (30 January 1830). The Duke of Cumberland had been in opposition to the Government since the passing of the Catholic Relief Act.
2 Portions of Knighton's Diary are printed in his *Memoirs*, II, 101–4. The first extract, there undated, was written on 2 February.
p. 101. After "literature" *add* "among books".
p. 101. Last line, for "hope" *read* "I have promised".

4th February 1830.

I SAW the Duke of Wellington this morning, he stated to me that the interview between the King & himself went off satisfactorily. H.M. wanted to make an alteration in the speech relative to the Greek question; in which the King wished to imply that what had been proposed he had consented to the introduction of making himself a mere cypher.[1]

The Duke very properly put this aside. His Grace then told me of a long conversation that he had yesterday with Prince Leopold.[2] This Prince has been in the hands of Huskisson who urged him to insist upon Candia—if he took possession of the Greek Government. Now this is inadmissible—inasmuch as it is the key to the Dardanelles; this may be known by reading Lord Collingwood's[3] correspondence published with his life—ergo—if Turkey is to be preserved as a Kingdom—Turkey must keep possession of it. His Grace then told Leopold, that he, as a Prince, was fix'd upon because it was a convenient political measure on account of his fifty thousand pr ann. & not for any other consideration. I think, said the Duke, you are foolish to go—but if you do so—you cannot have Candia. Get out of the country however, as fast as you can, to avoid intrigue & the deterioration of character which may be sure to take place, if you attach yourself to the influence of any Party; all men are sure to suffer, in public stations, from Party men—if they have the opportunity of fixing any thing to you. This is so true—that it really needs no illustration. Nothing in my opinion can be more contemptable than a politician; he dies & is immediately forgotten; such is the fate of Tierney who died some days ago. That man will not be remembered a week hence—& ought not....

1 The King's Speech at the opening of the Session on the 4th declared that "His Majesty has seen with satisfaction that the war between Russia and the Ottoman Porte has been brought to a conclusion. The efforts of His Majesty to accomplish the main objects of the Treaty of the 6th July 1827 have been unremitted. His Majesty, having recently concerted with his Allies measures for the pacification and final settlement of Greece, trusts that he shall be enabled, at an early period, to communicate to you the particulars of this arrangement, with such information as may explain the course which His Majesty has pursued throughout the progress of these important transactions".

2 Prince Leopold accepted nomination as Sovereign Prince of the new Greek State, but three months later, in May 1830, he resigned his claims.

3 Cuthbert Collingwood, first Baron Collingwood (1750–1810). Fought at Cape St Vincent and Trafalgar. Vice-Admiral, 1804.

6th February 1830.

I this day went down to Windsor for the purpose of having some communication with His Majesty on the subject of my visit to Dusseldorf to meet Lord Albert Conyngham.[1] The King seemed embarrass'd at the thoughts of my absence, not from any feelings towards myself, I am satisfied, but from the contention H.M. would have with Lady C. Under these circumstances I put the intention aside. I dined there. The King talk'd to me because he was opposite—but at night on his going to bed there was no desire to talk to me in preference to his eating his supper, which used to be the case when under the influence of his love concern. Lady C. has received a present of a handsome bracelet from Mr. Musgrave in return for her good offices for a living & a canonry of Windsor. Whether she received this gift I do not know, but she consulted Sir H. Taylor about it—*not me*!

> The Duke of Wellington to the King, 7 February 1830. (*W.N.D.* vi, 470.)
> The Duke of Wellington to the King, 8 February 1830. (*W.N.D.* vi, 471–2.)

8th February 1830.

An account of the melancholy catastrophe of Lord Graves having cut his throat.[2] The town was in an uproar. I do not believe that immediate jealousy made him commit the act but I believe the previous anxiety of this affair so enfeebled his mind that any previous thought brought back to his mind through the vile agency of the Press & caricatures made his feelings so intense, that a delirium, although momentary, overpowered his better judgment. Graves had a mind stuft full of the vice of conversation & few men had dipped deeper into the scenes (in early life) of immorality. One of his accomplishments was to recall them at the King's table.[3]

1 See No. 1493. The King, said Lord Aberdeen, the Foreign Secretary, in July 1829, "is very desirous for Lord Albert to go to Berlin as Secretary of Legation, in order that he may be with [Sir Brook] Taylor. He pressed this very strongly; and as Lord Albert has been Secretary of Legation at Florence for a year and a half, he may be moved without any impropriety." (*W.N.D.* vi, 13.) He was Secretary of Legation at Berlin, 1829–31.

2 Because of his wife's alleged infidelity. She was Lord Anglesey's sister, and had been separated from her husband for some time. "The King is horribly annoyed about the story which has come out of the Duke of Cumberland and Lady Graves", wrote Greville on 22 January. "They have been detected by Graves in an amour at the house of old Lady Lansdowne at Hampton Court...." (*Greville Diary* [1927], i, 93.) See Appendix, p. 505.

3 He was a Lord of the Bedchamber from 1813 to 1827.

Tuesday. [9th February 1830.] I went down to Windsor for the express purpose of recommending the King, if possible, to avoid seeing the Duke of Cumberland. Whatever might be his innocence as to intrigue with Lady Graves the public were in a state of mind not to believe it. The King, by seeing much of him would involve himself without doing any real benefit to the character of his brother. I succeeded in convincing the King that I was right, but only through the agency of the Duchess of Gloucester. The King did not seem in a very clear state of understanding. I left Windsor about 4 o'clock & returned to town.

Wednesday 10. I should have mentioned that in coming into town I call'd on the Duke of Wellington—he seem'd pleas'd that Genl. King[1] was dismissed the Household for not voting with the Governmt. The Duke is selfish & cares at this moment only that he may have the power of cooping [*sic*] with his political enemies. The Duke has strong sense, great resolution, but being wrong he has no power of setting himself right either from the advice of friends or the contemplation of his own reflections. In this respect he is Irish. There is much to admire in him, but a good deal to wish different. I mean as a Governor of a Kingdom. He has no humanity—no knowledge or power of judging that a man should be rewarded for civil service.

1578 SIR WILLIAM KNIGHTON's *Diary*

20th February 1830.[2]

Saturday 20. Went early in the morning to Windsor. The King was [not] particularly glad to see me. H.M. enquired for my daughter;[3] complained of his health. [It seem'd to me to depend on drink.] There
~~which was expressed also~~[4]
was great irritability in his frame—[& mark'd also very strongly] in his manner. [I conjecture that his heart is enlarged; much loaded with fat & that His Majesty's death will be sudden. He seem'd to think that the

---

1 Major-General Sir Henry King (d. 1839), fourth son of the second Earl of Kingston. He voted against the Government on 4 February, and the appointment of his successor as a Groom of the Bedchamber was gazetted on the 15th. See *W.N.D.* VI, 470, where the name is suppressed. "Others of your Majesty's Household in both Houses were absent."

2 This entry is printed in his *Memoirs*, II, 103–4, but, as it varies very considerably from the MS. at Windsor, part of the latter is worth printing. The words in square brackets are omitted in the published version which is wrongly dated "Friday, 19th". Knighton wrote nothing on the 19th.

3 Dorothea, who in 1829 married Captain Michael Seymour, son of Sir Michael Seymour.

4 The printed version.

Duke of Wellington was disposed to do nothing civil by him; complained that no communication had been made to him respecting the savings in the army. This however was all a mistake. I this day saw the Dss of Gloucester—spoke of the Duke of C[umberlan]d & wish'd him away. Discovered Watson not to be depended upon either from cunning or mistake. Perhaps both. Lord Conyngham friendly—her Ladyship much as usual. I] returned to town [at night]....

Sunday 21. Saw the Duke of Wellington in the morning—no particular political conversation. Talked of the state of the country—which he thinks suffering from every man's wishing to acquire capital—or in other words a great desire to save money. I afterw^{ds} saw the Chancellor —who look'd nervous & anxious—no cause explained....

1579 ROBERT PEEL *to the* KING

Whitehall, Feby. 23 [1830].
Tuesday night.

MR. PEEL presents his humble duty to your Majesty and begs leave to acquaint your Majesty that the House of Commons has been occupied this evening on a motion made by Lord John Russell to give representatives in Parliament to the towns of Manchester, Birmingham and Leeds.

The motion was supported by Lord John Russell, Mr. Huskisson, Lord William Powlett,[1] Dr. Lushington, Lord Morpeth and Mr. Brougham, and opposed by Mr. Twiss,[2] Mr. Charles Wynn, Lord Valetort,[3] Sir George Murray[4] and Mr. Peel.

On a division there were for the motion 140
Against it 188
majority 48

Sir Edward Knatchbull and a great majority of those members who usually act with him[5] left the House without voting.

1 William John Frederick Powlett, second son of the third Earl of Darlington (first Duke of Cleveland). He assumed the surname of Powlett in lieu of his patronymic, Vane. Originally a member of the Whig party, he went over to the Government with his father at the beginning of 1830, and voted against his former friends in the division on 15 November which decided the fate of the Wellington Ministry.

2 Horace Twiss (1787–1849), Under-Secretary for War and the Colonies, 1828–30; biographer of Lord Eldon.

3 Ernest Augustus Edgcumbe, Viscount Valletort (1797–1861); succeeded his father as third Earl of Mount Edgcumbe, 1839.

4 [1772–1846.] Succeeded Huskisson as Secretary of State for War and the Colonies, June 1828.

5 The Ultra Tories, who had been in opposition since the Government's surrender on the Catholic question.

Foreign Office, March 3 1830.

PRINCE LEOPOLD has informed me that it is his intention to leave England in the course of next week. He is naturally very desirous of an audience before his departure. Would you have the kindness to ascertain when it would suit His Majesty's convenience to receive him? You will oblige me also if you will let me know if I should attend, and in what manner.

I believe that Prince Leopold is going for a couple of months to Germany, and that he returns to England in May, for the purpose of taking his final departure in the course of that month. Upon this subject however he has not communicated his intentions to me.

1581 THE DUKE OF CLARENCE *to* SIR WILLIAM KNIGHTON

Bushy House, March 27th 1830.
Half past eight p.m.

YOURS of this morning from Windsor Castle has just reached me and I must begin by stating that not having a key I was under the necessity of breaking the lock which I have stated to the individual by the name of Baker who signed the order for the orderly to bring the bag to me from Pall Mall.

Certainly the season has been as extraordinary as severe and may therefore account for the embarrassment in the King's system not declaring itself at once to be gout. I shall be anxious to hear the sentiments of Sir Henry Halford.

I was astonished to see in the papers of this morning that the Duke of Cumberland had been yesterday morning by *nine* at Windsor and your account of *the* interview I am sure is correct and indeed stands to reason with any one that has common sense or with a person that would give himself the trouble to think for a moment when a visit is paid to one who is indisposed. However the conduct of the Duke of Cumberland is different from that of any one else whether to others or what concerns himself.

I trust your next account respecting the King will be such as you may wish to write. In the mean time I must be desirous of being informed how His Majesty finds himself and I leave entirely in your hands the propriety of delivering any message from me because I confide in your sound judgment as to the proper moment to make known to the King the anxious and sincere wish I must and do entertain to see him quite well and able to receive the world at the Levée and Drawing Room.

Robert Peel to the King, 13 April 1830. (*Parker*, II, 148; *W.N.D.* VI, 565.)

1582 THE DUKE OF CAMBRIDGE *to the* KING

Hanover, April 23d. 1830.

THOUGH this is not your birthday I can not let this day pass without writing you a few lines to assure you of the fervent prayers which I offer up to Heaven in conjunction with every one of your Hanoverian subjects for your welfare and happiness. Believe me, these are the sentiments of every one here, and I will answer for it that not even in England will this day be celebrated with more loyalty than here.

I feel particular satisfaction at the mail going out today, as it enables me to inform you, my dearest brother, of what I know will give you pleasure; that we have decided that our dear boy is to go to England this year for his education, and to request you will give me leave to bring him over myself in the course of the summer.

Dear William has been so kind as to say that he would receive him willingly under his roof, and my intention is to settle him at Bushy as soon as I return to the Continent.

Painful as the separation will be to the Duchess who is so excellent a mother, her mind is now relieved from the anxiety she felt at the idea of dear George not being under the same roof with some one of the family; and she now feels comfortable at the thought that he will be in perfect safe hands when he leaves us.

Knowing the kind interest you take, my dearest brother about our dear boy, and your wish that he should be educated in England, I have taken the earliest opportunity of informing you of our plan, which, I feel confident you will approve of.

I dare not trespass any longer on your patience, and therefore take my leave with the assurance of my ever remaining [etc.].

London, May 4th 1830.

You will have seen the Bishop of Chichester[1] this morning; who will have told you that I should be at Windsor tomorrow.

You will have seen that Goldburne [*sic*] was last night obliged to withdraw the vote for Windsor Castle. The question is a bad one. We are in the wrong for bringing forward for the third or fourth time a vote for a fresh grant without an estimate of the whole expence.[2] Then the King's tenacity upon the Carlton Garden passage, and the state of H.M.'s health added to the general state of the Govt. in consequence of the manœuvres of the King's brother[3] through the last summer and autumn rendered it impossible to risk this vote without previously ascertaining the total expence to be incurred; and laying open the whole case.

I inclose the note which Goldburne wrote me last night after the H. of Commons.

London, May 9, 1830.

I EARNESTLY recommend that Sir Henry Halford and Sir Matthew Tierney should see none of the noblemen and gentlemen who visit Windsor to enquire for H.M. One did I know at a dinner on Saturday report from one of these interviews and his enquiries what I did not understand to be true when I was there; and was certainly inconsistent with the official report in the bulletin.

1 Dr Carr attended the King during his last illness. (*Knighton*, II, 142–3.)

2 The original estimate of the expenses of the alterations and improvements of the Castle had been £300,000, but the expenditure had grown to £800,000 by 1828 and a further sum of £100,000 was now proposed. Goulburn agreed to have the vote referred to a committee of inquiry for the purpose of ascertaining what might be the ultimate expense necessary for the completion of the work. "He did so, he confessed, with considerable pain, but under the conviction that, at the present moment, he was taking that course which was best calculated to prevent a most painful discussion."

3 For the Duke of Cumberland's intrigues against the Government, see *W.N.D.* VI, 6, 36, 182, 323, 371, 455, 530, 533.

Hanover, May 18th 1830.

I HAVE many many thanks to return you for your three letters of the 1st 4th and 7th instant the two last of which I received on Sunday and yesterday.

The accounts of our beloved King are, I am grieved to find, no better; and though I am most anxious to put every confidence in the strength of his constitution, yet my dear Sr William at his age, and after many severe illnesses he has had, it is impossible for me not to see very black, and I can not deny to you that I do despair of his recovery.

No words can express how much I was affected by his very kind and gracious message which you communicated to me in your letter of the 4th. I entreat you if you can find an opportunity, to say how deeply I feel his goodness to me at all times, and how delighted I am at his approving of my dear boy being under the Duke of Clarence's charge; and that my most fervent prayers were offered up to Heaven that I may find him perfectly recovered on my arrival in England in August.

I have been rather puzzled by a passage in a letter of the 6th instant of the Duke of Cumberland, who after giving me an account of the dear King and stating that he had left him the day before in a less suffering state, adds "but with all this I think it will be a great relief to your mind to see him, as he told me he thinks you will set out directly upon getting Knighton's letter".

You know my affection for the King and therefore you will easily believe, that if I had the slightest idea that my going to England would be any comfort to my dear suffering brother I would travel night and day with the greatest pleasure: but as he has neither sent me a message through you nor through the Duchess of Gloucester I own I fear that my going immediately to England after having obtained his leave to go there at the end of July or beginning of August, might alarm him and then my visit would do more harm than good. I therefore have determined not to move from hence, and to wait till I hear from you, my dear Sr. William, what I had best do.[1]

1 Part of this letter is in *Knighton*, II, 134; also the postscript, dated the 20th.

1586 Sir F. Legatt Chantrey's *Receipt*

Received the 24th of August 1830, of his Grace the Duke of Wellington and Sir William Knighton Bart, executors of His Majesty King George the Fourth, deceased, the sum of one thousand pounds, being a further payment on account of the statue of His said late Majesty, whereof one thousand pounds more remain to be paid.

F. Chantrey

£1000.

1587 Richard Westmacott *to* Sir William Knighton

S. Audley St., Sep. 22, 1830.

Under very pressing circumstances I take the liberty of requesting yourself and the exors of His late Majesty will oblige me by a further payment on the equestrian statue.

The work was completed and ready for erection agreeable to His Majesty's commands and my promise but the position being changed and the granite not ready to receive the statue it still remains at my foundry.

You would oblige me exceedingly by complying with my request as the only fund I could now resort is India stock and by deducting from it I should lose my privilege of voting.

1588 Sir William Knighton's *Diary*

5th November 1830[1]

[I will endeavour to put down in detached bits all the occurrences that have happened during my residence or indeed my first acquaintance with His late Majesty George IV.]

My [first] acquaintance with His late Majesty ~~George the Fourth~~ began ~~thus~~ when H.M. was Regent[2]—after my return from Spain with Lord Wellesley. This must have been in the year [1811. Blank in M.S.].[3]

The Prince [Regent] had a lameness in his hand, arising [either] from an accident [that happened] in going to Oatlands, [or from the use of

1 The first part of this Memorandum, as far as "progress at court", is in *Knighton*, ii, 184–6, but I have reproduced it to show how prudential considerations affected the editing of Knighton's papers. Passages enclosed in square brackets are omitted from *Knighton*; passages scored out are in *Knighton* but not in the MS.

2 [Knighton's Note]: "This is a mistake. His Majesty was not Regent when I first knew him. He was then Prince of Wales."

3 There are some unimportant differences here between the MS. and the printed version.

laudanum or from his early habits of free living.] then the Duke of York's.
Lord Wellesley recommended the Prince to see me. I saw His Royal
Highness once; but as he was under the care [being in the hands] of
Home,[1] Cline,[2] and Sir Walter Farquhar, I had of course no opportunity
of recommending anything; and indeed if [had] I had [the opportunity]
I should have found myself without a remedy for his complaint.

When I entered the [his bed]room, I knelt down and kissed his hand.
Sir Thomas Tyrwhitt was in the room, but did not remain a minute.

It struck me then that the Prince was very intelligent, with a mind easily
roused to suspicion, [proud and overbearing,] but with a most fascinating
complacency of manner. [His skin appeared to me almost copper colour,
by which I mean a thick dusky hue. This I put down, in my own thoughts,
to the excessive free living of his early years. I was with him not more
than twenty minutes.] He inquired if I had been with Lord Wellesley in
India;[3] to which I replied no. I understood the praise bestowed on me
on this occasion by His Royal Highness was, that I was the best-
mannered medical man he had ever seen. This was told me [afterwards]
by Sir Walter [Farquhar]; and, being [he of course for the sake of
talking made known this which] made known did me no good, as it
[only] excited the jealousy of my medical brethren, who already supposed that my practice was beyond my deserts, and that at any rate it
came [in] too rapidly.

I saw no more of the Prince untill I was made his physician in ordinary
in the year 1818, when I [went to Court and][4] was presented. [H.R.H. was
then Regent][4] The Prince was then civil, spoke to me, and inquired for
Lord Wellesley. The second time I went, he said nothing, [scarcely
spoke] and his countenance betrayed displeasure. This I afterwards
found, arose from his having been [being] informed that I had spoken
offensively of him in regard to his conduct respecting the Princess of
Wales. This was a falsehood [lie], and, of course, carried to him [by
some one who was anxious] to stop my progress at Court.

Sometime afterwards when I was made a Baronet another story was
carried to him that I took part with Leigh Hunt the editor and writer of
the Examiner, who had been convicted of a libel on the P.R. This was
equally a lie, and I was enabled to give assurances of my conduct to the
contrary, by having refused to meet the Surrey Magistrates in the prison
in which Hunt was confined for the purpose of affording him more com-

---

1 Sir Everard Home.
2 Henry Cline (1750–1827), surgeon.
3 *Sic* in the MS. The printed version is "in India with Lord Wellesley".
4 These passages are scored out in the MS.

fort. I refused this because I was one of the physicians of the P.R. in ordinary and I thought it would be going out of my way in an offensive manner to lend myself to any proceedings of the kind. Perhaps I was personally wrong on the score of humanity, but a friend of mine Dr. Gooch went and did what was necessary in a medical point of view. During this period of my being made known to the P. [of] W.—or indeed at the time, I became personally acquainted with Col. McMahon and his wife,—their great object was then to be thought favorably of by Lord W. who being in power as Foreign Secretary of State, McMahon calculated upon some place or appointment—the P. [of] W. not having yet come to the Regency. McMahon was a thorough Irishman, a good heart, full of plausible professions, sensible and much more right headed than Irishmen generally are. He wrote well although his education had been of no regular kind.—His acquaintance was general—his manner conveyed to you that of friendship—he was a complete courtier. I have a great personal regard for him. It is a curious fact that when McMahon resigned he thought me better qualified to fill the station than anyone else then about his person. For some years after my appointment to the P.W., both as P. and P.Rt. I saw nothing of him, as his physician—Sir Henry Halford and Tierney were employed on all occasions—the former from the influence of the Princesses, the latter from that of Bloomfield, but I saw Col McMahon constantly both as his friend and physician. Upon one occasion McMahon was suddenly seized with a violent vomiting and faintness at Carlton House. This was when the Prince was Regent. I was immediately sent for as was Sir Walter Farquhar. The Regent was about to go to Brocket Hall to Lord Melborne's to dinner. He was long delayed. I then observed his manner to Bloomfield which was quite that of a master to an upper servant. I was ordered to write the next morning to give an account of McMahon's health. I did not do so but I left it to Blane[1] to write, upon which Dupasquier, the King's valet, observed that the P.Rt. desired me to communicate with him. In the hurry of McMahon's sudden seizure Mrs. McMahon arrived. I believe she had jumped out of the back window into the yard to get into Carlton House in order to avoid passing through the street. On her arrival H.R.Hss. immediately sent for sherry of which he made her drink a large glass. Mrs. McMahon was an ill educated woman. She had but two objects, that of making money and the adoration of her husband. She was impetuous—very violent in her temper—very jealous of McMahon and easily excited in all that related to him. She received all sorts of people, high and low. They all came to see her for places—some

1 Sir Gilbert Blane (1749–1834), the King's physician.

to solicit for bribes, some to offer her situations looking forward to some benefit for themselves in the form of title or the distinction of being noticed by the P.Rt. in some shape or other. I have often smiled at the adulation that was paid to this poor woman. McMahon was kind to all the servants and they were all ready to do their utmost to serve him. A strange fatality happened to this poor woman. She was suddenly seized at Bristol with an inflam[matio]n of her bowels and died in three days. There she was buried. She made a Will and left her savings to her husband which amounted to a large sum. This McMahon was much astonished at and knew not that she was possessed of anything untill after her death. I suspect that she was presented with slices of loans from Angerstein[1] and others at different times. This will explain everything and show the legitimacy of the transaction. It is a curious fact that no man is permitted in public opinion to have any right to wealth who happens to be engaged in public employment or placed under the influence of any Royal individual whom he may serve—whereas the loan contractor goes into the House of Commons, votes in favor of grants of the public money—gains his large or princely profits—without the slightest observation of anything derogatory to industry or the proper endeavors of a man who has done well for his family. This is no doubt the principle of justice and so is the other, for no man who has intellect but what should employ himself as it seems best and honest to guard his family against the misery of poverty. McMahon after the death of his wife exposed himself to all that wretchedness which the excess of drinking naturally induces. By degrees his mind became enfeebled untill at length it was absolutely necessary to make known the infirmities that were fast overtaking him to the P.Rt. I was called upon to undertake this errand and by a communication of Mr. now Sir F. Watson H.R.Hss. the P.Rgt. desired to see me. This brought me into confidential intercourse with the Regent. I found the Rgt. quick and intelligent, fond of hearing himself talk however, but with a thorough knowledge of human nature. I soon perceived that he cared but little respecting McMahon but he was uneasy at McMahon's situation lest there should be a disclosure of secrets which must of course have been reposed in him during so many years of confidential agency. I was therefore made the instrument to advise his resignation. I soon discovered also that Bloomfield was intended to fill his situation. B. was at this time the confidant of the P.Rt. and Lady Hertford and consequently was selected for this particular office, so necessary to the comfort and convenience of the P.Rt.

1 John Julius Angerstein (1735–1823), merchant and art collector. He retired from "the City" in 1811.

McMahon's health became so broken and his mind so shattered that he did all sorts of imprudent things. Amongst others he took a cottage in the neighbourhood of Blackheath which he called Cottage Institute. Here entered Mrs. H. Johnston and a Mrs. (I think) Frenwick at the same time. I had no great difficulty in persuading him to resign but the P.Rt. was desirous that I should prevail upon him to name his successor which the Rt. was anxious should be Bloomfield. This I also effected. My having the power to bring all this about so agreeably to the P.Rt's wishes made H.R.Hss. think and express himself very highly towards me, and from this moment I date his intention of having me constantly about him as soon as the opportunity should offer. All this took place in the summer of 18—[blank] and this year I went into Devonshire to pay a visit to my beloved mother whom I saw for the last time. Whilst I was at Salcombe an express reached me that poor McMahon was dead. It was agreed on my quitting London that he should proceed by slow journies to the Lands End, accompanied by a very faithful person of the name of Jutsham, one of the Regent's establishment. He just lived to reach Bath and there died and was buried at (I think) Clifton by the side of his wife. Thus ended the life of one who had for years been the confidant of the Prince that was to become the future King of these dominions. We have followed him through all his follies and licentiousness, through all his pleasures legitimate and illegitimate.

When McMahon was in the Prince's house (Carlton House) for the last time he waited two hours to take leave of his Prince but he did not see him. McMahon felt this very much but it probably arose on the part of the Prince from the pain such a meeting would have given him. I put this version on it at the time. I hope I was right. Nevertheless my experience of that class of life since, makes me feel, I know, that there is no affection, no friendship, but what is blended with hypocrisy; all their actions have their origin in selfishness. They scarcely ever seperate this from what they do or what they do not do. The love of self is always predominant. It is curious to observe how easily habit gets rid of principle untill at length the non-observance of this necessary Christian quality is so entirely seperated from what is called the man of the world, that in his conduct no trace of it is to be found. McMahon, although a great courtier, was an honest man and very sincere in his friendships. His great fault was a desire to please everybody without any enquiry into the merits of individuals. Hence he became embarrassed by the tricks and arts of wretches of the lowest description, more especially by that class of scoundrels connected with the daily Press, than whom there cannot exist a more despicable set of men. How marvellous, after a few years, appears the quickness of time. The past, the present, and the future are so near each other that one has scarcely the leisure or the opportunity to distinguish them. The year has but just begun its course when we are reminded of its end.

Upon receiving the news of McMahon's death I proceeded to Bath, took his Will and brought [it] to London. I saw the P.Rt. immediately in his bed; I was now beginning to be made his confidential friend in all those secret concerns which a life of pleasure and sensuality had exposed him to. McMahon's papers consisted principally of letters written to him by the Prince of Wales for a series of years, as well as those written by McMahon during this time. How those got back into his possession I know not, but they were all destroyed by the Regent himself as the trunks were examined. Amongst McMahon's papers were letters of Mrs. Fitzherbert's. The P.Rt. was anxious to retain those with a view of getting back those still in her possession, but she was too artful to comply with this proposition and so trumped up a story, in which the Duke of York joined her, that I had kept back those letters of hers to McMahon, when I had done no such thing. I went to Mrs. Errington[1] near Andover to make the proposition about this reciprocal interchange by the P.Rt's desire, but I had no other motive or interest in the affair. This Mrs. Fitzherbert is an artful, cunning, designing woman, very selfish, with a temper of the worst description and a mind entirely under the influence of Popish superstition. She is a woman never to be understood, but in all her actions self only predominates. I have seen her once and found her just as the late King George 4th. described her to me. He himself had a horror of her. In speaking of the subject of his marriage with her the P.Rt. said there was an artificial marriage; that a clergyman of the Church of England[2] read over a few lines just to satisfy her; that it was no marriage—for there could be none without a licence or some written document.[3] I think the P.Rt. said that this took place at night in Norfolk St.[4] Park Lane. He did not mention whether anyone was present beyond this clergyman. I suppose there must have been others.[5] The P.Rt. informed me that they soon lived very unhappily together; her temper was violent in the extreme and there was no end to her jealousies. It is very likely that she might have had much to complain of on the part of the Prince, but the moment a woman places herself in

1 Henry Errington was Mrs Fitzherbert's uncle.
2 The Rev. Robert Burt.
3 For this document see *Wilkins*, i, 99.
4 This should be Park Street.
5 The witnesses were Mrs Fitzherbert's uncle, Henry Errington, and her brother, John Smythe.

the position of mistress it is too late to complain of those miseries that follow as a natural consequence. To the eternal disgrace of the nobility and gentry of this country they all flocked in crowds to pay their homage to this mistress of the Prince—for in what other light could she be considered? An illegitimate wife can have no other name because in the eye of the law she must be so considered. It may be convenient for sensuality to give it a milder name, but lust is the foundation of the connection; and had there been children such children could only rank among the bastardy of the country. The Prince both as Regent and King never mentioned this woman but with feelings of disgust and horror. He told me that once in one of her fits of fury she flung her slipper at his head. They at last seperated from an attempt, either real or artificial, to make the Prince jealous. The Prince thought it real but it is very possible that he might have been mistaken.

1589 THE REV. SAMUEL SMITH *to* SIR WILLIAM KNIGHTON

Ch. Ch. [Oxford], 7 April 1831.

A COMMUNICATION to me from Mr. Chantrey respecting the bust of the late King, which is now in the Hall at Christ Church, obliges me to take the liberty of troubling you with a short explanation upon the subject.

When His Majesty (then Prince Regent) dined in the Hall in the year 1814 he was graciously pleased to signify his intention of giving his portrait to be placed there.

When I became Dean in 1824 I found that the picture had not been sent, and I took an early opportunity of mentioning the circumstances to the late Lord Liverpool, who did not give me any encouragement to hope that His Majesty would then be prevailed upon to sit for his picture.

He told me however that if I would write such a letter as might be laid before the King it was probable that His Majesty would be pleased to send his bust instead of the picture. I wrote accordingly, and received from Lord Liverpool an answer which led me to believe that His Majesty complied with my humble request and had given orders to Mr. Chantrey to prepare the bust and to forward it to Christ Church. This was done, but there seems to be now some doubt whether the order was to be considered as coming from the King or from the Dean and Chapter of Christ

Church by His Majesty's permission. It appears that Mr. Chantrey has not been paid for the bust, and it is in consequence of his representations upon the subject, that I have ventured to make this statement in the hope that it will shew that it was His Majesty's intention to present the bust to the society which had so many other marks of his gracious condescension and favour.[1]

1590 SIR JAMES KEMPT[2] *to* LIEUTENANT-GENERAL SIR HERBERT TAYLOR

O[rdnance] Office, 18 June [1831].

THE enclosed memorandum will give you the information which you required respecting the delivery of old brass ordnance to Mr. Westmacott.

Mem. On the 11th Oct. 1824 the Master General the Duke of Wellington authorised the issue of 10 tons of old brass ord^{ce} to be made to Mr. Westmacott for a statue of His late Majesty Geo 3^d. and on the 22^d Nov following, a further issue of 15 tons was authorised by the Master General for the *same purpose*, making together 25 tons.

On the 18 August 1828 the Master General Lord Beresford ordered 8 tons of old brass ordnance to be issued to Mr. Westmacott, without stating the purpose for which it was required.

Not any mention is made in any of these orders as to payment for the metal, nor has Mr. Westmacott been called on to make payment for the same.

Mr. Westmacott has therefore received 25 tons of metal for the

statue of Geo 3^d and
tons cwt. qr. lb
8 0 1 12 for a service not stated, which has not been paid for.

17 June 1831.

1 On 16 April 1831 Chantrey acknowledged the receipt of £210.
2 Governor of Nova Scotia, 1820–28; Governor-General of Canada, 1828–30; Master-General of the Ordnance, 1830–34. [1764–1854.]

(*Copy.*)

1st List	Large whole-length portrait of His Majesty in the Garter Robes, for the City of Dublin	630		*Payments*	
				1824	
				2nd June By cash from the Treasury £630	
	Hamlet at the grave of Ophelia (Mr. Kemble in that character)	525			
	Bishop's half-length portrait of His Majesty for Sir Chas. Long	315			
	Do. for Lord Francis Conyngham	315			
	Do. for the Duke of Devonshire (on the death of the Duchess)	315		19th May By payment from Sir Willm Knighton Bart.	1995
	Kit cat portrait of the late Mr. Angerstein	210			
	Bishop's half-length portrait of the Duchess of Gloucester	315			
		£2625			2625

May the 4th
    1824   (signed)
          Thomas Lawrence P.R.A.
          Principal Painter in Or-
          dinary to His Majesty.

	Pictures bespoken in 1824			*Payments*	
finished (d)	Kit cat portrait of the Lord Chancellor	210		1825 Feb 23 (a)	By draft to Sir Thos. Lawrence by Sir Wm. Knighton Bart £1050
(finished) a	His Majesty for the Duke of Wellington	525		Aug. 2 (b)	By Do. Do. 525
(finished) a	Kit cat copy of His Majesty for Sir William Curtis[2]	210		Dec. 16 (c)	£2000 paid to Sir Thos. Lawrence from the Treasury, which was repaid by Sir Willm. Knighton on 28th Janry 1826, and the receipt exchanged, for a Privy Purse receipt £2000
(finished) b	Kit cat portrait of His Majesty for Mr. Nash	210			
	Copy fm. the best remaing. materials or authority, of the late D. of Orleans (by Sir Joshua Reynolds)[3]	525			
(finished) a	Bishop's half-length portrait of His Majesty, for Sir William Knighton	315			
	Carr^d over £1995			Paym^ts carr^d over £3575	

1 For his scale of prices, at different dates, see *Williams,* I, 309.
2 The London banker, and friend of George IV (1752–1829).   3 See No. 296.

Paintings bespoken in 1825			*Payments*		
	Bro^t over	1995	1826	Paymts. bro^t over	3575
(finished)	Bishop's half-length portrait		August 15	By Sir W.	
b	of Her Rl. Highness the Prin-			(c) Knighton's	
	cess Sophia.	315		Draft	50
(e)	Copy of a picture by Sir			(d) Do.	210
	Joshua Reynolds of the				
(finished)	Duchess of Devonshire[1] and		Novr 27	Do.	945
	her child	420			
finished	Portrait of His Most Chris-				
(c)	tian Majesty—large whole				
	length	525			
Do.	Do. of H.R.Hss the Dauphin	525			
(c)					
(c)	Expenses and time in journey				
	to and stay at Paris, for the				
	last two portraits	1000			
(e)	Portrait of His Majesty—				
(finished)	large whole length—sent to				
	Count Munster for Hanover	525			
	Carried over £5305			Carried over £4780	

1 Georgiana, Duchess of Devonshire (1757–1806), eldest daughter of the first Earl Spencer, and wife of the fifth Duke. She left a son and two daughters.

		Brought over £5305
finished in March 1827	A Kit cat portrait of His Majesty for Sir William Knighton	210
finished in March 1828 (g)	Whole length portrait of the late Rt. Honble George Canning	525
finished Sept. 1828 (h)	Sept. 11th A kit cat portrait of His Majesty for the Rt. Honble William Adam	210
	A Bishop's half-length portrait of Jeffrey Wyatville Esq.	315
(i)	A Three quarters portrait of the Duke of Devonshire	157 – 10
finished Nov. 1828	(N.B. This price of a Three quarters portrait stated by Sir T. L. 9 Dec. 1828)	
finished (k)	June 2 1829 portrait of His Majesty for Lord Ravensworth Kit Cat	210
(l) finished	A kit cat portrait of Her Majesty the Queen of Portugal (1829)	210
		£7142 – 10

		Brought over £4780
1827 April 5 (f)	By Draft from Privy Purse (Separate Acct)	210
1828 April 7 (g)	By Sir William Knighton's draft	525
Sept. 20 (h)	By Do. Do.	210
Decr 13 (i)	By Do. Do.	157 – 10
1829 June 4 (k)	By Do. Do.	210
Sept. 9 (l)	By Do. Do.	210
		£6302 – 10

Charges   £7142 – 10
Payments   £6302 – 10

Difference   £ 840
which arises from the following pictures not being finished vizt the copy of the best remaining materials or authority of the late D. of Orleans by Sir Joshua Reynolds } £525

Bishop's half-length portrait of Mr. Wyatville } 315

£840

In the time of Col. McMahon

Large whole length portrait of His Majesty for the Viscount Castlereagh	£420
Do. for the Castle Dublin	420
Do. for the Marquess of Anglesea	420
Large whole length portrait of H.R.H. the Duke of York	420
Do. of F.M. the Prince Blucher	420
Do. of the Hetman Count Platoff	420
Large triumphal portrait of the Duke of Wellington	630
Half-length portrait of Lord Viscount Castlereagh	210

Total in the time of Col. McMahon £3360

In the time of Sir Benjn Bloomfield
(The Waterloo Collection)

Large whole length portrait of His Majesty in the Garter robes for the University of Oxford	630
Large whole length of the Emperor of Austria	525
Do. of the Emperor of Russia	525
Do. of the King of Prussia	525
Do. of the Arch-Duke Charles[1]	525
Large groupe whole lengths of Prince Schwatzenberg [*sic*] with his Hulan [*sic*] and horse	840
Large whole length of H.H. the Pope	525
Large whole length of Cardinal Consalvi	525
Half length of Prince Metternich	315
Do. of Prince Hardenberg	315
Do. of Count Capo d'Istria	315
Do. of Count Nesselrode	315
Do. of General Ouvaroff	315
Do. of General Czernicheff [Tchernitcheff]	315
Three quarters of Chevalier Grutz [? Gentz]	157 – 10
Half length portrait of Earl Bathurst	315
Do. of the Earl of Liverpool	315

Total Waterloo Collection £7297 – 10

1 Brother of the Emperor Francis I of Austria (1771–1847).

(Private Collection)

Whole length portrait of Her late Royal Highness the Princess Charlotte .	420
Large whole length portrait of H.R.H. the Duke of Cambridge	525
Large whole length portrait of the late King . . .	525
Do. of the late Benjamin West Esq.	525
Half length portrait of the Marchioness of Conyngham . .	315
Do. of the Lady Elizabeth Conyngham[1]	315
Kit cat portrait of the Lady Maria Conyngham . . .	210
Half length portrait of Sir Walter Scott	315
Large whole length portrait of His Majesty in the Garter robes for the Royal Palace Windsor	787 – 10
Large whole length portrait of His Majesty . . .	525

Total Private Collection £4462 – 10

Travelling expenses, compensation for time &c to Aix la Chapelle £1000—& the like to Vienna £1000[2] . .	2000

Total in the time of Sir Benjⁿ Bloomfield £13,760

In the time of Sir Wm Knighton

Portrait of Mr. Kemble, as Hamlet at the grave of Ophelia .	525
Bishop's half length portrait of His Majesty for Sir Charles Long	315
Do. for Lord Francis Conyngham	315
Do. for the Duke of Devonshire	315
Kit cat portrait of the late Mr. Angerstein	210
Bishop's half length portrait of the Duchess of Gloucester . .	315
Kit cat portrait of the Lord Chancellor (Eldon) . . .	210
Whole length portrait of His Majesty for the Duke of Wellington	525
Kit cat (copy) of His Majesty for Sir Wm Curtis . . .	210
Do. for Mr. Nash	210
Bishop's half length portrait of His Majesty for Sir William Knighton	315

[Carried over £3465]

---

1 Elizabeth (d. 1839) and Maria (d. 1843) were Lady Conyngham's daughters. They married the Earl of Aboyne and Sir William Meredyth Somerville respectively.

2 He painted the portraits of the Emperor of Austria and of Scharzenburg at Vienna, not at Aix-la-Chapelle. He wrote, from Vienna: "The terms on which I undertook this mission were, to be paid my usual prices for the portraits and £1000 for travelling expenses and loss of time. My journey to Rome will be on the same. These appear to be liberal terms, and I am sure are meant as such by the Prince. The first was of my own proposing, when the question was asked me; but I must still look to the honour I have received, and the good fortune of having been thus distinguished in my profession, as the chief good resulting from it, for many unavoidable circumstances make it of less pecuniary advantage." (*Williams*, II, 107.)

[*In the time of Sir Wm Knighton, cont.*]

[Brought over £3465]

Bishop's half length of H.R.Hss the Princess Sophia . . .	315
Copy of a picture by Sir Joshua Reynolds of the Duchess of Devonshire and her child	420
Portrait of His Most Christian Majesty—a large whole length	525
Do. of H.R.H. the Dauphin	525
Portrait of His Majesty—large whole length—sent to Count Munster for Hanover	525
Kit cat portrait of His Majesty for Sir William Knighton . .	210
Whole length portrait of the late Rt. Hble. Geo: Canning . .	525
Kit cat portrait of His Majesty for the Rt. Honble. William Adam	210
Bishop's half length of Sir Jeffrey Wyatville	315
A three quarters portrait of the Duke of Devonshire . . .	157 – 10
Kit cat portrait of His Majesty for Ld. Ravensworth . . .	210
Kit cat portrait of Her Majesty the Queen of Portugal . .	210
	7612 – 10

Expenses and time on journey to, and stay at, Paris to paint the
    portraits of His Most Christian Majesty and the Dauphin .   1000

                             Together   8612 – 10

Summary

Pictures painted in the time of Col McMahon .		£3360
Do. in the time of Sir Benjn Bloomfield vizt—		
The Waterloo Collection	£7297 – 10	
Private Collection	4462 – 10	
Travelling expenses and compensation for time	2000	
		13760
Pictures painted in the time of Sir Wm. Knighton	7612 – 10	
Travelling expenses and compensation for time	1000	
		8612 – 10
	Total	£25732 – 10

In the time of Col. McMahon	The first £1000	
	The second Payment, or in two Paymts of £500 each	1000
By Sir Benjn Bloomfield	1818 – September	1000
	—— December 26th	1000
	1819 – February 2d	500
	—— Do. 16th	1000
	1820 – January 18th	500
	—— October 10th	1000
	1821 – January 24th	2000
	—— September 19th	2000
By Sir Willm Knighton	1822 – August 8th	2000
	1823 – April 9th	1500
	—— July 29th	1500
	—— August 2d	500
	—— September 8th	620
	1824 – May 19th	1995
	1825 – February 23d	1050
	—— August 2d	525
	—— December 16th	2000
	1826 – August 15th	50
	—— Same day	210
	—— November 27th	945
	1827 – April 5th	210
	1828 – April 7th	525
	—— September 20th	210
	—— December 13th	157 – 10
	1829 – June 4th	210
	—— September 9th	210

Total Payments up to the period
of Sir T. L.'s death £25,417 – 10

Remaining due . . . . £. 315
(being for Portrait of Sir
Jeffrey Wyatville)

1594 Sir F. Legatt Chantrey's Receipt

Received the 26th of February 1834 of his Grace the Duke of Wellington and Sir William Knighton Bart, exors of His Majesty King George the Fourth, deceased, the sum of one thousand pounds, being the final payment on account of the statue of His said late Majesty and in full of all demands. F. Chantrey

£1000.

You will, I am assured, feel as I do upon the result of the late trials.[1] The Constitution is shaken to its foundation by the license of the Press, and the licentiousness of the Press is incited and upheld by the only means prescribed by the laws for its control. You will do me the justice to admit that my views upon the subject have been consistent and that all my anticipations have been unfortunately realised. I saw the dawning mischief in the first factious and unmanly libels upon the best of Princes. I hoped for a vigorous and powerful exertion to stem the torrent which threatened to accumulate from these beginnings. An opinion (I must still consider an erroneous one) that *silent contempt* was the best shield against the effects of the ribaldry prevailed. To me it appeared to be no shield, but on the contrary, the most ingenious mode of *sharpening the arrows* of the opposing party. If the public of this country hear only one side of the question the chances are always in favour of their adopting it, or if the opponents of it are only capable of making a weak defence, wit and talent, however prostituted, will confirm them in it. The selfish and unprincipled conduct of a disappointed faction at the commencement of the Regency, the part which certain individuals bore in it, and the conspicuous and obvious motives which influenced them, were all so many points in which they were *vulnerable*, and if skilful exertions had been *then* embodied and led boldly to the attack, the contest would soon have been decided and the example of success in a traitorous and licentious combination against the Throne and constituted authorities would have been wanting as a future incitement to still more degraded agents of sedition now rendered triumphant through their means. When, however, the evil had proceeded to a very great and injurious extent, when the regular journals of the country, it is too true, had outraged the decencies of life, and carried their unconstitutional insults to the foot of the Throne, still the law operated to inflict penalties because the influence of the Press had not been able to penetrate and poison the whole mass of the lower orders of society. The plague might have been stayed or, at least, mitigated in its effects whilst the law still continued to be in any degree a *terror* to the delinquents, but by an inconceivable oversight (I say inconceivable because to *me*, a very humble individual in the scale of society, it was obvious from the beginning) a new engine was suffered to erect itself in defiance of all usage and precedent and (as I must still

1 The reference is probably to the trial of William Hone (1780–1842) the Radical journalist and bookseller. In December 1817 he was prosecuted by the Attorney-General for writing and publishing a number of political satires directed against the Government, in which the Litany, Athanasian creed, and the church catechism were satirised. He was acquitted on all three charges.

believe) of all law, through whose machinery the price of political poison was reduced to the lowest possible scale, and therefore accessible to the very lowest orders of the people. Here no antidote (of any permanent effect) could be applied and the consequences, which were inevitable, displayed themselves in the course of a few weeks. The stream of public opinion was polluted, overt acts of insurrection and riot succeeded, justice in vain attempted to raise her sword, juries were either corrupted or intimidated, and every attempt and effort at control only added new power and efficacy to the traitorous and seditious attacks upon the public peace. Our Courts of Justice have been rendered mere Courts of record for triumphant sedition and the institutions of the country at this moment are laid open, naked and abandoned, to the insults and aggression of their avowed enemies.

There appears to me to be but one channel open to our security—a bold, steady, manly appeal from these innovations and breaches in the Constitution, to the sober sense of the country, a late but vigorous determination of adopting *preventive* measures, and Parliamentary interference for the purpose of enforcing existing laws; or if necessary of making new enactments to prevent the publication of *unstampt* journals. That there is nothing chimerical in the notions I have constantly entertained upon this subject may be inferred from the mere notoriety and popularity of men like Hone and Wooller. Had *preventive* measures been adopted a few months ago the public would not have known that such beings existed. By *penal prosecution* they are raised up and *armed* for any mischief to any extent they may think fit to carry it. The policy of Government which is expedient and applicable to *treason* is the very reverse of right when applied to *libel*. In the *first* instance the best security against ultimate success may be to suffer it to ripen into action; in the *latter* to nip it in the bud; although in both cases exceptions may be rendered necessary by the particular state or exigencies of the country. Libel it is true may go very far and no precautionary measures may have the power to affect it; still even in this case the Press is open as a means of counter action; but where preventive measures *can* be resorted to I must consider the policy more than doubtful which would reject them.

Had the penalties which Cobbett supposed himself to have incurred, and which the public was fully prepared to expect would be enforced, been actually levied against him, even as *an exile*,[1] these men whose names resound from one quarter of the country to the other, *as intended*

1 In March 1817, after the Habeas Corpus Suspension Act had been passed, Cobbett thought it prudent to emigrate to America, where he remained for two years.

martyrs to the liberties of the people, would never have been heard of. They would have been as much unknown as hundreds who now lost and absorbed among the mass of the people will hereafter rise up into notoriety if a different policy be not speedily adopted. Is not the sadness of the view, which the present posture of public affairs presents to the mind, severely enhanced by the recollection that their open resistance to the march of the Constitution is made even during the suspension of the *Habeas Corpus*! What are we to look to when all restraint is removed, when we find the laws impeded in their operation in the moment of their supposed greatest power?

Sedition and blasphemy are triumphant at a period in which the hands of Government are strengthened beyond the legitimate usage of the Constitution, overt acts are only *just* restrained within the strictest limits. If something be not done before the suspension be taken off what is to prevent the fearful encroachments of popular disaffection, heated by seditious harangues and drawn forth by new and *triumphant* leaders?

I trust and hope the impression of the late events has coloured this prospective view in my mind and that my apprehensions are more gloomy than future circumstances may warrant; still with every deduction of this nature the prospect before us is pregnant with alarm and presents, at least, difficulties of no ordinary magnitude.

We have a population divided by religious dissent which gives its own peculiar colour to civil institutions; we have, I grieve to say, a Church rent *internally* by a schism which threatens mischief and confusion; we have affiliated societies hostile to the Government in Church and State extending and corresponding through every part of the country; and to these *combustible* materials is held forth the torch of *triumphant sedition* and the scarcely concealed embers of recent insurrection and rebellion. If we suppose only partial success we must anticipate a powerful division in favor of the enemies of the Constitution and eventual victory over them may be ascertained only by a struggle that would shake the Empire to its foundation. Surely these are considerations which must awaken attention and strengthen every nerve in the ruling powers of the country. If such results are only possible (and who shall say that they are not so) no effort should be left untried to ward them off from the Constitution. I cannot then but revert to the system, which has been hitherto adopted, and ask what has been gained by *silent dignity* to the support and defence of the Throne and Government! What benefit has been derived to *these* by the forbearance of the public functionaries in not enforcing the preventive restraints upon the low Press? The answer is to be found in the present posture of affairs. And if it be denied that any *specific* measures of policy would have prevented such a result, still it cannot be assumed that those of forbearance have been effectual.

The Press is at all times a most powerful instrument in this country. It may be the safeguard of liberty, but it may also be the firebrand of sedition. It is a two edged sword which every knave or fool is at liberty to brandish. No man of common sense or common honesty will therefore deny that some *control* or counteraction is necessary for the common safety. But the law has so contrived its restraints that the parties concerned become the ultimate judges of their own submission to them. For the *law* and facts are *both* left to the interpretation of those who are avowedly ignorant of the rules by which they are to judge of *one* of *these*, and in times when circumstances require an appeal to this judgment in a more *particular* and *urgent* manner, the decision of Juries become arbitrary because the men composing them are identified (or at least suppose that they are) in interest with the delinquents who are brought before their tribunal. Thus the institutions of the country are laid open in their most vulnerable points and are *directly* assailable by the most formidable arms which their adversaries possess. And thus it is clear that the only effectual control upon the licence of the Press must be exercised through the *indirect* means of preventive laws, one of the most efficient and valuable of which arises out of the *stamp duties*, or by a vigorous and systematic union of wit and talent, subsidiary to the interests of Government and kept constantly active and operative in every stage, degree and department of literature and politics.

A man who has been observant of the change which has taken place in the tone and character of public opinion within these last twenty years cannot but perceive how infinite a portion of this change is *demonstrably* chargeable upon the influence of *two* publications only, the Edinburgh Review and the Morning Chronicle. If it be answered that the anti-Ministerial side of the question will, from the nature of things, be always more easily and readily served and that the assumed zeal on popular questions will invariably attract more admirers and proselytes than the defenders of specific measures, connected with revenue and taxation, it is only evading the general question, for, admitting the fact in its greatest latitude, it cannot be contended in sound policy that because an opponent enjoys certain advantages we are therefore to increase them by withholding the means of aggression or self-defence which we actually possess. But I refer to a matter of fact, and popular and fascinating as the principles of the French Revolution had been rendered in this country through the arts and machinations of the English reformers, I have no hesitation in affirming that a Revolution scarcely less important (if we calculate all possible consequences of the unimpeded career of Jacobinism) was effected in this country by the one single publication in the *Anti-Jacobin weekly paper*. This mean[s] of defence however has been rejected in the face of what appears to me to be the obvious policy of Governments in times like the present. Not only has an attempt been made to draw within the circle of Government influence the *loose talent* and *purchaseable* ability of the metropolis, but common support seems to have been systematically withheld from the efforts of voluntary auxiliaries and *independent* and *attached* partisans of the Constitution. And it is only within a few days that I have heard (from the man to whom I gave whatever advantage he might be able to derive from the publication of the *good old Times*, guaranteeing to him his expences) that on leaving the *penny numbers* at the door, even of Ministers of State, they were *rejected until* an assurance was given that no demand was intended to be made for them !

I know, humble and imperfect (from the variety of my professional duties and avocations) as was the little effort in the cause, that effectual good has been done by the combination of individuals to circulate it, and you would be surprised at the *bulk* of the correspondence communicated to the *unknown author* respecting the benefit derived from it in numberless instances in various parts of the country; and had a few official channels been opened to it (I say it without the smallest taint of vanity) I am satisfied from the *nature* of the *publication* it might have been rendered an effectual instrument of working considerable good upon the minds of the lower classes, who err more from the ignorance of facts, and the consequent impositions practised upon their credulity, than from any direct defect of perception when truth is laid before them or any inveterate viciousness of disposition.

Even so far back as the period of Mr. Pitt's Administration when Cobbett was in the zenith of his influence, I remember stating in conversation with that great man the policy of counteracting the mischief which was then in rapid progress. His observation was perfectly consonant with the practice which has ever since been followed. "It is better to leave him rope enough, he will hang himself. He will soon write himself out." *He has certainly written himself out*, but not before he has set the country in a flame, to which, from the example he has afforded, very inferior talents may add a perpetual supply of fuel.

It will not be disputed that in the present posture of public affairs something *ought*, something *must*, be done to rescue the country from the perils by which it is surrounded. The direct restraint upon the Press I may say is, for the present at least, *wholly lost*, and I apprehend it will be worse than fruitless for some time to come to bring a libeller into a Court of Justice, at least in London, for it is a curious fact that we have now in the County gaol in this town, Williams who was only the *re-publisher* of Hone's Parodies for which he is condemned to a twelve months' imprisonment. The remaining, the *only remaining*, restraint rests upon the indirect mode then of preventive laws which appears to me to be still open. If it is not, where is our abiding place? We are without hope or defence; for to expect forbearance from those who have attained power and influence in proportion to their defect of principle and patriotism is to look for fruit from the bramble. Such men will be as intemperate in the use of the advantages which they have gained as they have been unsolicitous concerning the means by which they have obtained them, and it must be recollected that the Press is *at this moment lawless*; that a revolution has taken place and that an avowal of *principles*, be their tendency what they may, is unshackled! How long *actions* can be controlled in such a state of things is the great question with which we have now to do, and a fearful one it is. Never was the union of *vigour* and *temper* more imperiously called for, and never, in my opinion, were these essentials more intimately combined than in the present Administration. They have only *not been* directed towards *one particular object*, which does not, however, lessen the importance of it.

Consciousness of deserving well of their country has, I fear, induced the conviction of securing it without the aid of representation; and the conviction is, I verily believe, well founded as far as the great body of the higher and middle classes of the country are concerned, but the most inflammable portion and those most open to delusion, combining and comprehending the vast mass of physical strength, has been left open to the operation of a new and malignant process of irritation to which no *one bar*, *let* or *restraint* has been opposed! Enforce the stamp duties without exception through the regular official channels and this Hydra is cut off at a single blow. Responsibility is created which these men cannot make good. *Capital* is *necessary* and *they have none*!

Thus at the trial of your patience have I, *without restraint*, poured out the result of those painful reflections which have arisen in my mind in consequence of the late events which have disgraced and degraded our Courts of Justice. The *war whoop* of the Morning Chronicle has proclaimed the victory of its subsidiaries! May the strength of Government yet prevail to snatch these *paper laurels* from its brow. In the hope that the same indulgence I have always experienced from you may be extended to this *magnified* offence.

I have the honour to be, Dear Sir, [etc.].

	£	s	d
17 July 1830—Paid to Richard Evans,[1] artist	52	10	0
26 July 1830—Paid to Mr. Maughan for destroying vermin in Windsor Great Park	23	14	9
6 May 1831 To Francis Chantrey for a bust of His late Majesty presented by the King to Christ Church College, Oxford	210		
28 May 1831 To Sir William Beechey, for restoring six portraits of the Princesses, by command of his late Majesty	63		
6 June 1831 To Richard Westmacott	390	9	
8 Dec. 1831 Do.	2,670		
16 April 1832 Do.	1,120		
26 Feb. 1834 To Francis Chantrey	1,000		

(These sums were paid by the Executors)

Subscriptions, Charities, and Donations (1822)

	£	s	d
British and Foreign School Society	100		
Marine Society	105		
Lying-in Charity	50		
Queen Charlotte's Lying-in Hospital	10	10	
Royal Infirmary for Diseases of the Eye	100		
Freemasons Charity	21		
Middlesex Hospital	105		
Adult Female Orphan Institution	100		
Foundling Hospital	52	10	
Medals for Winchester School	25	19	
Royal Cornwall Lunatic Asylum	25		
Seamen's Hospital Society	105		
Covent Garden Theatre, subscription for Box, half year to close of season, 29 June 1822	262	10	
Mr. Richard Kelly, gratuity on the occasion of his opera benefit	157	10	
Mr. Charles Mathews,[2] for private exhibitions of his professional talents	105		
Mr. J. Bellamy, in addition to £550, before advanced for subscriptions to his translation of the Bible, and in consideration of His Majesty's patronage being withdrawn	200		
Mr. Richard Westmacott, for expenses attending the casts from the Elgin Marbles presented to the Institution for the Fine Arts at Liverpool	509	14	

1 The portrait painter and copyist (1784–1871).
2 The comedian (1776–1835).

THE KING'S *Account with* MESSRS RUNDELL, BRIDGE & Co., *Jewellers*

Claims outstanding in April 1822

	£	s	d
Account dated 26 April to 27 August 1820	7,193	16	8
Whereon paid August 1821	2,000		
	5,193	16	8
Do. 6 May 1820 for Sword and Cap of State	15,906		
Do. 13 October 1820 to 27 March 1821	4,169	9	
Do. 27 March to 5 July 1821	8,090	2	6
Do. 9 July to 17 September 1821	4,933	15	6

Fixed Annual Charges upon the Privy Purse

	£
Annuities, Pensions and Allowances	19,915
Subscriptions, Charities, Donations and Bounties	4,340
Rates and Taxes at Windsor and Kew	1,200
The Band	6,000
	31,455

Among the annuities that were paid during the Reign were the following:

	£
Mrs. Fitzherbert[1]	10,000
Sir John Lade[2] (standing in the name of the Rev. Dr. Tolly)	500
Lady Douglas (standing in the name of the Honble. Miss Jeffreys by the direction of Colonel McMahon in April 1816, Miss Jeffreys' allowance being changed into a pension from Government)	200
Honble. Mrs. Fox ("Widow of the late Rt. Hon. Chas. Fox. Directions for this pension issued 1 July 1824")	500
John Byerley ("This originated in the late Sir John McMahon's time, as appears by a Memo. of Mr. Gray's, dated 11 August 1819, when it was ordered to be paid from the Separate Privy Purse Account")	200
Lieut. Col. George Fitzclarence	200
Lieut. Col. Fredk. Fitzclarence	200
Captain Fitzclarence, R.N.	200
Mrs. Phillis [*sic*] Wright ("Widow of Wright who was killed at the riots at Manchester")	10

1 In October 1801 the Prince increased Mrs Fitzherbert's pension from £3000 to £4000. Later it was increased to £6000, and finally, in April 1820, to £10,000.
2 See *Creevey Papers*, p. 677; Wilkins' *Mrs Fitzherbert and George IV*, I, 270.

[*Items from* GEORGE IV's *Accounts, cont.*]

The following items are taken from the 1827 Accounts:

24 March To rem^{r.} of Mr. Cooper's bill for clothing (Band)	1,104	17	6
6 April To President of the Royal Society of Literature, by command	1,155		
18 May To University Press, Cambridge, for printing Milton	665	11	6

Payments made to Mr. Hamlet, jeweller, from 6 March 1824 to 10 August 1829	22,231	9
Payments made to Messrs Rundell, Bridge & Co. from 13 Feb. 1821 to 14 January 1829	105,618 10	4

Samuel Cartwright's (Dentist) Bill for attendance upon the King from 1 Jan. 1829 to 17 Dec. 1829:

29 visits to Windsor by arrangement, 20 guineas per visit	609
8 visits to St. James's and with detention more than 14 hours at the Palace, 3 guineas per hour	42
Mechanical	50
	701
From 21 Jan. to 3 June 1830, 5 visits	105
	£806

[The Bill was paid by Wellington and Knighton on 14 July 1830.]

Rent of the King's Private Box at the Haymarket Theatre for the Season 1823:	£150
Subscription to the King's Theatre for the season 1829:	£367 10

SIR WILLIAM KNIGHTON'S MISSIONS
TO THE CONTINENT

The private Bagot MSS., and the Granville MSS. in the Public Record Office, throw additional light on the nature of Sir William Knighton's secret missions to the continent on behalf of his royal master. On 30 June 1826 the King wrote to Lord Granville, our Ambassador at Paris, informing him that Knighton was soon to call on him "for the purpose of communicating with Lord Granville on a subject upon which the King is most deeply anxious". "The business", wrote Canning, "is one which causes great disquietude in a quarter, in which I am sure it will be as much matter of inclination as of duty on your part, not only to lend yourself to any mode of removing uneasiness, but to devise means for that purpose if you can." (To Granville, 30 June.) In an undated letter, evidently written shortly after his arrival in France, Knighton told Granville that the Director of the Paris Police was to be asked to put "the individuals in question" under police surveillance, and to let "you confidentially know from time to time what their conduct and employments seem to be. If this could be done it would perhaps be a satisfactory auxillary [sic] to our own watchfulness! At any rate it would be a demonstration to those at home, who are so anxious on the subject".

On 2 September 1827 Lord Dudley, the Foreign Secretary, wrote to Granville: "You have just received a visit from a *great person* in the State. You need not be told how much importance is attached by a *still greater person* to the objects of his journey—particularly that with which you are best acquainted." A fortnight later, Knighton, who was on his way to Berlin, called on Sir Charles Bagot, our Ambassador at The Hague, at Aix-la-Chapelle, with letters from Dudley and the King. Fulfilling his promise that "no exertions shall be wanting on his part to give the earliest and most complete effect to His Majesty's wishes", Bagot met one of his secret agents at Frankfort, on the 24th, and sent him to Chimay, in Belgium, near the French frontier, with directions to obtain an interview with Mrs Rochfort, formerly Harriette Wilson. "I then directed him to acquaint Mrs Rochfort from me that from the moment of her first establishment in this country it had been, as she would readily conceive, a part of my duty to keep an eye fixed upon her proceedings—that the persons with whom she was in connexion—the characters with whom she was in correspondence, and all the steps which she had taken, were intimately known to me— that I had no wish to proceed to any extremities, or to take any harsh measures in regard to her if I could avoid it, but that I must have some positive security that she would discontinue immediately and for ever those annoyances which she had long and particularly of late been in the practice of directing against a quarter which she would perfectly understand, and in which it was not possible that they should be endured—that I would be perfectly content to accept her word of honour given to myself that these annoyances should cease—but that unless she was prepared to give me such a pledge, it would be necessary for me, under the instructions with which I was furnished, to take without delay such measures with the Government of this country in respect to her, and to those immediately connected with her, as would be infallibly attended with inconveniences to which she had probably never looked." Arriving at Chimay, the secret envoy found that Mrs Rochfort was away from home: she might be in Paris, she might be in England, he was informed; and she would not be back until the following summer. Mr Rochfort affected complete ignorance of any of his wife's proceedings which could give umbrage to the British Government, and said: "I know the Memoirs have made Mrs Rochfort...many enemies among what are called great people in England, and I will tell you besides that the same step which you are taking now has been tried with me before—it is nothing new—application was made to the French Government to turn *her* out of France and *they refused*...I know there is a determination to destroy her, and also know where they wish to send her to, but they never shall succeed... while I am able to protect her." He said it was impossible for anyone to pledge himself to so loose and general a proposition as that required. "The multiplicity of steps which she had taken for the last twelve months was so great that she could not by any possibility be certain of the quarter referred to—that she had been in correspondence with perhaps two hundred people, all in high quarters, for that she disdained the low ones." The envoy returned to The Hague, and Sir Charles Bagot confessed to having serious doubts "whether our démarche will be attended with the success which is to be desired". "If His Majesty", wrote Bagot to Knighton on 9 October, "should be of opinion that I might open myself confidentially upon the subject to some one member of this Government, the Minister for Foreign Affairs for example, or the Minister of the Interior, I think that I could rely upon their entire secrecy in the matter excepting so far as may regard the King their master, and it may perhaps be worth consideration whether, after what has passed between myself and Mr Rochfort, it might not be attended with the effect which it is desired to produce if a secret intimation should be given from the highest authority of the police that the attention of this Government has been awakened to Mrs Rochfort's proceedings. Thus much the Government would I think have no hesitation in doing, and such a step on their part would be the best confirmation of the truth and earnestness of all that I have already intimated....It might be doubtful whether the Government could be easily induced to do more than this." Nine days later Bagot received a letter from Harriette Wilson, to whom her husband had written an account of the interview at Chimay. As he forwarded it to Lord Dudley, and kept no copy, its precise contents are unknown; but he wrote to Dudley on the 19th: "They who have had to deal with her upon the subject of her publications are the best judges of the degree of reliance which is to be placed upon her promises; but, for my own part, I confess that I should be disposed to trust to the engagements which she declares herself ready to take upon the conditions which she states in her letter, and to accept those conditions without hesitation.... When you read her letter you will see that there are some things in it which make me desire...not to send it to Sir William Knighton. It might I think be more agreeable to his employers that they should never know that I have been put in possession of the statements which it makes —but I have no other reason than this for sending it to you rather than to him ...I am strongly tempted to submit to your consideration whether (assuming that H. Wilson is really in possession of facts the disclosure of which it may be an object to prevent) it might not be prudent to agree to her terms, and to accept her conditions precisely as she offers them. Her first object seems to be to obtain some situation for Mr Rochfort, but she appears to be quite aware that any appointment given to *him* would tell its own tale, and she therefore offers, in case no situation can be found for him, to accept £300 for what she calls her immediate difficulties, and £100 a year for her life conditionally—that is—so long only as the parties in question shall be no further troubled in any way by her letters, publications or otherwise, and so long only as the fact of her receiving such annuity shall be by her kept secret from all the world. Now it appears to me that these conditions, or some conditions *of this kind*, do afford the best and probably the only guarantee which can be obtained from a person of her character for her future silence, if there is any object in securing that silence. It seems evident from her letter that, unless she is to be defied, I must at last come to some arrangement of this nature. It is *very* doubtful whether I could carry into *complete* effect what it has been suggested to me to menace— and, if I could do so, it would be still more doubtful whether the result would be the prevention of all publication anywhere, anyhow, or at any time." Dudley's illuminating reply was written on 5 November. "I have seen the 'Iron Mask' as a friend of mine has nicknamed him. He seems inclined to defy the *heroine*, and for the present take no further steps about her. It is a doubtful question. For my part I think I should rather have been disposed to try the effect of money given from time to time during good behaviour. If none had ever been given, the case would be different, but having already to say with truth that she has been bribed, I don't see any additional evil from a continuance of the same system. It is altogether an ugly business, and what is more provoking is that the person who suffers by it most is not at all to blame, but is wounded through the sides of those to whom he is attached. What letters those of the young gentleman, and what a specimen of discretion of a person at that very moment filling a situation of the highest confidence! I had seen them before; they were shewn to me in the oddest way, and by a person *well acquainted* with the writer. I would not write on such a subject, even in cypher, but you would be amused if I were to tell you the story. You are quite right in not shewing the letter—it could only have produced unnecessary irritation." Knighton confirmed the Foreign Secretary's intelligence in a letter of the same date. "It is now thought that under all circumstances nothing further should be done at present: you will be pleased therefore, unless you should again hear from me, to remain quiet." Dudley wrote a final letter on 9 November. "When I saw Sir William Knighton last, he was still disposed to let the enemy do her worst. This is certainly the most courageous and perhaps the most prudent way. If any further steps are taken, I am clearly of opinion that it ought not to be through you. An exalted and conspicuous station disqualifies a man for a business the agent of which should work in the dark."

Knighton's letter to Granville dated from a Paris hotel, 8 March 1828, shews that his continental mission at that time centred round the De Beaume affair. "I am sure the King will feel most sensibly your dutiful attention to His Majesty's private affairs, about which His Majesty must naturally feel most anxious. You will be glad to learn that through my secret agency I have found out the individual in whose hands the *notorious copy* of the fraudulent bond is deposited. I have also, through the same agency, obtained an extract copy of the trial of J. J. de Beaune before the Criminal Revolutionary Tribunal. Your Lordship may be surprised at this, but in the low, despicable state to which human nature is reduced in this and every other country, it is in vain to wonder at anything. To make out the details of this affair (the stake of which for the King is three hundred thousand pounds) has been a matter of uncommon industry and management. Perhaps my feelings are at this moment more excited than usual, for whilst thus employed, a besotted scoundrel, with the grossest perceptions, of the name of T. Duncombe, has dared to vilify His Majesty's sacred name—through my humble person!"[1]

It is clear from Bagot's letter of 14 October 1828 to Knighton, written from The Hague, that Harriette Wilson's poison pen was still disturbing the King's peace of mind, for Bagot, acting doubtlessly on instructions from home, had again sent his secret emissary to Mr Rochfort at Chimay, again in her absence, a fortnight earlier. Again were presented the alternatives of an official situation for the husband and a life annuity of £100 for the wife, in return for an undertaking not to publish "certain facts". "What can I do?", asked Bagot. "I have of course not taken any notice of her letter, nor shall I now make any further move of any kind in the business till I hear again from you."

In May 1829 Lord Aberdeen, the Foreign Secretary, received a letter from Mr Rochfort which he naturally could not comprehend, and he forwarded it to Bagot with a request for an explanation. Having been sworn to secrecy, however, Bagot could only ask Aberdeen to see Lord Dudley in private. "It is in his power to give you all the information which you want if he shall feel at liberty to do so; if he shall not so feel, it is in his power to ascertain whether that liberty can be now given either to him or to myself.... You are aware, I conclude, that the Mr Rochfort is the husband, or the supposed husband, of Harriette Wilson.[2] His letter to me of which he transmits you a copy, is authentic, but I distinctly declare that no measures were taken or suggested or encouraged by me either directly or indirectly for the purpose, or which could possibly have the effect of injuring Mr Rochfort in any way publicly or privately in this country or elsewhere—that it is not within my knowledge that any such measures were taken by anyone else—and that to the best of my belief they never were taken at all. If Lord Dudley shall find himself at liberty to enter upon the whole matter with you, he will be able to show you a letter of mine

1 See his celebrated speech in the House of Commons, 18 February 1828 (*Hansard*, N.S. xviii, 540), and *Greville*, 25 February 1828.

2 Bagot's secret agent said there was something in Mr Rochfort's general manner and way of speaking that led him to think that they were not really married.

to him written on the 14th of October 1827, in which will be found the true meaning of the word Government of which Mr Rochfort has so dextrously availed himself for the purpose of extorting money from you."[1]

The Aberdeen MSS. in the British Museum give us a final glimpse of Harriette Wilson's husband. In December 1825 his house near the Champs Elysées had been ransacked by the Paris police, and property which he valued at not less than £150 had been seized. He was evidently regarded as a dangerous character, for he was known to have been A.D.C. to General MacGregor, the South American adventurer, "at that time detained in prison as was presumed at the instigation of His Catholic Majesty, under suspicion of organizing an auxiliary force to co-operate with the expedition then in the contemplation of the Colombian Government for the attack of Cuba". On 23 September 1830 Rochfort wrote to Wellington from a London address, asking him to use his influence with the French Government for the restitution of his property. The Duke pointed out that five years had elapsed since the alleged seizure, that a revolution had put an end to the Government under whose auspices the injury complained of had been done, and that he should have applied for protection to the English Ambassador at Paris. (Add. MS. 43059, ff. 187–91.)

THE DUKE OF CUMBERLAND AND THE LADY GRAVES SCANDAL [see No. 1577]

In fairness to the Duke it should be pointed out that he repudiated the allegation with the utmost vehemence. He wrote to Eldon on 14 February 1830: "...It is disgusting to live in a country where every man's character is at the mercy of hirelings who, to carry any purpose or gratify any Party motive, can insinuate the greatest lies [against] any one; but I own I treat such *vile* scoundrels with the contempt they deserve. I have some reason to believe that I *know* the source, at least if not the original one, at least the *abettor*. I have heard that some paragraphs appeared some time back in the public papers, but as they were in publications condemned in my house I have never read them, nor have I any one of them, as I cannot prevent them and I do not choose to be enraged by them; all I can say [is] that "The late Lord Graves never either by word or letter ever expressed himself towards me but amicably, that no later than Friday the 5th of February that [*sic*] he called on me at St James' while I was sitting with you as it was between 4 and 5 that evening, that I had been previously to calling on you here sitting I believe a full hour at my friend Anglesey['s], who received me just as ever in the most friendly and usual manner, nay that Lord Graves drove down to my house with Lady Mountcharles and Lady Graves, and *this* being the case, *what* can prove more clearly the fact that *he* believed no *such report*! But I really am sick of boring you with

1 The word Government was used in order to avoid any distinct mention of the King's name. "She affects to consider it as meaning the State, and would undoubtedly so treat it if means should not be eventually found of preventing her from publishing."

such trash, the invention of malice and what is worse, if not encouraged, at least countenanced by the papers in Downing Street, which that im[m]aculate nest has been crying so much against in their own case; but I am determined positively *not* to follow the example of the Duke of Wellington and his double faced Lord Chancellor and put myself into the hands of *Scarlett, never,* for I should only raise a host of newspaper writers against me...."

He wrote again, that evening: "I have just received your kind, friendly and most interesting letter, and have only to say in the first place that I am glad you agree with me that all idea of prosecuting or putting myself in the hands of that s[coundre]l the Attorney General is as foreign from your opinion as certainly it is and could be *thought* of or be *entertained* for one moment by me; the *idea* of my making any statement in the House of Lords, I own freely, seems to me at the first blush, but mind when I say this, and I merely give my opinion as it *first* strikes me, as *infra dignitatum,* for if every Peer is to be as foully attacked as I have been by some rascally hireling, and is to be forced to get up and contradict that which any man (*who knows me* and has as you now know me *all* the particulars I have stated, before them) must be convinced is false, this is really putting me in a strange position [*sic*]. How can I get up and state publickly all these particulars? It appears to me that Lord A[nglesey], the head of his family who must feel here (?) injured one of his own family, might distinctly put an end to the whole by his either calling openly on me, or my being seen publickly with him [*sic*]; and that this would be much more dignified than any public exhibition of the sort you hinted at, for it is not simply *what* may be the *effect* in this country but what it would have abroad, besides what *my own wife* must think, for thank God she has never *heard* any of these reports, and as I say and repeat that I myself had never heard one word till a short time ago, or *else* I should never *have called* as I did about six weeks ago upon Lord Graves which I told you, and when I sat with him a considerable time and perceived no alteration *whatever in his manner towards me.* It is only within these last days that I have heard (but when I say it, mind I may be incorrect) that some villainous rascal sent him a caricature under a blank cover; which I have never seen nor heard of. But really who is secure? Who is safe? For in times of violent political feelings as we have been living in for the last two years, there is none among us that is not liable to such attacks. As far as I am personally concerned, I treat the whole with the contempt it deserves, and as I am most perfectly happy in my interior domestic concerns, I should not like to cause any anxiety *here.* Had Lord A[nglesey] had the slightest idea of anything of the sort, he certainly would not have been so perfectly friendly and amicable with me as he was, nor could he have entered so fully as he did with me on political subjects as he did. So much was his manner perfectly the same, that it so occurred during our conversation, something was talked in which his sister's name was mentioned, and we talked just as if nothing had occurred, so that I feel perfectly persuaded that *he* at least never had had any such impression on his mind; and surely such a *step* as my explaining or defending myself in Parliament would rather confirm, if not exactly that, give it to understand that something *awkward* had occurred, which I can *positively deny* ever did taken place [*sic*]...."

On 17 February the Duke wrote again: "...I do believe your proposal of calling at Anglesey's tomorrow will settle the whole business completely and in a manner the most dignified and honourable to all parties, for I feel positive that Anglesey must feel confident that the *whole* is *a base calumny*, and that I am fully justified to be sure of this by the very *friendly* and kind reception he gave me when I called on him that morning at Uxbridge House, when *he and I* had a most *confidential* and *serious* conversation, which it would have been impossible for him to have had with a person that he thought capable of what I have been so basely accused; but it is evident that *party spirit* has been as active as it was formerly last year, and *just* at the identical period, the meeting of Parliament. As far as I am personally concerned I treat it with contempt, but when the character of a person for whom I have the highest *respect*, and the sincerest *attachment*, I feel I cannot act with too much delicacy, and I feel very horrified [*sic*]....The whole is the most infernal lie that ever was invented...."

Two days later the Duke wrote: "...I have *not* the slightest doubt that the other person[1] will affirm the same thing when you see him, as I feel convinced from my personal knowledge of his manly and open character that he never would have received me, or have talked to me as confidentially as we did that said Friday n.b. within *48* hours of the event's taking place, if his mind had been poisoned by those infamous lies that had been put about and invented by *those* who had the baseness for their private pique and vengeance against myself not to stick at trying to ruin their own dearest and nearest relative. Excuse my *speaking* or rather I mean *writing* thus *warmly* on the subject, but it is not for myself alone I think but for another most injured person. Wynford I related *all* to just as I had done to you, and he at last acknowledged to me *confidentially* (naturally) his authority; now *this* I smother (?) *completely*; it is an intrigue of a certain lady [Lady Conyngham], who is jealous of all that approaches that place, nay even of *her* own children, and as she finds that by honest and fair means she cannot poison his mind against me, it is to be done by false and artfull ones, but they may as well move St Paul's to this place, as get me to *flinch*. I trust and hope that you may have the conversation this day and send me this evening the result...." Eldon replied that Anglesey was not at home when he called to see him. Then on 21 February the Duke wrote: "...I have declared to you most sacredly and solemnly that neither *directly* or *indirectly* did Lord Graves ever hint at, or write to me anything even *leading* to such a *supposition*, and that *he called* in *person* and *wrote* down with his own handwriting which I *possess* and which I shewed Wynford, his name, having asked to see me, and finding me not at home, *on the day before his death*. Can any clearer proof exist of his being confident that there was *no truth* in all that had been (as I am told) instilled so industriously and maliciously into his mind? Nay more, I have been informed from pretty good authority, I believe, that *even after* some villain had sent him anonimously those caricatures, that he wrote to Lady Graves to tell her to *come to him*, that he was determined to *stand by her* and ward off from her such rascally and *infamous* attacks, and that she passed I believe one or two days with him, and that within an hour or so of *the act* he is said to have *written* her the most *loving* and *kind* letter, telling

[1] The one and the other: Lord Anglesey and the Duke of Richmond.

her to come to him and to accompany him to his daughter's, whom they were to join the very next day on a visit. Surely these are *proofs* as *strong* as can exist to confirm any assertion I make....Do they pretend to say that my calling repeatedly at an old and sincere friend's house, drinking tea there, with *all doors open*, and never remaining there later than 11 or 11½, that for that reason *I* and *she* are to be suspected? No, this is really too much. I *am most* happy you have had that confidential conversation with *Richmond*, the *nephew* of one of the parties concerned, and I feel confident that *he* will confirm the same, for that *his manner* and the perfect confidential conversation I had with him the *self-same day* n.b. that *Lady Graves called on* me, must *prove* to me most clearly that *he* is as confident of the *whole lie* as Richmond is....I feel that I have been most infamously used by a party of *political* enemies, and that *this* is in fact but a second volume of all that took place *last year* and at the self-*same moment* just as the meeting of Parliament took place."

The Duke repeated his charge against the ministerialists in another letter written on the 23rd: "...That Party thought to *frighten* me and make me *leave* the country, but by God *nothing shall*. And if (which has not occurred upon honour, such a proposal had come to me from that quarter which *you and* W[ynford] hinted at, my answer was ready prepared: 'If you can think me to be such a d—d coward as to run away, by God I am *not*, and will face that and every other false and infamous libell and cabal.' This is in fact but a repetition of their tricks last year, which the Duke of Wellington certainly had encouraged and moved Heaven and earth, not only trying his own persuasion, but even my brother's and at last that rascal the Lord Chancellor, talking to me of being assassinated, insulted, and God knows *what*. My reply was coolly, 'He who insults me openly shall not do it without meeting his deserts'. And I heard no more of it. Anonimous letters I received daily, but chucked them into the fire, as I have done now...."

The Duke went to see the King at Windsor on 1 March. "Nothing", he wrote to Eldon next day, "could be *more kind* or *friendly* than my brother was. He said I looked very ill and was grown very thin; he never *touched* upon this business, *not* in the *slightest degree*. He *talked* much about Prince Leopold, and that he had done *all* he could do, but that Ministers had used him ill...." (Private Eldon MSS.)

INDEX

The numbers refer to the letter, not the page

Abbas Mirza, Prince Royal of Persia, 176

Abbot, Charles, first Baron Colchester (1757–1829), 198, 247, 330, 461, 761

Abbott, Charles, first Baron Tenterden (1762–1832), 801, 939, 1550

Abercorn, John James Hamilton, first Marquis of (d. 1818), 736

Abercromby, James, first Baron Dunfermline (1776–1858), 1331, 1461

Aberdeen, George Hamilton Gordon, fourth Earl of (1784–1860), 364, 391, 406, 408, 412, 523, 1546
Letters from: 1538, 1554, 1559, 1580

Aboyne, George Gordon, fifth Earl of; later, Marquis of Huntly (1792–1853), 1228, 1303

À Court, Sir William, first Baron Heytesbury (1779–1860), 1256, 1258, 1260, 1267, 1416, 1552

Acton, 640

Adair, Sir Robert (1763–1855), 114

Adam, 1197

Adam, Prince, of Wurtemberg. *See* Wurtemberg

Adam, John (1779–1825), 405

Adam, William (1751–1839), 18, 23, 64, 203, 268–69, 405, 452, 469, 1591–92
Letters from: 52–53, 623
Letter to: 470

Adam, William George, 53

Addenbrooke, Colonel John Peter (? 1753–1821), Equerry to Princess Charlotte, 713

Addington, Henry. *See* Sidmouth

Addington, John Hiley (d. 1818), *Letter to*: 695

Adolphus Frederick, Duke of Cambridge (1774–1850), 70, 327, 344, 349, 356–57, 360, 381, 383–84, 440, 445, 454, 510, 542, 552, 555, 577, 590, 626, 697, 718, 882, 1282, 1285, 1373, 1529, 1534, 1540–42, 1552, 1562, 1566, 1592
Letters from: 354, 369, 376, 388, 397, 399, 404, 409, 421, 439, 495, 503, 546, 549, 620, 666, 683, 708, 711, 724, 744–45, 753, 776, 786, 1194, 1582, 1585
Letters to: 743, 746

Adult Female Orphan Institution, the, 1596

Ægina Marbles, the, 125

Ailesbury, Anne, Countess of (d. 1813), 224

Ailesbury, Charles Brudenell Bruce, second Earl and first Marquis of (1773–1856), 1413

Albani, Cardinal, 766

Albemarle, George Monck, first Duke of (1608–1670), 939

Albemarle, William Charles Keppel, fourth Earl of (1772–1849), 114, 1079

Alcudia, Count de, 1300

Alcudia, Manuel de Godoy, Prince of the Peace, and Duke of (1767–1851), 278

Alexander I, Tsar (1777–1825), 278–79, 282, 298–98A, 303, 315–16, 318, 335–36, 364, 381, 384, 394, 398, 403, 407, 411, 416–17, 419, 422, 429, 438, 442–43, 450, 454, 463, 479, 485, 491, 494, 500, 514, 533, 540–43, 545, 551, 554, 1200, 1592
Letter from: 1174

Alexander, Sir William, 1134

Ali, Pasha of Janina (1741–1822), 526

Allan, 563

Allen, William (1770–1843), 452, 543–44

Alopeus [Alopaeus], 278, 287, 523

Althorp, Viscount. *See* Spencer

Amalia, Princess, of Prussia, 440

Ambrossi, 901

Amelia, Princess (1783–1810), 361

Amherst, William Pitt Amherst, Earl (1773–1857), 761

Amir Khan, the Pathan leader, 521

Amory, Samuel, 749

Amshehl (?), Colonel, 411

Ancillon, 1529

Angerstein, John Julius (1735–1823), 1588, 1591–92

Anglesey, Charlotte, Marchioness of (d. 1853), 621, 714

Anglesey, Marquis of. *See* Paget

Angoulême, Duchess of, 438, 1260

Anne, Queen (1665–1714), 52, 789

Antaldi, Marquis, 766, 998

Antigallican, the, 148, 152

Anti-Jacobin, the, 1595

Arbuthnot, Dr Alexander, 1061
Arbuthnot, Charles (1767–1850), 41, 142, 149, 152, 156, 173, 650, 1005–6, 1065, 1085, 1102, 1116, 1124–25, 1233
    Letters from: 75, 94–95, 98–99, 109, 153, 155, 174, 177, 183, 208, 234, 323–24, 525, 568, 908, 911, 1117, 1119–20, 1274, 1291, 1304, 1370, 1537
    Letters to: 325, 760
Arbuthnot, Colonel Charles, Charles Arbuthnot's son, 525
Arbuthnot, Mrs Harriett (d. 1834), 1116, 1119–20
    Letter from: 1124
Arbuthnott, John, eighth Viscount (1778–1860), 1361
Arden, Margaret Elizabeth, Lady (? 1769–1851), 299
Argueilles, 816
Argyll, John Campbell, second Duke of (1678–1743), 215
Argyll, George William Campbell, sixth Duke of (1766–1839), 1362, 1487
    Letters from: 1363, 1365
Armagh, Archbishop of. *See* Stuart, William
Armstrong, Dr, 121
Arnscheldt, Major General, 1527
Artois, Count of. *See* Charles X
Ashe, Thomas, 860
    Letter from: 845
Asheton, Captain, 215
Aston, 231
Atholl, John Murray, fourth Duke of (1755–1830), 1403
Atkins, John Pelly, 155
Attersoll, John, 160
Atwood, 1145
Aubrey, Major, 678
Augereau, General (1757–1816), 201
Augusta, Princess of Wales (d. 1772), 185
Augusta, Princess Royal of England and Duchess of Brunswick (1737–1813), 669
Augusta, Princess of Saxony (b. 1782), 440
Augusta, Duchess of Mecklenburg-Strelitz (1822–1916), daughter of Duke of Cambridge, 1566
Augusta, Princess (b. 1804), daughter of Duchess of Cumberland, 798
Augusta Sophia, Princess (1768–1840), 394, 484, 640, 673, 739, 923–24

Augustus Frederick, Duke of Sussex (1773–1843), 55, 238, 288–89, 465, 717, 796
    Letters from: 675, 756
Austin, William, 508, 509, 529, 766–67, 827, 830, 839, 884, 998
Austin, Mrs (d. 1842), 767, 839
Austin, William's "father" (d. 1832), 767, 839
Austria, Emperor of. *See* Francis I
Austria, Empress of. *See* Maria Louisa
Austria, Prince Royal of. *See* Ferdinand, Emperor
Ava, Bodawpaya, King of (d. 1819), 765

Baden, Charles Frederick, Grand Duke of (d. 1811), 364
Baden, Louis, Grand Duke of (1763–1830), 1417, 1527
Bagot, Sir Charles (1781–1843), 794, 1174, 1372
Bagot, Richard (1782–1854), 1372
Bagot, William, second Baron (1773–1856), 1372
Bailey. *See* Bayley, Sir John
Baillie, Dr Matthew (1761–1823), 476–77, 482, 628, 698, 700, 783
    Letters from: 481, 488
Baji Rao, 742, 765
Baker, 1581
Baker, Anthony St John, 170
Baker, Sir Robert, 953
Balcarres, Alexander Lindsay, sixth Earl of (1752–1825), 438
Balmerino, Arthur Elphinstone, sixth Baron (1688–1746), 1358
Bankes, Henry (1757–1834), 66–67, 461, 466–67, 641, 649, 1348
Bar, M. de, 349
Barclay, David, 1337
Barclay, Sir Robert (1755–1839), 1088
    Letters from: 161, 401
    Letter to: 162
Barclay de Tolly, Michael, Prince (1761–1818), 152, 318, 514
Barclays, Tritton & Co., bankers, 161
Barham, Joseph Foster, 123, 461
Baring, Alexander, first Baron Ashburton (1774–1848), 1357, 1501
Barlow, Sir George Hilaro (1762–1846), 301
Barnard, Sir Andrew Francis (1773–1855), 572
Barnard, Lady Anne (1750–1825), *Letters from*: 438, 572
Barnes, Sir Edward (1776–1838), 984, 986

Barnes, Thomas (1785–1841), 821
  Letters from: 840, 844
Barrington, Dr Shute, Bishop of Durham
  (1734–1826), 1000
Barrow, Sir John (1764–1848), 649
Bates, 1119
Bath, Sir William Pulteney, Earl of
  (1684–1764), 1010
Bathurst, Benjamin (1784–1809), 523
Bathurst, Chas. Bragge (d. 1831), 461,
  565, 890, 972
Bathurst, Lady Georgiana (d. 1841),
  591, 982, 1088, 1272
Bathurst, Henry, third Earl (1762–1834),
  78, 337–38, 344, 401, 519, 522–23,
  537, 588–89, 593–94, 600, 613–14,
  698, 735, 982, 986, 1028, 1036,
  1099, 1109, 1170–71, 1197, 1199,
  1224, 1312, 1461, 1540, 1592
  Letters from: 180, 591, 703, 707, 984,
  1088, 1093, 1145, 1248, 1272
  Letter to: 985
Batley, Charles Harrison, 1341
Batoni [Battoni], Pompeo, 732, 781
Battescombe [Battiscombe], Robert,
  apothecary, 536
Bavaria, Maximilian Joseph, Elector
  and King of (1756–1825), 364, 424,
  500, 794, 1255
Bavaria, Lewis I, King of (1786–1868),
  463, 545
Bayford, John, *Letter from*: 288
  Letter to: 289
Bayley, Sir John (1763–1841), 1182
Beacon, the, 148
Beaufort, Henry Charles Somerset,
  sixth Duke of (1766–1835), 1292
Beaufort, Henry Somerset, Marquis of
  Worcester, seventh Duke of (1792–
  1853), 346
Beauharnais, Eugène (1781–1824), 533
Beaulieu, Colonel, 421
Beaumont, Thomas Wentworth (1792–
  1848), 1328
Beckendorff, 1364
Bedford, Francis Russell, fifth Duke of
  (1765–1802), 6
Bedford, John Russell, sixth Duke of
  (1766–1839), 23, 64, 106, 114, 355
  Letter from: 6
Beechey, Sir William (1753–1839), 38,
  59, 656, 1283, 1596
  Letters from: 218, 299, 459, 462,
  657–58
Belasyse, Thomas Edward Wynn,
  Letter from: 34
Belhaven and Stenton, eighth Baron
  (1793–1868), 1361

Bell's Dispatch, 148
Bell's Messenger, 148
Bellamy, J., 1596
Bellingham, John (*c.* 1771–1812), 73, 74
Benedict XIV, Pope (1675–1758), 732,
  779, 781
Benett, John, M.P., 1271, 1357
Benfield, Paul (d. 1810), 330
Bennet, Henry Grey (1777–1836), 45,
  648
Bennet, Richard Henry Alexander, 63
Bennett, 1001
Bennigsen, Count (1745–1826), 399,
  404, 421, 439, 514
Benoit, François, 403
Bentinck, Lady William (d. 1843), 121
Bentinck, Lord William Charles Augus-
  tus Cavendish (1780–1826), 171,
  1425
  Letter from: 173
Bentinck, Lord William Henry Caven-
  dish (1774–1839), 121
  Letter from: 446
Berenger, Charles de, 410
Beresford, Admiral Sir John Poo (1766–
  1844), 660–61
Beresford, William Carr, Viscount
  Beresford (1768–1854), 418, 1171,
  1258, 1284, 1414, 1590
Bergami. *See* Pergami
Berkeley. *See* Paget, Berkeley
Berkeley, Mary, Countess of (? 1767–
  1844), 52
Bernadotte, afterwards Charles XIV,
  King of Sweden and Norway
  (1764–1844), 145, 278–79, 287,
  303, 316, 318–19, 342, 344, 349,
  360, 376, 379, 384, 388, 397, 399,
  1085, 1165
Bernstorff, Count, 800, 1417, 1527–29,
  1534–35, 1542, 1552
Berolden. *See* Beroldingen
Beroldingen, Count de, 402, 406, 422,
  427–28, 431, 442, 455, 547
Beroldingen, Wurtemberg Minister at
  Vienna, 402
Berri, duc de (1778–1820), 796
Berri, Duchess of, 1260
Best, Baron, 795
Best, Colonel, 409, 439, 549, 620
Best, Thomas, *Letters from*: 158, 169
Best, William Draper, first Baron Wyn-
  ford (1767–1845), 737, 757
Bethell, Christopher (1773–1859), 1137,
  1139
Bexley, Lord. *See* Vansittart
Beyme, K. F. von, 798
Bhopal, Raja of, 521

Bianchi, Giuseppe, 844
Billinghausen, M. Münch de. *See* Münch
Binning, Lord. *See* Hamilton
Birnie, Sir Richard (? 1760–1832), 1263
Black Dwarf, the, 1522
Blackstone, Sir William (1723–1780), 1209
Blackwell, 524
Blackwood's Magazine, 1046
Blane, Sir Gilbert (1749–1834), 1588
Blomberg, Rev. Frederick William (? 1762–1847), 974–75, 977
Blomfield, Rev. Charles James (1786–1857), 1159
Bloomfield, Sir Benjamin, first Baron Bloomfield (1768–1846), 51, 290, 318, 356, 360, 369, 376, 386, 388, 393–94, 399, 403, 411, 414, 454, 472, 477, 486, 491, 541, 546, 574, 589, 593, 628, 641, 651, 690, 717, 722, 761, 804, 818, 829, 845, 849, 878, 881, 917, 921–22, 946, 958, 963, 965, 967–68, 972, 975, 981, 991, 997, 999, 1005–8, 1011–24, 1026, 1062, 1178, 1534, 1588, 1592–93
   Letters from: 357, 588, 595, 602, 660, 692, 706, 731, 734, 760, 769, 771, 785, 825, 956, 976, 978, 1009, 1027–28, 1030, 1032–33, 1049, 1055–56, 1069, 1165, 1167, 1173, 1179, 1193, 1294
   Letters to: 645, 661, 698–99, 702, 712–13, 730, 740, 759, 763, 768, 770, 781, 799, 812, 814, 821–22, 824, 858, 862, 884, 886, 893, 897, 898, 905, 908, 910–12, 914–16, 918–19, 925, 930–32, 937, 943, 944, 974, 980, 993, 1035, 1068, 1085
Bloomfield, Harriet, Lady, 1049, 1056, 1165, 1294, 1546
Bloomfield, John Arthur Douglas, second Baron Bloomfield (1802–1879), 717, 1032–33, 1056, 1085, 1165, 1167, 1173, 1178–79, 1193, 1294
Bloomfield, Lieutenant, 893
Blucher, Field Marshal (1742–1819), 315, 318, 399–400, 403, 429, 478–79, 519, 533, 541, 798, 1200, 1592
Blucher, Lieutenant Colonel, 318, 541
Bolivar, Simon (1783–1830), 1407
Bolton, Colonel John, 151
Bonaparte, Jerome (1784–1860), 349, 361, 1527
Bonaparte, Lucien (1775–1840), 73, 830
Bonaparte, Mme (d. 1822), 432
Bonaparte, Napoleon. *See* Napoleon I
Bone, Henry (1755–1834), 62

Bonelli, 670, 781
Bootle Wilbraham. *See* Wilbraham
Boscawen, Rev. John Evelyn (1790–1851), 975
Boswell, James (1740–1795), 1571
Bourne, William Sturges- (1769–1845), 1322, 1337, 1351, 1377, 1381, 1400
   Letters from: 1352, 1386
Bouverie, Edward (1760–1824), *Letter from*: 24
Bouverie and Antrobus, Messrs, 847
Bower, 352
Bowring, 1163
Bowyer, Robert (1758–1834), 478
Boyen, Major General von, 541–42, 798
Boyle, David, Lord Boyle, Lord Justice Clerk of Scotland (1772–1853), 939
Braddyll, Colonel Wilson (1755–1818), *Letter from*: 26
Bradshaw, Augustus Cavendish, M.P., 127, 173, 174
   Letters from: 150, 175, 209, 253, 474
Bradshaw, Mrs A. C., 150, 474
Bradshaw, Major, 521
Braithwaite, John (1797–1870), 1560
Brand, Thomas, Baron Dacre, 461, 878
Brandish's medicine, 723
Brazil, Prince of, 54, 60, 141
Bremer, the Hanoverian Minister, 282, 287, 342, 1527
Brent, Timothy (Groom and Clerk of the Robes and Deputy Comptroller of the Household), 1043, 1112
Breslau, Bishop of, 1533
Bridge, the jeweller, 640
Bridges [Brydges], George, 860, 884
Briggs, Captain Thomas, 830
British and Foreign School Society, 355, 433, 543–44, 1596
British Institution, the, 265, 296
British Museum, the, 1057–58
British Neptune, the, 148
British Press, the, 32–33
Broadhead, Theodore Henry, M.P., 461
Broadwood, Mrs, 1502
Brogden, James, M.P. (1765?–1842), 63, 145, 254, 518, 1271
Brogham. *See* Brougham
Bron [Brun], Mariette, 766, 830, 842, 847, 856, 998
Brooks, 155
Brougham, Henry Peter, Baron Brougham and Vaux (1778–1868), 178, 458, 466, 646, 799–800, 809, 821–23, 830, 833, 838–39, 842, 848, 857, 894, 901, 936, 1043, 1271, 1322–23, 1334–35, 1337, 1417, 1501, 1579

Brougham, Henry Peter (*cont.*)
　Letters from: 465, 653, 782, 801, 819,
　　834, 836, 841, 847, 851, 856, 889,
　　1374
　Letters to: 766–67, 820, 837
Brougham, James (1780–1833), 847, 891
　Letters from: 766–67, 838–40, 857
Brougham, John Waugh (1785–1829),
　766
Brougham, William, second Baron
　(1795–1886), 766–67
Broughton, C. R., 41, 136
Brown, 323
Browne, 1061
Browne, Anthony, M.P., 461
Browne, Denis (1763–1828), 913
Browne, Peter, 913
Browne, Lieutenant-Colonel Sir Thomas
　Henry, 766, 787, 847–48, 858, 891,
　898–900, 1088
　Letter from: 892
　Letter to: 748
Brownlow, the Rev. W., *Letter from*:
　1556A
Brownrigg, Sir Robert (1759–1833),
　984
Bruce, 749
Bruges, Comte de, 152
Brunswick, Duchess of (1737–1813),
　245, 257, 306, 508, 670, 998
Brunswick, Charles William Ferdinand,
　Duke of (1735–1806), 669–70, 845
Brunswick, Frederick William, Duke of
　(1771–1815), 207, 282, 287, 303,
　306, 407, 508, 583, 766
　Letter from: 510
Brunswick, Charles, Duke of (1804–
　1873), 1336, 1409, 1417, 1419,
　1527, 1529, 1566
Brunswick, William, Duke of (1806–
　1884), 1336, 1417, 1419
Brunswick Clubs, 1535
Bubna-Littiz, Count Ferdinand von, 523
Buccleugh, Charles William Henry Scott,
　fourth Duke of (1772–1819), 1361
Buccleugh, Walter Francis Montagu
　Scott Douglas, fifth Duke of
　(1806–1884), 1371
Buckingham, first Marquis of (1753–
　1813), 190, 818
Buckingham and Normanby, Catherine,
　Duchess of (d. 1743), 1010
Buckingham, second Marquis of, and
　first Duke of Buckingham and
　Chandos (1776–1839), 198, 881,
　969, 971, 973, 977, 979, 988–89,
　1086, 1222
　Letter from: 818

Buckinghamshire, Robert Hobart, fourth
　Earl of (1760–1816), 78, 84, 189–
　91, 308, 565–66, 633, 635
　Letter from: 89
Buckner, Rev. John (1734–1824), 1159
Bull, 845
Bull, Dr J., 1574
Buller, James, Clerk of the Privy Council
　(d. 1830), 1143
Buln (?), 479
Bülow, Baron, 791, 798
Burdett, Sir Francis (1770–1844), 241,
　461, 466, 509, 800, 811, 1271,
　1289, 1322–23
Burgess, Henry, 159
　Letter from: 1283
Burgess, Dr Thomas (1756–1837),
　1155
　Letters from: 1115, 1135, 1153,
　1349
Burghersh, Lord. *See* Fane
Burke, 730
Burke, Edmund (1729–1797), 213
Burnaby, Dr Sherrard Beaumont, 155
Burrell, William, 830
Burt, the Rev. Robert, 1588
Bury, Lady Charlotte Susan Maria
　(1775–1861), 508–9, 766, 830
Buxton, Sir Thomas Fowell (1786–
　1845), 1169
Byerly [Byerley], J., 1596
　Letters from: 285–86, 313
Byerly, Mrs, 313
Byron, Lord (1788–1824), 142, 1180

Cabala, 767
Cabinet, the, letters to, 2, 1187
　Minutes: 71, 78, 84, 806, 1170–71,
　1378, 1482
Cabinet, the *Great*, 648
Cabul, Afghan King of, 521
Calcraft, John (1765–1831), 641, 1271,
　1299
Callington election (1818), the, 749
Calvert, 1057
Calvert, Sir Harry (? 1763–1826), 1146–
　47
Cambridge, Adolphus Frederick, Duke
　of. *See* Adolphus Frederick
Cambridge, Augusta, Duchess of (1797–
　1889), 711, 718, 724, 753, 776,
　1566, 1582
Cambridge, George, Duke of (1819–
　1904), 776, 1562, 1566, 1582,
　1585
Cambridge, Rev. George Owen (?1756–
　1841), Archdeacon of Middlesex,
　1217, 1574

Cambridge University Press, the, 1596
Camden, John Jeffreys Pratt, second
    Earl, and first Marquis of (1759–
    1840), 78, 84, 136, 139, 761–62
Campbell, 336
Campbell, Lady, 401
Campbell, Lieutenant, 332
Campbell, Sir Alexander, 401, 573
Campbell, Lady Charlotte. *See* Bury
Campbell, Admiral Sir George (d. 1821),
    660–61, 784–85
Campbell, Sir Henry, 996
Campbell, John Frederick, second Baron
    Cawdor (1790–1860), 661
Campbell, Sir Neil (1776–1827), *Letter
    from*: 432
    Letter to: 526
Canning, Colonel George, first Baron
    Garvagh (1778–1840), 1448
Canning, George (1770–1827), 21, 75–
    76, 80, 84–93, 104–6, 132, 151,
    156, 198, 241, 633, 635, 733, 767,
    825, 862, 875, 877, 890, 893, 895,
    897, 930, 958, 959, 967, 1042–44,
    1049, 1055, 1085, 1087, 1094,
    1110, 1129–30, 1143, 1162, 1170–
    71, 1173, 1179, 1191–93, 1208,
    1222, 1235, 1238, 1282, 1289,
    1294, 1296, 1304, 1313–15, 1344,
    1354–55, 1363, 1365, 1369–70,
    1374–75, 1378–79, 1381, 1384–87,
    1393–95, 1397, 1400, 1403–4,
    1408, 1413, 1423, 1427, 1431,
    1440, 1442, 1445, 1448, 1454,
    1474, 1476, 1510, 1591, 1592
    Letters from: 111, 178, 188, 968,
    1047, 1053, 1090, 1092, 1103–5,
    1127–28, 1149, 1163, 1169, 1177–
    78, 1201, 1218–20, 1222A, 1230–
    31, 1233–34, 1243, 1246, 1252–54,
    1256, 1258, 1260, 1262, 1267,
    1270–71, 1279, 1292, 1299–1300,
    1305, 1316, 1318–24, 1326–28,
    1331, 1333, 1337, 1341–43, 1348,
    1351, 1353, 1356–57, 1359–62,
    1368, 1371–72
    Letters to: 1054, 1126–27, 1221
Canning, Mrs, afterwards Viscountess
    (d. 1837), 1246, 1384, 1395, 1423,
    1448
    Letters from: 1394, 1431, 1476
Canning, Stratford, first Viscount Strat-
    ford de Redcliffe (1786–1880), 126,
    793–94, 1559
Canova, the Abbate, 1210
Canova (1757–1822), 1113, 1210
Canterbury, Archbishop of. *See* Man-
    ners-Sutton

Canterbury, Dean of. *See* Percy, Hugh
Canton, Viceroy of, 654
Capel, General Thomas Edward (1770–
    1855), 660, 661
Capo d'Istrias, Count (1776–1831),
    1373, 1592
Cardigan, Elizabeth, Countess of (1758–
    1823), 640
Carhampton, second Earl of. *See*
    Luttrell
Carlisle, George Howard, sixth Earl of
    (1773–1848), 1331, 1465, 1469,
    1472, 1474, 1480
Carlisle, Georgiana, Countess of (d.
    1858), 1508
Carlisle, Bishop of. *See* Percy, Hugh
Carnoby (?), 549
Caroline, Queen (1768–1821), 45, 53,
    63, 133, 135, 139, 187, 195, 197,
    198, 208, 225, 238, 241–43, 245,
    247, 254, 263, 276–77, 279, 395,
    430, 437, 461, 467, 508–9, 526,
    529, 547A, 548, 552, 555, 562, 583,
    630, 653, 670, 717, 748, 766–67,
    782, 795, 799, 801, 809, 819–23,
    826–27, 831–33, 837–40, 842, 845,
    847, 848, 863–66, 868–75, 877, 879,
    882–84, 887, 889, 891, 893–95,
    899–901, 913, 931–34, 936, 950–
    54, 998, 1240, 1588
    Letter from: 830
    Letters to: 120, 694, 856, 861, 906,
    907
Carpenter, Charles, 749
Carr, Captain, 1522
Carr, Rev. Robert James (1774–1841),
    1063, 1139–40, 1159, 1164, 1353,
    1362, 1583
    Letter from: 1160
Cartwright, Samuel (1789–1864), den-
    tist, 1596
Cartwright, William Ralph (1771–
    1847), 251
Cashel, Richard Lawrence, Archbishop
    of (1760–1838), 1407
Castlereagh, Emily, Viscountess, 412,
    795, 1010, 1036
Castlereagh, Robert Stewart, Viscount,
    afterwards second Marquis of
    Londonderry (1769–1822), 21, 25,
    56, 78, 84–85, 87, 89, 132, 145,
    152, 179, 193, 278–79, 303, 308,
    319, 344, 391, 402, 404, 406–7,
    411–12, 424, 442, 455, 474, 491,
    514, 523, 537, 546–47, 619, 621,
    627, 629, 639, 669, 672, 726–27,
    730, 733, 771, 809, 834, 887, 895,
    898–899, 950, 960, 966, 973, 991,

Castlereagh (*cont.*)
1005, 1011–13, 1015, 1017–18,
1020–21, 1036, 1047, 1072, 1077,
1087, 1189, 1370, 1407, 1592
Letters from: 28–29, 57, 123, 170,
241, 247, 251, 382, 461, 466–67,
494, 550, 629–30, 634, 637–38,
641–44, 646–49, 697, 736, 764,
778, 793–95, 805, 894, 914, 933–
34, 936, 938, 957, 1004, 1022
Letters to: 415, 432, 958–59, 1014
Castlerosse, Lord, second Earl of
Kenmare (1788–1855), 129
Cathcart, Frederick, 794
Cathcart, Sir William Schaw Cathcart,
first Earl (1755–1843), 279, 282,
318, 364, 391, 398
Catherine, Grand Duchess of Oldenburg,
afterwards Queen of Wurtemberg
(1788–1819), 311, 381, 384, 407,
416–17, 425, 442, 463, 479, 484–
85, 510
Cattermole, Rev. Richard (? 1795–
1858), *Letter from*: 1155
Cavaletti, Baron, 830
Cave, Robert Otway, M.P., 1357
Cavendish, Henry (1731–1810), 763
Cawdor, John Campbell, first Baron
(d. 1821), 211, 661
Celtic Society, the, 1046
Chad, George William, 768
Chafy, Rev. William (1779–1843), 1427
Chamberlain, Sir Henry (d. 1829), 1430
Chambers, 155
Chantrey, Sir Francis Legatt (1781–
1841), 1293, 1586, 1589, 1594,
1596
Letters from: 1329, 1569
Charlemagne, Emperor (742–814), 438
Charles II, King of Great Britain and
Ireland (1630–1685), 813, 1106,
1209, 1254
Charles X, King of France (1757–1836),
399, 428, 539, 1176, 1220, 1253–
54, 1256, 1258, 1260, 1262, 1559,
1591–92
Charles XIII, King of Sweden (d. 1818),
278
Charles, Archduke of Austria (1771–
1847), 1592
Charles, Prince, of Mecklenburg-
Strelitz. *See* Mecklenburg-Strelitz
Charles Frederick William Ernest
(1804–1856), son of Duchess of
Kent, 1389
Charlotte, Queen (1744–1818), 63, 185,
206, 216, 219, 221–26, 228–29, 306,
310, 312, 361, 366, 391, 397, 406–

7, 422, 425, 428, 457, 463, 468,
479, 492, 508–9, 561, 577, 587–89,
591, 593–95, 598–600, 602, 604–6,
608, 611–14, 618, 624, 626, 651,
655, 664, 668, 676, 685–86, 697,
724, 727, 739, 753, 755–56, 759,
767, 813, 923
Letters from: 70, 73, 76, 197, 201,
207, 227, 239, 252, 257, 298, 341,
348, 368, 381, 389, 394, 413, 460,
476, 480, 484, 486, 520, 536, 540,
552, 555, 559, 584–85, 590, 603,
607, 617, 632, 640, 674, 705,
721
Letters to: 314, 319, 340, 346, 380,
393, 394A, 420, 477, 482, 504, 517,
537, 582, 586, 615, 672–73, 718,
720, 723, 725
Charlotte, Queen of Wurtemberg. *See*
Wurtemberg
Charlotte Augusta, Princess (1796–
1817), 73, 115, 120, 133, 135, 185,
197, 206–7, 216, 219–24, 229–30,
239, 244, 262, 310, 312, 314, 367–
68, 383, 386, 390–91, 396, 400,
411–12, 415, 425, 430, 434, 438,
442, 457, 460, 463–65, 467, 470,
472, 476–77, 481–82, 484, 486,
488, 492–93, 498, 504, 508–9, 511,
513, 515, 519–20, 522, 536, 547A,
552, 554, 602, 621–22, 630, 632,
640, 645–46, 651, 672, 679, 685–
86, 698–707, 709, 713, 716, 730,
738, 766–67, 838, 1592
Letters from: 217, 245, 436–37, 528,
530–31, 548, 562, 583, 625, 628,
694
Letters to: 277, 395, 471, 506–7, 510,
529, 532
Chatham, William Pitt, first Earl of
(1708–1778), 11, 12
Chaucer, Geoffrey (? 1340–1400), 1223
Chesterfield, Philip Dormer, fourth Earl
of (1694–1773), 1010
Chesterfield, Philip Stanhope, fifth Earl
of (1755–1815), 484
Chichester, Bishop of. *See* Carr
Chichester, Thomas Pelham, second
Earl of (1756–1826), 155, 207
Chinnery, William, 41, 253
Cholmondeley, George James, fourth
Earl and first Marquis of (1749–
1827), 121, 173–74, 469, 568,
670
Letter from: 171
Cholmondeley, Viscount Malpas, fifth
Earl and second Marquis of (1792–
1870), 121

Cholmondeley, Thomas, first Baron Delamere (1767–1855), *Letter from*: 147
Christ Church, Dean of. *See* Hall, C. H.; *and* Smith, Samuel
Christian VII, King of Denmark (d. 1808), 20
Christie, James (1773–1831), 20, 248
Churchill, Francis Almaric Spencer, Baron (1779–1845), 14
Clancarty, Richard Le Poer Trench, first Viscount (1767–1837), 768, 1036, 1090, 1092, 1103
Letter from: 1094
Letters to: 1087, 1104
Clanricarde, Ulick John de Burgh, Marquis of (1802–1874), 1235
Clanwilliam, Richard Charles Francis Meade, third Earl of (1795–1879), 1056, 1534
Letter from: 1200
Letter to: 909
Clare, John Fitzgibbon, first Earl of (1749–1802), 297
Clare, John Fitzgibbon, second Earl of (1793–1864), 333
Clarence, Duke of. *See* William IV
Clarence, Duchess of (1792–1849), 744, 753, 776, 1025, 1286
Clarendon, Edward Hyde, first Earl of (1609–1674), 896
Clarke, Rev. James Stanier (? 1765–1834), 781, 920–22
Letter from: 213
Clarke, Longueville, 749
Clarke, Mary Anne (1776–1852), 142, 508, 576
Clausewitz, Karl von (1780–1831), 798
Clerk, John, Lord Eldin (1757–1832), 1046
Clifford, Sir Augustus William James (1788–1877), 426, 1113
Clifford, Sophia, Lady de (d. 1828), 73, 115, 207, 216–17, 219, 222, 436, 482, 508–9
Letter from: 135
Letters to: 133, 220
Clifton, Lord, afterwards fifth Earl of Darnley (1795–1835), 1328
Cline, Henry (1750–1827), 1588
Clinton, Dr Charles Fynes (d. 1827), 1420
Clinton, Henry Fynes (1781–1852), 1446
Clinton, Robert Cotton St John Trefusis, eighteenth Baron (1787–1832), 171, 749
Clive, Viscount. *See* Powis, Earl of

Coats, Miss, 640
Cobbett, William (1763–1835), 242, 1595
Coburg, Prince. *See* Leopold
Cochrane, Basil (1753–1826), 770
Cochrane, Colonel, 953
Cochrane (?), Sir F., 781
Cochrane, Lord, afterwards tenth Earl of Dundonald (1775–1860), 461, 467, 1248
Cockburn, Alexander (? 1776–1852), 794
Cockburn, Admiral Sir George (1772–1853), 1529–30
Memo. from: 954
Cockburn, Henry Thomas, Lord Cockburn (1779–1854), 1046
Cockerell, Charles Robert (1788–1863), 126
Cockerell, Samuel Pepys (1754–1827), *Letter from*: 126
Codrington, Admiral Sir Edward (1770–1851), *Letter from*: 1257
Codrington, Edward (1803–1819), 1257
Codrington, Admiral Sir Henry John (1808–1877), 1257
Codrington, Lady, 1257
Coghlan, Dr, 408
Coke, Sir Edward (1552–1634), 757
Coke, Edward, M.P., 114
Coke, Thomas William, first Earl of Leicester (1752–1842), 114
Colbourne, General Sir John, first Baron Seaton (1778–1863), 1355
Colchester, Lord. *See* Abbot, Charles
Coleridge, Samuel Taylor (1772–1834), 1156
Colhoun, 166
Collier, Sir George Ralph, 339, 395, 396
Collingwood, Cuthbert, first Baron (1750–1810), 1575
Colloredo, the Austrian General, 318
Colman [Coleman], George, 1339–40
Colnaghi, Paul (1751–1833), 478
Colville, Sir Charles (1770–1843), 1361
Colville, ninth Baron (1768–1849), 1361
Conant, Sir Nathaniel (? 1746–1822), 670, 845
Concannon, Lucius, *Letter from*: 121
Concannon, Mrs, 121
Congreve, Sir William (1772–1828), 148, 164, 168
Letters from: 151, 379
Conroy, Sir John (1786–1854), 768
Consalvi, Cardinal (1757–1824), 494, 709, 738, 766, 1070, 1111, 1113, 1157, 1592

Constantine, the Grand Duke (1779–1831), 315, 384, 440, 621
  his wife, 311
Constitution, the, 148
Constitutional Association, the, 938
Conway, Henry Seymour (1721–1795), Field-Marshal, 215, 329
Conyngham, Lord Albert, afterwards Baron Londesborough (1805–1860), 1493, 1576
Conyngham, Lady Elizabeth (d. 1839), 1592
Conyngham, Elizabeth, Marchioness (d. 1861), 551, 1024, 1130, 1268, 1370, 1528–29, 1534, 1561, 1570, 1576, 1578, 1592
  Letter from: 1530
  Letter to: 1532
Conyngham, Lord Francis Nathaniel, later, Earl of Mountcharles, and subsequently second Marquis Conyngham (1797–1876), 1026, 1031, 1053–54, 1103, 1163, 1165, 1167, 1530, 1591–92
  Letters from: 1129, 1232, 1458, 1462, 1546, 1551
  Letter to: 1130
Conyngham, Henry, first Marquis (1766–1832), 1119, 1193, 1228, 1530, 1532, 1578
  Letters from: 181, 788
  Letter to: 1310
Conyngham, Henry Joseph, Earl of Mountcharles (1795–1824), 1193
  Letter from: 1112
Conyngham, Jane, Marchioness (d. 1876), 1530, 1546, 1551
Conyngham, Lady Maria (d. 1843), 1592
Cooke, Edward (1755–1820), *Letter to*: 58
Cooke, Lieutenant Colonel Henry, 278
Cooke, James Stamp Sutton, 939
Cooke, William (1757–1832), 766, 858, 899–900
  Letter to: 748
Cooper, 1596
Cooper, Sir Astley Paston (1768–1841), 1523
Copleston, Edward, Bishop of Llandaff (1776–1849), 1403–4, 1420, 1426–27, 1429–30, 1432, 1509
  Letter from: 1428
Copley, John Singleton (1737–1815), *Letter from*: 290
Copley, John Singleton, Baron Lyndhurst (1772–1863), 757, 858, 887, 894, 938, 1249–51, 1292, 1333, 1437, 1444–46, 1451, 1459, 1489,
1491, 1496, 1500, 1509, 1513, 1526, 1529, 1546, 1550, 1578
  Letters from: 1334–35, 1447, 1452, 1461, 1463–64, 1469, 1495, 1497, 1518
Cornwallis, Charles, first Marquis (1738–1805), 191
Cornwallis, Charles, second Marquis (1774–1823), 1078–79
Cornwallis, James, fourth Earl (1742–1824), 1137
Courier, the, 208, 501, 525, 681, 857
Courland, Duchess of (d. 1821), 411, 440, 500 n.
Court, A. *See* À Court
Courtenay, Thomas Peregrine (1782–1841), 308, 550
Courtenay, William, third Viscount, afterwards Earl of Devon (1768–1835), 1407
Coutts' Bank, 8, 748, 766, 1188
Coutts, Harriet, afterwards Duchess of St Albans (d. 1837), 845
Coutts, Thomas (1735–1822), 8, 482, 797, 1516
Covent Garden Theatre, 295, 1567, 1596
Cox, Henry, banker, 8
Cox and Merle, 1520, 1522
Cradock, Sir John Francis, first Baron Howden (1762–1839), 845
  Letters from: 143, 835
Crandon, Mary, 860
Cranstoun, George, Lord Corehouse (d. 1850), 1046
Craven, Richard Keppel (1779–1851), 508–9, 830, 847, 871, 873, 884, 998
  Letters from: 866, 872
  Letters to: 868–70
Crede [Credde], Maurice, 830, 847
Creevey, Thomas (1768–1838), 45, 178
Crespigny, Charles Fox, 31, 40, 43, 153, 155
  Letter from: 149
Crewe, Mrs Anna, *Letter from*: 1434
Croft, Sir Richard (1762–1818), 698–700
  Letter from: 701
  Letter to: 706
Croker, John Wilson (1780–1857), 179, 323, 410, 461, 649, 845
  Letters from: 740, 1010, 1387, 1571
Cromwell, Oliver (1599–1658), 148
Cross, Sir John (1766–1842), 1489
Crown Prince of Sweden. *See* Bernadotte
Cruise, 1407
Cumberland, William Augustus, Duke of (1721–1765), 20

Cumberland, Henry Frederick, Duke of (1745–1790), 8

Cumberland, Ernest Augustus, Duke of. *See* Ernest Augustus

Cumberland, Frederica, Duchess of (1778–1841), 279, 386, 391, 412, 468, 479–80, 486, 491, 499, 514, 533, 541, 552, 555, 561, 564–65, 577–78, 582, 587–88, 590–91, 602–5, 607, 611–13, 618, 624, 697, 790, 796–98, 800, 811, 874, 882, 1212, 1336, 1409, 1417, 1419, 1516, 1528–29, 1534–35, 1542, 1545, 1552, 1566

Curran, John Philpot (1750–1817), 323–25

Curtis, Patrick, Archbishop of Armagh (1740–1832), 1552

Curtis, Sir William (1752–1829), 1591–92

Curwen, John Christian (1756–1828), 165

Cust, the Rev., 1427

Dacre, Lord. *See* Brand

Dalhousie, George Ramsay, ninth Earl of (1770–1838), 434

Dallas, Sir George (1758–1833), *Letters from*: 301, 308

Dallas, Sir Robert (1756–1824), 301

Damas, Baron de, 1258, 1260, 1262

Damer, Lieutenant-Colonel. *See* Dawson-Damer

Damer, Lady Caroline, 1205

Damer, Mrs Lionel, 1205

Danvers, 1537

Darby, Admiral H. d'Esterre, 784, 815

Darlington, William Harry Vane, third Earl of, and first Duke of Cleveland (1766–1842), 371, 1289
Letters from: 13, 79

Darmstadt, Lewis I, Grand Duke of. *See* Hesse-Darmstadt

Darnley, fourth Earl of (1767–1831), 537

Dartmouth, Frances, Countess of (d. 1838), 640

Dartmouth, George Legge, Lord (1648–1691), 939

Dashwood, 524

Dashwood, Captain, 215

Dauphin, the. *See* Angoulême

Dauphiness, the. *See* Angoulême

Davies, Rev. Edward (1756–1831), 1156

Davis, Richard Hart, M.P. (? 1767–1842), 1165, 1167, 1193
Letter from: 1085

Davison, Dr, 1403–4

Davout, Marshal (1770–1823), 360, 428

Davy, Sir Humphrey (1778–1829), 763

Dawson, Alexander, M.P., 1271

Dawson, George Robert, M.P., 1322–23, 1509, 1531, 1533, 1540

Dawson, Rev. Henry Richard, Dean of St Patrick's (d. 1840), 1509

Dawson-Damer, Colonel George Lionel (1788–1856), 1202–3, 1205

Day, Alexander (1773–1841), 781
Letter from: 779

Day, Joseph, 781
Letter from: 763

"Dear Saint", the. *See* Tyrwhitt, Sir Thomas

Dearborn, General, 170

De Beaume [Beaune], John Jacques, 1518–19

Decken, Lieutenant General Baron, 342, 399, 549

De Duve, 1527

De la Warr, George John Sackville West, fifth Earl (1791–1869), 1360

Deerhurst, Lady Mary, 1070

Delicate Investigation, the, 51, 187

Demont [Dumont], Louisa, 766, 830, 842, 847

Denham, Sir James Steuart (1744–1839), 513, 516

Denison, John Evelyn, first Viscount Ossington (1800–1873), 1425

Denison, William Joseph (1770–1849), 1228
Letter from: 157

Denman, Thomas, first Baron (1779–1854), 695, 801, 833, 847, 851, 901, 934, 1543
Memorial from: 1526
Letter to: 1547

Denmark, King of. *See* Frederick VI

Denmark, Princess of, 718, 720, 730

Dent, John (d. 1826), 178

Desaguliers, Thomas (? 1725–1780), 349

Despenser, Hugh le (1262–1326), 69

Dessau, Frederica, Duchess of Anhalt- (b. 1796), daughter of Duchess of Cumberland, 1417

D'Este, Sir Augustus Frederick (1794–1848), 717

Deuxpont, Duchesse de, 484

Devonshire, Elizabeth, Duchess of (d. 1824), 1111, 1113, 1157–58, 1591
Letters from: 426, 709, 1070

Devonshire, Georgiana, Duchess of (1757–1806), 1591–92

Devonshire, William Cavendish, fifth Duke of (1748–1811), 709

Devonshire, William George Spencer Cavendish, sixth Duke of (1790–1858), 149, 1158, 1273–74, 1318 –21, 1471, 1474, 1508, 1591–92
Letters from: 1113, 1157, 1276, 1479
Letters to: 1275, 1465
De Witt, 1527
Dickie, Andrew (d. 1834), 1457
Dilke, 136
Dion Cassius, 1526
Disbrowe, Sir Edward Cromwell, 1082, 1215
D'Ivernois, Sir Francis, 523
Dixon, 749
Doble, 191
Dodson, Sir John (1780–1858), 894
Dodsworth, Rev. Frederick (? 1739–1821), 916
Domett, Sir William (1754–1828), 784
Donkin, Sir Rufus, 996
Donna Maria, Queen of Portugal (1819–1853), 1552, 1591–92
Donoughmore, Richard Hely-Hutchinson, first Earl of (1756–1825), 881
Letter from: 884
Doppieri, Monsignor S., 781
Letter from: 732
Dörenberg, M. de, 1534
Dörenberg, Mlle de, 1534
Dorset, George John Frederick Sackville, fourth Duke of (1793–1815), 1137
Dorset, Charles Sackville Germain, fifth Duke of (1767–1843), 1166
Letters from: 970, 1314
Douglas, Lady, 190, 251, 1596
Douglas, Sir John (d. 1814), 190–91, 848
Douglas, Lieutenant-General, 955
Dowdeswell, 405
Dowling, Vincent George (1785–1852), *Letter from*: 832
Downes, William, first Baron (1752–1826), 999, 1165
Downshire, Mary, Marchioness of (d. 1836), 179
Downshire, third Marquis of (1788–1845), 179
Doyle, Sir Francis Hastings (1783–1839), 521, 963, 965, 968, 978
Letters from: 962, 972
Letter to: 964
Doyle, Sir John (? 1750–1834), *Letter from*: 505
Drake, Francis (d. 1821), Minister at Munich, 407
Drummond, the banker, 410

Drummond, Sir Gordon, 996
Drummond, Sir John Forbes (d. 1829), 1440, 1442
Drummond, Sir William (? 1770–1828), 508
Drummond's Bank, 8, 1200
Drury Lane Theatre, 199, 205
Dublin, Archbishop of. *See* Troy
Dublin Evening Mail, the, 1407
Dublin Tabinet Ball, The, Article in *New Monthly Magazine*, 1244
Duckworth, Admiral Sir John Thomas (1748–1817), 240
Dudley, Sir Henry Bate (1745–1824), 142, 1001
Letters from: 114, 1125
Dudley, Earl of. *See* Ward
Duff, Sir Alexander, 1289
Duncombe, Charles, Baron Feversham (1764–1841), 1235
Duncombe, William, afterwards second Baron Feversham (1798–1867), 1322
Dundas, 206
Dundas, General Francis (d. 1822), 996
Dundonald, Anna Maria, Countess of (d. 1822), *Letter from*: 770
Dundonald, ninth Earl of (1748–1831), 770
Dunlop, Lieutenant-General, 996
Du Pasquier, 440, 1588
Dupaquet. *See* Du Pasquier
Durham, Bishop of. *See* Barrington, Shute; and Van Mildert, William
Dya Ram, 678
Dyneley, John, 330
Dyneley, Robert Peter (d. 1815), 330
Dynevor, George Talbot Rice, third Baron (1765–1852), 1430

Eben, Frederick, Baron, 290
Ebrington, Viscount, second Earl Fortescue (1783–1861), 467, 800
Edinburgh Review, the, 1046, 1283, 1595
Edmonstone, Neil Benjamin (1765–1841), 573
Edward Augustus, Duke of Kent (1767–1820), 433, 452, 513, 634, 640, 667, 707, 727, 778, 790, 799
Letter from: 768
Letter to: 769
Edwardina Kent, 509
Edwards, 827, 828
Edwards, an attorney, 1563
Eldon, John Scott, first Earl of (1751–1838), 5, 9–10, 71, 78, 84, 104–5, 114, 124, 198, 318, 414, 468, 470,

Eldon (*cont.*)
   479, 514, 524, 533, 545, 565, 577–
   78, 588, 594, 603, 613, 630, 639,
   644, 698, 748, 754, 767, 771, 797,
   801, 839, 858, 874, 882, 899, 1097,
   1106, 1143–44, 1170–71, 1181,
   1250, 1282, 1312, 1332, 1364,
   1491, 1494, 1497, 1500, 1512–13,
   1540, 1591, 1592
   Letters from: 90, 120, 259, 631, 726,
   737, 755, 757, 789, 923, 1038,
   1108, 1134, 1182–83, 1251, 1306–
   8
   Letters to: 863, 888, 924, 1044
   Minute on Coronation Oath, 1209
Elgin, Thomas Bruce, seventh Earl of
   (1766–1841), 1361
Elgin Marbles, the, 1596
Elizabeth, Princess (1770–1840), 229,
   380, 393–94, 500, 519, 536–37,
   673, 718, 721, 736, 1339, 1541,
   1566
Elizabeth Georgina Adelaide, Princess
   (1820–1821), 902
Ellenborough, Edward Law, first Baron
   (1750–1818), 164, 193, 537, 565,
   644, 795
   Letter to: 754
Ellenborough, Edward Law, first Earl
   of (1790–1871), 165, 1374, 1540
Ellenborough, Octavia, Lady (1772–
   1819), 764
Elliot, William, M.P. (d. 1818), 637
Elliott, Captain George, 352–53
Ellis, Charles Rose, first Baron Seaford
   (1771–1845), 155, 887, 894–5,
   1235, 1243
Ellis, Sir Henry (1777–1869), 1446
Ellison, Richard, 45
Elphinstone, George Keith, Viscount
   Keith (1746–1823), 395–96, 435,
   515–16, 1071
   Letter from: 547 A
   Letters to: 418, 434
Elphinstone, Margaret Mercer, Vis-
   countess Keith, Comtesse de Fla-
   hault (1788–1867), 486, 508–9,
   511, 515, 529, 531, 547 A, 679,
   1071
   Letters from: 339, 370, 395–96
   Letters to: 387, 435
Elphinstone, Mountstuart (1779–1859),
   1071
Elphinstone, Sir Robert Dalrymple
   Horn (1766–1848), 1423
Elphinstone, William Fullerton, 301,
   1105
Ende, Baron d', 874

Englishman, the, 148
Enniskillen, John Willoughby Cole,
   second Earl of (1768–1840), 1545,
   1551
Epaminondas (*c.* 418–362 B.C.), 1256
Erne, Mary, Lady (d. 1842), 1158
Ernest, Prince of Mecklenburg-Strelitz.
   See Mecklenburg-Strelitz
Ernest, Duke of Saxe-Coburg. *See*
   Saxe-Coburg
Ernest Augustus, Duke of Cumberland
   (1771–1851), 76, 298, 308, 357,
   369, 381, 384, 386, 388, 391,
   393–94, 397, 407, 412, 442, 486,
   552, 561, 564–65, 582, 587–88,
   590, 593–95, 598, 600, 602–3, 605,
   611, 614, 618, 621, 1212, 1216–17,
   1247, 1285, 1557, 1561, 1565,
   1574, 1577, 1578, 1581, 1583, 1585
   Letters from: 278–79, 282, 287, 298 A,
   303, 311, 315–16, 318, 327, 342,
   344, 349, 356, 360, 403, 411, 414,
   429, 440, 445, 454, 468, 479, 491,
   499, 500, 514, 533, 541–42, 545,
   577, 608, 613, 624, 626, 747, 790–
   91, 796–98, 800, 811, 874, 882,
   1282, 1336, 1364, 1366, 1373,
   1409, 1417, 1419, 1421, 1490,
   1516, 1527–29, 1531, 1533–35,
   1540–42, 1545, 1552, 1555
   Letters to: 152, 392, 480, 555, 578,
   591, 607, 612
Errington, Mrs, 1588
Erroll, William George Hay, eighteenth
   Earl of (1801–1846), 1358, 1360–61
   Letter from: 1346
Erskine, Thomas, Lord (1750–1823),
   80, 105, 269, 834, 1131
   Letters from: 19, 470–71, 473, 512
Essex, George Capel, fifth Earl of
   (1757–1839), 198
Esterhazy, Prince Paul Anton (1786–
   1866), 311, 315, 787, 1219, 1222 A
Esterhazy, Princess Paul (b. 1794), 311,
   787
Evans, G. W., 563
Evans, Richard (1784–1871), 1596
Evelyn, Lyndon, 177
Examiner, the, 148, 588, 1588
Exeter, Brownlow Cecil, second Mar-
   quis of (1795–1867), 1274
Exmouth, Sir Edward Pellew, first
   Viscount (1757–1833), 830
Eyre, 766

Fagel, Henry, 382, 430, 1087, 1090,
   1092, 1104
Falconet, 766, 830

Falkiner, Sir Frederick John, *Letters from*: 127, 134

Falmouth, Edward Boscawen, first Earl of (1787–1841), 975

Fane, 328

Fane, John, Lord Burghersh, eleventh Earl of Westmorland (1784–1859), 432, 1012

Fanna, 844

Farnborough, Lord. *See* Long, Charles

Farquhar, Sir Robert Townsend (1776–1830), 337, 401, 573, 1088

Farquhar, Sir Walter (? 1738–1819), 1147, 1588

Farrell, 1407

Fazel. *See* Fagel

Felici, 998

Fenn, Peter, 1550

Feodore, Princess (1807–1872), 1367, 1389, 1405

Ferdinand I, King of Naples and Sicily (1751–1825), 1022

Ferdinand VII, King of Spain (1784–1833), 816, 1253, 1256, 1258, 1262, 1300

Ferdinand, Archduke, and Emperor of Austria, 523, 545, 551

Ferguson, Sir Ronald Craufurd (1773–1841), 934, 1271

Fergusson, Robert Cutlar (1768–1838), 1271

Fesch, Cardinal (1763–1839), 432

Fielding, Lady, 640

Fife, James Duff, second Earl of (1729–1809), 52

Fife, James Duff, fourth Earl of (1776–1857), 1237, 1289, 1320

Finch, 821

Finlay, Councillor, 129

Fisher, John, Bishop of Salisbury (1748–1825), 216, 504
Letters from: 115, 492

Fisher, Major General (d. 1814), 492

FitzClarence, Adolphus (1802–1856), 1596

FitzClarence, Lady Amelia (d. 1858), 1539

FitzClarence, Frederick (1799–1854), 1596

FitzClarence, George Augustus Frederick, first Earl of Munster (1794–1842), 501, 573, 616, 662, 1596

FitzClarence, Lieutenant Henry (?1796–1817), 616, 652, 739

FitzErnest, George, 500

Fitzgerald, Captain, 1503

Fitzgerald, Lieutenant General Sir Augustine (d. 1834), 181

Fitzgerald, Maurice, Knight of Kerry (1774–1849), 30, 123

Fitzgerald, William Vesey, Baron Fitzgerald and Vesey (1783–1843), 466

FitzHenry, M., 1522

Fitzherbert, Maria Anne (1756–1837), 292, 1202–3, 1205, 1228, 1588, 1596

Fitzsimons, Edward, *Letter from*: 558

Fitzwilliam, William Wentworth, second Earl Fitzwilliam (1748–1833), 1407

Flahault, the Comte de (1785–1870), 1071

Fletcher, Joseph, 677

Flinn, Lieutenant John. *See* Flynn

Flint, Sir Charles (Resident Under-Secretary to the Lord-Lieutenant), *Letter to*: 816

Flynn, Lieutenant John, 830, 842

Foley, Sir Thomas (1757–1833), 784

Fonblanque, 821

Forbes, Sir Charles (1774–1849), 1169

Forbes, Lady Elizabeth, 830, 847

Forbes, eighteenth Baron (1765–1843), 1361

Forbes, Viscount (1785–1836), 30, 47
Letters from: 35, 39, 48

Forster [Foster], John, 1203, 1205

Foster, 563

Foster, the architect, 126

Foster, Sir Augustus John (1780–1848), 1011, 1179

Foundling Hospital, the, 1596

Fox, Charles James (1749–1806), 6–7, 148, 730, 1079, 1254, 1596

Fox, Mrs, wife of C. J. Fox, 1596

Fox, Henry Stephen (1791–1846), 1493

Fox, Joseph (? 1776–1816), *Letters from*: 433, 452, 543–44
Letter to: 441

Fox Club, the, 1046

Fox-Strangways, William Thomas Horner, fourth Earl of Ilchester (1795–1865), 1493

Francis I, Emperor of Austria (1768–1835), 316, 318, 335, 364, 419, 438, 443, 491, 510, 541–42, 551, 554, 766, 800, 830, 1031, 1222A, 1260, 1409, 1417, 1552, 1592

Francis, Sir Philip (1740–1818), *Letters from*: 293–94

Francis, Catherine, daughter of Sir Philip Francis, 294

Francomb, 155

Frankland, Colonel William, 466

Frederick II, King of Prussia (1712–1786), 839, 1373

Frederick, Prince, of Prussia. *See* Frederick William IV

Frederick William Louis, Prince, of Prussia. *See* Prussia

Frederick VI, King of Denmark (1768–1839), 388, 500, 718, 1167

Frederick Augustus, Duke of York and Albany (1763–1827), 6–7, 15, 23, 61, 210, 242, 292, 352, 368, 380, 479, 501, 517, 548, 576, 580, 725, 730, 744, 767, 815, 838, 947, 953, 1085, 1099, 1147, 1194, 1196–97, 1199, 1261, 1268, 1274, 1280, 1282, 1285–86, 1289, 1338–39, 1366, 1525, 1574, 1588, 1592

Letters from: 3–4, 185, 513, 516, 519, 761, 783, 996, 1096, 1114, 1123, 1205, 1265–66, 1269

Letters to: 1, 487, 515, 522, 762, 855, 1122, 1203, 1245

Frederick William III, King of Prussia (1770–1840), 279, 282, 287, 298–98A, 303, 316, 318, 364, 403, 407, 411, 414, 429, 438, 440, 443, 450, 454, 468, 479, 486, 491, 499–500, 514, 523, 533, 540–42, 545–46, 565, 577, 582, 585, 604–5, 613, 697, 791, 796, 798, 882, 1200, 1336, 1364, 1373, 1409, 1417, 1527–29, 1531, 1533–34, 1552, 1592

Letter to: 611

Frederick William IV, King of Prussia (1795–1861), 367, 468, 882, 1373, 1419, 1528

Free Masons, the, 55, 65, 288

Freeling, Sir Francis (1764–1836), 1502

Freeman's Journal, the, 27

Freemasons' Charity, the, 1596

Fremantle, Vice Admiral Sir Thomas Francis (1765–1819), 121

Fremantle, Sir William Henry (1766–1850), 45, 969

French, *Letter from*: 527

Frenwick, Mrs, 1588

Frere, Bartholomew (1778–1851), 795, 831

Frewin, Richard (1742–1822), 253

Friske, 1419

Fritz Louis. *See* Prussia

Fyson, Samuel, *Letter from*: 891

Gaekwar of Baroda, the, 765

Gagarin [Gagrin], Mrs (d. 1813), 207, 219

Gage, Lady (d. 1821), 640

Gainsborough, Thomas (1727–1788), 676

Galignani, Giovanni Antonio (1752–1821), 1521–22

Galitzin, Princess, 1252

Gallatin, Albert (1761–1849), 170

Gallatin, Count de, 306

Gandi (?), Major General, 499

Gangadhar Sastri (d. 1815), 765

Gardiner, Sir Robert, *Letters from*: 698–700, 702

Garrow, Sir William (1760–1840), 31, 40, 43, 461, 467, 565, 1491

Letter from: 36

Gascoyne, General Isaac (1770–1841), 177–78

Gaveston, Piers (d. 1312), 69

Gay, John (1685–1732), 1010

Gell, Sir William (1777–1836), 508, 766, 830, 847, 998

Letters from: 526, 848

Gentz, Friedrich von (1764–1832), 514, 1592

George I (1660–1727), 416, 813, 896, 905

George II (1683–1760), 20, 905

George III (1738–1820), 1–2, 6–8, 11, 20, 38, 49, 59, 61, 63, 73, 76, 88, 101, 124, 128, 148, 206, 229, 304, 306, 309, 328–29, 355, 361, 381, 390, 394, 404, 407, 413, 425, 428, 443, 449, 451, 454, 456, 482, 489, 493, 497, 503, 508, 535–37, 544, 564–65, 568, 584, 590–91, 596, 603, 647, 657, 664, 677, 697, 717, 761, 762, 767, 783, 788–92, 797, 813, 818, 872, 880, 903, 993, 1058–59, 1072, 1079, 1085, 1186–87, 1189, 1197, 1206, 1209, 1269, 1296, 1347, 1364, 1366, 1414, 1427, 1484, 1538, 1545, 1560, 1571, 1590, 1592, 1596

George IV (1762–1830), [1812], 4, 8, 10–12, 17–20, 22, 26–33, 35–41, 43–44, 47–56, 59–61, 63–65, 71–72, 75, 81–82, 94–98, 103, 110–13, 115–21, 124–25, 127–34, 136, 139–41, 143, 145–46, 148–50, 152, 154–55, 157, 159, 160, 163–64, 167–69, 171, 173–75, 181, 183, 187, 194, 196, 199–200, 202, 205, 208–9, [1813], 212, 214, 218, 226, 230, 232–33, 235, 237, 242–43, 248–50, 254–56, 260, 264–65, 267, 270, 272–73, 275–76, 278, 280, 283–85, 288–90, 292–93, 295–97, 299–303, 305–9, 316–17, 320–23, 325–26, 328–29, 332–34, 343, 347, 350–52, 355, 358, 363, 365–66, 372, 374–75, 377–78, [1814], 384–86, 391, 396, 401–2, 406–8, 412, 416, 423, 432–33, 436, 438, 441, 443, 447,

George IV (*cont.*)

450–53, 458–59, 462, 469–71, 474, 478, 480, 483, 489–90, 492, 496, 507, [1815], 509–10, 512, 518, 521, 523, 527, 534, 543–44, 555–58, 565, 569, 574–76, 580, 588, 591–92, 595–96, 599, 602–6, 609–10, 612–13, 616, 618, 621, 623, [1816], 626–27, 634, 645, 652, 657–58, 660–63, 668–70, [1817], 677–78, 681, 689, 691–92, 706, 712–13, 720, [1818], 730–31, 734, 740, 741, 746, 748, 750–52, 758–59, [1819], 760, 763, 766–770, 781, 785, [1820], 801–3, 812, 814, 819, 821, 824–25, 831, 838–39, 845, 858, 862, 870, 872, 874, 877, 884, 886–87, [1821], 893, 896–99, 901, 905–8, 910–12, 914–16, 918, 925, 927, 930–32, 937, 941, 943–44, 953–54, 956, 974, 978, 980, [1822], 988–89, 998, 1028, 1032, 1035, 1043, 1046, 1048–49, 1051–52, 1055, [1823], 1056–59, 1066–67, 1074–76, 1081–82, 1085–86, 1098–99, 1104, 1107, 1111–12, 1115, 1117, 1119, 1124–25, 1129–30, 1132, [1824], 1135–36, 1138, 1141, 1143, 1146–49, 1151, 1153, 1155–56, 1160–61, 1163–65, 1173, 1176, 1180, 1185, [1825], 1193, 1197, 1200, 1210, 1215, 1219, [1826], 1223, 1226, 1232, 1236, 1240–42, 1247, 1255, 1257, 1274–75, 1278, 1280, [1827], 1282–83, 1285, 1287–91, 1293–94, 1296, 1303, 1310, 1315, 1317, 1329, 1338–39, 1345, 1354–55, 1366, 1370, 1374, 1379, 1384–85, 1387, 1391, 1393, 1407, 1421, 1431, 1440–41, 1447, 1452, [1828], 1454–56, 1458, 1460–64, 1467, 1469–70, 1474, 1478, 1483–85, 1490, 1515–16, 1522, 1524–25, 1530–33, 1535–38, 1540, 1542, 1545–47, [1829], 1551, 1555–56 A, 1557, 1560–61, 1563, 1567, 1569, 1571, [1830], 1574–78, 1580–81, 1583–89, 1591–94, 1596

Letters from: [1812], 1–2, [1813], 210, 220, 277, 314, 319, 340, 346, [1814], 380, 390, 393–94 A, 420, 477, 482, 487, 504, 506, [1815], 511, 515, 517, 522, 529, 532, 537–38, 578, 582, 586, 593, 600, 611, 615, [1816], 635, 671–72, [1817], 673, 682, 686–87, 714, 718, 722–23, [1818], 725, 735, 738, 754, [1819], 762, 773–74, [1820], 804, 808, 810,

817, 826, 829, 843, 846, 855, 863, 867, 873, 875–76, 878–81, 885, 888, [1821], 902, 904, 917, 920, 922, 924, 928, 935, 942, 946, 948, 958–59, 961, 963–64, 977, 981, [1822], 982, 985–86, 990–91, 993, 997, 1008, 1013–14, 1017, 1020, 1029, 1031, 1042, 1044, 1050, 1054, [1823], 1068, 1073, 1087, 1110, 1116, 1122, 1126–27, [1824], 1139, 1186–87, [1825], 1188–89, 1191, 1195, 1198, 1203, 1206–8, 1211, 1221, [1826], 1228, 1238, 1245, 1263, [1827], 1295, 1297–98, 1325, 1365, 1375, 1380–81, 1388, 1390, 1395–96, 1400, 1404, 1422, 1427, 1429, 1432, 1435, 1437–38, 1445, 1450, [1828], 1465, 1468, 1471–72, 1475, 1480, 1487, 1489, 1496, 1500, 1509, 1514, 1519, 1523, [1829], 1562, 1565, 1572, [1830], 1573

Letters to: [1812], 3, 5–7, 9, 13–16, 21, 23–25, 34, 42, 45–46, 57, 66, 70, 73, 76–80, 83–93, 100–2, 105–7, 122–23, 135, 137–38, 142, 144, 147, 176, 180, 185, 190–93, 197–98, 201, 206–7, [1813], 211, 213, 215–17, 219, 221–25, 227–29, 231, 236, 238–39, 241, 245, 247, 251–52, 257–59, 263, 266, 278–79, 282, 287, 291, 298, 298 A, 303, 306, 310–12, 315–16, 318, 327, 331, 335–36, 341–42, 344–45, 348–49, 353–54, 356–57, 359–62, 364, 367–69, 371, 373, 376, [1814], 381–83, 388–89, 394, 397–400, 403–4, 409–11, 413–14, 419, 421–22, 425–31, 437, 439–40, 442, 444–46, 449, 454–57, 460–61, 463–64, 466–68, 472–73, 475–76, 479, 481, 484, 486, 488, 491, 493–95, 497–503, 508, [1815], 513–14, 516, 519–20, 525, 528, 530–31, 533, 535–36, 539–42, 545–54, 559–62, 564, 567, 570–73, 577, 579, 583–84, 587, 589–90, 594, 598, 608, 614, 617, 619–20, 622, 624–25, [1816], 628–33, 636–44, 646–51, 654–55, 659, 664–67, [1817], 674–76, 679–80, 683, 685, 690, 693, 696–97, 700, 703–5, 707–11, 715–17, 719, 721, 724, [1818], 726–28, 733, 736–37, 739, 742, 744–45, 747, 753, 755–57, [1819], 761, 764–65, 771–72, 775–78, 780, 783–84, [1820], 786–93, 795–98, 800, 805–7, 809, 811, 813, 815, 818, 823, 835, 842, 849–

George IV (*cont.*)
  50, 852–54, 871, 882, [1821], 890,
  894, 903, 913, 921, 923, 926, 929,
  933–34, 936, 938–40, 945, 947, 949–
  50, 952, 955, 957, 960, 962, 965–67,
  969–73, 975, 976, 979, [1822], 983–
  84, 987, 992, 994, 996, 999–1007,
  1009–12, 1015–16, 1018–19, 1021–
  27, 1033–34, 1036–41, 1045, 1047,
  1053, [1823], 1060–65, 1069–70,
  1072, 1077–80, 1083–84, 1088–97,
  1100–3, 1105–6, 1108–9, 1113–14,
  1118, 1120–21, 1123, 1127–28,
  1131, [1824], 1134, 1137, 1140,
  1142, 1144–45, 1150, 1152, 1154,
  1157–59, 1162, 1168–72, 1174,
  1177–78, 1181–82, 1184, [1825],
  1190, 1192, 1194, 1196, 1199,
  1201–2, 1204–5, 1212, 1214,
  1216–18, 1220, 1222–22A, [1826],
  1225, 1227, 1230–31, 1233–35,
  1237, 1239, 1243, 1248–54, 1256,
  1258–62, 1264–73, 1276–77, 1279,
  1281, [1827], 1284, 1286, 1299–
  1302, 1305–9, 1311–14, 1316,
  1318–24, 1326–28, 1330–33, 1335–
  37, 1341–43, 1346–48, 1350–53,
  1356–57, 1359–65, 1367–69, 1371–
  73, 1376–78, 1382, 1383, 1386,
  1389, 1392, 1394, 1397–99, 1401–
  3, 1405, 1408–12, 1414–20, 1423–
  26, 1430, 1433–34, 1436, 1439,
  1442–44, 1446, 1448–49, [1828],
  1453, 1459, 1466, 1473, 1476–77,
  1479, 1481, 1488, 1491–95, 1497–
  99, 1501–8, 1510–13, 1517, 1526–
  29, 1534, 1539, 1541, 1548–50,
  [1829], 1552–54, 1556, 1558–59,
  1566, [1830], 1579, 1582
George V, King of Hanover (1819–
  1878), 796–97, 800, 811, 1212,
  1216–17, 1282, 1417, 1516, 1528–
  29, 1534–35, 1542, 1545, 1552,
  1562, 1566
George, Prince of Hesse-Darmstadt.
  See Hesse-Darmstadt
George FitzClarence. *See* FitzClarence
George Fitz Ernest, 500
Gibbs, Dr, 721
Gibbs, Sir Vicary (1751–1820), 565
  Letters from: 32–33
Gifford, Sir Robert, first Baron Gifford
  (1779–1826), 757, 858, 859, 887,
  894–96, 938, 1062, 1249, 1251
Gillam, Robert, 265
  Letter from: 296
Gillespie, Sir Robert Rollo (1766–1814),
  502, 521

Gizziliere, Count, 830
Glaser, the Rev., 565
Glenbervie, Sylvester Douglas, Baron
  (1743–1823), 524
Glengarry, 1046
Globe, the, 17 n.
Globe and Traveller, the, 1522
Gloucester, Bishop of. *See* Ryder, Dr
Gloucester, Duchess of. *See* Mary,
  Princess
Gloucester, William Frederick, Duke of
  (1776–1834), 411, 513, 655, 767,
  1414–15
Gneisenau (1760–1831), 399, 533, 541,
  798
Goderich, Viscount. *See* Robinson, F. J.
Goldburne. *See* Goulburn
Goldsmith, Lewis (? 1763–1846), *Letter
  from*: 152
Golofkin [Golowkin], Count, 422, 424–
  25
Goltz, the Count de, 523
Gonomar (?), Madame de, 391
Gooch, Dr, 1588
Gooch, Thomas Sherlock, M.P., 649
Goodenough, Edmund (1785–1845),
  855, 1142
Gordon, Alexander, fourth Duke of
  (1743–1827), 1358, 1361, 1363
Gordon, George, fifth Duke of (1770–
  1836), 1411
  Letter from: 1410
Gordon, Sir James Willoughby (1773–
  1851), *Letter from*: 242
Gordon, Sir John, 616
Gordon, Lady, 242
Gordon, Robert (1791–1847), 176
Gordon, Lord William (1761–1823),
  1064, 1085
Gorringe, 155
Göttingen, University of, 1081
Goulburn, Henry (1784–1856), 401,
  968, 1030, 1045, 1261, 1407, 1461,
  1463, 1501, 1583
Gower. *See* Leveson-Gower
Grafton, Augustus Henry Fitzroy, third
  Duke of (1735–1811), 329
Graham, James, Marquis of, afterwards
  fourth Duke of Montrose (1799–
  1874), 940
  Letter from: 1313
Graham, General Sir Thomas, Baron
  Lynedoch (1748–1843), 394, 1414
Granard, George Forbes, sixth Earl of
  (1760–1837), 30, 343, 352, 408,
  423, 453
Granby, John Manners, Marquis of
  (1721–1770), 20, 215, 665

Grand Duchess Catherine. *See* Catherine
Grand Vizier of Persia, 42
Grant, Charles (1746–1823), 193, 1083–84
Grant, Charles, Baron Glenelg (1778–1866), 373, 466, 637, 643, 913
Grant, Sir William (1752–1832), 564
Grant, Sir William Keir (1772–1852), 352, 405
Grantham, Thomas Philip Robinson, third Baron, afterwards Earl De Grey (1781–1859), 1454
Granville, Lord Granville Leveson-Gower. *See* Leveson-Gower
Granville, Henrietta Elizabeth, Countess (1785–1862), 1252, 1508
Grattan, Henry (1747–1820), 247
Grattan, Henry, jun., 1271
Graves, Mary, Lady (d. 1835), 1577
Graves, Thomas North Graves, second Baron, Comptroller of Duke of Sussex's Household (1775–1830), 1289, 1577
Letter to: 1132
Gray, Francis, fourteenth Baron (1765–1842), 1361
Gray, Robert (d. 1823), 317, 326, 544, 980, 1017, 1026, 1085, 1596
Letters from: 441, 534, 656
Letters to: 433, 452, 657–58
Great Cabinet, the, 648
Greaves, 330
Greenough, George Bellas (1778–1855), 165
Greenwood, Charles, the banker, 8
Grenville, George (1712–1770), 11
Grenville, William Wyndham, Baron Grenville (1759–1834), 1, 3–4, 6–7, 12, 15, 23, 56, 80, 96, 100, 105, 107, 110, 116–17, 469, 636, 663–64, 669, 689–90, 818, 874, 875, 878, 881–82, 969, 971, 1079, 1142, 1151, 1235, 1283, 1466
Letter from: 903
Letters to: 876, 904
Greville, Robert Fulke (1751–1824), *Letter from*: 264
Grey, Charles, second Earl (1764–1845), 1, 3–4, 7, 12, 15, 23, 56, 63, 80, 96–97, 100, 101, 104–7, 110, 116–17, 379, 469, 612, 847, 878, 881, 1240, 1332, 1356, 1490, 1530
Grey, Sir Charles Edward (1785–1865), 1181, 1183
Grey, Rev. Edward, Bishop of Hereford (1782–1837), 1530
Grey, Sir George (1767–1828), 677

Grey, Sir Henry George, Viscount Howick, afterwards third Earl Grey (1802–1894), 1341
Grey, Mary, Countess (d. 1861), 63
Grieg [Greig], 953
Grolmann, General (1777–1843), 798
Grose, Sir Nash (1740–1814), 36
Grosvenor, Robert, second Earl, afterwards Marquis of Westminster (1767–1845), 1422
Grote, 1527
Guilford, Frederick North, fifth Earl of (1766–1827), 855
Gullet, 749
Gumpenberg, Mlle de, 391, 407

Hale, Sir Matthew (1609–1676), 896
Halford, Sir Henry (1766–1844), 219, 221, 298, 352, 394, 413, 481, 673, 721, 723, 783, 1070, 1195, 1245, 1288, 1450, 1540–41, 1581, 1584, 1588
Letters from: 222, 228, 310, 312, 792, 814, 1051–52, 1280
Letter to: 1166
Hall, 831
Hall, Dr Charles Henry (1763–1827), 1137, 1139
Halliday, Sir Andrew (1781–1839), 1025
Haman. *See* Hayman
Hamilton, Lady Anne (1766–1846), 820, 884, 998
Letters to: 831, 865
Hamilton, Lord Archibald (1770–1840), 461, 894–96
Hamilton, Lady (1761–1815), 901
Letters from: 236, 244
Hamilton, Terrick, 794
Hamilton, Thomas, Lord Binning, later ninth Earl of Haddington (1780–1858), 178
Hamilton, Sir William (1730–1803), 244
Hamilton, William Richard (1777–1859), 394, 630
Letter from: 1210
Hamlet, jeweller, 1596
Hamlet at the grave of Ophelia, Lawrence's picture, 1591, 1592
Hammersley, Charles, 8
Hammersley, George, 8
Hammersley, Hugh (? 1775–1840), 8
Hammersley, Thomas (? 1747–1812), 51
Letter from: 8
Hammerstein, 399
Hampden-Trevor, Thomas, second Viscount Hampden (1746–1824), 482, 504

Hannibal (247–183 B.C.), 419
Harcourt, William, third Earl (1743–1830), 1414
Hardenberg, Count, 311, 626, 1222 A
Hardenberg, Prince von (1750–1822), 479, 491, 514, 523, 798, 1592
Hardwicke, Philip Yorke, third Earl of (1757–1834), 249, 537
Hardy, Sir Thomas Masterman (1769–1839), 244
Harewood, Edward Lascelles, first Earl of (1740–1820), 537
Harewood, Henry Lascelles, second Earl of (1767–1841), 1332
Harris, Thomas, Letter from: 295
Harrison, Sir George (d. 1841), 323–24, 334, 1064, 1085, 1118, 1339, 1502, 1519
     Letters from: 1118, 1121
Harrison, William, 631
Harrowby, Dudley Ryder, first Earl of (1762–1847), 78, 84, 565, 761, 875, 950, 1143, 1170–71, 1332, 1425, 1444–45
     Letters from: 91, 1443
Hart, Sir Anthony (? 1754–1831), 1417
Hart, George Vaughan (1752–1832), 181
Hart, William Shakespeare, 1223
Harvey, Felton, 381
Harvey, Philip Whitfield, Letter from: 27
Hastings, Sir Charles (1752–1823), 662
Hastings, Francis Rawdon-, first Marquis of Hastings and second Earl of Moira (1754–1826), 7, 37, 63, 75, 80, 94, 105, 111, 114, 141, 150, 189–93, 214, 227, 229, 249, 262, 292, 308, 379, 505, 518, 566, 652, 962, 964–65, 967–68, 972, 975, 983–84, 1083–84, 1092, 1105, 1125, 1206, 1223, 1272–73, 1275
     Letters from: 18, 22–23, 30, 41, 47, 51, 55, 65, 82, 97, 102–4, 106–8, 112, 117, 130–31, 136, 139–40, 156, 166, 224–25, 238, 258, 261, 266–69, 274, 283, 331–32, 343, 352–53, 405, 408, 423, 475, 502, 521, 573, 654, 662, 678, 680–81, 742, 765, 780, 862, 893, 897, 930, 1075, 1086, 1150
     Letters to: 8, 19, 113, 226, 235, 692, 978
     Memorandum: 1133
Hastings, Marchioness of (d. 1840), 18, 140, 150, 190, 267, 405, 423, 573, 680–81, 780, 862, 930, 978
Hawker, Colonel, 1119

Hawkes, 440
Hawkins, Lieutenant, 429
Hay, Dr, 1574
Hayman, 52
Hayman, Miss, 508
Haymarket Theatre, 1091, 1596
Hayter, 1223
Healey, 352
Heaphy, Thomas (1775–1835), 246
     Letter from: 248
Heard, Sir Isaac (1730–1822), 194, 493
Heartrass [sic], Charles, 830
Heathfield, Francis Augustus Eliott, second Baron (1749–1813), 290
Heber, Reginald, Bishop of Calcutta (1783–1826), 1060, 1301
Heber, Richard (1773–1833), 994
     Letter from: 995
Hely-Hutchinson, John, first Baron Hutchinson, afterwards second Earl of Donoughmore (1757–1832), 881
     Letters from: 799, 821–22
     Letters to: 782, 801, 819
Henry IV, King of France (1553–1610), 666, 1253
Henry, Jabez, 847
Herbert, Henry Arthur, M.P. (d. 1821), 21
Hereford, Dean of. See Carr, R. J.
Hereford, Frances, Lady (d. 1864), 1151
Hereford, Henry Fleming Lea, fourteenth Viscount (1777–1843).
     Letters from: 1151–52
Herries, John Charles (1778–1855), 1085, 1292, 1381, 1392, 1400, 1437, 1447, 1463, 1490, 1504
     Letters from: 1278, 1288, 1391, 1441, 1451
Hertford, Francis (Ingram) Seymour, second Marquis of (1743–1822), 257, 311, 318, 656, 940, 945, 987, 990
     Letters from: 925, 941, 944, 988
     Letters to: 568, 989
Hertford, Francis Charles Seymour, Earl of Yarmouth, third Marquis of Hertford (1777–1842), 61, 117, 119, 152, 171, 208, 318, 323, 469, 525, 845, 1373
     Letters from: 179, 410
Hertford, Isabella, Marchioness of (1760–1836), 311, 318, 845, 1588
Hervey, Lady (1700–1768), 1010
Hervey, Lionel Charles, 794
Hesse, Princess Augusta of. See Cambridge, Duchess of
Hesse, Captain Charles (d. 1832), 395, 508–9, 547 A, 830

Hesse, Captain Charles (*cont.*)
Letters from: 387, 418, 434–35
Letters to: 339, 370, 396, 436
Hesse-Cassel, Caroline, Princess of, daughter of William II, Elector of Hesse-Cassel (b. 1799), 743
Hesse-Cassel, Landgrave Frederick of (1747–1837), 622, 711, 718, 724, 744, 1373
Hesse-Cassel, Landgravine of, 744
Hesse-Cassel, Princess Louisa of (b. 1794), daughter of Landgrave Frederick, 622, 718
Hesse-Cassel, Princess Maria (b. 1796), daughter of Landgrave Frederick, 718
Hesse-Cassel, William I, Elector of (1743–1821), 364, 411, 724, 744
Hesse-Cassel, William II, Elector of (1777–1847), 744
Letter from: 743
Hesse-Darmstadt, Prince George of, 279
Hesse-Darmstadt, Dowager Landgravine of, 279
Hesse-Darmstadt, Lewis I, Grand Duke of (1753–1830), 1527
Hesse-Homburg, Frederick Joseph, Hereditary Prince of (1769–1829), 318, 736, 1566
Hesse-Homburg, Louis, Hereditary Prince of (1770–1839), 1566
Heygate, Alderman William, 894
Heytesbury, Lord. *See* À Court
Hibernian Journal, the, 558
Hicks, 831
Hieronymus, John, 766, 830, 901, 998
Hildesheim, Major, 318
Hill, 1061
Hill, Sir George Fitzgerald (1763–1839), 1072, 1077
Hill, Rowland, first Viscount (1772–1842), 1414–15, 1436, 1449
Hill, William Noel-, third Baron Berwick (d. 1842), 1011, 1053, 1055, 1177
Hiller, Major-General, 542
Hippisley, Sir John Coxe (1748–1825), 664
Letters from: 669–70, 781
Letters to: 663, 668, 732, 779
Hippisley, Sir John Stuart, 670
Hippisley, Margaret, Lady (d. 1799), 732
H[is] C[atholic] M[ajesty]. *See* Ferdinand VII, King of Spain
H[is] M[ost] C[hristian] M[ajesty]. *See* Charles X, King of France

H[is] M[ost] F[aithful] M[ajesty]. *See* John VI, King of Portugal
Hislop, Sir Thomas (1764–1843), 616
Letters from: 566, 652
Hobart, Hon. Henry L., Dean of Windsor (1774–1846), 1097, 1106, 1144
Letter to: 1107
Hobhouse, Henry (1776–1854), 1368
Hobhouse, John Cam, Lord Broughton (1786–1869), 844, 884, 894–96, 1337
Hockin, 749
Hodrison, Mrs, 563
Hodson, Dr Frodsham (1770–1822), 994–95
Hoey, 1206
Holcombe, Dr, 975
Holderness, Robert D'Arcy, fourth Earl of (1718–1778), 1453
Holland, Sir Henry (1788–1873), 830
Holland, Henry Richard Vassall Fox, third Baron (1773–1840), 23, 80, 198, 205, 881, 1388, 1390, 1436, 1445, 1447, 1488
Holmes, Sir Leonard Thomas Worsley (1787–1825), 163
Holmes, Richard Fleming Worsley (d. 1814), 163
Holmes, William (d. 1851), 183, 525
Letters from: 132, 371, 373
Holroyd, Sir George Sowley (1758–1831), 1182
Holstein, Prince of. *See* Oldenburg
Home, Alexander, tenth Earl of (1769–1841), 1361
Home, Sir Everard (1756–1832), 393, 1588
Hone, William (1780–1842), 1595
Hood, Henry, second Viscount (1753–1836), 932, 951
Hook, Dr James (? 1772–1828), 1001, 1139–40, 1147
Hook, Theodore Edward (1788–1841), 1088
Letters from: 337–38, 1148
Hook, Walter Farquhar (1798–1875), 1147
Hope, Sir Alexander (1769–1837), 278
Hope, John (1794–1858), 1372
Hoper, 766–67
Hopetoun, John Hope, fifth Earl of (1803–1843), 1372
Hoppenstedt, 1527
Horn, A., 391, 406–7, 412
Horn, David, 407
Horton, Sir Robert John Wilmot (1784–1841), 1093, 1331

Howard, Major Frederick (1785–1815), 559
Howard, Henrietta, Countess of Suffolk (1681–1767), 1010
Howard, Henry (1769–1847), 62
Howard, Henry Charles, Earl of Surrey, afterwards thirteenth Duke of Norfolk (1791–1856), *Letter from*: 937
Howard, Lord Henry Thomas Molyneux (1766–1824), *Letter to*: 927
Howard, Lady, 463
Howden, Lord. *See* Cradock
Howick, Viscount. *See* Grey
Howley, 1407
Howley, William, Bishop of London and Archbishop of Canterbury (1766–1848), 686, 698, 919, 994, 1000, 1142, 1159, 1280, 1301, 1317, 1332, 1403–4, 1427, 1528, 1574
Letter from: 1217
Hownam, Lieutenant Joseph Robert, 830, 842
Hughes, Canon, 884
Hughes, Mrs, 884
Humboldt, Karl William von (1767–1835), 514, 697, 798
Hume, Dr, 798
Hume, Dr John Robert (? 1781–1857), *Letter from*: 1229
Hume, Joseph (1777–1855), 778, 796, 884, 1271, 1341, 1348, 1501
Hunt, Henry (1773–1835), 800, 811, 1046, 1422
Hunt, James Henry Leigh (1784–1859), 558, 1588
Hunter, Sir Claudius Stephen (1775–1851), *Letter from*: 74
Hunter, John (1728–1793), 393
Hunter, Orby (d. 1843), 121
Hunter, Sir Richard, 1524
Huntingdon, Hans Francis Hastings, eleventh Earl of (1779–1828), 1086
Hunton, Joseph, 1550
Hurlebusch, 1419
Huskisson, William (1770–1830), 106, 132, 524, 1109–10, 1160, 1170–71, 1304, 1357, 1368, 1374, 1397, 1399–1400, 1410, 1443, 1445, 1461, 1469–70, 1490, 1501, 1504, 1575, 1579
Letters from: 1408, 1411, 1444, 1517
Letters to: 1395, 1431
Hut, M. de, 440
Hutchinson, Lord. *See* Hely-Hutchinson

Ilchester, Countess of (d. 1842), 460, 476–77, 482, 486, 492, 504, 628, 640
Letter from: 472

Illingworth, 931
Impey, Archibald Elijah, 1156
Independent Whig, the, 148, 865, 868
Infantado, Duke of, 29
Inglis, Sir Hugh (d. 1820), 189, 193, 261
Inglis, John (1748–1822), *Letter from*: 302
Inglis, Sir Robert, 1556A
Institution for the Fine Arts, Liverpool, 1596
Ireland, Dr John (1761–1842), *Letters from*: 931–32
Isabella, Regent of Portugal, 1267

Jackson, Dr Cyril (1746–1819), 1142, 1146–47
Jacobi-Kloest, Baron von, 429, 523
Jagow, 533
Jaipur, Raja of, 681
James V, King of Scotland (1512–1542), 1303
James II (1633–1701), 1176, 1209
James, Francis Edward Stuart (1688–1766), the "Old Pretender", 732
James, Dr John Thomas, Bishop of Calcutta (1786–1828), 1301
James, William, M.P., 1004
Jamieson, Rev. Dr John (1759–1838), 1156
Jamieson, Sir John, *Letter from*: 563
Jayes, 845
Jeffrey, Francis, Lord (1773–1850), 1046
Jeffreys, Hon. Miss, 1596
Jegrondi, 830
Jelf, Richard William (1798–1871), 1217, 1282, 1542, 1574
Jell. *See* Gell
Jenkinson, Colonel (? 1783–1823), 1063
Jenkinson, Dr John Banks, Bishop of St David's (1781–1840), *Letter to*: 1349
Jenner, Dr Edward (1749–1823), *Letter from*: 485
Jersey, Frances, Countess of (1753–1821), 486, 504
Letters from: 232, 263, 307, 359
Jersey, Sarah Sophia, Countess of (1785–1867), 1530
Joachim, King. *See* Murat
Jocelyn, Robert, third Earl of Roden (1788–1870), 46, 257, 1513
John VI, King of Portugal (1767–1826), 1170–71
John Bull, 1148
Johnson, 523
Johnson, J., 269

Johnson, Samuel (1709–1784), 1571
Johnston, 812
Johnston, Major, 215
Johnstone, 183, 767, 1393
Johnstone, Andrew James Cochrane-
  (1767–1834), 241
Johnstone, Mrs, 1588
"Junius", 101
Jutsham, Benjamin, 1596
  Letter to: 656

Kaye, John (1783–1853), Bishop of
  Bristol and Lincoln, 1509
Keane, Sir John, first Baron Keane (1781–
  1844), 1408
Keate, Dr John (1773–1852), *Letters
  from*: 1066–67, 1241–42
Keate, Robert (1777–1857), 476, 481–
  82, 486, 488
  Letter from: 498
Keck, George Anthony Legh, 1337
Keir, Sir William. *See* Grant
Keith, Lord. *See* Elphinstone
Kellie, Earl of, 1361
Kelly, Richard, 1596
Kemble, Charles (1775–1854), 1568,
  1591
  Letter from: 1567
Kempt, Sir James (1764–1854), *Letter
  from*: 1590
Kenmare, Valentine Browne, first Earl
  of (1754–1812), 297
  Letter from: 129
  Letter to: 125
Kent, Duke of. *See* Edward Augustus
Kent, Duchess of (1786–1861), 768–69,
  790
  Letters from: 1367, 1389, 1405
Kenyon, George, second Baron (1776–
  1855), 1521–22
Keppel, Sir William (d. 1834), 234, 996,
  1085, 1294
  Letter from: 233
Kerrison, Edward, 330
Kerry, Knight of. *See* Fitzgerald, M.
Kerston, Charles T., 840
Ki[e]lman[n]segge, Count, 533
King, 121, 523
King, Captain, 416–17, 831
King, Sir Henry (d. 1839), 1577
King, Peter, seventh Baron (1776–1833),
  842
King, Sir Richard (1774–1834), 432
King's Theatre, the, 1596
Kingston, third Earl of (1771–1839),
  645
Kinnaird, Charles, eighth Baron (1780–
  1826), 630

Kinnaird, Douglas James William
  (1788–1830), 282
Kinnaird, George, seventh Baron (1754–
  1805), 8
Kirwan, 1457
Kleist, General, 318, 479, 499
Knatchbull, Sir Edward (1781–1849),
  1292, 1323, 1357, 1579
Kneisenau. *See* Gneisenau
Knight, Ellis Cornelia (1757–1837),
  221–25, 227–29, 244, 312
  Letter from: 226
Knighton, Sir William (1776–1836),
  788, 814, 1000, 1005, 1009, 1025,
  1033–34, 1064, 1068, 1073, 1085,
  1114, 1123, 1127, 1156, 1188, 1225,
  1234, 1269, 1398, 1409, 1492, 1508–
  9, 1511, 1522, 1534, 1541, 1552,
  1560, 1586, 1591–94, 1596
  Diary: 1574–78, 1588
  Letters from: 690–91, 717, 792, 1003,
    1024, 1026, 1035, 1057, 1130,
    1132, 1138, 1147, 1268, 1339,
    1457, 1485, 1502, 1566, 1568
  Letters to: 689, 804, 817, 878–80,
    902, 981, 1028–32, 1043, 1046,
    1048–52, 1055, 1056, 1059, 1066–
    67, 1071, 1075–76, 1081–82, 1086,
    1099, 1111–12, 1115, 1117, 1119,
    1124–25, 1129, 1135–36, 1141,
    1143, 1146, 1148–49, 1151, 1153,
    1155, 1160–61, 1165, 1167, 1173,
    1175–76, 1179–80, 1183, 1193,
    1195, 1200, 1206–8, 1211, 1215,
    1223–24, 1226, 1228–29, 1232,
    1236, 1238, 1241–42, 1244, 1246–
    47, 1255, 1257, 1263, 1274, 1278,
    1280, 1282, 1285, 1287–94, 1296–
    98, 1304, 1315, 1329, 1334, 1338,
    1340, 1344–45, 1354–55, 1358,
    1366, 1370, 1374, 1379, 1384–85,
    1387, 1391, 1393, 1396, 1406,
    1413, 1421–22, 1432, 1435, 1440–
    41, 1445, 1447, 1450–52, 1454–56,
    1458, 1460–64, 1467–72, 1474,
    1480, 1483, 1486–87, 1489–90,
    1496, 1514–16, 1518–19, 1523–24,
    1530–31, 1533, 1535–38, 1540,
    1542–46, 1551, 1555, 1557, 1561–
    65, 1569–72, 1580–81, 1583–85,
    1587, 1589
Knighton, Lady, 1561
Knoblauch, Lieutenant Colonel, 541
Knowles, Sir Charles Henry (1754–
  1831), 784
Köthen, Duchess of, 1364
Krackler, Philip, 830
Kraft, Major, 541

Kress, Barbara, 840
Kreutzer, Major General de, 514
Krishe, 440

Lacroix, 1177
Lade, Sir John, 1596
Laffitte, Jacques (1767–1844), 1176
Lake, Gerard, first Viscount (1744–1808), 8, 191
Lamb, Frederick James, third Viscount Melbourne and Baron Beauvale (1782–1853), 121, 794, 1253, 1256, 1258, 1260, 1416
Lamb, Peniston, first Viscount Melbourne (1748–1828), 576, 1588
    Letters from: 16, 167, 291
Lamb, Peniston (1770–1805), 121
Lamb, William, second Viscount Melbourne (1779–1848), 21, 466, 1318, 1320, 1337, 1393, 1407, 1461
    Letters from: 16, 1503
Lambton, John George, first Earl of Durham (1792–1840), 1423, 1448, 1453
Lancaster, Joseph (1778–1838), 355, 433, 441, 452
    Letter from: 677
Landgrave of Hesse. See Hesse-Cassel
Landseer, John (1769–1852), Letter from: 237
Lansdowne, Sir Henry Petty-Fitz-maurice, third Marquis of (1780–1863), 80, 149, 881, 1318–21, 1331–32, 1381, 1400–1, 1412–13, 1449, 1461, 1465, 1468, 1472, 1474, 1480
    Letters from: 1418, 1446, 1473, 1483, 1486
    Letters to: 1475, 1484–85
La Roche, Colonel, 541
Lascelles, Henry, second Earl of Harewood (1767–1841), 251
Lauderdale, James Maitland, eighth Earl of (1759–1839), 594, 834, 858, 874, 882, 1070, 1292, 1335, 1361
    Letters from: 15, 612, 621, 859, 864, 877, 1136
    Letters to: 613, 618
Lautour, 337
Law, Edward. See Ellenborough
Lawrance, Theodore, Letters from: 443–44
Lawrence, Mrs, 1423
Lawrence, Sir Thomas (1769–1830), 716, 722, 1591–93
    Letters from: 451, 478, 483, 713, 1111, 1255, 1532
    Letter to: 438

Leach, Sir John (1760–1834), 155, 623, 631, 717, 726, 801, 842, 881, 900
    Letters from: 748, 858, 886–87, 898–899
    Letters to: 859, 892
Leeds, Catherine, Duchess of (d. 1837), 206–7, 216–17, 219, 221–22, 227–29, 463
    Letter from: 223
Leeds, George William Frederick Osborne, sixth Duke of (1775–1838), 892, 1273–74, 1448, 1453
Lees, Rev. Sir Harcourt (1776–1852), 1244
Leger, Colonel St, 135
Legon, 399
Lehzen, Baroness (d. 1870), 1405
Leicester, Sir John Fleming, first Baron de Tabley (1762–1827), 1237
    Letter from: 255
Leiningen, Lieutenant General, 349
Leinster, Augustus Frederick Fitz-gerald, third Duke of (1791–1874), 297
Leiseck, Lieutenant Colonel, 401
Leitrey, General, 514
Leiven. See Lieven
Leman, James, 856
    Letter to: 857
Leningen. See Leiningen
Lennard, Thomas Barrett (1788–1856), 1341
Lens, John (1756–1825), 831
Leo XII (1760–1829), 1113, 1522
Leopold, Prince, of Saxe-Coburg (1790–1865), 621, 625, 629–30, 632, 634, 637, 639–40, 642, 645, 698, 700, 705, 713, 730, 767, 1516, 1573, 1575, 1580
    Letters from: 463, 651, 679, 685, 704, 716, 1168
    Letters to: 686, 722
Lestorg [L'Estocq], the Prussian General, 440
Lethbridge, 343, 352
Lethbridge, Sir Thomas Buckler (1778–1849), 1322, 1324, 1328
Leuthe, M. de, 344
Leuthe [Leuthes], Mme de, 391, 407
Leveson-Gower, George Granville, se-cond Marquis of Stafford and first Duke of Sutherland (1758–1833), 1433
    Letter from: 265
Leveson-Gower, George Granville, Earl Gower, afterwards second Duke of Sutherland (1786–1861), 800
Leveson-Gower, Lord Granville, first

Earl Granville (1773–1846), 1092, 1103–4, 1252, 1397, 1435
Letter from: 1508
Lewis, the Archduke, of Austria, 551
Lewis Ferdinand of Prussia, Prince (d. 1806), Frederick the Great's nephew, 839
Liddell, Henry Thomas, first Baron Ravensworth (1775–1855), 1591–92
Liddell, Henry Thomas, second Baron and first Earl, of Ravensworth (1797–1878), 1271
Liegnitz, Princess Augusta of, morganatic wife of Frederick William III of Prussia, 1529
Lieven, Count (1774–1839), 342, 431, 791, 1036, 1040, 1201, 1218, 1260, 1530
Letter to: 1219
Lieven, Princess (1785–1857), 477, 1113, 1530
Ligonier, first Earl (1680–1770), 215
Limerick, Bishop of. *See* Warburton
Lincoln, Bishop of. *See* Pelham, George
Lindsay, Lady Charlotte (1770–1849), 767, 830, 838, 847, 855
Linley, Elizabeth Ann, Sheridan's first wife (1754–1792), 1283
Lion, 207
Liston, Sir Robert (1742–1836), 794, 830
Litchfield, Henry Charles (1756–1822), *Letter from*: 695
Littleton, Edward John, first Baron Hatherton (1791–1863), 1335
Liverpool, Louisa, Countess of (d. 1821), 478, 660–61
Liverpool, Mary, Countess of (d. 1846), 1296
Liverpool, Robert Banks Jenkinson, second Earl of (1770–1828), 9, 75–76, 78, 80, 84, 86–87, 93–94, 96, 108, 111, 114, 116, 132, 135, 152, 156, 165, 185, 189–91, 193, 197, 216, 233, 239, 280, 285, 291, 301, 308, 334, 352, 362, 371, 382, 422, 447, 449, 469–70, 474, 501, 509, 512, 514, 522, 533, 552, 565, 569, 574, 581, 583, 603–5, 609–11, 613, 615, 617, 627, 637, 640, 669, 672, 690, 697, 718, 723, 726, 735, 748, 752, 758, 760–62, 771, 801, 821, 834, 858, 874–75, 882–83, 886, 898, 901, 908, 911, 914, 953–54, 957–58, 962, 964, 972, 976, 981, 985, 1011, 1013–15, 1022, 1044, 1058, 1061, 1085, 1134, 1146,

Liverpool, second Earl of (*cont.*)
1151, 1160–61, 1168, 1170–71, 1199, 1220–21, 1228, 1234, 1258, 1265–66, 1268–69, 1274, 1278, 1282, 1288, 1294, 1296, 1303, 1349, 1361, 1378, 1403–4, 1407, 1427, 1431, 1510, 1522, 1548, 1589, 1592
Letters from: 83, 137, 144, 194, 305, 321, 489, 553, 561, 587, 589, 594, 596, 598, 601, 614, 619, 633, 636, 639, 645, 647, 650, 661, 688–89, 712, 727–30, 733, 772, 775, 777, 805, 807, 809, 820, 823–24, 842, 869–71, 890, 905–7, 910, 912, 915, 919, 921, 926, 929, 940, 945, 947, 949–50, 952, 960, 965–67, 969, 971, 973–75, 979, 983, 987, 989, 992, 994, 999–1001, 1005–7, 1018–9, 1021, 1023, 1036–37, 1039–40, 1059, 1062–64, 1076, 1079–80, 1095, 1097, 1101–2, 1106–7, 1109, 1131, 1137, 1140–44, 1158–59, 1162, 1184, 1190, 1192, 1212, 1215, 1217, 1222, 1235, 1237, 1249–50, 1273, 1275, 1277, 1284, 1286
Letters to: 304, 309, 328, 524, 588, 592–93, 595, 597, 599–600, 635, 660, 684, 691, 731, 734, 773–74, 808, 825–26, 843, 846, 866–67, 872–73, 887, 917, 920, 922, 928, 935, 941, 942, 946, 948, 951, 961, 963, 968, 977, 982, 986, 988, 990–91, 995, 997–98, 1008, 1017, 1020, 1042, 1057, 1073, 1098, 1110, 1138–39, 1147, 1163, 1185–86, 1189, 1191, 1213, 1295
Llandaff, Bishop of. *See* Copleston, E.; Sumner, C. R.; and Van Mildert
Lloyd, Dr Charles (1784–1829), 1000
Loch, James (1780–1855), *Letter from*: 1071
Lock, 53
Locke, John (1632–1704), 1209
Lockhart, John Gibson (1794–1854), 1180
Lockhart, Mrs, 1180
Lockhart, John Ingram, M.P., 461
London, Bishop of. *See* Howley
Londonderry, Lady. *See* Castlereagh, Emily, Viscountess
Londonderry, third Marquis of. *See* Stewart
Long, Charles, first Baron Farnborough (1761–1838), 94, 171, 183, 550, 760, 1197, 1400, 1560, 1569, 1591–92
Letter to: 1210

Longman and Co., 1283

Lonsdale, William Lowther, first Earl of (1757–1844), 144

Lord Chancellor [Ireland]. *See* Manners-Sutton, Thomas

Lord Chief Baron of the Irish Exchequer. *See* O'Grady

Lord Chief Justice of England. *See* Ellenborough, first Baron

Lord Chief Justice of Ireland. *See* Norbury

Lord Lieutenant of Ireland. *See* Richmond, fourth Duke of; Whitworth, Earl; Wellesley, Marquis; Anglesey, Marquis of

Lothian, William John Kerr, fifth Marquis of (1737–1815), 512–13, 515–16

Lothian, John William Robert Kerr, seventh Marquis of (1794–1841), 1373, 1534

Loudoun, Lady. *See* Hastings, Marchioness of

Louis XVI, King of France (1754–1793), 471

Louis XVIII, King of France (1755–1824), 428, 438–39, 526, 540, 542, 545, 661, 666, 1176, 1220

Louis Ferdinand, Prince. *See* Lewis Ferdinand

Louis Philippe, King of France (1773–1850), 463, 634

Louisa, Queen of Prussia. *See* Prussia

Lovaine, Lady, 640

Lowther, William, Viscount, afterwards second Earl of Lonsdale (1787–1872), 151, 323, 1381, 1523

Letters from: 1043, 1289, 1454

Lowton, 190–93

Lucas, Matthias Prime, Lord Mayor of London, 1543

Lucca, Duke of, 1527–28

Luddites, the, 128

Lumley, General Sir William (1769–1850), 1414

Lushington, Stephen (1782–1873), 833, 847, 950, 952, 954, 1169, 1579

Letters from: 951, 998

Letter to: 1240

Lushington, Stephen Rumbold (1776–1868), 1085, 1292

Letters from: 895, 1296

Lushington, Mrs S. R., 1296

Luther, Martin (1483–1546), 1200

Luti, the Cavalier, 779

Luttrell, Henry Lawes, second Earl of (1743–1821), 489

Luttrell, second Earl of (*cont.*)

Letters from: 304, 309, 328–29, 449, 456, 496–97, 535

Letters to: 305, 321, 490, 538

Luttrell, Temple, 328–29

Lutzen, Colonel, 282

Lygon, Edward Pyndar (d. 1860), 749

Lying-in Charity, the, 1596

Lyndhurst, Lord. *See* Copley

Lynedoch, Baron. *See* Graham, Sir Thomas

Lyon, Mrs, 244

Lyon, General, 421

Lyttelton, William Henry, Lord Lyttelton (1782–1837), 508

Letters from: 68–69

Letter to: 67

Maberly, John, 1271

McCawdlish, Lieutenant, 332

Macclesfield, George Parker, fourth Earl of (1755–1842), 1360

Letter from: 1347

Macdonald, 678

Macdonald, Sir Archibald (1747–1826), 1197

Macdonald, Sir James (1784–1832), 1331, 1461

Macfarlane, General Sir Robert (? 1770–1843), 121

Mackenzie, 523

Mackenzie, A., *Letter from*: 230

Mackintosh, Sir James (1765–1832), 211, 213, 894, 1043, 1348

Letters from: 172, 212, 249

McMahon, Sir John (d. 1817), 7, 70, 77, 111, 132, 144, 260, 325, 380–81, 433, 444, 452, 473, 482, 497, 535, 570, 573, 592, 601, 614, 624, 631, 689–92, 781, 993, 1020–21, 1024, 1125, 1223, 1588, 1592–93, 1596

Letters from: 67, 105, 113, 125, 133, 142, 186, 190–93, 198, 211, 281, 289, 347, 375, 448, 490, 501, 557, 575, 580, 684

Letters to: 10–12, 17–18, 22, 26–33, 35–37, 39–41, 43–44, 47–48, 51–56, 60, 63–65, 68–69, 72, 74–75, 81–82, 94–99, 103–4, 108–10, 112, 114, 116–17, 119, 121, 124, 127–31, 134, 136, 139–41, 143, 145–46, 149–51, 153–61, 163–64, 166–75, 178–79, 181–84, 187–89, 194–96, 199–200, 202–5, 208–9, 212, 214, 218, 230, 232–34, 240, 242–43, 249, 253–54, 261–62, 264, 267–76, 280, 283–86, 288, 290, 292–95, 297, 299, 301–2, 307–8, 313, 317,

320, 322–24, 326, 330, 332–34, 337–
38, 343, 350–52, 355, 358, 373–74,
377–78, 401, 405, 408, 416–17, 423,
443, 447, 450–51, 453, 458–59, 462,
469, 474, 478, 483, 485, 489, 496,
505, 512, 518, 521, 523, 527, 543–
44, 556, 558, 563, 566, 569, 574,
576, 581, 601, 610, 616, 623, 626–
27, 634, 652, 662, 669–70, 677–
78, 681, 688
McMahon, Mrs (d. 1815), 11–12, 31,
43, 56, 63, 72, 81, 96, 110, 116,
129, 136, 141, 145, 214, 240, 243,
254, 262, 294, 323, 332, 401, 408,
423, 478, 483, 518, 563, 566, 1588
McMahon, Sir William (1776–1837),
297, 323–25
Letter from: 184
Macnamara, 323
Maconochie, Alexander, Lord Meadow-
bank (1777–1861), Letter from:
741
Macpherson, Sir John (1745–1821)
308
Macquarie, Major General Lachlan (d.
1824), 563
Madame Mère. See Bonaparte
Madison, President (1751–1836), 170
Mahommed Shah Khan, 521
Mai, the Abbate Angelo, 1156
Mainburg, Captain, 523
Majocchi, Theodore, 830, 842
Letter from: 861
Malby, 1373
Malpas, Viscount. See Cholmondeley
Malthus, Rev. Thomas Robert (1766–
1834), 1156
Manby, Miss, 509
Manby, Rear Admiral Thomas (1769–
1834), 508–9, 766–67, 839
Manchester, William Montagu, fifth
Duke of (1768–1843), 1408
Mandelsloh, Count, 391
Manners, Catherine Rebecca, Lady
(d. 1852), 576, 580, 610
Manners, Jane, Lady (d. 1846), wife of
the Lord Chancellor of Ireland,
1244
Manners, John (d. 1792), 597
Manners, Thomas Manners-Sutton, first
Baron (1756–1842), 184, 297,
323–24, 1316, 1407
Letters from: 325, 1317
Manners, Sir William (1766–1833), 569,
574, 601, 609, 610
Letters from: 271, 280, 447, 570, 576,
581, 592, 597, 627
Letters to: 281, 448, 575, 580, 596

Manners-Sutton, Charles, Archbishop of
Canterbury (1755–1828), 138, 686,
698, 1147, 1301, 1316, 1326, 1359,
1446
Letters from: 372, 556
Letters to: 557, 1317, 1325
Manners-Sutton, Charles, first Viscount
Canterbury (1780–1845), 94, 938,
1446, 1501
Manners-Sutton, Rev. Thomas (1795–
1844), 1420
Mansfield, Countess of, 1546
Mansfield, David William Murray,
third Earl of (1777–1840), 1325–
26
Maria Louisa, Empress of Austria (d.
1816), 407, 554
Marie, M., 1522
Marie-Louise, Archduchess, wife of
Napoleon I (1791–1847), 364
Marietti, 766, 847
Marine Society, the, 1596
Markham, 1372
Marlborough, John Churchill, first Duke
of (1650–1722), 972
Marlborough, Sarah, Duchess of (1660–
1744), 514, 1010
Marlborough, fourth Duke of (1739–
1817), Letter from: 14
Marley, Major General Bonnet, 502,
521
Marshall, Major General, 678
Marshall, John, M.P., 1271, 1337
Marshall, Mr Serjeant, 737
Martigny [Martigner], Fanchette, 856
Martin, 278
Martin, Colonel, 439
Martin, H., 653
Martin, John, attorney, 749
Martin, Lieutenant, 332
Martin, Richard, M.P. (1754–1834), 95,
913, 1271
Martindell, Major General Sir Gabriel
(? 1756–1831), 521
Mary Queen of Scots (1542–1587), 732,
767, 781
Mary, Princess, Duchess of Gloucester
(1776–1857), 207, 394, 484, 503,
518, 531, 549, 655, 673, 790, 882,
1336, 1415, 1529, 1552, 1577–78,
1585, 1591–92
Letters from: 206, 216, 219, 221, 229,
507–9, 739
Letter to: 511
Maryborough, Katherine, Lady (?1761–
1851), 1370
Maryborough, Lord. See Wellesley-
Pole

Mash, T. B. (Comptroller of Accounts, Lord Chamberlain's Department), 550
Letter to: 802
Masséna, Marshal (1758–1817), 432
Mathews, Charles (1776–1835), 1596
Mathias, Thomas James (? 1754–1835), 1156
Maughan, Mr, 1596
Maule, William Ramsay, Baron Panmure (1771–1852), 1045
Mawbey, Colonel, 502
Mecca, Shereef of, 343
Mecklenburg-Schwerin, Frederick Francis I, Duke of (1756–1837), 394
Mecklenburg-Schwerin, Princess Ulrica of (1723–1814), 393
Mecklenburg-Strelitz, Prince Charles of (1785–1837), 367, 376, 468, 491, 533, 582, 603, 811
Mecklenburg-Strelitz, Charles Louis Frederick, Grand Duke of (1741–1816), 279, 287, 298, 344, 376, 397, 403, 407, 468, 479, 491, 499, 514, 533, 541, 545, 552, 565, 577, 585, 590, 603, 613
Mecklenburg-Strelitz, Prince Ernest of (1742–1814), 279, 282, 348, 376, 394, 397, 407
Mecklenburg-Strelitz, Prince George, Hereditary Prince of, later Grand Duke of (1779–1860), 279, 468, 479, 491, 514, 577, 584, 587–90, 593–95, 598–600, 811, 1373, 1419, 1527
Letter to: 585
Mecklenburg-Strelitz, Maria, Grand Duchess of (1796–1880), 744
Meding (?), 1527
Meheux, J., 308
Melbourne, Elizabeth, Lady (1752–1818), 16, 291
Melbourne, Peniston Lamb, first Viscount. *See* Lamb
Mellish, Joseph Charles (d. 1823), 794
Melville, Anne, Viscountess (d. 1841), 982
Melville, Henry Dundas, first Viscount (1742–1811), 1163
Melville, Robert Saunders Dundas, second Viscount (1771–1851), 78, 80, 84, 98, 104, 109, 267–68, 332, 426, 565, 672, 820, 950, 952, 954, 982, 1170–71, 1302, 1361, 1371, 1448, 1523, 1540
Letters from: 44, 85, 450, 784, 815, 1041, 1303, 1309, 1525
Letter to: 785

Mercer, Miss. *See* Elphinstone
Merle, 1520–22
Merle, Gibbons, editor of the *Globe and Traveller*, 1521–22
Merle, Count, 1521
Merle, Mrs, 1521
Merveldt, 1417, 1419, 1527
Merveldt, General, 315, 318, 431, 440
Metcalfe, Sir Thomas Theophilus (d. 1813), 189
Methuen, Paul, M.P., 649
Metternich, Prince (1773–1859), 318, 364, 412, 494, 500, 514, 787, 795, 1222A, 1258, 1260, 1267, 1409, 1417, 1419, 1527, 1529, 1531, 1552, 1592
Metternich, Prince Victor de, 1222A
Meynell, Captain, 1373
Meynell, Mrs, 768
Middlesex Hospital, the, 1596
Middleton, Dr Thomas Fanshaw, Bishop of Calcutta (1769–1822), 1301
Miguel, Dom, 1258, 1260, 1267, 1279, 1458, 1460, 1462, 1467
Millingen, James (1774–1845), 1156
Mills, General, 391
Mills, George, *Letter from*: 523
Milton, John (1608–1674), 1596
Milton, Viscount, afterwards third Earl Fitzwilliam (1786–1857), 124, 128, 1337, 1341
Mina, General, 1126
Minto, Sir Gilbert Elliot, first Earl of (1751–1814), 189, 191, 332, 343, 352, 502, 678
Mirza Abdul Hassan Khan, 42
Mitford, William (1744–1827), 1156
Moira, Earl of. *See* Hastings
Money, William Taylor, 1169
Moniteur, the, 148, 542
Monitor and Recorder, the, 148
Monk, Rev. James Henry (1784–1856), 1001
Monmouth, Duke of (1649–1685), 1045
Monroe, President (1758–1831), 170
Monson, Rev. Henry (1796–1849), 1353
Montagu, George Brudenell, Duke of Montagu and fourth Earl of Cardigan (1712–1790), 14
Montagu, Henry James Montagu Scott, second Baron (1776–1845), 1361
Montagu, Matthew, Baron Rokeby (1762–1831), 21
Montceilli, 830
Montgomery, Sir Henry Conyngham, 163
Montgomery, Captain, 1061
Montmorency, Duc de, 1256

Montrose, James Graham, third Duke of (1755–1836), 939, 1085, 1287, 1293
Letters from: 1089, 1091, 1312, 1492
Moore, George, M.P., 1271
Moore, Peter, M.P. (1753–1828), 550
Moore, Thomas (1779–1852), 1180
Letter to: 1283
Morand [Morant], 414, 440, 479, 491, 514, 533, 549
Moray, Francis Stuart, tenth Earl of (1771–1848), 1361
Moreau, Jean Victor (1761–1813), 303
Morland, William (1739–1815), 8
Morland and Co., bankers, 669
Morning Chronicle, the, 32, 69, 142, 208, 525, 614, 617, 857, 1030, 1595
Morning Herald, the, 195, 251
Morning Post, the, 251
Morpeth, George William Frederick Howard, Viscount (afterwards seventh Earl of Carlisle) (1802–1864), 1357, 1579
Morris, Edward (d. 1815), 63, 124
Morton, George Douglas, Earl of (1761–1827), 1303, 1371
Mountcharles, Earl of. *See* Conyngham
Moustier, Marquis de, 1258
Mulgrave, Henry Phipps, first Earl of (1755–1831), 78, 84, 565
Letter from: 86
Müller, Adam, 1364
Münch, M. de, de Billinghausen, 1409, 1417
Munro, Sir Thomas (1761–1827), 1154
Münster, Count (1766–1839), 257, 278, 303, 314, 354, 369, 376, 388, 404, 463, 495, 503, 533, 546, 620, 697, 708, 718, 723, 725, 731, 744, 753, 795, 1222 A, 1255, 1409, 1417, 1419, 1591, 1592
Letters from: 1081, 1118
Münster, Countess, 1081
Murat, Joachim (1771–1815), 446, 547, 766, 830
Murray, Lady Augusta (d. 1830), 717
Murray, Sir George (1772–1846), 1579
Murray, George, Bishop of Rochester (1784–1860), 1403–4, 1430
Murray, Lord James, Baron Glenlyon (1782–1837), 72
Murray, John (1778–1843), 1180
Murray, John Archibald, Lord Murray (1779–1859), 1046
Murray, John, fourth Duke of Atholl (1755–1830), 1403
Murray, Captain, 214–15, 521
Musgrave, 1576

Nagle, Admiral Sir Edmund (1757–1830), 616, 785
Nagpur, the Bhonsla Raja of, 521
Napier, eighth Baron (1786–1834), 1361
Napoleon I, Emperor (1769–1821), 96, 110, 130, 148, 152, 201, 279, 298 A, 316, 341, 361, 364, 381, 398, 400, 403, 411, 413–14, 427, 429, 432, 442, 475, 514, 527, 539–42, 549, 560, 571–72, 766, 839, 880, 1200, 1224, 1226
Narischkin, Mme de, 415
Nash, John (1752–1835), 324, 504, 1225, 1227, 1278, 1502, 1514, 1563, 1591–92
Letters from: 163, 334
Nassau, Henry, Count and Lord of Auverquerque (1641–1708), 939
National Register, the, 148
National Society for the Education of Poor Children, 556–57
Natznen (?) [? Natzum], Lieutenant General de, 542, 1528
Nayler, Sir George (? 1764–1831), 522
Nelson, Horatio, first Viscount (1758–1805), 69, 148, 244
Nelson, Sarah, Countess (d. 1828), 244
Nelson, William, second Viscount (1757–1835), 244
Nepean, Sir Evan (1751–1822), 352
Nesselrode, Count (1780–1862), 1592
Netherlands, King of the. *See* Orange
Neuffer, General de, 547
Neumann, Baron Philip, Austrian Chargé d'Affaires in London, 1222 A
Neuville, M. Hyde de, French Ambassador in Portugal, 1171
New Monthly Magazine, the, 1244
Newborough, Thomas John Wynn, second Baron (1802–1832), 34
Newborough, Spencer Bulkeley Wynn, third Baron (1803–1888), 34
Newcastle, Henry Pelham Fiennes Pelham, fourth Duke of (1785–1851), 1045
Newport, Sir John (1756–1843), 123, 1337, 1341, 1357
News, the, 148, 208
Newspapers, List of Sunday, 148
Newspapers. See under
Antigallican *Constitution*
Anti-Jacobin *Courier*
Beacon *Dublin Evening*
Bell's Dispatch *Mail*
Bell's Messenger *Englishman*
Black Dwarf *Examiner*
British Neptune *Freeman's Jour-*
British Press *nal*

Newspapers (*cont.*)

Globe — News
Globe and — Observer
Traveller — Patriot
Hibernian Journal — Phoenix
Independent — Pilot
Whig — Portsmouth Journal
John Bull — nal
Moniteur — Review
Monitor and — Rifleman
Recorder — Sun
Morning — Sunday Advertiser
Chronicle — vertiser
Morning Herald — Times
Morning Post — Tribunal
National — True Briton
Register — White Dwarf

Ney, Marshal (1769–1815), 364
Nicholas I of Russia (1796–1855), 1218, 1220, 1373, 1479, 1559
Nicholl, Sir John (1759–1838), 330
Nicholls, Vice-Admiral, 815
Nipal, Raja of, 502
Nizam, the, 652
Noel, Rev. Mr, 1176
Norbury, John Toler, first Earl of (1745–1831), 297, 1333, 1343
Norfolk, Charles Howard, eleventh Duke of (1746–1815), 166, 190, 192, 458, 469
Letter from: 7
Norfolk, Bernard Edward Howard, twelfth Duke of (1765–1842), 937
Normanby, Constantine Henry Phipps, first Marquis of, and second Earl of Mulgrave (1797–1863), 1504
North, Lord (1732–1792), 309, 328, 329
Northey, William (d. 1826), 124
Northland, Thomas Knox, second Viscount (1754–1840), 1235
Northumberland, Duchess of (d. 1820), 11–12, 56, 63, 72, 81, 110, 141, 145, 240, 262, 518
Northumberland, second Duke of (1742–1817), 14
Letters from: 11–12, 31, 37, 40, 43, 56, 60, 63, 72, 81, 96, 110, 116, 124, 128, 141, 145, 182, 214–15, 240, 243, 254, 262, 518, 659
Letter to: 210
Northumberland, Hugh Percy, Baron Percy, third Duke of (1785–1847), 31, 40, 124, 659, 712, 728, 1359, 1553
Letter from: 17
Letters to: 729, 735
Nugent, Sir George (1757–1849), 190–91, 193, 332, 343, 405, 521, 566, 573, 1133

Nugent, Lady, 521
Nugent, Lavall, Count Nugent, 121

Oakes, Captain, 953
Observer, the, 148, 832
Ochterlony, Sir David (1758–1825), 502, 521
O'Connell, Daniel (1775–1847), 297, 1407, 1555
O'Donnell, Joseph, 816
Oertz, M. de, 514
Oglander, 830
O'Grady, Standish, first Viscount Guillamore (1766–1840), 297, 1061
O'Halloran, 184
O'Halloran, Mrs, 184
O'Hanlon, Patrick, 939
Oldenburg, Prince George of (1784–1812), 381
Oldenburg, Peter I, Grand Duke of (d. 1829), 381
Oldenburg, Grand Duchess of. See Catherine
Oldenburg, Paul Frederick Augustus, Hereditary Prince of, afterwards Grand Duke of (d. 1853), 367
Oldi, Countess, 766 n., 830, 856, 884, 901
Olivieri, Colonel Alessandro, 766
Olpherts, 1061
O'Meara, 831, 865
Ompteda, Baron von, 882, 1527
Ompteda, Baron von (d. 1819), 630, 767, 830
O'Neill, Charles Henry St John O'Neill, second Viscount and first Earl O'Neill (1779–1841), 1407
Opera House, the, 260, 1283
Orange, Prince of Orange, King of the Netherlands (d. 1843), 382–83, 1087, 1090, 1094, 1103
Orange, William, Hereditary Prince of [later, William II, King of Holland] (1792–1849), 180, 367–68, 390, 411, 425, 457, 463–65, 484, 509, 519–20, 528–29, 531, 707
Letters from: 400, 430
Orange, Princess of, sister of Tsar Alexander I, 707
Ord, 547 A
Orford, Horatio Walpole, third Earl of (1783–1858), 1362
Orleans, Louis Philippe Joseph, Duke of (1747–1793), 296, 1591
Orleans, Louis Philippe, Duke of (1773–1850). See Louis Philippe
Orloff, Count (1787–1862), 485
Orme, 1283
Ormonde, 127, 134

Ormonde, James, nineteenth Earl of Ormonde and Ossory, and first Marquis of (1777–1838), 939
O'Ryan, Dr John, *Letter from*: 837
 Letter to: 836
Oscar I, King of Sweden and Norway (1799–1859), 1165
Osmond, Marquis d', 629
Ossulston, Lady, 426
Oudh, King of, 1075
Oudinot, Marshal (1767–1847), 319
Ouseley, Sir Gore (1770–1844), *Letters from*: 42, 176, 336
Ouseley, Sir William (1767–1842), 1156
Ouvaroff, General, 1592
Owen, William (1769–1825), 414
Oxford, Jane Elizabeth, Countess of (1772–1824), 263
Ozarowski, Count, 1174

Paget, Berkeley (1780–1842), brother of first Marquis of Anglesey, 1154
Paget, Lord Clarence Edward (1811–1895), 714
Paget, Sir Edward (d. 1849), 983–86, 993, 1011, 1175
Paget, Henry, first Earl of Uxbridge (1744–1812), 34
Paget, Sir Henry William, second Earl of Uxbridge and first Marquis of Anglesey (1768–1854), 559, 594, 613, 712, 729, 735, 939, 950, 1315, 1364, 1388, 1447, 1503, 1536, 1544, 1551, 1555, 1592
 Letters from: 618, 710, 715, 719, 1154, 1281
 Letters to: 621, 714
Paget, Henry, Earl of Uxbridge, afterwards second Marquis of Anglesey (1797–1869), 1315
Pahlen, Count, 315
Palmella, Marchioness of, 1201
Palmer, Colonel Charles (1777–1851), 501
Palmerston, Henry John Temple, third Viscount (1784–1865), 643, 1355, 1392
 Letters from: 750, 752
 Letter to: 751
Pandolphi, 766
Parish, 1043
Parnell, Sir Henry Brooke, first Baron Congleton (1776–1842), 123
Parry, Edward (d. 1827), 1083–84
Pastorini, 1407
Patriot, the, 125, 129, 1407
Patterson, Mrs. *See* Wellesley
Paul I of Russia (1754–1801), 669

Paul, Prince and Princess of Wurtemberg. *See* Wurtemberg
Pauline, Napoleon I's sister (d. 1825), 432
Payne-Gallwey, Sir William (d. 1831), 513, 516
Pearson, Dr, 1057, 1059
Peat, Rev. Sir Robert, *Letter from*: 276
Pechell, Captain Samuel George, 830
Peel, Jonathan (1799–1879), 1327
Peel, Julia, Lady (d. 1859), 1224
Peel, Sir Robert (1788–1850), 177, 184, 890, 969, 1004, 1043, 1089, 1170–71, 1206–8, 1231, 1251, 1261, 1289, 1296, 1299, 1304–6, 1312, 1322–23, 1327–28, 1339, 1341, 1357, 1407, 1459, 1461, 1480, 1500, 1509, 1531, 1533, 1546, 1556
 Letters from: 1045, 1224, 1259, 1302, 1311, 1501, 1504, 1550, 1579
 Letters to: 1074, 1303, 1556A
Peichall. *See* Pechell
Pelham, Dr George, Bishop of Lincoln (1766–1827), *Letter from*: 1164
Pelham, John Cresset, M.P., 1337
Pembroke, Henry Herbert, tenth Earl of (1734–1794), 20
Pembroke, George Augustus Herbert, eleventh Earl of (1759–1827), 761, 1412–14
Peno. *See* Pino
Penrose, Vice-Admiral Sir Charles Vinicombe (1759–1830), 396
Perceval, Spencer (1762–1812), 4, 5, 13, 15, 23, 51, 53, 63, 72, 87, 143, 152, 156, 165, 218, 235, 291, 299, 524, 656–58, 767, 827, 839, 1400, 1431
 Letters from: 9–10, 21, 45–46, 66
Perceval, Mrs, 63, 299
Perceval, Bridget, Viscountess (d. 1826), 208, 509, 839
Percy, Hugh (1784–1856), Bishop of Rochester and of Carlisle, 1353, 1359, 1403–4, 1420
Percy, Lord. *See* Northumberland, third Duke of
Pergami, Bartolomeo (d. 1841), 766–7, 830, 837, 899, 901, 909
Pergami, Faustina, Pergami's sister, 766
Pergami, Lewis, 766
Pergami, Victorine, 766
Perry, 766
Perry, James (1756–1821), 69
 Letters from: 187, 195, 203–4, 883
 Letter to: 186
Persia, Shah of, 42, *Letter from*: 693

Persia, Prince Royal of. *See* Abbas Mirza

Peshwa, the. *See* Baji Rao

Peter, Richard, 749

Peter the Great, Tsar of Russia (1672–1725), 416

Peterborough, Deanery of, 1001

Peterborough, Charles Mordaunt, third Earl of (1658–1735), 1010

Petit, M., 1522

Pett, Rev. Phineas (? 1755–1830), 1397, 1403–4

Philips, George, M.P., 1337

Phillips, R., *Letter from*: 1223

Phillips, Sir Richard (1767–1840), 51

Phillpotts, Henry, Bishop of Exeter (1778–1869), 1429

Phiseldeck. *See* Schmidt-Phiseldeck

Phoenix, the, 148

Pigott, Sir Arthur Leary (1752–1819), 739, 838

Pilot, the, 242

Pindaris, the, 475, 652

Pino, General, 766, 830

Pino, Countess, 830

Pitt, William (1759–1806), 34, 328–29, 379, 449, 524, 669, 818, 988–89, 1110, 1189, 1431, 1433, 1595

Pius VII (1740–1823), 766, 781, 1070, 1592

   Letters to: 671, 682, 687, 738, 810

Planta, Joseph (1744–1827), 1446

Planta, Joseph (1787–1847), 619, 791, 887, 899, 1104, 1129, 1368

Platoff, Count (1757–1818), 478, 1592

Plowden, Edmund (1518–1585), 1209

Plumer, Sir Thomas (1753–1824), 259, 565

Plunket, William Conyngham, first Baron Plunket (1764–1854), 903, 971, 973, 1261, 1333, 1343, 1407

Pole. *See* Wellesley-Pole

Polignac, Prince Jules de (1780–1847), 1171, 1554

Pollock, Sir Jonathan Frederick (1783–1870), 1334

Ponsonby, Major General Sir Frederick Cavendish (1783–1837), 1272

Ponsonby, George (1755–1817), 45, 64, 105, 461

Ponsonby, John, second Baron and first Viscount (? 1770–1855), *Letter from*: 1570

Ponsonby, Major General Sir William (1772–1815), 559

Pope, a Quaker physician, 536

Pope, Alexander (1688–1744), 1010

Pope, the. *See* Leo XII *and* Pius VII

Popham, Sir Home Riggs (1762–1820), 269, 332, 343, 352, 405, 505

Popham, Lady, 405

Porter, Brigadier General George, *Letter from*: 154

Portland, third Duke of (1738–1809), 165, 524, 669, 1079

Portland, fourth Duke of (1768–1854), 173, 1381, 1436

Portsmouth Journal, the, 492

Portugal, King of. *See* John VI

Portugal, Queen of. *See* Donna Maria

Poten, Captain, 480, 565

Powell, John Allan, 766, 858, 887, 899
   Letter from: 900
   Letter to: 748

Powell, Major, 1503

Power, 337

Powis, Edward Clive, first Earl of (1754–1839), 1274, 1292, 1423, 1430, 1433

Powis, Edward Herbert, Viscount Clive, afterwards second Earl of (1785–1848), 1292, 1430, 1433

Powis, Henrietta, Countess of (d. 1830), 640

Powlett, Lord William John Frederick, later third Duke of Cleveland (1792–1864), 1579

Pozzo di Borgo, Count (1764–1842), 278, 1260

Praun, M. de, 1527, 1529

Press, Memorial respecting English Newspaper, 148

Press, Letter on the state of the, 1595

Prevost, Sir George (1767–1816), 170

Price, William, 366, 384

Prince of the Peace. *See* Alcudia, Duke of

Prince Regent, the. *See* George IV

Prince Royal of Austria. *See* Ferdinand

Prince Royal of Sweden. *See* Bernadotte

Prince Royal of Wurtemberg. *See* Wurtemberg

Princess of Wales. *See* Caroline, Queen

Pritzen [Prizen], Annette, 830

Privy Council's Report respecting Duke of Cumberland's Marriage, 564–65

Privy Council, Committee of, 939

Prudhoe, Lord Algernon Percy, Baron, afterwards fourth Duke of Northumberland (1792–1865), 659

Prussia, Prince Charles of (b. 1783), brother of Frederick William III, 1409

Prussia, Prince Charles of (b. 1801), third son of Frederick William III, 1336

Prussia, Princess Charles of (b. 1808), daughter of Grand Duke of Saxe-Weimar, 1336
Prussia, Prince Frederick William Louis (b. 1794), son of Duchess of Cumberland, 367, 533, 797, 1542
Prussia, King of. *See* Frederick William III
Prussia, Louisa, Queen of (d. 1810), 298 A
Prussia, Prince Royal of. *See* Frederick William IV
Prussia, Princess Royal of, 1528
Prussia, Prince William of (b. 1783), Frederick William III's brother, 542, 1409, 1534
Prussia, Prince William of (1797–1888). *See* William I, first German Emperor
Puller, 1182
Puller, Sir Christopher (1774–1824), 1181–82
Purkis, 1223

Quarterly Review, the, 1224
Queen Charlotte's Lying-in Hospital, 1596
Queensberry, Catherine, Duchess of (d. 1777), 1010
Queensberry, fourth Duke of (1724–1810), 244
Queensberry, Sir Charles Douglas, fifth Marquis of (1777–1837), 1361
Quentin, Sir George Augustus, 290, 501
Quintin. *See* Quentin
Quiroga, Lieutenant Colonel Antonio, 816

Radet, General, 1070
Radzivil, Princess, 440
Rae, Sir William (1769–1842), 939
Raeburn, Sir Henry (1756–1823), 1074
Raine, Jonathan, 31, 43, 63, 124, 128
Rancliffe, George Augustus Henry Anne Parkyns, second Baron (1785–1850), 1337
Ranjit Singh, 521, 765
Rastelli, 861
Ravensworth, Lord. *See* Liddell
Rawdon, Mrs, 139
Reck (?), M. de, 499
Reden [? General Wrede], 310, 335
Reden, Baron de, 1070, 1336, 1417, 1529, 1534, 1552
Redesdale, first Baron (1748–1830), 259, 1513
Regalia of Scotland, the, 740–41
Regent, Prince. *See* George IV

Reid, Sir Thomas (d. 1824), 968
Reiger [Rieger], Baron, 669
Reinagle, Philip (1749–1833), 62
Rennell, Rev. Thomas (1787–1824), 919, 922
Resident at Bussorah [Basra], East India Company's, 352
Restal, 830
Reventlow, Count de, 1529
Review, the, 148
Reynolds, Sir Joshua (1723–1792), 122, 265, 296, 438, 665, 1283, 1591–92
Rice, Dr Edward (1779–1862), 1430
Rice, Spring. *See* Spring-Rice
Richard II (1367–1400), 1223
Richards, Sir Richard (1752–1823), 695, 1043
Richardson, Sir John (1771–1841), 757
Richmond, second Duke of (1701–1750), 215
Richmond, third Duke of (1735–1806), 215
Richmond, Charles Lennox, fourth Duke of (1764–1819), 134, 181, 184, 284, 358
Richmond, Charles Gordon-Lennox, fifth Duke of (1791–1860), 1274
Ricketts, Vice Admiral Sir Robert Tristram (1772–1842), 1423
Ridgeway, James, the bookseller, 1289
Ridley, Sir Matthew White (1778–1836), 764
Riego, Don Raphael del (d. 1823), 816
Rifleman, the, 148
Rivers, George Pitt, second Baron (1751–1828), 1434
Robertson, 523
Robinson, Sir Christopher (1766–1833), 749, 939
Robinson, Eleanor Henrietta Victoria (1814–1826), 1264
Robinson, Frederick John, Viscount Goderich, and first Earl of Ripon (1782–1859), 21, 537, 733–34, 894–96, 1143, 1170–71, 1299, 1331, 1375, 1386, 1391, 1393, 1396, 1400, 1408, 1411, 1421–22, 1432, 1440, 1444–45, 1447, 1454, 1462, 1468, 1473–75, 1498–99, 1504, 1507, 1509–10
Letters from: 1196, 1199, 1225, 1227, 1264, 1287, 1293, 1332, 1350, 1376–77, 1382–83, 1392, 1397, 1399, 1401–3, 1412–13, 1420, 1423, 1425–26, 1430, 1433, 1436, 1439, 1442, 1448–49, 1453, 1455, 1466, 1477, 1506

Robinson [Viscount Goderich], *cont.*
  Letters to: 1198, 1380–81, 1388, 1404,
  1427–29, 1438
Robinson, Sir George Abercromby
  (1758–1832), 930
Robinson, George Richard, M.P., 1271
Robinson, Lady Sarah, afterwards Mar-
  chioness of Ripon, 1264
Robinson, Mary (1758–1800), 1223
Rochester, Bishop of. *See* Murray,
  George, *and* Percy, Hugh
Roden, third Earl of. *See* Jocelyn
Rolle, John, Baron (1750–1842), 1332
Romilly, Sir Samuel (1757–1818), 801
Roscoe, William (1753–1831), 1156
Rose, George (1744–1818), 550, 733
Rose, Sir George Henry (1771–1855),
  406–7, 412, 629, 697, 791, 798,
  811, 874, 882, 1430
Rose, the Hanoverian Cabinet Secretary,
  1527
Rosebery, fourth Earl of (1783–1868),
  1361, 1423, 1448
Rosenberg, 821–22
Rosenstirn [Rosenstein], the porcelain
  manufacturer, 1528, 1552
Ross, Sir Charles (d. 1814), 134
Rossini (1792–1868), 113
Rosslyn, Alexander Wedderburn, first
  Baron Loughborough and first Earl
  of (1733–1805), 669–70
Rosslyn, second Earl of (1762–1837),
  450, 513, 515–16, 1490
  Letter from: 1478
Rosslyn, Countess of (d. 1826), 460
Rothschild, Nathan Meyer (1777–1836),
  1026, 1118, 1566
Rothschild, House of, 1121, 1260
Rowley, Sir William (1761–1832), 537
Royal Academy, the, 38, 49, 59, 61–62,
  118, 246, 300, 320
Royal Cornwall Lunatic Asylum, the,
  1596
Royal Infirmary for Diseases of the Eye,
  the, 1596
Royal Society of Literature, the, 1115,
  1135, 1153, 1155–56, 1596
Rtischev, General de, 336
Rubens, Peter Paul (1577–1640), 61
Ruffo, Cardinal, 732
Rundell, Bridge and Co., Court Jewellers,
  766, 1596
  Letters from: 802–3
Russell, 170
Russell, Lord John, first Earl Russell
  (1792–1878), 1323, 1337, 1579
Russell, Lord William (1767–1840),
  1341

Russia, Emperor of. *See* Alexander I
  and Nicholas I
Russia, Tsarina of (1779–1826), 479,
  510
Russia, Sophia Dorothea, wife of Tsar
  Paul I of, 669
Rutland, John Manners, third Duke of
  (1696–1779), 939
Rutland, Charles Manners, fourth Duke
  of (1754–1787), 665
Rutland, John Henry Manners, fifth
  Duke of (1778–1857), 144, 271,
  323, 324, 1292
  Letters from: 665, 943
Rutland, Elizabeth, Duchess of (1780–
  1825), 665, 943
Rutland, Mary, Duchess of (d. 1831), 665
Ryder, Dudley, second Earl of Harrowby
  (1798–1882), 1337, 1425
Ryder, Lady Georgiana Elizabeth, after-
  wards Lady Wharncliffe (? 1804–
  1884), 1443
Ryder, Dr Henry (1777–1836), 1137,
  1139
Ryder, Richard (1766–1832), 78, 84, 761
  Letter from: 92

Sacchini [Sacchi], 830, 844, 847
Sagan, Duchess of (b. 1781), 500, 514
Saint, The. See Tyrwhitt, Sir Thomas
St Cecilia, 1283
St Cyr, General, 360
St David's, Bishop of. *See* Burgess,
  Thomas *and* Jenkinson, John Banks
St Leger, Colonel Anthony Butler
  (? 1759–1821), 509, 830
St Leger, Harry, 652
Salisbury, Bishop of. *See* Fisher, John
  and Burgess, Thomas
Saltoun, sixteenth Baron (1785–1853),
  1361
Salzas, M. de, 425
Sandon, Viscount. *See* Ryder, Dudley
"Sappio", 508
Sardanha, Baron, 900
Satchwell, 343, 352, 408
Saurin, William (? 1757–1839), 1244
Saxe, Marshal (1696–1750), 20
Saxe-Coburg-Gotha, Ernest, Duke of
  (1784–1844), 463, 685
Saxe-Meiningen, Princess of. *See*
  Clarence, Duchess of
Saxe-Meiningen, Duchess of (mother of
  Duchess of Clarence), 744, 776
Saxony, Frederick Augustus I, King of
  (1750–1827), 440
Saxony, Maria Amelia, Queen of
  (d. 1827), 440

Scarborough, Richard Lumley, second Earl of (d. 1740), 939

Scarlett, Sir James, first Baron Abinger (1769–1844), 831, 894, 1320, 1341, 1489, 1491, 1495, 1496

Scheele, 1527

Schérer, Messrs, bankers, 523

Schivini, Count, 830

Schmidt–Phiseldeck, Justus von (1769–1851), 1336, 1419

Schulte, 1527

Schultzheim, Major General Baron, 303

Schwarzenberg, Prince von, 315–16, 318, 414, 519, 545, 1592

Scindeah. *See* Sindhia

Scott, Miss, 206–7

Scott, Charles, Sir Walter Scott's son (1805–1841), 1424

Scott, Sir Walter (1771–1832), 740, 1424, 1592
  Letters from: 759, 1046, 1048, 1180

Scott, Sir William, Baron Stowell (1745–1836), 330, 565, 644, 1333

Seaford, Lord. *See* Ellis, C. R.

Seamen's Hospital Society, the, 1596

Sebright, Sir John Saunders (1767–1846), 1328

Sefton, William Philip Molyneux, second Earl of (1772–1838), 1530

Seguier, William (1771–1843), 1538

Senfft von Pilsach, Baron, 523

Serres, Mrs Olivia (1772–1834), 848

Seymour, Dorothea, wife of Captain [Sir] Michael Seymour (d. 1875), 1578

Seymour, Sir George Francis (1787–1870), 1373

Seymour, Lord George (1763–1848), 24

Seymour, Sir George Hamilton (1797–1880), 1490

Seymour, Captain James (1801–1827), 1355

Seymour, Mary (1798–1848), 1203, 1205
  Letters from: 345, 1202

Seymour, Sir Michael (1768–1834), 1147, 1352

Seymour, Richard, 1147

Seymour, Lord Robert (1748–1831), 114

Shakespeare, William (1564–1616), 1223

Sharp, Richard (1759–1835), 1289

Shawe, Colonel Meyrick (d. 1843), 812
  Letters from: 1236, 1244, 1344, 1354, 1393, 1406–7

Sheil, Richard Lalor (1791–1851), 1259, 1261, 1407

Shepherd, Sir Samuel (1760–1840), 461, 467, 565, 695, 757

Sheridan, Richard Brinsley (1751–1816), 80, 117, 188, 190, 377, 601, 1283
  Letters from: 64, 77, 101, 119, 159–60, 378, 458, 469, 609–10

Sheridan, Thomas (1775–1817), *Letters from*: 235, 292, 377

Shiel. *See* Sheil

Short, Dr William, 508

Shrapnel, Major General Henry (1761–1842), 148

Shrewsbury, Charles Talbot, Earl of (1753–1827), 939

Sicard, John Jacob, 508, 766–67, 830, 839

Sidmouth, Henry Addington, first Viscount (1757–1844), 78, 84, 134, 164, 168, 184, 285, 458, 469, 524, 565, 601, 610, 614, 698, 712, 740, 771, 926, 928–29, 952, 1170–71, 1184, 1186, 1448, 1521, 1522
  Letters from: 87, 138, 569, 574, 604, 606, 696, 849–50, 852–54, 916, 927, 1185
  Letters to: 165, 244, 605, 609, 741, 827–28, 885

Sidney, 845

Simon, M., 349

Sims, Dr John, 700
  Letter from: 701

Sinclair, Charles St Clair, thirteenth Baron (1768–1863), 1361

Sinclair, Sir John, first Baronet (1754–1835), *Letter from*: 1226

Sinclair, Sir George, second Baronet (1790–1868), 1226

Sindhia, 475, 521, 652, 678

Skelmersdale. *See* Wilbraham, E. B.

Slade, Rev. Samuel, 1137, 1139

Sligo, Howe Peter Browne, second Marquis of (1788–1845), 717
  Letter from: 913

Smirke, Sir Robert (1781–1867), 62
  Letter from: 1166

Smith, an attorney, 1263

Smith, F. C., 408

Smith, John (1749–1831), 264

Smith, John, M.P., 123

Smith, John Spencer, 402, 406–7

Smith, Rev. Samuel, 1142, 1147
  Letters from: 1146, 1589

Smith, Rev. Sydney (1771–1845), 1464

Smith, William (1756–1835), 461

Smith, Admiral Sir William Sidney (1764–1840), 148, 509

Smyth, John Henry, M.P. (d. 1822), 466

Sneyd, 1244

Society of Antiquaries, the, 1538

Sodor and Man, Bishop of. *See* Murray, George

Solms, Prince, 407, 412, 468, 479, 552

Solms, Princess Augusta of (b. 1804), 798

Solms, Princess of. *See* Cumberland, Duchess of

Somerset, Lord Charles Henry (1767–1831), 1086

Somerset, Charles Seymour, sixth Duke of (1662–1748), 939

Somerset, seventh Duke of (1684–1750), 215

Somaglia, Cardinal, 1113

Sondes, Lewis Richard Monson, third Baron (1792–1836), 1353

Sophia Dorothea of Celle, wife of George I, 896

Sophia, Princess (1777–1848), 257, 381, 394, 407, 411–12, 425, 739, 1591–92

Sophia Matilda, Princess, of Gloucester (1773–1844), 616, 622

Soult, Marshal (1769–1851), 346, 348

Souter, Ensign, 1355

Souter, Mrs, 1355

Southey, Robert (1774–1843), 717

Speaker of the House of Commons. *See* Abbot, Charles *and* Manners-Sutton

Spencer, Francis Almaric, Baron Churchill (1779–1845), 14

Spencer, George John, second Earl Spencer (1758–1834), 821

Spencer, John Charles, Viscount Althorp and third Earl Spencer (1782–1845), 466, 1337, 1504

Spencer, Lavinia, Lady (d. 1831), 821

Spenser [Hugh le Despenser] (1262–1326), 69

Spirit of the Book, the, 860

Spring-Rice, Thomas, first Baron Monteagle (1790–1866), 1169, 1461

Stadion, Count von, 364

Stafford, second Marquis of. *See* Leveson-Gower

Stallberg, Count, 1542

Stanhope, Captain, 742

Stanhope, Spencer, 386

Stanley, Sir John, 1182

Stapleton, Augustus Granville (1800–1880), *Letters from*: 1384–85

Staube, 1252

Stedingk, Field Marshal von, 344

Steiger, Major, 417

Stein, Baron von (1757–1831), 287

Stephen, James (1758–1832), 466

Stephenson, Sir Benjamin Charles (d. 1839), 758, 1095, 1101–2

Letter from: 1098

Stepney, Catherine, Lady (d. 1845), 1457

Stewart, Sir Charles William, third Marquis of Londonderry (1778–1854), 28, 303, 311, 316, 342, 376, 399, 407, 412, 442, 468, 483, 546, 630, 644, 795, 858, 899, 1011–12, 1015, 1027–28, 1036, 1068, 1315, 1335, 1374

Letters from: 787, 1072, 1077–78, 1310

Stewart, Professor Dugald (1753–1828), 573

Stewart, Frances, Lady (d. 1865), 787

Stewart, Frederick William Robert, fourth Marquis of Londonderry (1805–1872), 1324

Stewart, Sir James (d. 1827), 181

Stewart, Robert, first Marquis of Londonderry (1739–1821), 795

Stewart, Robert, Viscount Castlereagh, and second Marquis of Londonderry. *See* Castlereagh

Stewart, General, 438

Stewart, Major, 573

Stockdale, John Joseph (1770–1847), 1570

Stoddard, 901

Stothard, Thomas (1755–1834), 62

Stowell, Lord. *See* Scott, Sir William

Strahlenheim, 1527

Strangford, Percy Clinton Sydney Smythe, sixth Viscount (1780–1855), 37, 56, 60, 63, 81, 141, 145, 793–94, 1163, 1174, 1218, 1219

Letter from: 54

Strangways. *See* Fox-Strangways

Strathallan, Viscount (1767–1851), 1361

Strathaven, Charles Gordon, Lord, afterwards Marquis of Huntly (1792–1863), 1228

Street, Peter, 208, 501, 525

Stuart, Sir Charles, Baron Stuart de Rothesay (1779–1845), 629–30, 646, 1253, 1530, 1570

Letter from: 909

Stuart, Peter, *Letters from*: 146, 196, 200, 202, 270, 272–73, 275, 322

Stuart, William, Archbishop of Armagh (1775–1822), 358

Stuart-Wortley-Mackenzie, James Archibald, first Baron Wharncliffe (1776–1845), 81, 110, 114, 116, 461, 641, 1235

Stuart-Wortley, John, second Baron Wharncliffe (1801–1855), 1443

Stuart-Wortley, Edward, third Baron Wharncliffe and first Earl of Wharncliffe (1827–1899), 1443

Sturges-Bourne. *See* Bourne
Sublime Society of Beef Steaks, the, 50
Suchtelen, General de, 278
Sumner, Charles Richard (1790–1874), 910–11, 914, 917, 976, 1145, 1420
   Letters from: 918, 1558
   Letter to: 1164
Sumner, Dr John Bird (1780–1862), 1353
Sun, the, 898
Sunday Advertiser, the, 148
Surrey, Earl of. *See* Howard, Henry Charles
Sussex, Duke of. *See* Augustus Frederick
Sutton, Sir Thomas (d. 1813), 156
Sweden, King of. *See* Charles XIII
Sweden, Prince Royal of. *See* Bernadotte
Swift, Jonathan (1667–1745), 1010
Sylvester, a messenger, 422

Talbot, Sir Charles Chetwynd, second Earl Talbot (1777–1849), 913, 1433
Tarleton, General Sir Banastre (1754–1833), 178
Tatham, Charles Heathcote (1772–1842), 640
Tatischev, Mme de, 415
Taube, Count de, 407
Tauenzien, General Count, 440, 479, 541, 796, 798
Tavistock, Marquis of, afterwards seventh Duke of Bedford (1788–1861), 469, 894–95, 1328
Taylor, Sir Brook (1776–1846), 666, 794, 1255
Taylor, Lieutenant-General Sir Herbert (1775–1839), 598, 600, 614, 617, 624, 663–64, 669, 923, 993, 1020, 1085, 1274, 1339, 1528, 1530–31, 1576
   Letters from: 599, 605, 746, 758, 1082, 1099, 1215, 1355
   Letters to: 604, 606, 1590
Taylor, Michael Angelo (1757–1834), 157
Taylor, W., 260, 1283
Taylor, William, M.P., 178
Tchernicheff [Tchernitcheff], General, 303, 1592
Temple, Earl. *See* Buckingham, second Marquis of
Temple, Sir William (1788–1856), 1373
Terry, Daniel (? 1780–1829), 759
Thames Tunnel Company, 1446
Themistocles, 1256
Thomond, the Marchioness, *Letter from*: 122

Thomond, William O'Bryen, second Marquis of, 1235
Thomson, Sir Alexander (d. 1817), 565
Thornbrough, Sir Edward (1754–1834), 784
Thornton, Colonel Charles Wade, Equerry to Duke of Cumberland, 303, 308, 360, 393, 403, 411, 414, 514, 603, 1068, 1529
Thornton, Sir Edward (1766–1852), 25, 278
Thornton, Henry (1760–1815), 45
Thornton, Robert, 190–91, 193, 261, 301, 308
   Letter from: 189
Thorpe, John Thomas, 953
Thoughts on the State of the Country, pamphlet entitled, 200
Thurlow, Edward, first Baron (1731–1806), 451
Thynne, Lord George, second Baron Carteret (1770–1838), 761
Thynne, Lord John, third Baron Carteret (1772–1849), 761
Thynne, Lady John, 640
Tierney, Edward, 1061
Tierney, George (1761–1830), 21, 45, 53, 63, 114, 116, 251, 308, 501, 550, 878, 881, 1299, 1504, 1575
Tierney, Sir Matthew John (1776–1845), 504, 798, 1050, 1584, 1588
   Letters from: 792, 1051–52
Tighe, William (d. 1816), 21, 123
Times, The, 57, 412, 425, 953, 1522, 1574, 1595
Tindal, Nicholas (1688–1774), 896
Tindal, Sir Nicholas Conyngham (1776–1846), 833, 1250, 1491, 1495
Titian, 438
Todd, Rev. Henry John (1763–1845), 1156
Toler, Daniel, second Baron Norbury (d. 1832), 1333
Toler, Hector John Graham, second Earl of Norbury (1781–1839), 1333, 1343
Tolly, Rev. Dr, 1596
Tolstoy, General, 404
Tomkins, Peltro William (1759–1840), 49
Torlonia, 766
Torrens, Major General Sir Henry (1779–1828), 501, 576, 1099, 1530–31
   Letters from: 1100, 1330
Torrington, George Byng, sixth Viscount (1768–1831), 1505, 1509

Tour and Taxis [Turn und Taxis], Theresa, Princess of (b. 1773), 279, 311, 1534
Townsend, Lady, 839
Townshend, Lord John (1757–1833), 1115
Treasury Minutes, 1058, 1197
Trenck, Friedrich, Baron (1726–1794), 440
Tribunal, the, 148
Trimbuckjee Dainglia [Trimbakji Danglia], 765
Trinity College, Cambridge, 1076
Tritton, J. H., *Letter from*: 162
Trollope, Sir Henry (1756–1839), 815
Troupe, 713
Troy, John Thomas, Archbishop of Dublin (1739–1823), 297
True Briton, the, 1522
Tucker, 749
Tucker, Benjamin, 343, 352
Tugenbund, the, 523
"Tulipanos", the. *See* Hampden-Trevor
Turner, Sharon (1768–1847), 1135, 1156
Turner, Sir Tomkyns Hilgrove (?1766–1843), 290
    Letters to: 20, 38, 49, 59, 61, 115, 118, 126, 237, 246, 248, 250, 256, 265, 296, 300, 1085
Turntaxis. *See* Tour and Taxis
Turton, Sir Thomas (1764–1844), 21
Tweeddale, George Hay, eighth Marquis of (1787–1876), 1361
Twining, Richard (1749–1824), 308
Twiss, Horace (1787–1849), 1579
Tyrawley, second Baron (1690–1773), 141
Tyrwhitt, Sir Thomas (d. 1833), 44, 298 A, 315–16, 318, 327, 343, 361–63, 389–90, 393–94, 399, 414, 416–17, 425, 482, 484, 491, 673, 723, 725, 1588
    Letters from: 422, 424, 442
    Letters to: 255, 365–66, 384–86, 391, 402, 406–7, 412

Udney, Mrs, 436
United Service Club, 662
Ussher, Sir Thomas (1779–1848), 432
Uxbridge. *See* Paget

Valdes, Admiral, 816
Valletort, Ernest Augustus Edgcumbe, Viscount, and third Earl of Mount-Edgcumbe (1797–1861), 1579
Van Dyck, Sir Anthony (1599–1641), 61
Vandeleur, Sir John Ormsby (1763–1849), 513, 516

Van Mildert, William, Bishop of Llandaff (1765–1836), 1000, 1142, 1353
Vansittart, Nicholas, first Baron Bexley (1766–1851), 78, 84, 565, 672, 698, 950, 1004, 1170–71, 1447, 1463, 1545
    Letters from: 93, 647, 1083–84
Vassali, Colonel Carlo, 766, 830, 847
Vaughan, 352
Vaughan, Sir Charles Richard (1774–1849), 794
Vernon, 161
Vernon, Captain, 339
Victoria, Queen (1819–1901), 790, 1367, 1389, 1405
Villa Real, Count de, 1170–71
Villèle, 1253–54, 1256, 1258, 1260, 1262
Villiers, George (1759–1827), 24
Vimercati, 766, 900
Vincent, Baron, 795
Vindicio Gallicae, Sir James Mackintosh's pamphlet, 213
Vivian, Sir Richard Hussey, first Baron Vivian (1775–1842), *Letters from*: 1175, 1315
Vizard, William, 766–67, 857, 931–32
    Letters from: 831, 868
    Letters to: 653, 834, 840, 841, 844–45, 847–48, 851, 883, 891
Volkheim, Oberforstmeister von, 1527
Voltaire (1694–1778), 1373
Vulliamy, Benjamin Lewis (1780–1854), *Letter from*: 20
Vyse, Richard William Howard- (1784–1853), 318

Waithman, Robert (1764–1833), 884, 953, 1108, 1163, 1271
Wakeman, Sir Henry (1753–1831), 1423
Wales, Prince of. *See* George IV
Wales, Princess of. *See* Caroline, Queen
Walker, 1050
Walker, Sir Patrick, 939
Wallace, Thomas, Baron (1768–1844), 301, 308, 524, 733–34, 1079
Wallis, 318
Walmoden [Wallmoden-Gimborn], Count von, 287, 327, 342, 344, 349, 356–57, 360, 399, 409
Walpole, General George (1758–1835), 114
Walpole, Horatio, Lord, afterwards third Earl of Orford (1783–1858), *Letter from*: 415
Walter, John (1776–1847), *Letter from*: 58

Warburton, Dr Charles M., Bishop of Limerick (? 1755–1826), 130, 347, 351
Letters from: 284, 297, 333, 358
Warburton, Henry (? 1784–1858), 1337, 1341
Ward, 8, 51
Ward, James, 62
Ward, John William, first Earl of Dudley (1781–1833), 1381, 1435, 1442, 1445, 1447, 1461–62, 1502
Letters from: 1398, 1416, 1424, 1440, 1493
Ward, Lieutenant, 1204
Ward, Dr William, Bishop of Sodor and Man (d. 1838), 1429–30
Waring, 766
Warren, Sir John Borlase (1753–1822), 379
Warrender, Sir George (1782–1849), 1323, 1530
Warwick, third Earl of (1779–1853), 1528
Warwick, Countess of (d. 1838), 640, 1528
Watson, Sir Frederick Beilby (d. 1852), 565, 594, 666, 699, 781, 790, 845, 882, 1005, 1021, 1037, 1062, 1528, 1552, 1578, 1588
Letters from: 751, 1345
Letters to: 750, 752, 874
Watson, James (? 1766–1838), 816
Watteville, General, 523
Waverley Novels, the, 1180
Way, Rev. Lewis (1772–1840), *Letter from*: 1176
Webster, Sir Godfrey Vassal (1789–1836), 241
Webster, Sir James Wedderburn (1789–1840), 855
Weimar, Princess of, 311
Wellesley, Gerald Valerian (1770–1848), 1353
Wellesley, Sir Henry, first Baron Cowley (1773–1847), 1047, 1222 A, 1258, 1260
Wellesley, Richard, 163, 749
Wellesley, Richard Colley, Marquis Wellesley (1760–1842), 9, 23, 60, 75–76, 81–82, 84–87, 89–94, 96–99, 101–2, 104–6, 112–13, 131, 136, 140, 148, 156, 163, 198, 241, 301, 523, 749, 969, 971, 983, 999, 1015, 1084, 1214, 1232, 1236, 1244, 1333, 1343–44, 1354, 1381, 1393, 1406–7, 1418, 1430, 1436, 1445, 1449, 1588

Letters from: 5, 25, 80, 100, 812, 1034, 1061, 1213, 1261, 1369, 1379, 1524
Letters to: 829, 1365
Wellesley, Mary Anne, Lady [Mrs Patterson] (d. 1853), 1213–14, 1232, 1236, 1244, 1354, 1365, 1369, 1379, 1393
Wellesley, William Pole Tylney Long-, fourth Earl of Mornington and second Baron Maryborough (1788–1857), 1393
Wellesley-Pole, William, first Baron Maryborough (1763–1845), 94, 123, 649, 813, 1079–80, 1110, 1370, 1393, 1513
Wellington, Arthur Wellesley, first Duke of (1769–1852), 10, 56, 60, 69, 136–37, 139, 148, 180, 346, 348, 381, 419, 478, 541, 547, 549, 560, 672, 950, 972, 1014, 1017–18, 1036–37, 1040, 1061, 1068, 1077, 1110, 1117, 1124, 1165, 1170–71, 1189, 1193, 1207, 1220–22, 1229, 1232, 1258, 1260, 1268, 1274, 1277, 1289, 1291, 1294, 1296, 1304–5, 1312, 1349–50, 1355, 1361, 1366, 1370, 1373, 1393, 1421, 1436, 1438, 1461–63, 1468–72, 1477, 1480, 1482, 1487, 1489–90, 1495–97, 1502, 1504, 1506, 1514, 1523, 1525, 1530, 1537, 1540, 1542, 1545–46, 1551–52, 1555, 1562, 1574–75, 1577–78, 1586, 1590–92, 1594, 1596
Letters from: 231, 955, 1002, 1011–12, 1015–16, 1065, 1161, 1172, 1204, 1247, 1285, 1290, 1338, 1340, 1414–15, 1459, 1474, 1481, 1488, 1491, 1494, 1498–99, 1505, 1507, 1510–13, 1515, 1536, 1543–44, 1547–49, 1553, 1556–57, 1561, 1563–64, 1583–84
Letters to: 956, 1013, 1116, 1339, 1478, 1500, 1509, 1573
Wells, Vice-Admiral, 815
Wenlock, Anna Maria, Lady (d. 1850), 1530, 1534
Wesley, Charles (1757–1834), *Letters from*: 317, 326, 374
Wesley, Samuel (1766–1837), 65
West, Benjamin (1738–1820), 237, 248, 320, 438, 1484, 1592
Letters from: 38, 49, 59, 61, 118, 246, 250, 256, 300
West, Raphael Lamar (1769–1850), 1483, 1485
Letter from: 1484

Western, Charles Callis Western, Baron (1767–1844), 1271, 1357
Westmacott, Sir Richard (1775–1856), 62, 1457, 1560, 1590, 1596
Letters from: 980, 1456, 1587
Westmeath, George Frederick Nugent, seventh Earl of (1760–1814), 453
Westminster, Dean of, 1036
Westmorland, John Fane, tenth Earl of (1759–1841), 78, 84, 565, 950, 1143, 1170, 1171, 1463, 1537
Letters from: 88, 827–28
Weston, Dr (d. 1821), 974–75
Westphalia, King of. *See* Bonaparte, Jerome
Wetherell, Sir Charles (1770–1846), 330, 894–96, 1250, 1491, 1494–97, 1499, 1500
Wettier [Watier], John Baptiste, 56, 380, 403
Wharncliffe. *See* Stuart-Wortley
Wharton, Miss E., Housekeeper at Carlton House, 1263
Wharton, George, 1263
Wharton, Richard, 324, 371, 501
Whitbread, Samuel (1758–1815), 21, 45, 117, 225, 251, 258, 262, 433, 452, 461, 466, 469, 1283
Letters from: 199, 205, 355
Letter to: 375
Whitbread, Samuel Charles, 884, 938
White, Henry, 148 n., 356 n., 827, 828, 868
Letter from: 865
White, the London Magistrate, 953
White Dwarf, the, 1522
Whitelock, 974
Whiting, 1263, 1529
Whitmore, 1357
Whitmore, William Wolryche, 1354
Whitshed, Sir James Hawkins (1762–1849), 815
Whitworth, Earl (1752–1825), 280–81, 284, 291, 325, 333, 1137
Letters from: 351, 453
Letter to: 347
Wickham, Miss. *See* Wykeham
Wilberforce, William (1759–1833), 461, 466, 648
Wilbraham, Edward Bootle, Baron Skelmersdale (1771–1853), 466, 1448, 1453
Wilde, Thomas, Baron Truro (1782–1855), 831, 847, 951–52, 954, 998
Wilkes, Colonel, Governor of St Helena, 572
Wilkes, John (1727–1797), 329

Wilkie, Sir David (1785–1841), 62, 248, 250, 256, 300, 1180, 1255
Letters from: 320, 350, 1074
William I (1027–1087), 1294
William II (d. 1100), 1223
William III (1650–1702), 367, 1209
William IV (1765–1837), 310–11, 313, 354, 394, 412, 450, 477, 482, 484, 504, 584, 652, 718, 721, 723, 725, 727, 730–31, 739, 743–46, 753, 776, 831, 902, 933–34, 936, 1008, 1216, 1286, 1339, 1361, 1364, 1425, 1505, 1509, 1523, 1528–30, 1546, 1582, 1585
Letters from: 416–17, 616, 622, 720, 1025, 1358, 1460, 1467, 1470, 1539, 1581
Letter to: 1525
William I, first German Emperor (1797–1888), 797, 1419
Williams, Sir Edmund, 1355
Williams, Sir John (1777–1846), 833, 847, 851, 1289, 1334
Williams, R., 1422–23
Williams, Sir Thomas (? 1762–1841), 354
Williams, publisher, 1595
Willis, Dr John, 783
Wills, 407
Wilson, 161
Wilson, the Duke of Northumberland's steward, 40
Wilson, Harriette (1786–1846), 1263, 1471, 1570
Wilson, Lady, 1240
Wilson, Sir Robert Thomas (1777–1849), 834, 884–85, 1271, 1299, 1341
Letters from: 1239–40
Wimpfen, Baron de, 664, 667–68, 676
Winchester, Bishop of. *See* Sumner, C. R.
Winchester, Charles Ingoldsby Paulet, thirteenth Marquis of (1765–1843), 600
Winchester, Dean of, 1001
Winchester School, 1596
Windischgrätz, Prince (1787–1862), 500
Windsor, Dean of. *See* Hobart
Wintzingerode, Count de (d. 1818), 412
Wittgenstein, Count, 316, 318, 364, 533
Witzleben, Major General, 1417, 1527–29, 1534
Wodehouse, Edmond, 1328
Wood, Sir James Athol (1756–1829), 524

Wood, Rev. Sir John Page (1796–1866), 998
Wood, Mrs John Page (d. 1879), 998
Wood, Major General John Sullivan, 502, 521
Wood, Sir Mark (1747–1829), *Letters from*: 164–65, 168, 330, 524
Wood, Sir Matthew (1768–1843), 778, 821–22, 832, 841, 847, 884, 901, 1271
Wood, Colonel Thomas, M.P., 1357
Woodford, Colonel, 953
Wooler, Thomas Jonathan (? 1786–1853), 1046, 1522, 1595
Worcester, Marquis of. *See* Beaufort, Duke of
Woronzow, General (d. 1832), 545
Worsley, Colonel, 352
Wortley. *See* Stuart-Wortley
Wrede, Prince von, 310, 335, 364, 514, 545
Wright (d. 1819), 1596
Wright, Mrs Phyllis, 1596
Wrottesley, Henry (1772–1825), 45, 461
Wurtemberg, Prince Adam of (b. 1792), 367
Wurtemberg, Princess Augusta of, wife of Frederick I, King of Wurtemberg, 306
Wurtemberg, Princess Augusta of, 669
Wurtemberg, Charlotte Augusta Matilda, Queen of (1766–1828), 381, 389, 416, 422, 424, 442, 590, 666, 669–70, 1540–41
Letters from: 306, 335, 361–67, 383–86, 391–92, 398, 402, 406–7, 412, 419, 425, 427–28, 431, 455, 457, 464, 493, 539, 547, 551, 554, 560, 567, 571, 579, 655, 663–64, 667–68, 676
Letter to: 390
Wurtemberg, Frederick William Charles, King of (1754–1816), 306, 335, 361, 364–65, 367, 383–85, 389–93, 398, 402, 406–7, 412, 419, 422, 424–25, 428, 431, 442, 455, 457, 493, 500, 539, 547, 554, 560, 567, 571, 579, 663–64, 666–70, 676

Wurtemberg, Prince Royal of, afterwards William I (1781–1864), 391–92, 398, 419, 442, 455, 457, 479, 484, 510, 663–64, 667, 669–70, 794, 798, 1540, 1541
Wurtemberg, Princess Royal of, 484, 667
Wurtemberg, Princess Lewis of, 667
Wurtemberg, Prince Paul of (b. 1785), 392, 457
Wurtemberg, Princess Paul of, 384, 386, 391–92
Wurtemberg, Princess Sophia Dorothea of, 669
Wyatt, Benjamin Dean (1775–1850), 248
Wyatville, Sir Jeffry (1766–1840), 1514, 1591, 1592
Wykeham, Miss (d. 1825), 739
Wynn, Charles Watkin Williams (1775–1850), 45, 52, 56, 63, 461, 550, 643, 971, 973, 1170–71, 1183, 1337, 1466, 1498–99, 1506–7, 1509, 1579
Letters from: 1060, 1181, 1301
Wynn, Glynn, 34

Yarmouth, Earl of. *See* Hertford
York, Duke of. *See* Frederick Augustus
York, Duchess of (1767–1820), 479, 484, 767, 838
York, Henry Benedict Maria Clement, Cardinal (1725–1807), 494, 732, 781
York, Field Marshal, 479
Yorke, Charles Philip (1764–1834), 537
Yorke, Sir Joseph Sydney (1768–1831), 1271, 1328
Young, Admiral Sir William (1751–1821), 416–17

Zastron, Colonel, 541
Zeithen. *See* Ziethen
Zemrev, the little, 393
Zeppelin, Count, 335, 364, 391, 402, 407, 422, 424, 442
Ziethen, Hans Joachim von, Prussian General (1699–1786), 514
Ziethen, Count Hans Ernest Karl von, Prussian General, 315–16, 318

CAMBRIDGE: PRINTED BY WALTER LEWIS, M.A., AT THE UNIVERSITY PRESS